D1483811

STUDIES IN HEBREWS

STUDIES IN
HEBREWS

EDITED
BY
DUB MCCLISH

The Second ANNUAL DENTON LECTURES

November 13-17, 1983

PUBLISHED
BY
VALID PUBLICATIONS

A work of the
Pearl Street Church of Christ
312 Pearl Street
Denton, Texas 76201

STUDIES IN HEBREWS

Copyright 1983

by

Valid Publications

Printed and bound by Gospel Light Publishing Co., Delight, Ark., USA

Millard Smith   Harry Ledbetter

Dedication

This book containing the material delivered during the *Second Annual Denton Lectures*, November 13-17, 1983, is dedicated to Harry Ledbetter and Millard Smith, elders of the Pearl Street Church of Christ, Denton, Texas. This annual lecture series was initiated by these men because of their love for Christ, the gospel and the souls of men. Their love for the church of the Lord and their concern that it will not stray from the truth has been a constant source of encouragement. Their example of fidelity is one which is worthy of emulation by elders of the church everywhere.

Dub McClish
Editor, Director
Second Annual Denton Lectures

Table of Contents

SECTION I — EXPOSITIONS OF SELECTED TEXTS

THE LETTER TO THE HEBREWS — AN INTRODUCTION
Tommy J. Hicks 15

THE LETTER TO THE HEBREWS — A SURVEY
Roy C. Deaver 34

WHERE THE SCRIPTURES ARE SILENT WE MUST BE SILENT
(Hebrews 1:5, 13; 7:13-14) *Goebel Music* 43

LEST HAPLY WE DRIFT AWAY (Hebrews 2:1)
Larry Fluitt 56

THE CERTIFICATION OF THE GOSPEL (Hebrews 2:1-4)
Wendell Winkler 68

BUT WE BEHOLD JESUS (Hebrews 2:9)
Johnny Ramsey 87

EVERY HOUSE IS BUILDED BY SOMEONE (Hebrews 3:4)
Robert R. Taylor, Jr. 95

GOD HATH SPOKEN THE LIVING WORD (Hebrews 1:1-3; 4:12)
Dub McClish 108

AFTER THE ORDER OF MELCHIZEDEK (Hebrews 5:6-10; 6:20;
7:11, 15, 17) *Winfred Clark* 123

SPIRITUAL MATURITY (Hebrews 5:11-14)
Ira Y. Rice, Jr. 131

THE TRUE TABERNACLE WHICH THE LORD PITCHED
(Hebrews 8:1-2) *Hugh Fulford* 141

MAKE ALL THINGS ACCORDING TO THE PATTERN
(Hebrews 8:5) *Bill Jackson* 150

THE CLEANSING BLOOD OF CHRIST (Hebrews 9:14)
Avon Malone 163

THE APPOINTED JUDGMENT (Hebrews 9:27)
B. B. James 174

HE TAKETH AWAY THE FIRST THAT HE MAY ESTABLISH
THE SECOND (Hebrews 10:9) *J. Noel Merideth* 188

7

LET US PROVOKE UNTO LOVE AND GOOD WORKS
(Hebrews 10:24-25) *Charles R. Williams* 199

THE HEROES OF FAITH (Hebrews 11:4-40)
Hugo McCord 211

REFUSE NOT HIM THAT SPEAKETH (Hebrews 12:25)
Tom Bright 220

THE KINGDOM THAT CANNOT BE SHAKEN (Hebrews 12:28)
Bobby Duncan 232

THE CHRISTIAN'S CONCERN FOR OTHERS (Hebrews 13:1-3)
Norman Gipson 240

BE NOT CARRIED AWAY BY DIVERS AND STRANGE
TEACHINGS (Hebrews 13:9) *Garland Elkins* 252

THE BOOK OF HEBREWS: THE GREEK TEXT,
TRANSLATIONS, EXEGESIS — NO. I *Troy M. Cummings* 276

THE BOOK OF HEBREWS: THE GREEK TEXT,
TRANSLATIONS, EXEGESIS — NO. II *Troy M. Cummings* 290

SECTION II —
ANSWERING FALSE DOCTRINES RELATING TO HEBREWS

ANSWERING FALSE DOCTRINES RELATING TO HEBREWS —
NO. I
"The World to Come" a Millennial Kingdom (2:5)
"All Things Subjected" Refers to Millennial Kingdom (2:8)
"He Shall Not Tarry" Refers to Imminent Coming of Christ (10:37)
"Receiving a Kingdom" is Yet Future (12:28)
Jerry Moffitt 305

ANSWERING FALSE DOCTRINES RELATING TO HEBREWS —
NO. II
Is "Sanctification" a Second Work of Grace or a Second
Blessing? (2:11; 12:14; 13:12)
Is the Sabbath Law Still Binding? (4:9)
Is Salvation By Faith Only? (10:38-11:40)
Does the Mormon Priesthood Descend From Aaron
and/or Melchizedek? (7:11-17)
Frank Morgan 315

ANSWERING FALSE DOCTRINES RELATING TO HEBREWS —
NO. III
Jesus was Merely Human, a Creature (2:6-9)
Baptism May be Administered by Sprinkling (10:22)
"All" Marriages Includes Adulterous and Homosexual
"Marriages" (13:4)
James Meadows 325

SECTION III — DIFFICULT PASSAGES IN HEBREWS

DIFFICULT PASSAGES IN HEBREWS — NO. I
Who Wrote Hebrews?
Define "These Last Days" (KJV), "The End of These Days"
   (ASV) as to Beginning and Duration (1:2)
Do Christians Have Personal "Guardian Angels?" (1:14)
Is "A Little Lower Than the Angels" a Reference to Christ
   in Psalms 8:4-6 From Which it is Quoted or to Man in
   General? (2:6-8)
Carl B. Garner 341

DIFFICULT PASSAGES IN HEBREWS — NO. II
How Was Jesus "Made Perfect?" Does This Imply
   Imperfection Before His Death? (2:10)
Jesus Was Tempted, Yet God Cannot be Tempted (Jam. 1:13).
   Does this Mean that Jesus is Not Truly God? (2:18; 4:15)
Is There a Real or Only an Apparent Distinction Between the
   "Soul" and "Spirit" of Man? (4:12)
What Prayer of Jesus is Referred to, To Escape the Cross,
   To be Raised Up or Some Other? (5:7)
Roy H. Lanier, Jr. 353

DIFFICULT PASSAGES IN HEBREWS — NO. III
What are the "First Principles," Jewish or Christian? (6:1-3)
"Impossible to Renew" Apostates (6:4-8)
Gary Workman 365

DIFFICULT PASSAGES IN HEBREWS — NO. IV
Why is the Golden Altar in the Holy of Holies? (9:3-4)
How Does the Blood of Christ Redeem the Transgressions
   Under the First Covenant? (9:15)
What is "The Roll of the Book?" (10:7)
What is "The Day Drawing Nigh?" (10:25)
John Waddey 380

DIFFICULT PASSAGES IN HEBREWS — NO. V
What Does it Mean to Sin "Wilfully?" (10:26)
What is the Lord's "Chastening," and Does He Still do it?
   (12:5-11)
Whose Repentance is Referred to — Esau's or Isaac's? (12:17)
What is Meant by "Church of the Firstborn?" (12:23)
T. B. Crews 391

SECTION IV — CONTROVERSIAL ISSUES DISCUSSION FORUM

DISCUSSION FORUM NO. I-A: HOW THE WORLDS WERE
   FRAMED (HEBREWS 11:3). The Biblical Account of Creation
   Allows for a Very Ancient Earth. Jack Wood Sears 405

DISCUSSION FORUM NO. I-B: HOW THE WORLDS WERE FRAMED (HEBREWS 11:3). God Created the Universe and all that, is in it in a Mature State in Six Literal Days of Approximately 24 Hours each. He did not Employ a System Requiring Vast Periods or Long Ages of Time to Bring the Material World to its Present State. *Bert Thompson* 417

DISCUSSION FORUM NO. II-A: THE AUTHORITY OF ELDERS (HEBREWS 13:7, 17, 24). The Role of Elders is Best Defined as Spiritual Shepherds of the Flock Rather Than Authoritative Rulers. *Waymon D. Miller* 435

DISCUSSION FORUM NO. II-B: THE AUTHORITY OF ELDERS (HEBREWS 13:7, 17, 24). Elders have been Given Delegated, Decision-making Authority in Matters of Expediency in the Local Church by the New Testament and Members of the Local Church have a Responsibility to Abide by Their Decisions that are in Harmony with the New Testament. *Gary Workman* 449

DISCUSSION FORUM NO. III-A: THE NATURE OF BIBLICAL FAITH (HEBREWS 11:1-3, 6). In General Matters of Human Knowledge, Things Not Perceived Through the Senses are Matters of Faith and do not Provide the Certainty of Empirical Knowledge. *Arlie J. Hoover* 462

DISCUSSION FORUM NO. III-B: THE NATURE OF BIBLICAL FAITH (HEBREWS 11:1-3, 6). Some Non-Empirical Propositions may be Known with Greater Certainty than Empirically-perceived Things. *Dick Sztanyo* 472

DISCUSSION FORUM NO. IV-A: THE KINGDOM AND REIGN OF CHRIST (HEBREWS 10:12-13; 12:28). The Prophecies of the Messianic Kingdom and Throne Require a Literal Political Millennial Kingdom and Throne of Christ on Earth for Fulfillment. *Robert Shank* 484

DISCUSSION FORUM NO. IV-B: THE KINGDOM AND REIGN OF CHRIST (HEBREWS 10:12-13; 12:28). The Prophecies of the Messianic Kingdom and Throne are Fulfilled in the Establishment of the Church of Christ, the Ascension of Christ and the Present Reign of Christ in Heaven, Therefore There will be no Earthly Kingdom or Throne. *Wayne Jackson* 497

Preface

Even to the unbeliever, the Epistle to the Hebrews is a literary masterpiece. To the believer, it is an *inspired* literary masterpiece filled with both practical and doctrinal principles. It urgently exhorts Christians to "run with patience the race that is set before us" (12:1) and to "press on unto perfection" (6:1). What powerful lessons it contains to urge us to continue faithfully to the end! Perhaps no other portion of the Bible standing alone shows so clearly the superiority and utter exclusiveness of the religion of Christ. For these and other good reasons, the Hebrews epistle was chosen as the subject matter of the *Second Annual Denton Lectures*.

The reader will find four sections in this volume which at the same time give it a wonderful balance and provide a treasure of reference material that will not become obsolete this side of the Judgment. In the first section the authors were assigned some of the major themes of the epistle for expository treatment. In section two some of the false doctrines based upon misinterpretations of passages in Hebrews are dealt with. The third section deals with many of the difficult passages with which this profound epistle seems to be filled. Section four is composed of discussions between brethren of opposing views on four controversial issues that relate to the book of Hebrews. It is readily seen from the foregoing description that there is truly "something for everyone" who is a serious Bible student in this unique book.

Our authors (who were also speakers in the *Second Annual Denton Lectures*) were chosen in all but a few cases because they have distinguished themselves as true soldiers of the cross who can ably wield the "sword of the Spirit" with

11

both tongue and pen. Some of our authors/speakers were invited in spite of the fact that we believe that they hold erroneous, and in some cases, egregiously erroneous, views. However, they were invited to participate in the "Discussion Forums" and to make the strongest possible case for their respective positions. We believe that truth will be exalted and long-lasting good will result from the open discussion of such controversial issues. To all of our authors/speakers, including those with whom we differ, profound gratitude is expressed for their willingness to expend the time and trouble necessary to prepare the contents of this book which we believe will bless the lives of all who read it. Our 37 contributors have an average of approximately 30 years of preaching experience, representing the staggering figure of well over a millennium of preaching, teaching and scholarship in the production of this volume!

This book is a labor of love on the part of more than the authors. Our special gratitude is expressed to Bronwen Gibson, Andy McClish, Lavonne McClish and Nancy Smith for their able and willing assistance.

Studies in Hebrews is hereby sent forth with the expectation and prayer that it will truly be a significant contribution to the literature already extant on the epistle to the Hebrews.

Dub McClish
Editor, Director
Second Annual Denton Lectures

SECTION I

EXPOSITIONS OF SELECTED TEXTS

THE LETTER TO THE HEBREWS —
AN INTRODUCTION

By TOMMY J. HICKS

Born 1947, Lubbock, Texas. Married Nina Sue Cave; they have two daughters. Has attended several schools and colleges, and holds a Bachelor's Degree in Theology. Currently attending University of Texas at Arlington. Served churches in Arizona, California, Texas, and New Mexico. Meeting work for those states plus Oklahoma, Colorado, New York, Michigan, and Florida. Also speaks on lectureships and workshops. Has authored one book, and writes for several publications. Presently serves Handley church, Fort Worth, Texas, as a local preacher.

INTRODUCTION

E. F. Scott penned, "The Epistle to the Hebrews is in many respects the riddle of the New Testament."[1] Franz Delitzsch started a tradition nearly every Hebrews commentator has followed with his statement, "It is like the great Melchizedek of sacred story, of which its central portion treats . . ., we know not whence it cometh or whither it goeth."[2] Whether one characterizes Hebrews as a mystery or a riddle, there are three very simple, but most basic, questions which tantalize all who approach this book which has been called ". . . the greatest piece of exhortation found in the New Testament."[3] Those questions are: Who wrote Hebrews? What was its original destination? When was it written? Along with these, other questions must be answered before the mystery is unraveled and the riddle solved.

Acceptance by the Church: The first known use of the book of Hebrews was by Clement of Rome in his letter to the Corinthian church, written in 95 A.D. Unfortunately, Clement did not name the author. However, his use of it implies that Hebrews was recognized as being an authoritative writing. *The Shepherd of Hermas*, another early writing, reflects that its author knew of the book of Hebrews. Everett F. Harrison quotes Goodspeed as saying, "Hebrews left a marked impression upon the Roman church, and all the early writings of Rome after its appearance reflect its use."[4] Yet, a strange thing happens. Western churches, of which Rome had the greatest influence, did not accept the book as being canonical for several centuries. Eastern churches must have accepted Hebrews as inspired literature from its very first reception. A Western work, *The Canon of Muratory*, did not even mention Hebrews, but the Chester Beatty manuscript reveals that in the East, Hebrews was considered to be an important work of inspiration ranking with Romans and other works from the pen of the Apostle Paul. General acceptance of Hebrews as being canonical did not happen until about the fifth century in the West. What caused this division of thought between the East and West which lasted more than four centuries? The division revolved around one problem:

THE QUESTION OF AUTHORSHIP

Pantaenus, a second century scholar, teacher and elder in the church at Alexandria, is the first known to have attributed Hebrews to Paul. Clement of Alexandria was a student of Pantaenus. Of Pantaenus, Clement wrote,

> But now as the blessed presbyter used to say, "since the Lord who was the apostle of the Almighty, was sent to the Hebrews, Paul by reason of his inferiority, as if sent to the Gentiles, did not subscribe himself an apostle of the Hebrews; both out of reverence for the Lord, and because he wrote of his abundance to the Hebrews, as a herald and apostle of the Gentiles."[5]

Clement had no doubts about the Pauline authorship of Hebrews. F. F. Bruce stated, "Clement of Alexandria in his *Hypotyposes* said that it was written by Paul for Hebrews in the Hebrew language."[6]

Next, in the line of scholastic succession at Alexandria, came Origen, the student of Clement. Some modern commentators attempt to use Origen as a doubter of the

Pauline authorship of Hebrews. They take his statement, "But who it was that really wrote the epistle, God only knows," out of its context, making it appear as though Origen had no firm convictions. Here is what Origen actually said about Paul's authorship of Hebrews:

> . . . Again, it will be obvious that the ideas of the epistle are admirable, and not inferior to any of the books acknowledged to be apostolic. Every one will confess the truth of this, who attentively reads the apostle's writings. . . . But I would say, that the thoughts are the apostle's, but the diction and phraseology belong to someone who has recorded what the apostle said, and as one who noted down at his leisure what his master dictated. If then, any church considers this epistle as coming from Paul, let them be commended for this, for neither did those ancient men deliver it as such without cause. But who it was that really wrote the epistle, God only knows. The account, however, that has been current before us is, according to some, that Clement who was bishop of Rome wrote the epistle; according to others, that it was written by Luke, who wrote the gospel and the Acts. But let this suffice on these subjects.[7]

Clearly, Origen is saying Paul "dictated" Hebrews. When he says, "But who it was that really wrote the epistle, God only knows," Origen is speaking of Paul's amanuensis. Milligan explained, "By this remark, however, he evidently does not intend to express any doubt as to the authorship of the Epistle, but only as to the person who in this case acted as Paul's amanuensis."[8]

One statement in Origen's quote which seems to have been overlooked by many is, ". . . neither did those ancient men deliver it without cause." From this remark, it is implied that Pauline authorship of Hebrews had been taught for a considerable number of years before Origen's generation. Pantaenus, Clement and Origen were so proximate in time, Pantaenus and Clement could not have been the "ancient men" to which Origen had reference. Therefore, at least in the East, Pauline authorship of Hebrews was accepted and taught by those considered "ancient" — considered "ancient" by those living at the end of the second century and the beginning of the third. Bear in mind that little more than 100 years had passed from the time Hebrews was written until the birth of Origen. Men "ancient" to Origen must have lived very near the time of the writing of Hebrews. None would be in a better position to know who authored this great work.

Witness upon witness from the past could be called to give information about how the church in the East viewed Hebrews and its author. However, Albert Barnes said:

> But the most important testimony of the Eastern church is that of Eusebius, bishop of Caesarea, in Palestine. He was the well-known historian of the church, and he took pains from all quarters to collect testimony in regard to the Books of Scripture. He says, "There are fourteen epistles of Paul, manifest and well known: but yet there are some who reject that to the Hebrews, alleging in behalf of their opinion, that it was not received by the church of Rome as a writing of Paul." The testimony of Eusebius is particularly important. He had heard of the objection to its canonical authority. He had weighed that objection. Yet in view of the testimony in the case, he regarded it as the undoubted production of Paul.[9]

Strong evidence in the East kept the churches there from wavering in their conviction that Paul wrote Hebrews.

As the East was strong, the West was weak on evidence on the authorship of Hebrews. At first, the West seems to have viewed Hebrews as an anonymous work. Harrison revealed the error of this view when he said,

> Hebrews is not an anonymous epistle in the sense that the writer is unknown to the readers, but only in the sense that the name is not indicated. The writer asks prayer for himself, that he may be enabled to visit those to whom he is writing (13:18-19).[10]

At least until the fourth century there was no tradition of authorship for Hebrews in the West. There were denials of Pauline authorship. Irenaeus, Hyppolytus, Caius, Cyprian, Novatian and Victorinus were among the most influential Western church leaders who rejected Paul as being the author of Hebrews between 180 A.D. and 390 A.D. Only Tertullian offered another author for Hebrews; however, he may have gone so far as to deny its inspiration. Hewitt remarks,

> Tertullian in his opposition to the edict of forgiveness of Maximus quotes Hebrews vi. 4-8, and ascribes it to Barnabas. He thus clearly regarded the letter as un-Pauline, and it is possible that he also denied its canonicity.[11]

Neil Lightfoot shows his misunderstanding of Origen's statement about Clement of Rome and Luke. Lightfoot wrote, "Origen, as he discusses the problem of authorship, mentioned that some believed that the Epistle was the work of Luke, and others that it was the work of Clement of Rome."[12] From the context of the Origen quote it is evident that Origen was not saying some believed Luke or Clement had authored Hebrews. He was saying that some thought one or the other might have served as Paul's amanuensis.

Between 200 A.D. and 392 A.D. a definite shift can be seen in the West toward acceptance of Pauline authorship for Hebrews. By 392 Pauline authorship was acknowledged in the West. The Council of Hippo, 393, declared there to be "thirteen epistles of the apostle Paul, and one by the same to the Hebrews."[13] Just 26 years later, the Council of Carthage proclaimed there to be "fourteen epistles of the apostle Paul."[14] Even though Clement of Rome showed that the book of Hebrews was considered canonical in the West when he quoted from it in 95 A.D., it would take another 324 years before the church of the West would consider Hebrews to be Pauline and declare it canonical. Finally, the East and the West agreed and were united concerning Hebrews and its author.

Martin Luther is given credit for resurrecting the question of authorship for Hebrews. Rather than accepting Pauline authorship, Pfeiffer says, "Martin Luther suggested still another author — the eloquent Apollos of Alexandria (Acts 18:24-25)."[15] Bruce records,

William Manson, however, while conceding that "Apollos would ad-mirably suit the part in point of his Jewish-Alexandrian origin and training," finds it "difficult to think that the Alexandrian Church would not have preserved some knowledge of the fact in view of the distinguished role of this son of Alexandria in the world-mission, and that Clement would not have mentioned him writing to the Cor-inthians in whose history Apollos had played a notable part."[16]

Tenney correctly labeled Luther's choice of Apollos when he said, "Many other names have been suggested for the author, chief among them are Barnabas to whom Tertullian attributed it, and Apollos, *a guess* (emphasis mine, TJH) of Martin Luther."[17] After listing six of the most convincing arguments for authorship of Hebrews by Apollos, Lightfoot correctly ob-served,

. . . it must not be assumed that Apollos was the only man or the
only Alexandrian in the apostolic period who could fit Luke's description as one "eloquent . . . well versed in the scriptures." There
is further difficulty that Apollos' authorship is supported by no
ancient tradition. So far as is known, Apollos did not write anything.[18]

Going beyond Lightfoot's remarks, there may have been any
number of men who possessed the same abilities and qualities
as Apollos. Should one be willing to forget the evidence for
Pauline authorship, he might be willing to agree with Geoffrey
Wilson who candidly admitted, ". . . the modern attempts to
establish the author's identity have failed to pierce this veil of
anonymity (though Luther's choice of Apollos — cf. Acts
18:24-28 — still seems the likeliest guess!)"[19] Whenever
discussing Luther's choice of author, Luther's appreciation for
the book of Hebrews should be noted.

Luther did not like the Epistle to the Hebrews because he believed
that it taught that there was no second repentance. He placed it
with one or two others at the end of the New Testament, thus making a distinction between them and the rest.[20]

While Luther is not known to have rejected the canonicity of
Hebrews, it is apparent that he did question it. Since Luther
did not like the book his selection of another author may have
been less than objective. After all the evidence is considered,
there is no way any man can of a certainty say, "Apollos wrote
Hebrews." At the very best it would be but a *guess.*

Others have made guesses about the authorship of
Hebrews. Harnack theorized that Priscilla and Aquila wrote it.
Chapman's guess was that Aristion wrote Hebrews. Ramsay's
choice was Philip. Occasionally, Silas' name is mentioned.
Alas, the list could continue, but where is the evidence for the
claims? Robert Anderson boldly rejected Barnabas, Luke,
Apollos, and Clement of Rome as possible authors of Hebrews
and then said, "As for the other companions of the Apostle,
their claims rest on mere conjecture; there is not a scintilla of
evidence to connect them with the book."[21] Because all others
mentioned as possible authors for Hebrews are conjectural,
Milligan stressed,

. . . hence if it can be shown that Paul did not write the Epistle,
then indeed we may as well give up all further inquiry about its

authorship, and wait patiently for the revelations of the day of judgment.[22]

Pfeiffer says, "Neither external nor internal evidence is sufficient to solve the problem of identifying the author of Hebrews."[23] Bruce confesses, "If we do not know for certain to whom the epistle was sent, neither do we know by whom it was sent."[24] Wilson declares the authorship of Hebrews to be, "one of the unsolved mysteries of New Testament introduction."[25] The gist of modern scholarship seems to be, when it comes to Hebrews, we just cannot determine the author. Hence, the misuse of Origen's statement, "But who it was that really wrote the epistle, God only knows."

"It can't be Paul": Saying one cannot know who the author is, is not the same as saying we cannot know who the author is not. While denying that the author can be known, modern scholarship confidently affirms that Paul is not the author. Known as a superb reference work, the *International Standard Bible Encyclopedia* boldly declares, "We know enough about Paul to be certain that he could not have written Hebrews."[26] Consider this quotation from the "scholar" (?), William Barclay:

> At no time in the history of the Church did men ever really think that Paul wrote *Hebrews*. How then did it get attached to his name? It happened very simply. When the New Testament came into its final form there was of course argument about which books were to be included and which were not. To settle it one test was used. Was a book the work of an apostle or at least the work of one who had been in direct contact with the apostles? By this time *Hebrews* was known and loved throughout the Church. Most people felt like Origen that God alone knew who wrote it, but they wanted it. They felt it *must* go into the New Testament and the only way to ensure that was to include it with the thirteen letters of Paul. *Hebrews* won its way into the New Testament on the grounds of its own greatness, but it had to be included with the letters of Paul and come under his name. People knew quite well that it was not Paul's but they included it among his letters because no man knew who wrote it and yet it must go in."[27]

Never has such nonsense been sold to a wider market than today's so-called "Christendom." Barclay could not have written anything further from the truth. Yet, he has, in simple terms, expressed the view many "scholars" (?) advocate today, "Paul could not possibly be the author of Hebrews."

Objections to Pauline Authorship Considered: Without a doubt, there are legitimate scholars who honestly doubt the possibility of Pauline authorship for Hebrews, based on what they would consider "sound" objections. Some say they view a few of the objections as being "fatal" to Pauline authorship. "But as everyone who has had much experience in dealing with evidence is aware, a solution may often be found of difficulties and objections which at first seem 'fatal'."[28] Again, when "scholars" claim overwhelming evidence or reason for rejecting Pauline authorship for Hebrews, their objections must needs be objectively considered. In other words, just because a "scholar" says it, does not make it so. What are some of the "scholarly" objections to Paul's having written Hebrews?

"Paul does not identify himself in the address." "Pauline authorship is rendered difficult, if not impossible, by other considerations. (1) The author's name is not given."[29] Just because Paul's name does not appear at the beginning of or within Hebrews, some insist it could not be his work. This is a situation where what proves too much proves nothing. Barnes explains,

> If this fact will prove Paul was not the author, it would prove the same thing in regard to any other person, and would thus be ultimately conclusive evidence that it *had* no author.[30]

Answering this objection, Coffman remarked,

> Due to Paul's repudiation of Judaism and the fierce prejudice that existed against him throughout Jewry, it could easily have been that considerations of tact induced Paul to omit his name, in order to prevent stirring up unnecessary bias against the epistle, even before it was read. No such possible and plausible reason may be thought of as explaining why anyone, other than Paul, should have omitted his name. Who but Paul had a good reason for not signing such an epistle?[31]

Coffman, Barnes, Milligan and others who accept Pauline authorship, generally follow the explanation given by Pantaenus for the omission of Paul's name. However, there may be *another* reason for the omission.

Strictly speaking, Hebrews is not a letter. "Hebrews begins like an essay, proceeds like a sermon, and ends like a letter."[32] More precisely, "It is a midrash in rhetorical Greek prose — it is a homily."[33] A "midrash" is an expository sermon in written form or, as some would consider it, a commentary covering just a few passages of scripture. As such, it would be out of form if the writer had begun with an address comparable to those in Paul's thirteen other writings. Thus, when all the evidence is considered, there are more reasons why Paul should have omitted his name than can be garnered for any other proposed writer.

"Hebrews is written in a style very different from Paul's." To this objection Hewitt answers,

> Yet style and vocabulary should never be the decisive factor in settling questions of authorship. The Pauline authorship of Ephesians, Colossians, and the Pastoral Epistles has been questioned on the ground of style and vocabulary, although modern scholarship is, perhaps, more in favor of Pauline authorship of these Epistles than it was fifty years ago.[34]

Too many things come into play for critics to trust their "style" argument. Style is affected by the circumstances or the author, the readers, and the type of work. Milligan said of Hebrews, "It begins like a treatise, but it ends like an epistle. And hence we would naturally expect that its style would be somewhat more elevated and oratorical than that of an ordinary and formal epistle."[35]

Upon closer examination, some scholars are saying there is not *that much* difference, in style and vocabulary, between Hebrews and the other writings which are accepted as Pauline.

> Leonard deals very extensively with the peculiarities of vocabulary in Hebrews and shows that this difficulty is highly exaggerated. He also maintains that no other personal vocabulary that is known to us, not only in Christian literature, but in the whole range of Hellenistic literature, coincides so much in the vocabulary of Paul as do the 990 words which make up the lexicon of the Epistle to the Hebrews.[36]

Finally, on this point, the similarity between Hebrews 13 and the epistles of Paul is so very close that some "scholars" who reject Pauline authorship on the first 12 chapters of Hebrews want to claim that he actually did write chapter 13. From the text it is apparent that such speculation is not warranted. There is not a single clue that chapter 13 was not a part of the original text. Since Hebrews begins and continues for the most part as a sermon and then concludes like a letter, it is only natural that the author change his style. When the writer writes his "letter" section of the work, it compares with the "letters" Paul has written to others. Style here points to Paul.

"Hebrews 2:3 would disqualify Paul from being the author of Hebrews." That verse reads, "How shall we escape, if we neglect so great salvation; which at the first began to be spoken by the Lord, and was confirmed unto us by them that heard him." It is argued that Paul plainly revealed, "I conferred not with flesh and blood" (Ga. 1:16), when it came to his apostleship and preaching. Further, it is alleged that Paul could not have said such a thing because the apostles were eyewitnesses who had received their gospel directly from Jesus. How could Paul say the gospel was "confirmed unto us by them that heard" and still be correct in these other considered matters?

First, it should be recalled that even Paul had instruction from Ananias before his conversion and evidently had contact with other disciples immediately after his conversion.

> And Ananias went his way, and entered into the house; and putting his hand on him said, Brother Saul, the Lord, even Jesus, that appeared unto thee in the way as thou camest, hath sent me, that thou mightest receive thy sight, and be filled with the Holy Spirit. And immediately there fell from his eyes as it had been scales: and he received sight forthwith, and arose, and was baptized. And when he had received meat, he was strengthened. Then was Saul certain days with the disciples which were at Damascus (Acts 9:17-19).

Apostolic authority was not conferred upon Paul by Ananias, but it can be said that Ananias "confirmed" the "great salvation" to Paul when Paul was baptized. Paul definitely could have made the statement found in Hebrews 2:3.

Second, as an "untimely born" (cf. I Co. 15:8) apostle, Paul was not an eyewitness to the Messiah and his message as were the other apostles. Having this thought in mind, thinking too of the other apostles' work among the Hebrews, Paul may have chosen the language in question. On this point Coffman commented, "First, as regards Christ in his personal ministry,

Paul was not an eyewitness and might have appropriately used such language with that limitation in mind."[37]

Third, Paul could have used the language under question in order to identify with his readers. By placing himself in the personal plural, Paul knew his message of exhortation would be much more persuasive. Hebrews 2:3 needs to be considered in light of Hebrews 6:1-3 where a clear distinction can be made. There the author penned,

> Therefore leaving the principles of the doctrine of Christ, let *us* (emphasis mine, TJH) go on unto perfection; not laying again the foundation of repentance from dead works, and of faith toward God, . . . And this will *we* (emphasis mine, TJH) do, if God permit.

Coffman commented on this passage as follows:

> Now, should it be concluded that the author of Hebrews, speaking in this passage, intended to confess that he himself was lingering upon first principles, having made no effort to go on unto perfection? Such a conclusion would be ridiculous; and, in the same vein of reasoning, it is equally ridiculous to make the author of Hebrews forfeit his title to the apostleship merely because he made reference to the historical chain of witnesses that had delivered to that generation of believers the noble truths of the gospel.[38]

After considerable research, one might conclude that Hebrews 2:3 is a proof of Pauline authorship rather than an objection to it.

"We thus see that what appeared to be a fatal bar to the Pauline authorship of Hebrews admits of a solution which is both simple and adequate."[39] Other objections are sometimes raised, but they can be amply dealt with as have these. The three considered here are supposed to be the most conclusive and fatal objections to Pauline authorship.

Evidence for Pauline Authorship: As noted, it would appear from the critics that there is absolutely no evidence for Pauline authorship of Hebrews. In fact, however, there is no real evidence for anyone but Paul. If all the speculations and theories are removed and one is left only with the evidence, he will have no choice but to accept Paul as the author of Hebrews.

The earliest historical testimony affirms Pauline authorship. Pantaenus, Clement of Alexandria, and Origen proclaim Paul to have been the author. Eastern churches have permitted that no one other than Paul wrote Hebrews, as far back as history allows. While the West at first questioned the authorship of Hebrews, evidence brought the West to accept Paul as the author. Pauline authorship was universally accepted until Martin Luther. Luther did not like Hebrews; therefore, his motives for questioning its authorship are suspect. When considering authorship from the testimony of history two important items need to be observed. While not infallible in their provision of information, the early recorders of these views had an advantage in that they lived nearest the time when it was known who wrote the book. They studied, considered the pros and cons, weighed the evidence, and finally declared Paul to be the author. They were convinced.

The thoughts in the book of Hebrews are Paul's. Most modern scholars accept Origen's assessment. Hence, the reason for their selections of those close associates of Paul as possible authors. Not only are the thoughts Paul's, but so is the arrangement of the book. *"The general method and arrangement of this epistle and of the acknowledged epistles of Paul are the same."*[40] Even a novice cannot read Hebrews 13 without thinking of Paul as its author.

The author was a close associate of Timothy. "Know ye that our brother Timothy is set at liberty; with whom, if he come shortly, I will see you" (He. 13:23). From the beginning of his ministry (cf. Acts 16:1-3) until Paul's death (cf. II Ti. 4:9, 11, 13, 19, 21), Timothy was a constant and faithful helper to Paul. Coffman questions, "Who but Paul, in all that ancient world, could have commanded the attendance of Timothy upon some projected journey."[41] Milligan adds, "Indeed, it seems quite probable that none but Paul would presume to speak for Timothy, as our author does in this case."[42]

The author had been in bonds (or prison). "For ye had compassion of me in my bonds" (He. 10:34). Paul could certainly qualify to have made this statement. According to Luke's record, Paul had been placed in bonds in Jerusalem (cf. Acts 22:25), and was transported as a prisoner to Caesarea (cf. Acts 23:23) where he remained bound for two years (cf. Acts 24:27). No person in the Biblical or historical record would better fit this situation and rely upon Timothy while in bonds than the apostle Paul. Furthermore, Paul was not only in bonds in Palestine, he was in bonds in Italy (cf. Acts 28:16).

The author was acquainted with Italian Christians. "They of Italy salute you" (He. 13:24). Some have suggested that this has reference to a group of Italians away from Italy sending greetings back to Italy.[43] However, the language employed can also have reference to people from all around Italy who are acquaintances of Paul's as a result of his Roman imprisonment. "And Paul dwelt two whole years in his own hired house, and received all that came in unto him" (Acts 28:30). Jews were the first to come to him (cf. Acts 28:17-24). It is evident that these Jews of Italy were able to communicate with the Hebrews of Jerusalem. Therefore, it would be perfectly natural for Paul to say, "They of Italy salute you."

An inspired witness speaks. Generally, it is agreed that II Peter was written to Jews. In that letter an interesting statement is made. "And account that the longsuffering of our Lord is salvation; even as our beloved brother Paul also according to the wisdom given unto him hath written unto you" (II Pe. 3:15). Peter said Paul had written a letter to the Jews. Where is that letter? There is only one possibility in all of the New Testament. It could be none other than the book of Hebrews.

When one considers all the internal evidence (this treatise just touches the hem of the garment) and adds to its weight all the external evidence, the scales are balanced to the point of proof. *Paul is the author of Hebrews!*

DATE OF WRITING

The critics who will not accept Paul as the author of Hebrews admit that there is no way they can date the book. Just as they guess at authors, they guess at dates. Fudge would not even guess at a date, but did say, "The date of this epistle is also uncertain."[44] Barclay says, "If we take the date as A.D. 80 we shall not be far wrong."[45] Pfeiffer really "pinpoints" the date, stating, ". . . it is probable that the Epistle to the Hebrews was written some time during the decade A.D. 60-70."[46]

Noting the historical context set forth in the book of Hebrews, many scholars place its date of writing somewhere in the A.D. 63-65 time frame. Barnes suggests A.D. 63.[47] Bruce estimates the date to be shortly before A.D. 64.[48] Lightfoot calculates the date to be A.D. 65.[49] These dates would appear to be very close to correct, if one of them is not correct. Hebrews reveals the Temple to still be standing and animal sacrifices still being offered upon the altar. Jerusalem has not yet been destroyed. Barnes notes,

> It was evidently written before the civil wars and commotions in Judea, which terminated in the destruction of the city and nation. This is clear because there are no allusions to any such disorders or troubles in Palestine.[50]

Along this line it can be pointed out that the persecutions under Nero did not begin until A.D. 64. It would seem likely that if such persecutions were happening the writer would have mentioned them. Thus, A.D. 63 seems the most likely date, especially when Paul is believed to be its author.

Ephesians, Philippians and Colossians (the "Prison Epistles") reveal Paul's expectation to be released from Roman imprisonment. Paul told the Philippian church of his desire to send Timothy to them (cf. Ph. 2:19). The phrase "set at liberty" (He. 13:23) is most commonly understood to mean that Timothy had been sent on an errand. That same verse seems to indicate that Paul was not free to travel. Milligan shared this view. He wrote:

> From Phil. i:21-26, and ii.24, we learn moreover, that while Paul was a prisoner at Rome, in A.D. 62, he fully expected to be delivered from its confinement, and to make another visit to Philippi. . . . And again, it seems probable from ch. xiii.23, of this Epistle, that when it was written, Paul was then actually at liberty; and that it was his purpose to visit Jerusalem very soon in company with Timothy. Putting these facts together, then, it seems most likely that the Epistle to the Hebrews was written at Rome, in A.D. 63, soon after Paul's first imprisonment.[51]

If one accepts Pauline authorship for Hebrews, it is not difficult to date the book. From these points of reason, A.D. 63 is the date that should be accepted for the writing of Hebrews.

THE ORIGINAL READERS

Some have concluded that the recipients of Hebrews were living in the city of Rome because of the phrase, "They of Italy salute you" (He. 13:24). Also, those of this persuasion point to the fact that the first known use of the book was by Clement of Rome. Needless to say, this theory is built on a shaky foundation. First, the interpretation of the verse in question is just as likely to mean that the writer was in Italy sending greetings out as it is to mean that he is outside of Italy with Italian friends sending in greetings. Second, a work of inspired literature could travel a long distance in 32 years. The best reason for rejecting the idea that the book of Hebrews was originally sent to Rome is the book itself.

The title gives a clue. While it is improbable that the writer placed the heading, *"The Epistle Of Paul The Apostle To The Hebrews,"* on the book, its title was placed on it at an early time. All of the ancient manuscripts carried the heading. And, when discussing the book, the early uninspired writers called it by its "Hebrews" title.

The first verse gives another clue. "God, who at sundry times and in divers manners spake unto the fathers by the prophets" (He. 1:1). Who can deny that "the fathers" here mentioned were the Hebrews of old? These were the fleshly ancestors of the writer and readers of Hebrews. Verse two reveals that while the readers are of Hebrew descent, they have converted to Christianity.

The entire book gives a mass of clues. Details of the Temple are discussed. Animal sacrifices and other specifics of the Law of Moses are brought forth by the writer in such a way that it is easily seen that he expected his readers to have intimate knowledge of the Old Testament, something not all Gentiles would have. Hebrews, from beginning to end, sets forth the superiority of Christianity over Judaism clearly for the purpose of preventing the Jewish converts from returning to Judaism. Everything about the book shows that it was originally intended for the Hebrews who were Christians.

The focal point of all the clues is a city. ". . . only in Jerusalem and Palestine could the Judaizing influences have been felt in sufficient force to provoke the need of such a book as Hebrews."[52] Hebrews stresses the matters of Temple worship, the various rituals, animal sacrifices, *things that happened only in Jerusalem.* Constantly before the Hebrew convert, these centuries-old practices would tempt him to return to Judaism.

Does the term "Hebrews" mean something in particular?

Professor Stuart has endeavored to show that this was a term that was employed exclusively to denote the *Jews in Palestine,* in contradistinction from foreign Jews, who were called *Hellenists.* . . . Bertholdt declares that there is not a single example which can be found in early times of Jewish Christians outside of Palestine being called Hebrews.[53]

Quoting Delitzsch, Milligan writes,

"No traces," says Delitzsch, "are found of the existence of any such purely Jewish churches in the Dispersion, as the recipients of this Epistle must have been; while the Church of Jerusalem actually bore the title, *The Church of the Hebrews.*"[54]

Sometimes it is argued that this view will not stand up because the book was written in Greek; however, one should remember that some of the ancients thought Hebrews had been written in Hebrew and then translated into Greek. There are numerous valid arguments for a book's being written in Greek and being sent to a "Hebrew" congregation, but time and space will not allow such a venture here. Do not just accept the charge that it would not or could not be done. Ask, "Why not?"

All trustworthy evidence, external and internal, leads to Jerusalem as being the book's destination. No place on earth needed the book of Hebrews more.

THE PURPOSE FOR WRITING

"And I beseech you, brethren, suffer the word of exhortation: for I have written a letter unto you in a few words" (He. 13:22). Hebrews was written for the purpose of encouraging the Jewish Christians in Jerusalem. Some of the Hebrews were not developing as they should in spiritual maturation (cf. He. 5:12-6:3). Some were even forsaking the assemblies (cf. He. 10:25). Evidently, there was a danger of a great multitude of the Hebrews' falling away.

They had been Christians for some time. Christ had not returned and they were growing impatient. To them Christianity was new — perhaps a failing system. Judaism was, to them, God-ordained and proven true by its centuries-long existence. Unconverted Jews still benefited from Judaism, but the Christian Jews were ridiculed and persecuted. The pull back to Judaism was strong.

> All the traditional power of the Hebrew religion, the social excellence of its priests, the liturgical richness of the impressive ceremonial, together with the reverence of the sacred Scriptures in their custody, and all the passionate patriotism which pertained to the old ways and concepts — all these things exerted persuasive influence over the community of Christians then struggling with manifold trials.[55]

Such was the Hebrews writer's reason for the book. To deal with such a problem effectively would demand an approach and a presentation no Jewish Christian could deny. The manner in which Paul deals with the problem at Jerusalem represents the crowning glory of all of his writings.

Paul wrote a Hebrew *midrash*, an exposition of the Old Testament scriptures themselves. He used the Old Testament to prove the superiority of the New Testament and to show how much greater Christianity is than Judaism ever was. A basic outline of Paul's arguments is as follows:

I. Christ is superior to the angels (He. 1:1-2:18).

II. Christ is superior to Moses, the Lawgiver (He. 3:1-4:13).

III. Christ is superior to the priests of the Tribe of Levi (He. 4:14-7:10).

IV. The new covenant is superior to the old covenant (He. 7:11-8:13).

V. Christ is a superior sacrifice, greater than animal sacrifices (He. 9:1-10:39).

VI. The blessings of Christianity are superior to the blessings of Judaism (He. 11:1-40).

VII. Christian faithfulness should be superior to faith under the law (He. 12:1-13:25).

CONCLUSION

Hebrews explains the reasons and meanings of the Old Testament forms and shadows as no other work does. It sets forth the magnificence of the Christian system in a clarity and glory no other work can match. Written by a "Hebrew of Hebrews" whose prayer to God was that Israel might be saved, Hebrews stands as his monumental work, an effort to keep his people saved.

ENDNOTES

1. William Barclay, *The Letter to the Hebrews* (Philadelphia: Westminster Press, 1976), p. 5.

2. Everett F. Harrison, *Introduction to the New Testament* (Grand Rapids: Eerdmans, 1971), p. 367.

3. Neil R. Lightfoot, *Jesus Christ Today* (Grand Rapids: Baker Book House, 1976), preface.

4. *Ibid.*

5. *Eusebius' Ecclesiastical History* (Grand Rapids: Baker Book House, 1971), p. 234.

6. F. F. Bruce, *The Epistle to the Hebrews* (Grand Rapids: Eerdmans, 1979), p. XXXVI.

7. Eusebius, *op. cit.,* pp. 246-247.

8. R. Milligan, *The New Testament Commentary on Hebrews* (Nashville: Gospel Advocate, 1968), vol. IX, p. 8.

9. Albert Barnes, *Notes On The New Testament: Hebrews* (Grand Rapids: Baker Book House, 1966), pp. 8-9.

10. Harrison, *op. cit.,* p. 374.

11. Thomas Hewitt, *The Epistle To The Hebrews* (Grand Rapids: Eerdmans, 1960), p. 14.

12. Lightfoot, *op. cit.,* p. 24.

13. T. Rees, "Hebrews, Epistle To The:" *The International Standard Bible Encyclopedia,* (Eerdmans, 1939), Vol. II, p. 1357.

14. *Ibid.*

15. Charles F. Pfeiffer, *The Epistle To The Hebrews* (Chicago: Moody Press, 1962), p. 7.

16. Bruce, *op. cit.,* p. XL.

17. Merrill C. Tenney, *New Testament Survey* (Grand Rapids: Eerdmans, 1963), p. 358.

18. Lightfoot, *op. cit.,* p. 26.

19. Geoffrey B. Wilson, *Hebrews* (Banner of Truth, 1979), p. 11.

20. Hewitt, *op. cit.*, p. 24.

21. Sir Robert Anderson, *Types In Hebrews* (Grand Rapids: Kregel Publications, 1978), p. 1.

22. Milligan, *op. cit.*, p. 5.

23. Pfeiffer, *loc. cit.*

24. Bruce, *op. cit.*, p. XXXV.

25. Wilson, *loc. cit.*,

26. Rees, *op. cit.*, p. 1357.

27. Barclay, *op. cit.*, p. 8.

28. Anderson, *op. cit.*, p. 2.

29. Harrison, *op. cit.*, p. 376.

30. Barnes, *op. cit.*, p. 12.

31. James Burton Coffman, *Commentary On Hebrews* (Austin: Firm Foundation, 1971), p. 5-6.

32. Rees, *op. cit.*, p. 1355.

33. Bruce, *op. cit.*, p. XLVIII.

34. Hewitt, *op. cit.*, p. 17.

35. Milligan, *op. cit.*, p. 14.

36. Hewitt, *op. cit.*, pp. 17-18.

37. Coffman, *op. cit.*, p. 3.

38. *Ibid.*

39. Anderson, *op. cit.*, p. 11.

40. Barnes, *op. cit.*, p. 11.

41. Coffman, *op. cit.*, p. 7.

42. Milligan, *op. cit.*, p. 6.

43. Rees, *op. cit.*, p. 1359.

44. Edward Fudge, *Our Man In Heaven* (Grand Rapids: Baker Book House, 1974), p. 11.

45. Barclay, *op. cit.*, p. 6.

46. Pfeiffer, *op. cit.*, p. 8.

47. Barnes, *op. cit.*, p. 14.

48. Bruce, *op. cit.*, p. XLIII.

49. Lightfoot, *op. cit.*, p. 35.

50. Barnes, *op. cit.*, p. 13.

51. Milligan, *op. cit.*, p. 39.

52. Coffman, *op. cit.*, p. 15.

53. Barnes, *op. cit.*, p. 5.

54. Milligan, *op. cit.*, p. 28.

55. Coffman, *op. cit.*, pp. 12-13.

THE LETTER TO THE HEBREWS
A SURVEY

By ROY DEAVER

Native of Longview, TX. Graduate of Freed-Hardeman and Abilene Christian Colleges. Holds several graduate degrees. Author of numerous books, tracts and articles in several gospel papers. Editor, *Biblical Notes*. Founding President, Fort Worth Christian College. Long-time director and instructor in Brown Trail Preacher Training School. Has preached 43 years. Experienced debater. Married to Wilma Gibson and they have three sons. Instructor, Tennessee Bible College, Cookeville, TN. Speaker, *First Annual Denton Lectures*.

INTRODUCTION

As a matter of habit in Bible study, I work with "Skeleton Outlines," with "Brief Outlines," and with "Expanded Outlines." I suggest the following as the "Skeleton Outline" for the book of Hebrews.

HEBREWS — SKELETON OUTLINE

Note: It should be kept in mind that wonderful exhortations are interwoven into the very fabric of the book of Hebrews. These exhortations sometime interrupt the flow of thought, interfere with our seeing the outline, but are directly related to the purpose of Hebrews, and they emphasize the practical applications of the points established.

Throughout the book there is the evidence that the Hebrew Christians were in danger of apostasy — in danger of going back to the Jewish system. Severe persecution, improper spiritual growth, the temple and temple worship, and the condition of Christianity would all be contributing factors related to this danger. The Holy Spirit wrote, therefore, to emphasize the superiority of Christianity over Judaism, with the objective of precluding apostasy.

Purpose: To emphasize the superiority of Christianity over Judaism, and thus to preclude apostasy.

Theme: The Way of Christ — the Better Way.

The writer argues that Christians have:

   I. The Better Medium (1:1-4:13);
  II. The Better High Priest (4:14-10:18);
 III. The Better Way, the Way of Faith (10:19-13:25).

HEBREWS — BRIEF OUTLINE

In preparing the "Brief Outline" we take the Roman Numeral headings of the "Skeleton Outline," and add to these headings the outline of the related textual material. We suggest the following as the "Brief Outline" for the book of Hebrews.

The writer stresses that Christians have:

I. The Better *Medium* (1:1-4:13) — that is,
  1. The Christ is a better *Revealer* (1:1-2:18), better than:
    (1) Prophets, and
    (2) Angels;
  2. He is a better *Mediator* (chapter 3) — better than *Moses*;
  3. He is a better *Rest-provider* (4:1-4:13) — better than *Joshua*;

II. The Better *High Priest* (4:14-10:18) — that is, The Christ is High Priest
  1. Of a better *Order* (4:14-7:10);
  2. Of a better *Covenant* (7:11-8:13);
  3. Of a better *Tabernacle* (9:1-9:12);
  4. Of a better *Sacrifice* (9:13-10:18);

III. The Better *Way* — the Way of *Faith* (10:19-13:25) — the writer:
  1. Gives an *exhortation* to faithfulness (10:19-10:39);
  2. Discusses *faith* — its meaning, its importance, its nature, and certain examples (chapter 11);

3. Sets forth the *fruits* of faith — endurance, peace, love, obedience, steadfastness, prayerfulness (chapters 12 and 13).

CHRISTIANS HAVE THE BETTER *MEDIUM*
(1:1-4:13)

Christians have the Christ, as the better *revealer*. The fact is that God has spoken. He *has* revealed himself to man. He spoke long ago, and he has spoken in these last days. Long ago, he spoke to men by means of his *prophets*. He spoke in various portions, and he spoke in many ways. He gave to fleshly Israel the Mosaic Law, and this he gave through *angels* (cf. Ga. 3:19; Acts 7:38, 53). But, his divine message for all men *now* has been given through (by means of) his *Son*. And, this Son is greater than angels, and greater than prophets.

The writer, in beautiful and marvelous detail, continues to stress the greatness and the authority and the power and the position and the deity of the Son. His greatness implies the greatness and the importance of the message which came through him. The writer emphasizes that because of who he is and what he is we had better *listen* to what he has to say: We ought — we must — give the more earnest heed to this sacred message. Our very salvation depends upon our giving heed. We must be careful — we must give earnest heed to this divine message — lest haply we drift away from the things spoken. This obligation is clearly seen in consideration of a previous message. There was a previous message. It, too, was given by God. It was delivered through *angels*. This was the Mosaic Law. This previous message "proved steadfast." With reference to *it*, every transgression and disobedience received its just recompense (its just punishment). If the previous message demanded punishment proportionate to (commensurate with) the transgression, then obviously the greater message would have even more fearful consequences in the event of one's failure to give heed to it. There shall be no escape from fearful consequences for those who neglect the divine message spoken through God's Son.

The writer continues to stress the superiority of the Son over angels. He emphasizes that it never was God's plan to subject "the world to come" to angels, but it *was* God's plan to subject "all things" to the Son. But, at the time of the writing, not all things had as yet been subjected unto him. The writer says, what we see *now* is this: "We behold him who has been made a little lower than the angels, even Jesus, because of suffering and death crowned with glory and honor, that by the grace of God he should taste of death for every man" (He. 2:9). It was God's plan that through Jesus Christ many "sons" could be brought to glory. This perfect plan for perfect salvation necessarily demanded a perfect author. The author of this salvation was made perfect through sufferings. There is a beautiful unity and closeness between the saved and the author of their salvation: they are *brethren;* they are *one.* ". . . for which cause he is not ashamed to call them brethren" (2:11). This is according to Old Testament prophecy. He took upon himself a fleshly nature (a human nature) that he might be like those in whose behalf he came, lived and died. We have the privilege (and the obligation) to become like him. He became like us so we could become like him! He, therefore, is in position to *help* his brethren — to guide, to strengthen, "to succor them that are tempted." "Wherefore it behoved him in all things to be made like unto his brethren, that he might become a merciful and faithful high priest in things pertaining to God, to make propitiation for the sins of the people" (2:17). He knows what it means to be a human being. He knows what it means to suffer. He knows what it means to be tempted. "For verily not to angels doth he give help, but he giveth help to the seed of Abraham" (2:16).

The Son is indeed the better *revealer:* better than prophets and better than angels. He is the better author (the perfect author) of the better plan, the better message. Furthermore, he is the better *mediator* — better than Moses. He is the Apostle and High Priest of our confession. He was faithful to him that appointed him, as was Moses. But, he — the Christ — has been counted worthy of more glory than Moses. Just as the one who builds a house has more glory than the house, so it is that the Christ has more honor (more glory) than Moses. Moses was a part of the "house," but the Lord was the *builder* of the house. Moses was faithful "*in* all God's house" as a *servant;* but the Christ is faithful *over* God's house, as a *Son.* Moses related to the *type,* but the Son relates to the anti-type — "whose house are we, if we hold fast our boldness and the glorying of our hope firm unto the end" (3:6). Those who constitute this house of God, over which is the Christ: (1) must be diligent to maintain God's favor; (2) must exhort one another day by day; (3) must hold fast . . . firm unto the end; (4) must be characterized by an obedient faith. In Judaism Moses was the *mediator* (cf. Ga. 3:19), but now this Son is the mediator between God and man (cf. 1 Ti. 2:5). The Christ is the better mediator — better than Moses.

Further, the Christ (the Son) is the better rest-provider. There is a beautiful and wonderful rest to be had *in* the Christ, in the *church* of the Christ, upon the terms of the *gospel* of the Christ. "For we who have believed do enter into that rest . . ." (4:3). It is certainly true that God, through *Joshua,* gave Old Testament fleshly Israel rest in Canaan. But, that Canaan rest was but a *type* of the rest to be had *in* the Christ, and of the *final* rest — the heavenly rest. A long time after "Joshua had given them rest" David was still speaking of a rest to come: "There remaineth therefore a sabbath rest for the people of God." David spake of the rest to be had *in* the Christ and of the *heavenly* rest. Clearly, the Son is a better rest-provider — better than Joshua.

CHRISTIANS HAVE A BETTER *HIGH PRIEST* (4:14-10:18)

Christians have a great high priest. He has passed through the heavens. He is Jesus, the Son of God. He can be touched with the feeling of our infirmities. He has been in all points tempted like as we are, yet without sin. We can with boldness draw near to his throne of grace, and we can expect to receive mercy, and to find grace to help us in time of need (4:14-16).

He is High Priest after a better *order.* This point is stressed in 4:14 through 7:10. God who said "Thou art my Son; This day have I begotten thee" (Ps. 2:7), also said "Thou art a priest for ever after the order of Melchizedek" (Ps. 110:4). Having offered up prayers and supplications, and having been heard for his godly fear, and having been made perfect, and having been named of God *a high priest after the order of Melchizedek,* he became the author of eternal salvation to all them that obey him (5:7-10). The gospel plan enables us to have wonderful *hope,* ". . . which we have as an anchor of the soul, a hope both sure and stedfast and entering into that which is within the veil; whither as a forerunner Jesus entered for us, having become a high priest for ever after the order of Melchizedek" (6:19-20).

Melchizedek was *king* and *priest* at the same time. The greatness of Melchizedek is implied in the fact that to him Abraham paid tithes. Melchizedek's kingly and priestly genealogy cannot be traced — we know nothing of his ancestry. Further, ". . . through Abraham even Levi, who received tithes, hath paid tithes; for he was yet in the loins of his father, when Melchizedek met him" (7:9-10). Likewise, the Christ is Priest and King at the same time. He is greater than the Old Testament priests of the tribe of Levi. As there was no other priest-king like Melchizedek, so it is that there is no other Priest-King like the Christ. The Christ is High Priest after a better *order*.

The Christ is a High Priest after a better *Covenant*. This point is stressed in 7:11 through 8:13. "For the priesthood being changed, there is made of necessity a change also of the law" (7:12). The Lord could not possibly be a priest according to the Levitical system, for he came from the tribe of Judah, not from the tribe of Levi (7:13-14). The law made nothing perfect (7:19). There had to be a change. Jesus became the surety of a *better covenant* (7:22). "Wherefore also he is able to save to the uttermost them that draw near unto God through him, seeing he ever liveth to make intercession for them" (7:25).

Our High Priest is holy, guileless, undefiled, separated from sinners, and made higher than the heavens (7:26). He ". . . needeth not daily, like those high priests, to offer up sacrifices, first for his own sins, and then for the sins of the people: for this he did once for all, when he offered up himself" (7:27). ". . . the word of the oath, which was after the law, appointeth a Son, perfected for evermore" (7:28).

Our High Priest is ". . . a minister of the sanctuary, and of the true tabernacle, which the Lord pitched, not man" (8:2). He is not an earthly priest, and ". . . if he were on earth, he would not be a priest at all . . ." (8:4). "But now hath he obtained a ministry the more excellent, by so much as he is also the mediator of a better covenant, which hath been enacted upon better promises" (8:6), all according to God's prophecy through Jeremiah (chapter 31).

The Christ is High Priest of a better *tabernacle*. This point is stressed in 9:1 through 9:12. The Old Testament tabernacle was a *type* of the true tabernacle — the church of our Lord. It was "a figure for the time present" (9:9). Its priesthood and gifts and sacrifices could not "make the worshipper perfect" — could not forgive sins. It was "imposed until a time of reformation" (9:10). But the Christ,

> having come a high priest of the good things to come, through the *greater and more perfect tabernacle,* not made with hands, that is to say, not of this creation, nor yet through the blood of goats and calves, but through his own blood, entered in once for all into the holy place, having obtained eternal redemption (9:11-12).

The Christ is High Priest of a better *sacrifice*. This point is emphasized in 9:13 through 10:18:

> For if the blood of goats and bulls, and the ashes of a heifer sprinkling them that have been defiled, sanctify unto the cleanness of the flesh: how much more shall the blood of Christ, who through the eternal Spirit offered himself without blemish unto God, cleanse your conscience from dead works to serve the living God? And for this cause he is the mediator of a new covenant, that a death having taken place for the redemption of the transgressions that were under the first covenant, they that have been called may receive the promise of the eternal inheritance. For where a testament is, there must of necessity be the death of him that made it. For a testament is of force where there hath been death: for it doth never avail while he that made it liveth (9:13-17).
>
> It was necessary therefore that the copies of the things in the heavens should be cleansed with these; but the heavenly things themselves with better sacrifices than these. For Christ entered not into a holy place made with hands, like in pattern to the true; but into heaven itself, now to appear before the face of God for us; . . . but now once at the end of the ages hath he been manifested to put away sin by the sacrifice of himself (9:23-26).

There were the animal sacrifices made under the Mosaic system (and under the pre-Mosaic system), but these sacrifices did not and could not take away sin, "For it is impossible that the blood of bulls and goats should take away sins" (10:4). Therefore, there had to be the Lord's sacrifice of himself. "He taketh away the first, that he may establish the second. By which will we have been sanctified through the offering of the body of Jesus Christ once for all" (10:9-10).

. . . but he, when he had offered one sacrifice for sins for ever, sat
down on the right hand of God; henceforth expecting till his enemies
be made the footstool of his feet. For by one offering he hath perfected for ever them that are sanctified (10:12-14).

"Now where remission of these is, there is no more offering for
sin" (10:18). The Christ is High Priest of a *better sacrifice*.

CHRISTIANS HAVE THE BETTER *WAY* — THE WAY OF *FAITH* (10:19-13:25)

The way of the Christ, the way of the New Covenant, the
way of the new priesthood, is the better *way*. The better way is
the way of faith. This is the point stressed in 10:19 through
13:25 (the end of the book).

In 10:19-10:39 the writer exhorts those addressed to be
faithful. He says that because we have boldness, and because
we have this great priest over the house of God, let us: (1) draw
near, (2) hold fast, and (3) consider one another. In this connection, the writer stresses the importance of assemblies of exhortation — they are not to be forsaken. The writer discusses
the seriousness of willful sin, and sets forth a vivid description
of the fully-developed apostate. The writer refers to their
coming to know the gospel, their endurance, their sufferings,
their concern about others, their marvelous hope. He says,
"Cast not away therefore your boldness, which hath great
recompense of reward. For ye have need of patience, that,
having done the will of God, ye may receive the promise"
(10:35-36). The writer closes this section by saying: "But we
are not of them that shrink back unto perdition; but of them
that have faith unto the saving of the soul" (10:39).

In chapter eleven we have a beautiful and an amazing discussion of faith. The writer considers the *meaning* of faith,
refers to faith characteristic of *men of old*, and mentions
something about the *value* of faith. He stresses the *essential-
ity* of faith. He sets forth certain tremendous *examples* of
availing faith: the faith of Abel, Enoch, Noah, Abraham, Isaac,
Jacob, Sarah, Joseph, Moses, Israel, Rahab, Gideon, Barak,
Samson, Jephthah, David, Samuel, the prophets and countless
others "of whom the world was not worthy."

Then, in chapters 12 and 13 the writer considers the *fruits* of faith. We list these as follows: endurance, holiness, righteousness, peace, sanctification, and blessings, privileges and responsibilities of being members of the Lord's church (the kingdom that cannot be shaken) — brotherly love, compassion, respect for the elders of the churches, respect and love for the truth, praise, prayerfulness, perfection in every good thing and obedience. These are the marvelous fruits of faith (demanded and made possible by *the faith*).

CONCLUSION

Clearly it is the case that Christians have the better way. We have: (1) the better revealer, (2) the better mediator, (3) the better rest-provider, (4) the better rest, (5) the better High Priest, (6) the better covenant, (7) the better tabernacle, (8) the better sacrifice, (9) the better promises, (10) the better way — the way of faith, (11) the better life, (12) the better hope.

For early Jewish Christians to forsake the gospel and try to go back to the Mosaic system — to Judaism — would be for them to forsake the superior and attempt to return the the inferior.

Wherefore seeing we also are compassed about with so great a cloud of witnesses, let us lay aside every weight, and the sin which doth so easily beset us, and let us run with patience (stedfastness —ASV margin) the race that is set before us, Looking unto Jesus the author and finisher (perfecter—ASV) of our faith; who for the joy that was set before him endured the cross, despising the shame, and is set down at the right hand of the throne of God (12:1-2).

WHERE THE SCRIPTURES ARE SILENT WE MUST BE SILENT

HEBREWS 1:5, 13; 7:13-14

By GOEBEL MUSIC

Began Preaching in 1951, Taylor, Oklahoma. Holds degrees from Abilene Christian College and Vanderbilt University and has done additional study at Texas Tech, Peabody and Scarritt. Has served local churches in Texas and Arkansas. Author of two books and writes for several papers. Has conducted one debate. Directed Texas Tech Bible Chair 1956-58. Married to June Brownrigg in 1953 and they have four children. Speaker, *First Annual Denton Lectures.*

INTRODUCTION

It was an honor and privilege to be on your first Annual Denton Lectures last November, therefore, I am doubly honored to be on this, your second such effort. I believe our study on I Corinthians will, down through the years, perhaps be one of the finest of such books to be published. Indeed, it, too, was a book "Whose Time Had Come."

Our study of the book of Hebrews this year ought to be equally as great. I say this only because of the subject matter assigned, the men to whom they were given and the very fine team here at Pearl Street (the elders and brother Dub McClish) that has so carefully and precisely outlined this lectureship program. Of course, to God be the glory for such a study and for the internalization of this portion of the World's Most Marvelous Book, The Bible!

Indeed, the entire church at Pearl is to be highly compli-
mented on undertaking such an outstanding endeavor. Only
when local churches "study the Book," and that "in depth,"
will we have the type and kind that the Lord would desire us to
both have and be. To the end of showing ourselves approved
unto God (II Ti. 2:15), walking worthily of our calling (Ep. 4:1),
letting our manner of life be worthy of the gospel (Ph. 1:27) and
taking heed to ourselves and our teaching for salvation's sake
(I Ti. 4:16), do we come now to our study entitled "Where The
Scriptures Are Silent We Must Be Silent." Yes, we truly thank
God for Pearl Street and her religious backing of and commitment to such a tremendously important Biblical principle.

IMPORTANCE OF THIS SUBJECT

We need to give our utmost attention to this subject because of the nature and magnitude of the study. It is an extremely vital one and it is paramount that we understand that
with which we are dealing. In the fourth issue of *The Restorer*,
Gary Workman had this to say:

> People everywhere are in need of either an introduction or a remind-
> er as to how to deal with what has often been called "the silence of
> the scriptures." It is a failure to understand and respect such
> "silence" that is causing some erroneous deviations that are now
> creeping into the worship and work of many congregations. But this
> is not something new. It was this very same failure and lack of re-
> spect that caused musical instruments to be introduced into the
> worship in 1860 and ultimately to a massive split in the church.
> Those with the lax attitude formed what became known as the
> Disciples of Christ or Christian Church, the main body of which has
> now in recent times completely renounced the concept of New Testa-
> ment Christianity and voted itself into full-fledged denominational
> status. Such is the inevitable result of failing to respect the
> "silence" of the scriptures.[1]

Concerning our influence in this area, I want to share with
you the appraisal of what another said about us:

> Within the last generation, the Church of Christ has made a phe-
> nomenal growth. This is due to two things: (1) Its people have stood
> like the Rock of Gibralter for "the faith which was once delivered
> unto the saints," amid the doubt and confusion superinduced by
> liberalism. They have challenged the spirit of compromise and
> worldliness and dared to be a "peculiar" people teaching and prac-

ticing what they believe is the Bible way of life. (2) They have come to realize that the silence of the Scriptures must be respected as well as the commandments of Scripture, but that obedience to its silence permits freedom of judgment and action.[2]

All of us perhaps understand that the Bible prohibits by explicit prohibition. However, that is not the only way the Bible prohibits. Two terms ought to be familiar to us: (1) Explicit, which simply means "God says it," and (2) Implicit, which means "it is implied." Sometimes God uses a very explicit "thou shalt not" (Ro. 13:8-9; e.g.), but the Bible also restricts otherwise. In other words, the Bible does not have to say "thou shalt not" for a thing to be rejected. If it were otherwise, then the Bible would have to be as big as the world. This you will come to understand as we progress through this subject, as "the law of exclusion" (when God specifies a certain thing it excludes all other types of that item, e.g. gopher wood excluded oak, and vocal music excluded instrumental) will be clearly set forth. No place could this be better shown than in Genesis 6:14-22 or Leviticus 10:1-2, as they did not violate a stated prohibition but simply did not respect what it excluded, the silence of the statement. In simpler words you will come to appreciate and understand "When God says what a thing is, he does not have to say what it isn't."

This subject played a very significant part in the Restoration Movement. There was a motto used with which you are familiar, and it went something like this: "Let us call Bible things by Bible names, and let us do Bible things in Bible ways . . . Let us speak where the Bible speaks, and be silent where it is silent." Relative to this last statement, "be silent where the Bible is silent," there became a group within the Restoration Movement unhappy with it, therefore, a very serious division came about. However, a segment of the Restoration Movement maintained loyalty and dedication to the emphasis, "Let us speak where the Bible speaks and be silent where it is silent." Those unhappy with this taught that where the Bible is silent we are free to act, and thus we soon had the Missionary Society and instrumental music. They said that where we do not have a strict "thou shalt not" prohibition, then we are free to act.

It is interesting to observe that this matter of the authority of the Scriptures relative to respecting the silence of the Scriptures played an important role long before the Restoration Movement. Ulrich Zwingli who lived from 1484-1531 made a distinct contribution to the Reformation Movement (ultimately to the Restoration Movement). He was committed to the principle of having Bible authority for what we do in religion. In fact, the difference between Zwingli and Luther was on this very point. Luther thought you could have in religious practices that for which there was no strict prohibition. Of Zwingli we read: "He devoutly believed in the absolute authority of the Scriptures, affirming that what they did not expressly authorize is forbidden in worship."[3]

We do not have to go back to these movements to find men speaking out on this subject. One of the great guardians of the faith, during my lifetime, was our beloved Gus Nichols. In 1969, during the Forth Worth Christian College Lectureship, he said: "When a church brings in one single thing which is not authorized by the scriptures — and this means now the scriptures of the New Testament — it has opened the flood gate for complete apostasy."[4] Also, it was David Lipscomb who said that the New Testament is at once the rule and limit of our faith and worship to God. He went on to state the difference between us and others when he spoke of the distinction made between the idea of its being the rule but not the "limit" of their faith. In other words, we seek for things authorized and they seek for things not prohibited. I want us to observe what these are saying and that is simply that the safe ground is "what has God authorized."

ESTABLISHING THE PRINCIPLE OF RESPECT
FOR THE SILENCE OF THE WORD

"And whatsoever ye do, in word or in deed, do all in the name of the Lord Jesus, giving thanks to God the Father through him" (Col. 3:17). This verse says that regardless of our teaching or practice, it must come under the shelter of "doing all in the name of the Lord Jesus." "In the name of," means "by the authority of" and this is easily proven by Acts 4:7-10. Just as "in the name of the law" refers to the authority vested in a person as an instrument the law, so "in the name of

Jesus" refers to "the authority of Jesus." In Matthew 28:18 the Lord said, ". . . All authority hath been given unto me in heaven and on earth," therefore, all authority resides in him. In our government today we have various kinds of authority, executive (President), legislative (Congress) and judicial (Supreme Court). The Supreme Court's authority does not invade that of Congress nor does that of Congress invade the executive branch. But in the matter of the Bible, Christ has "all authority." He has the power to legislate, execute and judge, as the *King James* says, "All power is given unto me." Indeed, all authority abides and resides in the Christ of God, his chosen!

The authoritative Word, the New Testament, is that means by which his authority is executed today. This is easily seen by a host of verses, such as Jude 3; II Ti. 3:16-17; John 14:26; 16:13; Ga. 1:6-9; etc. Now in a study of the New Testament, we come to realize how the Word authorizes. I list four of various ways:

By An Explicit Statement. "And Peter said unto them, Repent ye, and be baptized every one of you in the name of Jesus Christ unto the remission of your sins; and ye shall receive the gift of the Holy Spirit" (Acts 2:38). Now here is an example of an explicit, direct, statement. If we respect the authority of Christ, as exercised through his word, we will do just as it says.

By An Implicit Statement. "He that believeth and is baptized shall be saved; but he that disbelieveth shall be condemned" (Mark 16:16). You see, you and I have been baptized by an implicit statement. No where did God ever say, "Goebel Music, you believe and be baptized . . ." The Bible does say, "He that believeth and is baptized . . ." It is implied that Goebel Music is part of the "he" in that verse! Yes, indeed, we baptize by implication. Everything the Bible teaches it does so either explicitly or implicitly. We teach the truth when we say that Lot went down into Egypt, although the Bible never states this specifically (cf. Ge. 13:1).

When geometry sets forth explicitly the axiom that the "whole of anything is the sum of its parts," then geometry sets forth implicitly that the whole of anything is larger than any of its parts, and that the part of anything is smaller than the whole to which it relates. And, that which is here taught implicitly is just as true as is that which is taught explicitly. Just so with the Word of God.[5]

By Expediency. In the great commission the Lord said: ". . . Go ye therefore, and make disciples of all the nations, baptizing them into the name of the Father and of the Son and of the Holy Spirit: teaching them . . ." (Ma. 28:19-20). I am explicitly commanded to "go," and implied in this word is a method or means I must employ. In this realm, I am left free to choose the method of going that would expedite the command. I choose to drive to Denton, as for me this was the most expedient method of traveling here for the lectureship. The same could be said about the generic word, "teach."

By An Approved Example. "And upon the first day of the week, when we were gathered together to break bread, Paul discoursed with them, intending to depart on the morrow; and prolonged his speech until midnight" (Acts 20:7). Here we have an approved happening, event or action, which, of course, is a large subject within itself, but the Word does authorize by the same.

We, therefore, have Bible authority in these four particular ways. Now, this being true, if we do that in religion for which we do not have at least one of the ways establishing Bible authority, then we do that thing "without Bible authority." We must ". . . walk by faith . . ." (II Co. 5:7) and that by which we must walk comes by hearing ". . . the word of Christ" (Ro. 10:17). If I cannot find an item in the word of God, then I cannot do it by faith and it takes that to be "well-pleasing" unto God (He. 11:6). Unless people respect the "silence" of the Scriptures, they will be exercising themselves without Biblical authority. To further emphasize this, let us note several specific passages on this very idea:

And Balaam answered and said unto the servants of Balak, If Balak would give me his house full of silver and gold, *I cannot go beyond the word of Jehovah my God, to do less or more* (Nu. 22:18, emphasis mine, GM).

"And Micaiah said, As Jehovah liveth, *what* Jehovah saith unto me, *that* will I speak" (I Ki. 22:14). Note the "what" is the "that," as this is respecting the silence of the Scriptures.

Now these things, brethren, I have in a figure transferred to myself and Apollos for your sakes; that in us ye might learn *not to go beyond the things which are written;* that no one of you be puffed up for the one against the other (I Co. 4:6, emphasis mine, GM).

Whosoever goeth onward and abideth not in the teaching of Christ, hath not God: he that abideth in the teaching, the same hath both the Father and the Son. If any one cometh unto you, and bringeth not this teaching, receive him not into your house, and give him no greeting: for he that giveth him greeting partaketh in his evil works (II John 9-11).

In Acts 15:7-9, we find how the early church, being bothered by circumcision, handled the situation. This is found in verse 24: "Forasmuch as we have heard that certain who went out from us have troubled you with words, subverting your souls; *to whom we gave no commandment"* (emphasis mine, GM). At one time God did command circumcision, but now under the new covenant he had not given any such legislation. Since there is no such legislation, the "silence of the Scriptures" must be respected.

In Hebrews 1:5, 13, we have the supremacy of Christ over Moses being introduced. Here in chapter one he addresses himself to the matter by showing that Christ was superior to the angels. The Jews had respect for angels and they even played a part in the giving of the law (Ga. 3:19). However, he speaks of Christ and says, "For unto which of the angels said he at any time, Thou art my Son, This day have I begotten thee?" and ". . . sit thou on my right hand, Till I make thine enemies the footstool of thy feet?" The author argued from the silence of God the supremacy of Christ.

In Hebrews 7:13-14, still discussing the supremacy of the Christian system over the old Mosaic system and now dealing with the Melchizedek priesthood's being superior to that of the Levitical (Aaronic system) one, he says:

For he of whom these things are said belongeth to another tribe, from which no man hath given attendance at the altar. For it is evident that our Lord hath sprung out of Judah; as to which tribe Moses spake nothing concerning priests.

He builds his argument upon the silence of the Scriptures. The kings came from Judah; the priests from Levi. He builds his argument of the supremacy of the Melchizedek priesthood upon the silence of the Scriptures.

ILLUSTRATING THAT THE SILENCE OF THE
SCRIPTURES MUST BE RESPECTED

I suppose there are a thousand ways a man might illustrate this, but everyone can surely appreciate and comprehend this illustration, especially since we are living in the days of "fast food service." Suppose I go down to one of these places and tell the lady that I want a hamburger with lettuce, tomatoes and mustard on it. The girl brings it out, I take a big bite but something is strange. I open it up and find out it has sauerkraut on it! I call the waitress and tell her she made a mistake. She said, "No, sir, I did not make a mistake." I said, "Lady, I ordered a hamburger with lettuce, tomatoes and mustard, and it has sauerkraut on it." She replies: Sir, you did not tell me not to put sauerkraut on it." If we do not respect the silence, then I would not have a "leg" to stand on in this. She could put anything in the world she desired on my hamburger and I could not do anything about it, not even reject it. Then, too, I would have to name every single item for her "not to put on it" and if I omitted one, she could have the freedom to put that one on it. Now I just believe that any one can see that, and the fellow who rejects the "silence" of the Word will support me on this point, that is, argue against the waitress. Why cannot we see this Biblically?

Now then, let us approach it from a Biblical viewpoint. In Leviticus 10:1-2 we have the story of Nadab and Abihu

> the sons of Aaron, who took each of them his censer, and put fire therein, and laid incense thereon, and offered strange fire before Jehovah, *which he had not commanded them* (emphasis mine, GM).

They did not respect the silence of God in this matter. They did that for which they had no divine authority, as God had not authorized such fire. They offered that which he "commanded not." The silence of the Scriptures is so strong here that they speak of it in terms of "which he had not commanded them." Their terrible state is related to us in verse two.

In Hebrews 11:7 we find that Noah "prepared an ark." Now remember that ". . . faith cometh by hearing" and that of "the word of Christ" (Ro. 10:17). According to the precise form that God had mentioned, thus he did (Ge. 6:22). However, what would have been wrong had he built it 800 cubits long? Would that have been a violation? Where did God ever say "thou shalt not build it 800 cubits long?" God did not say that. You cannot find it in the Biblical record. But God did tell him how long to build it. The divine instruction was "300 cubits." This is specific, not generic, and God's silence had to be respected. Furthermore, it was to be built out of "gopher wood" (complete text is Ge. 6:14-22). What would have been wrong had Noah wanted to use a little oak or a little pine? The thing wrong is that God did not authorize oak or pine. When God said "gopher wood" that in no way at all authorized anything else, and yet, God never did give a strict prohibition, "thou shalt not use oak or pine." But Noah did what? He did ". . . according to all that God commanded him, so did he" (Ge. 6:22b).

Perhaps one of the clearest ways to illustrate that the silence of the Scriptures must be respected is to read again of David and the ark of God as revealed to us in I Chronicles 13-15. Space does not permit this entire account to be given (chapter 13-15), but we do want to note that they carried the ark of God "upon a new cart" (13:7) and in this connection Uzza died. The ark was carried to the house of Obededom and remained there for three months. Soon David was anointed king over all Israel (14:8) and he "prepared a place for the ark of God" (15:1). Now then let us notice the following:

> And David called for Zadok and Abiathar the priests, and for the Levites, for Uriel, Asaiah, and Joel, Shemaiah, and Eliel, and Amminadab, and said unto them, Ye are the heads of the fathers' houses of the Levites: sanctify yourselves, both ye and your brethren, that ye may bring up the ark of Jehovah, the God of Israel, unto the place that I have prepared for it. For *because ye bare it not at the first, Jehovah our God made a breach upon us, for that we sought him not according to the ordinance.* So the priests and the Levites sanctified themselves to bring up the ark of Jehovah, the God of Israel. *And the children of the Levites bare the ark of God upon their shoulders* with the staves thereon, as Moses commanded according to the word of Jehovah (I Ch. 15:11-15, emphasis mine, GM).

This brief story about the ark of God and what is therein given for our admonition, should help to instruct us in the magnitude of this study. If we intend to save the church from apostasy, we had best get back to serving our God "after the due order" (*King James* of verse 13). God made a breach on these people because they did not seek him after the "due order" (according to the ordinance). Just what was this breach that God made upon them? Why? David made a "new cart" and they carried the ark of God upon it and while doing this the oxen stumbled and this is when Uzza put forth his hand to hold the ark and was smitten dead. What could possibly be wrong with David's making a "new cart" upon which the ark could be carried? Where did God ever give a prohibition against building a cart for it? The fact is that God never did. The problem is that they did not respect the silence of the revelation of God. One can read in Numbers 4:15 the following:

> And when Aaron and his sons have made an end of covering the sanctuary, . . . as the camp is to set forward; after that, the sons of Kohath shall come to bear it: but they shall not touch the sanctuary, lest they die.

One can easily see that this matter of "not seeking God after due order" becomes a very serious item. Therefore, it is extremely important that we do "according to the Word of God."

APPLYING THE PRINCIPLE OF RESPECTING SCRIPTURAL SILENCE

There are several major areas in which this principle could be applied, but I want to mention just three.

The Plan Of Salvation. Several years ago when I met the so-called Reverend Bob Harrington in a debate in Tennessee, he tried to force me about some men's being baptized in "sand." His case was one of emotionalism, sentiment and their last chance before being "killed" in war. However, regardless of the so-called emergency "circumstance," I would never baptize anyone in "sand." The reason is simple. I have no authority for doing that. God instructed us as to the element to be used in baptism and it is "water." "Can any man forbid water, that these should not be baptized, who have received the Holy Spirit as well as we" (Acts 10:47)? God legislated the element. No, God never did say, "Thou shalt not baptize in sand." But when God says what a thing is, he does not have to say what it is not!

Now the same idea could be applied to the matter of the so-called "infant baptism." Suppose a couple come up and describe, what is to them the most beautiful dedication service they have ever seen, and then they say, "We've been thinking about this in relation to our baby and have decided that we would like to have him baptized. We believe it would be a great thing for him and it would sort of mold our family in our religious beliefs. I know this is not common with you and I know that you always immerse adults, but would you please baptize our baby?" Do you want to know something? I would never baptize (?) their baby. They perhaps might say, "Well, where did God ever say 'Thou shalt not baptize babies?' " God never did say that. It is not in the Bible. However, God's Word legislates who is to be baptized and that must be respected. So must the silence be relative to the statement. ". . . And many of the Corinthians hearing believed, and were baptized" (Acts 18:8). Those old enough to hear (as faith comes from hearing, Ro. 10:17) and believe are those of this passage who can be baptized. Much, much more could be said on this subject, but this is enough to let all men see that the silence of the Scriptures must be respected.

The Worship Of God. How many times have we talked to people and they always bring up the thought of "instruments of music" in our worship to God. And they always say, "Well, where did God say we cannot have them?" "Where did God ever say 'Thou shalt not use mechanical instruments of music in worship?' " Of course, the legislation of God against such in explicit terms is not there. No where did God ever say, "Thou shalt not play a mechanical instrument of music in worship." In fact, God did not even say "make music," as that would have been "generic" and that would have included the instruments. God did authorize us to "sing." "Speaking one to another in psalms and hymns and spiritual songs, singing and making melody with your heart to the Lord" (Ep. 5:19). Now I need to see the principle clearly. God did not authorize pine in the construction of the Ark, therefore, Noah could not use it. Noah could only use what God authorized. I just believe anyone who wants to can see this point. Noah could only use gopher wood, as that was what God required. Noah respected the "silence" of the instruction of God. Today we sing because that is what God authorizes. We do not play because we respect the silence of God's authority.

Now this same thing could be discussed in relation to the Lord's Supper. Many times I have been asked, "Goebel, why don't you partake of the Supper on Thursday (certain ones out of the year) night?" Sometimes I have heard the answer, "Because the Bible speaks of its being done on the first day of the week" (Acts 20:7). However, I personally do not think that argument is as strong as it ought to be. Why? Simply because an example does not exclude. Paul traveled in his missionary work by ship, but that did not exclude his going on foot or by donkey. The very simple reason as to why we do not partake of the Lord's Supper on Thursdays is that we do not have any authority for so doing!

Many other areas could be covered just here, but this is perhaps sufficient to let us see the necessity of respecting the silence of the Scriptures.

The Christian Life. I heard brother Hugo McCord make reference about two or three years ago to a lesson he said he heard "up north" that was given by Wendell Winkler. He mentioned this particular subject with reference to the Spiritual Sword Lectureship and the lecture he was delivering. This was the genesis of some thoughts on it in relation to our present day problems of marriage, divorce and remarriage. Let me now share with you my findings.

In the book of Romans (7:1-4), we find that man and woman are married to one another until death. Then in Matthew 19:3-9 we find the Lord's giving the one exception to this rule and that is fornication. This tells us that the Bible authorizes the right of a person who has put away, on the ground of fornication, to contract a second marriage. I believe that the majority, if not all, in our great brotherhood believe and teach this. There seemingly is no problem here. However, there is a problem with the "put away" person's marrying again, as some are now teaching that the guilty party can remarry. I do not believe this and it seems that here is a principle of thought that has been perhaps overlooked relative to this paramount subject of marriage, divorce and remarriage. Why cannot he remarry? The answer is simple. God never gave to man any such authorization! Where is the passage that says he can? I submit to you that this thought alone, if truly we would respect the silence of the Scriptures here as we do on all these other subjects, would kill, embalm and bury such a false teaching! We need to do in this area what was spoken of in I Chronicles 15, and that is to seek God "after the due order."

CONCLUSION

"In those days there was no king in Israel: every man did that which was right in his own eyes" (Ju. 17:6; cf. 21:25). If there were no king, then this would and could be our situation, that is, "every man would be doing that which is right in his own eyes." However, we today do have a king, therefore, we must do that which is right. If we fail to respect the silence of the Scriptures, then the passage that says we have a king is useless (Acts 17:7). Not only do we have a king, but we also have a law (I Co. 9:21). We must abide by what the law says, not by what it does not say.

> We must realize two things: (1) Any statement that involves an obligation must be treated as a command, and (2) Implicit commands are just as authoritative and binding as explicit ones! In any positive command or statement, there is an implied opposite — an implicit negative command. As we read the positive, we draw an inference or make a deduction which leads to a conclusion about the negative. If we have correctly understood the positive statement, the inferred negative conclusion is decisive and inescapable. Therefore, do not begin by asking, "Where does the Bible say we can't do it?" First, see if it is excluded by what is specified. And if it is, respect the silence of the scriptures!"[6]

ENDNOTES

1. Gary Workman, "The 'Silence' of the Scriptures," *The Restorer* (Rowlett, Texas, 1981), Vol. 1, No. 4.

2. James DeForest Murch, *Christians Only* (Cincinnati, Ohio: Standard Publishing Company, 1962), p. 313.

3. Waymon Miller, *Survey of Church History* (Tulsa, Oklahoma: Plaza Press, 1959), p. 29.

4. Foy Kirkpatrick, "The Christian and Authority," *Fort Worth Christian College Tenth Annual Lectures* (Fort Worth, Texas, 1969), p. 248.

5. Roy Deaver, *Ascertaining Bible Authority* (Garland, Texas: Biblical Publishing Corp., 1977), pp. 16-17.

6. Workman, *op. cit.*

LEST HAPLY WE DRIFT AWAY

HEBREWS 2:1

By LARRY FLUITT

Born 1936 in Burnet, Texas; baptized at age 11. Married Linda Bradford in 1958 and they have two sons. Attended Abilene Christian University, the University of Texas at Austin, and North Texas State University. Began preaching in 1959 and served as local evangelist for churches in Mason, Decatur, Keller, and since 1968 the Lamar Street church in Sweetwater, Texas. Talented writer. Experienced radio preacher.

INTRODUCTION

Ours is a perilous world. We are surrounded by dangers of various kinds and degrees. Incurable diseases, nuclear accidents, raging storms and lawless men are only some of the forces that threaten us with suffering or death at any moment. Because of these, many are now living on the brink, if not in the throes, of paranoia. The Christian is not shielded from these dangers simply because he is a child of God. Jesus said, "In the world ye shall have tribulation . . ." (John 16:33).

The dangers that encircle the Christian are not all physical in their nature. The most to be feared are those that threaten the spirit. There is the danger of arrogantly renouncing one's faith in God! Some have lost their faith completely and embraced godless athiesm. Then there is the possibility of the Christian suddenly plunging into a life of gross immorality. Perhaps you know someone today who has done this very thing. However, I do not believe these pose the most serious threat to the child of God. Rather, it is my conviction that the greatest danger facing the church today is that of drifting slowly, almost imperceptibly, away from the moral and spiritual principles that have their roots in the Word of God, and have in every generation enabled Christ's church to shine

56

as a beacon in a world of darkness. It is the danger of becoming ever more like the world about us.

This matter of drifting is not a phenomenon about which we are ignorant. It is observed every day in society. Somewhere at this moment a man sits alone, staring at a half-empty bottle, shaking uncontrollably as he struggles to resist another drink. And he will fail—again! He didn't become an alcoholic deliberately, or even quickly. He began as a "social drinker." But day by day he continued to drink until he acquired an addiction that has destroyed him socially, economically, physically and, if continued, spiritually! Somewhere today a man and woman sit in the office of a lawyer, finalizing details of a divorce that years before neither would have believed possible. It was not infidelity that brought their marriage crashing down, nor cruelty on the part of either. They simply grew apart over the years and now they no longer love each other. At this moment a young girl, unmarried but bearing the child of a teenage lover, is pondering her future. Born into a Christian home, taught from her youth to love and honor God, she began to run with a questionable crowd. Warnings from parents and friends fell upon deaf ears. Then one night she fell into sin, and today she is trying to decide whether to abort the fetus, take her own life and end the torment she is now enduring or allow the child to be born and face the uncertain future. She didn't intend to do wrong. It just happened. How many other stories could be added to these, stories about real people who allowed themselves to become too deeply involved in the things of the world, and who can appreciate more than most the urgency in the warning of the Hebrews writer, ". . . lest haply we drift away . . .."

MAN BY NATURE A DRIFTER

The inclination of man has ever been to slip away from God and good and this is amply documented by the scriptures. Example after example is given for our admonition. Consider the case of Cain. The Bible says, "And in process of time it came to pass, that Cain brought of the fruit of the ground an offering unto Jehovah . . ., but unto Cain and to his offering he had not respect. And Cain was very wroth and his countenance fell" (Ge. 4:3-5). Notice the following points. First, Cain "brought . . . an offering." He worshiped. He didn't have to, but he did. Next, Cain "brought . . . an offering to Jehovah." He worshipped the true God. He was no idolator. Third, Cain "was very wroth and his countrnance fell" when his worship was rejected by God. These three facts tell us that Cain worshipped the true God expecting to be accepted, wanting to be accepted. He did not intend to fall away from God, but he did.

Another case in point is that of Solomon. Upon the death of his father David, he became king of Isreal, and for good reason. Scripture says, "And Solomon loved Jehovah, walking in the statutes of David his father . . ." (I Ki. 3:3). God blessed Solomon richly. He endowed him with unparalleled wisdom and overwhelmed him with wealth, glory and power. God them commissioned Solomon to build the magnificent temple in Jerusalem. The early days of Solomon's reign portrayed a beautiful relationship between the king and his God. But slowly things began to change. He married strange women in defiance to God's decree. His faith in Jehovah began to slip. The record says, "For it came to pass, when Solomon was old, that his wives turned away his heart after other gods . . ." (I Ki. 11:4). What a dramatic, and tragic, departure! And it occurred so slowly the king hardly noticed, until he found himself miserable, wretched and without God, and sought for the reason why.

These examples surely ought to remind us that man is a being that tends to drift away from his Maker. Perhaps Isaiah expressed it best: "All we like sheep have gone astray; we have turned every one to his own way . . ." (Is. 53:6).

WARNINGS FROM GOD

Because he knows man's inclination to stray, God has filled the Bible with admonitions and warnings, dircecting us to walk strictly by his Word. Moses instructed the children of Israel,

> And these words, which I command thee this day, shall be in thine heart: And thou shalt teach them diligently unto thy children, and shalt talk of them when thou sittest in thine house, and when thou walkest by the way, and when thou liest down, and when thou risest

up. And thou shalt bind them for a sign upon thine hand, and they shall be as frontlets between thine eyes. And thou shalt write them upon the posts of thy house, and on thy gates (De. 6:6-9).

The New Testament likewise sounds a warning to any who would drift away form the apostle's doctrine. Perhaps no book of the New Testament deals more pointedly with the problem of departure than Galatians. Listen,

> I marvel that you are so soon removed from him that called you into the grace of Christ unto another gospel: Which is not another; but there be some that trouble you, and would pervert the gospel of Christ. But though we, or an angel from heaven, preach any other gospel unto you than that which we have preached unto you, let him be accursed (Ga. 1:6-8).

Later Paul laments the precarious position of these same disciples,

> Howbeit, then, when ye knew not God, ye did service unto them which by nature are no gods. But now, after that ye have known God, or rather are known of God, how turn ye again to the weak and beggarly elements, whereunto ye desire again to be in bondage (Ga. 4:8-9)?

Then he inquires, "Ye did run well; who did hinder you that you should not obey the truth" (Ga. 5:7)? How subtle, yet sad, was their departure from the saving gospel! Believing themselves to be following God, they had turned aside unto a "gospel" of damnation.

The churches of Asia, like Galatia, were troubled by those who would lead God's flock away from the truth. Thus Paul summoned the Ephesian elders to Miletus, and warned,

> Take heed, therefore, unto yourselves, and to all the flock . . . For I know this, that after my departring shall grievous wolves enter in among you, not sparing the flock. Also of your own selves shall men arise, speaking perverse things, to draw away disciples after them. Therefore watch, and remember, that by the space of three years, I ceased not to warn every night and day with tears (Acts 20:28-31).

Despite the many warnings issued by God's watchman, departure became inevitable. Some were determined to ignore the truth in favor of a more appealing and appeasing message. Listen to God's man:

> Now the Spirit speaketh expressly, that in the latter times some shall depart from the faith, giving heed to seducing spirits, and doctrines of devils; Speaking lies in hypocrisy; having their conscience seared with a hot iron" (I Ti. 4:1-2).

In his second letter to Timothy, Paul continued to sound out the warning:

> Preach the word; be instant in season, out of season; reprove, rebuke, exhort with all longsuffering and doctrine. For the time will come when they will not endure sound doctrine; but after their own lusts shall they heap to themselves teachers, having itching ears; And they shall turn away their ears from the truth, and shall be turned unto fables (II Ti. 4:2-4).

History record that even as the first century moved toward its conclusion, apostasy was under way. The Thessalonian Christians had been told that the Lord would not return "except there come a falling away first," and that "the mystery of iniquity doth already work" (II Th. 2:3, 7). As the years passed and stalwart defenders of the faith took their places with the greats who had gone before, the gap between the gospel delivered and religion practiced grew ever wider. Apostasy swept over the church like a great tidal wave of destruction. The Spirit's prophecy, "some shall depart from the faith," had been fulfilled.

THE RISE OF "CALVINISM"

The main stream of the Lord's church became mired deeper and deeper in the doctrines of men and the apostate body came to bear little resemblance to the church of the first century. Even as this movement carried men farther and farther from God, a man by the name of Augustine stepped forth to proclaim the impossibility of apostasy, one of the most blatantly false doctrines ever conceived by the devil. This doctrine was taken up by John Calvin and others centuries later and became one of the bulwarks of the body of teaching known as "Calvinsim." Calvinism consists of five basic tenets. First, that man is born into the world a sinner, guilty of Adam's transgression, with a totally corrupt nature and destined for hell. Second, that God, before the world was formed or man created, predestined certain individuals to be saved and the rest to be lost. Third, that Christ's atoning blood was shed only for the saved. This is the doctrine of limited atonement. Fourth, that the sinner is saved wholly of grace, without any works of obedience on the part of the believer. God's grace irresistibly calls those who he has chosen unto salvation. Fifth, and finally, Calvinism contends that the Christian cannot fall away and be lost eternally, that he will somehow persevere unto the end and be saved.

The implications of this body of doctrine are staggering. It takes responsibility for human destiny completely out of the hands of man and places it squarely on the shoulders of God, and him alone. It contradicts everything the Bible teaches regarding the righteousness of God. It makes Him, at best, a respector of persons, and, at worst, a heartless tyrant! Calvanism says that man is responsible for something for which he cannot justly be held accountable, and is powerless to remedy the tragic situation. But let's take a closer look at the doctrine and its consequences.

Consider the claim of inherited sin. I propose these questions for the advocate of this doctrine: First, has God provided a means whereby the infant may be justified from guilt? If he can be forgiven, how is it possible and where is scriptural authority for it? Also, is man more righteous than God? We would not tolerate a system of government under which the new-born baby is convicted of his father's crime, sentenced and executed, as his father had been. Yet this is the very principle by which the Calvinist says God operates. Adam sinned, therefore every offspring of Adam must be condemned to hell for what Adam did!

This damnable doctrine has no basis in scripture. To the contrary, God's word clearly refutes any such notion. Consider the testimony of these inspired writers. Solomon stated, "Lo, this only have I found, that God hath made man upright . . ." (Ec. 7:29). Ezekiel denied inherited or imputed guilt also:

> The soul that sinneth, it shall die. The son shall not bear the iniquity of the father, neither shall the father bear the iniquity of the son: the righteousness of the righteous shall be upon him, and the wickedness of the wicked shall be upon him (Eze. 18:20).

Again, "Thou wast perfect in thy ways from the day that thou wast created, till iniquity was found in thee" (Eze. 28:15). David declared that the wicked "go astray as soon as they are born, speaking lies" (Ps. 58:3). Man is not born astray, he goes astray!

These facts are clear from the foregoing passages: man is born without sin, and God requires him to account only for transgressions he has committed. They forever destroy the basic premise of Calvinism, that God alone is in control of human destiny! We are not puppets with strings that are pulled daily by a Higher Being. God does not exercise arbitrary control over our lives.

Likewise, the doctrine of unconditional predestination as uprooted and destroyed by the word of God. It is both unbiblical and unreasonable. Jesus, in the great commission, clearly offers all men the gospel, and a choice regarding it: "He that believeth and is baptized shall be saved; but he that believeth not shall be damned" (Mark 16:16). To believe, or not to believe, that is the hearer's decision! Our Lord makes a final appeal to lost men in the closing verses of the New Testament: "And the Spirit and the bride say, Come. And let him that heareth say, Come. And let him that is athirst come. And whosoever will, let him take of the water of life freely" (Re. 22:17). The decision to follow Jesus is one that belongs to the individual.

I stated that unconditional predestination is unreasonable as well as unbiblical. Here is what I mean. If salvation is wholly of grace, arbitrarily bestowed by God without regard to man's wishes or the life he lives, then why will not all men be saved? It is God's avowed desire that all men should be saved, and that none should be lost (I Ti. 2:4; II Pe. 3:9). If God alone decides who is to be saved, and he does not wish any to be lost, why not just save everyone? This would make both God and man happy! Doesn't he love all men? Then why not save them all? The truth is, God provides the opportunity for man to be saved, but man must make the decision for himself.

The claim that Jesus died only for the elect, like the preceding doctrines, is inseparably related to the notion that everything that happens does so by the decree of God. Man is merely a pawn in the game of life. But Jesus dispelled this notion as he talked with Nicodemus. He said, "For God so loved the world, that he gave his only begotten Son, that whosoever believeth in him should not perish, but have everlasting life" (John 3:16). Jesus shed his precious blood for the sins of the world so that "whosoever believeth in him should not perish." Jesus died for the sins of the whole world. Listen to John as he writes to Christians: "And he is the propitiation for our sins: and not for ours only, but also for the sins of the whole world" (I John 2:2). Without doubt, Jesus tasted death "for every man" (He. 2:9). Friends, we can go to sleep tonight, confident in the belief that Jesus died for our sins, for we are a part of "the world."

That the sinner is saved by grace is indisputable. It is grace that is of God, that is wonderful and marvelous, but not irresistible! God appeals to the sinner's heart through the preaching of the gospel. And only through the gospel! He does not choose to convert lost men by means of dreams and visions and feelings, but by means of the most beautiful story ever told; the story of redeeming love! This was Paul's theme to the Corinthians.

> Moreover, brethren, I declare unto you the gospel which I preached unto you, which also ye have received, and wherein ye stand; by which also ye are saved . . . For I delivered unto you first of all that which I also received, how that Christ died for our sins according to the scriptures; And that he was buried, and that he rose again the third day according to the scriptures (I Co. 15:1-4).

They were Christians, had been saved and stood in the grace of God, because of the gospel they had heard and received! There was nothing mysterious about that. There was nothing miraculous about that. Marvelous certainly, but not miraculous.

The sinner is saved when his heart is touched by the gospel and his life turned to Jesus. Paul wrote, "Or despisest thou the riches of his goodness and forbearance and longsuffering; not knowing that the goodness of God leadeth thee to repentance" (Ro. 2:4)? Oh the awesome power in the gospel of Christ!

One by one the claims of Calvinism fall before the sword of God's Word. Hereditary depravity, unconditional predestination, limited atonement and irresistible grace, all are clearly exposed as heresy by the New Testament. With these also falls the doctrine of the impossibility of apostasy. As previously noted, all stand or fall together! All are tied to the claim that the eternal destiny of man is solely in the hands of

God. Of all the errors of Calvinism, perhaps none is more clearly exposed than the latter. The book of Hebrews renounces it time and again.

> Wherefore I was grieved with that generation, and said, They do always err in their heart; and they have not known my ways . . . Take heed, brethren, lest there be in any of you an evil heart of unbelief, in departing from the living God (He. 3:10-13).

The author here cites the tragic fall of the Israelites in the wilderness as an example of that which can befall the Christian. In a later passage, the writer makes an even stronger argument, for he discusses not only the possibility of falling away from Christ, but the impossibility of returning by those who became calloused. Listen to his warning:

> For it is impossible for those who were once enlightened, and have tasted of the heavenly gift, and were made partakers of the Holy Ghost, And have tasted the good work of God, and the powers of the world to come, If they shall fall away, to renew them again unto repentance; . . . (He. 6:4-6).

Had these of whom he writes been saved? No question about it! They had tasted of the many spiritual blessings God has provided for his children on earth, including the Holy Spirit, a blessing not enjoyed by those in the world (John 14:17). Yet they had turned away from the faith and embraced the rewards of the present world.

Despite these clear repudiations of the doctrine of perseverance, perhaps no book of the New Testament more forcefully exposes its folly than Galatians. In one brief statement, Paul announced, "ye are fallen from grace" (Ga. 5:4). The argument is made just here that those to whom he spoke were not really Christians. They appeared to some to have been saved, but were never actually in fellowship with God. To answer this fallacious argument one has only to scan this brief epistle, noting the following points. First, they had been "called into the grace of Christ" (Ga. 1:6). Second, they had "received the Spirit" (Ga. 3:2). Third, they were "children of God" (Ga. 3:26). Fourth, they had been "baptized into Christ" and had "put on Christ" (Ga. 3:27). Fifth, they were "Abraham's seed, and heirs according to the promise" (Ga. 3:29). And sixth, they had for a time "run well" the Christian race (Ga. 5:7). Now, tell me, were these Galatians saved? The conclusion is obvious: these were Christians! And it was some of these that Paul said, "Ye are fallen from grace" (Ga.5:4). Peter adds his word of warning to the others.

> For if after they have escaped the pollutions of the world through the knowledge of the Lord and Savior Jesus Christ, they again entangled therein, and overcome, the latter end is worse with them than the beginning (II Pe. 2:20).

The apostle was deeply concerned about the "latter end" of those who had "escaped the pollutions of the world" through a knowledge of the gospel, but were "again entangled therein, and overcome." And with good reason! For their souls were in jeopardy!

THE NEED FOR CONTINUED VIGILANCE

While the child of God can fall away and be eternally lost, he need not depart, for God's power to keep him from falling is always available (I Pe. 1:3-5; Jude 24). The power that keeps one in grace is the power that calls him into the grace, the gospel (Ga. 1:6-9; Ro. 1:16-17; I Pe. 1:5). It is through faith that the Christian is kept from the evil one, faith in Christ as revealed in the gospel. However, if we are to remain faithful to God, we must give diligent heed to his Word.

The history of man has been departure from God. The Gentile world turned away and would not retain God in their knowledge (Ro. 1:21-32). Israel also rejected God from time to time (Ro. 2:1-29). Even the church of Christ was let away by error of wicked men who sought their own advantage (Acts 20:28-30; II Th. 2:1-7; I Ti. 4:1-3; II Ti. 4:1-5). A period of spiritual darkness and oppression followed until a few religious leaders, weary of the gross errors of Catholicism, rose up to lead a movement aimed at reforming the church, an effort that resulted in the birth of Protestantism. Churches began to spring up, but with different names and creeds. People who had been united in error were now divided in error! After many years of religious confusion and division, a number of men on this continent resolved to try to lead others back to the religion of the New Testament and restore the church to the pattern laid down on Pentecost (Acts 2). Their efforts led to the Restoration Movement. Thousands of men and women left denominational ties for fellowship with one another in the body of Christ. Unity replaced division. But not for long.

Within fifty years of the dawn of the Restoration Movement, Christians began to divide. Issues such as the Missionary Society and the addition of instrumental music to the worship polarized brethren. Error had raised its ugly head once more. Since that time other points of doctrine have been debated and, in some cases, resulted in more division. The Bible class arrangement, located preachers, the method of congregational cooperation in preaching the gospel and church support of homeless children have become issues that splintered brethren.

Today we are further threatened by the errors of men. Unscriptural teaching regarding the role of women in the church, divorce and remarriage, the kingdom and the work of the Holy Spirit are being sounded out from pulpits and publications throughout the brotherhood. Add to these the attitude some have toward homosexual behavior, as well as other moral issues, and the social and recreational emphasis many are advocating today, and it is clear that the church of God, if it is to continue to be the church of God, must "give the more earnest heed to the things which we have heard" (He. 2:1).

CONCLUSION

In closing, may I make three pleas that I believe must be heeded if we are to avoid pitfalls of the past. First, that we renew our commitment to the absolute and final authority of the Scriptures! The Spirit guided the apostles into all truth (John 16:13-15). All that God wants men to know and do is revealed in his word (II Ti. 3:16-17). Let's go back to "chapter and verse" authority for every belief and practice. If we do this, we will not stray.

Second, let us commit ourselves to reject error of every kind! We are commanded to love the one who teaches false doctrine, but let us hate the doctrine itself. John gave instructions to govern our relationship with those who teach error. "If there come any unto you, and bring not this doctrine, receive him not into your house, neither bid him God speed: For he that biddeth him God speed is partaker of his evil deeds" (II John 10-11). We are to do nothing whereby we lend encouragement to him in propogating error! Paul makes it even stronger. "Now I beseech you, brethren, mark them which cause division and offences contrary to the doctrine which ye have learned; and avoid them" (Ro. 16:17). May we heed his advice.

Third, let us renew our faith in the fact that the gospel, and only the gospel, is the power of God to save the lost! It is his power to save the old and young, the rich and poor, the educated and illiterate. Nothing can take its place! Today there is an effort being made to teach and convert our young people with methods that seem to me to be more at home under the Big Top than in the church of God! Gimmicks may do a great deal to entertain the young, but they will do little to convict and convert them to Jesus! Somehow I cannot see Jesus dressed up like a circus clown or Timothy posing as some kind of feathered creature as they went about to save the young (Ma. 18:1-5; 19:13-15). The salvation of the human soul is serious business and every means we employ to accomplish this aim ought to be in harmony with the spirit of the gospel. The church today needs more sound, back-to-Bible, preaching, and less emphasis on entertainment if we are to make strong Christians of our children.

Drifting away from God and his word can happen so subtly and we need to watch night and day lest we depart from "the faith which was once for all deilvered unto the saints" (Jude 3). Drifting always jeopardizes souls and engenders strife and division within the body of Christ.

The scriptures have sounded a warning to Christians of all ages. Let us give diligent heed to it "lest haply we drift away."

THE CERTIFICATION OF THE GOSPEL

HEBREWS 2:1-4

By WINDELL WINKLER

Baptized by his father, M. P. Winkler, 1931. Married Betty Sue Hargrove and they have three sons. Attended Alabama Christian College and Lamar College of Technology. Since beginning his preaching work in 1944, has served local churches in Alabama, Texas, Missouri and Louisiana. Author of 10 books, editor of five others. Has served as staff writer for *Gospel Advocate*. Past director of Brown Trail Preacher Training School and the Fort Worth Lectures. Presently engaged in fulltime gospel meeting work. Speaker, *First Annual Denton Lectures*.

INTRODUCTION

The psalmist exulted, "Thy testimonies are very sure" (Ps. 93:5). Accordingly, how appropriate it is for us to study "The Certification of the Gospel." If the gospel has not been certified, the entire epistle of Hebrews — yea, the totality of the gospel revelation — is rendered invalid.

Our text for this study reads as follows:

Therefore we ought to give the more earnest heed to the things which we have heard, lest at any time we should let them slip. For if the word spoken by angels was stedfast, and every transgression and disobedience received a just recompence of reward; How shall we escape, if we neglect so great salvation; which at the first began to be spoken by the Lord, and was confirmed unto us by them that heard him; God also bearing them witness, both with signs and wonders, and with divers miracles, and gifts of the Holy Ghost, according to our own will? (He. 2:1-4).

68

Background to the text — The extended context: "The superiority of Christianity" is the theme of the book of Hebrews. This theme is developed in the following way:

1:1-3 — Christ is superior to the Old Testament prophets;
1:4-2:18 — Christ is superior to the angels;
3:1-4:16 — Christ is superior to Moses;
5:1-8:5 — Christ is superior to the Levitical priesthood;
8:6-9:10 — Christ's covenant is superior to the old covenant;
9:11-10:18 — Christ's sacrifice is superior to animal sacrifices; and
10:19-13:25 — Consequent exhortations.

Immediate context: Our text begins with the word "therefore." Thus, what the writer is about to say is based upon his immediate past observations. And, in chapter one Christ has been set forth as (1) *God's prophet* — "Hath in these last days spoken unto us by his Son;" (2) *God's priest* — "When he had by himself purged our sins;" and as (3) *God's king* — "Sat down on the right hand of the Majesty on high." Additionally, the writer affirms Christ's (1) *Authoritative power* — "Whom he hath appointedf heir of all things," 1:2 (cf. Ma. 28:18); (2) *creating power* — "By whom also he made the worlds," 1:2 (cf. John 1:1-3; Col. 1:16); (3) *illuminating power* — "Who being the brightness (shining forth, effulgence) of his glory," 1:3 (cf. John 14:9-11; Col. 2:9; II Co. 4:6); and (4) *upholding power* — "And upholding all things by the word of his power," 1:3 (cf. II Pe. 3:5). Now, what the inspired penman is about to discuss is based upon these majestic thoughts.

Identification and expansion of terms in the assigned topic — *"Certification:"* Etymologically, this word is from the Latin *certus* and means "certain." Webster defines the word "certify" as follows: "To attest authoritatively: confirm . . . to attest as being true or as represented or as meeting a standard . . ." Thus, a certified document is one that is not pseudo, not spurious; rather, it is genuine, authentic and truthful. In a day of attack, from within and from without, when with unquivering pens and unstammering tongues men deny divine revelation (*e.g.,* "Luke's gospel is from an uninspired document") and divine inspiration (*e.g.,* "The gospel accounts have within them clashes and jars"), it is so necessary that we discuss the certification of the gospel. *"Gospel:"* Contextually and exegetically, in identifying the gospel of this passage, we are beautifully, definitely and immediately led to Mark 16:15-20. Such can be seen in this parallel study:

He. 2:1-4 — The Great Salvation	Mark 16:15-20 — The Gospel
(1) "So great salvation"	(1) "The Gospel"
(2) "Spoken by the Lord"	(2) "And he said unto them"
(3) "Was confirmed unto us by them that heard him"	(3) "The Lord working with them, and confirming the word"
(4) "God also bearing them witness, both with signs and wonders, and with divers miracles"	(4) "With signs following"
(5) "How shall we escape" (implying there is no escape)	(5) "Shall be damned"
(6) "If we neglect"	(6) "He that believeth not"

Now, in the gospel accounts, the parallel passages to Mark 16:15-20 are Matthew 28:18-20, Luke 24:46-49 and John 20:21-23. And, from a brief analysis of Matthew's record we can conclude that the entire New Testament is involved in this gospel:

(1) "All power (authority, A.S.V.) is given unto me"	(1) Matthew through John (herein is established the Lord's deity and his consequent power and authority)
(2) "Go . . . and teach all nations, baptizing them"	(2) Acts of Apostles
(3) "Teaching them to observe all things whatsoever I have commanded you"	(3) Romans through Jude
(4) "Lo, I am with you alway, even unto the end of the world."	(4) Revelation

Notice that in column two we started with Matthew and ended with Revelation. Thus, the entire New Testament is involved and embraced in this "great salvation." No doubt the term "so great salvation" is used as a synecdoche (where a part is put for a whole) for the entire New Testament.

Notice now, especially, that the text describes the gospel as "so great salvation." But, why is salvation, why is the gospel, so great? (1) God "thought" it (I Pe. 1:18-20; Ep. 3:9;

II Th. 2:13; Tit. 1:2); (2) Christ "bought" it (I Co. 6:19-20; Tit. 2:13-14; I Ti. 2:6); (3) the Holy Spirit "brought" it (I Pe. 1:9-12; I Co. 2:9-13; John 14:26; 16:13); (4) the gospel "taught" it (Ro. 1:16-17; John 6:44-45; (5) Satan "fought" it (Ma. 4:1-11; 16:18-19); and (6) one must have "sought" it (Is. 55:6; Acts 17:26-27; 15:16-17).

With this background information in mind, let us now observe the three means by which the gospel has been certified.

SPOKEN BY THE LORD HIMSELF — MESSIANIC PROCLAMATION

"How shall we escape, if we neglect so great salvation; which at the first *began to be spoken by the Lord,* and was confirmed unto us by them that heard him." Such is the reading of verse three of our remarkable text.

It was not spoken by angels. Angels have always had a vital role to play in the divine economy; yea, in the earthly life of our Lord. In fact, they had an important function to perform in the giving of the old law. "It was ordained by angels in the hand of a mediator" (Ga. 3:19). Israel had "received the law by the disposition of angels" (Acts 7:53). But, in contradistinction, and to underscore the superiority of the gospel to the law of Moses, the gospel was spoken by the Lord himself. Concerning this we read in Mark 16:19, "So then after the Lord had spoken unto them." The Holy Spirit was to bring to the apostles' minds "whatsoever I (the Lord) have said unto you" (John 14:26).

Yes, it was spoken by the Lord; yea, by the Lord of Hebrews 1:1ff. And, the Lord of Hebrews 1:1ff is described as follows:

(1) *With relation to the Father:* He is God's prophet — "Hath in these last days spoken unto us by his Son" (v. 2). He is God's Son — "By his Son" (v. 2). He is God's heir — "Whom he hath appointed heir of all things" (v. 2). Being the Son, he is appropriately the heir. He is God's effulgence (brightness) — "Who being the brightness of his glory" (v. 3). He is God's image — "And the express image of his person" (v. 3).

(2) *With relation to the world:* He is creator — "By whom also he made the worlds" (v. 2). He is sustainer — "And upholding all things by the word of his power" (v. 3).

(3) *With relation to man:* He is our savior and priest — "When he had by himself purged our sins" (v. 3). He is our Lord and king — "Sat down on the right hand of the Majesty on high" (v. 3). Such is affirmed five times in Hebrews 1:3, 13; 7:1; 10:12; 12:2).

(4) *With relation to angels:* He is "so much better than the angels" (v. 4). This is true by virtue of his *name* — he is called "Son," whereas they are designated "angels" (vv. 4-6); by virtue of his *nature* — he is deity, worthy of receiving worship, whereas they are the ones rendering worship (v. 6); by virtue of his *position* — he is on the throne, being Lord, king and master, whereas they are servants or ministers (vv. 7-14).

Jesus Christ is God's prophet; thus, God's spokesman. The entire Old Testament revolves around three functions. The first one-third of the Old Testament relates primarily to the priesthood (Genesis through Deuteronomy). The second one-third relates to the kings primarily (Joshua through Song of Solomon). And the last one-third relates to the prophets (Isaiah through Malachi). In Christ all three functions merge and amalgamate. Since this present study has to do with his prophetic ministry, we will limit ourselves to observations related thereto. Christ is spoken of as prophet in several different places (De. 18:15, 18-19; Acts 3:22-23; John 6:14; 7:40; Luke 7:16; 24:19; Ma. 21:11). God's Son, as prophet, was superior to the Old Testament prophets in that they were several in number, whereas he was God's only begotten Son (John 3:16); they were servants, whereas he was Lord (Jer. 26:5; Ph. 2:11); they were temporal, whereas he is eternal (John 8:35); they were sinners, whereas he was perfect and sinless (Je. 5:31; I Pe. 2:23); and they pointed to the Son, whereas he pointed to himself (Luke 24:25-26, 44). Prophets operated through three mediums; and, our lord used all three: *teaching* (Matt. 5-7; John 3:1-2), *predictions* (Ma. 16:21; 24:1ff), and *miracles* (John 2:1-11; 4:46-54; 5:1-16; 6:1-14, 16-21; 9:1-41; 11:1-54). Concerning his *teaching*, "Never man spake like this man" (John 7:46), whether we are dealing with his message, method or manner. Concerning his *predictions*, they were verified by minute historical fulfillment (*e.g.*, the destruction of Jerusalem). And, concerning his *miracles*, even his enemies said, "What do we? for this man doeth many miracles" (John 11:47). His miracles met the test of indisputable evidence (which we will subsequently discuss in this lesson).

We have thus far observed that the gospel has been certified by Messianic proclamation — the gospel's being spoken by God's superior and incomparable prophet, his Son — with such proclamation being authenticated by the Lord's matchless teaching, the undeniable minute historical fulfillment of his predictions, and his irrefutable miracles.

CONFIRMED BY COMPETENT APOSTOLIC AND PROPHETIC WITNESSES — APOSTOLIC CONFIRMATION

Verse three of our text reads, "How shall we escape, if we neglect so great salvation; which at the first began to be spoken by the Lord, *and was confirmed unto us by them that heard him.*" The word "confirm" in this passage is a form of the same word rendered "stedfast" in verse two. Hence, God's word is affirmed as being sure!

The apostles and prophets were witnesses. Jesus said: "But when the Comforter is come, whom I will send unto you from the Father, even the Spirit of truth, which proceedeth from the Father, he shall testify of me: And ye also shall bear witness, because ye have been with me from the beginning" (John 15:26-27). Again we read, "Wherefore of these men which have companied with us all the time that the Lord Jesus went in and out among us, Beginning from the baptism of John, unto that same day that he was taken up from us, must one be ordained to be a witness with us of his resurrection" (Acts 1:21-22). Also, we read in Acts 4:33, "And with great power gave the apostles witness of the resurrection of the Lord Jesus."

They were reliable witnesses. The force of human testimony is dependent upon the integrity or honesty, the competency, and the number of the witnesses. Let us briefly study each of these.

The integrity or honesty of the witnesses: Such is determined by ascertaining the motives that prompted their testimony. Did fear prompt their testimony? Indeed not; for, since their lives were endangered by so testifying, fear would have prompted them to have remained silent. Did the love of money prompt their testimony? Again, indeed not; for, none of them "feathered their nests" by so testifying. Did pride prompt their testimony? Again, indeed not; for, as Paul later wrote, for so testifying they were counted "the offscouring of all things" (I Co. 4:13). What other ulterior motives could have prompted their testimony? Accordingly, only the irrefutable knowledge and conviction of the fact that they knew whereof they were so speaking could have prompted their testimony. Furthermore: Their testimony has all the appearances of being honest testimony. They do not stop to assert honesty, they do not eulogize, nor do they express utter amazement. They just seem to be totally unaware of the fact that their testimony will be otherwise than accepted and that they should be on their guard against detection; they differ in their testimony (though they never contradict) just as true witnesses do. For example, one gives a fuller account than the other, whereas in false testimony there is always exactness; their testimony appears to be against them. Impartially they record the denial of one, the doubting of another, the forsaking of them all, etc.; their extreme persecutions and sufferings for their testimony gives evidence of their honesty. As Harvey Everest, from whom these five observations were gleaned, says, "Martyrdom may not prove that a man is talented and learned, and therefore that his conclusions are correct; but it does prove that he is honest in that for which he dies. A bad man may be killed; but even a bad man will not suffer death, when he could save his life by giving up unprofitable deceit and falsehood." Their honesty can be further established by observing that they were either deceived, deceivers, or true witnesses. They were not deceived as is evident from the plainness and repetitiveness with which they spoke. They were not deceivers as is evident from their lives, their sufferings and their writings. Thus, inescapably we can conclude, they were true witnesses.

The competency of the witnesses: Concerning such, I John 1:1 states, "That which was from the beginning, which we have heard, which we have seen with our eyes, which we have looked upon, and our hands have handled, of the Word of life." Notice the ascending scale in this passage: heard, then seen, then looked upon (as if to gaze), then handled! Too, observe that three senses are appealed unto: hearing, seeing, and feeling! Then, in Luke 1:1-4, we read concerning the competency of the witnesses:

> Forasmuch as many have taken in hand to set forth in order a declaration of those things which are most surely believed among us, Even as they delivered them unto us, which from the beginning were eyewitnesses, and ministers of the word; It seemed good to me also, having had perfect understanding of all things from the very first, to write unto thee in order, most excellent Theophilus, That thou mightest know the certainty of those things, wherein thou hast been instructed.

Notice the "which from the beginning were eyewitnesses," and "having had perfect understanding of all things from the first," and "mightest know the certainty of those things" of this passage. Then in Acts 1:3, we are told, "To whom (the apostles, the witnesses) also he shewed himself alive after his passion by many infallible proofs, being seen of them forty days." Notice that they were *proofs* (plural), they were *many* (not just a few), and that they were *infallible* (irrefutable)! From these three passages alone we would know that the witnesses were competent.

Additionally, Peter affirmed:

> For we have not followed cunningly devised fables, when we made known unto you the power and coming of our Lord Jesus Christ, but were eyewitnesses of his majesty. For he received from God the Father honor and glory, when there came such a voice to him from the excellent glory, This is my beloved Son, in whom I am well pleased. And this voice which came from heaven we heard, when we were with him in the holy mount (II Pe. 1:16-18).

Commenting on this passage, Brother Guy N. Woods wrote in his commentary:

> In the verse immediately preceding this, Peter wrote of the things which he was doing; here, he passes from the singular "I" to the plural "we" as he describes matters which involved not only himself, but the other apostles, James and John (Ma. 17:1-8; Mark 9:2-9; Luke 9:28-36). The verb "follow" in the text, from the compound *ex-akoloutheo*, means to take the lead and follow the direction of

another; and as here used with the negative, is highly significant in that in it the writer clearly disavows secondhand sources of information regarding that about which he was testifying, affirming instead that he and those with him were eyewitnesses. "Fables" (*muthoi*) are myths, legends, fictitious stories without basis of fact. The words "cunningly devised" are from the verb *sophizo*, to invent artificially, to devise artfully. Thus, in making known the power and coming of the Lord, the apostles were not influenced by men who had deceived them by skillfully told fictitious stories, but were themselves eyewitnesses of the things alleged. The word translated "eye-witness" (*epoptes*) was current at the time Peter wrote of those who were initiated into the highest order of mysteries of the heathen religions. Such were styled "beholders" (from the word *epopteuo*) from the fact that they had attained to the highest degree possible. This word the apostle adopted to indicate that he, along with James and John, had been admitted to the highest degree of evidence in being privileged to see with their own eyes the glory and majesty of the transfigured Saviour.

Yes, they were competent. And, indeed, we shall momentarily see that they were not second-hand witnesses; but, rather, they were both "ear" and "eye" witnesses: "But were *eye*witnesses . . . this voice which came from heaven we *heard* . . ." (II Pe. 1:16-18).

Relating to this, Everest observes,

It is a rare thing that the eye-witness and the historian are the same person. Most writers of authentic history are compelled to collect their facts from former documents, from tradition, and from participants removed from them by several generations. A history is of the first-class and receives universal credence, if, like Xenophon's Anabasis and Caesar's Commentaries, it was written by an actor in the scenes described. Hence, the New Testament books must be placed in the highest class of reliable histories.

The number of the witnesses: There is certainly no lack of evidence in this particular. "And that he was seen of Cephas, then of the twelve: After that, he was seen of about five hundred brethren at once; of whom the greater part remain unto this present . . . And last of all he was seen of me (Paul) also" (I Co. 15:5-8).

More specifically, they were "ear" witnesses: "That which was from the beginning, which we have heard . . . and was manifested unto us" (I John 1:1-2). "And this voice (at the transfiguration) which came from heaven we heard" (II Pe.

1:18). For example: They heard his masterful discourses. He was a teacher come from God (John 3:2). "Never man spake like this man" (John 7:46). Never man spake with such authority, such originality, such variety, such methodology, such conviction, such love, and with such universal influence. His disciples were astonished at his teaching (Ma. 7:28); yes, his masterful discourses. What about the majestic sermon on the mount! In addition, the parables are insurmountable. They heard his incomparable logic. Remember how irrefutably he handled the Sadducees concerning the future resurrection (Ma. 22:31-32). He showed: God is the God of Abraham, Isaac and Jacob; God is the God of the living; therefore, Abraham, Isaac and Jacob are alive, though physically dead for centuries. They had heard his unassailable use of and response to questions. What about his beautiful response with the parable of the good Samaritan to the question, "Who is my neighbor?" (Luke 10:29-37)? Cannot we readily recall his response to the question asked of him, "By what authority doest thou these things?" by the chief priests and elders, by his asking, "The baptism of John, whence, was it? from heaven, or of men" (Ma. 21:23-27)? Seeing their dilemma, they were speechlessly answered by his amazing questioning. They heard his loving and gracious promise of salvation. Yea, they heard him present the "so great salvation" of our text (Mark 16:14-20). They heard the Father's comprehensive endorsement of him (II Pe. 1:17-18). Peter, James and John heard the Father's commending voice say of him, "This is my beloved Son (a statement of intimate relationship) in whom I am well pleased (a comprehensive statement of approval covering his entire earthly life); hear ye him (a statement of affirmative deity and superiority)" (Ma. 17:5).

Also, continuing, to be more specific, they were "eye" witnesses: "And many other signs truly did Jesus in the presence of his disciples" (John 20:30). Notice, that the signs were performed in their presence. Luke 1:2 reads, "Even as they delivered them unto us, which from the beginning were eyewitnesses." "Eyewitnesses" in this text means seeing with one's own eyes, according to Robertson. Too, the word is from *autoptai* from which we get the word "autopsy," a word used in medical circles of a personal examination of disease and/or

parts of the body, as noted by Vincent. John affirms in John
1:14, "And we beheld his glory." He said in I John 1:1-3, "We
have seen with our eyes, which we have looked upon . . . (For
the life was manifested, and we have seen it . . . and was manifested unto us;) That which we have seen . . ." Then, in I John
4:14, he stated, "And we have seen and do testify that the
Father sent the Son to be the Saviour of the world." Peter says
in II Peter 1:16 that he and the other apostles "were eyewitnesses of his majesty." Indeed, they were "eye" witnesses.

They saw his unique and undeniable miracles. They saw his
power over nature (stilling the sea), over material things
(multiplying the loaves and feeding the five thousand), over
disease (healing the woman with the issue of blood), over death
(he raised Lazarus), and over devils (he cast many out of
Legion). They saw the blind seeing, the dumb speaking, the
crippled walking with straightened limbs, the maimed walking
with restored limbs, and the dead living again. Even his
enemies said, "What do we? for this man doeth many
miracles" (John 11:47). As Homer Hailey observed:

> An interesting fact that adds weight to the testimony of miracles is
> that the enemies of Jesus never denied the miracles; however, they
> refused to accept them as being performed by divine power. Effort
> was never made by the Lord or by His disciples to prove that a
> miracle had been accomplished. The miracles were recognized and
> accepted by all; they spoke for themselves.

The evidences that our Lord's miracles are genuine are overwhelming. Accordingly, Jim McGuiggan lists the following
characteristics of the miracles: (1) they were performed in
public places; (2) they were performed over an extended period
of time; (3) they were performed in the presence of even his
enemies; (4) they were performed in great variety; (5) they were
performed without sensationalism; (6) they never made their
perpetrator extremely rich; (7) they were never successfully repudiated by his enemies; (8) none of them were absurd or silly;
(9) they did not always require faith on the part of the one
blessed by the deed; (10) they form an integral part of the narrative without being unduly prominent; and (11) the very nature
of the deeds witnessed that they were miraculous and thus
were indisputable evidence that Deity was at work. Add to
these thoughts the following additional evidence: (1) the credi-

bility of the book that reveals the miracles is unanswerably established; (2) Bible miracles have no marks of fakery — for example, a deceiver would work to obtain all the publicity possible, whereas Jesus forbade many of his deeds being publicized; (3) a deceiver would do everything to enhance the value of miracles, whereas Jesus at times leaned the other way (John 4:48; Luke 10:17-20); (4) the fact that no miracles were attributed to Christ before his public ministry indicates that the gospel writers were not inventing stories; (5) the fact that only a few instances of raising the dead are given shows that the writers were not fabricators; (6) that Jesus would not put on a show for Herod is worthy of note — would not a Simon the sorcerer have done so?; and (7) the miracles were always of a concrete nature — when the loaves and fishes were multiplied, men ate them; there was no trick to the feat.

They saw his transfiguration. Again, II Peter 1:16-18 reads,

> For we have not followed cunningly devised fables, when we made known unto you the power and coming of our Lord Jesus Christ, but were eyewitnesses of his majesty. For he received from God the Father honour and glory, when there came such a voice to him from the excellent glory, This is my beloved Son, in whom I am well pleased. And this voice which came from heaven we heard, when we were with him in the holy mount.

Observe that they "were with him" and "were eyewitnesses."

They saw his resurrection. That is, they saw him after he had been raised! What could be stronger evidence! The fact that no one saw him in the rising process is further evidence that the story is not fabricated by man; for, if so, no doubt such would have been affirmed. Yes, they saw him. Luke says, "To whom (the apostles) also, he shewed himself alive after his passion" (Acts 1:3). Also, he said, "And as they thus spake, Jesus himself stood in the midst of them" (Luke 24:36). "After these things Jesus shewed himself again to the disciples" (John 21:1). "This is now the third time that Jesus shewed himself to his disciples, after that he was risen from the dead" (John 21:14). "And that he was seen of Cephas, then of the twelve: After that, he was seen of above five hundred brethren at once. . . . After that, he was seen of James; then of all the apostles. And last of all he was seen of me also" (I Co. 15:5-8).

Now, we are aware that these witnesses to the resurrection are attacked thusly: "The witnesses assert that which is incredible. For example, it is incredible that Mary did not recognize Jesus but supposed him to be the gardner." Answer: This is proof that the story was not a made up one! Too, such can be accounted for on the basis that she was not expecting the resurrection and was still teary-eyed. We are further informed, "It was impossible for Jesus to enter through closed doors and vanish if he had a real body." Answer: he could if he arose! Such is no more incredible than the omnipresence of God. "But, the witnesses were incompetent, being demented; expecting the resurrection, they had an hallucination." Answer: They were *not* expecting the resurrection (Mark 16:1-3; John 20:13-14; 21:3). Too, it is sheer folly to suppose that above five hundred people (I Cor. 15:6) hallucinated at one time. Furthermore, the very nature of hallucinations calls for an increase of the same until the victim becomes irrational, or they decrease until the person is completely recovered. Neither happened in the case of the witnesses we are discussing. Too, what are we going to do with Saul of Tarsus who was a brilliant intellectual? "The witnesses contradict themselves. For example, the names of the women who went to the tomb differ." Answer: Neither writer said that the ones he mentioned were the "only" ones who went. An omission is not a contradiction. But, the attackers continue, "Matthew says one angel and Luke says two angels." Answer: Matthew mentions only the one who speaks while Luke mentions both without distinction between the two. Too, we are informed, "Matthew says the women were told to go and tell his make disciples that he had risen. Luke says they did, but Mark says 'for trembling and astonishment had come upon them; and they said nothing to any one, for they were afraid.' " Answer: Mark means that they said nothing to anyone except his male disciples. Fear was the motive for not telling; so, such would not have kept them from telling his disciples, only his enemies.

They saw his glorious ascension. "While they beheld, he was taken up; and a cloud received him out of their sight. And while they looked steadfastly toward heaven as he went up . . . why stand ye gazing up into heaven? . . . shall so come in like manner as ye have seen him go into heaven" (Acts 1:9-11).

The weight of this confirmatory evidence: Peter affirmed in II Peter 1:16-19 (especially verse 19) that because of such evidence, "We have also a more sure word of prophecy." Yes, prophecy, as sure and definite as it is in verification and confirmation (consisting of (1) the unveiling of the future so as to make certain that such could not have been guesswork, (2) a lapse of time sufficient in length between the prophecy and its fulfillment so as to preclude any possibility of the prophet so working as to bring about the fulfillment, (3) enough details so as to eliminate any possibility of an accidental fulfillment, and (4) the complete historical fulfillment of the same), as even made "more sure" with the evidence presented by the "ear" and "eye" witnesses! How weighty, then, such evidence becomes!

VERIFIED BY FIRST CENTURY MIRACLES — FIRST CENTURY ATTESTATION

Verse four of our text reads, "God also bearing them witness, both *with signs and wonders, and with divers miracles, and gifts of the Holy Ghost, according to his own will.*" Miracles attended the giving and delivering of the old law (Ex. 19, 20; Ga. 3:19). Thus, it should not be unexpected that the New Testament would be verified and attested by miracles.

Miracles were performed by the witnesses: The text says, "God also bearing them (the witnesses) witness, both with signs and wonders, and with divers miracles." Their designations: (1) From the standpoint of "purpose" they were called *signs,* since they signified that he who performed them was from God and that his message was genuine; (2) From the standpoint of "reaction" they were called *wonders,* for this was the reaction the miracles precipitated; (3) From the standpoint of "nature" they were called *miracles,* since they were supernatural acts; (4) From the standpoint of "source" they were called *"gifts of the Holy Ghost,"* since they were rooted in grace and brought blessings.

Their characteristics: They were performed in the presence of viewing auditors (II Co. 12:12; Acts 2:22; 3:16); instantaneously (Mark 2:12; Ma. 8:13-15; Acts 3:7-8; 9:18; 14:8-11); perfectly, with the healed ones being healed completely and wholly (Ma. 9:22; Acts 3:16; 4:9); on the lame (crippled) and maimed (amputees) (Acts 3:1-8; 4:22; Ma. 15:30-31); on the "all" (Acts 5:16; Ma. 12:15); without a single collection of money ever being taken; without faith being apparently possessed by the healed person (John 5:1-17; Mark 2:5; John 11:1ff); without any recorded relapses; without pre-screening; remotely (Acts 19:11-12); without the design of building up a personal or sectarian following; by raising the dead also (Ma. 10:8; Acts 9:36-43); by also predicting the future accurately (Ma. 24:1ff; Acts 27:10); and by striking false teachers blind (Acts 13:8-11). Bible miracles were not based on mere testimony, as is the case with so-called miracles today. Every so-called miracle worker can give as good a testimonial as the other. Now, are miracles being performed by them all? Are we to believe them all? Or, are we to believe one and not the other? If the latter, upon what grounds since one can give as convincing testimony as the other? Then, if God is working miracles through them all, he would be confirming contradictory doctrines since they all teach different and conflicting doctrines!

Their purpose: The primary purpose was confirmatory, not accomodative. Such is affirmed in our text. Then, Mark 16:20 reads, ". . . and confirming the word with signs following." Since they were not primarily accommodative in purpose, we read where Paul left Trophimus at Miletum sick (II Tim. 4:20). Now, since miracles confirmed the word (that is, verified it, proved it truthful, authenticated it), the testimony of the witnesses of the gospel ought to be unreservedly received. For, if they so performed miracles, the power admittedly came from God. And, such obtaining, what they taught was verified as true and genuine. Otherwise, God would be a party to evil. Hence, the complete trustworthiness of the word is established.

Also, there were gifts of the Holy Ghost in the early church. Again, our text reads, "God also bearing them witness, both with signs and wonders . . . miracles, and gifts of the Holy Ghost." I Corinthians, chapters 12, 13 and 14 contain the most detailed discussion of this subject to be found in the New Testament. Chapter 12 deals with the *presence*, chapter 13 with the *permanence* (lack of), and chapter 14 with the *practice* of these gifts of the Holy Ghost in the early church. Too, Ephesians 4:7-16 is a most comprehensive passage on this theme. Verse 8 deals with the *presence* of these gifts ("And gave gifts unto men"). Verse 11 deals with the *persons* who were enabled by these gifts ("And he gave some, apostles; and some, prophets; and some, evangelists; and some, pastors and teachers"). Verse 12 deals with the *purpose* of these gifts ("For the perfecting of the saints, for the work of the ministry, for the edifying of the body of Christ"). Verse 13ff deals with the *passing* of these gifts ("Till we all come in the unity of the faith . . ."). Now, more specifically, let us observe:

How were these gifts received? These spiritual gifts were imparted only by the laying on of the apostles' hands. Such can be seen by a study of Acts 8:12-24. Notice, per this passage, that even though Philip was present in the city of Samaria, and had the power to perform miracles himself (v. 6), that it was still necessary for the apostles (Peter and John) to come down to Samaria. And, "when they were come down, prayed for them, that they might receive the Holy Ghost (For as yet he was fallen upon none of them: only they were baptized in the name of the Lord Jesus.) Then laid they their hands upon them, and they received the Holy Ghost." Remember, also, that Simon, who desired to buy the gifts with money, was told, "Thou hast neither part nor lot in this matter." Now, if the gifts of the Holy Spirit could be conveyed through other means, why was it necessary for Peter and John to leave Jerusalem and go down to Samaria on this occasion? Call to mind also that Paul desired to *see* the brethren in Rome that he might impart some spiritual gift (Rom. 1:11). This shows that such things were not imparted through prayer alone, without the presence of an apostle.

How long were these gifts to last? According to Ephesians 4:8-16, these gifts were to last "Till we all come in the unity of the faith . . ." This text does not mean that the gifts were to last until everybody believes alike. The text does not say that the gifts were to last until we come to the "unity of faith." Rather, the text says that the gifts were to last till we come in "the unity of *the* faith." "The faith" refers to the gospel, as can be seen from Galatians 1:23 and Jude 3. Therefore, Paul is saying that the miraculous gifts were to last until we come to the unity of the gospel. The unity of the gospel, or of the faith, would obtain when faith, or the gospel, came into existence with all of its parts or units; that is, when it was complete. The New Testament, the gospel, the faith, was completed by A.D. 96. It was then that the faith with all its units was realized; thus, "the unity of the faith" had been reached. And, such obtaining, the miraculous gifts ceased!

Further evidence of the cessation of miraculous spiritual gifts can be seen from a study of I Corinthians 13:8-13. This text teaches us that something is to "fail," "cease," "vanish away," and "be done away." But, what? The text says "prophecies, tongues and knowledge." But, what are such things? By reading I Corinthians 12:8-10 we can see that these things are representative of the nine spiritual gifts existent in the early church. Now, Paul is saying in this text that these spiritual gifts are going to fail, cease, vanish away; yea, be done away. But when? Well, notice first that Paul speaks in verse 9 of these spiritual gifts (knowledge, prophecy) as being "in part." Then, observe in verse 10 that he says, "But when that which is perfect is come" *it is then* that the things that are "in part (spiritual gifts) shall be done away." The word "perfect" is used in contrast with "in part" and means *complete*. A perfect circle, for example, is a circle with all its parts. Furthermore, the "in part" things relate to divine revelation (prophecy and knowledge). Thus, what Paul is saying is this: that when the complete revelation of God's will (the perfect thing) is realized it is then that the spiritual gifts will fail, cease, vanish away, be done away. Hence, to affirm that these spiritual gifts are still in effect today is to also affirm that we have not received the complete and final revelation of God's will unto man! However, according to John 14:26; 16:13 and II Peter 1:3, we know of a certainty that we have received the complete and final revelation of God's will. Such obtaining, the things that were "in part" (the spiritual gifts) have ceased, failed, vanished away; yea, have been done away!

We now have the written miracles, with actual miracles no longer being performed. The written miracles are sufficient (John 20:30-31). That the actual miracles are not being performed is not because of a lack of divine power. Rather, it is a matter of the sovereignty of God. God has chosen not to thus exercise his power. Even our text says, "And gifts of the Holy Ghost, according to his own will" (He. 2:4).

Only new revelations need confirming. Thus, in the beginning of Christianity and the proclamation of the gospel, miracles were used for confirming the same. But, since there were to be no additional revelations after the days of the apostles (they were to be guided into *all* truth, John 16:13), there ceased to be a need for confirmation. And, since signs were for the purpose of confirmation (Mark 16:20), there ceased to be a need for such. So, when one affirms that signs are still being performed, he might as well affirm that we are still receiving revelations! This is the position of the Mormons. Such is a reflection on the established trustworthiness of the gospel. Too, remember that a document once sealed need not be sealed again and again; yea, from generation to generation.

Just as when a house is under construction, there is need for scaffolding, but when the house is completed, the scaffolding is removed, so in the beginning of Christianity there was a need for signs, miracles, etc., but when the New Testament was completed, there ceased to be a need for such and they ceased. Who would think of leaving scaffolding up on a newly constructed home?

All things started by means of a miracle. The first oak tree was the result of a miracle. However, after that, God placed the power of reproduction in the seed, the acorn. In like manner, the church of our Lord began, and for a while existed, in an atmosphere of the miraculous. However, thereafter matters were to obtain through prescribed law; that is, according to the New Testament (Ro. 10:17; John 20:30-31; II Pe. 1:3).

CONCLUSION

Recapitulation. Yes, "The Certification of the Gospel;" certified by (1) messianic proclamation, (2) apostolic confirmation, and (3) first century attestation. Accordingly, we read, "All his commandments are sure" (Ps. 111:7). "The testimony of the Lord is sure" (Ps. 19:7). "The grass withereth, the flower fadeth: but the word of our God shall stand forever" (Is. 40:8).

"This is the disciple which testifieth of these things, and wrote these things: and we know that his testimony is true" (John 21:24). "The foundation of God standeth sure" (II Ti. 2:19). So, though we live in a time of gross uncertainty, when financial institutions and political regimes rise, change, topple and fall, we can thank God for the certainty of the gospel! As Erdman said, "It is not want of evidence that turns one from the Christian faith; nor can it be discovery that Christianity lacks foundation in historic fact. Apostasy is caused by the failure to face evidence and by indifference to a divinely attested gospel."

Our relationship to this certified gospel. We are to believe it (Ep. 1:13), obey it (II Th. 1:7-8), live it (Ph. 1:27), preach it (Mark 16:15; I Co. 9:16), defend it (Ph. 1:7, 17), never change it (Ga. 1:6-9), and never forget that by it we will one day be judged (Ro. 2:16).

Consequent exhortation. With the certainty of the gospel having been unquestionably established, let us, with unwavering confidence, *believe* it, *obey* it, *live* it, *preach* it, *defend* it, *never change* it, and live in constant realization that we shall be *judged* by it! For, as the inspired writer asks, "How shall we escape" if we neglect it by doing otherwise than just outlined? And, with unquestioned assurance, let us contemplate the day when "the books will be opened" and by the certified gospel we shall be judged and, consequently, hear, "Well done, good and faithful servant" (Ma. 25:23). Yea, and between now and then, let us "hold fast the confidence and the rejoicing of the hope firm unto the end" (He. 3:6, 14). For, "Thy testimonies are very sure" (Ps. 93:5).

BUT WE BEHOLD JESUS

HEBREWS 2:9

By JOHNNY RAMSEY

Native Texan. Has preached 33 years. Graduate of Abilene Christian College, was class president two years. Has conducted more than 600 gospel meetings in 45 states and 15 foreign nations. Frequent speaker on major lectureships. Author of five books, 25 tracts. Staff writer for *Gospel Minutes*. Regularly writes for other gospel papers. Editor, *Christian Bible Teacher*. Mission work in Wisconsin and Australia. Married to Iris Baker and they have four children. Speaker, *First Annual Denton Lectures*.

INTRODUCTION

The Hebrews letter begins with the glory of Christ and closes magnifying "that great Shepherd of the sheep." In between 1:1 and 13:20 we are exhorted to keep our eyes on him (12:2) who is "higher than the heavens" (7:26). The epistle to the Hebrews was primarily an exhortation to faithfulness. Jewish Christians were leaving the gospel system and reverting to former allegiance toward the law given at Sinai. The inspired penman of Hebrews eloquently argues for the better things of Christianity. The heart and core of this powerful treatise is the beauty of Jesus, the only perfect One to live on the earth from creation to judgment day!

In Hebrews 2:9 we have one of the most definitive verses in all of sacred text regarding the way of redemption. Christians, then and now, are told to behold the Lord. By the grace of God, Christ tasted of death for every one of us. What loyalty we therefore owe to him. How foolish to even contemplate leaving the Savior! Rather, such consideration of the Redeemer's matchless love should naturally draw us nearer to him!

> Jesus, Jesus, Jesus, sweetest name I know
> Fills my every longing
> Keeps me singing as I go.

One ancient writer spoke these powerful words:

> Were the highest heavens my pulpit
> The innumerable angels my audience
> And eternity my time
> Jesus Christ would always be my text.

On the Mount of Transfiguration we read these graphic words in Matthew 17:8, ". . . they saw no man save Jesus only." After all, Christ is the only way to the Father (John 14:6) and the only name wherein salvation is found (Acts 4:12). It is significant that the Hebrews writer did not tell the recipients of this epistle to behold Abraham, Moses, David, Isaiah or John the Immerser. Jehovah gave Christ Jesus the name that is above every other name (Ph. 2:9) and the one name whereby we glorify God (I Pet. 4:16; Jas. 2:7). F. Whitfield wrote a song magnifying the sweet name of Jesus:

> There is a name I love to hear,
> I love to sing its worth:
> It sounds like music in mine ear,
> The sweetest name on earth.

In the opening stanza of the grandest life ever spent upon earth we learn that the name of the Master meant salvation (Matt. 1:21). He truly came to seek and save the lost (Luke 19:10). Paul wrote cogently of our desperate need and heaven's gracious gift in I Timothy 1:15 and II Corinthians 9:15: "Christ Jesus came into the world to save sinners. . . . thanks be unto God for his unspeakable gift."

CHRIST BEHELD IN PROPHECY

Many prophecies of the Old Testament foretold the coming of the One who had always been (Mi. 5:1-3). Yes, the very One on whom Jehovah would place the iniquities of us all (Isa. 53). The last book of the Old Testament promised that one in the spirit and power of Elijah would prepare the way for Messiah and then suddenly the Lord would come (Mal. 3; Isa. 40). In Luke 1:17 we learn that John the Baptist was the very man likened unto Elijah. His clarion call upon seeing Jesus Christ contained marvelous words: "Behold, the Lamb of God who taketh away the sin of the world" (John 1:29).

In Leviticus 16 the scape goat, in a metaphor, carried the sins of the people on the Day of Atonement into the wilderness, but our blessed Lord actually "gave himself for our sins that he might deliver us from this present evil world" (Ga. 1:4). When we compare John 1:1, 1:14 and 17:5 we can see the pre-earthly existence of our Savior set forth. Yes, *in the beginning,* the Word was *with* God and *was* God. That *Word* became flesh and tabernacled upon men. John 1:14 goes on to declare: "And we beheld his glory, the glory as of the only begotten of the Father, full of grace and truth." In John 17:5 our Lord prayed unto Jehovah: "And now, O Father, glorify thou me with thine own self with the glory I had with thee before the world was."

In Philippians, chapter two, we find the perfect commentary on our passage in Hebrews 2:9 and the verses just cited in the gospel account by John. The willingness Christ manifested to subjugate his roll to the ultimate redemptive plan of the Godhead and be made "a little lower than the angels for the suffering of death" is certainly cause for us to behold Christ, who by the grace of God, tasted of death for every man.

> There was one Who was willing
> To die in my stead
> That a soul so unworthy might live.

We thrill to the marvelous reminder in I Peter 2:24: "Who his own self bare our sins in his own body upon the tree."

CHRIST BEHELD IN CONTRAST

In the epistle to the Hebrews we also behold the Man of Galilee in contrast to others. His supremacy over angels is set forth in chapter one. In the second stanza of the book Christ is superior as the captain of our salvation. He is greater than Moses, according to Hebrews 3:1-6. The promise of rest attending Christianity (4:9; Re. 14:13) supersedes anything Joshua could provide in Canaan. The priesthood of the Levitical arrangements faded into oblivion when compared with the one High Priest of the gospel age — Christ Jesus our Lord. In fact Hebrews 7:26 and 9:26 forever form a tandem of thought that caused Judaism to fade away. Those verses tell us that the Savior is "holy, harmless, undefiled, separate from sinners, made higher than the heavens" and that "once in the end of the world he put away sin by the death of himself." In other words, our majestic Lord is both High Priest and sacrifice at the same time. Is it any wonder that we are told to constantly "look unto Jesus, the author and finisher of our faith" (He. 12:2)! Holland Boring wrote these beautiful sentiments in a gospel song:

> Twas Christ, my Lord, who came to share
> My greatest joy, my deepest care;
> I cast on Him my every fear,
> Content to know that He is near.

CHRIST BEHELD VICTORIOUS

In Isaiah 25:9, coupled with its fulfillment in I Corinthians 15:57, we rejoice to claim the victory in Christ our Savior, for whom mankind waited! Born of the virgin (Is. 7:14), Christ destroyed Satan's dominion (Ge. 3:15) when by the power of God the tomb could hold him no longer (Ro. 1:4). The miracles Jesus performed cause us to believe (John 20:31) and his perfect sojourn upon the earth gives us an example to follow (I Pe. 2:21). His simplicity in life, teaching, emphasis and selection of disciples gives us consolation, challenge and comfort. Truly never a man so spake or lived like the Master (John 7:46). His glorious life was consummated in his triumphal ascension and magnificent coronation in glory. Yes, Christ, whom we behold, "passed through the clouds unto the ancient of days and received a kingdom" (Da. 7:13-14). The everlasting doors of glory opened wide to receive him home in that supernal realm (Ps. 24).

> O Jesus, King most wonderful,
> Thou Conqueror renowned,
> Thou Sweetness most ineffable
> In whom all joys are found.

WE BEHOLD CHRIST

There are several areas or points of emphasis in which we need to behold Jesus today. Let us notice some of the more salient points:

As Church-Builder: In Matthew 16, as a result of Peter's confession that Jesus was the Christ, our Redeemer proclaimed the immortal words: "Upon this rock I will build my church." No other builder of churches has the authority of heaven to back him up. Last of all, *God sent his Son* is the message of Matthew 21:37. He is the only foundation (I Co. 3:11). Christ is the head of the body — the church — and has the pre-eminent position in the gospel system (Col. 1:18). God is glorified in the church now and forever is the dynamic message of Ephesians 3:21. May we ever behold the blessed Savior and his glorious church!

As King: Contrary to popular doctrine Christ is not coming back to earth to rule for he has been reigning as "King of kings" since the first century (I Ti. 6:15; Re. 17:14). His kingdom was preached as a reality nineteen centuries ago (Acts 8:12; 17:7; 28:31). His return will not be to earth to set up a kingdom but in the air to receive the kingdom and deliver it up to God (I Co. 15:23-25; I Th. 4:13-18). Yes, we behold Christ the King in all his authority (Ma. 28:18).

As Mediator: In Hebrews we learn that the New Covenant is a better arrangement than Moses could provide in Judaism. This was primarily true because of the superior nature of Christ who mediates the New Testament (He. 8:6; 9:15). In I Timothy 2:5 we learn that the Savior is *the one and only* mediator between God and man. We therefore must follow the testament he mediates. That rules out Joseph Smith and Mormonism and all other latter-day revelations. We are complete in Christ. Let us keep our eyes on him!

Our Righteous Judge: The Man of Calvary made it clear that the words he spoke would "judge us in the last day" (John 12:48). Paul told the Athenians in Acts 17:31 that a day would be appointed for judgment before that One who was raised from the dead. Romans 2:16 makes it clear that the gospel of Christ will be the standard of judgment and not the law of Moses. In a familiar setting that brave soldier of Christ, the apostle Paul, points to a final accounting when the Lord, "the righteous judge," would provide for all faithful servants a crown of glory (II Ti. 4:8). T. S. Teddlie wrote:

> Someday you'll stand at the bar on high,
> Someday your record you'll see,
> Someday you'll answer the question of life,
> What will your answer be?

As Creator: Yes, behold the One who made all things, even the Savior of mankind! In John 1 and Colossians 1:15-18 we learn that nothing was made unless Christ made it. All things were made *by* and *for* him! This forever establishes the deity of Christ. Truly, Jesus of Nazareth was the fellow-Jehovah, the Shepherd of the sheep, the One who shed saving blood at Golgotha that Zechariah 13:1-7 spoke concerning. What power!

As Dearest Friend: When one reviews the dramatic saga of Matthew, Mark, Luke and John he is bound to say with doubting Thomas concerning Jesus: "My Lord and my God." Realizing the personal touch Christ showed toward the individual will cause us to tell others "how great things the Lord has done" for us (Mark 5:19). A true friend comes to our aid, helps us when in need, challenges us to grow spiritually and provides sustenance for the future (Mark 10:30). All this — and much more — does Christ provide in the abundant life he bestows (John 10:10).

As Commander: In the struggles of this sojourn in a cruel and wicked world is it not grand, beyond description, to have a commander who never lost a battle and never gave an idle challenge? Tempted in all points like we are — yet Jesus never erred (He. 4:15). So, we follow his steps (I Pe. 2:21-22) unto ultimate victory. When we see Jesus in all his resplendent glory we exclaim with Revelation 19:6 . . . *Hallelulah — Praise God!* Fighting the good fight of faith (I Ti. 6:12) we follow "the captain of our salvation" all the way to the land of fadeless day (Re. 22:5).

As Redeemer: The Hebrews letter tells us from first to last to always gaze upon the Messiah. Fulfilling precisely the prophecies of the Old Testament Jesus Christ, our Redeemer, leads us to "the rest that yet remains" for true children of God. Into the grace of God, found in Christ, with eternal glory we march victoriously (II Ti. 2:1, 10). No wonder the song states so cogently:

> How I love the great Redeemer
> Who is doing so much for me;
> With what joy I tell the story
> Of the love that makes men free,
> Till my earthly life is ended,

I will send songs above
Then beside the crystal sea
More and more my soul shall be
Praising Jesus and his love.

Beholding Christ constantly will be all the consolation, joy, peace and challenge we need to make us grateful now and forevermore.

WHY MEN LOOK AWAY FROM CHRIST

It would be wonderful if we could state that the Hebrew Christians never wavered from that noble purpose, but that would be untrue to the sacred text. It would be thrilling to suggest that all members of the Lord's church today never took their eyes off Christ. But, again, such would be untrue. Why do so many who have received so much from God look away from divine mandates to worldly vanities? What caused the Hebrew brethren to take their eyes off the Christ? Perhaps the same problems that existed then exist today.

Persecution: Christianity, by the sixth decade of the first century, had finally raised the wrath of the Roman Empire. Jewish Christians did not wish to pay the price of duress and tribulation that accompanied the gospel (I Pe. 4:12), so they decided to turn back to the comfortable inherited religion of their fathers. The customs and traditions of Judaism appealed to them more than the challenge of Christianity. Jesus, in the Sermon on the Mount, referred to persecution such as the prophets endured as being a corollary of his system also (Ma. 5:10-12). Today, in our welfare society it is next to impossible to interest folk in anything that demands sacrifice. To follow the Savior means surrender and few today will deny themselves anything (Luke 9:23).

Demands of Spiritual Growth: The Hebrews were severely rebuked for being babes in the spiritual realm (5:12-14). They were on the verge of absolute apostasy (3:12; 6:4-9) due to indifference and malnutrition in the Scriptures. They were not assembling with the saints but rather backing away from loyalty to things divine (10:32-39). When we take our eyes off of the Lord to accommodate worldly pleasures and peer pressure we decline in spiritual service (I Pe. 2:1-3). Hosea bluntly said that such destroyed God's people in ancient times (Ho. 4:6). When we turn from godliness to the call of carnal pleasures we end up just like Esau did (He. 12:17-19). Perpetual infancy in the divine realm produces shallow congregations today as well!

Forgetting Our Blessings: Nothing hurts growth in eternal matters more than ingratitude. When our attention is constantly centered in Christ (Col. 3:1-3) we count our many blessings and press onward in Jesus' name (Ph. 3:14). But, becoming self-centered pushes us farther away from the beauty of holiness into a world of petty thoughts and sensual pleasures. In Hebrews 10:32-39, those weak brethren were told to "call to remembrance the former days" and thus not to turn back to the beggarly things of the world. Christians are commanded to be thankful in all things, pray without ceasing, rejoice evermore and not to murmur and complain (I Th. 5:16-18; Ph. 2:14). Keeping our affections centered on the Savior will produce grateful hearts and spiritual minds. Brethren who constantly feel sorry for themselves will never glorify God.

> A charge to keep I have,
> A God to glorify,
> A never-dying soul to save
> And fit it for the sky.

CONCLUSION

Instead of drifting away from the moorings of the gospel system (Heb. 2:1) we should offer unto the Lord the praise of our hearts continually (13:15). The love of God, in Christ Jesus, compels us to genuine fidelity in his service! Ephesians 3:17-21 is the best commentary on our subject.

> That Christ may dwell in your hearts by faith; that ye, being rooted and grounded in love, may be able to comprehend with all saints what is the breadth, and length, and depth, and height; and to know the love of Christ, which passeth knowledge, that ye might be filled with the fullness of God.

> Now unto him that is able to do exceeding abundantly above all that we ask or think, according to the power that worketh in us, unto him be glory in the church by Christ Jesus throughout all ages, world without end. Amen.

In all that we say, do and think, may we always look to Jesus!

EVERY HOUSE IS BUILDED BY SOMEONE

HEBREWS 3:4

By ROBERT R. TAYLOR, JR.

Baptized into Christ, 1944. Began preaching, 1949. Married to Irene Crump and they have two children. Graduate of Freed-Hardeman, David Lipscomb and George Peabody Colleges. Author of 12 books, over 20 tracts and several hundred articles in various gospel papers. Script writer for International Gospel Hour. Writes *Gospel Advocate* Adult Quarterly and has been *Gospel Advocate* staff member since 1969. Serves as local evangelist in Ripley, Tennessee. Speaker, *First Annual Denton Lectures.*

INTRODUCTION

The assigned verse for our study at this time is located in Hebrews 3:4 and contains these moving, marching and militant words, "For every house is builded by some man; but he that built all things is God." In somewhat of a larger context it reads,

Wherefore, holy brethren, partakers of the heavenly calling, consider the Apostle and High Priest of our profession, Christ Jesus; Who was faithful to him that appointed him, as also Moses was faithful in all his house. For this man was counted worthy of more glory than Moses, inasmuch as he who hath builded the house hath more honour than the house. For every house is builded by some man; but he that built all things is God. And Moses verily was faithful in all his house, as a servant, for a testimony of those things which were to be spoken after; But Christ as a son over his own house; whose house are we, if we hold fast the confidence and the rejoicing of the hope firm unto the end. (He. 3:1-6).

95

The astute student of Holy Writ will promptly and profitably perceive that our assigned statement, Hebrews 3:4, forms a vastly important link in the Hebrews penman's argument proving Christ's superiority over Moses in the immediate context of this great chapter. Note what is affirmed in these valiant verses: (1) Christ is Apostle and High Priest and must be duly contemplated by all holy brethren who are partakers of Jehovah's heavenly calling (v. 1). (2) Both Christ and Moses were faithful at their respective posts of heavenly callings (v. 2). (3) Just as the builder of the house has more glory than the house itself so Christ (the builder, creator and sustainer of all, including the Old Testament house or the Israelite Economy) greatly exceeds Moses in glory (v. 3). (4) Every house is built by someone. This is axiomatic and needs little or no proof to an intelligent mind (v. 4). (5) The builder of all is God (v. 4). Again, this is axiomatic and were it not for arrogant, blatant skepticism in our world, it would be of universal acceptation for a surety. (5) Moses was faithful in God's Old Testament house or the Israelite Economy but as *servant* (v. 5). (6) Christ is faithful to God in his own house (that of Christianity) and as *Son* (v. 6). Just as the Son is greater than the servant so Christ the Son in the house of Christianity is greatly superior to Moses the servant in the Old Testament house or the Israelite Economy.

This is the rich context in which the valiant verse appears that shall be the prized object of our study in Christian apologetics or evidences for the fervent fortification of our faith. The full verse affirms that earthly houses have men as builders but the builder of all is none other than God Almighty. Not only do earthly houses have builders, but religious orders or economies such as Judaism and Christianity have builders. It would have been foolish to the nth degree for any of the Hebrews readers to have denied that the Old Testament house in which Moses was situated as servant was minus a builder. Likewise, it would have been naiveness personified on their part to deny that the New Testament house (the Lord's church) wherein Jesus Christ served as Son had no builder. Matthew 16:18 states in crystal clear language, "And I say also unto thee, That thou art Peter, and upon this rock I will build my church; and the gates of hell shall not prevail against it." Hence, the church has a builder — the Christ. Both spiritual and physical houses have builders. They must, to exist! The builder of all is God. So affirms Hebrews 3:4.

SOME CLEAR POINTS INITIALLY OBSERVED

Hebrews 3:4 has set forth in crystal clear and plainly piercing logic the powerful principle of Cause and Effect. For every effect observed there must not only be a cause but the cause must be adequate to explain the effect it produces. The title of our study of this verse is that "Every House Is Builded By Someone." We travel down a street in any city of the United States for the first time. Facing the street on both left and right are beautiful and well-constructed houses on each building lot. We know that each of those houses had a builder. There was an architect that planned them initially and drew up the blueprints. Then came the corps of carpenters who began with footings and foundation and a few weeks later turned over the completed houses to the interested owners. We may never know the architect by name; we may never lay eyes of recognition on any of the carpenters but we know that the houses had such in their background of planning and building execution. In that same city we travel for the first time to downtown. There we behold skyscraper after skyscraper with some of them tens of stories high. Without exception each had talented architects who planned them and laboring men of skill who erected them. Every building on earth proclaims a crystal clear sermon which says, "I have a builder who caused me to be." The sight-seeing trip in that city is by car. The car had to be made. Behind it was engineering skill and know-how. Before the survey of the city was begun the trip to the city was made by plane. Somebody made that plane. The day after these lines were penned found my wife and me as we returned from a gospel meeting in the Northwest — in Idaho — her home state. We went out and returned by plane. As we flew over the snow-capped Rockies which rose up toward us in majestic beauty and observed the silvery clouds that formed a picture that no gifted artist could ever duplicate, the thought hit both of us that we have millions of people on earth who would say that the plane we were riding in had to have a maker, but not the majestic mountains just below us and the clouds that hovered about us and below us. It is amazingly amazing that such can be the observations of atheists and unbelievers. But back to that survey of that city again. During the survey of the city time was kept by a watch on the wrist. That watch had a maker. We do not have to see, touch or talk to the maker to know that he was responsible for the watch. A watch *demands* a watchmaker. Demanded also is a maker for the man or woman who wears the watch and determines time by perusal of its two hands.

What is said about houses, skyscrapers, cars, planes and watches as demanding makers will evoke no argument from an intelligent mind. Yet when God as Maker of the universe is declared many balk and become instant objectors. How amazingly amazing this is. How immeasurably sad it is that the Maker of all is denied by so many of his own human products!

AN ADEQUATE CAUSE DEMANDED
FOR EVERY EFFECT

The greater the building the greater the intelligence, the skill and the talents in its erection. There is a vast difference in a man with some building ability who constructs a garage for his two cars and a group of men who drew up all architectural blueprints and did all construction work on the Empire State Building in New York City or the towering Sears Building in Chicago, the world's tallest building. While I was in a meeting in the Chicago area some years back the local preacher showed me the sights of Chicago. We went to the top of the Sears Building. It is an imposing structure while on ground looking up at it; it is really imposing at its top when one sees so much of Chicago from this vantage point. A man would be a fool to look at that imposing structure and deny that it had architects, planners and builders. Chance did not build it; time did not erect it; a big bang in the middle of the Loop did not build it!

There is a certain amount of intelligence required in a child's building a model airplane, but how much more in a group of men who design and construct a mighty jet that can carry hundreds of passengers safely from location to location and even across our vast oceans. There is a vast difference between a man who constructs a simple machine to do a job for him and the people who have pioneered in building modern computers. It took intelligence to build our modern computers. But many in our world believe that the intelligence that was required to build computers in turn did not have any intelligence that produced it initially. Yet an IBM official has suggested that if a modern computer could be built to equal the mind of man, it would require a building to house it the size of the Empire State Building in New York City. Computers have not just happened; neither has our universe and all that therein is. Where there is an effect there must be a cause behind it that is competently and completely adequate in its production. This is a principle daily recognized and unusual would be the person who would call it in question relative to the man-made.

Yet take leave of what men have built and comprehend an entire universe and all the marvelous forms of variegated life therein and the masses of men will reject with rapidity what they accept without quibbling or question of their own works, labors, arts and productions. We live in a marvelous universe that works with precision and accuracy. We live amidst earthly surroundings and just under the two heavens. In the first heaven where birds fly, where clouds congregate, from where our moisture in forms of rain, sleet and snow fall and where man now flies with considerable ease, there is order and harmony. Who provided this order or harmony? Who made the air and its various components? Who formed and fashioned those clouds that are so beautiful to behold? Chance or Creator? Nature or the God of Nature? Then in the second heaven there are found stars, planets, sun and moon. So vast is immense space that stars are so many "light years" away from us. Light travels at a distance of about 186,000 miles per second! Think how far those stars are from the earth. The distance is beyond our ability to comprehend. The moon is some 240,000 miles from us. Men have now been to God's moon and human feet have walked on its surface. They returned to tell about it. It is amazingly amazing that some who worked on such projects would never deny that the space vehicles that took men there and successfully returned them to earth just happened as result of purposeless time and chance and yet they deny the moon had a maker or the men who went there had a maker.

The sun is 93,000,000 miles out there in space. Were it far more distant the earth would be a ball of ice with no forms of life possible. Were it far, far closer to us or we to it, the earth would be burned to a crisp — it would be a ball of fire. Our earth has been perfectly placed or poised in space. It does not rest on a body of water, upon a turtle's back or upon the shoulders of Hercules as formerly imagined. The great Uzzean patriarch Job affirms that Jehovah God "hangeth the earth upon nothing" (Job 26:7). God's gravity holds it in its proper orbit and in its planned position. Each twenty-four hours it rotates upon its axis. This makes possible day and night, alternations of time. Annually, it revolves around the sun which makes possible our various seasons of spring, summer, autumn and winter. The wonderful earth on which we live is tilted and positioned just right for the sun to warm us; the moon to protect us from high tides; and ocean and dry land to make possible all land, water and air forms of life. Suppose we were only 50,000 miles from the moon. Tides would then cover even the highest of mountains and do it daily. Who or what is responsible? A Creator — the *Who* — or an impotent *what* — *time* and *chance?* The man who has trouble with this question is to be pitied and pitied greatly!

No wonder Holy Writ says,

> The heavens declare the glory of God; and the firmament sheweth his handywork. . . . O Lord, how manifold are thy works! in wisdom hast thou made them all: the earth is full of thy riches. . . . For thus saith the Lord that created the heavens; God himself that formed the earth and made it; he hath established it, he created it not in vain, he formed it to be inhabited: I am the Lord; and there is none else (Ps. 19:1; 104:24; Is. 45:18).

Not only do the stars, planets, sun, moon and earth all exist as effects of an adequate cause that produced such and has maintained them across the ceaseless centuries but there are innumerable forms of life that inhabit our world. Some forms of life that inhabit our world are very simple; others on earth are very complex, such as man. David, Israel's Sweet Singer, observed, "I will praise thee; for I am fearfully and wonderfully made: marvellous are thy works; and that my soul knoweth right well" (Ps. 139:14). God has adapted the human eye to all the sights that it surveys with such marvel and wonder. He has adapted man's ear to all the sounds that abound in our world. He has adapted man's nose to the smells about him. He has adapted air with its proper and precise elements or ingredients of oxygen, hydrogen, nitrogen, etc., to our lungs. He has adapted food and water to our digestive needs. He has given us a marvelous system of nerves. He has adapted the feet to walk and run and the hands to feel and touch. He has adapted man and woman so they can mate and procreate the race as well as speak the extra language of love in marital sex. Mere Chance and Time — the two golden calves of silly, senseless evolutionary dogmas, could *never* explain the marvelous reproduction system of man and animals if they had a million, billion or trillion years to attempt this impossible feat. Anyone who can believe that evolution is the mastermind behind marvelous man and wonderful woman is using his God-given brain to *no* advantage at all.

Man's mind is marvelous beyond apt appraisal or accurate assessment. It is capable of thought processes, decision-making, emotional responses and either approval or disapproval within the realm of the conscience. We look at all that the mind of man has invented in this century alone and it staggers all our imaginations beyond their powers of expansion. Yet far greater than it all is the Mastermind in Heaven — Jehovah God — that gave man a mind in the first place. There are four billion plus of us on earth now. What if every piece of knowledge and wisdom possessed by *all* of us could be placed into just one gigantic mind? How fabulously marvelous and magnificent it would be. But take the matter a step further. What if every piece of knowledge and wisdom of every person now living and who has ever lived could be placed into just one gigantic mind? How great it would be! But what if every piece of knowledge and wisdom of every person now living, who has lived and who will ever live could be placed into just one gigantic mind? That would be even greater than the previous two. Yet not any of these three minds just described (or imagined) would be anywhere equal to the Mastermind in Heaven who bequeathed to every individual the marvels of his mind, the wonders of the wisdom he has accumulated or shall accumulate in the future. Could the aggregate equal God, then the aggregate would be on a par with God, which is unthinkable.

The mind and body of man are marvelous effects to behold and contemplate. Time and Chance are inadequate causes behind such. Time cannot produce what it never had the potential to produce in the first place. Random chance is not adequate as the great Prime Mover or the Cause that produced it all. Man has being. Time and Chance have no being. Who gave man his being? Man can think and act rationally. He can reason; he can change things; he can make things happen. Time and Chance do not think; they do not act rationally; they cannot reason; they do not act responsibly; they cannot change things from the better to the worse. What *Cause* conferred all this on man? It could not have been a Cause less intelligent or less powerful than man. Unquestionably, it had to be one far more intelligent and far more powerful than man. Does Time qualify? *No!* Does Chance qualify? *No!* Man did not make himself. Psalms 100:3 assures of this by stating in crystal clear language, "Know ye that the Lord he is God: it is he that hath made us, and not we ourselves; we are his people, and the sheep of his pasture." Without question or quibble it is certain that no lower forms of life could have made man. They cannot even make themselves, let alone one much higher and far more complex than are they. Non-living things like rocks, dust, mud, water, gasses and the like could not have made man. Nothing finite could have made him. Only the Infinite One in heaven fills all the necessary essentials as man's maker.

This is precisely what Moses affirms in Genesis 1:26-27; 2:7 and 2:21-23. This is exactly what Solomon affirms in Ecclesiastes 7:29. This is surely what the psalmist affirms in Psalms 100:3, a verse already quoted in this study. This is absolutely what Jesus the Christ affirms in Matthew 19:4 and Mark 10:6. This is what Paul affirms in Acts 17:28-29. This is what any truly reflective mind will conclude when all evidence has been duly collected, intelligently weighed, and logical conclusions have been drawn from the same.

WHAT SAY THE SKEPTICS?

In more than a third of a century of reading rather widely what unbelievers say about origins or in accounting for the existence of the universe and everything therein they have sought to avoid an acceptance of creation in Genesis in three ways.

First, a few have suggested that all is simply an illusion and no reality attaches to anything. Such people do not even acknowledge their own existence! They reject the proposition, "I think: therefore I am." Perhaps it reads this way, according to their views, "We refuse to think: therefore we deny that we exist!" One is made to wonder just what such people must think or feel if they take a hard fall to earth or a dangerous object collides with them and renders serious injury. Would a fall upon an illusionary earth that really had no existence produce pain and inflict injury? How could they collide with an object when neither they nor the object have any existence or reality? If all is nothing, then we have imaginary professors of *nothing*, lecturing to imaginary students of *nothing*, from imaginary books of *nothing*, about things of *nothing!* How ridiculous can people — though only a few — get? Logic, science and scripture all combined reject this as nothing but tomfoolery. Even labeling it as that gives it far too much credit! "I think: therefore I am" is sufficient to prove this to be a false philosophy. The Bible is a *real* book, that speaks of a *real* Godhead, that addresses *real* men who have *real* problems — sins — about the need to avoid a *real* hell and go to a *real* heaven. This illusionary philosophy will not square with *real* logic, *real* science, and *real* scripture. How could it?

A second stance that some skeptics have advanced is the eternality of Matter. They deny that the world has had a beginning. They affirm that it has always been and always will be. They do not believe that mind or man has always been and therefore have to conclude that non-living matter produced mind or man. Earlier in this century Charles Smith, a thorough-going atheist, an evolutionist who served as president of the American Association for the Advancement of Atheism, said this in a pamphlet called *Godless Evolution:*

> In the beginning was matter, which begat the amoeba, which begat the worm, which begat the fish, which begat the amphibian, which begat the reptile, which begat the lower mammal, which begat the lemur, which begat the donkey, which begat man, who imagined God. This is the genealogy of man.

Perhaps it was an oversight on Smith's part but it is interesting to observe that he uses "which" all the way through until he comes to man and then he changes to "who." Grammatically, *which* refers to things and *who* refers to humans. To Smith the "which" (things) produced the "who" (or that which is not a thing, but now a human)! This is amazingly amazing.

But none of this is really logical, for gas, rocks, dirt, etc., do not produce living creatures. Pasteur proved that, but evolutionists are anything but smart and plenty dense when it comes to accepting anything that upsets their organic evolutionary applecart. Spontaneous generation is not scientific. It never has been; it is not today; it never will be. Life does not come from non-life. Quite to the contrary, it comes from previous life. Rocks do not lay eggs that become little chickens! Dirt, mud, dust and sand do not breed pigs, cats, cows, horses and men! If there had ever been a time when just Matter existed and no Mind, then we could never had had Mind or men. Mind (God) acted upon matter to produce man as per Genesis 2:7 but Matter is absolutely impotent and incapable of acting upon itself so as to produce Mind. It is no longer scientific (it never really was but they call it such nevertheless) to believe that the Universe has always been here. The deeply respected second law of thermodynamics teaches that everything is wearing down and wearing out. The obvious implication of this is that anything that can wear down and out cannot be eternal. There is no way it can be. If so, how, How, *how?* This skeptical sentiment is at odds with both the Old and New Testaments. Genesis 1:1 speaks of the beginning. So does John 1:1ff. The universe is wearing down; it is getting older. It will one day be removed. Hebrews 1:11-12 in the New Testament and Psalms 102:25 so attest and affirm. Logic, science and scripture all oppose this senseless stance of the proud, defiant skeptic.

The third atheistic stance of the unbelieving world is that the universe came from nothing. But how could a great big nothing produce a great big something that sparkles with life, precision, harmony, etc.? Logic rebels at this; so does everything that is scientific; so does the entirety of God's Word — the Holy Bible. To claim a belief that somehow, somewhere and some way a *nothing* produced *something* is illogical, unscientific and totally unscriptural.

The so-called "Big Bang" theory cannot any more account for the precious precision and absolute perfection of our universe than that an explosion in a printing shop produced *Webster's Unabridged Dictionary* or a set of encyclopedias like *World Book* and *Brittanica.*

WHO BUILDED (MADE) MAN?

Not only do we have the marvelous world as God's house universal but we have man who inhabits a part of God's house universal — a body made by this God on high. Man is a soul who inhabits a body or house of clay. How came this creature to be? There are only two possible answers — evolution or creation. If anyone knows another alternative, just what would it be? Evolution has been a part of man's thinking (????) since the early Greeks nearly twenty-five centuries ago and maybe even before that. However, the movement of maliciousness has really enjoyed a heyday since Darwin and the publication of his *Origin of Species* in 1859. Millions of men and women reject all that God's Book teaches relative to creation in order that they might be the determined devotees of evolution. They prefer Darwin to Deity. They prefer what Huxley said to what Heaven said relative to origins. They prefer Simpson to the Savior as touching how things came to be. Simpson said, "Evolution;" the Savior of men — the Lord Jesus Christ — said, "Creation," in Matthew 19:4-5 and Mark 10:6. They prefer geology to Genesis and count Simpson and Sagan as greater authorities than Moses in Genesis 1 and Christ in Matthew 19.

But evolution has some real problems. They (the evolutionists) have a nothing that somehow, somewhere, and someway turned itself into a non-living something. This is illogical, unscientific and anti-scriptural. From nothing comes nothing. Something cannot come from nothing. In the second place they have this simple non-living something turning itself into a simple living something. This is nothing but spontaneous generation or living forms coming from non-living forms. Logic leaves them here. So does true science. So does every particle of Holy Writ that touches these momentous matters. Life comes from life — not non-living forms. In the third place they have simple living forms changing themselves into enough kinds (with each one's getting or growing just a little more complex) as ultimately to produce complex, complicated and intelligent man in all his majesty and marvel. And it all started with something that cannot be seen except by a microscope! Yet the best known law of reproduction is that everything brings forth after its own kind. Sows produce litters of pigs — not puppies. Mares produce horses — not honeybees. Cats produce kittens — not kangaroos. Women produce human babies — not non-human animals. Genesis 1 is filled with the well-established law that everything (both human and non-human) brings forth after its kind.

Evolution has lower forms of life here before man and by nearly one-half billion years between the first speck of life and man's arrival on the unplanned and disorganized scene of gradual development. Did man arrive here by birth or by transformation? These are the *only* two alternatives open to evolutionists. If a third one is open, just what would it be? If by birth, then a non-human mother gave birth to a human. The offspring took after neither the mother that bore it nor the father that begat it. And this is logical and scientific to believe? If not by birth, then it must have been by transformation. This would mean that somehow, somewhere, someway a non-human animal (a male) left his animal nature and suddenly became human. But for the system to have survived by procreation about that same time and not far away either a non-human animal (a female) somehow, somewhere and someway suddenly left her animal nature and became a woman. There she was about to make a step or move an inch as an animal and presto she became a human female by the time she had put her foot down or moved an additional inch! Then the two must have run into each other and that is why we have four billion plus of us here right now! And this is logical? And this is scientific? And this is philosophically sound? And this is intelligently sensible? It is not any of the foregoing. This I state as dogmatically as I am capable of doing!

CONCLUSION

Is it not ten million times easier to believe that God is the First Cause, the Eternal, Omnipotent, Uncreated One, who caused the universe to come into existence and all therein, than to account for it all with neither a Mind to formulate it nor the Accompanying Power to form it all? Yea, verily it is.

In a beautiful, striking tribute to the greatness of this God, Isaiah wrote, "Who hath measured the waters in the hollow of his hand, and meted out heaven with the span, and comprehended the dust of the earth in a measure, and weighed the mountains in scales, and the hills in a balance?" (Is. 40:12).

GOD HATH SPOKEN THE LIVING WORD

HEBREWS 1:1-3; 4:12

By DUB McCLISH

Native Texan, son of a gospel preacher, grandson of an elder. Married Lavonne James and they have three children. Graduate of Freed-Hardeman and Abilene Christian Colleges. Has done local work preaching in five states, gospel meeting work in 15. Has spoken on lectureships at several colleges and on several other major lectureships. Writes for several gospel papers. Radio speaker. Local evangelist, Pearl St. Church, Denton, TX. Director and speaker, *Annual Denton Lectures.*

INTRODUCTION

From his Roman prison cell, Paul wrote of the gospel, "Wherein I suffer hardship unto bonds, as a malefactor; but the word of God is not bound" (II Ti. 2:9). Paul wrote in recognition of the incomparable glory and power of God's Word. The messenger of God may be bound, but the message of God cannot be.

What is there about the Word of God that makes it so peculiar and unique? Of all of the many descriptions of the attributes of God's Word that one might compile from all of the Bible, the essential characteristics of that Word are found in two contexts of Hebrews. In the awesome, sweeping statement with which the letter begins, the writer speaks of the revealed Word as follows:

God, having of old time spoken unto the fathers in the prophets by divers portions and in divers manners, hath at the end of these days spoken unto us in his Son, whom he appointed heir of all things,

through whom also he made the worlds; who being the effulgence of
his glory, and the very image of his substance, and upholding all
things by the word of his power, when he had made purification of
sins, sat down on the right hand of the Majesty on high (He. 1:1-3).

In a subsequent passage the author describes God's Word
in the following terms:

For the word of God is living, and active, and sharper than any two-
edged sword, and piercing even to the dividing of soul and spirit, of
both joints and marrow, and quick to discern the thoughts and in-
tents of the heart (He. 4:12).

From these two passages let us now consider several facts
about God's Word.

SOURCE OF THE WORD

The Word of God is just that — *the Word of God.* It is not
the word of a man or of several men, except as men were used
as the mediums through which God revealed it. *"God* hath
spoken." Until he sent his Son to be his final spokesman, he
revealed his Word a piece at a time through many prophets in
various ways scattered out over many centuries. Then he sent
his Son and thundered from heaven that men were now to hear
him (Ma. 17:5). He preached and declared for three and one-half
years God's Word that would become effective with his own
death on Calvary. He continued speaking the new law of the
new spiritual kingdom, his church, through his inspired
apostles (John 16:13) and the prophets on whom they laid their
hands (Acts 6:5-8). Concerning the human agents through
whom God and Christ spoke, Peter says, "For no prophecy
ever came by the will of man: but men spake from God, being
moved by the Holy Spirit" (II Pe. 1:21).

Because *God* has spoken *his* Word it is an objective standard. It is objective truth as opposed to subjective opinion.
Webster defines "objective" in this sense as "expressing or
involving the use of facts without distortion by personal feelings or prejudices."[1] Conversely, that which is "subjective"
has to do with "experience or knowledge as conditioned by
personal mental characteristics or states."[2] It is clear from
these definitions that God's Word is objective because it came
from and stands outside of, above and beyond, man's personal
thinking, feelings and prejudices. All of the philosophies, reli-

gious ideas and doctrines outside of the objective Word of God are necessarily subjective — originating in the mind of man and colored by his experiences, opinions, feelings and prejudices. Perhaps we should move one step further back and give the "devil his due" for originating all false doctrine (John 8:44).

All truth resides in God, whether the specific revealed truth of his Word that can save our souls ("I am the truth," Jesus said — John 14:6), or the mathematical and scientific truths that relate to and result from the order of God's material universe. All matters that are truth or fact are such in and of themselves, independent of human mind or opinion. It matters not if man in his subjective prejudices refuses to accept the fact that $2 + 2 = 4$. Nor does it affect the truth of an objective proposition that all men are ignorant of it. $2 + 2 = 4$ was true from the beginning, even though man possibly did not discover it until several hundred years after creation.

What is true of objective mathematical truth is likewise true of objective, revealed spiritual truth. All men may reject, ignore, deny or even be guilty of violating God's truth on baptism, the church, marriage, divorce and remarriage or any other subject, but these remain true and unaffected. Man has more and more come to have a subjective approach to matters of religion. The way neo-Pentecostalism in the mid-1960's swept multitudes of people of all religious persuasions into its stream is a good demonstration of the foregoing observation. The feelings and opinions of men are the only authority in the subjective approach ("I wouldn't trade this feeling for a stack of Bibles."). Each person thereby becomes his own standard and the only thing worthy of being man's sole, universal standard — God's Word — is rejected. When the "testimony" of personal experiences is valued more than the testimony of God's Word one has adopted the subjective approach. The Word of God gives us the revealed and confirmed evidence of Christ and his gospel. It is objective truth because it is from outside of the minds and opinions of men.

We can easily fall into the subjective trap without realizing it. One of the spiritual songs we sometimes sing has the following words: "You ask me how I know he lives? He lives within my heart." I submit that this is pure subjectivism. If this is the proof of the living Jesus then we have no proof at all! The Moslems or Buddhists could make an equally strong case for their respective deities. We know Christ lives because of such testimony as the irrefutable evidence of an empty tomb, his post-resurrection appearances to hundreds of credible witnesses and his ascension into heaven in the presence of many witnesses. All of these are objective truths of God's Word. It is because God is the source of the Bible that it does constitute objective truth — that which is independent of the faulty and fickle feelings of man. We seriously damage the case of truth when we fall into the popular practice of appealing to subjective arguments in an attempt to establish objective truth.

THE LIVING WORD

We would expect the "living God" (He. 3:12) to produce the "living Word" (He. 4:12). The present participle form ("living") means that God's Word perpetually, continually lives. Vincent calls attention to the word order of the Greek text: "Note the emphatic position of *zon*, 'living.' 'Living' is the word of God . . ."[3] To be ever-living, ever-appropriate, ever-applicable is the very nature of God's Word. Roman Catholicism's doctrines of papal and church infallibility are rooted in their negation that the written word is ever-living: "The Scripture indeed is a divine book, but it is a dead letter . . .;" "a dead and speechless book."[4] Because they deny the life that is in the written word they justify the need for contemporary sources of an infallible and living message which they satisfy by their infallibility heresies. Many Protestant theologians have joined this attitude of relegating God's Word to the distant past as some sort of relic that is no longer relevant because of the technologies and sophistications of modern times. (What a convenient way of dispensing with the prohibitions, disciplines and requirements of the Bible!)

If the Bible is not a living message that will never be obsolete or outmoded, then it is certainly a fraud, because it claims such life for perpetuity. Peter wrote concerning the life that the Word of God possesses:

> Seeing ye have purified your souls in your obedience to the truth
> unto unfeigned love of the brethren, love one another from the heart
> fervently: having been begotten again, not of corruptible seed, but
> of incorruptible, through the word of God, which liveth and abideth
> (I Pe. 1:22-23).

Jesus plainly pictured the Word as seed: "The seed is the word
of God" (Luke 8:11). The efficacy, the essential quality of seed
is the life that is in it. Only by this quality does it produce life
and more seed containing more life. That which is non-living
can never produce life or living matter (although evolutionists
are forced to this utterly untenable position by their denial of
God). The conclusion follows that if the Word of God is dead
then the religion of Christ is dead. That which is dead cannot
produce life, whether it be animal, vegetable or spiritual. Man
cannot manufcture any seed with life in it. God alone holds the
secret of life and he alone is able to invest it in life-giving seed.
Herein is the secret of the living and abiding character of the
Word of God — it is full of life and can give life because it is
from God rather than man. Jesus' own summary statement of
this essential nature of his word proclaims: "the words that I
have spoken unto you are spirit, and are life" (John 6:63).

Cook's comments are well-stated and timely:

> That word did not speak to one generation and then die out. The
> "word" of the "living God" could not become a dead letter. As His
> creative word continues immanent in the natural world from age to
> age, so does His word of promise in the spiritual world.[5]

He who would make God's Word a "dead letter" or a mere
curiosity piece of more primitive times to be relegated to
a museum destroys not only that Revelation, but the God-
ordained religion it alone can produce. We will not let blind,
unbelieving, ignorant and evil men, regardless of how sophisti-
cated and scholarly they claim to be, rob us of our well-founded
faith in God's living Word!

THE ACTIVE WORD

God's Word is not only living, but "active" ("powerful" —
KJV). *Energes* is the word here used. It is rendered "effectual"
in Philemon 6 and I Corinthians 16:9. Harper's Lexicon defines
energes as follows: "Active, Phile. 6; efficient, energetic, Heb.
4:12; adapted to accomplish a thing, I Cor. 16:9."[6] From this

definition it is apparent that it carries the idea not only of
being active and working, but capable or powerful enough to
do what it is designed to do. Our English word, "energy," is
based upon this word. William Barclay comments on the
family of words of which *energes* is a member, as follows:

> The more we study this group of words, the more the same idea
> keeps recurring, the idea of action, strong and powerful, and above
> all effective. Again and again the idea of power and the idea of pur-
> pose achieved meet in these words. And that is most suggestive
> when we go on to see that in the New Testament these are the char-
> acteristic words for the action of God.[7]

God's Word is powerful with the sense of raw force or
ability: this seems to be Paul's meaning in his reference to the
power of the gospel in Romans 1:16. However, it is more than
raw force. It is force and ability with an end and with the
capability of accomplishing its design. What is the aim or
design of God's Word? There are actually several aims for
God's revealed truth.

Direction: "O Jehovah, I know that the way of man is not
in himself; it is not in man that walketh to direct his steps" (Je.
10:23). Since man does not know innately how he should live,
God gave his Word to direct us: "Thy word is a lamp unto my
feet, and light unto my path" (Ps. 119:105).

Prevention of sin: "Thy word have I laid up in my heart,
that I might not sin against thee" (Ps. 119:11). The person who
feeds on God's Word and constantly adds to the treasure-store
of that truth will be saved many a grievous and painful fault.

Correction of sin: In spite of the best the best of us can do
we will still sin and stand in need of correction. God's Word is
to be preached in such a way that it will ". . . reprove, rebuke,
exhort, with all longsuffering and teaching" (II Ti. 4:2). Scripture is profitable ". . . for reproof, for correction . . ." (II Ti.
3:16).

Sanctification, cleansing from sin: The means by which the
church is sanctified and cleansed is by its members having
received the ". . . washing of water with the word" (Ep. 5:26).
The Word is the means by which men are taught to be baptized
in water for their cleansing and sanctification in the blood of
Christ. Jesus' own words on this subject are "He that believeth and is baptized shall be saved" (Mark 16:16).

Salvation: Paul wrote, "For I am not ashamed of the gospel: for it is the power of God unto salvation to every one that believeth . . ." (Ro. 1:16). The gospel is the medium through which man is instructed in the means of appropriating the redeeming blood of Christ to his sinfulness. Did we not have its instructions we would have no means of knowing how our sins could be forgiven.

Spiritual maturity: I believe Peter has God's Word in view when he refers to the "spiritual milk" which will enable us to "grow thereby unto salvation" (I Pe. 2:2). The writer to the Hebrews also relates the spiritual diet of God's word to spiritual growth, discernment and maturity (He. 5:12-14).

Fight the enemies of truth: "The sword of the Spirit, which is the word of God" (Eph. 6:17), is to be used in fighting the "good fight of faith" (I Ti. 6:12), as faithful soldiers of the cross. The Word of God is our only weapon in this spiritual struggle for the minds and lives of men: "For though we walk in the flesh, we do not war according to the flesh (for the weapons of our warfare are not of the flesh, but mighty before God to the casting down of strongholds)" (II Co. 10:3-4).

God's Word has the energy, the capability, the effectiveness to accomplish all of these things that he has designed it to do. However, it cannot do its work if it is not allowed to. To say such implies that there are certain things which may destroy the power and effectiveness of God's Word.

Ungodly influence: Our lives should ". . . adorn the doctrine of God our Saviour in all things" (Ti. 2:10). Our behavior day by day will either make the gospel more attractive to others or it will cause men to despise it. If we live in ungodliness and worldly lusts (Ti. 2:12) we are destroying the power and effectiveness of the truth among those who know us. We are to live such pure lives that the doctrine and Word of God will not be blasphemed because of us (I Ti. 6:1; Ti. 2:5).

Silence: It matters not how good the salt may be, if it is left in the shaker it will not enhance the flavor of food — its effectiveness is neutralized. It matters not how potent a medicine may be, if it is never ingested or applied, its remedial power is wasted. Likewise, with all of the power the gospel has, if we keep it hidden by our silence we rob it of its potential and we prevent its effectual work. We must use every honorable medium at our disposal to publish and proclaim the blessed gospel. We must speak to one at a time or to 1,000 at a time, whichever opportunities are ours, so that the gospel can work, be activated and have its mighty power unleashed on the hearts of men.

"Helping God Out:" Ironically, the very ways in which some are presently trying to "help God" are ways which rob the gospel of its power. Some seem to believe that the gospel doesn't have the power it claims for itself, so they resort to secular and materialistic motivations to attract people. While granting that some may have a noble end in view in using such things as highly-structured social and recreational programs in the local church, the end has never justified the means in the Lord's work.

Others are trying to help God out of a "jam" by "streamlining" the truth as it is taught and preached. They live and are apparently ready to die by the credo "Make everyone feel good about themselves, don't arouse any guilt, don't preach anything controversial, emphasize only positive elements and never preach longer than 20 minutes." Unfortunately, the very things that some are now "streamlining" out of the gospel are its elements of reproof, rebuke and correction. These are all "negative" elements in their view (inspired men apparently never viewed them as such) and are to be passed over as completely undesirable. After all, we must never say anything, regardless of how true or needful, that might offend the most sensitive soul!

We have a new breed of preachers and elders the devil has raised up among us. They are either afraid of their own shadows or they don't know what the gospel is, or perhaps both in some cases. I am utterly amazed at the blind spots some of our preachers and elders have. For example, a preacher wrote me earlier this year to chastize me for being "caustic" and "rude" in a statement I had written in our church bulletin. Among other things, he said "Our Lord found frequent occasion to take the scribes and Pharisees to task for their ungodly stances. On none of those occasions did he ever stoop to rudeness." He also cited I Corinthians 13:5 which says that

love "doth not behave itself unseemly . . ." Now I doubt that
the scribes and Pharisees would have agreed that Jesus never
"stooped to rudeness" after the tongue-lashing of Matthew
23! I reminded my immature critic that the same apostle who
wrote I Corinthians 13:5, called Elymas the Sorcerer a man
". . . full of all guile and all villany, thou son of the devil,
thou enemy of all righteousness . . ." (Acts 13:10). Now I
suspect that Elymas considered Paul "caustic" and "rude"!
Yet, my words under criticism in no way approached the
severity of either Jesus' or Paul's denunciations. (All I did was
call the *Firm Foundation* the "flimsy foundation!") How is it
that supposedly intelligent people can see only what they want
to see in Christ and his faithful contemporaries — things that
agree with their spiritual disease of hypertolerance. Like
physical diabetics, their spiritual "sugar" level is so high that
they may be aptly labeled "spiritual diabetics."

If such brethren had constituted the company of the
apostles on Pentecost the murderous Jews would have left the
occasion feeling rather good about themselves. If the apostles
had been of the type of many of our elders and preachers they
would never have been imprisoned, beaten, and commanded
not to preach any more in the name of Christ because they
would never have preached anything to upset the San Hedrin
in the first place. Or, upon learning that they were doing so,
they would have apologetically ceased. Those poor old apostles
and Stephen! They just didn't know any better than to call
murder "murder" and rebellion against the Holy Spirit
"rebellion against the Holy Spirit" in such terms that they
could not be misunderstood! Think of all of the suffering,
humiliation and mistreatment they could have avoided had
they just been as smart as some of our present-day elders and
preachers!

Why can't we learn that the power and effectiveness is in
the Word *only* when we faithfully, boldly and lovingly declare
the "whole counsel of God" (Acts 20:27)? The more we try to
help God out by delivering polite little speeches full of
humorous stories so as not to offend anyone, the more we rob
the gospel of its power. The fact is, when we emphasize only
the soft, sweet and easy things, even if they are true to the
gospel, we are not preaching the soul-saving, living and active

Word. We are rather preaching a "different gospel" of which Paul warned in Galatians 1:6.

One of the saddest things about this "sweet and smooth" movement among us is the following: these suave, sweet-talking, promoter-type preachers have deceived themselves into believing that the large crowds some of them are able to draw are being attracted to the gospel and the Lord. But they are dead wrong! If they want to challenge me I dare them to do the following: preach one true-to-the-gospel sermon at least 40 minutes long on either "Marriage, Divorce and Remarriage" or on "The Sins of Drinking, Dancing and Wearing Immodest Apparel." It will be quickly seen that the crowds have not been drawn to the gospel or to the Lord, but to the "charisma" and "dynamism" of the men themselves or to the easy-come, easy-go, do-what-you-want-to message they have been preaching. I tell you, there is not enough power in such a message as I have described to lift a feather in a vacuum, much less to change men and women and fit them for heaven! Such effort is mainly spent in the attraction of people to things they are self-ishly pursuing. As a result I have the dreadful and sickening fear that some (if not many) of our congregations are nearer the spiritual cesspool of denominationalism than they are to New Testament Christianity. To say the very least, they have set their sails in that direction and if they don't change course soon that very destination is certain.

Brethren, I appeal for the return to preaching the truth, the whole truth, and nothing but the truth. This includes the parts that lift us up to heaven with hope and joy in the salvation and service of Christ. This also includes the parts that expose sin and error in all men (whether ourselves or those outside of Christ) and brings trembling souls to the foot of the cross, guilt-stricken, miserable, and ready to repent. Such was the power of this balanced message in the first century that its thrust was felt all the way to Caesar's household (Ph. 4:22). Such was the power of this rediscovered, restored message of truth in the first half of the 19th century in our nation that it dominated the religious skyline. Brethren, the power to accomplish its God-ordained ends is still in that Word because the life is still there. Why can't we be content to preach it faith-fully and fully and let it do its powerful work? Oh yes, it is

powerful: of that "shoot out the stock of Jesse" Isaiah prophesied, ". . . he shall smite the earth with the rod of his mouth;
and with the breath of his lips shall he slay the wicked" (Is.
11:4).

THE SHARP WORD

In a most expressive figure the writer compares the Word
of God to a sword, an offensive weapon of war. This is another
reminder that God's people are in a war, a death-struggle, and
our faithfulness in combat will determine not only our own
eternal victory, but that of many others. Therefore, we must
"war the good warfare" (I Ti. 1:18), as "good soldiers of Jesus
Christ" (II Ti. 2:3). In preparing for battle we have many
pieces of helpful armor, but only one weapon — the "sword of
the Spirit, which is the word of God" (Ep. 6:17). However, we
need none other, for it is abundantly adequate to teach,
reprove, correct, instruct, rebuke and exhort (II Ti. 3:16; 4:2).
God's Word, under the figure of a sword, is described as to its
mighty capabilities.

It is sharp. It is not merely a single-bladed instrument, but
one with a keen edge on both sides. Such an instrument is able
to pierce and cut in all directions and to do so deeply and
quickly. God's Word is even sharper than such a finely-honed
double-edged combat sword. This same striking figure was
seen in John's visions of Christ on Patmos: ". . . and out of his
mouth proceeded a sharp two-edged sword . . ." (Re. 1:16; cf.
19:15).

It pierces. Its penetrating power is due to its keen double-
edged "blade." Although a different word is used, the idea is
the same when Luke describes those on Pentecost and in
Stephen's audience as "pricked in their heart" and "cut to the
heart," respectively (Acts 2:37; 7:54).

It divides. As a literal sword partitions the living flesh of
its victim as it penetrates, so the Word of God is so powerfully
effective and sharp as to penetrate and divide matters within
the depths of man's spiritual nature. "Joints and marrow" are
obviously not to be taken literally for two reasons: (1) They are
not in contact with one another — the marrow is inside the
bones which are connected at the joints; (2) The spiritual
sword does not have any effect upon the physical structure of

man's body. "Joints and marrow" is a figurative reference to the innermost recesses of man's spiritual nature. "The word of God . . . divides and lays bare the soul and spirit even to the extent of their joints and marrows."[8]

It discerns. "Discern" is from *kritikos,* "skilled in judging,"[9]

> . . . the usual New Testament meaning being "to sift out and analyze evidence." In the word *kritikos*, the ideas of discrimination and judgment are blended. Thus, the Word of God is able to penetrate into the furthermost recesses of a person's spiritual being, sifting out and analyzing the thoughts and intents of the heart.[10]

The searching and judging power of God's Word is such that it penetrates and exposes the depths of the inner man. It is that "mirror of the soul" that does not deceive us when we gaze into it. It is only by knowledge of the Word of God that we have our ". . . senses exercised to discern good and evil" (He. 5:14).

When the sword pierces and discerns, either of two results will obtain. The sharp, piercing, dividing, discerning sword of God's Word did its work on Pentecost. Those who were "pricked in their heart" by it immediately realized their guilt and cried out, "What shall we do" (Acts 2:37)? The same sharp sword did its work on Stephen's audience and they were "cut to the heart" as the faithful words of the evangelist found their mark. However, rather than repenting of the sins of which Stephen's words convicted them, they violently seized the preacher and stoned him to death. Some who are pierced by the sword of the Spirit rebel, perhaps even violently, while others are brought to humbly seek peace with God by conformity to his will. However, in both reactions the discerning power of God's Word in the spirit of man is clearly demonstrated. Again, if we preach a spineless, diluted message, that is purposely designed not to stir guilt in the vilest sinner, we rob it of its discerning power.

The Lord's sharp sword does its work on man's spiritual nature. I agree with Milligan's summary of the sword's piercing and dividing work:

> The separation takes place within the region of the soul and the region of the spirit; not between them. The living word cleaves and lays bare all parts of the soul and all parts of the spirit, even to the

extent of their joints and their marrows; so that all the perfections and imperfections of man's spiritual nature are made perfectly manifest. And not only so, but even the thoughts and purposes of his heart are, by this infallible Judge, fully analyzed and perfectly classified.[11]

THE COMPLETED WORD

After summarizing how God had in earlier ages revealed his will to men, the Hebrews writer then said that God "hath . . . spoken unto us in his Son" (He. 1:1-2). The inspired writer makes it clear that the last medium of God's revelation to man was his Son. God's Son taught and preached constantly during the last years of his earthly life, ever conscious that he was revealing the Father's will ("For I spake not from myself; but the Father that sent me, he hath given me a commandment, what I should say, and what I should speak" — John 12:49). Moreover, Christ was aware that his word was God's final revelation. Thus he says that men who reject his word will eventually be judged by it (John 12:48).

In giving God's final revelation to men, Christ not only spoke much of it personally, but he also employed other worthy men through whom he spoke. The twelve apostles were granted at least some measure of inspiration to equip them for their very first preaching assignment: ". . . for it shall be given you in that hour what ye shall speak. For it is not ye that speak, but the Spirit of your Father that speaketh in you" (Ma. 10:19-20). As the Lord tried to prepare them for his fast-approaching departure from them, he promised them more specifically, "Howbeit, when he, the Spirit of truth, is come, he shall guide you into all the truth: for he shall not speak from himself; but what things so ever he shall hear, these shall he speak: And he shall declare unto you the things that are to come" (John 16:13).

Christ also empowered the apostles so that they could confer the gift of inspiration as well as other miraculous abilities on certain others (Acts 8:6-8; 8:14-19; II Ti. 1:6; etc.). Such explains how Mark, Luke and James could write by inspiration while not being apostles. Let it be clearly noted that the work of all of the New Testament writers is quite accurately termed the work of the Son, for it was work done by his command and power. Let it also be noted that all of the non-apostolic New

Testament books (Mark, Luke, Acts, James) were written no later than 70 A.D., giving them ample time to have been renounced and repudiated by the apostle John had they been uninspired. Yet, history shows that they were freely accepted as inspired accounts and for this reason are incorporated into the New Testament canon.

Perhaps the most significant thing to note about the promise of inspiration to the apostles is the phrase, ". . . when he, the Spirit of truth, is come, he shall guide you into all the truth" (John 16:13). This promise demands the following: (1) The Spirit was going to come upon the apostles at a certain time; (2) From the time of the coming of the Spirit upon them until sometime before all of the apostles died (Christ made this promise exculsively to them), he would guide them into all the truth; (3) Therefore, all of God's revelation through his Son was completed before the last apostle died. There are only three other possible conclusions, one or more of which must be accepted by those who deny that revelation ends with the book of Revelation: (1) Christ was sincere in his promise, but he was honestly mistaken; (2) Christ was a false prophet and knew that he was deceiving the apostles; (3) Christ's promise is true, but some of the original apostles are still living. If one accepts either of the first two possibilities then Christ is disqualified as man's Savior. If one accepts the third possibility he is insane.

We not only have the living, active, keen-edged Word of God through his Son, but we also have his completed, final Word. Just as God did not call any of the angels "Son" (He. 1:5), and Moses said nothing of priests in the tribe of Judah (He. 7:14), so he mentioned nothing of Mohammed, Joseph Smith, Mary Baker Eddy, the Roman popes, nor any others since the close of the apostolic age, as those through whom he would speak. The truth is, we have God's Word — his final Word, "the faith which was once for all delivered unto the saints" (Jude 3) — in the New Testament. There has been no further word from God and there shall be no further word. All who deny this truth are victims of infidelity!

CONCLUSION

The beauty, glory and power of the everlasting Word of God make it the marvel of all time. Let us handle it reverently, study it diligently, believe it hopefully, obey it faithfully and communicate it accurately. Only when we do so will we both save ourselves and those who hear us (I Ti. 4:16).

ENDNOTES

1. *Webster's Seventh New Collegiate Dictionary* (Springfield, Ma.: G. and C. Merriam Co., 1970), p. 581.

2. *Webster's, op. cit.,* p. 874.

3. M. R. Vincent, *Word Studies in the New Testament* (Mac Dill AFB, Fla.: MacDonald Pub. Co., n.d.), p. 1113.

4. O. C. Lambert, *Catholicism Against Itself* (Winfield, Ala.: O. C. Lambert, 1954), vol. I, p. 25.

5. F. C. Cook, ed., *The Bible Commentary* (Grand Rapids, Mich.: Baker Book House, 1981), vol. X, pp. 48-49.

6. *An Analytical Greek Lexicon (New York, N.Y.: Harper and Brothers,* n.d.), p. 139.

7. William Barclay, *New Testament Words* (London, Eng.: SCM Press Ltd., 1971), p. 81.

8. R. Milligan, *The New Testament Commentary* (Nashville, Tenn.: Gospel Advocate, 1963), vol. IX, p. 140.

9. A. T. Robertson, *Word Pictures in the New Testament* (Grand Rapids, Mich.: Baker Book House, 1932), vol. V, p. 363.

10. Kenneth S. Wuest, *Hebrews in the Greek New Testament* (Grand Rapids, Mich.: Wm. B. Eerdmans Publishing Co., 1956), p. 89.

11. Milligan, *loc. cit.*

AFTER THE ORDER OF MELCHIZEDEK

HEBREWS 5:6-10; 6:20; 7:11, 15, 17

By WINFRED CLARK

Born in Munford, Alabama, baptized by Gus Nichlos in 1937. Married to Edna Stephens and they have two children. Attended Alabama Christian College, Jacksonville State University, and Alabama Christian School of Religion (M.A.). Has preached for 37 years, serving local churches in Alabama and Georgia. Works with the West Hobbs Street church in Athens, Alabama. Director of Public Relations, Alabama Christian School of Religion.

INTRODUCTION

This phrase is found seven times in the Bible (Ps. 110:4; He. 5:6, 10; 6:20; 7:11, 17, 21). Such language focuses on the priesthood that would be peculiar to the Lord Jesus Christ in contrast to the priesthood under Aaron. This sets forth a different kind of priesthood to that of the Levitical. Thus, the nature and uniqueness should be clearly seen.

"After the order of" means such a priesthood is of a certain character and kind, or that which is of a certain arrangement. It has to do with rank or position. It refers to the likeness of. This is the reason the Hebrew writer refers to the fact that Melchizedek was "made like unto the Son of God" (He. 7:3). He is the type of Jesus as priest.

Thus, in our study we will be able to see some things typical of the priesthood of Christ and these will differ from the priesthood of the Levitical order. The priesthood of Jesus is of the order of Melchizedek and not of the order of Aaron.

We shall see it pictured, prophesied and perfected.

THE PRIESTHOOD PICTURED (Genesis 14:18-20)

This is the first account we have of the man in the Old Testament. He appears before us suddenly and is a king and priest when we first see him. He does not descend from Abraham as did Levi but rather descends from Adam. He is not restricted to a family nor is he limited by the law for he was before the law. In this same way, the promise to Abraham was given before the law was given (Ga. 3:16-17). He is pictured as blessing Abraham as he comes in victory from the conflict with the kings.

We, thus, see him pictured as one who is *eminent.*

One does not read these verses without noting that this is no ordinary person. He occupies positions of (1) *Power.* Notice, please that this man is king of Salem. Being a king he can exercise authority and power as such. He is also a priest of God and he has the power to bless Abraham, which thing he did. We see him occupying two positions and both of these are of power. (2) *Prominence.* One can measure the prominence of Melchizedek by the reaction of Abraham. Remember the place of Abraham was no small one. Yet, even Abraham shows his great respect to him in that he receives from him bread and wine and a blessing. He also gives a tithe of the best of the spoils of war (He. 7:1-3). You will notice that Abraham paid no such respect to the king of Sodom (Ge. 14:21-24).

He is also pictured as one who is *ethical.* One moves to the book of Hebrews and there learns from the writer what Melchizedek, king of Salem, means. In so doing we get a picture of the ethical import of his priesthood. Notice that we learn this from the (1) *Title of the King.* The name Melchizedek means "king of righteousness" (He. 7:2). This would set before us the standard used by such a one. Surely this is true of the Son of God and his priesthood (He. 1:8-9). (2) *Territory of the King.* He is called "king of Salem" which means "king of peace." Brought together in this great character are the ethical characteristics of righteousness and peace. Notice it is first righteousness then peace. It is in Christ our Lord that mercy and truth, righteousness and peace kiss each other (Ps. 85:10). The peace of which the Bible speaks can never be expected apart from righteousness. Any effort to gain such contrary to this order is sure to meet defeat. One would have to go against the grain of the priesthood of Christ to do so. The New Testament abounds with support for this principle (Rom. 14:17; II Ti. 2:22; He. 12:11). These writers would never try to divorce righteousness and peace and neither should we.

Furthermore, he is pictured as one who is *eternal*. Read Genesis 14:18-20 and you see Melchizedek appearing as if he had no father or mother nor does one see the beginning of his life or the end of it. In this way, as a priest, he looks to be eternal. He is in this way made like unto the Son of God. He is said to be without: (1) *Recorded Parents in the Priesthood*. In fact, the Hebrews writer says, "without father, without mother" (He. 7:3). This just means there is no record of his father or mother. We see him as a priest without a father and mother from the priestly line. In spite of this, he is still a priest. That did not disqualify him. His priesthood did not depend on such. (2) *Recorded Pedigree from the Priesthood*. The Hebrews writer says, "without descent" (He. 7:3). In a book like Genesis that records one descent or genealogy after another, this man differs. He has no such recorded genealogy. His priesthood is surely one that differs from the Levitical. A person would have to be able to show his descent or he could not serve as priest. Some found this to be true when they returned from Babylon (Ez. 2:62-63). (3) *Recorded Past or Passing*. He is one who stands before us continually. There is no record of his birth or death. There is no record of a past or his passing. Again, in this way he is made by this picture like unto the Son of God as a priest. God, who is the author of the Bible could in the distant past inspire the writer of Genesis to paint a word picture to fit a priesthood like the Son of God's from beginning to end. This surely must be another argument for inspiration.

In this section, we thus see a priesthood pictured that is eminent, ethical and eternal.

THIS PRIESTHOOD PROPHESIED (Psalms 110:1-4)

This is a Messianic psalm. In fact, it is quoted a number of times in the New Testament and applied to no less than Christ.

One should remember that the prophecy that refers to a priesthood to come after the order of Melchizedek was given while the Levitical was yet standing. This shows that the Levitical was a temporary one.

This psalm and prophecy first point to an *office*. One has but to read the first four verses and he will see an office to be occupied. Notice should be given that there is the (1) *Potentate.* "The Lord said unto my Lord, Sit thou at my right hand, until I make thine enemies thy footstool" (Ps. 110:1). Can one question the position of a potentate or a king? Surely not. Neither should one have any doubt as to whom this refers. The Lord quoted it to refer to himself (Mark 12:36; Ma. 22:44; Luke 20:42). Peter said it pointed to Jesus (Acts 2:29-34). The Hebrews writer speaks of it in reference to the Son (He. 1:13).

(2) *Priest.* The prophecy speaks not only of a potentate but also of a priest (Ps. 110:4). This prophecy shows that God will bring together both king and priest in one man. This was the way it was with Melchizedek and thus it would be like that arrangement. Remember that this is not true of the Aaronic. Uzziah, the king, tried to offer incense and became a leper because of this (II Ch. 26:16-21). He tried to become a priest because he was a king and this was not allowed.

This prophecy is also consistent with Zechariah.

> And speak unto him, saying, Thus speaketh the Lord of hosts, saying, Behold the man whose name is the Branch; and he shall grow up out of his place, and he shall build the temple of the Lord; . . . and he shall bear the glory, and shall sit and rule upon his throne; and he shall be a priest upon his throne: and the counsel of peace shall be between them both (Ze. 6:12-13).

This prophet speaks of one's being both king and priest. But this is exactly after the order of Melchizedek and as it would be fulfilled in Christ. So both of the prophets speak of the same thing. They see both king and priest as one person.

The psalm and prophecy also point to an *oath.* "The Lord hath sworn, and will not repent, Thou art a priest for ever after the order of Melchizedek" (Ps. 110:4). This, a solemn oath, is given to assure and establish this order of the priesthood. The oath makes this priesthood: (1) *Definite.* There can be no doubt about God's intentions concerning the priesthood. What he says concerning it is with an oath, making it definite that he will not change his mind. This is a fact upon which one can surely depend. There should be no uncertainty at all about this priesthood. (2) *Different.* This priesthood would differ from the Aaronic. There was no oath in connection with the Levitical. In fact, one of the differences pointed out by the Hebrews writer was this fact. "For those priests were made without an oath; but this with an oath" (He. 7:21).

The oath becomes a significant factor relative to this priesthood. The prophecy concerning the oath makes it definite and different.

The psalm and prophecy furthermore point to an *order.* Notice that this prophecy says it is to be "after the order of Melchizedek." That means it is not of the order of Aaron. Such an order then would be what kind? If it is after the order of Melchizedek we have seen that it would be: (1) *A Royal Order.* Wasn't Melchizedek a king? Doesn't this order then demand one who is a king? How would you have the same arrangement without such? The answer is, "You could not." (2) *A Religious Order.* Melchizedek's work as a priest had to do with man's approach to God. This is the nature of the work of any priest. One sees this in the blessings he bestows upon Abraham. This has to do with the religion.

Thus, we have a royal and religious order prophesied. This all the more makes the Levitical a temporary arrangement until this new type of priesthood arises under Christ.

THE PRIESTHOOD PERFECTED (Hebrews 7:1-28)

We have thus far seen this order of a priesthood pictured and prophesied. Now we are ready to move to the New Testament where we see this made complete in Christ, the Son of God.

The Hebrews writer will focus on the priesthood of Christ as no other writer of the New Testament does. He is well aware of the counter pull of the old order of Aaron on those to whom he wrote. He builds the case in a wonderful way as he moves through the epistle. He shows us the Son of God on the throne in chapter one. We see him as a merciful and faithful high priest in chapter two. If this raised doubts in their minds as to what sort of priest Jesus would be, he leads them to that point by saying, "Thou art a priest forever after the order of Melchizedek" (He. 5:6). He shows him to be "Called of God an high priest after the order of Melchizedek" (He. 5:10). He thus occupies the place of priest because God gives him that right. Jesus is no usurper of that position. He has every right to be a priest.

As we come to chapter 7 he will explain what he means by Jesus' being a priest "after the order of Melchizedek." We should remember that this is written by inspiration and is thus the Holy Spirit's answer to an interpretation of the picture and prophecy concerning this priesthood. Whatever we find in chapter 7 is not speculation but the truth concerning this very vital subject.

The writer sets before us a priesthood which is *superior* (He. 7:1-10). Let me hasten to say that the writer of this epistle to the Hebrews surely respects the Levitical priesthood. He found no fault with God's arrangement under the law. He will, however, show that the priesthood of Jesus is a superior one to that of the Levitical. This he will do in this section by setting before us: (1) *The Conduct of Abraham* (vv. 1-3). We are told of Abraham's meeting Melchizedek and how he was blessed of him (Ge. 14:18-20). His conduct in accepting such shows him to acknowledge the place and power of Melchizedek over him. His acceptance shows him to accept the maxim "the less is blessed of the better." One should also remember that Abraham had just enjoyed a great victory. He would have been considerably blessed by the victory but even then he receives a blessing from this royal priest. He would not accept anything from the king of Sodom. He wants no fellowship with him nor does he want to be in his debt. (2) *The Contribution of Abraham* (vv. 4-10). Abraham accords great honor by the giving to Melchizedek the chief spoils. He would offer him nothing less than the best. This would say that Melchizedek by his position had some claim upon him and he voluntarily gave the tithe. Also, his giving as the father of Levi argues the superiority of the priesthood after the order of Melchizedek over the order of the Levitical. Representatively, Levi paid tithes to Melchizedek through Abraham.

Thus, the conduct of one so great as Abraham and his contribution argues a higher order of priesthood.

The writer also sets before us a priesthood which *Supersedes* (He. 7:11-21). As the writer has shown one to be superior to the other he now moves to show that one supersedes the other. This just means one is taken away, the other is established. As to which one supersedes the other, the answer should be obvious. Surely the one that is superior would be established. (1) *Perfection Demands That It Should* (vv. 11-19). The writer assumes that all would know that perfection did not come by the Levitical priesthood. That system was never designed to accomplish this. It never did completely for man what God planned. It did not bring man to the point God wanted to bring him. Such demands a priesthood that would bring man to the place of reconciliation with God under the gospel. The Levitical priesthood was tied to a law and sacrifices that made nothing complete. Therefore, such must be superseded by a priesthood that could accomplish this. (2) *Prophecy Said That It Would* (vv. 20-21). We have already seen that the prophecy of a new order of priesthood would make the one then in existence old. Three times in this section (vv. 11-21) the writer quotes from Psalms 110:4. This prophecy would be fulfilled and was in the priesthood of Jesus. Thus, we find prophecy shows it would supersede and perfection demands that it should.

The writer finally sets before us a priesthood which is *suitable* (He. 7:22-28). If one order is going to supersede the other, then the one that is established will surely fit our needs. If it did not, we would be as well off with the old order of things. This priest becomes us (He. 7:26). He is suited to fit the place of a high priest in that he is: (1) *Changeless.* Under the Levitical order there were many priests by reason of death. A change would become necessary when one died and another took his place. One might be left to wonder what the next priest would be like. We like to stay with the same doctor. He has known us since we were born and he knows all about us and our illnesses. We just don't like to change when it comes to doctors. If our doctor dies we feel a great sense of loss because then we must change. Children dread the change of teachers because they don't know the new teacher's temperament or approaches. They have an uncomfortable feeling when change takes place. But what a joy it is to know that our high priest is changeless. "He continueth ever, hath an unchangeable priesthood" (He.

7:24). Our high priest is there on and on or to the uttermost and he ever lives to make intercession for us (He. 7:25). The One who stood by God's right hand when Stephen died is still there after two thousand years to help us. The ceaseless, changeless One abides.

(2) *Consecrated.* He is described as "holy, harmless, undefiled, separate from sinners, and made higher than the heavens" (He. 7:26). His character is above reproach and he will never prove to be unfit. This cannot always be said of men who were priests. Aaron proved to be weak and succumbed to the wishes of the people (Ex. 32:1-6). He wouldn't be much help to those who wanted to do right. How would you like to have as a priest either of the sons of Eli (I Sa. 2:12-17)? They would be no help in man's approach to the Lord. Their action disqualifies them before the Lord and incurs God's wrath. Godward, manward and selfward, he was consecrated as a priest. By character he is capable before God to handle the affairs of God that affect the souls of men.

(3) *Compassionate.* One might shy away from one who has no compassion but this is not true of Jesus. Our high priest can be and is touched with the feelings of our infirmities (He. 4:14-16). He could well say when we are tempted, "I know the feeling." He has been there. When we need help we have one who understands.

Thus, we see the priest after the order of Melchizedek perfected in Christ. He satisfies the needs of God and man.

CONCLUSION

Truly, a new order of priesthood is now in effect beginning on Pentecost. He is ours (He. 8:1). Our high priest is over the house of God (He. 10:21), whose house we are (He. 3:6).

What encouragement having a high priest who is on the throne offers us. We have somebody up there who intercedes for us. He has been down here among us and knows all our struggles. No wonder the Hebrews writer tells us to "hold fast the profession of our faith without wavering (for he is faithful that promised)" (He. 10:23). Thank God for Jesus the high priest pictured, prophesied, and perfected after the order of Melchizedek.

SPIRITUAL MATURITY

HEBREWS 5:11-14

By IRA RICE, JR.

Born 1917 at Franklin, Texas. Married Vada Ott in 1947; they have five children and five grandchildren. Trained in Bible by John P. Lewis at Bible Chair, Oklahoma School of Religion, University of Oklahoma. Graduated in Journalism. Local preaching in Oklahoma, Texas, California and Washington. Twelve years mission work in Singapore, Malaysia and Taiwan. Co-founder of Four Seas College of Bible and Missions. Publisher and editor of *The Christian Soldier* (1939-48) and *Contending for the Faith* (1970-). Author of several books. Lives in Memphis, Tennessee.

INTRODUCTION

Many years ago — sometime in the early '60's, as I recall — having been invited to speak at a chapel service of Harding College, in Searcy, Arkansas, I stopped by the office of George S. Benson, then president, to discuss a scholarship that he had arranged (paid for out of his own pocket) for one of our preacher students from Singapore.

After describing to him how brilliant this young Chinese brother was (how he had been able to carry a classwork load of from 18 to 24 college hours per semester with colors flying), I expressed the hope that his further studies at Harding College (and possibly later at Harding Graduate School) might *mature* him toward eventually heading up our Four Seas College of Bible and Missions, as president, in Singapore.

During that conversation, brother Benson expressed an astonishing truth. The maturing process, he pointed out, cannot be hastened. It has to develop at its own pace — *naturally*. We can *teach* a person, filling him full of facts and information. However, his ability to *apply* that knowledge depends upon his own inward growth; and there is absolutely nothing that you, or I, or anyone else can do to hurry it.

Introducing the general theme of spiritual maturity, Hebrews 5:11-14 puts it as follows:

> Of whom we have many things to say, and hard to be uttered, seeing ye are dull of hearing. For when for the time ye ought to be teachers, ye have need that one teach you again which be the first principles of the oracles of God; and are become such as have need of milk, and not of strong meat. For every one that useth milk is unskillful in the word of righteousness: for he is a babe. But strong meat belongeth to them that are of full age, even those who by reason of use have their senses exercised to discern both good and evil.

INTELLECTUAL BRILLIANCE NOT THE SAME AS MATURITY

We are living in a day when great numbers of our brethren seemingly equate intellectual attainment with spiritual growth. Scholastic brilliance, however, should not be mistaken for maturity. Brilliance, in fact, may be nothing more than evidence of a "sticky mind." One may be able to remember practically everything he either reads or hears; but until he has grown in understanding enough to make proper application of what he knows, he still is immature.

Never shall I forget my first acquaintance with dear old brother J. D. Tant, now dead for more than 40 years. My father, Ira Y. Rice, Sr., had been song leader for brother Tant in many a gospel meeting. We were in a Sunday afternoon song service at Combes, Texas. Someone pointed me out across the auditorium to brother Tant as the son of his old song leader. I was 20 years of age at the time. Tant rose to his feet and addressed the audience, saying, "We have young Ira Rice with us this afternoon. I think I never saw a more intelligent young man — but he hasn't got a lick of sense."

How right he was!

Later on, he invited me to visit him in Los Fresnos, Texas, where he then lived in the Lower Rio Grande Valley. One day I drove down, from Raymondville, Texas, where I was then editor of the *Willacy County Chronicle*. As I neared the front porch, where Tant was seated in a rocking chair, he grunted, "Sit down, Ira, on that top step and tell me all you know; before God, it won't take you a minute."

It was to be many a year before either he or anyone else would give me credit for spiritual maturity. Like brother Benson had said, maturity has to develop at its own pace — and there is nothing that any of us can do to rush it.

HINDRANCES TO MATURITY

The writer of Hebrews points out several things that retard the maturing process. He had "many things" that he wanted to tell his Hebrew brethren, but without sufficient background and development it would be difficult for them to understand.

Even a brief scan of the Hebrews letter demonstrates the necessity of some maturity in spiritual matters in order to grasp the content. After introducing how God had spoken "in time past unto the fathers by the prophets" and "in these last days" had "spoken unto us by his Son" (He. 1:1-2), the book goes on to point out the superiority of the Son to angels (1:3-2:18), the Son's superiority to Moses and Joshua (3-4), the high priesthood of Christ (5:1-10:18), and the superiority of the new covenant (10:19-12:29), concluding with some practical exhortations, in chapter 13.

With such detailed, involved information necessary to throw light on why the testament of the Christian dispensation was better, if they were not mature enough in Old Testament knowledge they should be unable to understand the Christian Scriptures either! I am reminded of what C. R. Nichol told a young questioner at a Pepperdine Lectureship back in the '40s. The young man had asked a question to which brother Nichol evidently thought the answer was obvious. "Young man," Nichol said, "when you study more you will know more."

The trouble is that, as Paul told Timothy, some are "ever learning, and never able to come to the knowledge of the truth" (II Ti. 3:7). Or, as the writer puts it in our text, these Hebrew Christians had had time enough that by then they ought to have been teachers; however, they had grown so little that they needed someone to teach them even the "first principles of the oracles of God" (5:12). Rather than being mature enough to teach others, they yet were so unskillful in the Word that they themselves needed to be taught the simple things of the gospel rather than being able to comprehend the more difficult matters of advanced learning.

NO SUBSTITUTE FOR STUDY

It is literally appalling how many supposed-to-be Christians manifestly stop studying the moment they are baptized. Sometimes we are made to wonder if they, in fact, were converted at all — or did they just go down into the water dry and come up wet!

The apostle Peter, in I Peter 2:2, teaches that "as newborn babes" we should "desire the sincere milk of the word" that we may "grow thereby." Also Paul, in II Timothy 2:15, admonishes, "Study to shew thyself approved unto God, a workman that needeth not to be ashamed, rightly dividing the word of truth."

When we quit studying we quit learning God's word, hence quit growing not only in the word itself but also in knowing how rightly to divide it. No wonder our text shows that such have need of milk and not of strong meat!

How many Bible classes have you ever attended wherein it was clear that neither the members of the class nor even the teacher had prepared the lesson? Many times, in such cases, even the simplest matters appeared beyond their comprehension. The teacher might ask the class (about some point of dubious consequence), "What does this mean?" Someone in the class, after much pondering, would reply, "It means what it says." To which the teacher (?) would exclaim profoundly, "There you are!" What is wrong with such exercises in futility is that there is no food for growth, whether of milk *or* meat.

And even some of our preachers are little better. Have you ever wondered why certain preachers seemingly have to move every year or two? Oh, in *some* instances, of course, there may be extenuating circumstances. However, it is my observation that great numbers of such preachers quit studying. Failing thus to grow they soon run out of anything to offer. Many appear to have built up a supply of possibly six months' or a year's worth of sermons. While these last, at least such preachers "get by." But when their stock of sermons runs out, because of a lack of fresh study, they have little more to say, hence soon are on their way. Once they are out of sermons, they either start tramping out the same old ground or else they just mouth words with almost no meaning. Failing to grow themselves, they also cannot help the congregation to mature either.

BASIS OF SPIRITUAL MATURITY IS KNOWLEDGE

If the object of spiritual maturity is to be more like God then we need to remember afresh that "the Lord is a God of knowledge, and by him actions are weighed" (I Sa. 2:3). "The heavens declare the glory of God; and the firmament sheweth his handywork. Day unto day uttereth speech, and night unto night sheweth knowledge" (Ps. 19:1-2). It is his will that "the earth shall be full of the knowledge of the Lord, as the waters cover the sea" (Is. 11:9). In Jeremiah's day, he told backsliding Israel, "I will give you pastors according to mine heart, which shall feed you with knowledge and understanding" (Je. 3:15).

We think of mature Christians as people of understanding. Proverbs 4:7 says that "wisdom is the principal thing; therefore get wisdom: and with all thy getting get understanding." King Solomon, who penned those words, is renowned to this day as the wisest man who ever lived. We read, in II Chronicles 1:7, how God appeared in the night unto Solomon, saying, "Ask what I shall give thee." And Solomon said unto God,

> Give me now wisdom and knowledge, that I may go and come in before this people: for who can judge this thy people, that is so great? And God said to Solomon, Because this was in thine heart, and thou hast not asked riches, wealth, or honor, nor the life of thine enemies, neither yet hast asked long life; but hast asked wisdom and knowledge for thyself, that thou mayest judge my people, over whom I have made thee king: wisdom and knowledge is granted unto thee; and I will give thee riches, and wealth, and honor, such as none of the kings have had that have been before thee, neither shall there any after thee have the like (II Ch. 1:10-12).

In his Proverbs, thus given to him by the Lord, Solomon said, "The fear of the Lord is the beginning of wisdom: and the knowledge of the holy is understanding" (9:10). "Wise men lay up knowledge . . ." (10:14). "Every prudent man dealeth with knowledge . . ." (13:16). ". . . the prudent are crowned with knowledge" (14:18). And, "The heart of him that hath understanding seeketh knowledge . . ." (15:14).

The children of Israel, like so many of us today, knew these proverbs; yet, like great numbers of us, they rebelled. Thus God said of them,

> . . . this is a rebellious people, lying children, children that will not hear the law of the Lord: which say to the seers, See not; and to the prophets, Prophesy not unto us right things, speak unto us smmoth things, prophesy deceits (Isa. 30:9-10).

As they "did not like to retain God in their knowledge, God gave them over to a reprobate mind" to do evil things, "who knoweth the judgment of God, that they which commit such things are worthy of death, not only do the same, but have pleasure in them that do them" (Ro. 1:28, 32). Hosea declared,

> My people are destroyed for lack of knowledge: because thou hast rejected knowledge, I will also reject thee, that thou shalt be no priest to me: seeing that thou hast forgotten the law of thy God, I will also forget thy children (Ho. 4:6).

And the Apostle Paul wrote:

> . . . Well spake the Holy Ghost by Esaias the prophet unto our fathers, Saying, Go unto this people and say, Hearing ye shall hear, and shall not understand; and seeing ye shall see, and not perceive: for the heart of this people is waxed gross, and their ears are dull of hearing, and their eyes have they closed; lest they should see with their eyes, and hear with their ears, and understand with their heart, and should be converted, and I should heal them (Acts 28:25-27).

MATURE CHRISTIANS NEED MORE THAN MILK

Back to our text, the Hebrews writer showed that "strong meat belongeth to them that are of full age" who "by reason of use have their senses exercised to discern both good and evil;" and that "every one that useth milk is unskillful in the word of righteousness for he is a babe" (5:13-14).

Truly, the gospel of Christ embraces far more than just faith, repentance, confession and baptism, yet how many times when mature preachers try to direct our attention to the deeper things, we hear some older (but still immature) Christian complain, "Why don't you just preach the gospel and leave those other things alone!" It never seems to dawn on such growth-stunted members that among those things that we are to "add" to our faith is "knowledge" (II Pet. 1:5). Note that Peter said to those of "like precious faith" that God's divine power "hath given unto us all things that pertain unto life and godliness, through the knowledge of him that hath called us to glory and virtue" (II Pe. 1:1, 3), continuing,

> And beside this, giving all diligence, add to your faith virtue; and to virtue knowledge; and to knowledge temperance; and to temperance patience; and to patience godliness; and to godliness brotherly kindness; and to brotherly kindness charity. For if these things be in you, and abound, they make you that ye shall neither be barren nor unfuitful in the knowledge of our Lord Jesus Christ. But he that lacketh these things is blind, and cannot see afar off, and hath forgotten that he was purged from his old sins. Wherefore the rather, brethren, give diligence to make your calling and election sure: for if ye do these things, ye shall never fall: for so an entrance shall be ministered unto you abundantly into the everlasting kingdom of our Lord and Saviour Jesus Christ (II Pe. 1:5-11).

Not only must we escape the pollutions of this world "through the knowledge of the Lord and Saviour Jesus Christ" (2:20), but Peter closes out his second book, exhorting that we should "grow in grace, and in the knowledge of our Lord and Saviour Jesus Christ" (3:18). Else, how shall we "sanctify the Lord God in your hearts: and be ready always to give an answer to every man that asketh . . . a reason of the hope that is in you with meekness and fear . . ." (I Pe. 3:15)?

When we think of the marvelous things God has prepared in his word for the mature Christian to learn, appreciate and enjoy, how wonderful it is! Things that pertain to the kingdom of God; to the indwelling and work of the Holy Spirit; to the design, nature, mission and destiny of angels; to marriage, divorce and remarriage; to the home as God would have it; to the love of God; to the sacrificial death of Christ as atonement for sin; to the place of suffering in the life of a Christian; to the two covenants; to the nature of man and the scheme of redemption; to the Bible doctrines of fellowship, of the church, the falling away and the restoration, as well as of final things. The catalog of fascinating things to add to knowledge seems endless when we get into the deeper things of God.

THE PRICE OF SHRINKING FROM SERIOUS STUDIES

On the other hand, consider the price we pay in spiritual maturity when Christians shrink from the study and discussion — especially in local pulpits — of serious issues and grave problems and dangers facing the church. The preacher for one of the largest congregations in the brotherhood was heard to boast, "Nothing controversial will ever be heard while I am the preacher here." He stayed for 20 years, and it wasn't; but the congregation finally divided anyway — over *Crossroadsism*, about which he, along with many others, refused to be warned.

How many elders have we heard who actually boast of not reading or even subscribing to any of our gospel papers? "Too much controversy," they say. So, when this or that controversial issue finally breaks out in the flock that they are supposed to be overseeing, they don't know what to do about it and can only wring their hands and mourn, "Why doesn't somebody *do* something!" If they were the kind of mature Christians that Titus 1:9-14 teaches that elders *must* be, they should have known that they *themselves* should be "holding fast the faithful word" that they may be able "by sound doctrine both to exhort and to convince the gainsayers." Paul goes on to show that

> there are many unruly and vain talkers and deceivers . . . whose mouths must be stopped, who subvert whole houses, teaching things which they ought not . . . wherefore rebuke them sharply, that they may be sound in the faith; not giving heed to Jewish fables, and commandments of men, that turn from the truth.

When the so-called Anti-Cooperation Movement got started on August 9, 1946, in the East Oakland Church of Oakland, California, I personally (along with some 400 others) was present. Roy Cogdill had been imported to make two speeches — one on "Inter-Congregational Cooperation," the other on "Church Government." His position that afternoon was that two congregations could not cooperate on *anything* without violating each other's local autonomy. Also, regarding the latter, he said, if your congregation has no elders, *appoint* some; if you have qualified men, appoint *them;* if no qualified men, appoint *the best you have*—that it is more scriptural to have *unqualified* elders than *no* elders; and if the church where you are will not *do* that, then *leave* that congregation and *go to one that will.*

Over the next two years, through a gospel paper that I then edited, called *The Christian Soldier,* I sounded out a warning brotherhood-wide what Cogdill and others he had persuaded were teaching and practicing on the West Coast. Instead of "being warned," naive brethren everywhere wrote for me to "quit lying about Roy Cogdill" — that they *knew* Roy and he didn't teach *that!* Well, he may not have been teaching "that" back in Texas, where he then lived; but he dead sure was teaching "that" up and down the West Coast where I lived. So many closed-minded elders, preachers and other Christians refused to be warned that by 1949 the Anti-Cooperation heresy had divided churches from California to New Mexico; by 1951 it had invaded Texas and Oklahoma; and by 1952 it was all the way to the East Coast.

When brother Gus Nichols, of Jasper, Alabama, found out what was happening, he tried to warn the churches in nearby Birmingham against inviting those Anti-Cooperation preachers for gospel meetings. For the most part they just hooted at him, said he was "seeing things," and they kept on inviting them. Then suddenly, when those elders finally woke up to the fact that their own congregations were being torn asunder and divided, they sounded an S.O.S. to brother Nichols to come over and help them save the churches. By then, of course, it already was too late. "Save them yourselves," he taunted; "when I warned you and there was still time, you didn't listen." He did not go. Those immature elders were unable "by sound doctrine . . . to exhort and to convince the gainsayers" — hence we lost approximately 40 congregations to Anti-Cooperation in the greater Birmingham area alone!

With the rise of Liberalism among us in the '60s and early '70s and the Crossroads Philosophy in the late '70s and '80s, responsible warnings by faithful brethren have gone out across the brotherhood once more. In certain instances, of course, concerned brethren *have* accepted warning and their congregations *have* been saved from these heresies. However, by far the majority of our brethren — elders, preachers and other members alike — have demonstrated their immaturity by refusing to listen. As a result, not just one or two but dozens, hundreds, even thousands of churches have been infiltrated, hence their value is no longer of any consequence in defending the truth against error.

CONCLUSION

Because our brotherhood, as a whole, no longer is interested in "earnestly contend(ing) for the faith which was once delivered unto the saints" (Jude 3), we have raised up a generation which, instead of teaching others, needs to *be* taught again "which be the first principles of the oracles of God." Feeding largely on "milk" or at most "pablum" rather than solid food, they are neither able to teach others nor any longer to discern between truth and error.

This widespread immaturity and Bible ignorance among brethren in general almost certainly traces directly to their demand to be fed only smooth, sweet, positive pep talks, preferably of no more than 20 minutes' duration. There is simply no way to delve into the deeper things of Christianity until brethren are willing to consider and appreciate the negative things of the gospel right along with the positive and to devote enough time and attention to master them.

Let us remember Paul's profound statement to the Ephesians that God had given some, apostles; and some, prophets; and some evangelists; and some pastors and teachers,

For the perfecting of the saints, for the work of the ministry, for the edifying of the body of Christ: till we all come in the unity of the faith, and of the knowledge of the Son of God, unto a perfect man, unto the measure of the stature of the fulness of Christ: that we henceforth be no more children, tossed to and fro, and carried about with every wind of doctrine, by the sleight of men, and cunning craftiness, whereby they lie in wait to deceive; but speaking the truth in love, may grow up into him in all things, which is the head even Christ: from whom the whole body fitly joined together and compacted by that which every joint supplieth, according to the effectual working in the measure of every part, maketh increase of the body unto the edifying of itself in love (Ep. 4:12-16).

THE TRUE TABERNACLE WHICH THE LORD PITCHED

HEBREWS 8:1-2

By HUGH FULFORD

Began preaching at age 15. Has preached for 31 years. Has worked with local churches in Kentucky, Alabama and Tennessee and has conducted gospel meetings in 13 states and North Ireland. Former staff writer for *Gospel Advocate* and presently writes for several gospel papers. Graduate of Freed-Hardeman College and has studied at several other colleges and universities. Married, father of two sons. Presently serves as evangelist with Skillman Avenue Church, Dallas, Texas. Speaker, *First Annual Denton Lectures.*

INTRODUCTION

One of the most truly fascinating studies of the Scriptures one can make is that of their types and anti-types. Several months ago I was preaching through the Bible book by book. When I came to the book of Exodus I chose to treat it primarily from its typical aspects — Moses a type of Christ, Egypt a type of sin, the Red Sea a type of baptism, the wilderness a type of the church, the Jordan River a type of death, and Canaan a type of heaven. The wife of one of our deacons who had come out of a denominational background had never before heard this kind of lesson — one so fundamental and one so familiar to most of us — and was literally thrilled over what she saw and heard. In that same sermon we showed how the tabernacle erected in the wilderness by Moses according to God's instruction was typical of the church and heaven. This, too, thrilled this Christian woman. She began to see for the first time the marvellous unity of God's Word and the connection between Old Testament persons, places, events, and institutions and New Testament Christianity.

141

It is this same kind of approach and emphasis that we shall be taking and making in this lecture entitled, "The True Tabernacle Which The Lord Pitched." The message is based on several passages from the great book of Hebrews, *viz.*, Hebrews 8:1-2; 9:11, 23-24; 10:1-6. Before reading these passages and developing our message from them let us make a few preliminary observations about types and anti-types.

TYPES AND ANTI-TYPES

The word "type" is from the Greek *tupos* and literally means "to strike." D. R. Dungan, in his excellent book, *Hermeneutics,* has a brief but excellent discussion of types beginning on page 389. Quoting from Webster, Dungan says that a type refers to "the mark or impression of something; stamp; impressed sign; emblem." It is "a figure or representative of something to come; a token; a sign; a symbol; correlative to antitype."

As an illustration, if a man should strike his fist into a ball of putty, he would leave, not his fist, but the image or type of his fist. The image or impression left in the putty is the type; the fist is the anti-type or the real thing. So it is with Biblical matters. Various Old Testament persons, places, events, and offices serve as the type, the image, the shadow of the "real thing" found in Christianity. Notice now the passages from the book of Hebrews stressing this very fact. Note: Hebrews 8:5; 9:9; 10:1. In a similar vein Paul wrote,

> Let no man therefore judge you in meat, or in drink, or in respect of an holyday, or of the new moon, or of the sabbath days [all Old Testament ordinances, HF]: which are a shadow of things to come; but the body [the real thing, HF] is of Christ (Col. 2:16-17).

Against this background let us turn our attention to the topic and passages assigned for this lecture.

THE TABERNACLE WHICH MAN (MOSES) PITCHED

In Hebrews 8:1-2 the writer emphasizes: (1) that Christ is the Christian's high priest; (2) that Christ is on the right hand of the throne of Majesty in the heavens; (3) that Christ is a minister of the sanctuary, and of the true tabernacle, which the Lord pitched, and not man.

The true tabernacle which the Lord pitched refers to the real tabernacle — the actual, the substance, the anti-type — as opposed to that which was but a shadow, the type, the tabernacle which man had pitched. The true tabernacle is the church of our Lord and its destiny in heaven, "the holy of holies" (He. 9:24; cf. I Co. 15:24; Ep. 5:27). It is the "greater and more perfect tabernacle, not made with hands" (He. 9:11).

The tabernacle which man pitched refers to the tabernacle set up in the wilderness by Moses under the instruction of the Lord (Ex. 36-40). While it was a sacred institution, constructed according to the divine pattern given Moses by the Lord (Ex. 25:40; He. 8:5), it was nevertheless a physical structure erected by man. It served "unto the example and shadow of heavenly things" (He. 8:5). It "was a figure for the time then present" (He. 9:9).

This tabernacle which man pitched was surrounded by an outer court 100 cubits in length (east to west) and 50 cubits in width (north to south) (Ex. 27:9-18). Inside this court in the eastern-most end stood the altar of burnt offerings, five cubits long, five cubits wide, and three cubits high. This altar was overlaid with brass (Ex. 27:1-2). Located a little to the west of the altar toward the tabernacle itself was the brass laver, a large vessel used by the priests for their various washings (Ex. 30:17-21).

In the western half of the court was to be found the tabernacle itself. The tabernacle, from all information available in the book of Exodus, was 30 cubits long and 10 cubits wide. It was divided into two compartments: the holy place and the most holy place or holy of holies. These two compartments were separated by a veil of blue, purple, scarlet, and fine twined linen (Ex. 26:31-32). In the holy place there were three pieces of furniture. On the north side was the table of shewbread (Ex. 40:22). This table was two cubits long, one cubit wide, and one and one-half cubits high. It was made of acacia wood and overlaid with gold (Ex. 25:23-30). On it were placed 12 loaves or cakes of unleavened bread which were renewed every week (Le. 24:5-9).

On the south side was the golden candlestick or lampstand consisting of a central stem, with three curved branches on each side (Ex. 25:31-39).

In front of the veil separating the holy place from the most holy place was the altar of incense. It was a cubit in length, a cubut in width, and two cubits in height. It, too, was made of acacia wood and overlaid with pure gold. On it was burned sweet-smelling incense.

Inside the veil in the most holy place was the ark of the covenant. It was two and a half cubits long, one and a half cubits wide, and one and a half cubits high. It was made of acacia wood and overlaid within and without with pure gold. Inside this ark was to be found the testimony of the Lord and, later, a pot of manna and Aaron's rod that budded (Ex. 25:10-16; He. 9:4).

On top of the ark of the covenant was the mercy seat. At each end of the mercy seat was a cherub. Their faces looked toward each other and their wings stretched forth and covered the mercy seat. The mercy seat represented the place where God met and communed with his people (Ex. 25:17-22).

Into the most holy place went only the high priest one day of the year to make atonement for himself and all the people (He. 9:7).

While all of this involved an extremely intricate and elaborate system, it was only temporal and temporary. It "stood only in meats and drinks, and divers washings, and carnal ordinances, imposed on them until the time of reformation [the gospel dispensation, HF]" (He. 9:10). It was but "a shadow of the good things to come, and not the very image of the things" (He. 10:1). It pointed to the "greater and more perfect tabernacle, not made with hands" (He. 9:11). It was but a type of "the true tabernacle, which the Lord pitched" (He. 8:2).

THE TABERNACLE WHICH THE LORD PITCHED

Jesus had said, "Upon this rock I will build my church; and the gates of hell shall not prevail against it" (Ma. 16:18). He did just exactly what he said he would do. Following his death, burial, and resurrection he appeared to his apostles and said to them,

Thus it is written, and thus it behoved Christ to suffer, and to rise from the dead the third day: and that repentance and remission of sins should be preached in his name among all nations, beginning in Jerusalem (Luke 24:46-47).

Under the influence of the Holy Spirit, the apostles began to do this on the first Pentecost following Christ's resurrection (Acts 2:1-4). As a result of their preaching, people were

. . . pricked in their heart, and said unto Peter and to the rest of the apostles, Men and brethren, what shall we do? Then Peter said unto them, Repent, and be baptized every one of you in the name of Jesus Christ for the remission of sins, and ye shall receive the gift of the Holy Ghost (Acts 2:37, 38).

"Then they that gladly received his word were baptized: and the same day there were added unto them about three thousand souls" (Acts 2:41). "And the Lord added to the church daily such as should be saved" (Acts 2:47). Thus, the "true tabernacle" was "pitched" by "the Lord"!

This "true tabernacle," the church, is found in an "outer court" — the world. God's people are located in the world, but they are not to be of the world. Jesus prayed with reference to his apostles, "I pray not that thou shouldest take them out of the world, but that thou shouldest keep them from the evil one. They are not of the world, even as I am not of the world" (John 17:15-16). God's people are not to be conformed to the ways of the world (Ro. 12:2). They are to "love not the world, neither the things that are in the world" (I John 2:15). Christians are to "come out from among them, and be ye separate" (II Co. 6:17).

Yet, the "true tabernacle" is in the world and is to influence the world. This influence is exercised through the preaching of the gospel of Christ to all the world. Jesus said, "Go ye into all the world, and preach the gospel to every creature" (Mark 16:15). The only thing that will bring people from the "outer court" into the "true tabernacle" is the blessed and powerful gospel of Jesus Christ (Ro. 1:16-17; I Co. 15:1-2)!

This influence on the world is exercised also by godly living on the part of those in the "true tabernacle." Paul exhorted Christians, "Do all things without murmurings and disputings: that ye may be blameless and harmless, the sons of God, without rebuke, in the midst of a crooked and perverse generation, among whom ye shine as lights in the world" (Ph. 2:14-15). Note also Matthew 5:13-16.

In the court of the tabernacle there stood the brazen altar on which the animal sacrifices were offered for sin. However, one could "never with those sacrifices which they offered year by year" be made perfect (He. 10:1). "For it is not possible that the blood of bulls and of goats should take away sins" (He. 10:4). "In those sacrifices there is a remembrance again made of sins every year" (He. 10:3). Thus, Christ had to become man's sacrifice for sin.

But Christ being come an high priest of good things to come, by a greater and more perfect tabernacle, not made with hands, that is to say, not of this building; neither by the blood of goats and calves, but by his own blood he entered in once into the holy place, having obtained redemption for us (He. 9:11-12).

"Christ was once offered to bear the sins of many" (He. 9:28). "For even Christ our passover is sacrificed for us" (I Co. 5:7). Indeed, Christ is "the Lamb of God, which taketh away the sin of the world" (John 1:29).

Also in the court before the door of the tabernacle there stood the brazen laver in which the priests washed prior to entering the tabernacle proper (Ex. 30:17-21). This properly typifies the cleansing that takes place in baptism before one can enter the "true tabernacle," the church, today. Baptism is clearly essential be being saved (John 3:3, 5; Mark 16:15-16; Acts 2:38; 22:16; Ro. 6:3-4; I Pe. 3:21). As the priests under the Old Testament could not enter the tabernacle until they had been washed, neither can we enter the church as "priests" until we have been washed in the waters of baptism (cf. I Pe. 2:9; Re. 1:6)!

Inside the tabernacle in the holy place, there stood the golden candlestick as a source of light for the tabernacle. In the church God has placed a source of light — his Word! David declared, "Thy word is a lamp unto my feet, and a light unto my path" (Ps. 119:105). He also said, "The entrance of thy words giveth light; it giveth understanding unto the simple" (Ps. 119:130). The Word of God is the only light for God's "true tabernacle" today and it gives all the light that is needed. It is inspired, inerrant, infallible, and all-sufficient (II Ti. 3:16-17). It is quick and powerful (He. 4:12). "Raccoon" John Smith, in one of the greatest sermons he ever preached, said,

God has but one people on the earth. He has given them but one book, and therein exhorts and commands them to be no longer Campbellites, or Stoneites, or New Lights, or Old Lights, or any other kind of lights, but let us all come to the Bible, and the Bible alone, as the only book in the world that can give us all the light we need.

In the holy place of the tabernacle there stood the table of shewbread, no doubt typical of the Lord's Supper which those who dwell in the "true tabernacle" eat every Lord's Day in memory of Christ their sacrifice. Matthew tells us,

> And as they were eating, Jesus took bread, and blessed it, and brake it, and gave it to the disciples, and said, Take, eat; this is my body. And he took the cup, and gave thanks, and gave it to them, saying, Drink ye all of it; for this is my blood of the new testament, which is shed for many for the remission of sins. But I say unto you, I will not drink henceforth of this fruit of the vine, until that day when I drink it new with you in my Father's kingdom (Ma. 26:26-29).

This memorial meal is to be observed in a worthy manner (I Co. 11:27). It is to be observed *ever* first day of the week and *only* on the first day of the week (Acts 20:7)! As the shewbread on the table in the tabernacle was renewed every week, even so those who eat at the table of the Lord in the "true tabernacle" are renewed spiritually as each week the sacrifice of Christ their passover is brought freshly to their minds!

Also in the holy place and very near to the most holy place, in front of the veil separating the two compartments, there stood an altar of incense. This typified the prayer and praise to be offered to God by the inhabitants of the "true tabernacle." In Revelation 5:8 we are told, "And when he had taken the book, the four living creatures and the four and twenty elders fell down before the Lamb, having each one a harp, and golden bowls full of incense, which are the prayers of the saints." In Revelation 8:3 it is said, "And another angel came and stood over the altar, having a golden censer; and there was given unto him much incense, that he should add it unto the prayers of all the saints upon the golden altar which was before the throne." Prayer, along with other forms of praise, such as singing, is a vital part of our life as a Christian. We are to "pray without ceasing" (I Th. 5:17). We are to "continue in prayer, and watch in the same with thanksgiving" (Col. 4:2). We are to "be careful for nothing; but in everything by prayer and supplication with thanksgiving let your requests be made known unto God" (Ph. 4:6). We need to remember that "the effectual fervent prayer of a righteous man availeth much" (Ja. 5:16). The writer of Hebrews exhorts, "By him therefore let us offer the sacrifice of praise to God continually, that is, the fruit of our lips, giving thanks to his name" (He. 13:15).

Passing from the holy place the high priest came into the most holy place where he offered blood for his own sins and the sins of the people. "But unto the second went the high priest alone once every year, not without blood, which he offered for himself, and for the errors of the people" (He. 9:7). The most holy place typified heaven into which Christ entered as our high priest.

> But Christ being come an high priest of good things to come, by a greater and more perfect tabernacle, not made with hands, that is to say, not of this building; neither by the blood of goats and calves, but by his own blood he entered in once into the holy place, having obtained eternal redemption for us (He. 9:11-12).

Since we know that Christ entered heaven "when he had by himself purged our sin" and "sat down on the right hand of the Majesty on high" (He. 1:3), then we know that we are correct in saying that heaven is the anti-type of the most holy place. "For Christ is not entered into the holy place made with hands, which are the figures of the true; but into heaven itself, now to appear in the presence of God for us" (He. 9:24).

Christ, unlike the priests of the Old Testament, had no sin; thus, he did not have to offer blood for his own sins. "He did not sin, neither was guile found in his mouth" (I Pe. 2:22). Further, he did not, like those priests, have to continually offer up sacrifices, "for this he did once, when he offered up himself" (He. 7:27). "Christ was once offered to bear the sins of many" (He. 9:28). Think of the marvellous superiority of Christ, our high priest, as compared to the high priests of the Aaronic order! Indeed, "for such a high priest became us, who is holy, harmless, undefiled, separated from sinners, and made higher than the heavens" (He. 7:26).

The abode of our high priest will become our abode if we remain faithful to his cause. When Stephen was being stoned to death for his loyalty to Christ he said, "I see the heavens opened, and the Son of man standing on the right hand of God" (Acts 7:56). A little later he piously requested of Christ, "Lord Jesus, receive my spirit" (Acts 7:59). Jesus promised such an abode for his faithful followers (John 14:1-3), and the apostle Paul assured Christians of that glorious place (II Co. 5:1).

As the holy place of the tabernacle stood between the outer court and the most holy place, just that surely does the church stand between the world and heaven. No one can enter heaven who does not pass through the church (Acts 2:47; I Co. 15:24; Ep. 5:27)!

Those who entered the holy place to carry out the service of God were the priests. Christians are priests (Re. 1:6), and in the "true tabernacle" we are to offer worship and service unto God" (I Pe. 2:9; He. 12:28-29).

CONCLUSION

With a few observations designed to encourage us and strengthen our faith we conclude this lecture.

First, God planned from eternity to save man through Christ (Ep. 3:8-12). This plan was clear in the mind of God from the beginning.

Second, this plan was gradually unfolded as God, through the ages, spoke to man and revealed his plan through patriarchs, prophets, priests, and kings (He. 1:1-2; 1 Pe. 1:10-12).

Third, this plan was revealed at first in dim, shadowy outlines, types, and figures (He. 8:5; 9:9; 10:1).

Fourth, "But when the fulness of the time was come, God sent forth his Son, made of a woman, made under the law, to redeem them that were under the law, that we might receive the adoption of sons" (Ga. 4:4-5).

Finally, now, "in the last days" God "hath spoken unto us by his Son" (He. 1:2). All who would be saved, therefore, must be saved by listening to his voice (He. 12:25), obeying his will (He. 5:8-9), and serving faithfully in "the true tabernacle, which the Lord pitched, and not man" (He. 8:2).

MAKE ALL THINGS ACCORDING
TO THE PATTERN

HEBREWS 8:5

By BILL JACKSON

Born in Sheffield, Alabama. He and his wife, Jean, have two sons. Career Marine Corps officer until 1956. Graduate of David Lipscomb College with a major in Bible. Served churches in Mississippi, Tennessee, and Texas. Mission work in South Caorlina and England. Director of annual Southwest Lectures, Austin, Texas. Writes for various publications. Regular television work for 3 years, radio for 15 years. Has had a number of debates. Currently preaches for the Southwest church in Austin, Texas, and teaches in their School of Bible Studies.

INTRODUCTION

In Hebrews 8, Jesus Christ is presented as our high priest, and a minister of the true tabernacle which the Lord pitched (vv. 1-2). In speaking of the priests who served under the Old Testament order, we're told this: They are those

> who serve that which is a copy and shadow of the heavenly things, even as Moses is warned of God when he is about to make the tabernacle: for, See, saith he, that thou make all things according to the pattern that was showed thee in the mount (v. 5).

We then have before us the picture so often seen in the epistle to the Hebrews — that of type and anti-type, shadow and substance, first covenant and second, and inferior covenant and better one. Beyond these things, there is also an important word in verse 5, a word that has been so much a part of our preaching down through the years, and which must continue to be a part of our preaching if we are to be faithful to God's word: that word is "pattern." No plea can be uttered that would better call us back to abide by the will of God than this: "See that thou make all things according to the pattern!"

A LOOK AT OUR TEXT

We've noted that Jesus Christ is the subject under consideration, and the fact that he is our high priest. He serves in that capacity as regards the true tabernacle, and not the tabernacle of shadow. The point is made that our Lord, if he were on earth, would not be high priest; the writer has shown earlier that Jesus, being of the tribe of Judah, would not qualify as priest (7:14). We, then, under the Christ, are subject to the new covenant, with the earlier covenant with its priesthood being taken away. We are then told that the Old Testament priests were serving within that which was merely a "copy" and "shadow." In the King James version, the words are "example" and "shadow." These matters of Old Testament concern pointed to the "heavenly things" — the things of substance, the things of the New Testament order.

Involved in the idea of "copy, example" is this: "a sign suggestive of anything, representation, figure, copy."[1] By "shadow" is meant just that, with the things of the Old Testament being merely a shadow, a shading, of those things of greater importance and permanence being brought to men through the New Testament of Christ. In this, we see these points:

(1) Even the things of shadow, copy and example were God's concerns.

(2) In approaching the making of the tabernacle, the instructions were given by God, and man was not left to his own devices.

(3) God called attention to the fact that he had established a pattern.

(4) And the commandment was, "See that thou make all things according to the pattern!"

That which stands out clearly to us is the fact that if, under the inferior covenant, God was concerned about the instructions he had given to man, and wanted these carried out with exactness, and bothered to command on this very point, then we dare not approach the New Testament law with any attitude of carelessness, looseness or presumption. Recurring throughout this epistle is the theme of the superiority of the Christ in all things. In that outline, the writer mentions also that disobedience was punished with certainty under the old covenant, and that a sorer punishment awaits those who disobey under this new one (10:29).

THE PATTERN CONCEPT IN THE OLD TESTAMENT

Our text directs us to the time of the building of the tabernacle, found in Exodus 25. This has been called a "Legal Type — a beautiful pictorial outline of the Christian System."[2] There, in great detail, God began to list those items to be gathered for use in the tabernacle, with the thrust that it was to be ". . . according to all that I show thee, after the pattern of the tabernacle, and the pattern of the instruments thereof . . ." (v. 9). The same point is made in verse 40, using the language now found in Hebrews 8:5.

Later in Israel's history, when David was not permitted to build the great house for God, he nevertheless was able to do some of the advance planning for it. Found in I Chronicles 28, there was the emphasis to abide by the pattern of David (vv. 11-12), and that all things were to be thus done, ". . . even all the works of this pattern" (vv. 18-19). In both Old and New Testaments, the idea is that of a "model." In the New Testament, the word is seen to be "a mark of impress made by a hard substance on a softer one; then, model, pattern, exemplar in its widest sense."[3] Surely then we can see what was intended in the use of the word "pattern." Men were to abide by it, and duplicate it, and could only be pleasing to God if they did so!

IN THIS, THE MATTER OF AUTHORITY!

In the history of the Lord's church, and especially in that history we've seen in the last few years, we've noted something concerning the word "pattern." It is a precious word, and used so often by brethren who love the truth, and who wish to give emphasis to the Old Paths. This was at the heart of the preaching done in the period known as the Restoration Movement. Men were called out of sectarianism, and ". . . back to the Christianity of the New Testament, and (to) make all things according to the pattern therein shown by Christ and his holy apostles."[4] So many were encouraged to break the shackles of denominationalism, and to return to the "pattern."

Very often, our text verse was the center of the appeal! That kind of preaching is urgently needed today, that men might once more love the idea of "the pattern."

But just as preaching on adherence to the pattern has been characteristic of those who love God and his will, we have also noted this: When turning away from the things of God, apostates move toward other fellowship and embrace other doctrines, and one of the first things they will turn to attack is the idea of "a pattern." They turn from the things they once embraced, and once preached, along with the rest of us, and now virtually everything is moved over to the area of "doubt," and just a little further down the road the doubt is removed, and they are now certain that sectarian views happen to be the correct ones! They reject the "pattern" concept, but in reality it is a rejection of the *authority of God!*

Once, when the Jewish leaders attempted to press the Lord as to the authority behind his actions, he placed them in a great dilemma on the baptism of John, and the matter of authority, with this question: "The baptism of John, whence is it? from heaven or from men?" (Ma. 21:25). This is the essence of it all, when we consider the patterns set forth by God. Do we abide by the will of heaven, or by our own wills? If we have the view that we are "free" men, in "free" congregations (as some now state), and therefore are "free" to do our own pleasure in all things, then there *is no pattern* for anything! Jesus calls us to remember that "He that rejecteth me, and receiveth not my sayings, hath one that judgeth him: the word that I spake, the same shall judge him in the last day" (John 12:48). And very near the end of the New Testament, John tells us that "Whosoever goeth onward and abideth not in the teaching of Christ, hath not God: he that abideth in the teaching, the same hath both the Father and the Son" (II John 9). Clearly, then, we are subject to authority, and must live within authority. The proper attitude of the child of God is to seek to know the authority of God, and to conform to it, and thus to abide by any pattern of the things of God set before him!

THE TENDENCY TO MOVE AWAY
FROM THE PATTERN

Actually, the idea of a pattern is seen in all matters wherein the Lord has spoken, and wherein he thus expects men to obey. By a statement of law, and at the same time his expectation that man will conform to that law, therein is a pattern to be followed. We find that, in the very beginning. In Genesis 2:16, the Lord specifies what manner of behavior constitutes obedience, and in verse 17 does the same regarding disobedience. Prior to the act of disobedience on the part of Adam and Eve, a pattern was set forth clearly indicating what was expected of them. Again, the classic case of disobedience is seen in examining Saul, in I Samuel 15. The Lord's instructions were very plain, and were summed up thusly: "Utterly destroy the Amalekites!" (v. 3). By that command, Saul had before him a pattern in words wherein obedience could be rendered by him. He did not choose this course, and was condemned. This picture, and the one above, is that of rejection of God's authority!

On the other hand, one of the finest examples of obedience is seen in the case of Noah, in Genesis 6. Beginning in verse 14, the Lord begins to instruct Noah as to the type vessel, the type wood, the type sealant, the dimensions, the openings and the animals to be gathered for transport. God's will has then been stated, and Noah has a pattern — a blueprint — to go by. He stands tall as one of the great heroes of the Bible by this statement concerning his fidelity: "Thus did Noah, according to all that God commanded him, so did he" (Gen. 6:22). He abode by the pattern he was given!

In sectarianism, the thrust has been to reject the authority of God, and for men to do their own pleasure in religious matters. In this, there has been a continuation on a course of denying any pattern, or simply refusing to abide by any that might be pointed out. Creedbooks have been produced in great abundance in order that followers of man-made systems might be directed in the sectarian paths and away from the idea of a New Testament pattern. We have been able to use that character of sectarianism down through the years in sermons dealing with first principles, in all lessons before audiences of non-believers and in all debates, as we have pressed home the matter of the authority of God. We have directed men to the word, and to the authority of it, and showed them the patterns set forth in the Bible, and urged that they conform to it. Regarding the church, as opposed to sectarian institutions, the point has been made that "the church (is) to be a divine institution (and) must be fashioned after that model."[5] Again, it was the idea that the Lord has given us a pattern, and men who deviate from it cannot be pleasing to him. There must be a change, and a return to the pattern! That has been a good and scriptural plea, and has served us well down through the years. It is so greatly regretted, today, that the rejection of, or deviation from, the pattern concept comes not just from sectarian sources, but that same rebellion to the things of God is seen today *in the church of the Lord!*

CHALLENGES TO THE PATTERN — IN THE CHURCH.

Having shown that denominationalism rejects the idea of the pattern concept, and that this is so because of a basic disposition to reject the authority of God and his word, we must say the same regarding some of the liberal trends in the church today. As stated before, one of the very first sounds coming from liberal brethren is the fact that they challenge the pattern concept. Again, the point is repeated on "free" men, in "free" congregations. The church as set forth in the New Testament, with all its identifying features, forms no pattern in their eyes. To these, the work of the church has no pattern; the worship of God has no pattern, and becomes mere "tradition" if men try to abide by any set order; and the plan of salvation is not given in such fashion as to set forth a pattern — rather, you are a "five-stepper" if you insist on steps in the plan of salvation, etc. This is rejection of the pattern! Yes, and it is rejection of God and his word!

In this section of our study, we want to focus on some of the areas wherein men choose to ignore the pattern concept. In the range of liberal trends in the church over these last several years, we will choose a few and examine them. With the charge from God to build according to the pattern, we want to see where some brethren are rejecting the idea. Some have well said that liberalism seeks to take the church Jesus built and turn it into a sectarian body. To do this, what more needs to be done than to reject the pattern concept, embrace the idea that we are "free" men with liberty to do our own pleasure in all things, and then to revamp New Testament doctrine to suit ourselves? The following, we feel, are areas wherein men attempt to move us from the purpose of making all things according to the pattern; we will emphasize these things with the charge to *build according to the pattern:*

First, we need to build according to the pattern of sound words! While another word, in the original, is used here for "pattern" or "form" (ASV), the idea is still that of "a delineating, an outline, a sketch or outline to be filled in." The instruction is found in II Timothy 1:13 — "Hold the pattern of sound words. . . ." The will of God has been given to us in words (I Co. 2:13), and surely children of God can express themselves in the language wherein God has addressed us. For many years, our brethren have illustrated departure from God's will in sectarianism by the unscriptural terminology used in those human systems. Now, we find that the same points are needed within the kingdom! More and more, we have evidence that our brethren are drinking from sectarian wells, and examining sectarian books, seeking sectarian counsel,. and expecting to learn something about the New Testament church from these sources. It is small wonder, then, that we have begun to speak like them, preach like them! More and more, we're hearing our people speak of "witnessing for Christ," giving "testimony," and speaking of "the *other* denominations." The men in our pulpits are speaking of the church as a denomination, uttering prayers asking for an infusion of the Spirit, speaking of "the miracle of baptism," and talking about "an umbrella of grace." All such indicates a departure from the terms in the New Testament. We pick up sectarian expressions, and endorsement of sectarian doctrine follows! Let us make all things according to the pattern, and let us begin with the pattern of *sound words* — words in keeping with the doctrine of Christ!

Second, let us make all things according to the pattern, and let us once more clearly show the distinguishing features of the church that Jesus built, and in contrast with all denominational bodies. Jesus promised to build *his* church (Ma. 16:18), and

he also declared that the heavenly Father would root up all else
(Ma. 15:13). The church is pictured as the body of the Lord
(Ep. 1:22, 23), and Paul stressed that there is but the *one*
body (Ep. 4:4). Down through the years men have been led
out of sectarianism because our brethren have been plain in
identifying the Lord's body by its distinguishing features —
features having to do with time and place of establishment, the
names given the church in scripture, the name "Christian" for
the members, the items of worship, the church's organization,
the plan of salvation that is taught, and the absence of human
creeds and doctrines of men. We have declared that herein —
right in the word of God — we find a pattern whereby any
person, in any place, and of whatever tongue, can take that one
standard of authority — the Bible — and thus be guided in a
fruitful search for that body of people making up the church
Jesus built! Liberalism would seek to remove all such ideas of
pattern, and render all men as "seekers" and some just a little
further down the road than the rest of us — the idea of
"brothers in prospect." Here, then, is room for the "umbrella
of grace" whereby error is really not seen as an ugly thing, and
room is made then for fellowship of all that is in sectarianism.
It is a rejection of God, and his authority; it is a rejection of the
word of God, and robs the church of a great and fruitful thrust
it has had for many years. We need to get back to the idea of
making all things according to the pattern, and we need to
establish before the eyes of all men the body of Christ, showing
its distinguishing features as those marks whereby we can be
certain we are pleasing to God. The absence of those marks
then renders men sectarian. We must return to emphasizing
the pattern of the New Testament church!

Third, let us make all things according to the pattern, and
let us focus once more on the church of our Lord, and the fact
that it is a *spiritual* institution! So many of the things disturbing to the people of God in recent years are in this very area —
the church delving into, and promoting that which is of a non-
spiritual nature. It has very often been pointed out to us that
the church has work to do in three scriptural areas: (a) Evangelism, (b) Edification — the building up — of the saints, and
(c) Benevolence. Before Pilate Jesus acknowledged that his
kingdom was *not* of this world (John 18:36). The church is sent

into the world by the orders found in the Great Commission (Mark 16:15-16), and concerns itself with seeking the lost, training itself in terms of Christian duty and service, and rendering aid to those in need. Those are areas wherein the church can be seen as a spiritual institution.

In recent days, there is the tendency for the church to become "all things to all men" in areas wherein there is very little or no connection with the matters of a spiritual nature. In some places the work of the church has centered on the social and economic spheres, with the church becoming more than anything else purely a community service organization. As an illustration of this, we think now of a very large congregation moving into new facilities in a metroplex area, and doing considerable advertising, and yet for all the programs, activities, facilities, and "outreach" programs mentioned, hardly anything at all was said about the lost, their need for the gospel, or the New Testament church as the body of Christ, and the family of the saved! All non-members who read these ads would get a picture of something akin to the YMCA or USO, and not the church of our Lord! The work of the church is not entertainment, and the Lord did not die that his body might act as a daily baby-sitting service for motherswho desire to work out of the home. Neither was the church designed as a "fitness center," and yet in some places this is a major "outreach"program of the church. It is amazing that some feel that this is the work of the kingdom, when the apostle Paul was plain in pointing out that exercise of the body profits little (I Ti. 4:8). Here is an instance of the church expending energies and resources in an area where the Holy Spirit himself declares there is *little profit!* At the same time, all gospel preachers know of newspaper sermons, radio and television programs, and other means whereby the gospel *was* proclaimed, and yet these were cancelled because brethren saw "very little benefit." Yet, here is a matter — development of the physical body — where the Spirit himself states there is *little profit,* and still it becomes a major part of the church's activity! Satan's joy must be boundless!

This area of activity is sometimes called "gimmickry," and that's a good term for it — activities wherein the church resorts to all means, of whatever source, of whatever fruit, and however unscriptural may be the tactics involved or the motivations used, in order to be busy "in the work of the Lord." One well-known preacher, in being questioned about such activities, and the criteria used, said he had just one criterion: "Whatever works!" Perhaps he has overlooked the fact that something might "work" as to the emotions, as to involvement, as to pleasure, and as to excitement, and still will not be the *working of the Lord's will!* In all of this, there is the sad fact that we have very often picked up these gimmicks only after the denominations have discarded them! The evident lesson from viewing denominationalism is the pattern of apostasy, and why should we obtain anything from them in expectation that it will further truth? Standing out clearly as we study the New Testament is this: The church of Jesus is a spiritual institution, armed with the gospel of God, and is to work to make that gospel known to all men. That *will work,* and it is not gimmickry! Let us make all things according to the pattern, and let us return to view the church as a *spiritual institution,* doing spiritual work!

Fourth, let us make all things according to the pattern, and let us once more very strongly emphasize the pattern of worship set forth in the New Testament. We have often stated that before the church are yet two great battles to be fought: (a) premillennialism and (b) the question of instrumental music. Regarding the latter, this is one of the first areas the liberal will begin to press, and all the while claiming that the church has been "too narrow" in rejecting the instrument, too dogmatic in our teaching on acceptable worship, and too restrictive in our fellowship of others when the matter of the instrument comes up. There is, among them, a denial that we can find a pattern in the New Testament, and by that they are simply opening the door for men to do as they please regarding their worship. All of these suggestions, and others along the same line, do not surprise us as we note their coming from men who have learned how to highly treasure just about anything they read and hear in sectarianism, and all the while are so anxious to reject what their brethren have said on all subjects!

The fact remains that the New Testament authorizes the study of the word — a continuing in the doctrine of the apostles (Acts 2:42). The book authorizes prayer, in the same verse. We find also authorized the giving of our means on the first day of the week (I Co. 16:2). Also authorized is the partaking of the Lord's Supper at that same time, the first day of the week (Acts 20:7). One other item, or avenue, remains, and that is the singing of praises to God (Ep. 5:19 and Col. 3:16). Repeatedly God has authorized the singing, and there has been the thunderous *silence* regarding the playing of any mechanical instrument. Our arguments in this matter have been proven down through the years in debates with sectarian preachers, and it is an awful tragedy when brethren decide they will vacate that ground so well defended in the past. We do find, we say, those five avenues of worship spelled out in the doctrine of Christ, and we find no other worship items authorized. By that, we declare the establishing of a pattern by God. Let us make all things according to the pattern, and let us return to strongly declare once more the pattern of New Testament worship!

Fifth, let us make all things according to the pattern, and let us return to hold the view of fellowship as set forth in the NewTestament. The idea of coming to God is that we thus belong to him, and have undergone a renewal in mind (Ro. 12:2), have become new creatures (II Co. 5:17), fully dedicated to God's truth in every way. Set apart for service to God, we value our fellowship in him, and cannot fellowship the unfruitful works of darkness (Ep. 5:11). In II John 10-11, we're told to have no fellowship with those who bring some other doctrine, else we are counted partaker of the false teacher's evil deeds. Yet men turn out to be false brethren, teachers of error, and all the while they continue to be used in meetings, lectureships, etc., and praised as sound and faithful men. Let us make all things according to the pattern, and let us return to the pattern regarding fellowship!

Sixth, let us make all things according to the pattern, and one pattern needing continual emphasis is that of the plan of salvation. When liberalism is at work, a clear and concise "plan" becomes "fuzzy" to some people, and those who adhere to the plan may be mocked as "five-steppers." Regardless of that, the Bible is the standard, and it plainly teaches that one must (a) Hear, Luke 8:18; (b) Believe, John 3:16; (c) Repent, Acts 17:30; (d) Confess, Romans 10:10; and (e) Be baptized, and for the remission of sins, Acts 2:38. The pattern so states, and those who love god and have respect for his authority will so teach. We'll also know that those who have not done these things are *not* children of God. Men today are trying to "enlarge" God's kingdom by ignoring this pattern. Let us build are things according to the pattern, and strongly proclaim the pattern that is the plan of salvation!

Seventh, and finally, let us make all things according to the pattern, and let us present the pattern of God with respect to the eldership. Some today are denying that elders have any authority at all, other than through their exampleship. There is, then, an ignoring of the word "rule" in Hebrews 13:17. The pattern is that of elders ruling, and we need to stress it. More "ruling" needs to be done, for the elders control the pulpits and the classrooms, and unsound teachers are given free course when elders consent to it. Let us teach concerning this pattern of elders ruling, and, elders, while we speak of the pattern, let's let the brethren see it in action! We need to make all things according to the pattern, and to follow what the pattern says about the eldership!

CONCLUSION

These points are made in order that we might see that, if God and his word are authoritative, then that word is filled with those things forming patterns by which we must abide. Non-spiritual men dislike the idea of "a pattern," and unfaithful brethren begin to attack this as they move toward rebellion. If we, as God's children, are faithful in his sight, we will note the pattern of God's things, and we will teach these things repeatedly — yea, never ceasing to teach that men must abide by the pattern. Then, and only then, will we be faithful. Here is a lifetime work for us in teaching and in living: "Make all things according to the pattern!" Our salvation depends on it!

ENDNOTES

1. Joseph H. Thayer, *Greek-English Lexicon of the New Testament* (New York: American Book Company, 1889), p. 642.

2. R. Milligan, *The Scheme of Redemption* (St. Louis: The Bethany Press, 1962), p. 118.

3. Ethelbert Bullinger, *A Critical Lexicon and Concordance to the English and Greek New Testament* (London: Bagster and Sons, Ltd., 1957), p. 575.

4. H. T. Morrison, "Twelve Reasons Why Disciples of Christ Are Right," in *New Testament Christianity*, Vol. II, ed. Z. T. Sweeney (Columbus: New Testament Christianity Book Fund, Inc., 1926), p. 189.

5. J. W. Shepherd, *The Church, the Falling Away, and the Restoration* (Nashville: Gospel Advocate Company, 1954), p. 7.

THE CLEANSING BLOOD OF CHRIST

HEBREWS 9:14

By AVON MALONE

Born in Dallas, TX. Bachelor's and Master's degrees from Abilene Christian College. Has done local preaching in Colorado, Texas, Illinois and Arkansas. Taught at Bear Valley and Preston Road schools of Evangelism in Abilene, TX. Author of four tracts. Has video-taped lessons on some of the epistles of Paul. Now in his ninth year of teaching at Harding University. He and his brother David co-authored *Drawn to Christ*, portraying the life and work of their father, Joe Malone.

INTRODUCTION

The magnificent Hebrews letter begins majestically:

God, who at sundry times and in divers manners spake in time past unto the fathers by the prophets, hath in these last days spoken unto us by his Son, whom he hath appointed heir of all things, by whom also he made the worlds; who being the brightness of his glory, and the express image of his person, and upholding all things by the word of his power, when he had by himself purged our sins, sat down on the right hand of the Majesty on high (He. 1:1-3).

The Hebrews writer, early in the letter, lays heavy stress on a major theme: The saving death of Jesus. The thrust of this truth rings through the words, "When he had by himself purged our sins." The note struck here reverberates through the whole letter.

A number of years ago I was in the studio of a radio station in Waukesha, Wisconsin. There was a placard on the wall that captured my attention. This poster simply said, "There is no substitute for blood." The poster stated a physiological fact about our bodies, but the language might be used to state a great spiritual truth: "There is no substitute for blood." Hebrews 9:22 says: "I may almost say, all things are cleansed with blood, and without the shedding of blood there is no remission." One of the great unchanging, immutable, principles of the Divine Government is the truth that, "without the shedding of blood there is no remission." There is no substitute for blood.

When we sing "I Shall Ne're Get Sight of the Gates of Light If the Way of the Cross I Miss," we communicate a great truth. The Bible teaches very clearly that man himself could never be good enough to enjoy the favor and fellowship of a holy, sin-hating God. For this reason the cross is at the heart of God's eternal purpose (I Pe. 1:19-20; Re. 13:8). This great predictive statement finds fulfillment in the death of Christ:

> Since then the children are sharers in flesh and blood, he also himself in like manner partook of the same; that through death he might bring to nought him that had the power of death, that is, the devil; and might deliver all them who through fear of death were all their lifetime subject to bondage (He. 2:14-15).

Without his death, we would be hopelessly in the power of the Evil One. No wonder Paul would write, "God forbid that I should glory, save in the cross of the Lord Jesus Christ by whom the world is crucified unto me and I unto the world" (Ga. 6:14). Again Paul writes, "I determined not to know anything among you save Jesus Christ and him crucified" (I Co. 2:2). The cross is the heart of the gospel message.

"The word of the cross is to them that perish foolishness" (I Cor. 1:18). Later in that chapter Paul writes, "the Jews ask for signs and the Greeks seek after wisdom, but we preach Christ crucified unto the Jews a stumbling block . . ." Paul uses the Greek word *scandalon* for "stumbling block." *"Scandalon"* may be kin to our word "scandal." It literally means "a snare, a trap, the trigger of a trap," and thus the Jews looked upon the cross as a stumbling block, a *scandalon*, and the Greeks "foolishness." Paul adds, "But unto them who are called both Jews and Greeks, Christ the power of God and the wisdom of God" (I Co. 1:23-24). From then until now the cross has been to each person either "the stone of stumbling" or the "Rock of Ages."

It is unspeakably tragic when any would refuse or reject the cross of Jesus Christ. Walter Martin, a great religious writer, tells of a young lady who came into his office and said very bluntly and flippantly, "There is no need for Jesus to climb up on any cross and die for me, for I am already perfect as I am the reflection of the Divine Ideal." In the book, *Science and Health With the Key to the Scriptures,* a statement is made on page 25 to the effect that "the material blood of Jesus was no more efficacious to cleanse from sin when it was shed upon the accursed tree than when it actually flowed within his veins as he walked about the earth doing the Father's business." This young lady who told Walter Martin that there was "no need for Jesus to die for me," was a devotee of the system reflected in the book that we have just mentioned.

None of you would say what that young lady said. You would not verbalize a rejection of the cross — a refusal of the blood shed for you. However, what you would not say with your lips, you may be saying with your life.

Let me mention three great blessings or benefits that can accrue to you through the blood of Jesus. If you don't enjoy these blessings, if you cannot with certainty lay claim to these benefits, you're wasting the blood of Jesus. Blessing number one: The blood was shed for the remission of sins. Jesus tells us that in Matthew 26:28. Blessing number two: The blood was shed for our reconciliation. We have reconciliation through the blood of Christ. In Romans 5:10, Paul tells us we are "reconciled to God by the death of his Son." A third great and related blessing or benefit, "we have redemption through his blood" (Ep. 1:7; He. 9:12). So the remission of sins, reconciliation, redemption — all of these blessings — come through the blood of Christ. If you do not enjoy those blessings, you are wasting his blood. Let us look at the blessings.

REMISSION OF SINS THROUGH CHRIST'S BLOOD

Blessing number one: The remission of sins! Look with me at Matthew 26:28. Jesus said, "This is my blood of the covenant which is poured out for many unto the remission of sins." The preposition appearing here also appears in Acts 2:38,

"Repent and be baptized everyone of you, in the name of Jesus Christ unto the remission of sins." In both places the preposition looks forward and not backward. It is "in order to obtain" the remission of sins. Without that blood, friend, your sins are not remitted.

In Ephesians 1:7, Paul writes, "in whom we have redemption through his blood, the forgiveness of sins, according to the riches of his grace." So the forgiveness of sins comes through his blood. Revelation 1:5 says: "unto him that loved us and loosed us from our sins by his blood." In one familiar translation the passage is rendered "washed us from our sins in his blood." In Revelation 7:13-14, the question is asked, "who are they, and whence came they?" John responds, "Thou knowest, Sir." And now we hear the answer to the question asked. "These are they that come out of the great tribulation, and they washed their robes and made them white in the blood of the lamb." Question: what really washes robes? Now, you and I can assemble on a Sunday morning, stiffly starched and clean, and that's good, but the only thing that really washes robes is blood. And regardless of how immaculate and apparently clean we may be externally, we are altogether unclean, defiled within, unless we have been cleansed by the blood. What animal blood could not do (He. 10:1-4), Christ's death accomplished once for all (He. 9:28).

In Romans 5:9, Paul says, "being now justified by his blood, shall we be saved from the wrath of God through him." The word "justified" means to be acquitted. It is a forensic term or a court term. It is the term that would be used when it is found that the accused is not guilty. When one is acquitted he is rendered guiltless; he is "justified." In practical terms, "justified" means "just as if I'd never sinned," and the Bible says we are justified by his blood. So we see in a number of passages (Ma. 26:28; Ep. 1:7; Ro. 5:9) that the remission of sins, the forgiveness of sins, comes through the blood of Christ.

The great Hebrews letter emphasizes the finality and completeness of Christ's death as the sacrifice for sins as powerfully as any portion of scripture:

Nor yet through the blood of goats and calves, but through his own blood, entered in once for all into the holy place, having obtained

eternal redemption (He. 9:12). So Christ also, having been once offered to bear the sins of many, shall appear a second time, apart from
sin, to them that wait for him, unto salvation (He. 9:28). By which
will we have been sanctified through the offering of the body of
Jesus Christ once for all. And every priest indeed standeth day by
day ministering and offering oftentimes the same sacrifices, the
which can never take away sins: but he, when he had offered one
sacrifice for sins for ever, sat down on the right hand of God; henceforth expecting till his enemies be made the footstool of his feet. For
by one offering he hath perfected for ever them that are sanctified
(He. 10:10-14).

Someone might say, "Well, I know the Bible says that he
died for our sins and that his sacrifice is final and complete,
but I want to know why! Why did Jesus have to die? Why was
such a sacrifice necessary for the remission, the forgiveness of
our sins?"

God's being who he is; sin's being what it is; man's being
the sinner that he is, someone who is qualified had to do for
man what he could not do for himself. God is holy! In Isaiah
6:3, the Seraphim, heavenly creatures, incessantly cry, "holy,
holy, holy is Jehovah of Hosts, the whole earth is full of his
glory." In the Old Testament frequently God is referred to as
"the holy one." Growing out of his holiness is his intense
hatred of sin. "Thou hast loved righteousness and hated
iniquity . . ." (He. 1:9). The statement is made of God the Son
and it can be said of the Father as well. Because of his holiness
he is the sin-hating God. He hates iniquity because he loves
righteousness. God, then, being who he is, and sin's being what
it is — spiritual leprosy, anarchy against God, the "transgression of the law" (I John 3:4) — and man's being the sinner that
he is ("we have all sinned and come short of the glory of God"
— Ro. 3:23), someone who was qualified had to act in man's
stead. Because of the sinfulness of man, Jesus had to pay the
price for man. The boot-strap method will not work. It is not
by human attainment but by Divine atonement that we are
saved. It is not by humanly achieving, but by obediently
believing in the Christ and his cross that we have our forgiveness.

God saw the problem of man from before the foundation of
the world. He had a plan that Bible writers call "the eternal
purpose" (Ep. 3:10-11). At the heart of that purpose was the

cross. It is that purpose which is reflected in the profound prediction of Genesis 3:15. Peter writes,

> knowing that ye were redeemed, not with corruptible things, with silver or gold, from your vain manner of life handed down from your fathers; but with precious blood, as of a lamb without blemish and without spot, even the blood of Christ: who was foreknown indeed before the foundation of the world, but was manifested at the end of the times for your sake (I Pet. 1:18-20).

Notice that the Lamb was "without blemish and without spot." His sinless life (He. 4:15; 7:26) is vital to his saving death. It is because of the blood that God is able to say "For I will be merciful to their unrighteousness, and their sins and their iniquities will I remember no more."

An illustration might be helpful here. Back in the days when severe corrective discipline — even corporal punishment (bodily punishment) — was common in the classroom, a teacher had a problem. Severe corrective discipline has gone out of style. In the past when Johnny was in the principal's office, that meant that Johnny was in trouble. It now may mean that the teacher, or the school board, or Johnny's parents or the principal is in trouble. But I am talking about a day many, many years ago when severe, corrective discipline was common, and a teacher dealing with a class of unruly boys said, "Boys, this is the law, no stealing, and every theft will be punishable by a sound beating." The very first boy caught in the breaking of the law was a pale, frail, weak, sickly looking young man. It looked as if he could hardly endure that beating. But the teacher understood the nature of the law. The price must be paid or the majesty and dignity of the law is dissipated. So the teacher reluctantly made ready to administer the beating that he knew had to be given. And suddenly from the back of the room a tall, vigorous man came forward and he said, "He took my lunch but he's not able to take that beating, so I'll take it for him," and his back was bared and he became the substitute for the other. And Jesus through his death, in effect, is saying of all of us, "He's not able to take that beating so I'll take it for him."

Eight centuries before the birth of our Lord, Isaiah wrote,

he was wounded for our transgressions, he was bruised for our iniquities; the chastisement of our peace was upon him, and with his stripes, we are healed. We all like sheep have gone astray. Everyone has gone into his own way. And Jehovah laid upon him the iniquity of us all (Is. 53:5-6).

The Lord, Jehovah, laid upon him the iniquity of us all. Friend, if you bear the guilt of your sins, if you are now separated from God because of your sins, if your sins have not been forgiven, you are wasting the blood of Jesus.

RECONCILIATION THROUGH CHRIST'S BLOOD

Jesus shed his blood to reconcile us to God (Ro. 5:10). Paul writes,

for when we were yet without strength in due time Christ died for the ungodly. For scarcely for a righteous man will one die: yet peradventure for a good man some would even dare to die. But God commendeth his love toward us, in that, while we were yet sinners, Christ died for us. Much more then, being now justified by his blood, we shall be saved from the wrath of God through him. For if, when we were enemies, we were reconciled to God by the death of his son, much more, being reconciled we shall be saved by his life (Ro. 5:6-10).

We are reconciled to God by the death of his Son.

In Ephesians 2:12-17, Paul makes it very clear that not only does the cross reconcile man to the maker, but it is the cross of Christ that brings together the two great warring segments of humanity, Jews and Gentiles. In Ephesians 2:16, Paul writes, "that he might reconcile both unto God, in one body by the cross, having slain the enmity thereby." And so, Jew and Gentile are reconciled to God through Christ's cross, and reconciled to each other in one body by the blood shed for you and me.

The Hebrews writer emphasizes the reconciling work and the priestly ministry of Jesus in a moving passage:

Wherefore in all things it behoved him to be made like unto his brethren, that he might be a merciful and faithful high priest in things pertaining to God, to make reconciliation for the sins of the people. For in that he himself hath suffered being tempted, he is able to succour them that are tempted (He. 2:17-18).

A little boy was lying right at death's door. On one side of his bed stood Mommy, and on the other side, Daddy. Mommy and Daddy had been seperated, alienated, estranged, and it was breaking the heart of this little fellow. With the last surge of strength that he could summon, in his very death, he reached out and grabbed his Mommy's hand and he reached over and grabbed his Daddy's hand, and he brought those hands together in his death in the effort to bring about reconciliation. Jesus Christ, the God-man, hangs suspended at Golgotha. He reaches up to the Father who in his holiness has been offended by the anarchy of man, and he reaches down to man, deeply marred and scarred by sin, and he brings the two together in his death, bringing about reconciliation. If you have not been reconciled to God, friend, you are wasting the blood of Christ.

REDEMPTION THROUGH CHRIST'S BLOOD

Jesus died to redeem us. "In whom we have redemption through his blood, the forgiveness of sins, according to the riches of his grace" (Ep. 1:7). Peter said,

> knowing that ye were redeemed, not with corruptible things, with silver or gold, from your vain manner of life handed down from your fathers, but with precious blood, as of a lamb without blemish and without spot, even the blood of Christ: who was foreknown indeed before the foundation of the world, but was manifested at the end of the times for your sake (I Pe. 1:18-20).

The Hebrews writer affirmed that Christ "through his own blood, entered in once for all into the holy place, having obtained eternal redemption" (He. 9:12).

It is through the blood that we are reconciled, brought back to God. It is through the blood that we are redeemed, bought back. And in the process of redemption we are freed, emancipated, liberated, and thus "we have redemption through his blood."

Back in the dark days when cruel and indefensible slavery prevailed in this country, a slave girl working faithfully for her master was allowed to work for others. She received remuneration for her efforts. Because of her hard work and her frugality, she amassed, for a slave, a remarkable sum. Her master came on hard times financially and he put a price on some of his slaves. She was among that number. In an unprecedented transaction her freedom was granted on the condition of meeting of the price, which she was well able to do. Shortly after that the old "massa" died and her younger brother was brought to the auction block. Men began to bid on his fine body as you might bid on a horse, cow or other livestock. The bids rose higher and higher, and finally, the auctioneers gavel was raised and he was saying, "Going, going," when suddenly the shrill voice of a woman pierced the air with a bid so high that none dared to top it. It was his sister's voice and she had now saved enough to redeem, to ransom the brother that she loved. Could that young man to his dying day forget the redemptive love of that sister? You know the answer.

Can those of us who are in Christ ever forget we have been "bought with a price?" We are his — mind, muscle, money; time, tongue and talent — because we are redeemed (I Co. 6:19f). But, friend, if you have not been redeemed, ransomed, bought back, and liberated, you are wasting the blood of Christ.

CONCLUSION

Question: how do we contact the cross? How do we appropriate the blood of Christ? At what point are we cleansed by the power of his death? Look at Romans 6:1-4:

> What shall we say then? Shall we continue in sin, that grace may abound? God forbid. How shall we, that are dead to sin, live any longer therein? Know ye not, that so many of us as were baptized into Jesus Christ were baptized into his death?

How and when do we appropriate the saving power of his blood? The Bible teaches we are baptized into his death. Paul is here writing to people who have already been baptized. He is reminding them of the spiritual, moral and ethical implications of the death they died. You cannot continue in sin that grace may abound. Why? Well, how shall we that are dead to sin live any longer therein? When you see a body buried in the earth, you don't expect to see that person in that body walking the streets of your city the next day. Why? Death has transported that person into another realm. Now Paul is saying, "You died to sin." When? "When you were baptized into his death."

We are washed by the blood of Christ when we are
Biblically baptized. Later in Romans 6, Paul said in verse 17,
"God be thanked that ye were the servants of sin, but ye have
obeyed from the heart that form of doctrine which was delivered you. Being then made free from sin, ye became the servants
of righteousness." You obeyed from the heart that form of doctrine, that pattern of teaching. "Obedience from the heart"
involves what? Solomon said, "as he thinketh in his heart, so is
he" (Pr. 23:7). Paul spoke of "my heart's desire . . ." (Ro.
10:1). Obedience from the heart is intelligent, willing obedience, involving trust in Jesus and a turning from sin. What
happens when one thus obeys from the heart that form of doctrine and is Biblically baptized? That one is baptized into
Christ's death (Ro. 6:3). That answers the question, "When are
we cleansed by the blood?"

Jesus said the blood is shed unto remission of sins (Ma.
26:28). Peter said, "Repent ye and be baptized every one of you
in the name of Jesus Christ unto the remission of your sins"
(Acts 2:38). Someone may ask, "Now if the blood was shed for
the remission of sins, how could Peter say, 'Repent and be
baptized for the remission of sins?' " The answer is quite clear,
and it is very simply stated in God's word. "You are baptized
into his death" (Ro. 6:3). We sing, "What can wash away my
sins?" The answer is, "Nothing but the blood of Jesus."
Ananias said in Acts 22:16, "Arise and be baptized and wash
away thy sins, calling upon the name of the Lord." How can
that be? The answer is quite clear. It is very simple and
apparent in God's word: "Know ye not that so many of us as
were baptized into Jesus Christ were baptized into his death?"
(Ro. 6:3). When one is Biblically baptized, according to God's
word, that one is baptized into Christ's death. To argue that
one might be saved before and without Bible baptism is to
argue for salvation before and without the blood of Jesus
Christ. It is through the blood of the "eternal covenant" that
we have our help and hope. Remission of sins; reconciliation
and redemption come through — and only through — the blood
of Christ.

Hear the Hebrews writer: "Now the God of peace, who
brought again from the dead the great shepherd of the sheep
with the blood of an eternal covenant, even our Lord Jesus

. . ." (He. 13:20). His blood — the blood of the everlasting covenant — is our only hope.

One poet has pictured graphically the saving scene:

Under an eastern sky,
  Amid a rabble cry,
A man went forth to die for me,
  Thorn-crowned his blessed head,
Blood-stained his every thread,
  Cross-laden on he sped for me
Thus wert thou made all mine,
  Lord, make me holy thine,
Give grace and strength divine for me.

My friend, he has grace and strength divine for you. Purging and pardon, cleansing and clemency can be yours. But these blessings come only through his blood. Refuse his terms for pardon and his blood to you is wasted blood. I am urging you to come to him because "there is a fountain filled with blood drawn from Emmanuel's veins, and sinners plunged beneath that flood lose all their guilty stains."

THE APPOINTED JUDGMENT

HEBREWS 9:27

By B. B. JAMES

Humphreys, County, TN native. Obeyed gospel, 1931. To him and his wife, Mildred Dunagan, four children have been born. Has been preaching since 1934, serving local churches in Tennessee, Alabama and Virginia. Attended Freed-Hardeman College. Debated L. H. Brown (Baptist) on the church and salvation. Radio preacher for many years. His articles have appeared in several periodicals. Conducts eight to ten gospel meetings annually. Serves as local evangelist, Marlboro, Tenn. Speaker, *First Annual Denton Lectures.*

INTRODUCTION

An unalterable decree of God is that men must die, and they must be judged. The writer of the Hebrews letter states:

> For we know him that hath said, Vengeance belongeth unto me, I will recompense, saith the Lord. And again, The Lord shall judge his people. It is a fearful thing to fall into the hands of the living God (He. 10:30-31).

In the last two verses of Hebrews 12 he says: "Wherefore we receiving a kingdom which cannot be moved, let us have grace, whereby we may serve God acceptably with reverence and godly fear: For our God is a consuming fire."

It is appointed for man, not only to die, but also that he must stand before the Lord in judgment. These are Bible truths that must be believed and seriously considered.

It is my purpose in this lecture to show that preparation to meet God in peace in this life prepares one to meet him in peace at the last day. The prophet Amos cries, "Prepare to meet thy God" (Amos 4:12). There will be no chance for preparation after death. The rich man of Luke 16 tried to alter his situation in Hades but was unable to do so. Jesus taught a great lesson there. If the rich man could not make preparation after death neither can we. We need to feel the urgency of making necessary preparation ourselves and also of persuading others to do the same. In all of our preaching, whether it be to saint or sinner, this idea should be uppermost in our minds. If people are unaware of the judgment or are indifferent toward preparation, they will stand condemned in that awful and final day. None of us can hope to hear him say, "Well done," unless we have "done well," that is, made preparation for the Judgment Day.

GOD KEEPS HIS PROMISES

A most important question for us to consider is, *"Will God keep his promises?"* The entire lesson relates to this question. Everything depends upon God's keeping his promises. If the Bible is true, then God keeps his promises. If God keeps his promises then we know that the Bible is true. If the Bible is true, and it is, then his Word can be relied upon. If we cannot depend upon God and his Word then we are like a mariner lost at sea without chart or compass.

However, we believe the Bible, and when we turn to it we find that God has always kept his promises. There can be no doubt in our minds. With Paul of old we can say, "For I know whom I have believed, and am persuaded that he is able to keep that which I have committed unto him against that day" (II Ti. 1:12b). He had no doubt. From Genesis to Revelation we are impressed with the faithfulness of God. Paul put it this way, "If we believe not, yet he abideth faithful: he cannot deny himself" (II Ti. 2:13). In the great book of Hebrews we read:

> That by two immutable things, in which it is *impossible for God to lie*, we might have strong consolation, who have fled for refuge to lay hold upon the hope set before us: Which hope we have as an anchor of the soul, both sure and steadfast, and which entereth into that within the veil (He. 6:18-19).

God's promise and his oath surely would be the "two immutable things." We have the promise, the warning, and the threat of the judgment by him who cannot lie. Titus informs us, "In hope of eternal life, which God, *that cannot lie,* promised before the world began" (Tit. 1:2). We can depend upon God because he cannot lie.

One of the first lessons we learn is that we can depend upon God in *nature.* After the great Genesis flood, God said, "While the earth remaineth, seedtime and harvest, and cold and heat, and summer and winter, and day and night shall not cease" (Ge. 8:22). We rightly expect that harvest will follow seedtime. We expect that winter will follow summer and that day will follow night. It never fails.

The Psalmist said:

> The heavens declare the glory of God; and the firmament sheweth his handiwork. Day unto day uttereth speech, and night unto night sheweth knowledge. There is no speech nor language, where their voice is not heard (Ps. 19:1-3).

God has never failed to keep his promises in nature. His "law of nature" is immutable. Fire burns even the innocent, water drowns. If we violate the laws of nature we pay the penalty. We know we can trust God in nature.

We can also trust his word. When he tells us, "And it is appointed unto man once to die," we believe him. We see death almost every day and on every hand. The same God who said that, also said, "But after this the judgment." Death is certain. The judgment is just as certain. He has never failed to keep a promise. Concerning the fruit of the tree of the knowledge of good and evil, God said to our first parents, "For in the day that thou eatest thereof thou shalt surely die" (Ge. 2:17). They ate and God kept his promise. He told Noah to build an ark because he would send a great flood of waters (Ge. 6). Noah built the ark and God sent the flood. After the flood he set a rainbow in the cloud as a token of the promise that he would not destroy the earth by flood again. He has kept his promises these several millennia and I know that he will continue to do so.

> And the Lord said to Abram, Get thee out of thy country, and from thy kindred, and from thy father's house, unto a land I will shew

thee: And I will make of thee a great nation, and I will bless thee, and make thy name great; and thou shalt be a blessing: And I will bless them that bless thee, and curse him that curseth thee: And in thee shall all families of the earth be blessed (Ge. 12:1-3).

Again, "And in thy seed shall all the nations of the earth be blessed; because thou hast obeyed my voice" (Ge. 22:18). Did God keep his word? Read where Paul tells of the fulfillment of this promise. "Now to Abraham and his seed were the promises made. He saith not, And to seeds, as of many; but as of one, And to thy seed, which is Christ" (Ga. 3:16). There's no doubt about it, God kept the promise he made to Abraham.

When Joshua had called the people together he said:

And behold, this day I am going the way of all the earth: And ye know in all your hearts and in all your souls, that not one thing hath failed of all the good things that God spake concerning you; and all are come to pass unto you, and not one thing hath failed thereof (Josh. 23:14).

God keeps his promises!

Notice another promise that God kept. "Therefore the Lord himself shall give you a sign: Behold, a virgin shall conceive, and bear a son, and shall call his name Immanuel" (Is. 7:14). He didn't say that a "young woman" shall conceive and bear a son, he said a "virgin" shall conceive and bear a son. I may not know much about the Hebrew language but I assume Matthew did. Hear him:

Now all this was done, that it might be fulfilled which was spoken of the Lord by the prophet, saying, Behold, a virgin shall be with child, and shall bring forth a son, and they shall call his name Emmanuel, which being interpreted is, God with us (Ma. 1:22-23).

He kept the promise that he made through Daniel concerning the kingdom (Da. 2:44). Compare that promise with Acts chapter 2.

GOD'S THREATS ARE NOT IN VAIN

We need to remember that God has also made some threats. In this he cannot lie. God decreed that he would destroy Sodom and Gomorrah. Abraham asked him if he would destroy the righteous with the wicked. God agreed that if even ten righteous men could be found he would not destroy those wicked cities. Abraham asked the question, "Shall not the Judge of all the earth do right?" (Ge. 18:25). May I point out that God was doing right when he condemned those wicked cities. He permitted Abraham to search for some righteous persons but when none could be found he carried out the threat to destroy those wicked cities. In the New Testament we read, "But we are sure that the judgment of God is according to truth against them which commit such things" (Ro. 2:2). In the midst of Mars' Hill, Paul said to the Athenians, "Because he hath appointed a day, in the which he will judge the world in righeousness by that man whom he hath ordained . . ." (Acts 17:31).

Notice, please, the consistency of his judgment:

> Therefore we ought to give the more earnest heed to the things we have heard, lest at any time we should let them slip. For if the word spoken by angels was steadfast and every transgression and disobedience received a just recompense of reward; how shall we escape, if we neglect so great salvation; which at the first began to be spoken by the Lord, and was confirmed unto us by them that heard him (He. 2:1-3).

Even during the Old Testament system when the law was temporary and could not give life, every transgression received a just recompense of reward. They paid the penalty for sin even though the covenant was faulty (He. 8:7-8). How do we think we can escape today if we neglect the "so great salvation?" He always kept his promises in Old Testament times and will keep his promise with us. "How shall we escape?" There is no escape!

The idea prevails that God is good and that God is love and, so being, he will not judge us harshly. There must be a characteristic of God that some have not learned. "Behold therefore the *goodness* and *severity* of God: on them which fell, severity: but toward thee goodness, if thou continue in his goodness: otherwise thou also shall be cut off" (Rom. 11:22). When John saw many of the Pharisees and Sadducees coming to his baptism, "He said unto them, O generation of vipers, who hath warned you to flee from the wrath to come? Bring forth therefore fruits meet for repentance" (Ma. 3:7-8). This is another example of the severity of God. Listen to Paul:

Therefore thou art inexcusable, O man, whosoever thou art that judgest; for wherein thou judgest another, thou condemnest thyself; for thou that judgest doest the same things. But we are sure that the judgment of God is according to truth against them which commit such things (Ro. 2:1-2).

God is just but he is also severe. He could not be God if he promised to punish and failed to do so. Some parents will threaten the child but the child is not afraid because he knows the parent will not punish. God is not like that.

GOD HATES SIN

When we think of God's judgment for man and his punishment for sin, we must consider that the sinless nature and perfect justice of God require him to hate sin. It is true that he loves the sinner but he hates the sin of the sinner. When God finished the creation he looked upon his work and pronounced it to be very good. Then Satan and sin entered the picture. It was sin that drove Adam and Eve from their first and most beautiful home. Sin was responsible for physical death's being appointed. Because man was driven from the garden he was separated from the tree of life; hence, man dies. Sin was and is to blame for it all. Sin caused Cain to kill his brother Abel. Sin caused that great flood of waters to destroy every creature on earth that breathed air. Sin destroyed Sodom and Gomorrah and the other cities of the plain. Sin caused Israelites to drop like flies in the wilderness. Sin kept Moses from crossing the river Jordan and enjoying the Land of Promise. Sin cut off John the Baptist's head. Sin caused God to send his son to die on the cross for us. God hates sin. It is so completely out of harmony with the very sinless nature of God. God would not be God if he were not just. Justice demands that he hate sin and punish the impenitent.

JUDGMENT AT CHRIST'S COMING

What about this Appointed Judgment, this great Judgment Day? There is a great deal of speculation about it. Several years ago we had some brethren in Arkansas who started preaching that there will be no Judgment Day. Their contention was that when one died that was his Judgment Day. It is very true that when one dies his doom is fixed, his fate is sealed. I have shown before that it is too late to prepare after death. However, that is not the judgment of our text. A brother in Ohio, whom I have known and with whom I have worked in a gospel meeting, began some years ago to preach that the second coming, the end of the world, the resurrection, and the judgment occurred in A.D. 70, when the city of Jerusalem was destroyed. I wonder why they have the Lord's Supper in which, according to Paul, we do "show forth the Lord's death till he come" (I Co. 11:26). The judgment didn't occur in A.D. 70. The end of the world didn't occur then, either.

There is much knowledge for which we sigh about that day. I suppose we will have to wait until that day to have the knowledge that we might want. However, scattered throughout the Bible, there are a number of things described which will take place when he comes. We can know what the Bible teaches us on this subject and no more.

Jesus said, "And if I go and prepare a place for you, I will come again, and receive you unto myself: that where I am, there ye may be also" (John 14:3). On that day Jesus is coming. As Jesus was pronouncing the very last benediction upon the apostles, he was received up in a cloud. They stood gazing after him. Two men in white apparel stood beside them and said, "Ye men of Galilee, why stand ye gazing up into heaven? This same Jesus, which is taken up from you into heaven, shall so come in like manner as ye have seen him go into heaven" (Acts 1:11). The angels said that Jesus would return. Jesus said he would come again. Paul said, "For the Lord himself shall descend from heaven with a shout, with the voice of the archangel, and with the trump of God: and the dead in Christ shall rise first" (I Th. 4:16). Our text states,

> And as it is appointed unto man once to die, but after this the judgment: So Christ was once offered to bear the sins of many; and unto them that look for him shall he appear the second time without sin unto salvation (He. 9:27-28).

Jesus will come in the glory of his Father. His second coming will be much different from the first. He came first in humiliation. He had no place he could call home, even though it was by him that the worlds were created. Then he was despised and rejected and finally crucified. The second advent will be in glory. But that Judgment Day, the day God audits his books, will occur when he comes in the clouds of glory, and every eye shall behold him.

TIME OF COMING UNKNOWN

Concerning the fact of the judgment, there is no doubt. As to the time, no man knows. Somewhere I read a statement from Pat Boone to the effect that we don't know the exact time of the Lord's coming, but we do know that it will be in our lifetime, for Jesus said, "This generation shall not pass until all these things be fulfilled." Of course, whatever Jesus was speaking of in Matthew 24:34 would come to pass during the lifetime of those people to whom he was speaking. Hear what he said:

> Verily I say unto you, This generation shall not pass, till all these things be fulfilled. Heaven and earth shall pass away, but my word shall not pass away. But of that day and hour knoweth no man, no, not the angels of heaven, but my Father only (Ma. 24:34-36).

Listen to Jesus again: "A wicked and adulterous generation seeketh after a sign; and there shall no sign be given unto it, but the sign of the prophet Jonas. And he left them and departed" (Ma. 16:4). While Jesus was upon earth even he didn't know the time of the second coming and the judgment; only the Father knew. Hear him again: "Watch therefore: for ye know not what hour your Lord doth come" (Ma. 24:42).

It's the height of folly to predict the time of the second coming of Christ. However, people continue to do it. Denominations have been established, based upon predictions of the time of the second advent of Christ, notably, the Seventh Day Adventist church and the Jehovah's Witnesses. If we know the Bible, we know that Jesus is coming again. If we believe the Bible, we understand that no one knows when. The Bible does teach that he is coming in person. He will not send an angel nor anyone else. "For the Lord *himself* shall descend . . ." (I Th. 4:16). The angels told the apostles that he would "so come in like manner as ye have seen him go into heaven" (Acts 1:11b). We also know that when he does come every eye shall see him. Some have taught that he has already come and that only a select few were able to see him. This, the Bible does not teach.

WHY IS CHRIST COMING?

Study with me some of the reasons why Jesus Christ is coming back to earth, *not on* the earth. I know it isn't to establish a kingdom. That was one of the reasons why he came the first time. The Jews were disappointed in Jesus because he didn't build an earthly kingdom. He reminded them, "My kingdom is not of this world" (John 18:36). Premillennialists make the same mistake today the Jews made then. They are expecting Jesus to return upon earth and establish an earthly kingdom. His first advent was not for that purpose, neither will his second advent be to set up an earthly kingdom. He is already reigning as Lord of lords and King of kings. What then will be the purpose of his second coming? The answer may be found in his own words:

> Marvel not at this: for the hour is coming, in which all that are in the graves shall hear his voice, and shall come forth; they that have done good, unto the resurrection of life; and they that have done evil, unto the resurrection of damnation (John 5:28-29).

The grave does not end it all; there will be a general resurrection. Man cannot avoid this any more than he can avoid death. When Jesus returns and the great resurrection takes place, then will be the judgment. This will be the Appointed Judgment of our text. This Judgment Day will not be a time to determine guilt or innocence. That will have been determined beforehand. When this life comes to an end, none of us will be able to cross the great gulf in the Hadean world. The Judgment Day will be the final separation of the wicked from the righteous.

> When the Son of man shall come in his glory, and all the holy angels with him, then shall he sit upon the throne of his glory: And before him shall be gathered all nations: and he shall separate them one from another, as a shepherd divideth his sheep from the goats (Ma. 25:31-32).

Guilt or innocence will have already been established. However, the Judgment Day is an Appointed Day.

> Because he hath appointed a day, in the which he will judge the world in righteousness by that man whom he hath ordained; whereof he hath given assurance unto all men, in that he hath raised him from the dead (Acts 17:31).

In the very last book in the Bible we have this striking statement, "And behold I come quickly: and my reward is with me, to give to every man *according as his work shall be*" (Re. 22:12). Evidently we are going to be judged according to our lives, according to our works. As I have said before, he will not say, "Well done," if we have not "done well." According to the inspired Word, none of us will be able to escape this great day which God has appointed. "For we must *all* appear before the judgment seat of Christ; that every one may receive the things done in his body, according to that he hath done, whether it be good or bad" (II Co. 5:10). The Judgment Day is an Appointed Day and Christ is to be the Judge. Christ, the Judge, knows all about us. We can stand before a judge in this world and plead "Not Guilty." We can't do this before God and Christ. He already has the facts, he has the evidence. He knows us better than we know ourselves. "The Lord is in his holy temple, the Lord's throne is in heaven: his eyes behold, his eyelids try, the children of men" (Ps. 11:4). Again the Psalmist said, "He ruleth by his power for ever; his eyes behold the nations . . ." (Ps. 66:7). He knows what we do and what we say. He knows if we remain quiet when we ought to speak out. Not only that, but he also knows why we do and say things. While Jesus was upon the earth he knew exactly why people asked certain questions. He knew when one was hypocritical and deceitful. Many times he exposed them on the spot.

One very important thing we must remember is that there is no way we can escape this great Appointed Day. Also there is no way we will be able to hide anything from the All-Seeing Eye. Our life on earth is an open book before him (He. 4:13). The most important thing that we can do in this life is to prepare to meet him in peace at the Judgment. If we fail in that our entire lives have been miserable failures. Some are expecting God to extend his mercy on that day. Beloved, *this* is the day of mercy. We cannot hope for mercy then. God is extending his mercy to us even now. If we waste away the day of God's mercy now, here in this life, we should not expect it to be extended then. At the Judgment Day we will receive *justice.*

THE STANDARD OF JUDGMENT

God even tells us what the standard of judgment is going to be:

> And I saw the dead, small and great, stand before God; and the books were opened; and another book was opened, which is the book of life: and the dead were judged out of those things which were written in the books, according to their works. And the sea gave up the dead which were in it; and death and hell delivered up the dead which were in them: and they were judged every man according to their works (Re. 20:12-13).

Here we learn two things: We learn that we are going to be judged according to our works. We also learn that the standard will be the "books," that is, the law, the spiritual government under which we have lived. People who lived from Adam till Moses will be judged by the law under which they lived. Those who lived from Moses till Christ will be judged by the Law of Moses. We will be judged by the "perfect law of liberty." Evidently the "book of life" is a register of names. Names may be added to that roll book and names may be taken away from it. Jesus tells us what the standard of judgment will be. "He that rejecteth me, and receiveth not my words, hath one that judgeth him: the word that I have spoken, the same shall judge him in the last day" (John 12:48). Is it not sad when we realize that all of us will be judged, and many of us are not even acquainted with the standard by which we will be judged? Only the Bible tells us what we need to know about that great day. As preachers and teachers we must do more to make people aware of this great Appointed Day.

WHO SHALL BE ABLE TO STAND?

The last time I heard brother W. A. Bradfield preach, he conducted a gospel meeting for us in Paris, Tennessee. His last sermon was, "Some Scenes At The Judgment." We had about 85 responses in that meeting and many of them came forward that last night. I have heard brother Bradfield criticized for playing on the emotions of the audience too much. I don't know whether he did or not. One thing I know, many came forward who had needed to for a long time. None of the rest of us had been able to move them. I have wished many times that I had some of the power of persuasiveness that he had. I recall the five points in that great sermon. He said there would be the *Greatest Crowd* ever assembled. "For we must *all* appear." From Adam and Eve to the very last person who will live upon the earth, will be there. There's no way that we can imagine how many that will be. His second point was the *Greatest Judge.* That judge, of course, will be Jesus Christ. He lived here in the flesh himself. He was man! Even though he was tempted as we are, he didn't sin. His judgment will be just. He knows all about us. He will not be ignorant of the facts and he will not be prejudiced. Then brother Bradfield would say, *The Greatest Books* will be opened. Of course, he was speaking of the standard of judgment, the Bible. We have that book now, and we can study it. We can make our lives harmonize with it. That's the only standard about which we must be concerned. The fourth point of his lesson was the *Greatest Separation.* This is the separation of the sheep from the goats. Husbands and wives may be separated. Parents and children, brothers and sisters may be separated. The best of friends may be separated. Those on the right hand will hear him say, "Come, ye blessed of my Father, inherit the kingdom prepared for you from the foundation of the world" (Ma. 25:34). "Then he shall say also unto them on the left hand, Depart from me, ye cursed, into everlasting fire, prepared for the devil and his angels" (Ma. 25:41). Surely, this will be the greatest separation of all time. The final point was, *The Greatest Verdict* ever pronounced. "Come, ye blessed of my Father, inherit the kingdom prepared for you from the foundation of the world." And, "Depart from me, ye cursed, into everlasting fire, prepared for the devil and his angels." Our eternal destiny depends upon this verdict. Will we be one of those on the right hand or the left? It's the difference between heaven and hell. You and I will make that difference. We may order our lives so that we will be on the right hand of Jesus in that great and final day. The Appointed Judgment.

Many will not be able to stand in judgment.

> Enter ye in at the strait gate: for wide is the gate, and broad is the way, that leadeth to destruction, and many there be which go in thereat: Because strait is the gate, and narrow is the way, which leadeth unto life, and few there be that find it (Ma. 7:13-14).

Not only does Jesus say that some are in the "broad way" and will be on the "left hand" but he says "many." Many will not stand the test in the Judgment Day. Some are going to be lost who think they are saved.

> Many will say to me in that day, Lord, Lord, have we not prophesied in thy name? and in thy name have cast out devils? and in thy name done many wonderful works? And then will I profess unto them, I never knew you: depart from me, ye that work iniquity (Ma. 7:22-23).

Think of those who do not believe in God! What about those who reject Jesus Christ as Lord and Master? What about those who deny the inspiration of the Bible? Many do not believe in the hereafter or the Judgment Day. Will they be able to stand? I sometimes feel that most people of my acquaintance do not believe that God means what he has said in his word. Suppose we live and die in that condition? Some believe that ignorance will excuse them and they remain willfully ignorant. Think of those who make fun of baptism and refuse to obey Jesus in this act of submission. Will they be on the right hand or the left? What about those who believe that a child of God cannot fall away and be lost? What about the five foolish virgins and those whom they represent? They represent all who do not make sufficient preparation. Think of the church members who walk after the flesh rather than after the Spirit. Think of the worldly church member. Think of the hypocrite, the careless and unconcerned, the indifferent. Or think of that one who knows to do good and does it not. These are some sobering thoughts.

CONCLUSION

We need to understand that the Judgment is just as sure as *Life, Death* and the *Resurrection.*

One great question for us to consider is, in that Appointed Judgment, will we be on the right hand or the left? Where will we live in eternity?

Another important question for us is, where will our children live in eternity? The following poem asks a sobering question:

WHAT THEN?

When all the great plants of our cities
Have turned out their list finished work,
When our merchants have sold their last yard of silk,
And dismissed the last tired clerk;
When our banks have raked in their last dollars
And paid the last dividend;
When the judge of the earth says,
"Closed for the night,"
And asks for a balance . . .*What Then?*

When singers have sung their last anthem,
And the preacher has made his last prayer;
When the people have heard their last sermon
And the sound has died out on the air;
When the Bible lies closed on the pulpit
And the pews are all empty of men,
And each one stands facing his record,
And the great Book is opened . . . *What Then?*

When the actors have played their last drama,
And the mimic has made his last fun,
When the film has flashed its last picture,
And the billboard displayed its last run;
When the crowd seeking pleasure has vanished,
And gone out in the darkness again,
When the trumpet of ages has sounded,
And we stand up before him . . . *What Then?*

When the bugle's call sinks into silence,
And the long marching columns stand still,
When the captain repeats his last orders,
And they've captured the last fort and hill,
When the flag has been hauled from the masthead,
And the wounded afield checked in,
And the world that rejected its Saviour,
Is asked for a reason . . . *What Then?*

J. Whitfield Green.

HE TAKETH AWAY THE FIRST THAT HE
MAY ESTABLISH THE SECOND

HEBREWS 10:9

By J. NOEL MERIDETH

Born in 1941, Humphreys, County, Tenn. He and wife Betty have five children. Educated at Freed-Hardeman, Bethel, Scarritt Colleges and Vanderbilt University. Author of book of sermons and a commentary. Editor of *Christian Light* and owner of Christian Light Publishing Co. Frequent contributor to gospel papers. Speaks on numerous major lectureships each year. Experienced debater. Serves as local evangelist in Lawrenceburg, Tenn. Speaker, *First Annual Denton Lectures.*

INTRODUCTION

Psalms 40 is a psalm of David that is a thanksgiving for deliverance and a plea for help. In the middle is a pledge to do God's will. Psalms 40:6-8 says,

> Sacrifice and offering thou didst not desire; mine ears hast thou opened: burnt offering and sin offering hast thou not required. Then said, I, Lo, I come: in the volume of the book it is written of me, I delight to do thy will, O my God: yea, thy law is within my heart.

The author of Hebrews finds these words fulfilled in Christ who, during his work on earth, did God's will as it was written of him in the book (Ma. 5:17; Luke 24:44). The psalm is thus a kind of conversation between the Son and the Father, with the Son as the speaker. Hebrews 10:5-7 says,

Wherefore, when he cometh into the world, he saith, Sacrifice and offering thou wouldest not, but a body hast thou prepared me: in burnt offerings and sacrifices for sin thou hast had no pleasure. Then said I, Lo, I come (in the volume of the book it is written of me) to do thy will, O God.

Following the quotation from the psalm the author draws conclusions: "Above when he said [in the quotation — JNM], Sacrifice and offering and burnt offerings and offering for sin thou wouldest not, neither hadst pleasure therein; which are offered by the law" (He. 10:8). The words are those of the Son. He knew that the sacrifices of the Old Covenant were not adequate to completely remove sin (cf. He. 10:1-4). He was willing to come personally to the earth and give himself. "Then said he, Lo, I come to do thy will, O God" (He. 10:9a). So Christ came to the earth to do the will of God and provide for man a loving sacrifice. He gave himself as an offering that was "once for all" (He. 10:10). Consequently, "He taketh away the first, that he may establish the second" (He. 10:9b). The thing taken away is not merely the Levitical sacrifices, but the whole arrangement under which they were offered, the Old Covenant. The thing established is the more gracious and perfect arrangement, the New Covenant, which has the once-for-all sacrifice of Jesus. This is seen: (1) by the use of the abstract neuters, "the first" (to proton) and "the second" (to deuteron); and (2) by what follows in Hebrews 10:10, "By the which will we are sanctified through the offering of the body of Jesus Christ once for all."

The primary purpose of the author of Hebrews was to persuade his Hebrew brethren in Christ to remain faithful and not to fall back again to Judaism. For this purpose, he wrote the epistle to the Hebrews, in the course of which he clearly demonstrates the superiority of Christianity over Judaism. Moreover, he shows that the gospel plan is really the only plan by which one can now be saved. The writer clearly sets forth the relations that exist between the Old and the New Covenants. A proper understanding of this subject is of immense importance to everyone. This was a subject that agitated the early church and it is a subject which is often discussed in other books of the New Testament. It is the theme of this book. The author says the Old Covenant was, in fact, but a shadow of the New and there was therefore nothing in it to take away the sins of man. It was not possible that the blood of bulls and goats could take away sins; sin was remembered year by year. But, in Christianity, the blood of Christ takes away sins completely (it even reaches back for the sins of those under the first covenant, He. 9:15). The Old Covenant simply offered to the people typical pardon, through a typical mediator, a typical high priest, and typical sacrifice, until the Seed should come to whom the promise was made.

THE NEW COVENANT IS "BETTER"

In comparing the two covenants, the Old and the New (He. 8:13) there are certain words characteristic of the Old: "daily" (*kath' hemeran*, He. 7:27; 10:11); "often" (*pollakis*, He. 9:25-26; 10:11); "shadow" (*skia*, He. 8:5; 10:1); "example" or copy (*hupodeigma*, He. 8:5; 9:23); the "first" (*protos*, He. 8:7, 13; 9:1-2, 6, 8, 15, 18; 10:9); "worldly" or earthly (*kosmikos*, He. 9:1); "made with hands" (*cheiropoietos*, He. 9:11, 24). But the New Covenant is vastly different and better. With the New Covenant go the terms "better" (*kreitton*), "once" (*hapax*), "once for all" (*ephapax*), and "eternal" (*aionios*). In place of the many sacrifices of the old, there is the once-for-all sacrifice of Jesus.

Jesus is presented as being so much "better" than the angels (He. 1:4). He is the mediator and guarantee of a "better" covenant which offers "better" promises and a "better" hope (He. 7:19, 22; 8:6. And inherent in the better covenant are "better" sacrifices (He. 9:23), a "better" possession (He. 10:34), a "better" country (He. 11:16), "better" things (He. 11:40), and the blood of Jesus that has "better" things to tell than the blood of Abel (He. 12:24; cf. 6:9; 7:7; 11:35). The comparison of the two covenants is the main part of the epistle to the Hebrews and takes up most of the book (He. 1:1-10:18), the remainder of the epistle consisting of encouragements to faithfulness and warnings against apostasy (He. 10:19-13:25).

The author sets out, in the contrast of the covenants, the priesthood of Jesus Christ and its eternal consequences. For religion to do its job it must cleanse the conscience from sin. The law of Moses was never intended to stand alone to do that job. The law of Moses was to make sin exceedingly sinful (Ro. 7:13) and it was a schoolmaster to bring the people to Christ (Ga. 3:24) that we might be justified by the gospel system.

Jesus Christ is our High Priest. Ten times the author of Hebrews calls Jesus our "High Priest" (He. 2:17; 3:1; 4:14-15; 5:5, 10; 6:20; 7:26; 8:1; 9:11) and several times more he refers to Jesus as "priest" (He. 7:11, 15, 21; 8:4; 10:21). Christ is not only high priest but he is superior to the Aaronic priests. This principle is developed in numerous ways. One important feature is that Christ's priesthood is of a different kind. His priesthood did not go back to the tribe of Levi; his priesthood went back to the time of Abraham — a priesthood like Melchizedek's, not based on genealogical descent but specially designed by God (a priesthood, incidentally, to which Levi paid tribute through Abraham). Christ's priesthood is based on an unchangeable, eternal oath of God (He. 7:1-14, 20-22). Now, since the priesthood has been changed, "there is made of necessity a change also of the law" (He. 7:12). The Lord sprang out of Judah; he did not come from the tribe of Levi. So in the New Covenant there has been a change in the priesthood. It follows that the law has been changed; we are now under the New Covenant, the New Law!

RIGHTLY DIVIDING THE COVENANTS

We are to rightly divide the Word of God (II Ti. 2:15). In doing this we must make the distinction between the Old Covenant and the New Covenant. We are not under the Old Covenant, and if anyone goes back to the Old Covenant for one thing he is duty-bound to keep all of the law, a thing which he cannot do. Paul says if one goes back to the law for circumcision he is debtor to do the whole law (Ga. 5:3). If one goes back for the Sabbath or any other part of the law he is debtor to do the whole law. But man cannot be justified by the law.

> Be it known unto you therefore, men and brethren, that through this man is preached unto you the forgiveness of sins: and by him all that believe are justified from all things, from which ye could not be justified by the law of Moses (Acts 13:38-39).

In the Old Covenant they had the blood of animals and "it is not possible that the blood of bulls and of goat should take away sins" (He. 10:4). In order for us to have remission of sins we must be cleansed by the blood of Christ (Ma. 26:28).

The Old Covenant has been taken away and we are now under the New Covenant. Paul's allegory in Galatians 4:21-31 shows that we are not under the Old Covenant. The two women (Hagar and Sarah) represent two covenants, the Old and the New. The two sons (Ishmael and Isaac) represent two nations, fleshly and spiritual. Hagar and Ishmael were different from Sarah and Isaac; National Israel is different from Spiritual Israel, the church. The verdict was, "Cast out the handmaid and her son: . . . So then, brethren, we are not children of the bondwoman, but of the free" (Ga. 4:30-31). Paul continues in Galatians 5:4, "Christ is become of no effect unto you, whosoever of you are justified by the law; ye are fallen from grace." Romans 7:4 gives another statement of the same character: "Wherefore, my brethren, ye also are become dead to the law by the body of Christ; that ye should be married to another, even to him who is raised from the dead, that we should bring forth fruit unto God."

II Corinthians 3:6-14 is another passage that shows we are not under the law of Moses, but under the New Testament. The thing done away was that instrument "written and engraven on tables of stone," identified by Paul as the law that was given when Moses' face did shine so that the children of Israel could not look upon the face of Moses for the glory of his countenance, the glory of which covenant was to be done away. That identifies it with the Ten Commandments and the time that the law was given. In Exodus 34:29-33 we read that when Moses came from Mount Sinai with the two tables of testimony the skin of his face shone while he talked with God. There can be no mistake about what covenant was meant: it was the "two tables of stone," or "tables of testimony," the Ten Commandments. Repeatedly in II Corinthians 3, after identifying the covenant as the one containing the sabbath commandment, that which "was written and engraved on tables of stone" at the time Moses' face shone — Paul said that covenant was done away. Paul says of the law: "Which was done away;" "Which is done away;" "Which is abolished;" and "Which is done away in Christ." To try to escape the force of this it is sometimes argued that Paul refers to the memorial stones set up by Joshua when Israel crossed the Jordan (Jos. 4). The attempted objection will not work. The stones mentioned in II Corinthians 3 were engraved ("written and engraved on tables of stone") and there is no record of engraving on the stones in the Jordan. Also, the stones in II Corinthians 3 were given when Moses' face shone "so that the children of Israel could not steadfastly behold" his face "for the glory of his countenance." When the memorial stones were set up at the Jordan Moses was not there — he was dead!

In another attempt we are told that the Ten Commandments were not abolished but that it was the ceremonial law which was abolished. This is an effort to try to distinguish between the "law of God" and the "law of Moses." A reading of the Bible will show that this is not correct. Ezra 7:6 says that God gave the law of Moses. Then in II Chronicles 34:14 we read that the law of God was given by Moses. So God gave the law of Moses and Moses gave the law of God. In II Chronicles 31:3 we read that the burnt offerings, sabbaths, new moons and the like were a part of "the law of the Lord." These are things we are told are in the ceremonial law, but II Chronicles put them in God's law. In Luke 2:22-23 we read of the purification of Mary according to the law of the Lord. The sacrifice according to the "law of the Lord" was a pair of turtledoves, or two young pigeons. This teaches that the "custom" of the law and the law of the Lord are the same (Luke 2:24-39).

Ellen G. White claimed that the sabbath commandment was not done away. She said,

> In the holiest I saw an ark . . . in the ark was the golden pot of manna, Aaron's rod that budded, and the tables of stone which folded together like a book. Jesus opened them and I saw the ten commandments written on them with the finger of God . . . the holy sabbath looked glorious — a halo of glory was all around it. I saw that the sabbath was not nailed to the cross.

This statement from the so-called visions of Ellen G. White is the source of the sabbath doctrine of the Seventh-day Adventists. Ellen White claims that she was caught up into heaven where she saw that the sabbath was not nailed to the cross. She said a "halo" of glory was all around the holy sabbath which would over-shadow everything else. Here is the all-important part of it: "The holy sabbath looked glorious and I saw the sabbath was not nailed to the cross." But in Colossians 2:14-16 Paul said the sabbath *was* nailed to the cross! Paul wrote,

> blotting out the handwriting of ordinances that was against us, which was contrary to us, and took it out of the way, nailing it to his cross; and having spoiled principalities and powers, he made a show of them openly, triumphing over them in it. Let no man therefore judge you in meat, or in drink, or in respect of a holy-day, or of the new moon, or of the sabbath days.

Paul said the sabbath was nailed to the cross; Ellen White claims she took a trip to heaven and saw the sabbath was not nailed to the cross. We will take what Paul said about the matter.

Ellen G. White claims to have taken a trip to heaven and came back to tell what she saw. But Paul took a trip to heaven and he said he "heard unspeakable words, which it is not lawful for a man to utter" (II Co. 12:4). What made it unlawful for Paul, the apostle, but lawful for Ellen G. White? Was it because she was a woman and he was a man? Of course not. Inasmuch as Paul said it was not lawful to tell about these things it repudiates the claims of all pseudo-seers, both male and female, concerning "visions and revelations." Joseph Smith claims that he got his revelations out of the ground; Ellen White claims that she got her visions out of the air. But neither got it from God. Paul said, "But though we, or an angel from heaven, preach any other gospel unto you than that which we have preached unto you, let him be accursed" (Ga. 1:8).

THE TWO COVENANTS CONTRASTED

One of the best ways to see the difference between the two covenants is to see the contrast between them. Jeremiah predicted that God would make a new covenant with the house of Israel and with the house of Judah. It would not be according to the covenant that was made with their fathers. It will be a covenant where the law is put in the inward parts and written upon the heart (Je. 31:31-34; He. 8:8-12). "For the law was given by Moses, but grace and truth came by Jesus Christ" (John 1:17).

The law of Moses is the "letter" of the law; the gospel is the "Spirit" bringing life (II Co. 3:3; He. 8:8-12). The law was given at Mt. Sinai; the gospel at Mt. Zion. The law was given by Moses; the gospel was given by Christ. The law was for the nation of Israel; the gospel is for all nations (De. 5:2-3; 5:15; Ex. 20:1; Mark 16:15-16). The old law had the blood of animals; the new has the precious blood of Christ (He. 10:1-4). The old law had fleshly circumcision; the new law has circumcision of the heart (Col. 2:11-12). The old law had the sabbath; the new law has the Lord's day (Ex. 20:8; Re. 1:10; John 20:1; Acts 20:7). The old law was temporal; the new is eternal. The old law had divers washings; the new has baptism. The old law had anointing with oil; the new has the Holy Spirit. The old law had the Passover feast; the new law has the Lord's supper. The old law was the shadow; the new is the substance. The law was a schoolmaster to bring people to Christ; the gospel has Christ. The law was nailed to the cross; the gospel abides.

The contrast between the law and the gospel is seen especially in such books as Romans, II Corinthians, Galatians, Colossians and Hebrews. Paul deals with the problem of Judaizers who were trying to get Christians to keep the law of Moses. Paul shows clearly that we are not under the law of Moses. We are free from the law of Moses; it has served its function. We are now under the gospel law. The law of Moses has been done away and anyone who leaves the gospel and goes back to the law of Moses has fallen from grace.

ANGLO-ISRAELISM — HERBERT W. ARMSTRONG

The cult of Anglo-Israelism has existed for more than a century in the United Staes, having come to this hemisphere from England, where it first gained adherents shortly after the close of the Elizabethan era. The largest of all the Anglo-Israelism promulgators is Herbert W. Armstrong, founder of the "Radio Church of God" and "The World Tomorrow." Armstrong is also the founder of Ambassador College in Pasadena, California, and is by far the most well-known and widely-heard and read of all Anglo-Israelism cultists. Armstrong is editor of *The Plain Truth*, a monthly magazine with a wide circulation. The basic premise of the Anglo-Israelism theory is that ten tribes were lost (Israelites) when they were captured by the

Assyrians under Sargon and that these so-called "lost" tribes are, in reality, the Saxae, or Scythians, who surged westward through Northern Europe and eventually became the ancestors of the Saxons, who later invaded England. The theory maintains that the Anglo-Saxons were the "lost" ten tribes of Israel, and are substituted, in Anglo-Israelism interpretation and exegesis, for the Israel and the Bible. They maintain that Ephraim is Great Britain, and Manasseh, the United States.

The period of the divided kingdom was a period of separate kingdoms of Israel and Judah. Israel was carried away into Assyrian captivity. They did not return nationally, although there were groups of them who did return. The southern kingdom of Judah was carried away into Babylonian captivity in 606 B.C. and they returned nationally in 536 B.C. In the New Testament we read that the message of redemption was to Jews and Gentiles. The New Testament speaks in a way to equate Israel and Judah as one nation and they are described alternately and interchangeably as the Jews and Israel. Paul in Acts 26:6-7 speaks of the promise to the twelve tribes. "And it shall come to pass, that as ye were a curse among the heathen, O house of Judah, and house of Israel, so will I save you, and ye shall be a blessing" (Ze. 8:13). When the captivity was over, the peoples were considered as one nation (Je. 50:4; cf. Eze. 37:15-25).

PREMILLENNIALISM

The word "premillennialism" has four ideas: "pre" means before, "mille" means thousand, "annum" means year, and "ism" means the philosophy or doctrine of. Premillennialism is the doctrine which says that Jesus is yet to reign literally upon this earth for a thousand years. But before this reign begins he must return to earth and establish himself upon the throne of David, in the city of Jerusalem, in the land of Judea, after which he will exercise dominion over all the earth for one thousand years in a revived state of Old Testament Judaism.

All of the land promises to Isreal were fulfilled, as is seen by reading the book of Joshua in the conquest and the books of Ezra and Nehemiah after the Babylonian captivity. The promise of the Messiah was fulfilled in the coming of Christ (Acts 2). The promise of the kingdom (Da. 2; Is. 2, 11; II Sa. 7) was fulfilled when Christ set up the kingdom. In Mark 9:1 we learn that it would be established in the life-time of the people then present. If the kingdom was not estabslihed then there must be someone on earth nearly 2,000 years old! The kingdom of Christ is not a worldly kingdom (John 18:36); it is a spiritual kingdom which one enters by the new birth (John 3:5). Those who were in the church were also in the kingdom, for the body of Christ is the same as the church and the kingdom (Col. 1:13-18). John was in the kingdom (Re. 1:9) and this kingdom is one that cannot be moved (He. 12:22-28).

The hope of Israel is fulfilled in Christ and his kingdom (Acts 23:6). Paul's message was that which Moses and the prophets had spoken of (Acts 26:22-23). The Jews in unbelief were looking for a kingdom of earthly greatness with material wealth and national superiority. They were blind to the truth of their own scriptures and prophets that the kingdom of God was spiritual, to be entered and seen by a birth from above — a birth of the water and Spirit. Romans 11:7 says, "What then? Israel hath not obtained that which he seeketh for; but the election hath obtained it, and the rest were blinded." What has the election obtained? The salvation of God in the kingdom of God, the church. The book of Acts closes with this significant description of Paul's work: "Preaching the kingdom of God, and teaching those things which concern the Lord Jesus Christ . . ." (Acts 28:31).

Foy E. Wallace, Jr. in his excellent work, *God's Prophetic Word,* gives a thorough refutation of premillennialism. He shows that the church is the kingdom of the prophets, that Christ is now reigning in his kingdom and that there is no need to bring Christ back to reign on the earth. The "postpone-ment" theory is shown to be false and an impeachment of the power of God. He shows that Jesus is now king on David's throne and that God's promise to David is fulfilled in Christ. In one of his best chapters entitled "Consequences of Premil-lennialism" he gives the serious problems of this false doctrine. (1) It denies that Christ is now reigining, (2) annuls the gospel dispensation, (3) makes God false to his promise, (4) adulterates Christianity and Judaism, (5) minimizes the gospel and belittles the church, (6) revokes the Great Commission, (7) denies that salvation is given to the Gentiles now, (8) demotes Jesus Christ, (9) makes the first coming of our Lord a failure, and (10) denies the scriptures which teach that the Second Coming will also be the end of the world. There are no New Testament prophecies of a Jewish Kingdom out in the future! In fact when Christ comes back the righteous will live with him forever in heaven (I Th. 4:13-18; I Co. 15).

LET US PROVOKE UNTO LOVE AND GOOD WORKS

HEBREWS 10:24-25

By CHARLES R. WILLIAMS

Born in Oklahoma City 1915; baptized in 1935. Married Mary Jo Barnett in 1937, and four daughters were born to them. Trained at Freed-Hardeman College, Union University, East Texas State University, and Harding Graduate School of Religion. Served churches in Oklahoma, Tennessee, and Texas. Chairman of English department and member of Bible faculty at Freed-Hardeman 1957-63. Has done much work in radio and television and speaks on many lectureships. Local evangelist, Rose Hill Church, Texarkana, Texas.

INTRODUCTION

The burden of the Hebrew letter is that of apostasy. It is difficult to understand how one could read the book with any degree of comprehension and still cling to the doctrine of the impossibility of apostasy. The letter was written to members of the church with Jewish background who were in danger of abandoning Christianity. Judaism, although a God-given religion, was at the time of the writing of this epistle an obsolete religion. When it was in effect it was binding only on Jews and those who had become proselytes to the Jewish faith. It could "never with those sacrifices which they offered year by year continually make the comers thereunto perfect" (He. 10:1). To turn from the blood of Christ as a meritorious basis for redemption (Ep. 1:7) to the "blood of bulls and goats" (He. 10:4) which could never take away sins, was to face the future without valid hope of salvation (He. 10:26). There would be nothing but "a certain fearful looking for of judgment and fiery indignation, which shall devour the adversaries" (He. 10:27). To reject the *cross* would mean their eternal doom, for "there remaineth no more sacrifice for sins" (He. 10:26).

The letter was written to encourage faithfulness. A series of comparisons is presented to indicate the superiority of Christianity to Judaism. One does not readily give up the superior for the inferior! There may have also been a lingering feeling that in accepting Christ they had been disloyal to Moses. Peter dealt with this in his second sermon — recorded in Acts chapter three. He applied Moses' language in Deuteronomy 18:18 to prove that disloyalty to Moses would be involved in rejecting Christ rather than in accepting him. He applied Moses' statement, "another prophet," to Christ. In readily admitting the greatness of Moses' position as a "servant" in God's house, and then exalting Christ as a "son over his own house," he enforces the need for holding "fast the confidence and the rejoicing of the hope firm unto the end" (He. 3:3-6). It has always been difficult for man to worship a God which he cannot see or touch — experience through the senses. One of the reasons for the incarnation was that man might have a clearer conception of God (John 1:14, 18). The rituals, the ceremonials, the material temple versus the church, a visible high priest as opposed to an invisible one — all of these and many more appealed to the less spiritual. The hungry heart of Philip cried, "show us the Father and it sufficeth us" (John 14:8).

The problem of God's people has always been one of "worldly-mindedness." On its lowest level it manifests itself in a desire to satisfy the lusts of the flesh (Ga. 5:19-21), on a higher level by seeking to "live by bread alone" — material *things* — (Ma. 4:4). Brethren today sometimes make the mistake of trying to encourage faithfulness to Christ by *buildings* and *entertainment* rather than by a diet of scriptural admonitions (Ma. 4:4; II Ti. 3:16-17; II Pe. 1:3). It is in the light of this background that the verses assigned to me — Hebrews 10:24-25 — must be considered.

HEBREWS 10:24-25

These verses are part of a sentence that begins with verse 19 and concludes with verse 25. To understand the thought of gospel, and their wills must willingly bow in loving obedience to the Lord! He sought to motivate them by the Word of the living God! This is the method employed by the Old Testament prophets and the New Testament apostles. We would do well to heed their example.

Let us note the following quotation:

> Having completed his elaborate argument, and concluded the doctrinal part of the treatise, the author warmly exhorts the Hebrews to maintain their Christian steadfastness. The appeal contained in these verses (19-25, CRW) collects into a focus of intense light and heat the main teaching of this weighty book. The paragraph before us may be regarded as the centre of gravity of the Epistle. It is also the key-note of the representations and loving counsel which occupy the remaining pages.[1]

The main teaching of the book centers in the long sentence of Hebrews 10:19-25. This section may be easily divided into the *privileges* of the child of God and the *responsibilities* of the child of God.

PRIVILEGES OF THE CHILD OF GOD

The first privilege is that of enjoying complete forgiveness of sins. This marvelous privilege results from the fact that an acceptable sacrifice has been made. There are four great Servant Songs in the book of Isaiah (Is. 42:1-9; 49:1-12; 50:4-11; 52:13; 53:11-12). In the fourth of these (Is. 53:11) the author states, "He shall see the travail of his soul and be satisfied." Jesus through his death provided a meritorious basis that enabled God to forgive the sins of man and yet uphold the majesty of his divine government. Thus, the redeemed can enjoy the privilege of absolute forgiveness. This theme is developed in thoroughness in the first 18 verses of chapter 10, thus the writer is able to say, "Their sins and iniquities will I remember no more" (He. 10:17).

In addition to the privilege of forgiveness, heaven has been opened to the faithful by "a new and living way, which he hath consecrated for us, through the veil, that is to say, his flesh" (He. 10:19-20). Christ has entered into heaven itself and has made manifaest the way into the "holiest of all." At Jesus' death the magnificent veil separating the holy place from the most holy place was rent asunder from the top to the bottom these verses one must consider the context. The immediate context must be considered in the light of a larger context. There are thirteen passages in the book of Hebrews which have been called "Let Us" passages. A close study of these passages indicates a progression of thought which is not at first apparent. All of these are designed to encourage faithfulness and to "provoke unto love and good works." The limits of this paper will allow only a cursory glance at these verses.

Four of the "Let Us" passages are in the fourth chapter of Hebrews — verses 1, 11, 14, and 16. The writer admonishes the Hebrew Christians to fear, labor, (give diligence, ASV), hold fast their profession, and to come boldly unto the throne of grace. Fear of failing to enter into the "rest that remaineth to the people of God" should prompt them to action. Because of their great high priest who had "passed into the heavens" they should "hold fast their profession." This high priest could be "touched with the feeling of their infirmities" and thus they could with assurance come boldly unto the throne of grace.

Another "Let Us" passage is found in the sixth chapter. The Hebrew Christians had not grown spiritually as they should have. They were in need of being re-taught the "first principles of the oracles of God" (He. 5:12). The writer encourages them to "go on unto perfection" (He. 6:1). The seriousness of their condition is emphasized by the warning that they could reach a point where they could not be renewed "again unto repentance." However, the warning is tempered by the statement, "But, beloved, we are persuaded better things of you, and things that accompany salvation, though we thus speak" (He. 6:9).

The admonitions in chapters 4, 5 and 6 provide the background for the admonitions to follow. The author seeks to encourage, strengthen, and challenge them to greater spiritual heights. It is interesting and instructive to note how the author seeks to do this. He does not try to accomplish his objective by gimmicks, pep talks or shallow emotionalism. His appeal goes straight to the heart — the spiritual heart — of his readers. For them to remain faithful and to be provoked "unto love and good works" their spiritual heart must be changed. Their intellect must be instructed in divine truth, their emotions must be touched by the story of redeeming love in the

(Mark 15:38). In accordance with Jesus' statement to Nathaniel (John 1:51) heaven had been opened.

The third blessing referred to is that man has a glorious high priest to intercede with God on his behalf. The Levitical priesthood had served its purpose. Now a great high priest after the order of Melchisedec is at God's right hand to intercede for the Hebrew Christians. Paul said, "For there is one God, and one mediator between God and men, the man, Christ Jesus" (I Ti. 2:5). What unique privileges the child of God enjoys! He has a sacrifice that satisfies divine justice; a heaven that has been opened; and an intercessor at God's right hand. How could the Hebrew Christians or any of God's children possibly turn away from faithfulness in worship and service to God? And yet, at the time of the writing of this book some were in danger of doing so. These privileges alone should suffice to "provoke them unto love and good works."

RESPONSIBILITIES OF THE CHILD OF GOD

In Hebrews 10:22-25 we have three more of the "Let Us" passages. Whether or not Paul is the author of Hebrews, and I believe that he is, in these verses we see Paul's great triad — Faith; Hope; Love.

Faith:

The readers have been encouraged to fear; to labor; to hold fast; to come boldly to the throne of grace and to grow into spiritual maturity. They are now urged to "draw near." But they must draw near in sincerity — with a true heart; and it must be in full assurance of *faith!* It is especially significant that faith should be emphasized in view of the fact that the besetting sin of the Hebrews was that of unbelief, and without faith they could not be well pleasing to God (He. 12:1; 11:6). Every step that is taken, whether in becoming a child of God or in living the Christian life, must be taken in faith (II Co. 5:7). They must also have their "hearts sprinkled from an evil conscience." This is obviously an allusion to the sprinkling of blood in the Old Testament, but their hearts were to be cleansed by the precious blood of Christ. Of this passage, Milligan says,

Every act that we perform contrary to the known will of God
defiles our conscience and also our consciousness; we have them
both in evil conscience and an evil self-consciousness. And this, so
long as it continues, must seriously interrupt our union, communion and fellowship with God. . . . But "if we confess our sins, he is
faithful and just to forgive us our sins, and to cleanse us from all
unrighteousness" (I John 1:9). And this he does in all cases by
applying to our hearts the blood of sprinkling; for it is this, and only
this, that can cleanse from sin (I John 1:7). And when our hearts are
thus purified, we have then "confidence toward God" (I John 3:21).[2]

Their bodies were to be "washed with pure water." This
refers to their having been baptized into Christ (Ro. 6:3-5; I Pe.
3:21). Thus, faith and baptism are prerequisites to "drawing
near" to God (Ga. 3:26-27; I Pet. 1:18-20; Ro. 5:17-18).

Hope:

In verse 23 we have another of the "Let Us" passages, and
the second of Paul's great triad — Hope. "Let us hold fast the
confession of our hope that it waver not" (He. 10:23, ASV).
Paul wrote, "We are saved by hope" (Ro. 8:24). "Faith is assurance of things hoped for, a conviction of things not seen" (He.
11:1, ASV). Without faith there can be no hope! Without hope
there is no incentive to remain faithful. Without hope there
would be no "provoking unto love and good works." "Faith
cometh by hearing, and hearing by the word of God" (Ro.
10:17).

One of the reasons we are not growing numerically as a
people today is because of weakened faith that results in weakened hope. Faith in God, in his word, and in his church has
been weakened. Faith is to be strengthened by "hearing God's
word" and the "uncertain" sound from many pulpits simply
aggravates the problem. We should preach with conviction
and boldness, and with the clarity of the prophets and apostles
to strengthen faith. This cannot be accomplished by twenty-
minute "pep-talks" and "sermons" that "smack" more of
human philosophy than of the Word of God. Human philosophy apart from divine revelation has been defined as, "The
search of a blind man in a dark alley for a black cat that isn't
there!" The substitution of "programs" for preaching and
"methods" for message has further weakened faith and hope.
When faith and hope are weakened then resistance to compro-

mise and to the attraction of the world becomes increasingly difficult. It should be evident that the means employed by the author of Hebrews to encourage steadfastness on the part of his readers is vastly different from the means employed by some today.

In Hebrews 10:24-25 is brought to bear the numerous admonitions in previous chapters, and the heart of the task assigned to me.

LET US CONSIDER ONE ANOTHER

Wuest says " 'Consider' is the translation of *katanoeo* which speaks of attentive, continuous care. The exhortation is to take careful note of each other's spiritual welfare."[3] This comment is in agreement with Vincent, "Take careful note of each other's spiritual welfare."[4]

The passage emphasizes the mutual responsibility for one another's condition. Cain's question, "Am I my brother's keeper?" is answered in the affirmative. Lack of concern for one another can cause us to lose our souls. Paul said, "Brethren, if a man be overtaken in a fault, ye which are spiritual, restore such an one in the spirit of meekness; considering thyself, lest thou also be tempted" (Ga. 6:1). James said, "Brethren, if any of you do err from the truth, and one convert him; let him know, that he which converteth the sinner from the error of his way shall save a soul from death, and shall hide a multitude of sins" (Jam. 5:19-20).

Some of the Hebrew Christians were in spiritual danger. Other Christians needed to be aware of their danger and be concerned. Such consideration requires time and patience. This is not a responsibility limited to elders and preachers. It must be shared by every member. One of the greatest tragedies in the church today is our neglect of one another. Members may begin to miss services and no inquiry is made as to the reason. New converts are often welcomed and then forgotten. If infants in families were neglected as we often neglect babes in Christ the welfare department would take them away from their families. Much of the neglect is caused by selfishness. Some become so concerned with their own affairs that they have no time for the affairs of others. The admonition of Paul goes unheeded, "Look [to view, inspect, CRW] not every man on his own things, but every man also on the things of others" (Ph. 2:4). Adam Clarke wrote, "Let us diligently . . . consider each other's trials, difficulties, and weaknesses; feel for each other, and excite each other to an increase of love to God and man; . . ."[5]

In view of the danger of apostasy on the part of the Hebrew Christians, they were in special need of understanding and concern. There are two words in English which are very much alike and yet vastly different — empathy and sympathy. Empathy says, "I understand how you feel." Sympathy says, "I feel as you feel." Sympathy is not possible without empathy. Paul said of Jesus, ". . . we have not an high priest which cannot be touched with the feeling of our infirmities; but was in all points tempted like as we are, yet without sin" (He. 4:15). Jesus truly experienced both empathy and sympathy!

TO PROVOKE UNTO LOVE AND GOOD WORKS

Wuest says, "The word 'provoke' is the translation of *paraoxusmos* which means 'an incitement, a stimulation.' The word is also used in a bad sense, for instance, 'irritation.' Here it is used in its good sense, that of a stimulation."[6] How, then, are we to incite or stimulate one another?

Any effort to motivate one another must be within the framework of scriptural authority. We cannot accept the implications of pragmatism and simply say, "If it works — do it!" Satan sought to incite or stimulate Eve to eat of the forbidden fruit. He was successful, but dare we employ his method? He appealed to the "lust of the flesh, and the lust of the eyes, and the pride of life." But such is "not of the Father, but is of the world" (I John 2:16). Our major thrust must be to the spirit of man (Ro. 8:1, 4).

The principal ways to motivate one another are by example and by the word of God. One of the darkest chapters in the life of David was his affair with Bathsheba. In Psalms 139:23 David said, "Search me, O God, and know my heart." To provoke David to repentance God searched him by holding up the life of another before him by means of the parable of Nathan (II Sa. 12). David was brought to repentance and as a result wrote two of the most beautiful of the Psalms (Ps. 32; 51). God searches mankind by holding up before man the perfect life of his Son. Jesus seeks to motivate (provoke) by appealing to his example, "I, if I be lifted up from the earth, will draw all men unto me" (John 12:32). Paul wrote, "Be ye followers of me, even as I also am of Christ" (I Co. 11:1). The Hebrew Christians were to provoke one another by example.

One of the greatest appeals ever made by Paul is found in Romans 12:1-2. Paul appeals to the "mercies of God" to motivate to greater dedication. This is an appeal to the *cross!* The *cross* is the greatest demonstration of love the world has ever known. The *cross* involves the church purchased by the blood of Christ (Acts 20:28). The *cross* involves the memorial of the cross — the Lord's Supper (I Co. 11). The *cross* made redemption possible (Ep. 1:7). The *cross* demands separation from the world (Jam. 4:4; I John 2:15-17). The *cross* makes salvation possible — past; present; and future (Mark 16:16; I John 1:7; I Pe. 1:3-9). Can there be a greater means of motivation than an appeal to the *cross*?

How shallow by comparison are the methods often employed today. Paul said, "For I determined not to know anything among you, save Jesus Christ and him crucified" (I Co. 2:2). It is obvious that the author of Hebrews appeals to the word of God and the sacrifice of Jesus. When we learn to rely on the wisdom of God rather than on the wisdom of men; realize that the gospel of Christ is still the power of God unto salvation; and let our pulpits ring with the old Jerusalem message we will wield a greater influence over our brethren and the world!

PROVOKE TO LOVE

"Let us . . . provoke unto love." In this great "Let Us" passage we reach the third word in Paul's triad — *love*. It is impossible to fully define love! To define a word means to "fix the boundary." God is love (I John 4:8). Finite mind cannot fix the boundary of an infinite God. The "love chapter" of the New Testament (I Co. 13), which sets forth nine elements of love, is a serious indictment against the Corinthians because they had failed to manifest these characteristics.

The love spoken of in the Hebrews text is not a "mushy" sentimental "umbrella" which would condone false teachings. It is not the "New Unity" approach which ignores God's law of exclusion. It is a love for God which induces reverence for his word and his church (Ma. 22:37; I John 5:3; John 14:15). Such love will cause one to seek first the kingdom of God and his righteousness (Ma. 6:33). Such love was needed by the Hebrew Christians to keep them from apostasy to Judaism. It is needed today! It was a love for man that caused concern for the lost.

PROVOKE TO GOOD WORKS

Good works provide a means for demonstrating our love to God and man. There are many avenues of service open to those who really want to do "good works."

> To teach a class well . . .; to visit the neglected, the sick, and the dying; to comfort some troubled heart or cheer some depressed spirit; to perform common duties with diligence and fidelity, or irksome duties with cheerfulness; to bear physical pain or social trial patiently; to suffer long by reason of the faults of others, and still be kind to them; — these are "good works," beautiful works. . . . Perhaps the best way to stimulate others to love and good works is to set a good example in respect to these things. Learn here the most effective method of preventing strife and securing unity amongst Christian brethren. Kindly mutual consideration, love, and good works preclude disagreement, and unite hearts in sacred and blessed fellowship.[7]

NOT FORSAKING THE ASSEMBLY

"Not forsaking the assembling of ourselves together, as the manner of some is; . . ." (He. 10:25). Milligan says, "The apostle refers here, not to apostasy from the Church, as some allege, but simply to the neglect of public and social worship."[8] James Thompson gives three possible reasons for some "Forsaking" the assembly: a feeling of superiority; persecution; and the appeal of Hellenistic Judaism.[9]

To neglect attending services indicates a lack of dedication and concern for the things of the Lord. It suggests that one's priorities are not right. To neglect is not to "abandon" but can easily lead to such. Worship and fellowship with fellow Christians are needed to replenish our supply of "spiritual oil."

Worship is designed by a benevolent God to meet the basic spiritual needs of man. We should leave the assembly with our minds instructed by God's word and our emotions stirred by remembrance of the Lord's sacrifice; and with our lives rededicated and a zeal that seeks an acceptable outlet in service to God and man.

BUT EXHORTING ONE ANOTHER

"But exhorting one another: and so much the more, as ye see the day approaching" (He. 10:25). Not only did the apostle Peter present evidence on Pentecost to change unbelievers in the deity of Jesus into believers, but he also sought to "exhort" them to act on the truth they had learned (Acts 2:38ff). Barclay wrote:

> It is easy to laugh at men's ideals, to pour cold water on enthusiasm; to discourage them. The world is full of discouragers; we have a Christian duty to encourage one another. Many a time a word of praise or thanks or appreciation or cheer has kept a man on his feet. Blessed is the man who speaks such a word.[10]

AS YE SEE THE DAY APPROACHING

Another speaker has been assigned the task of discussing the "day approaching." I must, however, give brief attention to it because of its relationship to the subject assigned to me. Whatever the identity of that "day" may be, it obviously was a day they could "see" approaching. It would be a time of severe testing. They would need the encouragement and spiritual strength that their assembling together would provide in order to survive spiritually.

No doubt those who were "forsaking the assembly" should be admonished to return to their "first love." Those who were still assembling could be exhorted in their assemblies to remain faithful.

The author closes the chapter by reminding them that if they reject the atoning blood of Jesus and return to Judaism there "remaineth no more sacrifice for sins." He warns them of a "certain fearful looking for of judgment . . ." They are urged to remember the "former days," and not cast away their confidence, "which hath great recompense of reward." The chapter closes with this final encouragement, ". . . we are not of them who draw back unto perdition; but of them that believe to the saving of the soul."

CONCLUSION

Hebrews 11 demonstrates the nature and sustaining power of faith. Hebrews 12 presents two more of the "Let Us" passages for exhortation. In Hebrews 13:13, 15, are presented the last appeals and exhortations to prevent their apostasy and to "provoke them unto love and good works." If the exhortations presented in the book of Hebrews will not "provoke unto love and good works" then God's people cannot be motivated in a way pleasing to God!

ENDNOTES

1. H. D. M. Spence and J. S. Exell, eds., *The Pulpit Commentary* (New York, NY: Funk and Wagnalls Co., 1950). vol. XXI, Hebrews, p. 272.

2. R. Milligan, *The New Testament Commentary* (Nashville, TN.: Gospel Advocate, 1963), vol. IX, pp. 281-282.

3. K. S. Wuest, *Hebrews in the Greek New Testament* (Grand Rapids, MI: Wm. B. Eerdmans Pub. Co., 1956), p. 182.

4. M. R. Vincent, *Word Studies in the New Testament* (Mac Dill AFB, FL: MacDonald Pub. Co., n.d.), p. 1147.

5. Adam Clarke, *Clarke's Commentary* (New York: NY and Nashville, TN: Abingdon Press, n.d.), vol. VI, p. 757.

6. Wuest, *loc. cit.*

7. Spence and Exell, *loc. cit.*

8. Milligan, *op. cit.*, p. 283.

9. J. Thompson, *The Living Word Commentary* (Austin, TX: R. B. Sweet Co., 1971), vol. XV, p. 140.

10. W. Barclay, *The Letter to the Hebrews* (Philadelphia, PA: Westminster Press, 1956 — revised edition), pp. 122-123.

THE HEROES OF FAITH

HEBREWS 11:4-40

By HUGO McCORD

Baptized by L. L. Brigance in 1923. Th. D. from New Orleans Baptist Seminary. Retired professor of Bible and Biblical languages, Oklahoma Christian College. Adjunct professor, Alabama Christian School of Religion, Montgomery, AL. Author of nine books. Lectures and conducts meetings in the U.S. and several other nations. He and his wife, Lois, have a son and a daughter. Speaker, *First Annual Denton Lectures.*

INTRODUCTION

On the human side faith (*pistis*) is the greatest word in the New Testament. It is that which stands under (*hupostasis*) the things hoped for (as, heaven). It is the proof, the sure persuasion (*elenchos*), of things not visible (as, God — He. 11:1). By it human beings are able to go beyond empirical knowledge to faith-knowledge, and have an assurance that is as certain and reliable as sense perception. A deduction from things that are made (*poiemata*) leads one into faith-knowledge of an eternal power and deity that is so sure men who refuse to entertain it are without excuse (Ro. 1:20). By faith we understand that the worlds were framed by God's word (He. 11:3).

Faith-knowledge is a mental conviction springing from an observance of things that are made. Those made things may be inarticulate but their testimony is overwhelming. "There is no speech nor language" (Ps. 19:3) from the sun and the moon but they speak loudly of their Maker. A voice "is not heard" from the stars, but they sing "as they shine, the hand that made us is divine."

Not only does faith arise from human reasoning about the things that are made, but it also comes from a hearing of God's word (Ro. 10:17). Faith born in the human heart from God's word then properly leads one into an obedience of faith (Ro. 1:5; 16:26). An obedient faith is the theme of Hebrews 11:4-40.

OLD TESTAMENT HEROES

In Hebrews 11:4-40 is a long list of people who have heard God's word and then by faith have obeyed that word. Heroes and heroines, named and unnamed, are set forth as an inspiration to living Christians. The writer of the book of Hebrews pictures them as spectators in a stadium, having finished their races successfully, who are now looking down on more recent racers, watching intently and encouragingly, with the spirit of "we did it; you can too!" They have become a "cloud of witnesses" giving valuable testimony.

This dramatic scene should cause every Christian runner to lay aside every weight and the sin which easily besets and to run with patience the race that is set before him, looking to Jesus the leader and finisher of the faith, who for the joy set before him endured the cross, despising the shame, and has sat down at the right hand of the throne of God (He. 12:1-2). When today's Christians spend time in Hebrews 11:4-40 they are entering the stadium and visiting with Old Testament worthies who have completed their races.

Abel's sacrifice (He. 11:4). One of those successful racers is Abel. Though dead, he is yet speaking. From what Paul tells us, Abel's faith arose from his hearing God's word as he commanded that a lamb be used in a sacrifice (Ro. 10:17). Without that word from God Abel would not have known with what kind of sacrifice God would have been pleased. Conscientious trust in God's word led him to do "exactly" that which was "commanded by the God of heaven" (cf. Ezra 7:23). That kind of faith Cain had refused to allow an entrance into his heart. On the contrary Abel had witness borne to him that he was righteous because of an obedient faith.

Enoch's translation (He. 11:5-6). Whereas faith-knowledge or mental conviction springs from solid even though non-speaking evidence, and whereas the obedience of faith springs from a hearing of God's word, the faith that would cause God to work a miracle might properly be called miraculous faith (cf. Ma. 17:20; 21:21). Since by nature every man has an appointment with death (Ro. 5:12; He. 9:27), only a miracle could make Enoch an exception. But the miraculous faith evident in his exceptional case in no wise lessens his deep trust that God is and that he is a rewarder of them that seek him. Further, his miraculous faith in no wise detracts from his obedience of faith evident in his walking with God for three centuries (Ge. 5:21-24).

Noah's ark (He. 11:7). "Every one that hath heard from the Father, and hath learned" (John 6:45), is prepared by faith to do the Father's will. Noah had heard God's word that a flood was coming. That word induced a confidence in his heart that that flood would be real, a confidence deep enough to cause him to build an ark to prepare for the announced deluge. Thus he saved himself and seven others of like faith and became an heir of righteousness.

From Abraham to Joseph (He. 11:8-21). Though Abraham's father was an idolater (Jos. 24:2), Abraham's reliance on God was firm enough to change the world's history (Ga. 3:29), a reliance that led to "steps" (Ro. 4:12) of faith over hundreds of miles for a hundred years. Abraham has become a special example, for only one man is called "the father of us all" and "the friend of God" (Ro. 4:16; Jam. 2:23).

Moses' choice (He. 11:23-29). Since faith comes as a result of hearing, Moses' life shows that he believed what had been told him by Amram and Jochebed, and he ordered his life accordingly. So he too changed the history of the world and among all heroes of faith he is a giant.

The walls of Jericho (He. 11:30). Assurance was certain in Joshua's heart that God intended to give Israel the city of Jericho. That assurance led him and the Israelites into seven days' marching, an obedience of faith. Since walls normally do not fall by being encircled no matter how strong is the faith of the marchers, this incident has to be marked as another example of miraculous faith.

Rahab's deliverance (He. 11:31). What Rahab had heard about God's blessing Israel induced faith in her heart to risk her life to protect two spies (Jos. 2:1-24), and apparently caused her to repent of immorality and so to become a heroine of faith (Jam. 2:25).

Samson and others (He. 11:32-40). What apparently was true of Rahab's penitence must also be true of Samson, else the Hebrew writer would not have listed him as a hero of faith.

EARLY CHRISTIAN HEROES

Stephen (Acts 6:5-7:60). "Stephen, a man full of faith," after apostolic hands had been laid on him, had a miraculous faith so that he was full of "power" and able to work "great wonders and signs among the people." As the first Christian martyr he must be placed in God's record as a hero of faith along with the Old Testament men and women "of whom the world is not worthy."

Paul. An undoubting conviction led Paul into such an active obedience of faith that he changed the lives of untold hundreds while he lived and of thousands since his death. The life he lived in the flesh he lived in the faith of the Son of God, because he believed that Jesus had loved him, even him the chief of sinners, and had died for him (I Ti. 1:15; Ga. 2:20). Much he endured, and gladly, for Jesus' sake. The scars on his body were brand marks of Jesus (Ga. 6:17). Prematurely he was "Paul the aged" (Phile. 9), at about the age of sixty-two. At sixty-seven, on death row in Mamertine prison, awaiting the executioner's sword, he could triumphantly say, "I have fought the good fight, I have finished the course, I have kept the faith" (II Ti. 4:7).

Polycarp. In 108 A.D., when Ignatius visited Smyrna, one of the bishops there was Polycarp. Tertullian wrote that the apostle John had appointed him to that office. When the letter to the church at Smyrna was delivered, it could very well be that in the Lord's day service there, it fell the lot of Polycarp to read Jesus' letter to that church. From what happened later we know that the message was faith-building and fortifying to the whole church, and in particular to Polycarp:

> Fear not the things which thou art about to suffer; behold, the devil is about to cast some of you into prison, that ye may be tried; and ye shall have tribulation ten days. Be thou faithful unto death, and I will give thee the crown of life. (Rev. 2:10).

As it turned out, Polycarp had the cold reality of that letter on his mind from 96 A.D. until Saturday, February 23, 155 (Barclay), when he suffered a martyr's death. He could have saved his life by renouncing the name of Jesus. The Jews joined with the heathen in demanding Polycarp's death by being thrown to the lions (Fausett). When something prevented that bloody death, the Jews brought logs for a fiery death. Given a last chance to deny his Lord, even as the flames began to arise around him, he was heard to say, "Eighty and six years have I served him, and he has never done me wrong. How can I deny him now?"

TWENTIETH CENTURY HEROES

Sarah Andrews. The parents of Sarah Andrews (1890-1961) lived so far out in the country from Dickson, Tennessee, they decided to start a neighborhood congregation. On a visit to Dickson, after she was baptized at the age of fourteen, she heard a visiting missionary speak about the work in Japan: J. M. McCaleb on a furlough from his work in Tokyo. Her heart was deeply stirred. She determined, God willing, that she would be a missionary to that far away land. Prayerfully and diligently she pursued her plan. At age 25, single and alone, she boarded a ship in San Francisco bound for Japan. For many years she was largely supported by her parents, and the Dickson church and others kept her work going.

For a young lady to arrive in a foreign land, to learn a new and difficult language, to begin house Bible classes with neighborhood children, and then with their mothers, these were no small accomplishments. With the passing of the years the children became teen-agers, and were baptized along with some mothers and fathers. Sarah's extended and tireless work saw four congregations established by people whom she had taught, and property acquired for places to meet.

However, when the war started she was interned in 1942 as an enemy alien. Her internment camp was a houseboat, where the dampness and a starvation diet brought on tuberculosis. Authorities, giving her up for dead, sent her back to her Numachu home, but also sent 17 wounded Japanese soldiers for her to nurse. At times she had to crawl from cot to cot. Neighborhood children, whom she had taught and who loved her, supplemented her meager diet. But the task was too much. She fainted, and never knew how long she was unconscious. On coming to, perhaps two days later, all the soldiers had been moved out, and she had been left to die. Again, little children with handouts saved her life.

Over in America her sister in the flesh, Myrtle Thompson, at Tyler, Texas, regularly invited Air Force men for Sunday dinners. To each one Myrtle gave the last address known for Sarah. For three years only one message had come about Sarah, and that through the Red Cross. When General Douglas MacArthur had entered Tokyo, a Christian soldier, with an address given him by Myrtle, drove a jeep 70 miles to find Sarah nearly dead. Weighing only 75 pounds, her body swelling showed imminent death because of starvation. The soldier left her his emergency rations, returned to Tokyo, and came back with his jeep full of groceries and supplies. He had saved her life.

Years later, on a furlough back to her Tennessee home, only three years prior to her death, her family, including Mack Wayne Craig (a vice-president of David Lipscomb College), begged her to stay at home. Her reply was, "It is as near heaven from Japan as from America." In her beloved adopted country, where she had lived 46 of her 71 years, she died and was buried by loving Japanese Christians, who erected a beautiful memorial at her gravesite. Truly, all of God's great souls of faith did not live in the Old Testament days, nor even in the early years of Christianity.

When Mack Craig, visiting at Dickson with his aunt Sarah, expressed a desire to be a missionary in Japan, she said, "You can serve God as well in America as in Japan." Yes, there are heroes and heroines of faith in America whose names the Lord knows and whom he loves. "The Lord knoweth them that are his" (II Ti. 2:19). Their names, men and women who labor in the gospel, "are in the book of life" (Ph. 4:3).

Johnny Pepper. In a brief tract Jim Bill McInteer has memorialized another heart-touching example of 20th century faith:

"Johnny Pepper!" That name itself is fascinating, isn't it? But Johnny Pepper has more of a claim for fame than just the existence of a good Irish-American name.

As we assembled under a tent in Athens, Alabama, Clinton Brackeen, the song leader, said at an appropriate spot in the service, "Now Brother Johnny Pepper will lead us in prayer."

We bowed together and one of the petitions that came from the lips of Johnny Pepper was this: "Help Brother McInteer to preach like he ought to preach, and help us who sit here to hear like we ought to hear." That is a sobering responsibility, is it not?

Johnny Pepper was totally unknown to the visiting evangelist. At the end of the service Doyle Banta said, "This is Johnny Pepper."

After a cordial exchange of customary greetings the local evangelist said, "And this is the eighty-seventh different gospel meeting he has attended this year!" Eighty-seven meetings in the course of one year! Eighty-seven preachers had enjoyed his support. Eighty-seven churches had been encouraged by his presence. Eighty-seven different congregations within a radius of fifty miles had shared in his expressions of gratitude for the work that they were attempting to do.

And that wasn't all. In forty-eight years of service since he has become a Christian only five times has he missed the public assembly on the Lord's day. Those five absences were caused by his illness. Otherwise he has always been there.

That gave rise to these questions as suggested by Doyle Banta: "Doesn't it rain at Johnny Pepper's house? Doesn't it get cold out Johnny Pepper's way? Doesn't the road get bad that leads by Johnny Pepper's house? Doesn't it get hot where Johnny Pepper lives? Aren't there duties he needs to attend to? Sometimes doesn't he need to be at other places? Doesn't Johnny Pepper ever get tired? Does Johnny Pepper have relatives? What about those eleven children he has — aren't they trouble to get ready to bring to Bible school?" (Incidentally, every one of his eleven children is a faithful Christian.)

Every excuse that you hear offered by every one of the brethren who has been an absentee brother could also come to Johnny Pepper. Yet eighty-seven gospel meetings in one year have been graced by his attendance, and for forty-eight years he has attended the worship faithfully. *Quite a man — this Johnny Pepper!*

No, not all heroes of faith are recorded on the pages of the Bible, and they are not all overseas. This Johnny Pepper was an elder of the Bethel congregation (on U.S. 72 east of Athens, Alabama), a church, due to the effective preaching by Howard Blazer, that contributes thousands of dollars to mission work and to Childhaven. Brother Pepper has now gone to his reward, but he lives on in the better world, and still in this one. Three of his sons make up the eldership of the Bethel church, and one son is a deacon. Blessed are the dead who die in the Lord from henceforth: yea, saith the Spirit, that they may rest from their labors; for their works follow with them (Re. 14:13). "This is the victory that hath overcome the world, even our faith" (I John 5:4).

Willie Fayette. A Christian young lady married a non-Christian, and in much grief paid for it. He hated the church and church people. His language was of cursing and bitterness, even in the presence of their young son and daughter, and when visitors were present. Wisely, Willie stopped asking Al to go to church, though she and the children never missed. At home she went out of her way to be a kind and thoughtful wife.

With no spiritual leadership from Al, Willie decided meals would not be eaten unless thanksgiving was expressed, and she led the prayers. She subscribed for that worthwhile magazine of daily devotionals, *Power for Today,* and at the breakfast table she read a selection each morning. This Al tolerated with a frown and tried to ignore it.

One day their son, seeing a baptism at services, went home and asked his father if he had been baptized. Al's reply was coldly negative. But apparently the lad's question was not forgotten. Soon Al volunteered to go to church on Sunday morning only, but told Willie, "Don't ask me to go at any other time." Wisely, she agreed.

At a Sunday morning service, while they were standing up for the invitation song, Willie was weeping, which Al noticed. At home he asked her why she cried. She said, "Sit down, Al, I want to talk to you." When they had sat, she continued,

> Al, you have taken out a large insurance policy on your life to take care of me and the children if you die. You have assigned your eyes to the eye bank that others might see when you are dead. You have assigned your body to the Tulane Medical School for research to help others when you are gone. You have taken care of everything but your soul, and you ask me why I am crying!

That was enough. Shortly Al was baptized. He went through quite a struggle to quit using habitual curse words. He became a daily Bible reader and never missed a service at church. Such amazing growth he made in a knowledge of the word (reading it morning and night on long bus rides to and from work) the elders asked him to supervise the Bible school. Now, in retirement, he works diligently with correspondence work and in a jail ministry.

CONCLUSION

No, all the names of God's heroes of faith are not inscribed in Hebrews 11:4-40, but they are written in the heart of God.

REFUSE NOT HIM THAT SPEAKETH

HEBREWS 12:25

By TOM L. BRIGHT

Born 1939, Shidler, Oklahoma. Married Mary Jane Jelsma; two children. Graduated from Elk City School of Preaching, presently working toward degree in philosophy through University of Oklahoma CLS program. Has preached in Oklahoma, Louisiana and Texas; conducted meetings in same; spoken on lectureships in California, Florida, Tennessee and Oklahoma. Instructor in Owasso School of Biblical Studies in Owasso, Oklahoma. Staff writer for *Contending for the Faith*. Writes for other gospel papers. Local evangelist, Sapulpa, Oklahoma.

INTRODUCTION

The purpose underlying Paul's writing of this majestic epistle was twofold: (1) encouragement in the face of trials and tribulation; (2) to exhort his Jewish readers to faithfulness. The theme of this book is: Jesus is the Christ, the long-awaited Messiah; he was the "heir of all things" spoken by the prophets (He. 1:2) and the pivot around which God's mystery of the ages revolved.

Within the context of the superiority of Christ's system of righteousness, as opposed to Judaism, Paul encouraged his readers, "See that ye refuse not him that speaketh" (He. 12:25). Certainly, this singular admonition is limitless in magnitude and sobering in its implications. Indeed, who would want to refuse Him that speaks? It seems, however, that Paul's readers had already lost some of their brethren in a reversion to Judaism, and the distinct possibility existed that others might follow the road of apostasy. With this background, then, the apostle takes pen in hand to encourage them to remain faithful to their profession (He. 10:23).

Paul, having directed his readers' attention to the great entourage of Old Testament worthies in chapter 11, encourages them to lay aside every hindrance and patiently run the race before them, all the while with their eyes upon "Jesus, the author and finisher of our faith" (He. 12:2).

He then quotes Proverbs 3:12 to show that God chastens those whom he loves, exhorting them by this to keep their paths straight (vv. 6-18).

In verses 18-24, Paul contrasts two "mounts," one to which "ye are not come" (v. 18), and one to which "ye are come" (v. 22). The first, the mount "that might be touched, and that burned with fire . . ." was Mt. Sinai and was a direct allusion to the law of Moses received there. The second was:

> . . . mount Sion, and unto the city of the living God, the heavenly Jerusalem, and to an innumerable company of angels, to the general assembly and church of the firstborn, which are written in heaven, and to God the Judge of all, and to the spirits of just men made perfect, and to Jesus the mediator of the new covenant, and to the blood of sprinkling, that speaketh better things than that of Abel (vv. 22-24),

which referred to that system of righteousness instituted by Christ, summed up in the familiar phrase, New Testament Christianity.

Interestingly enough, in verses 18 and 22, the word translated "come" is of such significance in the original language as to denote the present results of a completed action. Thus, Paul's thoughts are that these Christians had not come, and were not yet, at the mount that burned with fire (the law of Moses), but that they had come, and were yet, at mount Sion, the heavenly Jerusalem.

It is at this juncture that we come to our text, "See that ye refuse not him that speaketh. For if they escaped not who refused him that spake on earth, much more shall not we escape, if we turn away from him that speaketh from heaven" (He. 12:25). That the one who "speaketh from heaven" is Christ cannot be denied in light of "God . . . hath in these last days spoken unto us by his Son . . ." (He. 1:1-2). This is an argument from the less to the greater. If those who refused him that spoke on earth (Moses and the law) did not escape, how much more will those not escape who refuse Him who speaks from heaven, "For this man was counted worthy of more glory than Moses, inasmuch as he who hath builded the house hath more honour than the house" (He. 3:3).

To fully appreciate Paul's admonition to "refuse not him that speaketh" (He. 12:25), let us consider the meaning of "refuse." A noted authority, J. H. Thayer, defines it as "to refuse, to reject."[1] Cremer adds "to decline, refuse, avoid,"[2] while another recognized authority says "decline . . . reject, refuse someone or refuse to do something to someone."[3]

Paul magnifies the meaning of this word by using the term "turn away" in our assigned text. The same word is used in II Timothy 1:15: "This thou knowest, that all they which are in Asia *be turned* away from me; of whom are Phygellus and Hermogenes." It appears also in Titus 1:14: "Not giving heed to Jewish fables, and commandments of men, that *turn from* the truth;" and in the familiar II Timothy 4:4: "And they shall *turn away* their ears from the truth, and shall be turned unto fables" (all emphasis mine, TLB). Certainly, anyone can grasp the implications of the apostle's statement.

THE PERPETUAL PLIGHT OF MAN

Refusing to hear God was not limited to the first century. It can be truthfully said that man, from the very beginning, has exemplified this malady. When Eve ". . . took of the fruit thereof, and did eat, and gave also unto her husband with her; and he did eat" (Ge. 3:6), the first act of refusing to hear the Lord was perpetrated. And we need not remind you of the drastic consequences of this sin.

The acceptance of Abel's offering by God, while rejecting his brother's, was due to Cain's refusal to hear God. Since Abel's offering was by faith (He. 11:4), and ". . . faith cometh by hearing, and hearing by the word of God" (Rom. 10:17), we know that God had told Cain and Abel what they were to offer; Cain refused to hear, and his offering was rejected.

Another excellent example of refusal to hear God is seen in the world-wide flood which was brought upon the earth because ". . . God saw that the wickedness of man was great in the earth, and that every imagination of the thoughts of his heart was only evil continually" (Ge. 6:5). It is sad, yet true, that of all the people who then lived upon the earth, only eight were willing to hear the One speaking from heaven. This certainly is a distressing picture of mankind in general.

The book of Judges stands as a silent sentinel of a refusal to hear him who speaks from heaven. The Israelites, after finally taking possession of the long-awaited promised land, were punished by God with captivity after captivity, simply because they refused to hear him.

When we take all the previously mentioned examples and couple them with the fact that almost all of the Old Testament prophecies were uttered against God's people with the intention of bringing them to repentance, it becomes clear that our heavenly Father has always had to contend with this attitude of his own people.

Looking beyond the borders of his selected people, we can see that mankind, in general, has fared no better. The general refusal of man to hear God, from the beginning, has already been cited. This is presented most conspicuously in Genesis 15:12-15. Here God promises Abram that even though his descendants would go into a strange land for some four hundred years, Jehovah would bring them out with great substance. In verse 16, he was told, "But in the fourth generation they shall come hither again: *for the iniquity of the Amorites is not yet full*" (emphasis mine, TLB). With this setting, let us consider God's message to Israel:

> Speak not thou in thine heart, after that the Lord thy God hath cast them out from before thee, saying, For my righteousness the Lord hath brought me in to possess this land: but for the wickedness of these nations the Lord doth drive them out from before thee. Not for thy righteousness, or for the uprightness of thine heart, dost thou go to possess their land: but for the wickedness of these nations the Lord thy God doth drive them out from before thee, and that he may perform the word which the Lord sware unto thy fathers, Abraham, Isaac, and Jacob (De. 9:4-5).

Certainly, these verses show that even though God is long-suffering, there comes a time when a people become so wicked, that their "iniquity is full," even to overflowing; they must pay the consequences (cf., De. 18:9-14; 12:31; Le. 18:24-30; 20:1-5; Nu. 31:15-16).

The attitude and subsequent behavior of man, when he refuses to hear God, is vividly presented by Paul in Romans 1:18-32. One needs only to read this passage to see the depths of degradation to which man will fall when he rejects God.

Indeed, this is a pitiful picture. It makes one wonder how much pain, anguish, and suffering could have been prevented if man had given heed to God's call to righteousness. The deterioration of man from that high and holy state in which he was created, to the level of depravity pointed out by Paul, is frightening, especially when we realize that it is a result of man's refusing to hear Him who speaks from heaven. How true are the words of Jeremiah: "O Lord, I know that the way of man is not in himself: it is not in man that walketh to direct his steps" (Je. 10:23).

THE JEWS REFUSE GOD

A sad spectacle it is when we picture a great mob exiting from the city of Jerusalem on the way to a place called Golgotha, the place of a skull. This mob is preceded by the Roman soliders and a man bearing his own instrument of death. Upon their arrival at Golgotha, the soldiers crucify the man named Jesus. There is no doubt that this one incident is *the* classic example of refusing to hear Him who speaks from heaven.

It is incontestable; if anyone ever lacked an excuse for refusing to hear God, it was the Jews of the first century. Their Old Testament Scriptures amply foretold of the one who was to come, the promised Messiah. Moses spoke most forcefully on the subject (De. 18:15-19). The Old Testament prophets, as they sent forth their clarion call of repentance in an attempt to bring Israel back to God, blended into their messages the promise of the coming Messiah and his kingdom.

When John the baptizer came preaching ". . . Repent ye: for the kingdom of heaven is at hand" (Ma. 3:2), the Jews knew exactly what he meant. They understood his reference to be to that Messianic kingdom the Israelites had been eagerly awaiting for some fifteen centuries.

But Jesus did not fit their own prejudiced ideas as to what this long-awaited Messiah was to be like. They expected an earthly kingdom, with an earthly king, whose throne would be in Jerusalem. It was not that they could not understand divine prophecy; it was that they would not. They refused to hear Him who speaks from heaven.

Jesus told his antagonists that ". . . had ye believed Moses, ye would have believed me: for he wrote of me. But if ye believe not his writings, how shall ye believe my words?" (John 5:46-47). Obviously, they thought they had a proper understanding of the Scriptures, but Jesus affirms the contrary. In this same conversation, Jesus told them, "Search the scriptures; for in them ye think ye have eternal life: and they are they which testify of me" (John 5:39). It is implied here that they could understand the Scriptures and, in so doing, they would be pointed to Christ; in other words, they could understand them *exactly* alike!

Another reason the Jews had no excuse was that the miracles proved his divinity. Peter affirmed that ". . . Jesus of Nazareth, a man approved of God among you by miracles and wonders and signs, which God did by him in the midst of you, as ye yourselves also know" (Acts 2:22). Before his crucifixion ". . . many of the people believed on him, and said, When Christ cometh, will he do more miracles than these which this man hath done?" (John 7:31).

The Jews' refusal to hear God on this occasion was catastrophic for them as a nation. By rejecting Jesus while he was here and, subsequently, rejecting his message of salvation (Ro. 1:16-17), they ceased to exist as a nation some forty years after this classic example of rejection. Without question, Paul's exhortation to "See that ye refuse not him that speaketh . . ." is both appropriate and meaningful.

THIS ATTITUDE EXISTS TODAY

It would be absurd to limit this philosophy or its consequences to the first century Jews. Roman Catholicism and denominationalism stand as silent witnesses to this agelong malady of man. Unequivocally, modern-day "Christendom"flies in the face of that oneness for which Jesus prayed in John 17:20-21. It exists because man still refuses to hear the One speaking from heaven.

Certainly, this same attitude is present in the New Testament Church today. Everywhere we turn, this philosophy is evidenced. Today, so much is heard about "positive"preaching. At first sight, it seems so comforting, but when one is asked what is meant, the answer is less than inviting . To many, "positive" preaching does not mean to be "positively" opposed to sin and those advocating it, nor does "positive" preaching mean to be "positively" in favor of truth, righteousness, and holiness, regardless of who might be offended.

In essence, those who advocate "positive"preaching are saying, "Don't say 'don't'." They do not want anything said which might be of a negative nature. They do not want sin pointed out as "sin." To some, preaching should be a "don't-rock-the-boat" kind of sermon; do not cause any ripples.

The similarity between brethren today and those of Jeremiah's day is striking: both desiring to hear ". . . Peace, peace; when there is no peace" (Je. 6:14; 8:11). Many today desire to come to the service satisfied with their sin, and depart the same way! Indisputably, some desire a license for worldliness, or unscriptural doctrines and practices, and they want to feel good about it.

Isaiah condemned the same philosophy: "Woe unto them that call evil good, and good evil; that put darkness for light, and light for darkness; that put bitter for sweet, and sweet for bitter!" (Is. 5:20). Indeed, these today, just as those of centuries past, are of the same heart and mind,

> Which say to the seers, See not; and to the prophets, Prophesy not unto us right things, speak unto us smooth things, prophesy deceits: Get you out of the way, turn aside out of the path, cause the Holy One of Israel to cease from before us (Is. 30:10-11).

Those who want a wholly "positive" message should consider that eight of the ten commandments (Ex. 20:1-17) are preceded by a "negative." They should remember that God's prophets preached, in part, messages that would be classified as "negative" by today's standards. Interestingly enough, seven times the phrase, "Woe unto you, scribes and Pharisees, hypocrites!" is used by Jesus (Ma. 23:13-29). Indeed, today's "positive preaching" devotees would make our Lord a very negative preacher! Moreover, they should not be unmindful that Paul exhorted Timothy to mix the positive with the negative: "Preach the word; be instant in season, out of season; reprove, rebuke, exhort with all longsuffering and doctrine" (II Ti. 4:2). The same apostle told Titus, "Wherefore rebuke them sharply, that they may be sound in the faith" (Tit. 1:13). And can anyone read the second chapter of Peter's second epistle and not see "negativism" everywhere?

Unquestionably, many today want their ears tickled with soothing "sermonettes" and "after dinner" speeches which do not describe sin with the ugliness with which our heavenly Father views it, and which could be preached in the most liberal denomination in town without offending a single person.

Sermons on God's love, mercy, grace, kindness, longsuffering, care for each individual, etc. are certainly needed, but in preaching on these valuable themes, we should not be unmindful that none of these are unconditionally promised; thus, each implys a negative.

It borders on absurdity to say "Preach the gospel, but don't mention the 'issues'." We need to realize that sin is the issue. Sin is the ever-changing chameleon, appearing in different forms. But when sin rears its ugly head, an "issue" is present. The "issue" may be either moral or doctrinal, but nonetheless, it is an "issue" which must be faced. To imitate an ostrich is not the way to deal with such an "issue."

THE GOSPEL VERSUS "ANOTHER" GOSPEL

In Galatians 1:6-9, Paul, in no uncertain terms, speaks of "another" gospel which is not "another." Paul originally used two different words (each translated here as "another") in painting a beautiful thought not noticeable in our English versions. The basic thought is that some were preaching "another gospel of a different sort" which is not "another gospel of the same sort I delivered unto you." Certainly, if Paul were alive today, he would quickly see that this basic problem has not changed. He would in all probability, still write:

> I marvel that ye are so soon removed from him that called you into the grace of Christ unto another gospel: which is not another; but there be some that trouble you, and would pervert the gospel of Christ (Ga. 1:6-7).

There is today, among our brethren, the advocacy of the same denominational doctrines that our forefathers in the faith have met and resoundingly routed on the polemic platform. Through the ridiculous philosophy of subjectivism, the church is now being moved to accept with open arms, the denominational doctrines of premillennialism, instrumental music in our worship, the direct operation of the Holy Spirit in conviction, conversion and sanctification, etc.

After all, if the truth of any proposition is to be subjectively determined (If in your study of the Bible, you come to the conclusion that the Bible teaches "thus and so," then the Bible does teach "thus and so"; however, "thus and so" is binding only upon you and nobody else, unless they personally grasp such from their own study), then whatever one teaches is true and acceptable to God, whether it be premillennialism, instrumental music, direct operation of the Holy Spirit or any other denominational falsehood.

The doctrine of "once saved, always saved" is from man and not from God. This false doctrine has always been opposed by faithful Christians. Now, out of Lubbock (and possibly from other schools, as well) is a teaching on the subject of "Grace," which is bringing us to the same camp as the denominational doctrine of "preseverance of the saints." One such devotee, when questioned by a personal friend of mine as to how often one had to confess his sins to God, responded, "About every three months." How long, my friends, will it be before we hear the same deniminational doctrine of "once saved, always saved" that now emanates from Baptist pulpits? Not long, I fear.

Grace is not some better-felt-than-told experience. The term, "the grace of God" encompasses all that God has done in order that he might offer salvation to the fallen creature. First, there was the "gracious disposition"[4] by our heavenly Father towards the fallen creature, which moved him to offer the remission of sins to man, which he made possible through the sacrifice of his only begotten Son, Jesus the Christ. All of this was by "grace," by unmerited favor; that is, nothing meritorious in nature was done.

However, man appropriates this "grace" by obedience. The very fact that salvation can be enjoyed bespeaks the grace of God, but the appropriation of such *does not* constitute meritorious works. We *do not* earn this salvation; we *do not* place God in the position wherein he is obligated to save us when we comply with those conditons which he, himself, has established as prerequisites to participating in this free offer. And to affirm otherwise is the apex of ridiculousness.

MODERN-DAY KORAHS

When man is determined to refuse Him that speaks from heaven, it is always necessary to circumvent, in some way, God's delegated authorities.

Korah, and his band of rebels, is an excellent example of the philosophy permeating the brotherhood today. The liberals today rebel against the elders, saying the same thing that the rebellious Korah said in the long ago: ". . . Ye take too much upon you, seeing all the congregation are holy, every one of them, and the Lord is among them: wherefore then lift ye up yourselves above the congregation of the Lord?" (Nu. 16:3). Unquestionably, the seriousness of this rebellion is seen in their destruction: "And the earth opened her mouth, and swallowed them up . . ." (Nu. 16:32). Does this not irrevocably show the abomination in which God holds rebellion against his authourity! The principle expressed by Jesus in Luke 10:16 is certainly applicable here: "He that heareth you heareth me; and he that despiseth you despiseth me; and he that despiseth me despiseth him that sent me."

"Example," say the modern-day Korahs, "is the only authourity elders have." In other words, we are to be persuaded to follow them because of their godly example. And this, in the light of such passages as Acts 20:28, Hebrews 13:17, and I Peter 5:1-3! Indisputably, the exemplary life of elders is an absolute necessity, without which they would be unqualified. But to limit their authority to "example only" is to go beyond what is written (I Co. 4:6).

Certainly, they have no authority to bind things that are optional, nor to make optional those things that are binding; the Lord has already done this through the apostles (Ma. 16:18-19). But, this does not remove their obligation before God, to function as overseers and shepherds (Acts 20:28), to watch (Acts 20:31), to "superintend" and "care for" (I Ti. 3:4-5), to admonish (I Th. 5:12), and to rule over the church (He. 13:17), but not as "lords" (I Pe. 5:3).

Even though Paul named false teachers (I Ti. 1:20; II Ti. 1:15; II Ti. 2:17) and commanded that they be marked (Ro. 16:17), such actions are "taboo" in the liberal mind today. It would be "judgmental and unscriptural" for me to mark Robert Shank as a false teacher or to mark Pat Boone, James Bales, W. Carl Ketcherside, Leroy Garrett, and a host of others as false teachers.

Even with the plain and pointed examples of the Old Testament and with the plain teaching from the pen of Paul that false teachers are to be withdrawn from, when it is attempted, loud rings the cry of "foul." It is better, in the minds of some, to allow these false teachers to have an open and unrestrained influence upon the unlearned and unsuspecting, than to point out the heresy they openly advocate. To some, it is more "Christian" to allow man to be drawn to error than it is to expose that error and those propogating it.

CONCLUSION

What, then, are we to do? We must take the whole armor of God (Ep. 6:11-17) and, having unsheathed the sword of the Spirit, we must confront this terrible malady of refusing to hear Him who speaks from heaven. We must boldly proclaim the once and for all delivered faith of Jude, verse 3, without fear or favor.

Let us so conduct ourselves so that we can say, just as confidently as did Paul, "Wherefore I take you to record this day, that I am pure from the blood of all men. For I have not shunned to declare unto you all the counsel of God" (Acts 20:26-27). May this be our lot in life.

ENDNOTES

1. John Henry Thayer, *Greek-English Lexicon of the New Testament* (Grand Rapids, MI: Zondervan, 1977), p. 482.
2. Hermann Cremer, *Biblico-Theological Lexicon* (Edinburgh: T. & T. Clark, 1954), p. 74.
3. William F. Arndt and F. Wilbur Gingrich, *A Greek-English Lexicon of the New Testament and Other Early Christian Literature* (Chicago, IL: University of Chicago Press, 1973), p. 621.
4. Cremer, *op. cit.*, p. 573.

THE KINGDOM THAT CANNOT BE SHAKEN

HEBREWS 12:28

By BOBBY DUNCAN

Born in Jacksonville, AL, 1934; baptized into Christ, 1945. Married Lois Ann Elliott and they have two children. M.A. degree from Alabama Christian School of Religion, Montgomery, AL. Serves as local evangelist, Adamsville, AL. Daily radio preacher several years. Editor of *Vigil* three years. Editor of *Words of Truth* six years. Author of booklet and tract. Frequent speaker on major lectureships. Listed in *Personalities of the South,* 1977. Speaker, *First Annual Denton Lectures.*

INTRODUCTION

When the Jews, following the Babylonian captivity, read the words recorded in Daniel 2:44, they had to be impressed:

> And in the days of these kings shall the God of heaven set up a kingdom, which shall never be destroyed: and the kingdom shall not be left to other people, but it shall break in pieces and consume all these kingdoms, and it shall stand for ever.

They had heard of the glory of their nation during the lives of their ancestors while David and then Solomon reigned over the kingdom. They knew something of the humiliation their nation had suffered in the Babylonian captivity. Actually, from the time of the captivity right on down to the time of Christ the Jewish nation never was free from domination by more powerful kingdoms than were they. No doubt the Jews would thrill to read the promise that God would some day set up a kingdom which should not be ruled over by another people, but which would consume all other kingdoms, and would stand forever.

This is the very kingdom the writer of Hebrews has in mind in our text for this lecture: "Wherefore we receiving a kingdom which cannot be moved, let us have grace, whereby we may serve God acceptably with reverence and godly fear" (He. 12:28).

THE KINGDOM THAT CANNOT BE SHAKEN IS THE CHURCH

That the kingdom of this passage is the church of Christ is abundantly taught, both in this chapter, and in numerous other passages. Beginning in verse 22 of this chapter, the writer said:

> But ye are come unto mount Sion, and unto the city of the living God, the heavenly Jerusalem, and to an innumerable company of angels, to the general assembly and church of the firstborn, which are written in heaven, and to God the Judge of all, and to the spirits of just men made perfect, and to Jesus the mediator of the new covenant, and to the blood of sprinkling, that speaketh better things than that of Abel.

Notice the expression, *church of the firstborn.* The "kingdom which cannot be moved" of verse 28 is the "church of the first-born" of verse 23.

Our Lord made it plain in Matthew 16 when he said in verse 18, "I will build my church," and then in verse 19, "I will give unto thee the keys of the kingdom of heaven," that the church is the kingdom and the kingdom is the church.

But go back for a moment to the prophecy of Daniel 2:44: "And in the days of *these kings* . . ." What kings? An examination of the context will reveal that Daniel had interpreted a dream of Nebuchadnezzar, and had told him the dream had to do with a succession of kings and kingdoms. Babylon was the first, followed in order by the kingdom of the Medes and Persians, then by the Grecian kingdom under Alexander the Great, and then by the mighty Roman Empire. It was in the days of these Roman kings that the God of heaven was to set up a kingdom which would stand forever. Jesus was born, lived his lifetime, and died during the days of the Roman kings. When Jesus began his preaching during the days of the Roman kings, he said, "The time is fulfilled, and the kingdom of God is at hand . . ." (Mark 1:15). Since Daniel had prophesied that the kingdom of God would be set up in the days of the Roman kings, we should not be surprised to learn that Jesus preached, "The time is fulfilled, and the kingdom of God is at hand."

A little later, Jesus said, "Verily I say unto you, That there be some of them that stand here, which shall not taste of death, till they have seen the kingdom of God come with power" (Mark 9:1).

John the Baptist also preached: "Repent ye: for the kingdom of heaven is at hand" (Ma. 3:2). When the twelve were sent out to preach to the "lost sheep of the house of Israel," they were told to say, "The kingdom of heaven is at hand" (Ma. 10:6-7). When Jesus sent out the seventy, he told them to preach, "The kingdom of God is come nigh unto you" (Luke 10:9).

Now the question is, was the kingdom set up in the days of the Roman kings, as was prophesied by Daniel, and as preached by John the Baptist, by Christ, by the twelve, and by the seventy? Or did they all miss it? The Premillennialist says they all missed it, and that the kingdom still has not been set up. He says Christ really meant to do what Daniel prophesied, what he himself promised, and what John the Baptist, the twelve, and the seventy preached, but because the Jews rejected him, he was not able to do so. So he set in operation Plan B, and set up the church instead. Such teaching as this borders on blasphemy, and makes Christ and inspired writers of both Old and New Testaments false teachers.

What the Jew of Jesus' day and the Premillennialist (or Zionist) of our day never learned is that the kingdom is the church. Every single prophecy concerning the kingdom of God is fulfilled in the church. The church was not established according to "Plan B," but was established "according to the eternal purpose which he purposed in Christ Jesus our Lord" (Ep. 3:10-11). In Acts 2:23, on the day of Pentecost, Peter declared that Jesus was "delivered [to be crucified] by the determinate counsel and foreknowledge of God." In other words, everything went according to God's plan. In that same chapter, Peter quoted a prophecy from Psalms 132:11 concerning Christ on the throne of David, and then made it clear to his hearers that David, in that prophecy, was referring to the time when Christ would be raised from the dead and exalted to the right hand of the Father.

Another prophecy of Daniel is interesting in this connection:

> I saw in the night visions, and, behold, one like the Son of man came with the clouds of heaven, and came to the Ancient of days, and they brought him near before him. And there was given him dominion, and glory, and a kingdom, that all people, nations, and languages should serve him: his dominion is an everlasting dominion, which shall not pass away, and his kingdom that which shall not be destroyed (Da. 7:13-14).

Notice that this one "like the Son of man" was given this dominion — this kingdom — when he "came with the clouds of heaven," and when he "came *to* [not *from*] the Ancient of days." To what could this possibly refer except to the Lord's ascension back to the Father in the clouds to become king over his kingdom, the church? The church is the "kingdom that cannot be shaken."

REIGN OF CHRIST TO END WHEN HE COMES AGAIN

We have shown clearly that Christ is now reigning as King over his kingdom, which is his church. We will now show that this reign of Christ as king will end when he comes again. Notice carefully the following:

> But now is Christ risen from the dead, and become the firstfruits of them that slept. For since by man came death, by man came also the resurrection of the dead. For as in Adam all die, even so in Christ shall all be made alive. But every man in his own order: Christ the firstfruits; afterward they that are Christ's at his coming. Then cometh the end, when he shall have delivered up the kingdom to God, even the Father; when he shall have put down all rule and all authority and power. For he must reign, till he hath put all enemies under his feet. The last enemy that shall be destroyed is death" (I Co. 15:20-26).

These verses show: (1) that Christ is now reigning, (2) that he will continue to reign until all enemies have been destroyed, (3) that the last enemy to be destroyed will be death, (4) that death will be destroyed when the dead are raised and (5) that the dead will be raised "at his coming." In other words, he will reign until he comes again, at which time he will have overcome all enemies, and will then deliver up the kingdom to the Father.

THE MAJOR ERROR OF THE PREMILLENNIALIST

The major error of the Premillennialist (or Zionist) of our day is the same as the error of the Jews who rejected Christ in the first century. The Jews rejected Christ because they were expecting their Messiah to set up a material, fleshly, earthly kingdom, and they refused to accept the fact that the church was and is the kingdom foretold by the prophets. One reason this was then, and is today, a problem is the fact some have never learned that spiritual things are far superior to fleshly things. Is not the burden of Hebrews to show the superiority of Christianity, a spiritual system, over Judaism, a fleshly system? When we read in Hebrews 12:28 about a "kingdom which cannot be moved," we are reading about a spiritual kingdom, the church, which is put in contrast to a fleshly system, Judaism. And the emphasis in the latter part of the chapter is upon the fact that the ecclesiastical system of Judaism was to be shaken and removed, and that the spiritual system of Christianity could not be shaken, and would remain.

In the first five verses of Galatians chapter 3 there are six questions, all of them asked for the purpose of challenging the thinking of those who were about to go back under the law of Moses. One of these questions is in the latter part of verse 3: "Having begun in the Spirit, are ye now made perfect by the flesh?" This question and the discussion surrounding it should be given serious consideration by all those who are expecting the Lord to return to the earth for the purpose of establishing an earthly kingdom, with headquarters in Jerusalem, and with the Jews returning to Palestine. If such were to take place, it would be a giant step backward for God and his people.

The church of Christ is a *spiritual* house (I Pe. 2:5), composed of people who mind *spiritual* things (Ro. 8:5-6), walk after the *spirit* (Ro. 8:1-4), sow to the *spirit* (Ga. 6:8), offer up *spiritual* sacrifices (I Pe. 2:5), and enjoy *spiritual* blessings (Ep. 1:3). Their citizenship is in heaven (Ph. 3:20), and even those faithful in Old Testament times "confessed that they were strangers and pilgrims on the earth" (He. 11:13). Are we then to believe that all this will be culminated by the establishment of an earthly kingdom, with an earthly throne, and in which we enjoy material blessings, and offer up material sacrifices to our earthly king? Will our citizenship then by upon this earth? Will we then be no longer strangers and pilgrims on the earth? Will we then be taught to mind earthly things, and walk after the flesh? "Having begun in the Spirit," will we then be "made perfect by the flesh?" This, my dear brother, is what Premillennialism and related theories demand.

But someone may say, "What about the promise to Abraham and his seed?" Well, it is true that the promise to Abraham involved a fleshly nation and a material territory — the Jews and the land of Palestine (Ge. 15:13-21). But this part of the promise found its fulfillment many years before Jesus was born into the world. Nehemiah 9:7-8 says:

> Thou art the Lord the God, who didst choose Abram, and broughtest him forth out of Ur of the Chaldees, and gavest him the name of Abraham: and foundest his heart faithful before thee, and madest a covenant with him to give the land of the Canaanites, the Hittites, the Amorites, and the Perizzites, and the Jebusites, and the Girgashites, to give it, I say, to his seed, and hast performed thy words; for thou art righteous.

These words show that the promise concerning the fleshly seed of Abraham in the land of Canaan had already been fulfilled in the days of Nehemiah. If every fleshly descendant of Abraham in Palestine today should leave, and never another set foot on that soil, the promise to Abraham concerning his fleshly seed and the land of Canaan has been fulfilled. Furthermore, if every Jew in the world should move to Palestine, and if Israel should become the world ruler, such would not be in fullfillment of any promise made to Abraham, because Nehemiah, by inspiration of the Holy Spirit, said that, with reference to the fleshly seed and the land, God had performed his words.

The land of Canaan and the Jewish nation, like the law of Moses, were only secondary and temporary elements of God's promise to Abraham. They were only vehicles through which the ultimate fulfillment of the promise could come to pass. Look at Paul's statement in Galatians 3:7: "Know ye therefore that they which are of faith, the same are the children of Abraham." Look also at verse 9: "So then they which be of faith are blessed with faithful Abraham." Verse 14 says, "That the blessing of Abraham might come on the Gentiles through

Jesus Christ; that we might receive the promise of the Spirit through faith." These verses show that the primary fulfillment of the promise to Abraham has to do with salvation through faith in Christ, and not with some material blessing on a fleshly nation.

When God made the promise to Abraham he was looking beyond the fleshly nation, and the land of Canaan, and the law which was given at Sinai. He was looking to the coming of Christ into the world so that men could be forgiven of sins and become the children of God by faith in Christ Jesus. He was looking to the time when men could become citizens in that "kingdom that cannot be shaken." Is this not the force of the statement in Galatians 3:16? "Now to Abraham and his seed were the promises made. He saith not, And to seeds, as of many; but as of one, And to thy seed, which is Christ." In view of all this, how can one expect a return to that which is fleshly, earthly, and material? "Having begun in the Spirit, are ye now made perfect by the flesh?"

Then what was the purpose of the law of Moses and the fleshly nation to which it was given?

> It was added because of transgressions, till the seed should come to whom the promise was made. . . . Wherefore the law was our schoolmaster to bring us unto Christ, that we might be justified by faith. But after that faith is come, we are no longer under a school-master (Ga. 3:19-25).

You see, it never has been God's intention for Jesus to be an earthly king on an earthly throne. Jesus himself said,

> My kingdom is not of this world: if my kingdom were of this world, then would my servants fight, that I should not be delivered to the Jews: but now is my kingdom not from hence (John 18:36).

Now look at Galatians 3:26-29:

> For ye are all the children of God by faith in Christ Jesus. For as many of you as have been baptized into Christ have put on Christ. There is neither Jew nor Greek, there is neither bond nor free, there is neither male nor female: for ye are all one in Christ Jesus. And if ye be Christ's, then are ye Abraham's seed, and heirs according to the promise.

Can the establishment of an earthly kingdom improve on this arrangement?

CONCLUSION

We would like the Premillennialist to answer the following questions: (1) When Jesus reigns from his throne in Jerusalem, and the Jews are returned to their native Palestine, who will then be Abraham's seed? (2) When that time comes, who will then be "heirs according to the promise?" (3) Will God at that time recognize a distinction between Jew and Greek? Between bond and free? Between male and female? (4) Will this earthly kingdom that will be set up be superior to the Lord's spiritual kingdom over which he now reigns as king?

THE CHRISTIAN'S CONCERN FOR OTHERS

HEBREWS 13:1-3

By NORMAN GIPSON

Born 1918 in Estelline, Texas. Married Annice Teurman in 1938, and they have four children and seven grandchildren. Served as local preacher for several churches in Texas, as well as Bangor, Maine and Melrose, Massachusetts. Director of Bear Valley School of Preaching in Denver, Colorado 1970-75, instructor from 1968-76. Instructor Sunset School of Preaching, Lubbock, Texas 1976-79. Presently preaches for the Bear Valley church in Denver.

INTRODUCTION

Care for one's fellow Christians runs like a golden thread through the New Testament. Among other things it has done for us, it gave us a word in our language: "Philadelphia," given by William Penn to the city he founded in his new world colony. He wanted it to be forever the City of Brotherly Love. And that is precisely what the Lord meant for his church to be.

This section assigned to me for examination is Hebrews 13:1-3. Here is the reading from the American Standard Version:

> Let love of the brethren continue. Forget not to show love unto strangers: for thereby some have entertained angels unawares. Remember them that are in bonds, as bound with them; them that are ill-treated, as being yourselves also in the body.

This is not only a brief outline of Christians and their reciprocal duties; it is a kind of commentary on the lives of the early saints. They often had to flee their homes, as when Claudius made all the Jews leave Rome (Acts 18:2). As a result, they were strangers, wanderers, seeking rest in some new city where they could live "a quiet and peaceable life in all godliness and honesty" (I Ti. 2:2). They were at times unjustly put in prison. They were often treated badly. As Paul was remembering the way he had misused the Lord's people before he knew the Lord Jesus, he used some very strong words: "I was before a blasphemer, and a persecutor, and injurious" (I Ti. 1:13). He inflicted suffering upon the saints that robbed them of their dignity and degraded them in the eyes of the beholders. For this he was forgiven, but he seemed to have found it hard ever to forgive himself — a problem we all have in some degree. Such things are implied in the brief text assigned to me.

USES OF "PHILADELPHIA"

Sometimes we study subjects which involve dozens or even hundreds of uses of some word. This time we have fewer occurrences, although we have many related ideas in the Scriptures. Here are the passages which speak of "brotherly love":

In love of the brethren be tenderly affectioned one to another; in honor preferring one another (Ro. 12:10).

But concerning love of the brethren ye have no need that one write unto you: for ye yourselves are taught of God to love one another; for indeed ye do it toward all the brethren that are in all Macedonia. But we exhort you brethren, that ye abound more and more . . . (I Th. 4:9-10).

Yea, and for this very cause adding on your part all diligence, in your faith supply virtue . . . and in your godliness brotherly kindness; and in your brotherly kindness love (II Pe. 1:5-7).

These verses, along with our present text, constitute all the New Testament uses of the word "philadelphia." However another term is so close it must be quoted here:

Finally, be ye all likeminded, compassionate, *loving as brethren,* [*philadelphoi*] tenderhearted, humbleminded: not rendering evil for evil, or reviling for reviling; but contrariwise blessing; for hereunto were ye called, that ye should inherit a blessing (I Pe. 3:8-9).

SOME SURFACE FACTS IN HEBREWS 13:1-3

With these words from the Lord warming our hearts, let us now put them through a sort of spiritual extractor and see what lessons are easily apparent on this theme of Christian concern for each other.

Hebrews 13:1 is a beautiful contrast to the last statement of the previous chapter:

> Wherefore, receiving a kingdom that cannot be shaken, let us have grace, whereby we may offer service well-pleasing to God with reverence and awe: for our God is a consuming fire (He. 12:28-29).

These climactic truths convey clearly that the kingdom of God will outlast the wreck of the worlds! How marvelous to be a citizen of the only kingdom that will survive the centuries and endure unto eternity! And then with no break our writer says, "Let love of the brethren continue." Shall we say it like this: Be absolutely certain you worship the great God in a reverent way, understanding what is involved in his kingdom; and be just as sure that you keep right on loving one another. Sadly, we may often emphasize pure worship without proper stress on loving our fellow-worshippers.

This brotherly concern will extend even to strangers. One of the most amazing things to the pagan world of the first two centuries was the treatment of fellow Christians by those who had never seen them before. By contrast, one of the many terms which uses the word "phobia" (fear) is the word *xenophobia*, which means "fear of strangers." My father-in-law once related how his mother, having been left a widow, put her children in a wagon and started across the plains of Kansas toward the home of relatives, many miles away. As night drew near she stopped at a lonely farm house. The man of the house was bearded, sombre, severe; and she was a bit frightened. But having no choice, she asked shelter for the night. They seated her and her children at the supper table, where everyone ate in a rigid silence (the fashion of many homes in those long ago days). When the meal was ended, the patriarch got up, reached for his Bible, and said in a very careful tone: "Will you worship with us?" Gone was all fear! She said she never slept better any night of her life. And that might well express the willingness with which the early saints entertained each other.

The name of Gaius shines like a beacon in the annals of such saints. When the aged John wrote that beloved one, he commended him:

> Beloved, thou doest a faithful work in whatsoever thou doest toward them that are brethren and strangers withal; who bare witness to thy love before the church: whom thou wilt do well to set forward on their journey worthily of God: because that for the sake of the Name they went forth, taking nothing of the Gentiles. We therefore ought to welcome such, that we may be fellow-workers for the truth (III John 5-8).

This touching tribute to a saint who was himself in poor health tells us of the joy the Christians found in helping each other, especially — let me use the word — ʼmissionaries. To set them forward on their journey (give them food, lodging, money or other help) was to act worthily of God. Christian concern for others is not unnoticed in the courts of glory. And isn't it sad that now such men (as Gaius helped) have to drive tens of thousands of miles even to find enough help to go to the field they have chosen! No wonder the world waits in darkness while we hold our goods greedily and ignore the cries of the lost.

When Christians go to prison for their faith, as they still do in many lands in our time, we should never abandon them to a prayerless fate — prayerless on our part, that is. We are taught to remember them as if we shared their cells and their suffering. And when others are ill-treated, we should consider their hurt and their need as if the injuries were being inflicted upon us.

SOME SURFACE FACTS IN HEBREWS 13:4-7

Here I venture beyond my brief section, because the context demands it: concern for my fellow-Christians will insure that I respect everything he owns, including his wife. Repeat: including his wife. Emphasis: *especially his wife.* Here in your city as well as in mine, laxity sometimes sets in among church members. Carelessness and a bit of flirting start a train of events that gathers momentum. Soon or late, there is dissatisfaction with one's own mate and home; and under the pretense of love — which in this case is spelled L-U-S-T — homes are broken, children marred for life, the church downgraded before the community, the word of God is disgraced and souls made unfit for eternity. Surely the writer has not changed the subject from brotherly concern when he says we must "Let marriage be had in honor among all" (He. 13:4). Not only is it right in God's sight for the marriage bed to be kept undefiled; a day when all sophistry will vanish, all excuses disappear, all pretenses be stripped away — such a day is coming, for "fornicators and adulterers God will judge." And we had better not ever forget it.

Still pressing on, concern for my brother will guarantee that I will not covet his possessions. Love of money *is* a root of all kinds of evil. It may be the hallmark of worldly success; but a man was coming close to fact when he wrote, "Money is the hottest crucible into which the soul of man can be put." Brethren will have differences and even sue one another over money; then palliate their deeds before the tribunal of truth by saying, "I know the Bible says not to go to law with a brother; but anybody who would treat me that way is no brother of mine!" It will not do, Christians — not now, not on Judgment Day. Being content with such things as I have will make it certain that I will have concern for my brother, and keep my hands off his belongings — I will not covet anything that is my neighbor's — especially when my neighbor is my brother in the Lord.

And on we go: If I love my brethren, I will remember those who *had* the rule over me and spoke the word of God to me (v. 7). I will obey them that *have* the rule over me and be submissive (v. 17), since they are the guardians of my soul, and will have to account for that soul on the Day of Days.

SURFACE FACTS IN OTHER TEXTS

Lest I infringe too much on the brother who will discuss more of this 13th chapter, let me extract a lesson from another text on our great theme: How about some "tender affection" between brethren? In Romans 12:10 we have this exhortation: "Be tenderly affectioned one to another" — but it is explained that this is "in love of the brethren," and it follows that we will in honor prefer one another. Maybe you have heard that "feelings cannot be commanded;" apparently Paul had not read that book! How do we feel about our brethren? Many times when even a few of us get together in some social meeting, we would more resemble the book of Judges and the act of judging than tender affection and honorable preferment. And in case you are not reading me, let me give you the passage from Judges: "And they went out into the field and gathered their vineyards, and trod the grapes, and held a festival, and went into the house of their god, and did eat and drink and cursed Abimelech" (Ju. 9:27). That gathering in Shechem resembles some gatherings I have been in! There was much eating and joking and praising each other — and speaking evil of those who were not present. It is not right!

And what about that part which reads "in honor preferring one another?" That is simply love for the brethren in action. When love prevails, the heart seeks for, looks for, even longs for, the things that will help our brethren. We come to be more like the words which tell us, "Not looking each of you to his own things, but each of you also to the things of others" (Ph. 2:4).

Further, we already know what we ought to do about this theme of brotherly love. At least the Thessalonians did: "But concerning love of the brethren ye have no need that one write unto you: for ye yourselves are taught of God to love one another" (I Th. 4:9).

Loving our brethren is not "an optional course in the Christian curriculum," as Avon Malone likes to say. It is a requirement — and there will be no graduation to glory without it on the transcript of life. But, we learn, those Thessalonians already loved all the brethren in Macedonia — and that's great. Do you love every brother in Texas? Oklahoma? Any other state? Even that is not enough! "But we exhort you that ye abound more and more." Love more, abound more! What else, Paul? "And that ye study to be quiet, and to do your own business, and to work with your hands, even as we charged you." One version reads, "Make it your ambition to have no ambition." A writer put it this way long ago: "Mind your own business, and you will succeed — you will have so few competitors." He was right; and this is one of the basics of brotherly love; for if I do not mind my own business, I am absolutely certain to be meddling in that of my brethren. And love of this kind has its effect not only within the body of Christ, it reaches out: ". . . that ye may walk becomingly toward them that are without, and may have need of nothing" (I Th. 4:9-12).

This loving brethren is a personal duty — no one else can fulfill it for us. In the great section of admonitions from the apostle Peter, he tells us about supplying things. We start as partakers of the divine nature, we add all diligence, and each good quality supplies another: faith supplies virtue; virtue supplies knowledge; knowledge supplies self-control; self-control supplies patience; patience supplies godliness; godliness supplies brotherly kindness (*philadelphian*—an objective case form of *philadelphia*), and brotherly kindness supplies love. Peter also used an intensive form of the word meaning "to supply" — *epichoregesate*, which indicates abundance, plenty, fullness of the thing being supplied. He is saying, in your faith supply an abundance of virtue. In your virtue supply stacks and stacks of knowledge. In your knowledge pile up self-control. In your self-control supply plentifully patience. In your patience produce a great amount of godliness. And in this abundance of godliness supply a ton of love of the brethren. Having done that, you can reach on out and supply — pile up — increase — stack up — love. Then our prayer we sing will be answered; we will really have "a soul so large that all mankind can be embraced therein; the good, the bad, the high, the low be counted all akin."

The company it keeps — this is often an easy way to determine character. Look at the company kept by the *philadelphoi* — the lovers of brethren. Here we find a wondrous list! Such people will be likeminded, compassionate, tenderhearted, humbleminded, not returning good for evil, but blessing instead. All these are listed in I Peter 3:8-9. For a grand exercise in discerning what is *really* love of the brethren, take your concordance and work through each of these tremendous qualities. Or, just get downright practical: Say to yourself, "Today, I will with the help of the Savior, be a compassionate person. I will overlook as many flaws as I can in the people I meet, when doing so will not compromise my attitude toward sin. I will, even when I discern sin in another, try to take a sympathetic view of the person who is caught in that sin. As a guideline for this, I can also look carefully at the standards set by Paul as he wrote Timothy about the work of the evangelist:

> And the Lord's servant must not strive, but be gentle towards all, apt to teach, forbearing, in meekness correcting them that oppose themselves; if peradventure God may give them repentance unto the knowledge of the truth, and they may recover themselves out of the snare of the devil, having been taken captive by him unto his will (II Ti. 2:24-26).

A careful application of such texts might cure some of us from "roaring on the mountains and pawing in the valleys." It might even help us to understand what James was discussing when he said, "And the fruit of righteousness is sown in peace for them that make peace" (Jam. 3:18). Compromise? Softness? Not in the least; no such thing is recommended in Scripture where truth is concerned. But in our dealings with each other over matters of judgment (where most of our problems occur), the application of this powerful potion from the Word would assuage the wounds of many a soul, and make us all more like the Master.

THE SUPREME EXAMPLE

It is a thrilling truth that Jesus is my brother. The writer to the Hebrews commented on this glorious truth when he wrote, "For both he that sanctifieth and they that are sanctified are all of one: for which cause he is not ashamed to call them brethren, saying, I will declare thy name unto my brethren, In the midst of the congregation will I sing thy praise" (He. 2:11-12). *"My brethren!"* That's what Jesus called his people. And if we want to know how to treat one another, we simply need to consult the guidebooks called the gospel accounts, and act toward our brothers now as he acted then. Superbly simple to understand — undeniably difficult to practice. The reason is stated in a bit of verse by some unknown genius:

> To dwell with saints above
> Will be eternal glory;
> To dwell with saints down here —
> Well, that's another story.

THE "LIMITATIONS" OF BROTHERLY LOVE

When we speak of the limitations, we are not saying that we should ever cease to love a brother. But even the Scripture indicates that there is a limit to what can be done for others. As time grew lean and the latest depression began to deepen, the calls for help increased. City churches in particular were (and are) hard put to keep up with requests for help. Anyone who has been in the work of the kingdom for long begins to recognize some patterns of the unworthy.

They are always on the way from one place to another, usually by some road that has little connection with either origin or destination. I remember a late night phone call from a man who had started to Denver and got only as far as Albuquerque; he was desperate. Inquiry determined that he was coming to Denver from Missouri by way of Arizona! You know the kind.

In Grand Prairie, Texas, the church building was located one block off Highway 80 — then the main road from Savannah to Los Angeles. We had an astonishing number of calls for help — until the day I took a caller over to my neighbor's rocky garden plot, put him on the business end of a hoe handle, and kept him there for a period of plentiful perspiration. It was amazing how the callers stopped coming! Some people have communcation networks and marks, they pass notes under bridges where they meet on their travels — they know who will give them a meal, who will furnish lodging, and all other salient details. For all such deadbeats, there is an appropriate text: "If any will not work, neither let him eat" (II Th. 3:10).

These problems existed very early in Christianity. Here is a fascinating quotation from a document called *The Didache* — which means *The Teaching*. The formal name is *The Teaching of the Twelve Apostles,* although reading it will soon convince one that the apostles had nothing to do with it. Dating as scholars think it does, from near the end of the first century, it does furnish some valuable insights into what happens when men try to compose a creed. But it also tells how the saints were to deal with those who wanted help from them.

And with regard to apostles and prophets, do with them according to the ordinance of the Gospel. Let every apostle who cometh to you be received as the Lord. He shall not overstay one day, though, if need be, the next; but if he remain three days he is a false prophet. And let not the apostle, on departing, take aught save bread till he come to a stopping place; and if he ask money he is a false prophet. . . . And no prophet who in the spirit appointeth a feast eateth thereof, unless he be a false prophet . . . and whosoever saith in the spirit, give me moneys or other things; you shall not hearken to him; but if for others in straits he say give, let no one judge him. . . . Let everyone that cometh in the name of the Lord be received, and then by testing you shall know him, for you shall have understanding right and left. . . . If he that cometh be a wayfarer, help him as much as you may; he shall not tarry with you save two or three days if need be. But if he would abide among you, being an artisan, let him labor and eat; but if he have no trade provide according to your judgment, that no idler live as a Christian among you. If he will not act thus he is a trafficker in Christ. Beware of such.[1]

We are often torn inside by the requests of those who come for help. It is amazing to me how many babies are allergic to cloth diapers; at least the mothers want us to buy the expensive disposable ones. And in some of those cases it appears that the mothers are allergic to soap! One such family came and asked me to help; I took them to the store and bought groceries; went to the station and bought gasoline for them; then decided I would go by their house. Miles away across the city, I found that the number they had given me did not exist. Yet this same man came back later and insisted that I help him more.

Then there are the forgetful types. One young man called telling me that he had to have help to repair his car. He described a transmission job that would have cost not less than $400; then said he could go and buy the parts for $12.50 if only I would supply the money. He too gave an address. When I arrived there, I found that there was not one house on that side of the street — I was facing a cliff! So I went on home. A few months later the same man called, gave the same name, and the same address, and described a different car with other ailments. He had forgotten — but I had not. He seemed very startled when I reminded him of his former attempted rip-off.

WHAT TO DO WHEN IN DOUBT

But with all the vagabonds and rascals in the world, there are often real people in real trouble. Of course we should check — get a number, make the phone calls; find out (I suddenly recalled the family, averaging 40 pounds overweight, who move from Oklahoma to Oregon every year at brotherhood expense, pulling a U-haul trailer with old tires in it, which they "sell" along the way to get enough to eat. They are good salesmen, judging by their corpulence!) But in Denver last winter, people were found dead on the streets — they had frozen for lack of shelter. There is suffering, real and terrible. And I confess that whenever I do not try to give some help, however much no help seems to be proper, I usually go around with a knot in my stomach. So, on the matters where no real determination can be made, surely we ought to err on the side of mercy. In those cases, the people who have misused the Lord's church and the brothers are the ones who are in trouble! And the Lord will know how to deal with them, whether we do or not.

MONEY OR NOT?

Many elderships have been forced to make a policy that no cash will be given. They have a supply of food available at the building — and our brethren are always unfailingly generous in keeping such supplies on hand. Usually there is a clothing room — and in our case we get more clothing than we can handle. Some of it is even good clothing! Sadly, I must confess that some is not. And our gracious ladies who take care of it can tell by the first two or three garments they take out of the bag whether the rest is worth keeping or not. Giving away old shoes that would cost more to repair than they are worth; giving away clothing which has had the buttons taken off (oh, yes!); using old garments to paint the barn or the fence and then putting those wretched remnants of raiment up as if they would help the poor, is a crass commentary, an insult to the one whose wardrobe was divided among those who nailed him to the tree.

Sometimes — to get back to where that last paragraph started — giving money is not really very helpful. But the happiest people I have known were those who helped, and helped, and helped, giving to their power and beyond their power. Listen to the Word of God:

> Blessed is he that considereth the poor: Jehovah will deliver him in the day of evil. Jehovah will preserve him, and keep him alive, and he shall be blessed upon the earth; and deliver not thou him unto the will of his enemies. Jehovah will support him upon the couch of languishing; thou makest all his bed in his sickness (Ps. 41:1-3).

Job was accused by his "friend" Eliphaz of having "sent widows away empty, and the arms of the fatherless have been broken" (Job 22:9). That touched a nerve! Job's angry reply was,

> . . . I delivered the poor that cried, the fatherless also, that had none to help him. The blessing of him that was ready to perish came upon me; and I caused the widow's heart to sing for joy. . . . I was eyes to the blind, and feet was I to the needy; and the cause of him that I knew not I searched out. And I brake the jaws of the unrighteous, and plucked the prey out of his teeth (Job 29:12-17).

And of all the things that could be said about concern for others, nothing can surpass the sweet summary given by the Holy Spirit when Luke recorded the words of Simon Peter concerning Jesus: "Who went about doing good" (Acts 10:38). Let us go and do likewise! It will greatly multiply the power of our teaching when our hearts show compassion for those who need us. There is truth in the aphorism of George Bailey, "The world will not care how much we know, until it knows how much we care."

CONCLUSION

May the Lord bless us in caring — and letting our hands match the hearts which have been touched by the love of the Lord.

ENDNOTE

1. *The Didache (The Teachings of the Twelve Apostles)*, Chapters XI and XII.

BE NOT CARRIED AWAY BY DIVERS AND STRANGE TEACHINGS

HEBREWS 13:9

By GARLAND ELKINS

Native Tennessean. Baptized in 1939. Married to Corinne Smith and they have three daughters. Attended Freed-Hardeman College, Middle Tennessee State University and University of Tennessee. Has worked with local churches in Virginia and Tennessee. Author and editor of several books and tracts, co-author of *Elkins-Ross Debate.* Radio preacher for many years. Associate editor of *Spiritual Sword* and co-director of annual Spiritual Sword Lectures. Local evangelist, Getwell Church, Memphis, Tenn. Speaker, *First Annual Denton Lectures.*

INTRODUCTION

"Be not carried away by divers and strange teachings: for it is good that the heart be established by grace; not by meats, wherein they that occupied themselves were not profited" (He. 13:9). By "divers" is meant "different; various." By "strange" is meant "not previously known." The word "teachings" means "things taught," "doctrines." So, by "divers and strange doctrines" we simply are referring to the many different teachings which are not taught in the truth.

The warning to "be not carried away by divers and strange teachings" was badly needed by both Jews and Gentiles in the first century. It is as much needed in our day, and this doubtlessly will be true as long as time continues.

When the Hebrews writer warns, "Be not carried away with divers and strange doctrines," it seems apparent that he is, in this metaphor, thinking of a ship that is taken out of course and driven to and fro by the tempestuous winds of a storm. Paul uses this same type figure: "That we may be no longer children, tossed to and fro and carried about with every wind of doctrine, by the sleight of men, in craftiness, after the wiles of error" (Ep. 4:14). The immature and unstable are pictured as running after every new false teacher. When people are unstable, easily persuaded or excitable, they fall a ready prey to the multiplicity of false teachers of our day. The Holy Spirit did not fail to warn us of this very thing.

> Now I beseech you, brethren, mark them that are causing the divisions and occasions of stumbling, contrary to the doctrine which ye learned: and turn away from them. For they that are such serve not our Lord Christ, but their own belly; and by their smooth and fair speech they beguile the hearts of the innocent (Ro. 16:17-18).

If time and space permitted, I would in this lecture discuss such "divers and strange doctrines" as "Humanism," "Values Clarification," "The New Morality," et al. I will discuss three "strange doctrines" as follows:

THE "STRANGE DOCTRINES" CONCERNING SECTARIANISM

Sectarianism is as foreign to New Testament Christianity as the East is from the West. Not only do denominationalists misapply Scripture in an effort to justify the existence of the various sects, but currently some among us are doing the same thing. Some are misapplying Mark 9:38-40 which says,

> John said unto him, Teacher, we saw one casting out demons in thy name; and we forbade him, because he followed not us. But Jesus said, Forbid him not: for there is no man who shall do a mighty work in my name, and be able quickly to speak evil of me. For he that is not against us is for us.

The key to understanding these passages is that John says that the man was casting out demons "in thy name," and Jesus speaks of a man's doing a mighty work "in my name." To do a thing in the name of Christ means to do it by his authority (Col. 3:17; Acts 4:12). Hence, the man that John forbade was, like John, a true follower of Christ, and this is evident from the fact that Jesus said he authorized the work that the man was doing, *i.e.,* he was working by Christ's authority. Jesus said, "In my name." There are many followers of Christ that have obeyed the gospel in countries around the world whom I do not know, yet if they are faithful, they are as much approved as those whom I do know.

Through the years denominationalists have misapplied Mark 9:38-40 and Luke 9:49-50. They have contended that these passages authorize acceptance and fellowship of any and all denominational groups regardless of their various differences and false doctrines. The only time I have personally heard a man who claims to be a member of the church misapply these passages was when I heard the editor of an ultra-liberal magazine attempting to convince a man that these passages teach that the church should fellowship the denominations. I took issue with him, pointing out the truth set out in the passages. I have never heard in person any other member misapply these passages. However, recently, it was called to my attention that another man has misapplied them.

Of all the preachers that I have ever known I consider brother N. B. Hardeman to be one of the most outstanding of them all. Though he was not perfect, I consider him to have been faithful. It is my judgment that his series of five *Tabernacle Sermons* and brother J. W. McGarvey's single volume entitled *Sermons* are among the best books of sermons every preached and then put into print by uninspired men.

The report has come to me that there is an effort being made among us which implies that brother N. B. Hardeman in some way intimated some sort of sympathy for denominationalism. Nothing could be further from the truth!

I have always considered the privilege of being one of brother N. B. Hardeman's students one of the truly great blessings of my life. He was my teacher, fellow Christian and trusted friend. I know what he taught. I sat in his classes. Through the years I heard him preach on numerous occasions on a wide variety of subjects. I have never known a man who was more opposed to denominationalism. In private, in the classroom, in the pulpit, in articles and books and on the

polemic platform, brother Hardeman opposed denominationalism as the greatest curse known to man!

For one to take statements of brother Hardeman's out of
context to make it appear that he in any way, shape, form or
fashion endorsed denominationalism would be comparable to
someone's taking an isolated statement from the pen of
brother Foy E. Wallace, Jr., and misapplying it in an effort to
make it appear that he endorsed premillennialism! Or, to
someone's taking some isolated statement from the pen of
brother Thomas B. Warren and seeking to make it appear that
he endorsed atheism! Or, to someone's taking an isolated
statement from the pen of brother Robert R. Taylor, Jr., to
make it appear that he endorsed the perverted translations!

Regardless of what anyone may ever say or do with the
writings of these men, brother N. B. Hardeman opposed
denominationalism! Brother Foy E. Wallace, Jr., opposed
premillennialism! Brother Thomas B. Warren opposes atheism! And, brother Robert R. Taylor, Jr., opposes the perverted
translations!

Brother Hardeman was not pleading for Christians to
fellowship the denominations nor was he endorsing the denominations, but rather he was pleading for members of the
church, Christians who had left the church and gone into
denominationalism into what he called "a state of confusion,"
to renounce denominationalism and return to the truth, to
return home!

Following are a few of the many quotes from brother N. B.
Hardeman on this subject:

> I want you to join no organization, no body, no party unknown to
> the book of God. I want you to wear no name other than the name
> "Christian." I want you to accept no creed other than the Bible,
> which is a lamp unto our feet and a light unto our path. . . . The
> creeds of the land are a curse to the cause of Christ. They ought to
> be cast aside, not because of prejudice, not that they were not
> written by honest, earnest, good men, but because we have God's
> word, which needs no revision, no amendments, no repealings. The
> creeds of men hinder the progress of Christianity, divide believers in
> the Lord, and engender a party and sectarian spirit. In the language
> of the great English evangelist, I can truly say that if I had my way,
> and all of them were in a pile before me, I would be glad to strike the

match and see them light up the heavens in their final destruction and annihilation. I really believe I would be doing that which would advance primitive Christianity in our beloved land. . . . The greatest tool that the devil has obtained is not direct talk against the Bible, but the most effective weapon in the hands of sinners to-night, in the hands of atheists and skeptics, is the fact that people who claim to be religious are divided into parties, sects, denominations, and orders unheard of and absolutely unknown to the book of God.[1]

The time ultimately came when men rose up above the clouds of Catholicism and denominationalism and said: "Jesus Christ is not in Catholicism; Jesus Christ is not in denominationalism. . . . Believe the gospel, repent of your sins, publicly confess your faith in the Christ, be buried with him in the name of the Father, Son, and the Holy Spirit. That will make of you nothing on earth but a Christian, and right there stop your religious affiliation. . . . When I talk about the church of God, I am not talking about some human denomination; for be it remembered that the church of God is not even the distant relative of human organizations, which are unknown to the book of God. . . . I regret that there is such teaching abroad as this — for instance, that a man does not have to become a member of the church in order to be saved; that there are just as good people outside of the church as there are in it. Now, I do not believe either one of those statements. . . . The thing I now want to emphasize is the fact of its unity and its oneness. That very statement of itself denies and opposes the idea of its being a denomination. I know it is as common as can be that wherever you talk with men and meet with people they speak about different denominations all over the city, all over this land and country of ours. But put it down, friends, for further study and for earnest consideration, that when you are reading in the Bible about the church, never get it in your minds that you are reading about some denomination; for no man ever did or ever can read from the book of God a single, solitary statement or even a hint at anything that smacks of denominationalism. That thing is modern, recent, and unknown to the book of God as certain as in your midst I stand, and there lives not a man in all the city of Nashville who can take God's book and turn to a single, solitary passage therein and find anything that even looks like a distant relation of modern denominationalism. . . . The greatest curse on this earth tonight is religious division. The greatest hindrance to the cause of Christ is denominational rivalry. The greatest handicap and the greatest discouragement unto faithful, godly men is the fact that people who claim to be members of the body of Christ are torn asunder, riven, by human opinions, popular preference, rather than submit to God's will, all speak the same thing, and be of one mind and one judgment, as the Lord prayed and for which the apostles pleaded. . . . Well, well, what a picture! One great body of all professed Christians, and from that body, projecting in various directions, about two hundred heads! What a monster! Friends, I cannot accept that. The judgment and the reason that I have absolutely rebelled and cannot accept such a ridiculous presentation; and while I love to be kindly disposed toward my fellows and yield every possible point, I cannot accept such. . . . Friends, in all candor, what better is the picture when you present one head over about two hundred different bodies? . . . The church of the New Testament Scriptures was governed purely and solely by God's law. I think nobody would question that. But those denominations to which reference has been made are governed, guided, and controlled by creeds, disciplines, and rules not found in the book of God. . . . The word of God — the seed of the kingdom — lay buried for hundreds of years under the rubbish of popery and denominationalism. . . . Friends, just as certain as it is that we have the same seed used by the apostles, we can have the same product and the same church. No one will deny that we have the same soil — "good and honest hearts." The crop produced then was Christians. The seed, the word of God, did not and will not produce Mormons, Methodists, Baptists, Presbyterians, or Campbellites. These must come from other plantings. Let us cut loose from all such and stand on the original ground. . . . And we might as well get right down to the point and admit that if the Christian forces of the city of Nashville ever get together on the question of a creed, it will be by the elimination, the wiping out, of all human books and booklets and the adoption of the Bible, and the Bible alone. May God speed the day when this shall be done. We can never unite on a human name. You can't get the religious people of the world to be Campbellites, Methodists, Baptists, or Presbyterians; and if we ever present a solid phalanx against the devil and all the agencies that threaten the peace, happiness, and highest estate of human beings here upon this earth, we must stand simply as Christians, and as Christians alone. . . . If you believe there will be no Mormons, Methodists, Baptists, Presbyterians, or Campbellites over there, why not try to get rid of all such here? . . . If there are those who have subscribed to human creeds and human affairs, I beg you to lay aside these, that there be no divisive things to mar the peace and unity of those who really love the Lord. . . . So, then, in answer to the query from another point of view, allow me to say that Alexander Campbell didn't "pick up the church." It was not in existence in its organized form. What did Campbell do? Seek to organize something different from the Bible? O, no; not at all. Did he want to establish a church or a denomination and become the head of it? Just the opposite. He and Stone and others believed from the great depths of their souls that denominationalism was of human origin, and they pleaded with all to take the Bible, and the Bible alone. They said: "Let us march out of denominationalism, cast off denominational ties, and become and be just what they were back in the days of inspiration." The

Bible was their creed, Christ was their leader, the church of God was their home, and Christianity was their life work. Upon these principles they begged the world to unite. Such is what the world calls "Campbellism." My friends, that was not establishing anything; but the effort was to restore that which had been buried under the rubbish, under denominationalism, in the generations that are gone by.[2]

We must stand together against the powers of denominationalism, of all kinds of error, and as Jude said, "earnestly contend for the faith once for all delivered unto the saints."[3]

You can study the history of all denominations and find that not one of them meets the demands of the New Testament. . . . With the distinct understanding that all denominations are purely of human origin, I would subscribe to the statement that one is as good as another or that one is as bad as another. But if you refer to things sacred and things found in the Bible, all such expressions are absolutely foreign to anything that God Almighty ever authorized.[4]

Denominationalism has always been an enemy of New Testament Christianity. Advocates on the outside of the church do great harm. As great as this damage is, perhaps the damage is minor when compared to what a member of the church who has been faithful does to the church when he compromises with denominationalism. In speaking of the restoration theme, the statement was made, "*Somewhere along the line, maybe fifty years ago, we abandoned that theme. And we crystallized, and we became to a large measure what we set out to oppose*" (emp. mine, GE). I deny the above statements, and I am prepared to do so publicly or privately. Fifty years ago (as we now do) we opposed denominationalism. I deny that we became a denomination fifty years ago or at any time.

The Church of Christ is Not A Sect! In one of our older journals dated January 12, 1982, there appeared a most disturbing and revealing editorial. Among other things the following statements were made.

We do not usually advocate that churches observe special occasions, but we believe it would be a commendable thing if all sects among us gave some thought to trying to reenact the famous "unity meeting" held in Lexington, Kentucky, in 1832. All our sects are justly proud of that meeting, and the part it played in our history. It just could be that another one like it might give us more reason to rejoice.

Then, in the same journal on March 2, 1982, pictured on the front page was the chairman of the Bible Department of one of "our" Christian colleges shaking hands with the preacher of the Christian Church. Underneath the picture it read, *"The 'handshake'* of Barton W. Stone and 'Raccoon' John Smith at the famous 'unity meeting' in Lexington, Kentucky, on January 1, 1882 (the date was actually 1832, GE) is reenacted . . ."* Then, the names of the two preachers are given. The gospel preacher in an article in the same issue of the previously mentioned periodical referred to the editor's January 12, 1982, editorial and stated,

> Without knowing that this editorial would appear this happened in Los Angeles, California, on Sunday, January 19, 1982. Sponsored by the Disciples of Christ Historical Society a "Celebration of Heritage" reenacting the famous Lexington meeting of New Year's, 1832, was held in the large Wilshire Christian Church auditorium at 3:00 p.m. A capacity crowd of between 800 and 900 attended. The crowd was composed of large number from the three major groups recognizing the Restoration Movement: the Christian Church (Disciples of Christ), Christian Churches and Churches of Christ (instruments) and churches of Christ.

The gospel preacher stated further in the article, "The famous handshake was reenacted and passed to the audience and 'a song arose.' Since communion had already been observed by the people in their churches, it was symbolically reenacted by the two men."

When an editor and a gospel preacher who was also a chairman of a Bible Department can advocate a meeting of the type described above, one wonders if the editor and the chairman of the Bible Department have either forgotten or do not believe the following Scriptures:

> And have no fellowship with the unfruitful works of darkness, but rather even reprove them (Ep. 5:11).

> Whosoever transgresseth, and abideth not in the doctrine of Christ, hath not God. He that abideth in the doctrine of Christ, he hath both the Father and the Son. If there come any unto you, and bring not this doctrine, receive him not into your house, neither bid him God speed: For he that biddeth him God speed is partaker of his evil deeds (II John 9-11).

In the interest of Christian fairness and accuracy let it be made known to all that the editor of the journal from which these statements have been quoted is no longer editor of that paper. Thanks be unto God that journal has been purchased by sound brethren, and a faithful brother is now its editor. If I am correctly informed, the chairman of the Bible Department under consideration has retired.

The above referred-to men are not the only ones who have made statements that have shocked faithful brethren. If a man were brought up to believe denominational teaching and thus became a member of a denomination but later learned the truth and obeyed it, the following statements would not only be expected but also appreciated. However, when a man has been reared by godly, Christian parents, became a member of the church, attended Christian schools, and preached for faithful churches of Christ, the following statements are incredible: "I am trying to think my way out of a sectarian attitude. I grew up in the context of one. I learned a sectarian spirit. I breathed a sectarian spirit. I exhibited a sectarian spirit, and I taught a sectarian spirit. I am embarrassed. I am ashamed. I have repented."

The church of Christ is not a sect, and, therefore, the man does not live (and none who are dead could do so either) who can prove the charge that the church of Christ is a sect. Paul, though a member of the church, denied that he was a member of a sect (Acts 24:5, 13-14).

It is a fact easily established from the Scriptures and corroborated by history that the church of Christ was established and existed in the world for centuries before either Catholicism or Protestantism was known. This was before the followers of Christ were divided into various denominations (Acts 2:22-47; Ro. 16:16).

When the true gospel of Christ is preached and obeyed in any given community, the church of Christ will be reproduced. The seed of the kingdom is the word of God (Luke 8:11). The good soil is the "honest and good heart" (Luke 8:15). When the word of God was planted in the first century, it produced Christians (Acts 11:26; 26:28) and churches of Christ (Ro. 16:16). Since seed always produces after its kind (Ge. 1:11-12;

Ga. 6:7-8), *it will produce in this century what it produced in the first century!*

"STRANGE DOCTRINES" RELATIVE TO
MARRIAGE—DIVORCE—REMARRIAGE

Multitudes are seeking to rationalize and justify adultery because it affects so many people and is apparently very widespread. When one compares the kingdom of Israel and America of our day, there is a passage that should strike home:

> Hear the word of the Lord, ye children of Israel: for the Lord hath a controversy with the inhabitants of the land, because there is no truth, nor mercy, nor knowledge of God in the land. By swearing, and lying, and killing, and stealing, and committing adultery, they break out, and blood toucheth blood (Ho. 4:1-2).

According to *Time* magazine, September 7, 1981, there are professors in prestigious universities in our land who are carrying some of these doctrines to their implied extremes. There is the rationale that every person has the right to do with his or her body what they please. They contend that no nation has a right to enact a law, nor do others have a right to bind any kind of a rule as to how they use their bodies. Therefore, they argue that if a man decides to have a sexual relationship with another man, that is his business and nobody else's. If a woman decides to have a sexual relationship with another woman, they contend that that is her right, as is also the matter of abortion. There are those who are contending that as soon as an infant is born his body belongs to him or her, and he or she has the right to full sexual relations. There are those who are saying that incest between a father and his daughter is right. Such gross immorality is an insult to the holy God whom we serve (Hab. 1:13). We are to strive to be pure like God (I Pe. 1:15-16). God condemns homosexuality and adultery and makes clear that those who practice such cannot enter heaven (Ro. 1:26-27, 29; I Co. 6:9-11; He. 13:4; Ga. 5:19-21; Re. 21:8).

What has brought us to this state? How did all of this come to pass? The atheistic philosophy which is so generally held in high places of our day has brought much of this to pass. It was correctly stated by a French philosopher, Jean Paul Sartre, who died a short time ago, when he said, "If there is no God, then everything is permitted." If there is no God, then there is no such thing as right and wrong. Hume, Kant, Russell, and men like them have contributed greatly to the widespread compromises, both in doctrine and morals of our day.

It is a fact that we live in a world where this philosophy exists. We see it on television, in magazines and newspapers, in movies, on the radio, and we hear it from pulpits. The philosophy in effect says, "If it brings fun, if it feels good and if it brings pleasure, then it is right." I own a copy of the Methodist Discipline. John Wesley said (and Methodists continue to believe and teach it) that the doctrine of "faith only" is "a doctrine very full of comfort." Even so, our permissive society is saying that the immorality of our day is "a doctrine very full of comfort." It is deplorable, dangerous and sad when error is taught outside the church; however, many false doctrines relative to the subject of divorce and remarriage are presently being taught among those who are members of the body of Christ. These doctrines of men are "very full of comfort" to those who desire to rationalize and thus to convince others or to be convinced themselves that one can live in an adulterous state with God's approval and inherit heaven when this life is over.

As incredible as it is, one brother has written a book in which he contends that one passage "countermands" another passage, i.e., it cancels, revokes the first! There are those who teach that "the guilty have the same right to remarry as the innocent," thus flying in the face of and denying what the Lord said in Matthew 19:9. If their contention were true, then Christ would have no law on divorce and remarriage. Again, I emphasize that Jesus refutes such a false doctrine in Matthew 19:9. The guilty forfeit their right to marriage while the innocent do have a right to put away the guilty party because of fornication and remarry (Ma. 19:9). Just as amazing and revolting is the affirmation of another brother in public debate in which he has affirmed, "The scriptures teach that unscripturally divorced and remarried people may continue in the remarriage without further sin." How distressing and disturbing that a man would actually believe, and even publicly affirm by implication, that people can enter adultery and live and die in adultery with God's approval. Such a one needs to read and believe Galatians 5:19-21 and in fear and trembling repent!

Another brother of prominence has now espoused a view of Matthew 19:9 that is built upon a foundation of false doctrine, that denies the very fundamentals of the gospel. His doctrine that Matthew 19:9 is a "covenant passage," *i.e.,* applies "to the church only," would by implication mean that nobody could be saved. I debated a Baptist preacher who affirmed that "the scriptures teach that salvation comes at the point of faith alone before and without any further acts of obedience." The implication of such a doctrine is that salvation is by a dead faith (Jam. 2:26). He denied the implication, but it still followed. Likewise, the doctrine that Matthew 19:9 is "a covenant passage," applying to "the church only," implies that no one can be saved, for if the alien sinner is not amenable to the law of Christ, he cannot obey it (Ro. 3:19; 4:15). However, he cannot be saved unless he becomes a Christian, but if he cannot obey the very law that makes him a Christian, and since he is condemned if he does not obey the gospel, it follows that given this brother's view on Matthew 19:9 then nobody could be saved. Thus, this brother's doctrine implies universal damnation.

I thought that I had heard false theories as foreign to New Testament teaching on the subject of marriage, divorce and remarriage as could be advanced. I had concluded that no one could equal or surpass the aforementioned errors. As incredible as it is, another brother in debate affirmed, "The Scriptures teach that one must continue in any marriage he is in when called, whether it be his 1st, 2nd, 3rd, or any number." The man does not live who can prove this proposition, and I stand amazed that anyone (especially a member of the church and a preacher of the gospel) would attempt to do so! Imagine a man's taking the position that one "must continue in any marriage!"

The instructions and teaching of Christ on the subject of marriage are so simple that it takes but a short time for an honest person to learn the truth on divorce and remarriage as set out by Christ in Matthew 19:9. Jesus said, "And I say unto you, Whosoever shall put away his wife, except it be for forni-

cation, and shall marry another, committeth adultery: and
whoso marrieth her which is put away doth commit adultery."
Jesus taught that marriage is of universal application. The
word "whosoever" makes that abundantly clear. Jesus gave
one and *only one* exception that would give anyone the right to
put away his partner, that is, the innocent is permitted to put
away the guilty and marry an eligible (in God's sight) partner.
But Jesus plainly teaches that the guilty *cannot* marry a
second time with his approval (Ma. 19:9). If Jesus had given no
exception, then every person who puts away his companion
and marries another would be guilty of adultery. However,
Jesus did give an exception, thus making it clear that one
whose companion has been guilty of physical fornication may
put him or her away and marry another eligible partner with
God's approval. When our hearts are open for information, we
can easily see the meaning of an exception. John 3:5 teaches,
"Except a man be born of water, and of the Spirit, he cannot
enter into the kingdom of God." Even so, in Matthew 19:9
Jesus uses the same sort of language. John 3:5 gives the *one*
and *only* door into the kingdom of God, and Matthew 19:9
gives the *one* and *only* door into a second marriage while
one's first partner lives.

THE "STRANGE DOCTRINE" OF PREMILLENNIALISM

Nothing could be further from the truth than premillennialism. This false doctrine is widely believed and taught in denominational circles. A few years ago a preacher in the church
of Christ by the name of R. H. Boll embraced premillennialism
and created great havoc in the church with his error. A few of
the many faithful and able preachers who opposed him were
brethren H. Leo Boles, N. B. Hardeman, Foy E. Wallace, Jr.,
E. R. Harper, et al.

While professing to be devoting much of his time to the
converting of denominational preachers to pure New Testament Christianity, a brother of some influence and ability was
himself subscribing to one of the rankest tenets of denominationalism. Do you ask what denominational doctrine it was
that he held? The answer is premillennialism, one of the most
popular, erroneous, and dangerous denominational doctrines
ever invented by Satan!

During those years that he was financially supported by faithful brethren, I never heard him in a public, explicit way teach premillennialism. Why did he not do so? Could it be that he knew that if he honestly admitted to the brethren that he was a premillennialist that they would drop his financial support and, if he did not repent of holding to a false doctrine and being a false teacher, mark him publicly as a false teacher? *No one knows the answer to this question better than this brother!* In this action he was not following Jesus (John 18:20; I Co. 11:1).

Because I have pointed out that this premillennial brother did take his salary from good and honest but unsuspecting brethren (who would not have supported him had they known that he was premillennial), this premillennial brother has charged that I have slandered him. Such a charge would be ludicrous if it were not so serious. The word "slander" is defined as "the utterance or spreading of a false statement or statements harmful to another's character or reputation." I have simply told the truth about him. Since when did the truth become slander?

Though not daring to teach his doctrine explicitly, I did on one occasion hear him teach it implicitly. Through the years this brother has often spoken during the Blue Ridge Encampment. During one of those lectures the late and inimitable brother B. C. Goodpasture, one of the truly great Bible scholars of this generation, and I were sitting together. As we listened to his remarks, we turned to each other and said, "That is premillennial teaching!"

This brother has written a book in which he advocates and defends the false doctrine of premillennialism. His name could be removed from the book and any well-known, full-fledged, and admitted denominationalist's name put there, and you could tell no difference in the error advocated. The only difference in the fact that this brother's name is there as the author of the book is that naive and unsuspecting brethren will be the more easily deceived!

In addition to his book this brother has written an article entitled "Israel And The Church." In the article he says, "In the light of Bible prophecy the world today is filled with signs of the end of the age and the coming of Christ. Foremost among signs is the little nation of Israel struggling for existence." He is dead wrong, for there are positively *no* signs pointing to Christ's near coming and the end of this age. To say there are repudiates the whole scope of such passages as Matthew 24:36, Mark 13:32, I Thessalonians 5:1-2, and II Peter 3:10ff.

There were two sets of prophecies touching Israel and Canaan. One set has to do with all the prophecies from Abraham through Moses about their initial inheritance of the land. This was fulfilled under Joshua. "And the Lord gave unto Israel *all* the land which he sware to give unto their fathers; and they possessed it. . . . *There failed not aught of any good thing* which the Lord had spoken; *all* came to pass" (Jos. 21:43-45, emp. mine, GE). After they had been in the land for almost a thousand years, they were removed from it. Prophecies relative to their return were *all* given before Cyrus' decree that permitted their return from Babylonian exile. Neither this brother nor any other premillennialist can find a prophecy promising Palestine to the Jews of our day or in any future time from the New Testament scriptures. A few references to the land subsequent to Pentecost are historical references such as Acts 7:4ff and Acts 13:19ff. If he cites a scripture from the Old Testament in an effort to prove his point, he misapplies it. The restoration prophecies were fulfilled when the Israelites returned to the land. They never refer to modern Israel and Palestine. The United Nations put Israel on the map as a nation with the United States as financial upkeeper and military protector — not God Almighty! It is incredible that this brother advocates a restitution of Judaism with temple worship and its sacrifices. Incidentally, the Levitical priesthood was an essential part of the Mosaic system. This priesthood cannot be restored to the Jews for many reasons, one of which is that *all* tribal distinctions have been lost among the Jews for nineteen centuries plus! *Further, the Levitical priesthood could not be restored unless the priesthood of Christ was first abolished!*

His Argument on Deuteronomy 32: This premillennial brother refers to Deuteronomy 32:21 which reads, "They have moved me to jealousy with that which is not God; they have provoked me to anger with their vanities: and I will move them to jealousy with those which are not a people; I will provoke them to anger with a foolish nation." He then misapplies this passage in a vain effort to prove that *fleshly* Israel (as well as spiritual Israel, the church) is also God's people today. However, this premillennial brother refutes his own argument when he says,

> Fifteen centuries after Moses, Peter wrote to the faithful of the Church, "You are a chosen race, a royal priesthood, a holy nation, God's own people. . . . Once you were no people, but now you are God's people; once you had not received mercy, but now you have received mercy" (I Pe. 2:9-10). As foretold in Moses' prophecy, the Church is now "a holy nation, God's own people" (cf. Ro. 10:19).

It is crucial to note that this brother has admitted that Peter taught that Moses' prophecy was fulfilled in the church. On this point this brother and Peter agree; however, when he attempts to prove that the nation of Israel in our day is a fulfillment of Moses' Old Testament prophecy, not only does he part company with Peter, but also with Paul. I agree with Peter and Paul for they were inspired (John 16:13; 14:26; I Co. 2:13; II Pe. 1:20-21); *this premillennial brother is not!*

As just stated when I proved this point his entire argument fell of its own weight. Since my reply to his "Israel and the Church" article, he wrote another article in which he explicitly stated, "I agree that 'the Israel of God' (Ga. 6:16) has reference to the church, God's spiritual 'Israel' for the present age." *Exactly, and that is what I have said all of the time!* This premillennial brother has now conceded that the church is "God's spiritual Israel" for the present. *Since the Bible teaches that there will be no age following this one and that both the earth will be burned up with fire and time will end, therefore, this premillennial brother's error, i.e., that Christ will reign over the Jews in Palestine, has now gone down, world without end!* Note the proof that the earth will be burned up and that time will end when Christ returns the second time: "But the day of the Lord will come as a thief in the night; in the which the heavens shall pass away with a great noise, and the elements shall melt with fervent heat, the earth also and the works that are therein shall be burned up" (II Pe. 3:10). "And sware by him that liveth for ever and ever, who created heaven, and the things that therein are, and the earth, and the things that therein are, and the sea, and the things which are therein, that there should be time no longer" (Re. 10:6). Even though after making the above-stated admission, *i.e.*, that the church is the fulfillment of Moses' prophecy in Deuteronomy 32, he then contends that Christ will return to reign over the Jews, his argument has *absolutely no weight as I have just shown, and have proved it both by the Bible and his own admission!*

Further, when reviewing his article on "Israel and the Church," I said, "When he attempts to prove that the nation of Israel in our day is a fulfillment of Moses' Old Testament prophecy, not only does he part company with Peter but also with Paul." He has since replied,

> Contrary to bro. Elkins' assertion, I have not affirmed that "the nation of Israel in our day is a fulfillment of Moses' prophecy." Instead, I said that Israel's present "existence as a nation sets the stage for events associated with the end of the age and the coming of Messiah" — an altogether different matter. The little nation of Israel today, struggling for survival, is not the promised restoration of Israel, but rather a harbinger of the coming restoration at the coming of Messiah.

The truth is, whether he contends that the nation of Israel in our day is a fulfillment of Moses' prophecy or "rather a harbinger of the coming restoration at the coming of Messiah," he is just as wrong as wrong can be!

What does Paul teach on this subject? He teaches that an individual Jew has no advantage over an individual Gentile.

> For he is not a Jew who is one outwardly; neither is that circumcision which is outward in the flesh: but he is a Jew who is one inwardly; and circumcision is that of the heart, in the spirit, and not in the letter; whose praise is not of men, but of God (Ro. 2:28-29).

Peter taught the very same thing.

> And when there had been much questioning, Peter rose up, and said unto them, Brethren, ye know that a good while ago God made choice among you, that by my mouth the Gentiles should hear the word of the gospel, and believe. And God, who knoweth the heart, bare them witness, giving them the Holy Spirit, even as he did unto us; and he made *no distinction* between *us* (the Jews) and *them* (the Gentiles), cleansing their hearts by faith (Acts 15:7-9, emp. mine, GE).

So, both Peter and Paul taught that God makes "no distinction" between Jew and Gentile as individuals. *Paul not only corroborates what Peter said in I Peter 2:9-10, i.e., that the church is "a holy nation," but Paul emphatically shows that it is "the," not "an," Israel of God. Once I prove this point, this premillennial brother's entire argument falls of its own weight.* Please read the proof: "For neither is circumcision anything, nor uncircumcision, but a new creature. And as many as shall walk by this rule, peace be upon them, and mercy, and upon *the* Israel of God" (Ga. 6:15-16, emp. mine, GE). *His argument is refuted on this point alone.*

Paul sees nothing in what Moses said or what Isaiah penned that even remotely relates to some so-called wholesale conversion of infidelic Jews to Jesus Christ in a moment of time (Ro. 10:18ff). Further, Paul sees nothing in Moses' statement or Isaiah's prediction that even remotely resembles this premillennial brother's false doctrine of the nation of Israel in the Palestine of our day having God's special favor simply because they are *fleshly* Jews!

A Remnant Restored: The prophecies of the restoration make clear that only a remnant would be restored. Isaiah said, "Only a remnant of them shall return" (Is. 10:22). Jeremiah likewise prophesied, "And I will gather the remnant of my flock out of all countries whither I have driven them" (Je. 23:3). Paul reminded the Jewish Christians in Rome that "it is the remnant that shall be saved" (Ro. 9:27).

Some Jews did not choose to be restored to Palestine. Some twenty years after the return under Cyrus God pleaded through Zechariah for more of the Jews to return home. He said, "Ho, ho, flee from the land of the north" and "Ho Zion, escape" (Ze. 2:6-7, 12).

Some of all the ten tribes remained in Judah when the northern kingdom was taken into captivity. Even after the kingdom was divided during the reign of Rehoboam and Jeroboam, many of the northern kingdom joined the southern kingdom. Thus we read, "And after them, out of *all the tribes of Israel* . . . set their hearts to seek Jehovah the God of Israel" (II Ch. 11:1-17).

Not all of the people of the ten tribes were taken to Assyria (Amos 5:1-3). Some years after the fall of the northern kingdom Hezekiah sent letters to Judah and to all Israel.

> So the posts passed from city to city through the country of Ephraim and Manasseh, even unto Zebulun: but they laughed them to scorn, and mocked them. Nevertheless certain men of Asher and Manasseh and of Zebulun humbled themselves, and came to Jerusalem (II Ch. 30:10-11).

During Asa's time there was a gathering of people from all the ten tribes who rallied to Judah. "And he gathered all Judah and Benjamin, and *them that sojourned with them out of Ephraim and Manasseh and out of Simeon:* for they fell to him out of Israel in abundance, when they saw that Jehovah his God was with him" (II Ch. 15:9).

Amos clearly prophesied that the captivity of Israel, the remnant, would return to Palestine and would rebuild the destroyed cities and live in them.

The evidence that people of the ten tribes were restored to Palestine after the time of the Babylonian captivity is abundant! Isaiah prophesied the fall of Babylon (Is. 13:19), and Cyrus the Persian, king of Medo-Persia, is named by God (Is. 44 and 45). Isaiah prophesied of Cyrus, "And he shall let my exiles go free" (Is. 45:4, 13).

Brother Curtis A. Cates, faithful and able gospel preacher, has commented:

> When one understands that the territory of Assyria, who had carried Israel into captivity, was conquered by and became a part of the Babylonian Empire, he can understand why Ezekiel 3:1-15 refers to the "house of Israel" being in captivity with Judah in Babylon. When Babylon took over Assyria, the exiles had been there over one hundred years. Thus, the "house of Israel" would be brought back into "the land of Israel." God said, "I will place you in your own land" (Eze. 37:11-14). This would fulfil Jeremiah's promise, "As Jehovah liveth, who brought up and who *led the seed of the house of Israel out of the north country, and from all the countries* whither I had driven them. And they shall dwell in their own land" (Jer. 23:8).[5]

Restoration of the Ten Tribes — A Matter of History: Ezra records that people of all twelve tribes returned and resettled their native lands (Ezra 2:70). Further, the sacrifices were made in Jerusalem for people of each of the twelve tribes (Eze.

47:13-14; Ezra 6:16-17). People of all of the tribes were recognized in Israel (Ezra 8:29; cf. 9:1). Some of Ephraim and Manasseh were in Jerusalem; therefore, people from all ten tribes were restored (I Ch. 9:1-3).

We have proved beyond doubt that there were people from all of the ten tribes restored. I have presented abundant proof, and more could be presented; however, if a person would not believe what has already been set out, it is not likely that he would believe additional passages. It is proper at this time to make some observations.

First, if an inspired writer states that a particular prophecy is fulfilled in a particular manner, that settles it — it was fulfilled that way!

Second, if an inspired writer states that certain events have already been fulfilled, then neither this premillennial brother nor any other person has a right to insist on a later fulfillment.

Third, neither this premillennial brother nor any other person can postpone a prophecy's fulfillment. Such action puts him in the position of implicitly teaching that the great and true prophets were false prophets.

Cates properly states:

Jeremiah prophesied that the Lord would "make a *new covenant* with the *house of Israel and with the house of Judah.*" IIe further quoted Jehovah, "*If those ordinances depart from before me, saith the Lord, then the seed of Israel also shall cease from being a nation* before me *for ever*" (Je. 31:31-36). Paul proved conclusively that the prophecy of Jeremiah had been fulfilled (He. 8:8-10). In addition, since the ordinances had departed (He. 9; Col. 2:14-16; Ro. 7:1-4), then *Israel had also ceased* as a nation *for ever.* Too, unless the errorists can find a *fault* in the *second covenant*, they cannot defend a *third covenant* for the "millennium."

Isaiah prophesied that after a branch would rise out of Jesse's roots and bear fruit, "the wolf would dwell with the lamb, and the leopard shall lie down with the kid; and the calf and the young lion and the fatling together; and a little child shall lead them." At the same time would God "*recover the remnant of his people*, that shall remain, from *Assyria*, and from *Egypt*, and from *Pathros*, and from *Cush*, and *from Elam*, and *from Shinar*, and *from Hamath*, and from the islands of the sea." The Gentiles would also seek the Lord, as well as "the *outcasts of Israel* and . . . the dispersed of Judah from the *four corners of the earth*" (Is. 11:1-12). This prophecy was literally fulfilled on the day of Pentecost of Acts 2. The Holy Spirit revealed, "Now there were dwelling at Jerusalem Jews, devout men, out of *every nation under heaven*" (Acts 2:5; cf. vv. 8-11). Indeed, the mountain of Jehovah — the kingdom — was established on Pentecost when Israel was gathered from every nation (cf. Acts 13:22-24; 13:46-47).[6]

Some years after Pentecost James addressed all twelve tribes. "James, a servant of God and of the Lord Jesus Christ, to the *twelve tribes* which are of the Dispersion, greeting" (Jam. 1:1). James could not have addressed Christians among all twelve tribes if they were lost, *i.e.*, not restored, at the time of Cyrus. Further, this explains how Anna, a prophetess and a descendant of Asher, came to be in Jerusalem (Luke 2:36). Further, Paul carried "the hope of the promise made of God unto our fathers; unto *which promise our twelve tribes*, earnestly serving God night and day, hope to attain" (Acts 26:6-8; cf. 26:22-23; 28:20-28).

Hosea prophesied that the children of Judah and the children of Israel would be gathered together under one head (Ho. 1:10-11). Paul stated that this prophecy had been fulfilled in the church, "the Israel of God" (Ro. 9:24-27; Ga. 6:16), the partition having been broken down (Ep. 2:12-16; Ga. 3:28).

Brother Curtis Cates correctly, concisely, succinctly sums up this matter in the following splendid way:

A "remnant" of the ten tribes who went into Assyria and of the Jews who went into Babylon returned from captivity to Palestine, and by the time of Christ, the remanent had grown substantially, into millions of "Jews." People of all twelve tribes were present on Pentecost. Many from each tribe, both in Palestine and among the Diaspora, became Christians. Millions are today being deceived by the heretical fantasy of premillennialism and thus are not honoring Christ as he presently sits on the throne of his kingdom.

The Old Testament prophecies *did not fail*, neither were they postponed, which is tantamount to failing. Everything has gone according to God's infallible and immutable plan and promise (He. 6:13-20; Acts 2:22-24; 4:27-28). The so-called "mystery parenthesis" is a renegade doctrine, which strikes at the very nature of God. Whether Jew or Gentile, a person must be saved by entering the kingdom established on Pentecost, over which Christ reigns as king, and which he shall have delivered up to God at his second coming (I Co. 15:20-28). "Except one be born of water and the Spirit, he cannot enter into the kingdom of God" (John 3:5). "For ye are *all*

sons of God through faith in Christ Jesus. For as many of you as
were baptized into Christ did put on Christ. There *can be neither
Jew nor Greek*, there can be neither bond nor free, there can be
neither male nor female; for ye are *all one man in Christ Jesus*. And
if ye are Christ's, then are ye Abraham's seed, heirs according to
promise" (Gal. 3:26-29).[7]

Acts, chapter 2, is a spiritual "Gibraltar" which neither
this brother nor any other premillennialist can answer. It de-
vastatingly destroys and overthrows their every argument. In
two issues of *The Spiritual Sword* we exposed the errors of premillennialism (Vol. 9, No. 1 and Vol. 9, No. 2). While this premillennial brother admits that he has read these issues of *The
Spiritual Sword,* he cannot live long enough to refute the truth
set out therein. Thomas B. Warren's great editorial in Volume
9, Number 1, entitled "Acts 2 — The *Death* of Premillennialism" is unanswerable for this brother or any other premillennialist. I strongly urge all to read it. Note the following part of
that editorial:

1. *The basic argument stated.* The basic argument here being
used (1) to set forth the truth about Christ and his kingdom and (2)
to refute the essential doctrine of premillennialism is as follows:

(1) If the *death*, the *burial*, the *resurrection*, the *ascension*,
and the *coronation* of Christ all occurred in fulfillment of
prophecy, then premillennialism is false, and Christ has
been reigning as king since the first day of Pentecost following his resurrection from the dead.

(2) The death, the burial, the resurrection, the ascension,
and the coronation of Christ all occurred in fulfillment of
prophecy.

(3) Therefore, premillennialism is false and Christ has been
reigning as king since the first day of Pentecost following
his resurrection from the dead.

2. *The argument explained.* This argument is unquestionably
valid since it is a hypothetical syllogism in which the antecedent of
the first premise is affirmed. Thus, if the premises are true, the
conclusion must be true. Since it is necessary (if premillennialism is
true) for certain sub-doctrines to be true, if even *one* of these sub-
doctrines can be shown to be false, then it will have been shown that
premillennialism itself is false. Thus, if it can be shown that the
prophecies relating to the *death* of Christ or to his *burial,* or to his
resurrection, or to his *ascension,* or to his *coronation* involve such
facts as to show that even one sub-doctrine of premillennialism is
false, it will have been shown that premillennialism is false. Along
with other matters, it will also be shown that Jesus is now reigning
as king over his kingdom.

CONCLUSION

Brother Robert R. Taylor, Jr., a great and good man, and one of the most prolific writers of our day, has, in a most thorough manner and with penetrating accuracy, analyzed and summed up this brother's premillennial error in these words:

> His premises do grave damage to type and antitype, to shadow and substance. Ancient Israel was type; Spiritual Israel the antitype. Now he calls for a revival of the type again after the antitype has been here for nearly 2,000 years! This is amazingly amazing. Ancient Israel was the shadow. Spiritual Israel is the substance. He calls for a restoration of the shadow after the substance has been here for nearly 2,000 years. In fact, when his restoration of physical Israel occurs and the church exists by the side of such, he actually has physical Israel (the restored shadow) as in a place over Spiritual Israel (the continuing substance). He prefers *shadow* over substance![8]

As Christians we are taught to love the sinner but to hate his sin (He. 1:9; Ro. 12:9; Re. 2:6). *Few men — if any — in this generation have done the church of the Lord a greater disservice in teaching the false doctrine of premillennialism than has this premillennial brother!* This is true for several reasons. I mention only two. *One,* he has for years enjoyed the fellowship of faithful brethren who thought that he believed the truth while all the while he was a premillennialist.[9] And, *two,* he has now written a book of more than five hundred pages in which he militantly teaches and pushes his false doctrine. *If this brother would repent of his error, faithful brethren would gladly forgive him (Luke 17:3-4); however, until and unless he does so, he will be marked and avoided by faithful brethren (Ro. 16:17-18; II Th. 3:6).*

ENDNOTES

1. N. B. Hardeman, *Hardeman's Tabernacle Sermons — Volume I* (Nashville, TN: Gospel Advocate Company, 1953), pp. 87, 263-264.

2. N. B. Hardeman, *Hardeman's Tabernacle Sermons — Volume II* (Nashville, TN: Gospel Advocate Company, 1958), pp. 118-120, 162, 174, 177-178, 183, 195-197, 250-251, 262-263.

3. N. B. Hardeman, *Hardeman's Tabernacle Sermons — Volume III* (Nashville, TN: Gospel Advocate Company, 1960), pp. 139, 148, 157.

4. N. B. Hardeman, *Hardeman Tabernacle Sermons — Volume IV* (Nashville, TN: Gospel Advocate Company, 1975), p. 233.

5. An unpublished article by Curtis A. Cates, Memphis, TN.

6. *Ibid.*

7. *Ibid.*

8. A note from Robert R. Taylor, Jr., to author.

9. A conversation with Guy N. Woods.

THE BOOK OF HEBREWS:
THE GREEK TEXT, TRANSLATIONS,
EXEGESIS — No. I

By TROY M. CUMMINGS

Born and reared in Hillsboro, Texas. Attended Freed-Hardeman College. Bachelor's and master's degrees in New Testament Greek and English Bible, Abilene Christian College. Taught Greek for 14 years, mostly in Southern California School of Evangelism. Preached 48 years, in 11 states; last 19 years in the Los Angeles area. Extensive radio preaching in Oregon. Now retired; spends time writing and in appointment preaching, Los Angeles area.

INTRODUCTION

It is a real spiritual blessing to me to be here with you in this lectureship, and also to have a part in the speaking. I want to thank Dub McClish and the elders of the Pearl Street Church for their invitation.

I hope that the title of my two lectures in this series did not scare off some of the people. The title, "The Book of Hebrews: Greek Text, Translations, Exegesis," admittedly is quite generalized, and the subject could easily become too lengthy. But the subject also sounds rather technical, which it really is, in part. But I have made a careful effort to make this lecture interesting and useful, even if it does necessarily have some technical aspects. As to the word "exegesis" in the title, I believe that this rather theological term is widely known by this audience; it is simply a formal word for "exposition," or "explanation," or "bringing out the meaning of."

276

So, the title simply means that I want to deal briefly with some points concerning the original Greek language in which the book of Hebrews was written, and also make a comparison of the literal or exact meaning of the Greek with some of the major translations in English. Finally, I want to give a brief exegesis, or discussion of the meaning, of the various words or verses under consideration.

TRANSLATIONS

Since this discussion involves the use of various English translations of God's Word (originally given in Hebrew, Aramaic, and Greek), it seems to me almost necessary to make a number of preliminary statements about the various translations in general. Those of you who are well-informed as to what is currently being written in the brotherhood (and for some years in the past), know that there is much controversy regarding the use of the many English translations (or alleged translations). This is really a vast subject, but I cannot now allow myself to stray from my chosen topic and to plunge into the details of the many English versions. I will say that I believe, after much study in this area, that some extreme positions and attitudes are manifest.

In these two lectures I am going to quote from a number of translations, some of which are admittedly liberal and too loose and flatly erroneous in *many* places, in both the Old Testament and in the New Testament. But, in certain passages, some of these liberal versions are correct in their translation, as measured by the original language, the final authority. Some of my fellow-conservative preachers hardly give me the right to quote from these liberal versions, in *any* place, approvingly.

Right at this point, I believe that it is logical and wise to make these personal comments. Those who know me well, especially my former students in the Southern California School of Evangelism, where I taught Greek and hermeneutics for thirteen years, know that I am a thoroughgoing "conservative," in opposition to all forms of "liberalism," or looseness in handling the word of God. My liberal brothers consider me as a full-fledged "legalist," with a bad connotation. But they are wrong. I believe in salvation by the grace of God as much as they do, only I insist on taking the *"whole* counsel of God" on this and all other Biblical subjects, and not just seizing one or two pet passages and hammering on them to the exclusion of others.

I am leading up to the matter of the translations. When I say that I am "conservative," that does *not* mean that I automatically, without thorough study, take the conservative position. There are *some* conservative ideas held by some, which I do not and cannot accept. Truth and facts will not allow me to accept them. My earnest purpose has always been to *let the facts be the facts,* regardless of whether these facts are considered to be conservative or liberal. Honesty and fairness *demand* this course of action. Correspondingly, wherever there may be actual *errors,* let the errors be errors, and point them out as such, whether held by conservatives or liberals.

Some people in the brotherhood are so extreme in their concept of the place the King James Version has, that they virtually deny others the right to appeal to and use and teach the truth of the word of God as found in the original Hebrew or Greek languages. They say that appealing to the original language, or referring to several other English translations besides the King James, casts doubt on the King James and destroys their confidence. Brethren, it is simply absurd to say that it is hurtful to appeal to the very original language that God himself used in giving us the Bible! It is also another man-made law that would deny us the right to study and to compare various English translations other than the King James, to see which one more closely adheres to the original Hebrew or Greek.

Brethren, I exhort you now to listen very closely to this statement which I want to make concerning references to various translations in my two lectures: When I call attention to a certain translation of some particular word or verse, and approve of that particular verse, that does *not* mean that I thereby approve of that translation *as a whole, for general use among brethren.* That particular version may have many serious errors of translation *elsewhere* in it, which would make it unsafe for use by the average person who does not know the original languages or who does not know how to check up and find out about these errors.

The true, exact, and full meaning of any verse of Scripture, as God gave it in the original, is so *important* that we have the right and the obligation, where needful, to appeal to the original language or to some English translation where that exact and full meaning is best brought out. That should be obvious to any thoughtful and fair-minded person.

These comments which I have made in the last few minutes are not off the subject; they are right on it, because I am discussing the book of Hebrews with reference to the Greek text, the translations, and the exegesis of that book. Please remember these points all the way through my two lectures, so that you will not misunderstand what I am doing.

Right here I want to give a clear illustration of what I have been talking about: Profesor Edgar J. Goodspeed was a liberal, modernistic professor of Greek in the University of Chicago many years ago. In 1923 he published his translation of the New Testament, which, in general, is too liberal and loose with the original language to be approved. It is not safe to use, as a whole. Yet, here is how he translated Acts 2:38: "Peter said to them, 'Repent, and be baptized every one of you in the name of Jesus Christ, in order to have your sins forgiven; then you will receive the gift of the holy Spirit.' " While this is not exactly literal, the statement, "in order to have your sins forgiven," is an excellent practical translation that is really better than either the American Standard Version of 1901, or the King James, as measured by the original Greek. Also, it eliminates the English preposition "for" which has been the subject of endless debate and quibble by those who are determined to try to break the force of what Peter said about the necessity of baptism as well as of repentance. The Greek literally reads in part: "be baptized . . . *into* remission of your sins," meaning that they were commanded to be baptized *into* the spiritual state or realm where they would have remission of sins.

Now then, for my point: Shall we reject Goodspeed's translation of Acts 2:38 because he was a modernist? Shall we deny that Goodspeed is correct in Acts 2:38 because we can find many errors he made *elsewhere* in his translation? Certainly *not*. Does my approval of Goodspeed in Acts 2:38 necessarily force me into saying that I approve of Goodspeed's translation *as a whole?* Certainly *not*. Why can't we accept *truth* where we find it, and reject *error* where we find it? Any other course of action would, to me at least, be dishonesty, unfairness, and prejudice.

Now a few words on the relative value of some of the translations of Scripture into English: I still believe that the two safest, the two most accurate, as a whole, are the American Standard Version of 1901, and the King James Version in the edition which is in use today. Also, from what I have observed, I believe that the *New* King James Version of the New Testament is, as a whole, good and safe, with great improvement over the old King James in modernized wording and spelling, plus some other changes that make it more accurate measured by the original language.

The *New* American Standard Version, so-called, is not truly a new edition of the ASV of 1901; it is mostly a *new* translation that is marred by many imperfections, along with a number of good points. Overall, the quality of the NASV falls far short of the ASV.

But the worst blunder of the NASV that I have observed is the deliberate mistranslation of the clear Greek of II Peter 1:10. I say "deliberate mistranslation" carefully; it could not be otherwise, since these translators are men who know Greek reasonably well at least. All of the conservative and accurate translations read in part: ". . . give the more diligence to make your calling and election sure." The Greek is very clear, and also there are no textual variants in this verse that in any manner support the false translation of the NASV: "be all the more diligent to make certain about His calling and choosing you." They change the Greek from "*your* calling and election," to "*His* calling and choosing you." Their Calvinistic bias just would not allow them to accept Peter's words as he wrote them. In their Calvinistic perverted thought there is simply no place whatever for what Peter actually said, "*your* calling and election;" they believe that the "calling and election" belong *entirely* to God, and that man has absolutely nothing to do with that calling and election, and can do nothing to make them sure. The translators also changed the "make sure" your calling and election, to "make certain *about* His calling and election." This changes the meaning to fit their Calvinism.

The same translation butchery is shamelessly committed by the following translations: J. B. Phillips,[1] Charles B. Williams,[2] William F. Beck,[3] *Good News for Modern Man (Today's English Version)*,[4] Edgar Goodspeed,[5] and *The New English Bible*.[6]

So far as I am personally concerned, such deliberate mistranslation in order to hold to their false doctrine completely disqualifies these translators as being worthy to translate Scripture.

Now I can almost hear some shallow-thinking person say to me about this: "Bro. Cummings, you don't believe that *God* calls and elects us, do you?" That question would be entirely beside the point; off the subject. Of course, *God* calls and elects us; *but that is not what Peter is talking about in II Peter 1:10!* In this particular text Peter is dealing with the *human* side of salvation, and is commanding the brethren "to make *your* calling and election sure," and then says: "for if ye do these things, ye shall never stumble." Peter is not here talking about *God's* part; he is commanding us to do *our* part about making *our* calling and election sure. The Calvinist cannot tolerate such truth; he will dare to take his sectarian knife and cut these words out of holy Scripture! They have done that very thing on this verse!

The *New International Version* and the *Revised Standard Version* have a number of good points about them, but they also have a number of serious errors that teach false doctrine, such errors that make them unworthy to be your main study Bible. They are *not* safe guides in the hands of the average person who does not know the original languages nor how to find their errors. I have already admitted their *good* points; but I have also pointed out their dangerous and false points.

In addition to the translations mentioned before as mistranslating the crucial passage of II Peter 1:10, I want to mention the fact that neither Weymouth's[7] nor Moffatt's[8] translation is reliable in many places; and that the so-called *Amplified Bible*[9] and *The Living Bible*[10] are far too loose and even wild in various places. They are just paraphrases, not translations, and corrupt ones at that.

In view of the controversy in the brotherhood at present about the use of the various translations, and of my use of some of them in these two lectures, I have felt it necessary to say what I have said so that you will know exactly where I stand.

In the book of Hebrews there are dozens of places where the original Greek text presents interesting, useful, and even vital information, beyond what is revealed in the standard translations. In my lectures I can discuss only certain selections from among many.

HEBREWS 1:1-2

In reading the very first two verses I notice the *aorist* tense participle *lalesas* ("having spoken," ASV), and the *aorist* indicative verb *elalesen* ("hath spoken," ASV). The writer, as you know, is saying that God, having of old time spoken to the fathers in the prophets, at the end of these days has spoken to us in his Son. Just a little thought makes it plain that the writer is referring to many different occasions of speaking in the prophets of the Old Testament, and likewise, to many different occasions in New Testament times when the Lord spoke to his disciples. But all of the many times of God's speaking in the Old Testament are *summarized* by the use of the *aorist* participle; and all of the many occasions when Jesus spoke are *summarized* by the *aorist* verb. The widespread idea that the Greek aorist tense means "point" action, "momentary" action, "instantaneous" action, and only *one* verbal action, and even a "once for all" action only, is shown in these two verses, and in literally hundreds of other verses in the Greek Testament, to be false. The Greek aorist tense is seriously misunderstood and misused countless times by many who try to use it in various Scriptural arguments.

As mentioned, the aorist in Hebrews 1:1-2 is simply used to *summarize* many verbal actions, which actually extended over some period of time. Certainly the idea that all of these actions were only *one* action, and a "momentary" action at that, is totally false.

For a full discussion, with many citations, of the meaning of the aorist tense throughout the New Testament, see my article in *The Spiritual Sword,* Vol. 13, July, 1982, Number 4, pp. 37-42. I know that many who are reading these words studied Greek, and would be interested in this point.

HEBREWS 2:1-2

It is useful to compare the different translations on these two verses, especially v. 1 in part: "lest at any time we should let (them) slip" (KJV). But the ASV reads: "lest haply we drift away (from them.)" The NKJV almost changes over to the ASV: "lest we drift away." The NIV agrees substantially: "so that we do not drift away," and the RSV likewise has "lest we drift away from it."

So modern Greek scholars agree that the basic idea in the Greek verb is "drifting," rather than the KJV's "let them slip." The Greek verb is *pararuomen (pararruomen),* found only here in the New Testament. Here it is the second aorist passive subjunctive. It means literally to "flow by" or "flow past," and Xenophon in ancient Greek literature uses it of the river flowing by.[11] Robertson further notes that "here the metaphor is that 'of being swept along past the sure anchorage which is within reach' (Westcott), a vivid picture of peril for all . . ." Note that Robertson correctly brings out the passive voice meaning. So the *exact* idea in the original is not the KJV's "we should let *them* (the things having been heard) slip," but rather, "lest we ourselves be swept along past" these truths from God.

This vivid metaphor of Christians being on a flowing river, the river of the pressure of everyday living, and trying to pull us downstream away from the solid anchor of God's revelation, is so true to the constant temptations of life in the fleshly body.

This is just one sample out of many hundreds in the Greek Testament that make the word of God come alive and be loaded with the full spiritual cargo of all that God brought to us in his original language. It is very difficult to bring out all of this flavor and force and exactness of meaning in the translations. This is exactly what Dr. A. T. Robertson, who wrote a 1,454 page Greek grammar, meant when he wrote on p.

xix: "The Greek New Testament is the New Testament. All else is translation."[12] Now he did *not* mean, nor do I mean, that we do not have the substantial message of God in the best English translations; we do. And certainly anyone who studies carefully a good translation will get the basic truths necessary to know what to do to be saved, and how to live the Christian life. Let this point be remenbered. At the same time, my preceding remarks about the extra riches and the additional exactness found in the original language stand true.

Another rich comment from Prof. Robertson is found in the preface to the fourth edition of his large grammar (already cited). "I have never gone to the Greek New Testament without receiving fresh illumination on some point. The charm lures one on forever," p. xx. I know exactly what he means; I feel the same way. Since I first started studying Greek thirty-eight years ago in Abilene Christian College, my desire for it continues to increase. The richness of God's inspired Greek New Testament is simply inexhaustible.

HEBREWS 10:26-31

One of the most important passages in the book of Hebrews where the Greek Testament sheds valuable light in understanding exactly what the writer means and does not mean, is in chapter 10, vv. 26-31.

In addition, the failure of most of the translations to bring out the *full* and *exact* meaning of the Greek has resulted in much confusion even among preaching brethren in really understanding just what inspiration is saying. Likewise, some commentators whom I have consulted fail to bring out this exactness. Right now I wish to concentrate on verse 26.

In the ASV we read: "For if we sin wilfully after that we have received the knowledge of the truth, there remaineth no more a sacrifice for sins." The KJV is identical except for not having the article "a" before the word "sacrifice." The New KJV is substantially the same. The 1971 second edition of the *Revised Standard Version* reads: "For if we sin deliberately after receiving the knowledge of the truth, there no longer remains a sacrifice for sins."

One point of crutial importance in understanding verse 26 is this: Is the writer speaking of committing one act of sin, or is he referring to a continued practice of sin? The preceding translations are ambiguous on this point; the English used *could* refer to one act of sin, or it *could* refer to a continued practice. This is unfortunate, because the original Greek is *not* ambiguous on this point. This is *not* just my arbitrary notion; Greek scholars who really know their advanced grammar, and pay close attention to the grammatical construction here, and the context, must agree that the writer is not referring to an isolated act of sin; rather he carefully uses his mastery of Greek grammar to emphasize strongly that he is picturing a continued state of willful or willing sin. *This fact vitally affects the proper exegesis of the passage.*

Brethren, it is simply impossible to understand this passage correctly without in some manner finding out just what the Greek is really saying, either by knowing the Greek for yourself, or by help from some translation or commentary or individual who knows the language.

Do we have any well-known scholars or commentators or translations that recognize the fact that I am pointing out? Yes, we do; I'll give you these in a short time. But first I want to call attention, for the benefit of you who have studied Greek sufficiently, to the grammatical construction in this verse 26.

(Right here, parenthetically but I believe importantly, I want to give friendly warning to Greek students: Do not depend upon the commonly used Greek-English interlinear Testaments to give you a full and accurate literal translation of the Greek; there are many places both in Berry's[13] interlinear and in Marshall's[14] where plain errors of grammar are found, and also many places where the interlinear is scarcely more literal than the standard English version. Berry's is especially weak and unsatisfactory on Hebrews 10:26 which we are now studying.)

Now for the grammar of verse 26; transliterated the Greek is: *Hekousios gar hamartanonton hemon meta to labein ten epignosin tes aletheias, ouketi peri hamartion apoleipetai thusia.* Very literally, in Greek word order except for the postpositive *gar*, it reads: "For willingly sinning us after the receiving the full knowledge of the truth, no longer concerning sins is being left a sacrifice." But to get the force of this in English we have to use additional words and arrange the words, to something like this: "For if we willingly keep on sinning after we receive the full knowledge of the truth, there no longer remains a sacrifice for sins."

Several points need to be made: First, it is important to observe that the very first word in this Greek sentence is the adverb *hekousios*. Thayer[15] defines this adverb as meaning "voluntarily, willingly, of one's own accord," citing Hebrews 10:26. There is no doubt that the Hebrews writer placed this word first in the sentence for emphasis. He is not talking about just any sin, some sin of the moment, or of ignorance, or of weakness; it is sin indulged in "willingly," with reckless unconcern for God or his will; arrogantly, defiantly, with no restraint. This is the kind of sin that the humble, God-fearing Christian *never* indulges in; his *attitude of heart* will not allow it. He will sin occasionally through ignorance or weakness or being overcome by the passion of the moment, but never will the devoted child of God *willingly* and *deliberately* turn over his soul to the devil with *intentional* rebellion to God.

In the second place, the Greek words *hamartanonton hemon* hold the key as to whether the Hebrew writer is referring to *one* sin as an isolated act, or to a continued practice or state of sin. This Greek construction is the *present* active participle, genitive masculine plural, from the verb *hamartano*, used along with the genitive plural of the first personal pronoun. The whole construction is called a "genitive absolute," consisting of an adverbial or circumstantial participle, with its noun or pronoun, and expressing one or more of these ideas: time, condition, concession, cause, purpose, means, manner or attendant circumstance.[16]

Greek *tense*, in its advanced phases, is indeed complicated, and widely misunderstood, measured by the actual examples in the Greek Testament. Often the New Testament writers would use different tenses to describe the same verbal action, under certain grammatical conditions. But when it comes to the genitive absolute construction which we have in Hebrews 10:26, the Greeks could not arbirtarily and rhetorically switch from tense to tense at will. In this specialized construction, the Greeks had to have, idiomatically speaking, a clear means of distinguishing *simultaneous* participial action going on at the time of the main verb, from *antecedent* participial action that was *not* going on, but was complete, completed, summarized, in relation to the main verb. The latter thought would be expressed by the aorist tense, and the time indicated would usually be prior to the time of the main verb.

Remember that the participle in our text is *present* tense, without a doubt here in this context, with the adverb, and the main stream of thought in the discussion, expressing strongly the duration concept, the going-on action, the continued practice. No Greek scholar known to me has ever argued otherwise.

Even though the ASV, KJV, NKJV, and RSV do not translate the full force of the duration concept in this verse, other translations do. It is one of the good points about the NIV (remember the bad points I warned you about) that it gives an excellent translation here: "If we deliberately keep on sinning." Also the NASV is good here: "For if we go on sinning willfully . . ." Even the wild TEV does a good job on this verse: "For there is no longer any sacrifice that will take away sins if we purposely go on sinning after the truth has been made known to us." And the ordinarily reckless NEB gets the correct idea here: "For if we persist in sin . . ." Even the unreliable Jehovah's Witnesses Version (New World Translation) reads in part: "For if we practice sin willfully . . ." Again, even the usually radical and wild Amplified version gets the idea in this verse. Isn't it amazing and strange and inconsistent how these generally unworthy translations suddenly decide to get serious and to stick closely to the Greek in certain passages?

Marcus Dods, in *Expositor's Greek Testament*,[17] Robert Milligan, in his commentary on Hebrews,[18] J. Barmby, in *The Pulpit Commemtary*,[19] Henry Alford, *The Greek Testament*,[20] and A. R. Fausset, *Commentary*,[21] are some of the scholars who point out the meaning of the Greek as I have done, agreeing with the Greek exegesis I gave.

CONCLUSION

It is my purpose to continue in my second lecture in this series to examine closely the Greek text, the translations, and the exegesis of various passages in the book of Hebrews, which have not been dealt with in this first lecture.

ENDNOTES

1. J. B. Phillips, *The New Testament in Modern English* (New York: The Macmillan Co., 1962).

2. Charles B. Williams, *The New Testament In the Language of the People* (Chicago: Moody Press, 1963).

3. William F. Beck, *The New Testament In the Language of Today* (St. Louis: Concordia Publishing House, 1964).

4. Robert G. Bratcher, *Good News for Modern Man (The New Testament in Today's English Version)* (New York: American Bible Society, 1966).

5. Edgar J. Goodspeed, *The New Testament, An American Translation* (Chicago: The University of Chicago Press, 1951).

6. *The New English Bible, New Testament* (Oxford and Cambridge: University Press, 1961).

7. Richard Francis Weymouth, *The New Testament In Modern Speech* (New York: Harper & Brothers, 6th ed., n. d.).

8. James Moffatt, *The New Testament, A New Translation* (New York: Harper & Brothers Pub., 1950).

9. *The Amplified New Testament* (La Habra, Calif.: The Lockman Foundation, 1958), used in *The Layman's Parallel New Testament* (Grand Rapids: Zondervan Pub. House, 1970).

10. Kenneth N. Taylor, *The Living New Testament* (Wheaton, Ill.: Tyndale House Foundation, 1967), used in *The Layman's Parallel New Testament* (Grand Rapids: Zondervan, 1970).

11. A. T. Robertson, *Word Pictures In the New Testament*, Vol. V, (New York: Harper & Brothers, 1932), p. 342.

12. A. T. Robertson, *A Grammar of the Greek New Testament In the Light of Historical Research* (Nashville: Broadman Press, 4th ed., 1923), p. xix.

13. George Ricker Berry, *The Interlinear Literal Translation of The Greek New Testament* (Chicago: Wilcox & Follett Co., 1948).

14. Alfred Marshall, *The Interlinear Greek-English New Testament (London: Samuel Bagster and Sons, Ltd., 1958).*

15. Joseph Henry Thayer, *Greek-English Lexicon of the New Testament* (Grand Rapids: Zondervan Pub, House, rpt. 1969), p. 198.

16. See, for examples, Ernest DeWitt Burton, *Syntax of the Moods and Tenses in New Testament Greek* (Chicago: Univ. of Chicago Press, rpt. 1943), pp.169-75; F. Blass and A. Debrunner, *A Greek Grammar of the New Testament and Other Early Christian Literature,* trans. and rev. by Robert W. Funk (Chicago: Univ. of Chicago Press, 1962). pp. 215-19; Robertson, *Grammar,* pp. 1124-32.

17. Marcus Dods, *The Expositor's Greek Testament.* ed. by W. R. Nicoll, Vol. IV, (Grand Rapids, Mich.: Eerdmans Pub. Co., n.d.), p. 348.

18. Robert Milligan, *The New Testament Commentary,* Vol.IX, *Epistle to the Hebrews* (Des Moines: Eugene S. Smith, rpt. n. d.), p. 285.

19. J. Barmby, in *The Pulpit Commentary,* ed. by H. D. M. Spence and Joseph S. Exell, Vol. 21 (Grand Rapids: Eerdmans, rpt. 1962), pp. 267-68.

20. Henry Alford, *The Greek Testament,* Vol. IV, Part I, 2nd ed. (London: Rivingtons, 1861), pp. 198-99.

21. A. R. Faussett, in *A Commentary On the Old and New Testament,* by Jamieson, Fausset, and Brown, Vol. VI (Grand Rapids: Eerdmans Pub. Co., rpt. 1948), pp. 563-64.

THE BOOK OF HEBREWS:
THE GREEK TEXT, TRANSLATIONS,
EXEGESIS — No. II

By TROY M. CUMMINGS

(See picture and biographical sketch at beginning of author's previous chapter.)

INTRODUCTION

This second lecture on this subject is closely tied to the first one; so much so that the one now is really incomplete without studying the first one beforehand. I want to avoid repetition so far as I can wisely do so.

In the first lecture I set forth my attitude toward and use of the many translations in English which we have of the Scriptures, and it is very important that you review that material. Basically and very briefly, I approve, in *any* translation, only that which is clearly correct and accurate, as measured by the original language in which God gave us the Bible. Likewise, I do *not* approve, in *any* translation, any word or passage which can be proved to be a wrong or inadequate translation. This is the only honest and scholarly course to pursue.

I now continue with the discussion of specific verses in the book of Hebrews:

HEBREWS 1:1-2

If you read these two verses carefully in the KJV, the NKJV, the ASV, or the NASV, you will notice that the word "his" is italicized in the reading "his Son," indicating that the word "his" is not actually found in the Greek. The ASV footnote reads: "Gr. a Son." Since there is no indefinite article in the New Testament Greek, it could also literally be read simply "Son," without the "a."

English-speaking readers might wonder why the Greek writer would say: "hath at the end of these days spoken unto us in Son," rather than "in *his* Son," or even "in *the* Son." The translators of the four versions previously cited added "his" in italics as best expressing, in their view, the idea to us in English. But the exact Greek meaning was of course best expressed by the Greek writer, who knew exactly what he was doing. Incidentally, the book of Hebrews in Greek, as all scholars agree, is a beautiful literary monument, expressed in polished and therefore, to us, difficult Greek. In our colleges the study of the book of Hebrews in Greek is usually delayed until the third, fourth, or fifth year of study. One of the high-lights of my years of teaching Greek in Southern California School of Evangelism was in taking my third year Greek students *slowly* through all the entanglements and complexi-ties of the Greek grammar. I freely admit that even I as the teacher was forced to review, study hard, and do additional grammatical research in order to satisfy myself and my students in solving the problems. But as I said in the first lecture, the spiritual *richness* of God's inspired Greek Testa-ment is simply inexhaustible and continually refreshing to the mind and heart of the Christian scholar.

In our item now being discussed, chapter 1, verses 1 and 2, the Greek writer omitted the definite article "the," and also the pronoun "his," in referring to the Son, for a specific gram-matical purpose. Namely, it was to stress the nature, the quality, of the divine revelation, rather than the *identity* of the Son. In other words, it was a comparison of the in-the-prophets revelation in the Old Testament, with the in-Son revelation of the New Testament. Still further, the writer is showing the *superiority* of the revelation in the Son, by so much as God's *Son* is greater than God's *prophets*.

Since so many of those who read these words have studied Greek, I hope you will be interested in these grammatical details. Dana and Mantey in their Greek grammar give a good summary of this point: "When identity is prominent, we find the article; and when quality or character is stressed, the construction is anarthrous (that is, without the article)."[1]

Marcus Dods,[2] Marvin Vincent,[3] and A. T. Robertson[4] are some of the scholarly commentators who discuss the point I am making.

HEBREWS 1:3

The KJV reads: "Who being the brightness of his glory, and the express image of his person." The ASV reads in part: "the very image." It is interesting to observe that the Greek word behind this is *charakter,* which you can easily see is the source of our English word "character." (Many people do not realize just how many hundreds of English words are directly from the Greek language.) Robertson[5] has some interesting comments on *charakter.*

HEBREWS 1:7

It is useful and thought-provoking to compare some of the translations of this verse. The KJV: "And of the angels he saith, Who maketh his angels spirits, and his ministers a flame of fire." The ASV in part has: "Who maketh his angels winds, And his ministers a flame of fire." This is a quotation from Psalms 104:4, which in the KJV reads: "Who maketh his angels spirits." The ASV in Psalms 104:4: "Who maketh winds his messengers," with a marginal reading: "Who maketh his angels winds." Compare also the NASV, the RSV, and the NIV.

The scholarly commentators have interesting discussions about the uncertainties involved in knowing for sure exactly how to translate these passages. The technical discussion of all the alternatives is too lengthy for our study at this time. But a careful comparison of four or five of the major translations in both the Old Testament passage and in Hebrews 1:7 gives one a good foundation for sizing up the possible meanings of this verse.

HEBREWS 1:11

The ASV reads: "They shall perish; but thou continuest." The KJV: "They shall perish; but thou remainest."

While both the ASV and the KJV are what you could call correct, yet neither one really translates *fully* just what the Greek says: "They *themselves* shall perish, but *you* are remaining throughout." The Greek is more emphatic; the intensive pronoun *autoi* ("themselves"), and the second personal pronoun *su* ("you") are added to the pronouns already in the Greek verbal endings. The Hebrews writer is emphasizing a contrast between the perishable created physical world, and the eternal existence of God the Son. The Greek is simply richer, more flavorful, more forceful, than the translations.

HEBREWS 1:12

In this verse you have the same situation I have just discussed in verse 11. The Greek has "But *you* are the same," with the emphatic pronoun *su* added, to glorify Christ as the one who will remain forever, even after the created world will dissolve.

HEBREWS 2:2

(I have already dealt with verse 1 in the first lecture.) This verse is a good example of one of the quaint and amusing means the Greeks used to create *emphasis* in their statements. It sounds strange and mixed-up to some people who have not studied foreign languages, but to long-time Greek students who love the language that God used in giving us the New Testament, it is not only quite understandable, but also amusingly flavorful and forceful and loaded with meaning. Let me give you a literal reading, in Greek word order, of verse 2: "For if the-through-angels-having-been-spoken word came to be steadfast, and every transgression and disobedience received a just recompense of reward." Certainly the Greek here gives special emphasis to the *kind* of word he is talking about; he is actually contrasting sharply the word of God which came through angels, with (v. 3) the salvation-words which came "through the Lord." When the Greek hearer or reader listened to the word "the through-angels-having-been-spoken word," he felt the power of the vivid description of the *kind* and *quality* of word in mind. In Greek class we would analyze this grammar as being an articular attributive adjectival participle modifying the Greek noun *logos*, "word." I guess such descriptions are one of the reasons why Greek grammar scares off many students. In Abilene Christian College the number of Greek students when I was there got to be so few, the higher you would go, that finally, in one of my graduate courses, I was the *only* student! One fellow called me a "Greek-freak." I guess he's right.

HEBREWS 2:3

We see some more emphasis in this verse. The first part of the verse literally reads: "How *we* shall flee out so great having neglected salvation?" This is typical Greek-talk, with quite different word-order from English. To express the same or similar thought in English we would say: "How shall *we* escape, having neglected so great a salvation?"

The point right now is the emphasis upon the word "we," from the Greek *hemeis*. Again, the flow of thought in the context makes it clear why he stresses the word "we."

If the violators of the Mosaic law received punishment for "every transgression and disobedience," he asks, "how shall *we* escape" punishment if we have neglected *so great* a salvation which has been spoken through *the Lord*, not Moses?

Brethren, this point, this passage, Hebrews 2:1-3, properly understood, really believed, whole-heartedly accepted, would in itself put a stop to all of this false teaching going on right now in the brotherhood about these perverted concepts concerning salvation by grace! I have been reading in our gospel papers and hearing teaching concerning "grace" that is nothing more than the old sectarian false teaching of salvation by grace alone, or by faith alone. Now I have been believing in and preaching salvation by the grace of God for forty-eight years, straight from the "*whole* counsel of God," but I have *not* been preaching the false ideas that are now being unloaded on the brotherhood in *many* places all over the nation!

Now what is Hebrews 2:1-3 clearly saying? I have just given it to you a minute or two ago, straight from verses 2 and 3. Earnest Bible students who can think well should know and admit that the Hebrews writer is certainly saying that if the violaters of God's law through angels, the Mosaic law, received a just recompense of reward for "every transgression and disobedience," then "how shall *we* escape" punishment if *we* neglect the so-great salvation which has come to *us* "through the Lord," that is, the gospel of Christ! This *fact* is absolutely clear if we really *believe* what God has said *here* in this text. What good does it do, brethren, to isolate a few pet passages on the "grace" of God and hammer on them constantly *without*, at the same time, using *all* of the passages that relate to the subject? I believe *every* passage in God's word about "grace," "law," "works," "faith," "commandments," "obedience," "punishment," "fear," "love," but I am not going to isolate certain texts and make them *contradict* what God has clearly taught *elsewhere* in his word! We *must* get *all* the evidence, *all* the testimony of God together, study it all thoroughly and then draw conclusions about each Biblical subject that will *not* contradict the other subjects! This *can* be done; it *has been* done by hundreds of sound, God-fearing, scholarly gospel preachers for a long time in the brotherhood.

If the brotherhood in general does not rise up in moral courage and Bible wisdom and put a stop to all of this false teaching, we are going to see a wholesale falling away to where many "churches of Christ" will become nothing more than just soft stand-for-nothing sectarian congregations, with a "grace-only" banner. Now, I have documentary proof in my files of these charges and can produce it when necessary.

The idea that our salvation today is wholly by grace, and that our works or obedience or lack of obedience have nothing *essential* to do with being saved by grace, is *flatly contradictory* to this plain teaching in Hebrews 2:1-3 — and incidentally, contradictory to *many* other passages in the New Testament.

We *know* that the Hebrews writer is saying that we today cannot escape punishment for our sins under the gospel, if we neglect so great a salvation. Whatever is true about "grace" and "works" in the New Testament *cannot* mean that we *can* escape punishment if we neglect this salvation. This *fact* positively does *not* fit into the false ideas about "grace" that we are hearing more and more.

The membership as a whole in many congregations does not know Scripture deeply enough to *detect* the gradual and smooth and fair speech of these false teachers. And, sad to say, many *elders* do not know Scripture deeply enough to detect these subtle errors. I say this thoughtfully. I have served as an elder in two congregations, so I speak with proper respect for qualified elders. But so many elders across the land cannot really carry out with any effectiveness what God has told them they must do in Titus 1:9-13, which reads in part, ASV:

> that he (the elder) may be able both to exhort in the sound doctrine, and to convict the gainsayers (contradicters). For there are many unruly men, vain talkers and deceivers, specially they of the circumcision, whose mouths must be stopped. . . . For which cause reprove them sharply, that they may be sound in the faith. . . .

While we are still on Hebrews 2:3, I want to make mention of a point that I spoke of in my first lecture, namely, that you cannot depend on the accuracy of these commonly used Greek-English interlinears, Berry's and Marshall's, in every case. In fact, there are quite a few types of errors. In the particular case of Hebrews 2:3, Berry's is correct (basically) in its translation of the first aorist active articular participle *ton akousanton;* he renders it "by those that heard."[6] (More literally and exactly, "by the ones having heard.") But Marshall here makes an error in his translation that he makes many dozens of times throughout the New Testament. He renders it: "by the ones hearing,"[7] as if it were a *present* participle instead of the aorist. The aorist participle can, in a few cases, under special grammatical circumstances, be translated by the English present participle. But predominantly, and certainly here in this construction, the past participle must be used. In the Greek Testament the aorist participle's principal use is to denote antecedent (past) action in relation to the main verb. The reason for this is that the aorist tense pictures the verbal action in summary, as a single whole, complete, *not* going on. This fact caused the Greeks to use the aorist participle predominantly to represent a preceding and past action in relation to the main verb. If they wanted to picture the verbal action in the participle as currently going on, in its process or duration, they used the *present* participle.

I have made these comments about Berry's and Marshall's interlinears, not primarily to find fault but to do my part in warning against errors in Biblical concepts. We need to understand *exactly* what God has taught in his word.

HEBREWS 2:6

In my first lecture I called attention to an article I wrote on the aorist tense of Greek, which was published in the July, 1982, issue of *The Spiritual Sword*, Vol. 13, Number 4, pp. 37-42. I dealt at length with this because of its doctrinal importance in understanding the Greek Testament, and in making doctrinal arguments on Scriptural subjects. Very few Greek students and even Greek teachers seem to have a complete grasp of the significance of the vital facts I set forth in the article.

Right here in Hebrews 2:3 is one of literally hundreds of places in the Greek Testament that confirm the facts I am talking about. Many Greek students think that when the Greek aorist tense is used, it *necessarily* means that the verbal action is only "point" action, that is, in their concept, "momentary," very short duration, and that being such, a duration-concept tense, like the present, simply could not properly be used to describe that action. But that is all wrong. (The genitive absolute construction, dealt with in the first lecture, is somewhat of an exception.) Greek tense does not *control* the verbal action; tense merely *pictures* the particular mental concept of that action which the Greek wanted to set forth at any given moment. He often switched from tense to tense, very quickly, in order to present a different mental picture of that verbal action. We do the same in English.

In our present text, Hebrews 2:6, the master scholar of Greek who wrote the book of Hebrews, illustrates my point exactly. He wrote: *diemarturato de pou tis legon.* Literally, that says: "But fully testified somewhere one saying." In smooth English: "But somewhere one fully testified, saying."

The point now is this, for you Greek students: *diemarturato* is *aorist* middle indicative verb; but the *present* active participle immediately following, referring to *the same verbal action*, is *legon!* So the Greek writer used *both* the aorist and the present tenses, in the same sentence, to describe the same verbal action! Now suppose some brother tries to make an argument on the aorist verb, claiming that the aorist means only "point" or "momentary" action. In the same sentence his argument would be shot down, because the same action is described by the *duration*-concept *present* tense participle! And remember that all grammarians agree that the present *participle* always pictures the verbal action in its *duration*, progressive, on-going concept.

So be very careful, brethren, about making doctrinal arguments on Greek tenses; the subject is very complex.

HEBREWS 4:1

The ASV reads: "Let us fear therefore, lest haply, a promise being left of entering into his rest, any one of you should seem to have come short of it." Our grace-only, fear-not, "always-feel-good-about-yourselves" brethren are here *contradicted* by the Holy Spirit in this verse, if only they could see and admit it.

HEBREWS 4:8

The KJV reads: "For if Jesus had given them rest . . ." The *context* makes it absolutely clear that it is not *Jesus* to whom the writer refers, but to the *Joshua* of the Old Testament. The whole verse 8 would not make sense if it referred to Jesus, our Lord. The NKJV, the ASV, the RSV, the NASV, and the NIV all translate "Joshua," not "Jesus."

It is true that the Greek word is *Iesous,* the common term for Jesus our Lord; but all of the Greek lexicons (dictionaries)[8] agree that the term means "Joshua" in this context. The Greek used the term *Iesous* to translate the Hebrew word for "Joshua," which is *Yehoshua.* The reference to "Joshua" in this context should never have been translated "Jesus" in the KJV.

HEBREWS 6:4-8

This is an especially important text in this book, dealing in general with the subject mentioned so much in this epistle: the danger of falling away.

The ASV reads as follows:

For as touching those who were once enlightened and tasted of the heavenly gift, and were made partakers of the Holy Spirit, and tasted the good word of God, and the powers of the age to come, and *then* fell away, it is impossible to renew them again unto repentance; seeing they crucify to themselves the Son of God afresh, and put him to an open shame. . . .

In the KJV the reading is, v. 6, "If they shall fall away." The ASV has "and *then* fell away." The NKJV stays with the KJV, but the NASV reads: "and *then* have fallen away." The RSV has: "If they then commit apostasy." The NIV has: "if they fall away."

If Greek scholars will just stay consistently with the Greek construction in this text, there is no doubt that they will translate substantially as both the ASV and the NASV have it, "and *then* fell away." More literally: "and having fallen away." *In the Greek there is no "if," either stated or implied. There should not have been any "if" inserted in any of the translations.* I personally believe that it was Calvinistic bias that put the "if" in the versions, to try to soften the very strong warning about the danger of falling away.

I recently read an article by some brother who was trying to defend the "if" in the KJV at all costs, by arguing that a close study of the context will make plain what the writer really intended. But this is dodging the point; off the subject. We are not discussing what the whole context is teaching; we are asking the specific and exact point: *"Is there Greek in the passage to support the English word 'if'?"* The answer is *"No."* We ought not to try to deny this grammatical fact of the Greek Testament. (It is also an error to appeal to other Greek constructions where the grammar is different.)

The most important grammatical facts that the Greek scholar notices as he reads this text in the Greek are the list of *aorist* participles in verses 4, 5, and 6. Note them as follows:

photisthentas, "having been enlighened"
geusamenous, "having tasted"
genethentas, "having become (been made)"
geusamenous, "having tasted"
parapesontas, "having fallen away"

All of these aorist participles are in the same grammatical relations. None of the translations put an "if" to modify any of the first four aorist participles in the list, but several of them did insert the "if" to modify the *last* participle in the list. Why? There is no grammatical justification for the "if" anywhere in the list. As is true so often, the ASV did not make this mistake, but stayed closely to the Greek, translating, "and (then) fell away." As mentioned previously, more literally it is: "and having fallen away."

There is no "if" about the reality of whether or not they fell away; the Hebrews writer is picturing an *actual* falling away, not an "if" situation. Of course this whole text, chapter 6:4-8, is one of the strongest in the New Testament to show the reality of apostasy, or falling away, when we do certain things.

Be it said to the credit of the NASV, in this particular place, that it too correctly translates, "and (then) have fallen away." This is true, even though the same version in II Peter 1:10 shamefully mistranslated that passage, as I discussed in my first lecture.

This shows how *inconsistent* many of these translations are, doing a good job on much of the material, and then jumping the track on other passages.

It is quite possible — I would say probable — that the same translator or translators that handled II Peter 1:10, did *not* do the translating in Hebrews 6:4-8. The glaring Calvinistic bias manifested in II Peter 1:10 does not appear in Hebrews 6:4-8.

So, to be honest and fair, I point out both the good and the bad points about any or all of the translations under consideration. Advanced Bible and language scholars can separate the wheat from the chaff, but the average member of the church cannot, and therefore it is *not safe* for that person to use and depend upon many of these modern versions.

Many people ask: "Since I don't know the original languages of the Bible, there is no way for me to know just which version is accurate in any given verse of Scripture. What should I do?"

Again, I remind you to review what I have said on this general subject in lecture number one. There is no doubt that any earnest student of Scripture can take either the KJV or the ASV or the NKJV and find the substantial message of God concerning salvation. In these lectures I have especially been talking about the more *exact* and *precise* and *literal* meaning of the original language.

For serious Bible students in the church, the first step I recommend is that they have and study carefully both the ASV and the KJV; the NKJV is now even better, as a whole, so far as I have observed, than the old KJV.

In this manner you can get the very best of both, or all three standard, conservative, reliable versions.

HEBREWS 7:25

The KJV reads in part: "Wherefore he is able also to save them to the uttermost that come unto God by him." I am sure that many people in reading this suppose that the meaning is that God is able to save to the uttermost in the sense of anyone anywhere in all the world, or anyone in any spiritual condition. While this is true, I do not believe that is what the Hebrews writer had in mind just here.

While the ASV reads about the same, it has a valuable footnote explaining the expression "to the uttermost," and says that the Greek is "completely." In other words, Christ is able to save *completely.* A. T. Robertson comments on the Greek here, the words *eis to panteles,* literally: "to the all-complete," and says that "the common meaning is completely, utterly," putting his approval of the footnote of the ASV.[9]

Why would the writer say that Jesus saves us "completely?" This point fits in exactly with the general tenor of the book of Hebrews, because he is contrasting the inadequate and the *temporary* cleansing of sins under the Old Covenant, since it was based on the shed blood of *animals,* with that *permanent* taking away of sins by the blood of the divine God-man Jesus Christ.

Also, and even more closely to the exact point, the writer in verses 23 and 24 is pointing out that under the Old Law there were many priests necessary, because of their continuing death and replacement. But in contrast, Jesus is our high priest who "abideth forever," and "seeing he ever liveth to make intercession for them."

Out of the six translation, KJV, NKJV, ASV, NASV, RSV, and NIV, the only one to translate "he is able to save *completely,* " in the main text, is the NIV! Be it said to the credit of the ASV, as I have already mentioned, they put the literal meaning in the footnote.

I am sure myself that the NIV is the best of all of them, on this particular word "completely." That is the Greek exactly. No matter what errors the NIV makes elsewhere (and they are considerable), it is right in Hebrews 7:25 and superior to the others. Honesty and fairness absolutely force the scholar to say this.

CONCLUSION

There are many other places in Hebrews that we could have studied, but we do not have time. "Grace be with you."

ENDNOTES

1. H. E. Dana and Julius R. Mantey, *A Manual Grammar of the Greek New Testament* (New York: The Macmillan Co., 1944), p. 138.

2. Marcus Dods, in *The Expositor's Greek Testament* (Grand Rapids, MI: Eerdmans Pub. Co., n.d.), Vol. IV, p. 249.

3. Marvin Vincent, *Word Studies In The New Testament* (New York: Charles Scribner's Sons, 1908), Vol. IV, p. 379.

4. A. T. Robertson, *Word Pictures In The New Testament* (New York: Harper & Brothers, 1932), Vol. V, p. 335.

5. *Ibid.,* p. 336.

6. George Ricker Berry, *The Interlinear Literal Translation of the Greek Testament* (Chicago: Wilcox & Follett Co., 1948), p. 561.

7. Alfred Marshall, *The Interlinear Greek-English New Testament* (London: Samuel Bagster & Sons Ltd., 1958), p. 855.

8. For example: Walter Bauer, *A Greek-English Lexicon of the New Testament and Other Early Christian Literature,* 2nd ed., rev. and augm. by F. Wilbur Gingrich and Frederick W. Danker (Chicago: The University of Chicago Press, 1979), pp. 373-74; Joseph Henry Thayer, *Greek-English Lexicon of the New Testament* (Grand Rapids: Zondervan Publ. House, rpt. 1969), p. 300; G. Abbott-Smith, *A Manual Greek Lexicon of the New Testament* (Edinburgh: T. & T. Clark, 3rd ed., rpt. 1968), p. 215.

9. Robertson, *op. cit.,* Vol. V, p. 386.

SECTION II

ANSWERING FALSE DOCTRINES
RELATING TO HEBREWS

ANSWERING FALSE DOCTRINES RELATING TO HEBREWS — No. I

HEBREWS 2:5	**"THE WORLD TO COME" A MILLENNIAL KINGDOM**
HEBREWS 2:8	**"ALL THINGS SUBJECTED" REFERS TO MILLENNIAL KINGDOM**
HEBREWS 10:37	**"HE SHALL NOT TARRY" REFERS TO IMMINENT COMING OF CHRIST**
HEBREWS 12:28	**"RECEIVING A KINGDOM" IS YET FUTURE**

By JERRY MOFFITT

Holder of B. S. from Southwest Texas State University, candidate for M. A. Graduate of Preston Road School of Preaching. Author of three books: *Is Baptism Essential to Salvation?*, *Non-Boring Preaching*, and *Bales' Position Explained and Denied*. Editor of *Thrust*, a quarterly journal devoted to refuting false doctrine. Director of the Southwest School of Bible Studies, Austin, TX. Debater. Mission work in Vermont and Michigan.

INTRODUCTION

Premillennialism is the belief that Christ will return to earth before he starts a 1,000 year reign from Jerusalem. The view holds that the kingdom was rejected, so Christ could not set it up at his first coming. He will set it up (usually it is supposed to be set up in the near future) and rule from Jerusalem. During this 1,000 year reign the earth, they say, will be reconditioned and perfect in every way. They give Isaiah 11:6ff as proof. The final abode of those in Christ, they teach, is a literal new earth.

All we intend to do in this study is try to understand four passages in Hebrews which influence our understanding of "last things." They all relate to the study of Premillennialism. Let us begin.

"THE WORLD TO COME" (2:5)

"For not unto angels did he subject the world to come, whereof we speak."

This fits into the premillennialists' picture because they believe this is the renovated earth subject to man in its fullest sense. Shank writes:

> But the Messianic kingdom will indeed be "of this world" in the sense that Christ will personally reign (present bodily) over the nations here on earth. "The world to come" (Heb. 2:5) which God has "put in subjection" to his Son is the *oikoumene*, the inhabited earth.[1]

Is It A Renovated Earth? Milligan says it is "the habitable world under the reign and government of the Messiah."[2] Lenski says it is "the new earth (Re. 21:1)."[3]

I know that the passage seems, at first glance, to speak of the next world or age — heaven. Truly that is *a* world to come, and it is not impossible that it could be heaven in the sense of "new heavens and a new earth" (II Pe. 3:13). But Peter, there, uses another word for earth — *ge* (earth) — while the Hebrews writer here uses *oikoumene*. Vine says this word means "the inhabited earth."[4] The word is used fifteen times in the New Testament, and every time it is used of *this* inhabited world. Never is it used in the sense of "age." Flender says it means the "inhabited earth,"[5] as does Arndt and Gingrich.[6] Thayer thinks that in Hebrews 2:5 it means "the universe, the world . . . that consummate state of all things which will exist after Christ's return from heaven."[7] But Thayer is unusual in that definition, and even he admits that the primary meaning is "inhabited earth." And that also seems to be what Thayer had in mind even in the above quote — a world and universe existing after the second coming.

Actually, I reject the idea that the Holy Spirit uses *oikoumene* (inhabited earth) to talk of heaven. But if I do that, do I say that the premillennialists are correct, and that this inhabited world will be renovated under Christ's subjection, and that that is "the world to come"? No! Notice a few quotes. Robertson says *oikoumene* is "The new order, the salvation just described."[8] Barnes says, "the world under the Messiah — the world, age, or dispensation which was to succeed the Jewish, and which was familiarly known to them as 'the world to come.' "[9]

According to the above, it refers to the world of the Messiah we are all now in. It is the inhabited world which Christ now rules (Ma. 28:18-20). Paul calls it "the world to come," not because it was future to him, but because that is the way they designated it for so long. Although Bruce believes that the world-order has not come in its fulness, he says on 2:5:

> the new world-order inaugurated by the enthronement of Christ at the right hand of God, the world-order over which He reigns from that place of exaltation, the world of reality which replaces the preceding world of shadows . . . [10]

Notice Paul in verse 3 says, "how shall we escape, if we neglect *so great a salvation.*" This great salvation was contrasted with the Jewish system, *i.e.,* "the word spoken through angels" (verse 2). Then in verse 5 he talks of "the world to come, *whereof we speak.*" Where did he just *speak* of the "world to come?" In the immediate context he neither speaks of a renovated earth or heaven itself. He did speak, however, of the new order of things on this inhabited earth when he talked of "so great a salvation." This new system was contrasted with the old Jewish system which existed when Christ was not yet crowned King over the world, the inhabited earth. It is this new system Paul was afraid the Hebrew Christians might leave, and he is trying to get them to hold on to it. Under the old system, the earth may have been governed by angels (Da. 10). But in this new system, the inhabited earth is ruled by Christ (Ma. 28:18-20). But in any case, whether the world to come is heaven or the Christian age, premillennialism is left out in the cold.

"ALL THINGS SUBJECTED" (2:8)

"But now we see not yet all things subjected to him."

The above passage is in a context which shows the superiority of Christ over the angels. There are two ways to misunderstand this passage. Premillennialists sometimes say it refers to Jesus, and that Jesus is not now ruling as king, so all things are not yet subjected to him. Notice what Shank writes:

> He whom the Father has "appointed heir of all things" (He. 1:2) now shares the Father's throne in heaven. To him the Father has "subjected the world to come" (He. 2:5), but "we do not yet see everything in subjection to him" (He. 2:8), and shall not *until* . . . Jesus will return to earth in power and glory . . . [11]

Of course, what Paul quotes here in Hebrews 2:8 is from Psalms 8:4ff. And that psalm *seems* exclusively to be speaking of man, not the Son of God. That is another way to abuse the passage. Premillennialists say that only when the earth is made new, in the millennium, will man subdue the earth. But some say the passage talks of mankind and not of the Messiah. Notice what some of the commentators state. Robertson takes it in the sense of the creation subjected to mankind. He says, "Not even today in the wonderful twentieth century with man's triumphs over nature has he reached that goal."[12] Notice Lenski:

> but in the rest of the quotation, in fact, through verse 8 the pronouns refer to "man" and "son of man" without change. The whole ancient Jewish exegetical tradition understood David to refer to "man" and not to the Messiah.[13]

Now the premillennialist will try to make the point that only in the perfect age of the millennium will man fully subjugate the earth. And in that age even the wild beasts will be subject to him. Then they quote Isaiah 11:6-9. Notice:

> And the wolf shall dwell with the lamb, and the leopard shall lie down with the kid; and the calf and the young lion and the fatling together; and a little child shall lead them. And the cow and the bear shall feed; their young ones shall lie down together; and the lion shall eat straw like the ox. . . . They shall not hurt nor destroy *in all my holy mountain* . . . etc.

This is surely a description of things under the reign of the Messiah. But it is not to be taken literally. These events take place in Jehovah's holy *mountain* (v. 9). In Isaiah 2:2 Isaiah, in talking of the establishment of the kingdom, called it the *"mountain* of Jehovah's *house."* Well, what is the house of Jehovah? Paul wrote to Timothy, "but if I tarry long that thou mayest know how men ought to behave themselves in the house of God, which is the church of the living God" (I Ti. 3:15).

So Isaiah 11:6-11 is only talking of the peace and security Christians have in the church. It is symbolized by the harm-lessness of wild beasts. When the Messiah was born the angels sang to the shepherds, "Glory to God in the highest, and on earth *peace* among men in whom he is well pleased" (Luke 2:14). So Paul said of Christ, "For he is our *peace"* (Eph. 2:14).

So we are now in the golden age which Isaiah prophesied about. It was symbolized by the figure of animals in Isaiah 11, and by a lack of warfare in chapter 2, where they beat their swords into plowshares and their spears into pruning-hooks (Is. 2:1-4). Besides, if the passage is really talking of the earth and mankind, it is not ever said to be a renovated earth. It is the earth as it now is. Why should they be allowed to assume that it is a renovated earth?

We believe, with many premillennialists, that the passages (Ps. 8:4ff; He. 2:8) need not be talking of mankind in general, but of the rule of the Messiah. They are wrong, however, when they say that the Messiah, when he rules, will have all things subject to him. First, Jesus now rules the earth. Notice a few passages (emphasis mine, JM):

> All authority hath been given unto me in heaven and on earth (Ma. 28:18).

> The word which he sent unto the children of Israel, preaching good tidings of peace by Jesus Christ (*He is Lord of all*) (Acts 10:36).

> Of whom is Christ as concerning the flesh, *who is over all,* God blessed forever (Ro. 9:5).

> And from Jesus Christ, who is the faithful witness, the firstborn of the dead, and *the ruler of the kings of the earth* (Re. 1:5).

See also, for similar sentiment, the following: Psalms 18:43-44; Psalms 72:11; Ephesians 1:20-22; Philippians 2:9-11;

Luke 6:46; I Peter 3:22; Revelation 17:14; Revelation 19:15; Psalms 2:8-9; Isaiah 42:3; Acts 17:31; and Matthew 25:31-32. So he is now reigning over the earth.

But the premillennialist would question, "How do you explain that some things are not subject to him if he is reigning?" Well, we have showed that Jesus is now reigning as king, but the best commentary on Hebrews 2:8, "But now we see not yet all things subjected to him," is I Corinthians 15:24-27. Notice:

> Then cometh the end when he shall deliver up the kingdom to God, even the Father; when he shall have abolished all rule and all authority and power. For he *must reign, till* he hath put all his enemies under his feet. The last enemy that shall be abolished is *death.* For, He put all things in subjection under his feet.

So to sum up: Yes, Christ is the one spoken of in Hebrews 2:8; yes, he now rules as king; yes, *all things* are not yet subject to him; yes, one of those things not subject to him is "death" (I Co. 15:24-27). Premillennial assumptions wither in the light of the above scriptures. And did you notice that I Corinthians 15:24-27 said Christ would reign *till* his enemies are put under his feet, not *after* they were put under his feet?

"HE . . . SHALL NOT TARRY" (10:37)

"For yet a very little while, He that cometh shall come, and shall not tarry."

Paul tells the Hebrew Christians to have patience, for the coming one will come soon. The passage is probably from Habakkuk 2:3 and Isaiah 26:20. Shank applies it to the "rapture," that supposed coming of Christ in the air to catch the living saints away before the "great tribulation."[14] And he, again, applies it to the end of the age.[15] Hoekema also uses it that way.[16] Boettner also mentions it in that respect, that it is a reference to the second coming of Christ which precedes the millennium.[17] Bruce says on 10:37, "our author, then is dotting the i's and crossing the t's of the Septuagint interpretation when he applies the prophecy to the second coming of Christ."[18] Others disagree with that interpretation.

Notice two commentators, Milligan, then Barnes:

Many say, "To his second personal coming." But this is plainly inconsistent with the scope of the apostle's exhortation, as well as the truth itself. His obvious design in the passage is to encourage the Hebrew brethren to persevere in their begun Christian course, on the ground that the coming of Christ was then near at hand.[19]

Barnes says, "Most probably the idea is, that the Messiah who was coming to destroy Jerusalem, and to overthrow the Jewish power (Ma. 24), would soon do this."[20]

Following are some reasons why we believe the destruction of Jerusalem is under discussion here:

First, the apostle knew that the second coming was not imminent, for he had already told the Thessalonians that it was not at hand, and that a "falling away" had to come first (II Th. 2:1-3).

Second, what comfort from persecution could Hebrew Christians get from the second coming which was at least 1900 years up in the future? How could that give immediate relief?

Third, though not called a "coming" in the sense of the second coming, the destruction of Jersualem was prophesied about (Luke 21:20; Ma. 24:15-22).

But if this arrival is the destruction of Jerusalem, is Max King right when he claims the second coming of Christ is over, having already occurred in the destruction of Jerusalem? No, for there are many passages which teach the second coming has not yet come. For example, notice Revelation 1:7: "Behold, he cometh with the clouds; and every eye shall see him, and they that pierced him; and all the tribes of the earth shall mourn over him. Even so, Amen" (Re. 1:7).

Brother King, where are the clouds at the destruction of Jerusalem? Did *every* eye see him then? Josephus didn't mention it! Did those who pierced him see him then? Did all the tribes then mourn for him? No! And we could multiply passages and problems for Max King's novel view.

Our conviction is that Hebrews 10:37 is not speaking of the rapture or the second coming of Christ. The Lord tarries, but will soon destroy Jerusalem, breaking the back of the Jewish persecution in that area. But lest Max King thinks his position is strengthened because he is right on *one* passage, we alluded to the fact that he is woefully wrong on so many others.

"RECEIVING A KINGDOM" (12:28)

"Wherefore, receiving a kingdom that cannot be shaken, let us have grace, whereby we may offer service well-pleasing to God with reverence and awe."

It is difficult to believe that premillennialists would try to use this passage to support a future kingdom, but some do. Hoyt says,

> The message of the kingdom did not entirely disappear. For God's purpose in this age was to form an aristocracy for the kingdom; the church was to be associated with Christ in ruling and reigning over that kingdom (I Co. 4:8; 6:2; He. 12:28).[21]

But Hebrews 12:28 does not say that saints are associated with Christ in reigning. It says that in the first century they received the kingdom! Let us look further at the passage.

Reasons Why It Does Not Teach A Future Kingdom:

First, this kingdom cannot be shaken, and the church or kingdom we claim has that same characteristic. Notice that the church and the kingdom are used interchangeably in Matthew 16:18-19: "And I also say unto thee, that thou art Peter, and upon this rock I will build my *church;* and the gates of Hades shall not prevail against it. I will give unto thee the keys of the *kingdom . . .*"

The church and the kingdom are the same. The gates of Hades shall not prevail against it (Ma. 16:18), and so it cannot be shaken (He. 12:28). Too, notice that in Hebrews 12:23 Paul says we have come to the church of the firstborn. Then Hebrews 12:28 says we have received the kingdom. If you have come to the church, you have received the kingdom! Both are aspects of the same thing and cannot be destroyed.

Second, "receiving" is a present active participle. The Holy Spirit could have used a future tense had he wanted to, but he used the present. So Paul is telling the Hebrew Christians that they possessed the kingdom in their day.

Third, since the kingdom is present in the first century, premillennialists cannot help their case by saying a "phase" of it existed in the first century. Nowhere does the Bible show that we are to receive the kingdom on the installment plan or in increments.

Fourth, Hebrews 12:28 is in a great group of passages, all of which teach the kingdom as present in the first century. Let us notice a few of them: "Who delivered us out of the power of darkness, and *translated us into the kingdom* of the Son of his love" (Col. 1:13). "To the end that ye should walk worthily of God, *who calleth you into his own kingdom* and glory" (I Th. 2:12). "For the kingdom of God *is* not eating and drinking" (Ro. 14:17). "I John, your brother and *partaker with you in the tribulation of the kingdom"* (Re. 1:9).

So premillennialists cannot take Hebrews 12:28 and other passages which speak of a present kingdom, and apply them to a future kingdom. The kingdom and the church are the same and are unshakeable. The Hebrew Christians came unto the church in the first century, and in doing so received an unshakeable kingdom. Premillennialists cannot say it was present in some form or phase, for the scriptures know nothing about that. And Hebrews 12:28 falls in step with a great body of passages, all of which say the kingdom was present in the first century. So, let premillennialists and dispensationalists give it up, and return the passage back to us so we can speak the message that Christ is on his throne, and that he now reigns over us in his glorious kingdom.

CONCLUSION

What have we seen? First, we have investigated four passages claimed by premillennialists, and have returned them to those who believe that the kingdom is present, and that Christ now rules. We have contended that the "world to come" (He. 2:5) does not speak of a future millennial reign, but talks of the present age, the world of the Messiah which we are now in. We have argued that "not yet [are] all things subjected to him" (He. 2:8) does not speak of a future reign of Christ on the earth, but it speaks of death and Hades not yet subjected to Christ in his present rule. We insisted that "yet a little while, He that cometh shall come" (He. 10:37) does not speak of the imminent second coming, but that it speaks of an act of providence when Jesus will destroy Jerusalem. Finally, we have put Hebrews 12:28 back in with those passages which speak of the kingdom as present. That is where it belongs.

All in all, the book of Hebrews presents many problems to the premillennialists, and offers them no comfort at all. It is a valuable book for what it teaches, but isn't it also a grand book for what it refutes!

ENDNOTES

1. Robert Shank, *Until* (Springfield: Westcott Publishers, 1982), p. 445.

2. Robert Milligan, *Commentary on Hebrews* (Delight: Gospel Light Publishing Company, n.d.), p. 84.

3. R.C.H. Lenski, *The Interpretation of the Epistle to the Hebrews and the Epistle of James* (Minneapolis: Augsburg Publishing House, 1966), pp. 71-72.

4. W. E. Vine, *An Expository Dictionary of New Testament Words*, 4 vols. (Old Tappan: Fleming H. Revell Company, 1940), 2:13.

5. *Dictionary of New Testament Theology*, s.v. "Earth," by Otto Flender.

6. W. F. Arndt and F. W. Gingrich, *A Greek-English Lexicon of the New Testament and Other Early Christian Literature* (Chicago: The University of Chicago Press, 1957), pp. 563-564.

7. Joseph Henry Thayer, *Greek-English Lexicon of the New Testament* (Grand Rapids: Zondervan Publishing House, 1962), p. 442.

8. A. T. Robertson, *Word Pictures in the New Testament*, 6 vols. (Nashville: Broadman Press, 1931), 5:344.

9. Albert Barnes, *Notes on the New Testament*, (Grand Rapids: Baker Book House, 1949), p. 58.

10. F. F. Bruce, *The New International Commentary on the New Testament, The Epistle to the Hebrews* (Grand Rapids: Wm. B. Eerdmans Publishing Co., 1964), p. 33.

11. Shank, *Until*, p. 24.

12. Robertson, *Word Pictures*, 5:345.

13. Lenski, *The Epistle to the Hebrews*, p. 75.

14. Shank, *Until*, p. 337.

15. *Ibid.*, p. 392.

16. Anthony A. Hoekema, *The Bible and the Future* (Grand Rapids: Wm. B. Eerdmans Publishing Company, 1979), p. 126.

17. Loraine Boettner, *The Millennium* (Grand Rapids: Baker Book House, 1957), p. 248.

18. Bruce, *Epistle to the Hebrews*, p. 273.

19. Milligan, *Commentary on Hebrews*, pp. 292-293.

20. Barnes, *Notes*, pp. 246-247.

21. Herman A. Hoyt, "Dispensational Premillennialism," in *The Meaning of the Millennium*, ed. Robert G. Clouse (Downers Grove: InterVarsity Press, 1977), p. 90.

ANSWERING FALSE DOCTRINES RELATING TO HEBREWS
No. II

HEBREWS 2:11; 12:14; 13:12	IS SANCTIFICATION A SECOND WORK OF GRACE OR A SECOND BLESSING?
HEBREWS 4:9	IS THE SABBATH LAW STILL BINDING?
HEBREWS 10:38 - 11:40	IS SALVATION BY FAITH ONLY?
HEBREWS 7:11-17	DOES THE MORMON PRIESTHOOD DESCEND FROM AARON AND/OR MELCHIZEDEK?

By FRANK MORGAN

Born 1934, attended high school in Spiro, Oklahoma. Married Jacqueline Sue Hayes in 1952. Attended college at Eastern Oklahoma A & M and Harding College. Has worked with churches in Arkansas and Texas. Presently serves as local evangelist with West Side church in Muskogree, Oklahoma. Writes for brotherhood papers, weekly articles for local newspaper. Has done radio preaching. Meetings in Arkansas, Oklahoma, Texas, Kentucky, California and Virginia.

INTRODUCTION

Jesus warned, "Beware of false prophets" (Ma. 7:15). No doubt, the reason for such warning was, and still is, that false teachers "deceive many" (Ma. 24:11), and "seduce, if it were possible, even the elect" (Mark 13:22).

Unfortunately, all of the false prophets/teachers with whom we have to contend are not outside of the church, nor has it ever been so. Paul's difficulties with false brethren are documented in II Corinthians 11:26 and Galatians 2:4. The apostle did not give "place by subjection, no not for an hour; that the truth of the gospel might continue" (Ga. 2:5), and neither should we.

By inspiration, no doubt, Peter was able to see what many seem to deny; that the active presence of false teachers would continue, and that the end result of their work would be destruction, and that "many shall follow their pernicious ways; by reason of whom the way of truth shall be evil spoken of" (II Pe. 2:1-2). We must take seriously, therefore, the admonition of John: "Beloved, believe not every spirit, but try the spirits whether they are of God: because many false prophets are gone out in the world" (I John 4:1).[1]

IS SANCTIFICATION A SECOND WORK OF GRACE OR A SECOND BLESSING?

In brief, the idea of sanctification's being the result or the product of "a second work of grace" or "a second blessing" arises out of the theology "that man by nature is depraved," and "that regeneration begins the process of cleansing, but . . . does not complete it."[1] The Book of Discipline of The United Methodist Church states:

> Original sin standeth not in the following of Adam, but it is the corruption of the nature of every man, that naturally is engendered of the offspring of Adam, whereby man is very far gone from original righteousness, and of his own nature inclined to evil, and that continually.[2]

It is then explained that "Sanctification is that renewal of our fallen nature by the Holy Ghost . . . whereby we . . . are enabled, through grace, to love God with all our hearts and to walk in his holy commandments blameless."[3] Again,

> We believe sanctification is the work of God's grace through the Word and the Spirit, by which those who have been born again are cleansed from sin . . . and are enabled to live in accordance with God's will . . .[4]

In summary these examples set forth the proposition that sanctification follows regeneration, or being born again, and that it is an act of God's grace by which one already regenerated, or born again, is finally set free from the natural inclination to evil and empowered to "walk in his holy commandments blameless." I confidently affirm this doctrine to be false. Having so affirmed I shall seek to prove the same as we review the passages assigned for this discussion.

It is needful just here that we define the term sanctification. Vine says it "is used of (a) separation to God; (b) the course of life befitting those so separated."[5] Thayer says it means to "render or declare sacred or holy, consecrate . . . to separate from things profane and dedicate to God."[6]

In support of these definitions we refer to Paul when he said, "this is the will of God, even your sanctification, that ye should abstain from fornication" (I Th. 4:3), and "God hath not called us unto uncleanness, but unto holiness." He therefore that despiseth, despiseth not man, but God" (I Th. 4:7-8). Here the word holiness is translated from the same word rendered sanctification in I Thessalonians 4:3, and means the same thing. With this in mind we shall consider the designated passages.

Hebrews 2:11:

"He that sanctifieth" refers to Christ (cf. 9:13-14; 10:10). "They who are sanctified" denotes those referred to as his brethren in the context (cf. verses 11, 12 and 17). We have only to refer to Matthew 12:48-50 to learn who were, and still are, his brethren. "Are all of one" seems to me to refer to the "flesh and blood" of verse 14. When "he that sanctifieth," who is Christ, "was the Word, and the Word was with God, and the Word was God" (John 1:1), he was not "of us" with "they who are [or might become — FM] sanctified." Not until "the Word was made flesh, and dwelt among us" (John 1:14), and was "made like unto his brethren" (He. 2:17), able to suffer and be tempted (He. 2:18) "like as we are" (He. 4:15), could "both he that sanctifieth and they who are sanctified" be "all of one."

Hebrews 12:14:

"Holiness" is translated from the Greek *hagiasmos* which is rendered "holiness" five times (here and in Ro. 6:19, 22; I Th. 4:7; I Ti. 2:15), and sanctification five times (I Co. 1:30; I Th. 4:3-4; II Th. 2:13; I Pe. 1:2). "Follow" holiness/sanctification denotes something we do, not something done to us (cf.

Ro. 6:19, 22). To do so is essential to seeing the Lord (cf. Ma. 5:8).

Hebrews 13:12:

Jesus is the sanctifier. "His own blood," shed when he "suffered without the gate" is both the means and the element whereby "he might sanctify the people" (cf. He. 9:13-14; 10:10, 29).

From these observations we draw the following conclusions:

Since the concept of "original sin" or "inherited sin" is itself false (Eze. 18:20), sanctification cannot relate to the removal of such a depraved nature.

Since sanctification is by the blood of Christ (He. 13:12), his blood was shed in his death (John 19:34) and we are "baptized into his death" (Ro. 6:3), man is, therefore, sanctified (separated from things profane, dedicated to God and set upon the course of life befitting those so separated) when he is baptized according to the scriptures.

Sanctification has no inherent enabling power such as would enable the sanctified "to live in accordance with God's will" or "to walk in his holy commandments blameless." It is instead a course of life unto which one is called (I Th. 4:7), to which one must personally yield (Rom. 6:19) and after which one must consciously follow (He. 9:13-14; 12:14).

IS THE SABBATH LAW STILL BINDING?

The Seventh-Day Adventists are, I suppose, the foremost proponents of keeping and recognizing the seventh day of the week (Saturday) as a holy day, and of binding the Sabbath Law as recorded in Old Testament scriptures upon people today, besides the Jews themselves.

The law regarding the Sabbath day is found in Exodus 20:8-11. Of this law it is said by some: "The law of God still remains in force. That law requires the observance of the seventh day of the week."[7]

Though I am not aware of any direct statements using Hebrews 4:9 as a proof-text for sabbath keeping, there probably are some. I do find in Mr. Haynes' book, quoted in the preceeding paragraph, a statement on page 16 as follows:

> Sabbath means rest. It was given not merely for physical rest but as a sign of spiritual rest and deliverance from sin. Hence he who keeps the Sabbath understandingly has entered into the rest of God, and 'he that is entered into his rest, he also hath ceased from his own works, as God did from his' (He. 4:10).

This would certainly indicate that author's conviction that the "rest" of verse 9 refers to Sabbath Day keeping. Such, we declare, is a gross misunderstanding of the passage, and any such doctrine is, therefore, false. In attempting to prove that Hebrews 4:9 does not teach Sabbath Day keeping or the binding of the Sabbath Day Law we must go back to the writings of Moses and come forward to the Hebrews text. To the children of Israel Moses wrote saying:

> For ye are not as yet come to the rest and to the inheritance, which the Lord your God giveth you. But when ye go over Jordan, and dwell in the land which the Lord your God giveth you to inherit, and when he giveth you rest from all your enemies round about, so that ye dwell in safety; Then there shall be a place which the Lord your God shall choose to cause his name to dwell there . . .(De. 12: 9-11; cf. Jos. 1:14-15; 21:43-45; 22:4; 23:1).

Clearly, the promised rest (v. 9) was from their enemies (v. 10), and was to be enjoyed when they had crossed over Jordan to dwell in the land God was to give them as an inheritance. But something went wrong! David summarizes the problem in Psalms 95:8-11. The Hebrews writer quotes David in 3:7-11, further explaining:

> But with whom was he grieved forty years? was it not with them that had sinned, whose carcases fell in the wilderness? And to whom sware he that they should not enter into his rest, but to them that believed not? So we see that they could not enter in because of unbelief (He. 3:17-19).

This bit of history becomes relevant in view of a continuing promise of "rest to the people of God" (He. 4:1, 9) which they, too, may "come short of . . . after the same example of unbelief" (He. 4:1, 11). The question is, "What is the promised "rest" of Hebrews 4:1, 9?" Is it Sabbath Day rest according to the law given through Moses, or is it something else? As already indicated, I believe it is something else for the following reasons.

First, the "rest" of Hebrews 3:11, 18, is "a shadow of good things to come" (He. 10:1), while the "rest" of Hebrews 4:1, 3,

9, 11 is "the very image [or exact reality — FM] of the things" foreshadowed (He. 10:1). Since the shadow does not refer to the Sabbath Day rest nor the law establishing it, neither does the "very image."

Second, the "rest" of Hebrews 3:11, 18 — the shadow — clearly refers to a condition to have been enjoyed by Israel in the promised land of inheritance (De. 12:9-10). The "very image" would, therefore, have to include a similar condition and a similar inheritance.

Third, it is important to notice that the "shadow" rest of Hebrews 3 and Deuteronomy 12 was to come in conjunction with the inheritance, not before. Harmony would demand the same of the "rest" of Hebrews 4:9.

Fourth, today "the people of God" (He. 4:9) anticipate a similar, yet far superior, inheritance (cf. Acts 20:32; Ep. 1:11; Col. 1:12; 3:24; He. 9:15; I Pe. 1:3-5).

Fifth, today "we which have believed" (He. 4:3) anticipate a similar, yet far superior, "rest" in conjunction with our inheritance. Israel's "rest" was to be from their enemies (De. 12:10; Jos. 21:44). Our "rest" is to be like that of God who rested "from all his works" (He. 4:4-5; Ge. 2:2; Rev. 14:13). The Greek word translated "rest" in Hebrews 4:9 is *sabbatismos* meaning "keeping sabbath"[8] or "a sabbath keeping,"[9] and denotes, not the day of rest, but rather the type of rest to be enjoyed.

IS SALVATION BY FAITH ONLY?

In Hebrews 10:38 the scripture says, "Now the just shall live by faith." As is well known, some religionists seize upon all such statements in a vain attempt to prove the false doctrine that salvation comes by faith only. Thus, the following statements from a selection of denominational creed and discipline books: "We believe the scriptures teach that . . . justification . . . is bestowed, not in consideration of any works of righteousness which we have done, but solely through faith in Christ . . ."[10] "Faith, thus receiving and resting on Christ and his righteousness, is the alone instrument of justification."[11] "Wherefore, that we are justified by faith only is a most wholesome doctrine, and very full of comfort."[12]

Of course, the people and churches who espouse these statements do not like the language of James 2:24 because it once-and-for-all destroys the aforementioned position. However, James 2:24 is in the Bible, has always been there, will always be there and should settle the question for all time. In support of James are the examples cited in Hebrews 11. Consider two of these for additional study.

In Hebrews 11:4 we read, "By faith Abel offered unto God a more excellent sacrifice than Cain, by which he obtained witness that he was righteous, God testifying of his gifts." Now observe: Abel had faith, and Abel worked in that he offered a sacrifice. "By which," note it carefully, "he obtained witness that he was righteous." God is obviously the one who witnessed that Abel was righteous. On what grounds did God witness that Abel was righteous? The scripture says, "God testifying of his gifts." God, then, testified that Abel was righteous on the basis of his "excellent sacrifice" (his work) offered "by faith," and James 2:24 is proven true.

In Hebrews 11:7 we read:

> By faith Noah, being warned of God of things not seen as yet, moved with fear, prepared an ark to the saving of his house; by the which he condemned the world, and became heir of the righteousness which is by faith.

Observe: Noah had faith, and Noah worked in that he prepared an ark. The result was "to the saving of his house." Was the saving of Noah's house the result of his faith only, apart from any work of righteousness which he did? Peter said Noah prepared an ark "wherein few, that is, eight souls were saved by water" (I Pe. 3:21). If anyone can get Noah and his family saved without the ark, then they can get them saved by faith only without works. Otherwise, James 2:24 stands firm and true.

The fact is that faith is made perfect by works (Ja. 2:22), as is evidenced in every example in Hebrews 11 and elsewhere in the Bible.

DOES THE MORMON PRIESTHOOD DESCEND FROM
AARON AND/OR MELCHIZEDEK?

Mormonism says, "There are, in the church, two priest-hoods, namely, the Melchizedek and Aaronic."[13] Much stress is laid on apostolic succession as the basis of authority and priesthood by Mormons. Since the basic view of Mormonism is that apostolic succession was broken when the church went into apostasy in the middle ages, it was necessary for apostolic authority to be conferred anew. Joseph Smith, founder of the Mormon Church, related how he and another of the early Mormon leaders, Oliver Cowdery, supposedly received priest-hood authority on May 15, 1829. He claimed that John the Baptist descended from heaven and conferred on him and his friend, Cowdery, the Priesthood of Aaron, and ordained them saying:

> Upon you my fellow servants, in the name of Messiah, I confer the Priesthood of Aaron, which holds the keys of the ministering of angels, and of the gospel of repentance, and of baptism by immersion.[14]

Smith further said that at the time of the bestowal of the Aaronic Priesthood, he and Cowdery were promised the Melchizedek Priesthood, the keys to which were held by Peter, James and John.[15] "The Mormon Apostle LeGrand Richards admitted that the exact date of this ordination is not known: 'we do NOT have the date that Peter, James and John conferred the Melchizedek Priesthood upon them'."[16] *The Doctrine and Covenants* is cited as proof that the Melchizedek Priesthood was conferred at a very early date: "And also with Peter, and James, and John, whom I have sent unto you, by whom I have ordained you and confirmed you to be apostles . . ." (27:12). Since this statement did not appear in the "revelation" when it was published in the Book of Commandments in 1833, it would seem to have been added at a later date; a practice that is very convenient for anyone who believes in and practices continuing revelation. Regardless, it can be demonstrated from the Bible that the claims of the Mormon Church to the Aaronic and/or Melchizedek Priest-hoods are false and must be rejected.

First, the Aaronic or Levitical Priesthood, and the law establishing it, has been changed (He. 7:11-12). The change in the priesthood is from "the order of Aaron" (Ex. 28:1; Nu. 18:1-5), to the priesthood of all "people of God" (I Pe. 2:9-10; Rev. 1:6). The change in the law is reviewed in Hebrews 7:18-19. The "better hope" which replaced the disannuled commandment/law that "made nothing perfect" must surely be the same as the "better testament" of 7:22. It is called a "better covenant which was established upon better promises" (He. 8:6). Both the first and the second are further reviewed in Hebrews 8:7-13.

Second, none can doubt that the order of the Priesthood of Melchizedek was passed unto Jesus Christ (He. 5:5-6, 10). In Hebrews 3:1 we are admonished to "consider the Apostle and High Priest of our profession, Christ Jesus." When we do we observe that he:

1. Is able to "make reconciliation for the sins of the people" and "to succor them that are tempted" (He. 2:17-18; 4:15).

2. Is "over his own house, whose house are we" (He. 3:6).

3. Is entered within the veil as a forerunner for us (He. 6:17-20; 4:14; 9:11-12, 24).

4. Is "made . . . after the power of an endless life" and is "unchangeable" (He. 5:6; 6:20; 7:15-17, 21, 24, 25).

5. Is "able also to save them to the uttermost that come to God by him" (He. 7:25).

6. Is "holy, harmless, undefiled, separate from sinners, and made higher than the heavens" (He. 7:26).

7. Is once offered for the people's sins (He. 7:27; 9:25-26, 28).

8. Is "consecrated for evermore" by an oath of God (He. 7:21, 28).

Can any Mormon lay claim to even one of these characteristics? If not, and they cannot, then they should forevermore cease to insult our intelligence and heaven's host by attempting to place themselves into such an exalted position as is reserved for the Lord Jesus Christ, and none other!

ENDNOTES

1. John McClintock and James Strong, *Cyclopedia of Biblical, Theological and Ecclesiastical Literature* (Grand Rapids, MI: Baker Book House, 1968), vol. IX, p. 333.

2. *The Book of Discipline of the United Methodist Church,* "The Articles of Religion of the Methodist Church" (1784), Article VII, p. 56.

3. *Ibid.,* p. 62.

4. *Ibid.,* p. 65.

5. W. E. Vine, *An Expository Dictionary of New Testament Words* (Westwood, NJ: Fleming H. Revell Co., 1966), p. 317.

6. Joseph Henry Thayer, *Greek-English Lexicon of the New Testament* (New York, NY: American Book Co., 1889), p. 6.

7. Carlyle B. Haynes, *From Sabbath to Sunday* (Washington, DC: Herald Publishing Assoc.), p. 11.

8. Vine, *op. cit.,* p. 288.

9. Thayer, *op. cit.,* p. 565.

10. Edward T. Hiscox, *The Standard Manual for Baptist Churches* (1951), p. 62.

11. *The Confession of Faith of the Presbyterian Church* (John Knox Press, rev. ed.), pp. 78-79.

12. *Discipline of the Methodist Church* (Nashville, TN: Methodist Publishing House, 1960), p. 32.

13. *The Doctrine and Covenants* (Salt Lake City, UT: The Church of Jesus Christ of Latterday Saints, 1952), 107:1-3, 5, pp. 191-192.

14. *The Pearl of Great Price* (Salt Lake City, UT: The Church of Jesus Christ of Latterday Saints, 1952), 2:69-71, p. 56.

15. *Ibid.,* 2:72, p. 56.

16. Jerald and Sandra Tanner, *Mormonism — Shadow or Reality?* (enlarged ed., 1972), p. 180.

ANSWERING FALSE DOCTRINES RELATING TO HEBREWS

No. III

HEBREWS 2:6-9	JESUS MERELY HUMAN, A CREATURE
HEBREWS 10:22	SPRINKLING FOR BAPTISM
HEBREWS 13:4	"ALL" INCLUDES ADULTEROUS AND HOMO-SEXUAL MARRIAGES

By JAMES MEADOWS

Born in 1930, Cuba, KY. Attended Freed-Hardeman College, Harding Graduate School and Union University. Has been preaching since 1953. Has worked with local churches in Kentucky, Tennessee and South Carolina. Has written 25 books for classroom work. Author of Senior Quarterly for *Gospel Advocate*, 1980-82. Writes for several gospel papers. Frequent speaker on major lecture programs. Presently engaged in full-time gospel meeting and lectureship preaching. Speaker, *First Annual Denton Lectures*.

INTRODUCTION

In every age there have always been those that misused the scriptures to uphold false doctrines. Satan, the master of all such, set the example by misusing the scriptures in leading Adam and Eve away from God (Ge. 3:1-6). At the time of our Lord's temptation Satan quoted scripture and tried to lead the Lord astray by misapplying them (Ma. 4:1-11).

Peter wrote that some people "wrest" the scriptures unto their own destruction (II Pe. 3:16). "Wrest" means ". . . to twist, to torture (from *streble*, a wrench or instrument of torture, and akin to *strepho*), is used metaphorically in II Pe. 3:16, of wresting the scriptures on the part of the ignorant and unsteadfast."[1] "It is used here of those who twist the scriptures from their intended purpose in order to make them teach things never intended by the sacred writers."[2]

Who are some people that twist, pervert, and misuse the scriptures? *First,* Peter says those that are "unlearned" (ignorant) and "unstable" twist the scriptures (II Pe. 3:16b). *Second,* some twist the scriptures when they are trying to keep their "time-honored" traditions going (Ma. 15:1-9). *Third,* there are those that are trying to deceive the hearts of the simple (Ro. 16:17-18). *Fourth,* some are trying to preach what people want to hear (II Ti. 4:1-5). *Fifth* are those that are making merchandise of the souls of men (II Pe. 2:3). *Sixth,* some people have no real love for the truth (II Th. 2:10-12).

The theme of this lectureship is "Studies in Hebrews" and this particular lecture will discuss some false doctrines based on certain passages in Hebrews.

JESUS MERELY HUMAN, A CREATURE (2:6-9)

But one in a certain place testified, saying, What is man, that thou art mindful of him? or the son of man, that thou visitest him? Thou madest him a little lower than the angels; thou crownedst him with glory and honor, and didst set him over the works of thy hands: Thou hast put all things in subjection under his feet. For in that he put all in subjection under him, he left nothing that is not put under him. But now we see not yet all things put under him. But we see Jesus, who was made a little lower than the angels for the suffering of death, crowned with glory and honour; that he by the grace of God should taste death for every man (He. 2:6-9).

Psalms 8 clearly sets forth the exalted position of man. The Psalmist contemplated the greatness of God's creation and was amazed that man, who was made a little lower than the angels, had been exalted so highly. But in consequence of sin man, to a great extent, lost his high position, and there was no hope of regaining it on his own.

The leading thought of Hebrews 2 is Christ's *oneness* with us. The Hebrew writer quotes Psalms 8 and shows that Jesus himself "was made a little lower than the angels" (He. 2:9a).

For verily he took not on him the nature of angels; but he took on
him the seed of Abraham. Wherefore in all things it behoved him to
be made like unto his brethren, that he might be a merciful and
faithful high priest . . . (He. 2:16-17a).

It "was necessary that he too should, as a man, be made 'a little
lower than the angels.' For otherwise, indeed, he would not be
a man. . . ."³ Christ assumed our nature that through his sufferings and varied experience, he might himself be made
perfect as our high priest and mediator (He. 4:14-16; 5:8-9).

As a man Christ lived above sin (He. 4:15; II Co. 5:21), died
on the cross and was ". . . crowned with glory and honour
. . ." (He. 2:9a). Since Christ, the one that "sanctifieth" (He.
2:11) and Christians, ". . . they who are sanctified are all of
one . . ." (He. 2:11b), then what Christ enjoys Christians
enjoy. Thus through Christ man may once again be exalted to
the position that God intended him to have.

The charge that Jesus was merely a man, and not Deity, is
shown to be false in a number of ways. *First,* Jesus did not
forfeit Deity when he became man. If Satan or some other
force had imposed humanity on the Lord then he would have
surrendered his Deity, but he took the nature of man by his
own choice.

Let this mind be in you, which was also in Christ Jesus: Who, being
in the form of God, thought it not robbery to be equal with God: But
made himself of no reputation, and took upon him the form of a servant, and was made in the likeness of man: and being found in
fashion as a man . . . (Ph. 2:5-8a).

Hence, "being in the form of God," describes our Lord's essential, and therefore, eternal, being in the true nature of God;
while the "taking on Him the form of a servant" similarly
refers to his voluntary assumption of the true nature of man.

Second, "In Isaiah 7:14 the prophet declared that the
virgin would conceive, bear a son, and that his name would be
called 'Immanuel,' which means *God is with us!* This prophecy
was fulfilled in the birth of Christ (cf.: Ma. 1:22-23). Subsequently, Isaiah referred to this Son as 'Mighty God' (9:6). In
fact, in the year that King Uzziah died, Isaiah saw 'the Lord'
sitting upon a throne (cf.: Is. 6:1ff); overpowered by the scene,
the prophet exclaimed: 'Woe is me . . . mine eyes have seen
the King, Jehovah of hosts' (6:5). In the New Testament, we

are informed that: 'These things said Isaiah, because he saw his (Christ's) glory' (cf.: John 12:36-41)."[4]

Third, the rich young ruler called Jesus "Good Master" (Ma. 19:16). Jesus said: "Why callest thou me good? there is none good, but one, that is God . . ." (Ma. 19:17). Some say that Jesus was denying Godhood, but he was actually asserting it. He knew that he was God, but he also knew that the young ruler was not recognizing the significance of what he was saying. "Do you know the meaning of this word you apply to me and which you use so freely? There is none good save God; if you apply that term to me, and you understand what you mean, you affirm that I am God."[5]

Fourth, Jesus forgave sins which is a prerogative of God alone (Mark 2:5-7). Worship is due only to God (Ma. 4:10), yet Jesus accepted the worship of men (John 9:38).

Fifth, there are a number of scriptures in which Jesus claimed Deity or equality with God (Ma. 26:63-66; John 5:17-20; 8:56-59; 10:30-36; 17:5; 19:7), and a number of scriptures in which he is called God (John 1:1; 20:28; Col. 1:15; He. 1:8-9).

SPRINKLING FOR BAPTISM (10:22)

Having therefore, brethren, boldness to enter into the holiest by the blood of Jesus, By a new and living way, which he hath consecrated for us, through the veil, that is to say, his flesh; And having an high priest over the house of God; Let us draw near with a true heart in full assurance of faith, having our hearts sprinkled from an evil conscience, and our bodies washed with pure water (He. 10:19-22).

Arguments For Sprinkling

Hebrews 10:22; Ezekiel 36:25 and Isaiah 52:13-15 are verses that are often used to prove that sprinkling is baptism. The Methodist Discipline reads: "Let every adult person and the parents of every child to be baptized, have the choice of sprinkling, pouring or immersion."[6] The Catholic Church states that, "Baptism may be validly administered in either of three ways, *viz.* by *immersion,* or by plunging the candidate into the water; by *infusion,* or by pouring the water; and by *aspersion,* or sprinkling."[7]

The Teachings of Hebrews 10:22:

Under the law of Moses when the Israelites were ceremonially polluted, they were to be cleansed by sprinkling with the water of separation. A red heifer without spot or blemish (Nu. 19:1-2) was to be burned and the ashes were to be laid up ". . . without the camp in a clean place, and it shall be kept for the congregation of the children of Israel for a water of separation: it is a purification for sin" (Nu. 19:9). The water of separation consisted of a mixture of the ashes of the heifer and pure water (Nu. 19:17) and was to be sprinkled on an unclean person (Nu. 19:13). The blood of bulls and goats could not take away sins (He. 10:1-2, 4). On the day of atonement each year all the sins an individual had ever committed were remembered and atonement had to be made (Le. 16:1-34), thus the conscience was never free from the distress and burden of sin.

". . . but the sprinkling or cleansing here recommended is not of the body from ceremonial pollution, but of the soul from the guilt and distress of an accusing conscience."[8] "Perfect passive participle of *rantizo* with the accusative retained in the passive, an evident allusion to the sprinkling in the old tabernacle (9:18-22) and the shedding of Christ's blood for the cleansing of our consciences (10:1-4)."[9] The sprinkling in the New Testament is the sprinkling of the blood of Christ. That which is to be sprinkled is the heart; and it is to be sprinkled from an evil conscience by the blood of Christ. The sprinkling of the blood of Christ then refers to the remission of sins which a person receives at the time of his baptism into Christ (Mark 16:16; Acts 2:38).

Why Sprinkling Cannot Be An Acceptable Act For Baptism:

First,

the first law of sprinkling was obtained in the following manner: Pope Stephen II, being driven from Rome by Adolphus, King of the Lombards, in 753, fled to Pepin, who, a short time before, had usurped the crown of France. Whilst he remained there, the monks of Cressy, in Britany, consulted him whether, in the case of necessity, baptism poured on the head of an infant would be lawful. Stephen replied that it would. But the truth of this fact be allowed — which, however, some Catholics deny — yet pouring or sprinkling was admitted only in cases of necessity. It was not until 1311 that the legislature, in a council held at Ravenna, declared immersion or sprinkling to be indifferent."[10]

Second, the word sprinkling (and related expressions) appears sixty-one times in the Bible. Pure water, unmixed with other matters, was never sprinkled upon anybody, at any time, for any purpose. Furthermore, when the water of separation was sprinkled upon an individual it was for the purpose of cleansing him (Is. 52:13-15; Ez. 36:25), not because he was already clean as taught by those that practice sprinkling today.

Third, the actual meaning of baptism proves that sprinkling cannot be an acceptable act for baptism. There are three different words in the Hebrew, Greek and English languages for the three different acts of pouring, sprinkling and dipping. Moses, in connection with the work of the priest under the Old Testament, used these three words, and made a distinction between each one.

> And the priest shall take some of the log of oil, and *pour* it into the palm of his own left hand: and the priest shall *dip* his right finger in the oil that is in his left hand, and shall *sprinkle* of the oil with his finger seven times before the Lord (Le. 14:15-16).

Approximately two hundred eighty years before Christ, the Hebrew Old Testament was translated into the Greek language in Alexandria, Egypt. When the words in Leviticus 14:15-16 were translated, *pour* was represented by the word *keo*, *dip* by the word *baptidzo*, and *sprinkle* by the word *rantidzo*. When the word baptism is mentioned in the New Testament, the word *baptidzo* is used, and never the words that mean to sprinkle or pour.

Fourth, there is no mention in the New Testament of baptism being used in connection with sprinkling or pouring. The first mention of pouring for baptism is found in an uninspired work of the second century called *The Didache*. The author is unknown; and since it is uninspired, it does not carry the authority of God with it. Even the Catholic Church admits that "for several centuries after the establishment of Christianity Baptism was *usually* conferred by immersion; but since the twelfth century the practice of baptizing by infusion has prevailed in the Catholic Church as this manner is attended with less inconvenience than Baptism by immersion."[11]

Fifth, many Bible verses clearly teach that baptism is a

burial. John the Baptist baptized ". . . in Aenon near to Salim, because there was much water there . . ." (John 3:23). When Philip baptized the eunuch they ". . . went down both into the water; both Philip and the eunuch; and he baptized him. And when they were come up out of the water . . ." (Acts 8:38, 39a). "Know ye not, that so many of us as were baptized into Jesus Christ were baptized into his death? Therefore we are buried with him by baptism into death . . ." (Ro. 6:3). "Buried with him in baptism, wherein also ye are risen with him through the faith of the operation of God, who hath raised him from the dead" (Col. 2:12).

"ALL" INCLUDES ADULTEROUS AND HOMOSEXUAL MARRIAGES (13:4)

"Marriage is honourable in all, and the bed undefiled: but whoremongers and adulterers God will judge" (He. 13:4).

What Hebrews 13:4 Teaches:

The American Standard Version reads: "Let marriage be had in honor among all, and let the bed be undefiled: for fornicators and adulterers God will judge." The institution of marriage is as old as the family of man. It is honorable, for God instituted it for man in the garden of Eden, knowing that it is not good for man to be alone (Ge. 2:18-24). Christ honored marriage with his presence and first miracle at Cana of Galilee (John 2:1-11). Marriage is honorable as a means to prevent fornication and a defiled bed (I Co. 7:1-5). The honor of marriage is never to be defiled by fornication and adultery, because God will bring all such into judgment and just punishment will follow. Thus the institution of marriage is by *all means* and in *all respects* honorable, but not all marriages are honorable and approved by God.

What Hebrews 13:4 Does Not Teach:

First, it does not teach the doctrine of the Essenes "who held marriage in little repute, totally abstained from it themselves as a state of comparative imperfection."[12]

Second, it does not uphold the doctrine of the Catholic Church that celibacy is a purer and more holy state. James Cardinal Gibbons wrote: "Our Savior and His Apostles,

though recognizing matrimony as a holy state, have proclaimed the superior merits of voluntary continency, particularly for
those who consecrate their lives to the sacred ministry."[13]

Third, it does not lend support to all the views that are being
taught about marriage today. Jim E. Waldron sets forth some
of these views under the following heads: (1) The divorced
fornicator is also free to remarry; (2) Christ's law doesn't even
apply to non-Christians; (3) a believer deserted by an
unbeliever is free to marry another; (4) baptism sanctifies an
adulterous marriage; (5) adultery is a one-time act in the
'consummation' of an adulterous marriage, and succeeding
similar acts are sanctified because of the new 'marriage;' (6)
the legal acts of divorce and remarriage equal adultery, and are
one time actions, thus the resulting marriage itself is not
sinful."[14]

Jesus Christ allows divorce and remarriage on the ground
of fornication.

> The Pharisees also came unto him, tempting him, and saying unto
> him, Is it lawful for a man to put away his wife for every cause? And
> he answered and said unto them, Have ye not read, that he which
> made them at the beginning made them male and female, and said,
> For this cause shall a man leave father and mother, and shall cleave
> to his wife: and they twain shall be one flesh? Wherefore they are no
> more twain, but one flesh. What therefore God hath joined together,
> let not man put asunder. They say unto him, Why did Moses then
> command to give a writing of divorcement, and to put her away?
> He saith unto them, Moses because of the hardness of your hearts
> suffered you to put away your wives: but from the beginning it was
> not so. And I say unto you, Whosoever shall put away his wife, ex-
> cept it be for fornication, and shall marry another, committeth
> adultery: and whoso marrieth her which is put away doth commit
> adultery (Ma. 19:3-9).

The word "except" introduces a condition which sets aside the
rule which has been given elsewhere. Language means nothing
if this is not an exception. "Committeth" indicates a continu-
ance of the action described. "Thus the expression
'committeth adultery' would indicate that such activities are
continued during the time these people remained married"
(William Woodson). Colossians 3:5-7 clearly states that one
can live in adultery despite the claim of some that it is a one-
time act.

Fourth, Hebrews 13:4 does not sanction homosexual marriages as some are now contending. The Hebrews writer condemns heterosexual immorality.

> Does his silence concerning homosexual relations imply ignorance of such things, unconcern about them, or their tacit inclusion under 'marriage'? He could not have been ignorant of something so common in the Greco-Roman world. He could hardly remain silent because of unconcern; in such a case he would certainly have had to state that homosexuality was of no moral significance. And we have no reason to assume that *gamos* (marriage) could have been understood by his readers to include a same-sex union."[15]

The Bible makes it very clear that *men* and *women* are to marry (Ge. 2:18-24; I Co. 7:2; Ma. 19:5; Ep. 5:22-33), but it no where speaks of a "same-sex union." The idea of homosexual marriages is a misuse of the Biblical use of the term marriage.

Fifth, homosexual marriages are a sin because homosexuality is a sin. Sexual perversity on the part of the men of Sodom led to that city's destruction. Two angels came to Lot's house and

> before they lay down, the men of the city, even the men of Sodom, compassed the house round, both old and young, all the people from every quarter: and they called unto Lot, and said unto him, Where are the men which came in to thee this night? Bring them out unto us, that we may know them. And Lot went out at the door unto them, and shut the door after him, And said, I pray you, brethren, do not so wickedly (Ge. 19:4-7).

First, the terms "sodomite" and "homosexual" across the centuries have been synonymous. *Second,* the men of Sodom wanted Lot's visitors brought out "that we may know them." The word *know* (He. *yada;* Grk. *ginosho)* is sometimes used as a euphemism for "to have sexual relations with."[16] Genesis 4:1 says Adam *"knew"* Eve his wife; and she conceived." Joseph *knew* not Mary until after she had given birth to Jesus (Ma. 1:25). The men of Sodom clearly wanted to engage in homosexual activities. Lot knew their design and begged them to "do not so *wickedly.*" The Lord said their sin was "very grievous" (Ge. 18:20). *Third,* Isaiah denounced those who "declare their sin as Sodom, they hide it not" (Is. 3:9). *Fourth,* Ezekiel also alluded to the iniquity of Sodom (Ez. 16:49). *Fifth,* Peter said God

turning the cities of Sodom and Gomorrha into ashes condemned
them with an overthrow, making them an ensample unto those that
after should live ungodly; and delivered just Lot, vexed with the
filthy conversation ["lascivious life" ASV] of the wicked. (For that
righteous man dwelling among them, in seeing and hearing vexed
his righteous soul from day to day with their unlawful deeds;) (II
Pe. 2:6-8).

Peter describes the homosexual activities (along with other
sins) of Sodom and Gomorrha as "ungodly," "filthy conversation," "wicked," and "unlawful deeds." *Sixth*, Jude declares
that "Sodom and Gomorrha, and the cities about them in like
manner, giving themselves over to fornication, and going after
strange flesh, are set forth for an example, suffering the
vengeance of eternal fire" (Jude 7). "Fornication" here is the
Greek word *ekporneuo*. The prefix *ek* strengthens *porneuo* and
"implies excessive indulgence" (Abbot-Smith, Manual
Lexicon, p. 141) or "to commit much fornication." (Young's
Analytical Concordance to the Bible, p. 368). The word
"strange" or "other" flesh here means "out of the order of
nature" (Macknight); "that which was unnatural" (Alford); "a
departure from the law of nature" (Salmond); "contrary to
nature" (Barnes). The word "strange" in Leviticus 10:1 means
"strange to the law" or that which God commanded. God has
commanded and approved sexual relations between men and
women in marriage (I Co. 7:1-5) but men seeking after men and
women after women is "strange flesh," *i.e.,* flesh which God
has not commanded. It is contrary to "that appointed by God
for the fulfillment of natural desire" (Alford, cf. Ro. 1:26-27).
This clearly reveals that *homosexuality is a form of fornication!* The men of Sodom were destroyed because they were
guilty of homosexual activities. *Seventh,* a listing of all the
terms used to describe the people of Sodom are (1) "wicked"
(Ge. 13:13); (2) "sinners" (Ge. 13:13); (3) "sin is very grievous"
(Ge. 18:20), (4) "wickedly" (Ge. 19:7), (5) "declare their sin" (Is.
3:9), (6) "iniquity" (Eze. 16:49), (7) "ungodly" (II Pe. 2:6), (8)
"filthy conversation" (II Pe. 2:7), (9) "unlawful deeds" (II Pe.
2:8), (10) "fornication" (Jude 7), (11) "strange flesh" (Jude 7).

Homosexuality was strongly condemned in the law of
Moses. "Thou shalt not lie with mankind, as with womankind:
it is abomination" (Le. 18:22). "If a man also lie with mankind,
as he lieth with a woman, both of them have committed an

abomination: they shall surely be put to death . . ." (Le. 20:13). There was to be no "sodomite" or "dog" (euphemism for "a male prostitute") "of the sons of Israel" (De. 23:17, 18). "And Juda did evil. . . . And there were also sodomites in the land . . ." (I Ki. 14:22-24). Asa and Jehoshaphat, both righteous kings, removed the sodomits from the land (I Ki. 15:11-12; 22:46). Josiah broke down "the houses of the sodomites" (II Ki. 23:7) during his reformation. During the Patriarachal and Mosaical ages, while God was revealing his law gradually and progressively, he tolerated certain human weaknesses (cf. Acts 14:16; 17:30) but "there was never a time in any age when he tolerated homosexuality."

Christ condemned homosexuality despite the claim of some to the contrary. "Jesus specifically stated that God created *male* (Hebrew, *zakar*) and *female* (Hebrew, *neqevah*) (Ma. 19:4). We find no mention of a third or fourth type of human sexual being."[17] He condemned fornication (Ma. 19:9) and homosexuality is a form of fornication. "Every form of unchastity is included in the term fornication." In antiquity "fornication" (*porneio*) was used in a generic sense "of every kind of unlawful sexual intercourse."[18] *Porneio* includes "any kind of extra-marital sexual intercourse" and "all kinds of unnatural sexual intercourse."[19]

Paul describes homosexuality in Romans 1:26-27, as

> . . . their women did change the natural use into that which is against nature: and likewise also the men, leaving the natural use of the woman, burned in their lust one toward another; men with men working that which is unseemly, and receiving in themselves that recompense of their error which was meet.

Sodomy

> is characterized as: (a) the result of *vile* passions; passions of dishonor (ASV f); (b) a change from the natural to that which is against *nature* (note Jude's reference to the Sodomites going after "strange flesh" vs. 7); (c) *lust* causing males to burn for males and females for females; (d) *unseemliness;* and (e) *error* that was due to recompense.[20]

Paul characterizes homosexuality as abandoning "natural relations," that is, "the normal and normative heterosexual responses and behavior. The phrase 'natural relation' (Greek, *fusike ckresis*) refers directly to God's creation order, nature

(Greek, *fusis*), here meaning the way he intends man and woman to relate sexually."[21]

> . . . Paul cites these sexual violations of nature as marking the depth of immorality to which godlessness descends, because sexual degradation always constitutes such a mark. The moment God is taken out of the control in men's life the stench of sex abberration is bound to arise. It is so the world over to this day. Without God sex runs wild.[22]

Paul's plain language to the church at Corinth shows that a *practicing* homosexual cannot enter heaven.

> Know ye not that the unrighteous shall not inherit the kingdom of God? Be not deceived: neither fornicators, nor idolaters, nor adulterers, nor effeminate, nor abusers of themselves with mankind, nor thieves, nor covetous, nor drunkards, nor revilers, nor extortioners, shall inherit the kingdom of God . . . (I Co. 6:9-11).

"The word 'effeminate' found here is from the Greek *malokos,* which means '*soft.*' The secondary meaning is: of persons, soft, effeminate, esp. of catamites, men and boys who allow themselves to be used homosexually."[23]

> The phrase in verse 9, 'abusers of themselves with men' is translated from the Greek word *aranskoites,* which means: a. One who lies with a male as with a female, a sodomite (I Co. 6:9; I Ti. 1:10, 11); b. a male homosexual, pederost, sodomite (I Co. 6:9; I Ti. 1:10). [25-26]

CONCLUSION

Hebrews 2:9 does not teach that Christ was merely a man or creature. Advocates of sprinkling for baptism find no support in Hebrews 10:22. False views about marriage come from man's fertile imagination, not Hebrews 13:4.

ENDNOTES

1. W. E. Vine, *An Expository Dictionary of New Testament Words,* (Westwood: Fleming H. Revell Co.) 1962, p. 239.

2. Guy N. Woods, *A Commentary on the New Testament Epistles— Peter, John and Jude,* (Nashville: Gospel Advocate Co.), 1954, p. 191.

3. R. Milligan, *The New Testament Commentary, Epistle To The Hebrews,* (Nashville: Gospel Advocate Co.), 1953, p. 88.

4. Wayne Jackson, *Reason and Revelation,* April, 1983, Vol. III, No. 4, p. 16.

5. R. C. Foster, *Studies In The Life of Christ,* (Baker Book House), 1971, p. 1022.

6. *Doctrines and Discipline of The Methodist Church,* The Methodist Publishing House, 1952, p. 519.

7. James Cardinal Gibbons, *The Faith of Our Fathers,* (Baltimore: John Murphy Co.), 1976, p. 277.

8. Joseph Benson, *Romans To The Revelation,* (New York: Carlton and Phillips), 1854, Vol. V, p. 547.

9. A. T. Robertson, *Word Pictures In The New Testament,* (Nashville: Broadman Press), 1932, Vol. V, p. 411.

10. John F. Rowe, *The History of Apostasies,* (Rosemead: Old Paths Book Club), 1956, p. 202. Quoting from the Edinburgh Cyclopaedia, *Article on Baptism.*

11. Gibbons, *op. cit.,* p. 277.

12. Adam Clarke, *Clarke's Commentary,* (New York: Abingdon Press), Vol. VI, p. 785.

13. Gibbons, *op. cit.,* p. 399.

14. Jim E. Waldron, *Contending For The Faith,* "Enemies of the Cross," April, 1983, Vol. XIV, No. 4, p. 10.

15. Charles W. Keyson, *What You Should Know About Homosexuality,* (Grand Rapids: Zondervan), 1979, p. 95.

16. Colen Brown, *Dictionary of N. T. Theology,* Ed. II, p. 396.

17. John M. (Kim) Batteaw, "Sexual Differences: A Cultural Convention," *Christianity Today,* July 8, 1977, p. 8 (1064).

18. W. I. Arndt and I. W. Gingrich, *A Greek Lexicon of The New Testament and Other Early Christian Literature,* University of Chicago Press, p. 699.

19. Brown, *op. cit.,* p. 497-501.

20. Wayne Jackson, "Homosexuality," *Sound Doctrine,* Jan./Feb., 1978, Vol. III, No. I.

21. Batteaw, *op. cit.,* p. 9.

22. R. C. H. Lenski, *Commentary on Romans,* p. 115.

23. Arndt and Gingrich, *op. cit.,* p. 489.

24. *Thayer's Greek English Lexicon of the New Testament,* (Grand Rapids: Associated Publishers), p. 75.

25. Arndt and Gingrich, *op. cit.,* p. 489.

26. Several of the notes on *Homosexuality* are taken from a lesson delivered by James Meadows at the 1979 Spiritual Sword Lectureship. Permission has been granted to use it in this lecture.

SECTION III

DIFFICULT PASSAGES
IN HEBREWS

DIFFICULT PASSAGES IN HEBREWS

No. I

	WHO WROTE HEBREWS?
HEBREWS 1:2:	**DEFINE "THESE LAST DAYS" (KJV), "THE END OF THESE DAYS" (ASV) AS TO BEGINNING AND DURATION.**
HEBREWS 1:14:	**DO CHRISTIANS HAVE PERSONAL "GUARDIAN ANGELS?"**
HEBREWS 2:6-8:	**IS "A LITTLE LOWER THAN THE ANGELS" A REFERENCE TO CHRIST IN PSALMS 8:4-6 FROM WHICH IT IS QUOTED OR TO MAN IN GENERAL?**

By CARL B. GARNER

Born in 1936 in Fort Worth, Texas. Graduated from Abilene Christian College in 1958, master's degree from North Texas State University in 1965. Taught in Fort Worth public schools from 1959-66. Directed Bible Chair at Navarro Junior College in Corsicana 1966-76. Now director of McCarty Student Center and Instructor of Religion at Southwest Texas State University in San Marcos, Texas. Editor of *Sound Doctrine*, a quarterly journal. Writes for *Christian Bible Teacher*. Married Janice Sowards in 1963 and they have two children.

INTRODUCTION

When first-century Christians failed to grow and mature as they should, they were told, "I have fed you with milk, and not with meat: for hitherto ye were not able to bear it, . . . for ye are yet carnal . . ." (I Co. 3:2-3). It may be that in avoiding the difficult and controversial passages in Scripture, many of us have deprived ourselves of the rich "meat" that God has provided as food for our spiritual health.

A distinct danger, however, deserves our consideration. We are often tempted to give definitive answers to questions for which God has not provided those answers. Such questions as, "Why did Nicodemus approach Jesus at night?" and "Was the apostle Peter ever in Rome?" may provoke diligent study. Such difficulties may eventuate in our increased knowledge of a context or a critical analysis of an important subject, but if God has not "revealed" these matters (De. 29:29), either explicitly or implicitly, then we should acknowledge our limitations and not allow pride to force a conclusion that is not warranted by God's revelation.

WHO WROTE THE BOOK OF HEBREWS?

There are several good reasons for studying this question, and several good results can come from contemplating all these facts, but it is a mistake to spend an inordinate amount of limited Bible class time on authorship to the neglect of textual study and practical applications.

Having said that, I address the subject of the authorship of this great book. Men of scholarship have presented a diverse list of possibilities with varying degrees of fervor. Tertullian claimed Barnabas, an unsung hero of the New Testament, as the author. The eloquent Apollos was suggested by Martin Luther. Paul's loyal and faithful associate, Luke, is suggested by Origen as the possible penman. Clear parallels can be seen in Hebrews and the writings of Clement of Rome, although serious problems belie this choice. Others suggested are Priscilla and Aquila, Silas, Stephen and Jude.[1]

However, the preponderance of scholarly study has centered around Pauline authorship. Strong arguments for Paul are as follows:

First, the oldest evidence on the authorship of Hebrews seems to be at the end of the second century when Clement of Alexandria named Paul as the writer of Hebrews in the Hebrew language, and that Luke translated it into Greek for the Gentile Christians.[2]

Second, the sixth Synod of Carthage (A.D. 419) specifically attributes "fourteen epistles" to the apostle Paul, as did the Synod of Hippo (A.D. 392).[3]

Third, the Chester Beatty papyrus lists Hebrews as having Pauline authorship, placing it immediately after Romans.[4]

Fourth, the anonymous nature of the epistle points to Paul because of the prejudice in the mind of the Jews toward Paul, and the false rumors that had been spreading concerning his life and teaching.

Fifth, Lightfoot lists several favorable comparisons between passages in Hebrews and passages from Paul's epistles: Hebrews 13:18, 20, 23, 25 are similar in expression to Romans 15:30; II Corinthians 1:11; Philemon 22; Philippians 1:24-25; I Thessalonians 5:28; and II Thessalonians 3:18. Descriptions of Christ's being in the "image of God" (He. 1:3; Col. 1:15), Christ as Creator (He. 1:2-3, 10-12; Ro. 11:36; I Co. 8:6; Col. 1:16-17) and Christ's offering of himself for the sins of mankind (He. 7:27; I Co. 15:3; Ep. 5:2; I Ti. 2:6) are comparable in Hebrews and in the known writings of Paul. The emphasis on the changing of the covenant in Hebrews 7-10 complements similar statements in Ephesians 2, Colossians 2 and Romans 7. Only in Acts 13:33 and Hebrews 1:5 is the Psalmist's statement "thou art my son, today I have begotten thee" applied to Christ. See Psalms 2:7.[5]

Other similarities include: Hebrews 2:4 "signs and wonders," cf. I Corinthians 12:4, 11; Romans 12:6. Hebrews 2:16 "descendants of Abraham," cf. Galatians 3:29; Romans 4:16. Hebrews 4:12 "word of God is . . . sword," cf. Ephesians 6:17. Hebrews 10:19 "confidence to enter the sanctuary," cf. Romans 5:2; Eph. 2:18; 3:12.

Equally convincing arguments are presented opposing Paul's authorship. Such arguments, while not conclusive, certainly are sufficient to suggest a justifiable caution in our ultimate resolution of this matter.

First, if Paul authored this book, why is his name not only omitted from the text, but also why was his name attributed only after many years? There is little *historical* basis for Pauline authorship.

Second, in Hebrews 2:3-4 the writer states the gospel had been "confirmed" unto him by the "signs and wonders." However, in Paul's writings, he always claimed that his message came directly from the Lord without the intervention of the apostles (Ga. 1:12-20).

Third, the pronounced style of Paul is not as obvious in Hebrews as in his other epistles.

According to Wikenhauser, there are 168 words in Hebrews that do not occur elsewhere in the New Testament, and an additional 124 words which are not found in any of Paul's epistles. While such "word-counting" is often a favorite ploy of modernist writers in attacking the authenticity of the scriptures, such may be worthy of mention in this study.[6]

Fifth, strong claims for the authorship of Apollos, Barnabas, etc., would seem to weaken the traditional view of Pauline authorship.

What shall we conclude from this study? This writer has always been impressed with the strength of the arguments for the authorship of Paul, but the only plausible conclusion for those of us with deep respect for the Bible's silence is that we do not know the human author. However, if the book of Hebrews is scripture, and it most certainly is, then we *can* be assured of the Holy Spirit's authorship (II Ti. 3:16-17), and that is more significant than all of these other points combined. Is such a conclusion in reality a non-conclusion, a "straddling" of the theological fence? What fence is there for us to "straddle"? We concur with Origen's familiar observation: "But who wrote the epistle God only knows certainly."[7]

Perhaps our ignorance lends to our strength in this one matter. B. F. Westcott concluded:

> In this case the confession of ignorance is really the confirming of an inspiring faith. We acknowledge the divine authority of the epistle . . . we measure what would have been our loss if it had not been included in the Bible; and we confess that the wealth of spiritual power was so great in the early church that he who was so empowered to commit to writing this view of the fulness of truth has not by that conspicuous service even left his name for the grateful reverence of later ages.[8]

DEFINE "THESE LAST DAYS" (KJV), "THE END OF THESE DAYS" (ASV) AS TO BEGINNING AND DURATION (1:2)

Jesus set the tone for this great text when he took his disciples up on the mount of transfiguration (Ma. 17; Mark 9; Luke 9). There, with Moses and Elijah, the great law-giver and the loyal prophet in company with them, the voice of Jehovah declared, "This is my beloved Son, in whom I am well pleased; hear ye him" (Ma. 17:5). In the past, God had directed man through the law and the prophets and by direct means, but now we are directed to give our attention to Jesus — to God's final revelation through his Son.

F. F. Bruce comments:

> The earlier stage of revelation was given in a variety of ways: He spoke in storm and thunder to Moses, in a still small voice to Elijah. To those who would not heed the gently flowing stream of Shiloah (Is. 8:6ff), He spoke by means of the Euphratean flood. Priest and prophet, sage and singer, were in their several ways His spokesmen; yet all the successive acts and varying modes of revelation in the ages before Christ came did not add up to the fulness of what God had to say. His word was not complete until Christ came; but when Christ came, the word spoken in him was indeed God's final word.[9]

For those with some dispensational doctrine to defend, this passage, along with Acts 2:16-17 and others, becomes difficult. Premillennialists have taken a perfectly good, Biblical term and given to it an entirely *un*biblical application. Just like their abuse of other words, such as *tribulation* and *rapture*, the world has become accustomed to thinking of some period just prior to, or just after, Jesus' second coming when they hear the term "last days." Fifty years ago, upon hearing words like "pot," "gay" and "bread," we would have been thinking of "cast-iron," "happy" and "Mrs. Baird's." Today these words are used to speak of marijuana, homosexuality and money. A similar distortion is now seen even in Bible words and phrases.

There are at least two things we must not do. (1) We must not let false teachers make their own rules. We must teach, both positively and negatively, correcting false doctrines even when we ourselves are weary of giving such warnings. We must "read in the book of the law of God distinctly, giving the sense, and causing them to understand the reading" (Ne. 8:8).

(2) We must make sure that we do not fall victim to the same deception, by misusing passages just because they have the catch phrases that sound as if they either strengthen or weaken the dispensational view. Misusing a passage is inexcusable regardless of the person who does it or the purpose for which it is done.

In using the phrase "these last days" (or "the end of these days," ASV), the emphasis is on contrasting the revelation of "old time" or "time past" with the new and final revelation of God through Jesus.

> The last days are in contrast to the days of old. The Old Testament often speaks of "the last days" (Ge. 49:1; Nu. 24:14; Is. 2:2; Ho. 3:5), by which is meant the future in general or the messianic age in particular, the time when when prophecy would find its fulfillments. . . . *These last days* denotes the final phase of history, brought on by the entry of the Son into the world and continuing until the consummation of all things.[10]

The Jews never attempted to carefully delineate the exact beginning of this period, but by letting the inspired New Testament writers do so, we can come to a rather strong conclusion. The Old Testament prophets had said that some things would happens in the last days:

First, *God would pour out his Spirit upon all flesh* (Joel 2:28). In desribing the events of the day of Pentecost, Peter was inspired to say "this is that" (Acts 2:14-17). This writer submits that it is somewhat presumptuous for man to say "this is *not* that."

Second, *the last days were to be characterized by the Lord's House being established, which would bring an era of genuine peace to the world, and for the law of God to proceed from Jerusalem* (Is. 2:2-3; Mi. 4:1-3). This peace came to be enjoyed by those who knew how to behave themselves "in the house of God, which is the church of the living God, the pillar and ground of the truth" (I Ti. 3:15). In Acts 2, with "men out of every nation" (Acts 2:5) present, the law of the Lord did proceed from "Jerusalem, and in all Judea, and in Samaria, and unto the uttermost part of the earth" (Acts 1:8).

Third, *God promised to "make a new covenant"* (Je. 31:31-34) *with his people,* and that not only the Jews but the Gentiles would be "called by a new name, which the mouth of the Lord shall name" (Is. 62:2). In Antioch, under this new covenant and with Jews and Gentiles now called by the name "Christian" (Acts 11:26), God's people enjoyed the blessings promised for those in the last days. Since the law was nailed to the cross (Co. 2:14), this would establish the beginning and project the duration of this prophetic era, "the last days."

Note carefully the additional New Testament usage of this and similar terms:

First, I Timothy 4:1: "In the latter times some shall depart from the faith . . ." The actions described and the doctrines mentioned were prevalent in the first century as well as today. As Wallace says, "the 'latter times' did not mean that a general departure from the faith, or a mass apostasy, portends the end of time."[11] It meant the last age — the Christian age.

Second, II Timothy 3:1: "In the last days perilous times shall come." That these days were to be in Timothy's lifetime is obvious since Paul then warns Timothy that he must "turn away" from those who possessed these wicked qualities. See also Jude 18 for a similar warning.

Third, II Peter 3:3-4: "There shall come in the last days scoffers, . . . saying, Where is the promise of his coming?" These scoffers are then described as being "willingly ignorant" (present tense) of the facts, and Timothy is warned to *not* be ignorant. This spoke of a problem current to Paul's and Timothy's work, not some fanciful age thousands of years in the future. See also I John 2:18.

Let it be noted that Christ is *now* in the kingdom, and that we look forward to a rest at God's side, not on his footstool.

DO CHRISTIANS HAVE PERSONAL "GUARDIAN ANGELS"? (1:4)

In Hebrews 1:13, the writer does two things. First, he makes an argument based upon the silence of the scripture. Just as God asked Nathan, "Spake I a word with any of the tribes of Israel, . . . saying, Why build ye not me an house of cedar?" (II Sa. 7:7), now he says that he never gave such honor to angels that he now gives to Christ. In this, and other arguments, we find that such silence is often as profound as are the explicit commands of the Bible.

Second, the writer begins to perfect a series of arguments in which the supremacy of Christ is established by placing him in contrast with various persons of honor and prestige. Jesus is said to be superior to the prophets (1:1-3), to angels (1:4-14), to Moses (3:1-6), to Joshua (4:3-13), and to Aaron (4:14-10:18). In keeping with the theme of the book, this is one of several attempts to dissuade Jewish Christians from departing from the faith and going back to Jerusalem. Why go back to the Mosaic Law or the Aaronic priesthood when Christ is far superior to them?

The mention of angels as "ministering spirits" is not intended so much as a description of what they *do* as to what they *are*. Here he speaks of their position as *servants* as contrasted with the authority of Jesus as a *Son* (1:2). Only in a supportive or corollary role would this passage be used to discuss angels as "guardian angels," but not in a primary role because that is not its place in the context. The context contrasts Jesus and the angels and establishes Jesus' supremacy.

The question of "personal guardian angels" is an interesting one, however, and warrants our consideration. Among the passages alluding to this subject are: Psalms 34:7, "the angel of the Lord encampeth round about them that fear him, and deliver them;" Matthew 18:10, ". . . despise not one of these little ones, . . . in heaven their angels do always behold the face of my Father which is in heaven;" Psalms 91:10-16, (quoted by Satan and meant to tempt Jesus, Luke 4:10-11), "There shall no evil befall thee, . . . for he shall give his angels charge over thee, to keep thee in all thy ways;" Matthew 26:53, "Thinkest thou that I cannot now pray to my Father, and he shall presently give me more than twelve legions of angels?" and our text, Hebrews 1:14, "Are they not all ministering spirits, sent forth to minister for them who shall be heirs of salvation?"

From these and other references, we learn that (1) God cares for and watches over his people; (2) God stands ready to deliver his people in times of trouble; (3) that even though these promises are true, a child of God will not be shielded from all trials (see Acts 4-5; Ma. 26:39f; and II Co. 11:21-27); and (4) the angels are "in heaven" and not on earth.

For one to conclude, as do many, that these scriptures teach "personal" guardian angels, that somehow God is "pulling the strings" on every event, thereby preventing harm from ever falling upon Christians today, would be taking from the scripture that which is not there. Many of the same arguments for rejecting the direct operation of the Holy Spirit upon Christians today are also strong reasons for rejecting the individual and personal direction and protection of "guardian angels."

One area that has puzzled man for ages has been the question of God's providential care for man. How is this providence shown? Why are there times when God allows difficulties and troubles? Even Paul said "perhaps" (Phile. 15) when speaking of Onesimus' departure from his master. The faithful Mordecai, when referring to Esther's responsibility to her people, said "Who knoweth whether thou art come to the kingdom for such a time as this?" We dare not presume to know and to bind upon others that which God has not revealed by inspiration. God will be with us! His angels will constantly keep watch over us! He will limit Satan's power of temptation (I Co. 10:13)! But even the Son had to "suffer many things" (Mark 8:31), and "all that will live godly in Christ Jesus shall suffer persecution" (II Ti. 3:12). Therefore, let us be strong!

IS "A LITTLE LOWER THAN THE ANGELS" A REFERENCE TO CHRIST IN PSALMS 8:4-6 FROM WHICH IT IS QUOTED OR TO MAN IN GENERAL (2:6-8)?

There are well over thirty direct quotations from the Old Testament in the book of Hebrews. This not only shows the significance of those scriptures to the recipients of this book, but also indicates a healthy respect for their value and usefulness to Christians in general.

One such quotation is from Psalms 8:4-6. This quotation is found in Hebrews 2:6-8a. The difficulty we address is the identify of the "son of man" in the Psalms' quotation and its application in our text. Was Psalms 8 speaking of man in general? Was the psalmist speaking only in a prophetic way of the coming Messiah? Was the Hebrew writer giving a divine *commentary,* making Jesus the psalmist's "son of man"? Is there some form of comparison, in which Psalms 8 is used to illustrate again the supremacy of Jesus?

Some preliminary observations, which can help us to grasp the meaning of this entire section, are appropriate at this point;

First, the term "son of man" is a term often used to describe Jesus (Ma. 16:13; Acts 7:56).

Second, however, "son of man" is also used to describe man in general (Ps. 146:3; Job 25:6).

Third, Psalms 8:4-6 is a familiar form of Hebrew parallelism in which two similar terms (man, son of man) are used in a poetic way to describe the same person or thing.

Fourth, at the time of creation, man *was* given dominion over the earth and "every living thing that moveth upon the earth" (Ge. 1:26-28). This dominion was taken away because of man's sin (Ge. 3:17-19).

Fifth, the word "little," in both Hebrew and Greek, can denote either a brief period of time (*i.e.,* "for a short time man was made lower than the angels" ASV, RSV, NEB, TEV), or a position of rank. In this context it is very difficult to determine its usage by grammar alone.

Sixth, the original Hebrew word translated "angels" in Psalms 8:5 is the word *elohim,* a term used to describe God in Genesis 1:1 and to angels or divine beings in Psalms 82:1. Most Bible students are in agreement that the Septuagint was correct in translating "angels" in Psalms 8:5.

Now let us see how all these factors can be fused together into something not only comprehensible but also edifying.

The psalmist's description of "man . . . son of man" was primarily a statement of man's delight at receiving the attention of God. Man had been given this honor and this dominion but had lost it through sin. Barnes explains:

> What is *man* that he should have attracted the attention of God, and been the object of so much care? The question would not have been appropriate to David if the Psalm be supposed to have had reference originally to the Messiah.[12]

Therefore, what he lost in Adam, he regained in Christ. But this was accomplished by Christ when he also was made "a little lower than the angels," so that he could be capable of suffering death for every man and be the loyal, understanding high priest who can sympathize with our infirmities, as he had dealt with his own (He. 4:14-16). I admit to my inability to comprehend deity and humanity in the same person, but Jesus, who was "equal with God" (Ph. 2:6-11) became also "in the likeness of man" (see also He. 2:16-18; John 1:14; I Ti. 2:5).

Therefore, a Psalm with man as the subject, is now quoted and used to honor the authority, supremacy and glory of the Messiah himself. Man was given a great opportunity, but he did not live up to it. But through Christ, he can regain the place he had before sin separated him from God. Lightfoot says:

> The drift of the quotation and the author's meaning may be summarized as follows: God, mindful of man from the beginning, gave him a high place. He bestowed on him glory and honor and made him lord of creation (Ge. 1:26-28). All things were put under his feet. But man rebelled and lost his universal dominion. Man originally was given dominion. He is still destined to achieve it. But this dominion can only be realized, as the author goes on to say, through the ideal or representative man, Jesus Christ. Not everything is under man's control, but, the author says, we do see Jesus, crowned with glory and honor. That is to say, in Christ the complete fulfillment of the Psalm is realized and true dominion is conferred.[13]

Did the psalmist have the Messiah in mind when he wrote Psalms 8:4-6? Probably not. Was the redemptive work of Jesus thrust back into this text, giving it a poetic beauty even deeper than it had known before? Yes, at least indirectly by the Hebrews writer. Is man capable of overcoming the Evil One by his own strength? Of course not! However, we can see that our ultimate victory over sin and Satan will be through the Son of God who voluntarily became the Son of Man, "that he . . . should taste death for every man" (He. 2:9). "Thanks be unto God for his unspeakable gift" (II Co. 9:15).

ENDNOTES

1. James Orr, editor, *The International Standard Bible Encyclopedia* (Grand Rapids, Mich.: Wm. B. Eerdmans Pub. Co., 1939), vol. II, pp. 1356-1358.

2. Eusebius, *Ecclesiastical History*, 6.14.

3. F. F. Bruce, *The Epistle to the Hebrews* (Grand Rapids, Mich.: Wm. B. Eerdmans Pub. Co., 1964), p. xxxix.

4. F. G. Kenyon, *The Chester Beatty Biblical Papyri* (pub. n. a., 1936), fasc. III, p. viii.

5. Neil Lightfoot, *Jesus Christ Today* (Grand Rapids, Mich: Baker Book House, 1976), pp. 20-22).

6. Alfred Wikenhauser, *New Testament Introduction,* translated by Joseph Cunningham (New York, N.Y.: publisher n. a., 1960), p. 467.

7. Eusebius, *op. cit.,* 6.25, 11-14.

8. B. F. Westcott, *The Epistle to the Hebrews* (Grand Rapids, Mich.: Wm. B. Eerdmans Pub. Co., 1973), p. lxxix.

9. Bruce, *op. cit.,* pp. 2-3.

10. Lightfoot, *op. cit.,* p. 54.

11. Foy E. Wallace, Jr., *God's Prophetic Word* (Fort Worth, Tex.: Foy E. Wallace, Jr., Pub., 1946), p. 66.

12. Albert Barnes, *Notes on the New Testament, Hebrews* (Grand Rapids, Mich.: Baker Book House, 1949), p. 60.

13. Lightfoot, *op. cit.,* p. 74.

DIFFICULT PASSAGES IN HEBREWS
No. II

HEBREWS 2:10:	HOW WAS JESUS "MADE PERFECT?" DOES THIS IMPLY IMPERFECTION BEFORE HIS DEATH?
HEBREWS 2:18; 4:15:	JESUS WAS TEMPTED, YET GOD CANNOT BE TEMPTED (JAM. 1:13). DOES THIS MEAN THAT JESUS IS NOT TRULY GOD?
HEBREWS 4:12:	IS THERE A REAL OR ONLY AN APPARENT DISTINCTION BETWEEN THE "SOUL" AND "SPIRIT" OF MAN?
HEBREWS 5:7:	WHAT PRAYER OF JESUS IS REFERRED TO, TO ESCAPE THE CROSS, TO BE RAISED UP OR SOME OTHER?

By ROY H. LANIER, JR.

Born in Abilene, TX. Married Patricia Boswell and they have one daughter. Attended Freed-Hardeman, Florida Christian and Abilene Christian Colleges. Has served local churches in Iowa, Florida, Oklahoma and Colorado. Has served as instructor at Bear Valley School of Biblical Studies. Past editor, *Rocky Mountain Christian Newspaper*. Author of several tracts and study guides. Time now divided between gospel meeting and lectureship preaching and publishing writings of his father. Speaker, *First Annual Denton Lectures*.

INTRODUCTION

Four assignments have been given for this study, two of which will encompass similar areas. The four passages and questions involved are: (1) 2:10, "How is Jesus made perfect?;" (2) 2:18; 4:15, "How could Jesus be tempted if he is truly God?;" (3) 4:12, "Is there a distinction between 'soul' and 'spirit'?;" (4) 5:7, "Was Jesus praying to escape death, or what?"

Since three of the questions involve the nature of the Incarnate Christ, it would be well to see something first about the nature of Jesus, who was both man and God. Upon a basic understanding of some of these principles, it will be easier to consider several of the assigned topics.

Jesus was in every sense God. Jesus was in every sense human. The blending of these two natures in the one man has offered a puzzle for students, and will continue to do so till eternity. That he was God, the Only Begotten, is declared (John 1:18), as is also declared he was Very God, ". . . the Word was God" (John 1:1). That he "shared in flesh and blood" (He. 2:14) is known, as well as is the full humanity he took upon himself, ". . . emptied himself, taking the form of a servant, being made in the likeness of men; and being found in fashion as a man . . ." (Ph. 2:7-8). How can he be both human and divine? Earthlings may never comprehend the vastness of this subject, but notice some further enlightenment.

> In the incarnation our Lord added to His divine nature, not another person (which would have given Him a double personality), but impersonal, generic human nature, so that He was and continues to be God and man, in two distinct natures and one person forever. . . .
> This human nature had no personality apart from the Divine nature.
> . . . In this union the Divine nature was basic and controlling, so that this was not the case of a man being exalted to Deity, but of God voluntarily humbling Himself and descending to the plane of man in such manner that he shared equally with us the experiences which are common to men.[1]

Yet another expresses it:

> The possession of two natures does not involve a double personality in the God-man, for the reason the Logos takes into union with himself, not an individual man with already developed personality, but human nature which has had no separate existence before its union with the Divine.[2]

Again,

> An incarnate life is an enfleshed life. It is not a divine coupled with a human life. This is the old Nestorian theory. It is not two consciousnesses and two wills, much less two personalities. It is not that Jesus did certain things in his divine, and others in his human nature, as if he were sometimes God and at other times man. . . .
> It was constituted by the indissoluble union of a divine and human factor. These factors were not merely placed side by side, or in rela-

tions of fellowship. They were rather in relations of mutual inter-penetration and vital union. All sense of dual consciousness and dual life is absent. We are not to think of the divine imparting its qualities to the human and vice versa, as if there were an interval between to be bridged over. We are to think rather of a personality constituted by the vital union of two factors and qualified and conditioned by the action of both.[3]

The possibility of such a union is staggering. Human minds cannot comprehend such a thing, but it has happened. It is possible:

> . . . in the fact that man was originally made in the image of and likeness of God. The human spirit is the offspring of God (Acts 17: 29); God is the Father of the human spirit (He. 12:9). This being true, there could be no union of the divine spirit with the brute beast.[4]

Scriptures do not seem to speak of Jesus in first one and then the other nature. It may well be a mistake to speak of Jesus doing something "only as a man," or "only as God," for the Bible does not speak of such. He did the miraculous actions as a "God-man," and he did the ordinary human things as a "God-man." The Bible only speaks of him as one person, one consciousness, one will.

Certainly, this "dual-oneness" was conditioned by both natures. He voluntarily limited his knowledge when becoming a God-man, for he grew in wisdom (Luke 2:52), and said that he did not know the time of the coming (Ma. 24:36). While he retained all the attributes of Deity, such as omnipotence, omnipresence, omniscience, eternity, etc., he chose not to exercise them. His emptying himself (Ph. 2:7) must have included this; he gave up the right to exercise divine powers on his own determination. He evidently exercised such powers through the Holy Spirit, after his descent upon him (John 1:33; Ma. 12:28). Thus it may be said:

> It is one of the mysteries which the Scriptures reveal but which they make no effort to explain. Christ is an absolutely unique person. . . . His personality . . . remains a profound mystery, in some respects as baffling as the Trinity itself. All we can know are the simple facts which are revealed to us in the Scripture, and beyond these it is not necessary to go. As a matter of fact we do not understand the mysterious union of the spiritual and physical in our own natures; nor do we understand the attributes of God. But the essential facts are clear and are understandable by the average Christian.

These are that the Second Person of the Trinity added to His own nature a perfectly normal human nature, that His life on earth was passed as far as was fitting within the limits of this humanity, that his life remained at all times the life of God manifest in the flesh, that his action in the flesh never escaped beyond the boundary of that which was suitable for incarnate Deity . . .[5]

HOW WAS JESUS "MADE PERFECT?"
(2:10)

The Scriptures state,

For it became him, for whom are all things, and through whom are all things, in bringing many sons unto glory, to make the author of their salvation perfect through sufferings (He. 2:10, ASV).

Does this imply imperfection of our Lord prior to such suffering? How then could he be True and Very God?

The key to this question of the nature of Jesus is found in the words "to make . . . perfect." It simply means that through suffering Jesus was brought to completion, fully qualified now to be the author, cause of eternal salvation for humanity. It does not imply prior imperfection of character, only prior incompletion of his assigned task.

The word under study is *teleiosai,* an aorist 1, infinitive, active from *teleioo.* Thayer says it includes, "make perfect or complete . . . to bring to the end (goal) proposed . . . *i.e.,* to raise to the state befitting him: so of God exalting Jesus to the state of heavenly majesty."[6] Arndt and Gingrich speak of this word's meaning, ". . . bring to an end, bring to its goal or accomplishment."[7] Vine adds, ". . . to make him perfect, legally and officially, for all that he would be to his people on the ground of his sacrifice."[8] Lightfoot adds an interesting note to such a word study when he mentions this meaning is "determined by the Septuagint which regularly uses the term in the Pentateuch to refer to the consecration of priests."[9]

Commentators add some light though, as does Delitzsch, when he says, ". . . mainly refers to ethical perfection, the putting into a state completely answering to his destination and commission."[10] Barnes adds, ". . . Christ was not made better . . . he was completely endowed for the work which he came to do, by his sorrows."[11]

The author of Hebrews comes to this same thought again in 5:8-9, teaching that Jesus learned obedience by suffering and then was made "perfect." So, this is not an uncommon use of the term "perfect." It often means "to complete" or "finish." Hebrews 6:1 speaks of "going on unto perfection" in the same sense, a growing, a completing action. And then in 13:21, it speaks of God's making Christians "perfect" in doing his will.

So, it is accurate to conclude that Jesus was not made perfect in character, but rather made perfect in the sense of completion of his goal and work on this earth.

JESUS WAS TEMPTED, YET GOD CANNOT BE TEMPTED (Jam. 1:13). DOES THIS MEAN THAT JESUS WAS NOT TRULY GOD? (2:18; 4:15)

If Jesus be God, how could he be tempted? The Bible says that "God cannot be tempted" (Jam. 1:13). Does this mean Jesus was not True God?

> The fact that he could be tempted has led some to deny that Jesus was God, since God cannot be tempted with evil. If he had been God alone, he could not have been tempted; if he had been man alone, he would have given in to temptation. But since he was neither God alone, nor man alone, but was God-man, he was subject to temptation and he could overcome temptation.[12]

Another interesting thought comes from Lenski:

> Neither the Father nor the Spirit would be tempted by Satan because both are only God. The Son could be tempted because he became man. He alone of the three persons, by assuming our human nature, could suffer human hunger and could be asked to appease that hunger in a sinful way. He alone, by his human nature, was made dependent on his Father and could thus be asked to abuse his dependence by a false trust in his Father. He alone, in his human nature, faced the cross, and could thus be asked to evade it and follow an easier course.[13]

Then also, a large part of this puzzle hinges on the definition of a word. When the Bible says, "For in that he himself hath suffered, being tempted," and ". . . one that hath been in all points tempted like as we are, yet without sin" (He. 2:18; 4:15), it uses a Greek word *peirastheis,* an aorist passive participle from *peirazo.* Conybeare and Howson state, "This verb does not mean usually to be tempted to sin, but to be tried by affliction — I Corinthians 10:13, James 1:2."[14] Bagster suggests this means, "to make proof or trial of, put to the proof."[15]

Could Jesus have sinned? This has been a hard question through the years, but the more obvious thought of it all, simplest of all, seems to be that surely he could have sinned. Though his sinless character was untouched by the slightest imperfection, nor tainted with the barest of evil desires, the fact must remain that he could have done so. If not, the world is faced with a series of serious conclusions: (1) he is not man's *example,* for he does not really know the agony of temptation and the fight of desires to go contrary to God's will; (2) all stories and statements about such in the Bible are just sham, *playacting* for the benefit of gullible man; (3) he is not the "last Adam," the head of a new spiritual race of victorious mankind (I Co. 15:22, 45); (4) he has not conquered and *destroyed* the work of the devil (I John 3:8; He. 2:15).

So, accuracy demands that one conclude Jesus was truly God, and was also truly tempted in all points as are men. (Additional thoughts concerning this subject will be given in answer to "Jesus Praying.")

IS THERE A REAL OR ONLY AN APPARENT DISTINCTION BETWEEN THE "SOUL" AND "SPIRIT" OF MAN?
(4:12)

The text reads,

> For the word of God is living, and active, and sharper than any two-edged sword, and piercing even to the dividing of soul and spirit, of both joints and marrow, and quick to discern the thoughts and intents of the heart (He. 4:12, ASV).

Just what is the distinction, if any, between "soul" and "spirit?" Is there any real distinction, or is it only apparent?

The complexity of such a study in words is interesting and almost endless. Consulting Greek authorities can be by the dozens, and definitions by the dozens of both words will pop right out. One may take one of many choices about words that are used both literally and figuratively. Many such authorities give over one dozen definitions of each word, so such an inquiry can easily be bogged down in confusion.

Vine gets to the heart of the matter about as quickly as any, when he states succinctly:

> The language of Heb. 4:12 suggests the extreme difficulty of distinguishing between the soul and the spirit, alike in their nature and in their activities. Generally speaking, the spirit is the higher, the soul the lower element. The spirit may be recognized as the life principle bestowed on man by God, the soul as the resulting life constituted in the individual, the body being the material organism animated by soul and spirit. . . . Apparently, then, the relationships may be thus summed up, *soma*, body, and *pneuma*, spirit may be separated, *pneuma* and *psuche*, soul, can only be distinguished (Cremer: from *Notes on Thessalonians*, by Hogg and Vine, pp. 205-207).[16]

Milligan gives a full note of explanation about the Grecian philosophers' ideas of the trichotomy of man: body (material substance of flesh), soul, *psuche*, animal life, and spirit, *pneuma*, being the immortal spirit. He takes this as the answer to I Thessalonians 5:23, but then gives doubt as to whether this be the object of this particular verse in Hebrews 4:12. For, says he, "The separation takes place within the region of the soul and spirit; not between them."[17] Delitzsch adds an interesting thought, as he states, "*Pneuma* is the spirit, which proceeds immediately . . . from God Himself, and therefore carries in itself the divine image. . . . The *psuche*, on the other hand, is the life emanating from the *pneuma*, when united with the body. . . ."[18] Lenski emphasizes the context well, when he states, "The Word of God is the only power that can penetrate so deeply and expose so completely the inwardness of our being."[19]

The context of the chapter does not lead one to delve very deeply into the puzzles of such word studies; rather, it is as Lightfoot states, "The author is merely heaping up terms to show that the divine word cuts sharp through everything that is in man. No segment of human personality can escape its keen edge."[20]

There may be times for keen and sharp distinctions between *psuche* and *pneuma*, but probably not in this context.

WHAT PRAYER OF JESUS IS REFERRED TO,
TO ESCAPE THE CROSS, TO BE RAISED UP
OR SOME OTHER? (5:7)

The last text for study offers one of the most perplexing inquiries. The text reads,

> Who in the days of his flesh, having offered up prayers and supplications with strong crying and tears unto him that was able to save him from death, and having been heard for his godly fear, though he was a Son, yet learned he obedience by the things which he suffered (He. 5:7-8).

The questions come to be answered: (1) did he pray to escape the cross; (2) to be raised up; (3) to not die in the garden; or what?

First of all, keep in mind the context. This whole section is given to show how well Jesus is qualified to serve as the Messiah. His suffering, his temptations, his obedience all show him to have a total sharing in the humanity: the passions, pathos, and problems therein. If Jesus be thus qualified this well, who then could charge him with being unable to sympathize with all men as High Priest, Savior, Offering, Atonement, Testator? That he is God is not the question of this context; rather, the question might be, "Is he truly enough acquainted with the problems of man?" "How does he really know the agonies of mankind?"

The answer comes through clearly: "He, too, has suffered, has been tempted. And, he, too, has relied on prayer to the Father."

"In the days of his flesh" — This must refer to the days of his earthly life, prior to the death on the cross. This is an appeal to remember a suffering man, not the King of all kings on the Right Hand of God now exalted. The author is telling them to remember Jesus as a human.

"Strong crying and tears" — It is interesting to notice this is not mentioned in the gospels. Some say this "crying" is an "outcry," or earnest petition, and may be what is meant by praying "more earnestly" (Luke 22:44). But this is doubtful. The author of Hebrews adds to the rich color of the agony of our Lord, as we can now know how agonized was this God-man in the Gethsemane experience.

"Unto him that was able to save him from death" — This implies the petition was to save him from death. Cutting through all the froth presented by all the scholars, let us just here consider why it is stated that the petition was sent to the one able to save Jesus from death. If Jesus' prayer did not involve such a petition, there would have been no reason to include this phrase. It takes some imagination to ignore this implication. Now, as to whether it means the death on the cross, or an untimely death in the garden will be another question to settle.

"Having been heard for his godly fear" — The KJV says "was heard in that he feared," helping to raise a question of possibility that Jesus was merely praying to be relieved from fear of death. This seems, however, to have been translated more correctly by the ASV and RSV, which tend to strengthen the idea that Jesus' prayer was heard because of his cautious reverence for the Father.

Jesus' prayer was heard and answered, but the "cup" remained! Jesus told Peter to put up the sword, for, ". . . the cup which the Father hath given me, shall I not drink it?" (John 18:11)? Jesus thus implied he was still to drink the "cup," evidently the death on the cross. Now, look at some of the prior uses of this "cup":

(1) The cup which the sons of Zebedee would partake, evidently a cup of suffering (Ma. 20:22-23); (2) The cup of suffering and death, for which he prayed three times that it might be removed (Ma. 26:39-42); (3) The cup of suffering and death, which could be removed by him to whom "all things are possible" (Mark 14:36); (4) The cup of suffering and death during which time an angel strengthened him and his sweat became as it were great drops of blood (Luke 22:42-44). He was said to be "in agony" and prayed "more earnestly;" (5) Yet, finally, he said to Peter that he was still to drink the cup (John 18:11).

Therefore, it seems to be the most evident that Jesus was praying that he might not have to die and suffer on the cross. He was still willing to do so, but it was not his desire to do so. He did pray that the will of the Father be done, and in this sense, his prayer had an affirmative answer. The Father's will was done, Jesus suffered and died.

Many questions about this conclusion can still be raised. And, they may not all be answered satisfactorily. But, in all other positions examined, there seem to be even more unanswerable questions. So, we shall opt for the position that is the *least unsatisfactory!*

Lightfoot gives a brief sketch, very germane, of four positions about this verse: (1) Jesus was heard on the basis of his godly fear, that he prayed for the cup of death to be removed, but the Father's will was done; (2) Jesus was delivered from the fear of death; (3) Jesus was delivered from death by means of resurrection; (4) Jesus prayed that he might not die then and there in the garden, and thus frustrate his life's mission.[21]

His conclusion about this is well put: "In Gethsemane . . . like all men, Jesus needed to pray: he needed to submit absolutely to God's will and feel firsthand the frustration of not giving in to his own human desires."[22]

Coffman makes a cogent remark that the Father "sends not a lighter burden but a stronger heart to bear it."[23] Bruce gets poetic when he phrases it as a "career of public obedience which was inaugurated in the earlier baptism . . . crowned by the second baptism . . ."[24] (Obviously this was in reference to the baptism of suffering: Mark 10:38; Luke 12:50). Barnes puts it as concisely as any when he says, ". . . if human redemption could be accomplished without such sufferings, it might please his Father to remove that cup from him."[25]

CONCLUSION

So, the best conclusion about this God-man and his prayer in the garden may well be that his humanity shrank from suffering and death, as does all humanity. He prayed as any man would pray, for any other possible and consistent conclusion. But, he prayed, as any other dedicated man would pray, that the Father's will would be done. And it was.

Milligan's position was that Jesus prayed that he might be relieved from the fear and apprehensions of death and be able to satisfy the claims of Divine Government. This corresponds to number two above, but his further note about the death of our Lord is most worthy:

. . . he had nevertheless now to meet and endure the solemn and awful reality. He had to pass through such a spiritual ordeal as no creature had ever before experienced. The nails that pierced his hands and feet were but as nothing. Persons of ordinary strength generally lived on the cross from one to four or five days, and sometimes even longer. But Jesus, though in the prime of manhood, survived but six hours after his crucifixion. The weight of our indebtedness to the Divine government fell like a mountain avalanche on his soul. The light of God's countenance was withheld; and a horror of appalling darkness overwhelmed his spirit. He could bear no more. He said, "It is finished." His heart broke under the weight of his mental agony; and he meekly bowed his head and expired![26]

ENDNOTES

1. Loraine Boettner, *Studies in Theology* (Grand Rapids, MI: Wm. Eerdmans Pub. Co., 1957), pp. 197, 199-200.

2. A. H. Strong, *Systematic Theology* (Philadelphia, PA: Judson Press, 1907 — reprint 1946), p. 649.

3. E. Y. Mullins, *The Christian Religion in Its Doctrinal Expression* (Philadelphia, PA: Judson Press, 1949), p. 186.

4. Roy H. Lanier Sr., *The Timeless Trinity for the Ceaseless Centuries* (Denver, CO: Roy H. Lanier, Sr., 1974), p. 268.

5. Boettner, *op. cit.*, p. 202.

6. J. H. Thayer, *A Greek-English Lexicon of the New Testament* (New York, NY: American Book Co., 1889), p. 619.

7. W. F. Arndt and F. W. Gingrich, *A Greek-English Lexicon of the New Testament and Other Early Christian Literature* (Chicago, IL: University of Chicago Press, 1957), p. 817.

8. W. E. Vine, *Expository Dictionary of New Testament Words* (Iowa Falls, IO: Riverside Book and Bible House, 1952), p. 846.

9. N. R. Lightfoot, *Jesus Christ Today, A Commentary on the Book of Hebrews* (Grand Rapids, MI: Baker Book House, 1976), p. 76.

10. Franz Delitzsch, *Commentary on the Epistle to the Hebrews* (Edinburgh, Scot.: T. & T. Clark, 1857), vol. I, p. 119.

11. Albert Barnes, *Notes on the New Testament — Hebrews* (Grand Rapids, MI: Baker Book House, 1868 — reprint 1949), p. 66.

12. Lanier, *op. cit.,* p. 260.

13. R. C. H. Lenski, *Interpretation of St. Matthew's Gospel,* (Minneapolis, MN: Augsburg Pub. House, 1961), pp. 160-161.

14. Conybeare and Howson, *The Life and Epistles of St. Paul* (New York, NY: George H. Doran Co., n.d.), p. 858.

15. H. K. Moulton, *The Analytical Greek Lexicon Revised* (Grand Rapids, MI: Zondervan, 1978 — revision and reprint of *Bagster's Analytical Greek Lexicon,* 1852), p. 314.

16. Vine, *op. cit.*, pp. 1067-1068.

17. R. Milligan, *The New Testament Commentary — Hebrews* (Dallas, TX: Eugene S. Smith — reprint of 1875 edition), pp. 139-140.

18. Delitzsch, *op. cit.*, p. 213.

19. Lenski, *op. cit.*, p. 143.

20. Lightfoot, *op. cit.*, p. 99.

21. *Ibid.*, p. 114.

22. *Ibid.*, p. 109.

23. J. B. Coffman, *Commentary on Hebrews* (Austin, TX: Firm Foundation, 1971), p. 109.

24. F. F. Bruce, *The Epistle to the Hebrews, The New International Commentary on the New Testament* (Grand Rapids, MI: Wm. Eerdmans Pub. Co., 1964), p. 104.

25. Barnes, *op. cit.*, p. 116.

26. Milligan, *op. cit.*, p. 159.

DIFFICULT PASSAGES IN HEBREWS
No. III

HEBREWS 6:1-3:   "FIRST PRINCIPLES" — JEWISH OR CHRISTIAN?
HEBREWS 6:4-8   IMPOSSIBLE TO RENEW APOSTATES

By GARY WORKMAN

Native Californian. Local preaching work in California, Nevada, Texas. Served in Beirut, Lebanon for three and one-half years where he established a congregation and served as Dean of Middle East Bible Training College. Served as instructor in Bible and Biblical languages in Preston Rd. School of Preaching, Dallas, TX. He and his wife, Sunny, have four children. Founder and editor of *The Restorer*. Author of booklet on I Corinthians 13. Is presently devoting his time to Christian journalism and preaching in gospel meetings and special lecture programs. Speaker, *First Annual Denton Lectures.*

INTRODUCTION

The two connected passages treated in this chapter have occasioned much difficulty for the interpreter. The second section (vv. 4-8) has been described as "one of the fiercest theological battlegrounds of the centuries."[1] This is due partly to doctrinal bias and partly to a failure to rightly understand the first section (vv. 1-3). The first six verses of this chapter are admittedly difficult no matter how one views them. But it is the opinion of this writer that most commentators have viewed them wrongly. We offer the following discussion with an admonition to the reader to test our conclusions for himself — "prove all things; hold fast that which is good" (I Th. 5:21).

"FIRST PRINCIPLES" — JEWISH OR CHRISTIAN?
(6:1-3)

This passage is usually thought to mean that the readers should leave the ABC's of Christianity (in the sense of building on them) in order to go on to Christianity's deeper matters. It is interesting to read the remarks of various commentators *who hold this view but who are candid enough to admit the lack of evidence for it.* For example, Bruce notes "how little in the list [of first principles] is distinctive of Christianity, for practically every item could have its place in a fairly orthodox Jewish community."[2] And Lightfoot observes, "What is striking about the list is how little that is specifically Christian it contains."[3] Why then do these and many other such writers go ahead to interpret them as the basics of Christianity? Perhaps Hughes provides the answer when he admits that it would "ease some of the exegetical problems of the passage if the readers are being encouraged to abandon beliefs that are distinctly Jewish rather than Christian," but thinks that the expression "the elementary doctrines of Christ" (as he renders it), the tenor of the immediate context, and the long history of Christian interpretation of the passage make it "impossible" to do so.[4] We believe, however, that the weight of the evidence swings to the other side — *that the readers are not being urged to leave the basics for the deeper things of Christianity but rather to leave Judaism behind in order to really go on fully into Christianity as the finality or "perfection" of God's redemptive plan.*

The context. The word "therefore" (KJV) or "wherefore" (ASV) at the beginning of verse 1 indicates a conclusion and points back to the preceding section of 5:11-14. But going back even further, chapter 5 began by demonstrating that Jesus qualified to be a High Priest. He was therefore "made perfect" (cf. 2:10) or qualified through his atonement to be (1) the author of eternal salvation (5:9) and (2) a divinely called, permanent High Priest after the order of Melchizedek (v. 10). It was this Melchizedekan high priesthood of Christ that these readers needed to be convinced about. But they had become so "dull" or sluggish in their spiritual understanding that they needed for someone to take them back to the Old Testament scriptures — "the beginning of the oracles of God" (v. 12, literal reading) — and show them how Jesus was qualified to be their Savior and High Priest so that they would not be inclined to revert to the Jewish system. They had not studied those Old Testament "oracles" (cf. Acts 7:38; Rom. 3:2) enough and so had not really understood the basic "principles" (KJV) or "rudiments" (ASV) of the Old Testament system — its types, ordinances and ceremonies that pointed to the Messiah (5:12). Therefore, they wanted to remain in that now abrogated covenant.

"*Leaving.*" The basic meaning of this word *aphiemi* is derived from its two parts: *apo* — "away from" and *hiemi* — "to send." Hence, it indicates separation — to send away. Occurring 142 times in the New Testament, it means to *let go, remit, send away, cancel, leave, divorce or forsake.*[5] In a literal sense, it was used of the sending away of the multitudes (Matt. (13:36), the leaving of a spouse (I Cor. 7:11-13), and the leaving behind of an object (Mark 1:18) or thing (v. 20). The Arndt-Gingrich lexicon gives its figurative use as "give up, abandon."[6] For example, the Ephesians had "left" or abandoned their first love (Rev. 2:4). Homosexuals had been "leaving" the natural use of the woman (Rom. 1:27). Jesus rebuked the Pharisees, saying, "Ye *leave* the commandment of God, and hold fast the tradition of men" (Mark 7:8). To "leave" is here explained by Jesus as to "reject" the commandment of God (v. 9). They also had "omitted" (KJV) or "left undone" (ASV) the weightier matters of the law (Matt. 23:23).

Arndt and Gingrich render the word *leave* in Hebrews 6:1 as "leave behind."[7] Also, Bultmann in the *TDNT* assigns it as "to leave behind."[8] It is clear that the word does not mean to *build upon,* as many have supposed. In our passage, the word "leaving" is an aorist participle, which serves as an imperative preceding the action of the main verb. One must leave one thing before he can go on to another. The Hebrew Christians needed to abandon or leave behind "the doctrine of the first principles of Christ" in order to "go on to perfection" (He. 6:1).

"*The first principles of Christ.*" "The doctrine of the first principles of Christ" is more literally "the word of the beginning of Christ," as the ASV margin renders it and according to the word order notated in Marshall's interlinear. The

KJV has "the principles of the doctrine of Christ," whereas the ASV reverses the order of the first two key terms and gives it as "the doctrine of the first principles of Christ."

Actually, there is no word for "principles" in this verse at all. The Greek word is *arche,* which means "beginning, origin." It is the same word translated in 5:12 as "first" (KJV) or "beginning" (ASV mg.). That passage should therefore be rendered "the rudiments of the beginning of the oracles of God" or "the beginning rudiments of the word of God." While some think the word *arche* means "elementary" in 5:12, it more likely refers to past revelation. The same is true for the word as used in 6:1. Thayer renders 6:1 as indicating "the instruction concerning Christ such as it was at the very outset,"[9] thus "the beginning word of Christ."

"The beginning word of Christ" (6:1) is equivalent in meaning to "the beginning elements of the oracles of God" (5:12). Both point back to the Old Testament. Pink says that the expression "has reference to what God has made known concerning His Son under Judaism," such as the prophecies of his coming and the types and figures of the work he would do.[10] Wuest remarks, "The tabernacle, priesthood, and offerings all speak of Him in His Person and work. And this interpretation is in exact accord with the argument of the book."[11]

"Let us press on unto perfection." The word "perfection" (*teleiotes*) is found only here and in Colossians 3:14. But the verb *teleioo* is used several times in the argument to the Hebrews, and a noun synonym (*teleiosis*) is used once. Let us notice the application of these key terms:

7:11 — There was no "perfection" under the Levitical priesthood.
7:19 — The law made nothing "perfect."
9: 9 — The tabernacle system could not make the worshippers "perfect."
10: 1 — The law could not "make perfect" the offerers through its sacrifices.
10:14 — Jesus' atonement "perfected" those who are sanctified.
11:40 — Old Testament saints could not be "made perfect" without us, but now their spirits have been "made perfect" (12:23).
12: 2 — Jesus is the "perfecter" of our faith.

It is obvious that the "perfection" the writer is concerned with in this book is the Christian system and its consequences.

Whereas the Hebrew Christians were inclined to revert to the Old Covenant, or at least straddle the fence and try to be Jews and Christians at the same time, the writer urges them to "leave" (fully) the Jewish system in order to "go on" (fully) into the Christian system.

"Not laying again a foundation." Next the writer presents six foundational elements not to be laid again (vv. 1b-2). This section is an explanation or elaboration of what it means to abandon the beginning word of Christ. Contrary to the assumption of most commentators, these six items are not fundamentals of Christianity but rather of Judaism. Some of the six are also relevant to Christianity, but *none are exclusively Christian!* On the other hand, *all* of them are to be found in the Old Testament and some pertain *only* to the Old Testament system. Let us look at each of the six items.

"Repentance from dead works." The writer did not say "repentance from sins" which would be characteristic of conversion to Christianity (Luke 24:47). "Dead works" are mentioned only here and once again in Hebrews 9:14. Numerous writers think that these "dead works" refer to the Old Testament Levitical rituals — "the works-righteousness of man without Christ," as some conceive of it.[12] But these cannot be the ceremonial works of a Jewish worshipper, for one was never called upon to repent of having obeyed the Law of God! Therefore, this expression does not speak of conversion from Judaism to Christianity.

"Dead works" were sins that remained upon the conscience even after the Levitical ceremonies were able to "sanctify" the Jew in a limited sense (9:14), because the respondent was never fully "cleansed" by animal blood from the "consciousness of sins" (10:2). They are "dead works" because they belong to the realm of death — spiritual death which is the result of sin (Eze. 18:20; Ep. 2:1). These sins needed to be repented of by the Jew under the Old Covenant as well as by the Christian under the New.

"Faith toward God." Whereas Gentiles were for the most part ignorant of the one true God (Acts 17:23; Rom. 1:25, 28), the first-century Jews believed in God (John 14:1). They were instructed about God from early childhood (He. 8:11a; II Ti. 3:15). The Old Testament saints listed in the honor roll of

chapter 11 all had faith toward God (cf. 11:6). But what Jewish hearers needed to heed was Christ's plea to "believe also in me" (John 14:1) in order to become Christians.

The New Testament faith is predominantly connected with Jesus in New Testament references (Ga. 2:16, 20; 3:22, 26; Ep. 1:15; Ph. 3:9; Col. 1:4; 2:5; I Ti. 3:13). "Faith toward our Lord Jesus Christ" was preached by Paul as the Christian message to Jews and Gentiles (Acts 20:21). Jesus is "the originator and finisher of the faith" which pertains to the New Testament age (He. 12:2). But "faith toward God" was characteristic of the Old and was therefore a foundational element of Judaism.

"The teaching of baptisms." The English noun "baptism" is found 22 times in the KJV New Testament. John's baptism is mentioned 13 times; Jesus' suffering is figuratively referred to as a baptism five times; and Christian baptism is mentioned four times. In all of these instances the Greek word is *baptisma*, a neuter singular noun. But in Hebrews 6:2 the English word "baptisms" is not from that same Greek word. Instead it is *baptismos*, a masculine word occurring here in the genitive plural — *baptismon* instead of *baptismaton*. It is elsewhere found only three times in the New Testament (four in the *Textus Receptus*). In every case (except a doubtful manuscript variant in Col. 2:12) it is translated "washings" and refers to Jewish cleansing rites. It thus had to do with the "washings of cups and pots and brasen vessels" (Mark 7:4; cf. v. 8, KJV), and such like. The word is found again in Hebrews 9:10 where it is likewise used in reference to "divers washings," defined as "carnal ordinances, imposed until a time of reformation."

Since *none* of the occurrences of *baptisma* refer to Jewish washings, and since *all* of the occurrences of *baptismos* do refer to those washings, this makes a strong case for the word in Hebrews 6:2 to also refer to those same washings of the Levitical rituals. Trench, in his famous work on New Testament words, says: "By *baptismos* in the usage of the N.T. we must understand any ceremonial washing or lustration . . . while by *baptisma* we understand baptism in our Christian sense of the word," and he adds that "all explanations of Heb. 6:2 . . . which rest on the assumption that Christian Baptism is intended here, break down before this fact."[13]

Commentators labor hard to try to think of a reason why the plural term for "washings" should be used here to refer to, or at least include, Christian baptism. Space prohibits a refutation here of these various notions, except for one of the more popular ideas. It has been thought by some to refer to both Christian baptism and Jewish washings collectively, with the "teaching" or "doctrine" about them relating to a proper distinction between the two. John's baptism might even be thought to be included. Hughes takes this as the most viable explanation, with Paul's instruction to the Ephesian disciples (Acts 19:1-7) and Apollos' new insights from Priscilla and Aquila (Acts 18:24-26) cited as prime examples of such needed "teaching."[14]

Such a conclusion, however, is imaginative and speculative. Why would not the "laying on of hands" (mentioned next) also be plural in order to distinguish between Jewish and Christian uses of it? Hughes has to candidly admit that "it is not obvious that baptism is intended" in Hebrews 6:2.[15] It appears that this commentator, as well as many others, argues that Christian baptism is involved here simply because he assumes at the outset that the writer was discussing a "foundation" of Christianity, and therefore to him "it seems impossible . . . to remove Christian baptism from the center of the picture."[16]

All of this reasoning begs the question. One cannot assume that which he is trying to prove. The fact is that the Greek word for "washings" is never used in the New Testament as these writers conjecture, but only of Jewish ceremonial rituals. And this is strong evidence for understanding the word the same way in this passage. Besides, the whole context of the book of Hebrews is to convince these Jewish Christians not to go back to the Levitical system but rather to proceed fully into Christianity. The reader should take note that if our understanding of "washings" here is correct, this point alone is decisive for the "first principles" being Jewish rather than Christian.

"*Laying on of hands.*" The majority of commentators, thinking the previous foundational item a reference to Christian baptism, have interpreted this to be the apostolic laying on of hands in order to confer supernatural gifts of the Holy Spirit. Reference is therefore usually made to such passages as Acts 8:17; 19:6; and II Timothy 1:6. Laying on of hands to initiate miraculous healing is sometimes thought to be included (Mark 16:18; Acts 9:12, 17; 28:8). Some even imagine the writer to also encompass the imposition of hands as an act of blessing or commissioning someone to a particular task (Acts 6:6; 13:3; I Ti. 4:14).

These latter purposes for the laying on of hands were certainly exceptional and not even distinctively Christian. But even the apostolic conferring of spiritual gifts followed baptism only on occasions when an apostle happened to be present (Acts 8:16-17; 19:5-6), which often was not the case (Ro. 1:11). This question immediately comes to mind: if the writer is listing basic elements of Christianity, common to all Christians, why mention the laying on of hands and omit the Lord's supper? After all, newly baptized converts were continually involved in "the breaking of bread" (Acts 2:42) as a key element of Christianity.

It appears that a better interpretation than that above can be given for the "laying on of hands." If these six items refer to Judaism rather than Christianity, reference to the laying on of hands seems much more natural. Such imposition of hands was fundamental to Jewish religion. It was repeatedly prescribed in the Levitical ritual for the offerers to lay hands on their animal sacrifices. Such was true of priests (Le. 4:4), elders as representatives of the whole nation (v. 15), rulers (v. 24) and every common person (Le. 1:4; 3:2, 8, 13; 4:29, 33). The laying on of hands was extremely important in the consecration of priests (Ex. 29:10, 15, 19; Le. 8:14, 18, 22, 27-28). And in the case of every individual's burnt offerings, "his own hands" had to be involved (Lev. 7:30).

Not only this, but the prescribed ritual concerning the high priest on the annual Day of Atonement was for him to "lay both his hands upon the head of the live goat," the scapegoat which representatively bore "all the iniquities of the children of Israel" (Le. 16:21). This action immediately followed the sacrifice of "the goat of the sin offering" for all the people of God (vv. 15-19). Every Jew was involved in the blood offering of the one goat and the laying on of hands in connection with the other.

It is important also to observe that our passage in Hebrews 6 where the laying on of hands is mentioned occurs in the section of Hebrews where Jesus, our "great high priest," is set in contrast to the high priest of the Levitical system (He. 4:14-10:18). The offerings of the Day of Atonement were alluded to already in Hebrews 5:3. However, Jesus needed to offer only one sacrifice — himself (7:27). It was thus demonstrated in the argument of the book that there was no "perfection through the Levitical priesthood" (7:11). The Day of Atonement offerings of the Jewish high priest (9:7), those "goats and calves" (9:12), were only "carnal ordinances" (9:10). Since it was "impossible that the blood of bulls and goats should take away sins" (10:4), or that a scapegoat could really carry sins away, the "blood of Christ" was offered (9:14), and Jesus "put away sin by the sacrifice of himself" (9:26).

The "laying on of hands" was a foundational element, therefore, which must not be laid again. It had to do with the Old Covenant which the writer urges his readers to *abandon* in order to really *press on* into the "perfection" of the New Covenant. These two middle items in the foundation list — washings and laying on of hands — make it conclusive to this writer that the interpretation here advocated is correct.

"Resurrection of the dead." Teaching about the "resurrection of the dead" was also revealed in Old Testament times (Job 19:25-27; Is. 26:19; Dan. 12:2; Ps. 17:15). It was commonly believed by all Jews (Acts 24:14-15; 26:6-8) except Sadducees (Acts 23:6-8; Ma. 22:23). Jesus proved it by a quotation of Exodus 3:6 (Luke 20:37-40). Martha therefore knew that her brother would "rise again in the resurrection at the last day" (John 11:24). But she needed to learn more about Jesus as "the resurrection and the life" (v. 25).

The preliminary resurrection of the Messiah had been hinted at by implication in the Old Testament (Is. 53:10, 12; Ps. 24). But it took the personal teaching of Jesus to make known that his rising "out of the dead" (Mark 9:9-10; Ma. 17:9; I Co. 15:20) was primary. Jesus' resurrection as the "firstfruits" (I Co. 15:20, 23; Col. 1:18; Re. 1:5) is the specific contribution of New Testament teaching, as well as elaboration on the nature of our resurrection bodies (I Co. 15:35-54; Ph. 3:21; I John 3:2). No, knowledge of the resurrection of the dead was not new to these Christian converts from Judaism. This foundation stone had been laid long ago.

"Eternal judgment." The doctrine of the final judgment of mankind was also known far back in the Old Testament period, even in pre-Mosaic days (Jude 14-15; Ps. 1:5; 50; 96:13; 98:9; Ec. 11:9; 12:14; Mal. 3:16; Da. 7:9-11, 22; 12:1-2; De. 32:22, 36; Is. 26:21). It is not the readers' understanding of this item, or indeed of any item in this list, that the writer urges them to abandon. Rather it is allegiance to the Mosaic Covenant as an ongoing system of religion — to which these elements were central — that must be given up.

Summary. While the majority of commentators on record have interpreted the foregoing passages as having to do with basic Christian doctrines, the view here espoused has had a fair representation. It has been defended vigorously by some (*e.g.,* Pink, Wuest, Vine, Camp) and moderately by others (*e.g.,* Clarke, MacKnight, Stibbs). We trust that the reader will give due consideration to the evidence presented.

IMPOSSIBLE TO RENEW APOSTATES
(6:4-8)

This section of chapter six has been one of the most hotly debated passages of the book — and even of the New Testament. Much twisting of terms and circuitous reasoning has been practiced by commentators in order to evade the apparent meaning of the passage: (1) that Christians can fall away from the faith and ultimately be lost, and (2) that certain ones who do this cannot come back into God's favor again. Let us first clear up some misinterpretations. Our discussion in this chapter has to do with the second of the above two items — why we cannot "renew them again unto repentance" — and, in particular, what the word "impossible" is intended to convey.

Two false views. Some think that the discussion in these verses about a person's falling away is only a hypothetical case that could never happen in real life to real Christians. This has been a favorite dodge of Calvinists and of those who retain the Calvinistic doctrine of the perseverance of the saints. Beza and the early English versions beginning with Tyndale inserted an "if" into verse 6. This was imitated by the KJV translators, and many commentators have followed suit. But there is no conditional element to the Greek construction, and it is therefore unjustifiable regardless of reasoned efforts to the contrary. Moulton traces the influence back to Erasmus and Luther.[17] The appearance of the "if" is probably due to doctrinal bias, though some have denied this. As MacKnight commented (himself a Calvinist), "no translator should take upon him to add to or alter the Scriptures for the sake of any favourite doctrine."[18] Clarke commended MacKnight for being "a thorough scholar and an honest man" who, "professing to give a *translation of the epistle,* he consulted not his creed but his candour."[19]

Others think the apostasy describes only "professing" rather than real Christians. Vine says, "The warning in verses 6 to 8 is not applied to actual Hebrew Christians."[20] Wuest agrees that "an unsaved person" is in view here and adds that "this sin cannot be committed today."[21] Some have resorted to the note of confidence expressed in verses 9-12 to support this view. But the five blessings enumerated in verses 4 and 5, plus their initial state of repentance alluded to in verse 6, cannot be ascribed to any but actual Christians. The sublime terms used obviously demonstrated to the Hebrew Christians that "apostasy from the highest degrees of grace was possible."[22]

Explanations about "impossible." Those who admit to the possibility of apostasy often attempt to find some way to explain away the word "impossible" in connection with a renewal to repentance. One idea is that "impossible" does not describe the apostates' ability to return but only the preachers' ability to re-convert them. So Westcott says, "It is impossible for man to renew . . . those who have fallen from the Faith," though he concedes that the fallen might, with some special help from God, ultimately come back.[23] This idea commonly speaks of what is not "impossible for God" but only "impossible for the ministers of Christ."[24] Often Mark 10:27 is incorrectly used to support the notion. In other words, they could not be re-convinced by man unless God supposedly performs some supernatural work on their hearts. This concept is foreign to the teaching of the New Testament, for "belief cometh of hearing, and hearing by the word of Christ" (Ro. 10:17).

Another idea was developed early in the Christian centuries — that this passage prohibits a repetition of baptism. Many therefore concluded that for sins committed after baptism (or at least for some sins) there could be no forgiveness. The names of Chrysostom, Clement of Alexandria, Tertullian, Ambrose, Jerome, the Montanists, and the Novations are all connected with this idea in one way or another. It is forthrightly refuted by such passages as Acts 8:22 and I John 1:9.

Still another misinterpretation is to soften the word "impossible" to just mean *difficult.* The Latin version of the sixth-century Codex D actually inserted the word *difficile* into the text. But this evasion does violence to the original language, which Robertson says "bluntly denies the possibility of renewal for apostates from Christ" and "cannot be toned down."[25] The Greek word for "impossible" is *adunaton.* It occurs ten times in the New Testament, including three other passages in Hebrews (6:18; 10:4; 11:6). In all other places the word plainly means nothing less than *absolutely impossible,* and that must be its meaning in 6:6 also.

It has also been suggested that it is impossible to renew them unto repentance "the while" (ASV mg.) they crucify to themselves the Son of God afresh. This view emphasizes that "crucify" is a present participle and that the impossibility lasts only as long as the apostates continue their figurative crucifying. Both Bruce and Hughes repudiate this view as a simplistic truism. They take the crucifying as the *cause* for the impossibility rather than a temporal modifier for how long the state would continue.

A further explanation supposes a hardening of the apostates' senses to the point where it is a moral impossibility for them to return to Christ. This would therefore be the ultimate result of the process warned against in Hebrews 3:12-13. Thus, Bruce comments that "it is possible for human beings to arrive at a state of heart and life where they can no longer repent."[26] Woods likewise speaks of these fallen Christians as having "gone beyond the point of no return."[27] But while such a condition may be possible, as Scripture seems to attest (II Co. 4:3-4; Ep. 4:17-19; I Ti. 4:2), this does not appear to be the correct explanation of the passage in Hebrews 6.

One final view to be mentioned is that God simply will not accept back a fallen Christian who has once deliberately and wholeheartedly repudiated his Savior and his salvation. Hughes therefore suggests "a particular disposition involving a repudiation of grace so grave that it has the effect of permanently severing those who display it from the body of Christ." He equates it with the "sin unto death" (I John 5:16) and the "eternal sin" of blasphemy against the Holy Spirit (Mark 3:29). In this view our passage in Hebrews describes an "irremediable state" where a person "places himself beyond forgiveness and renewal."[28] But while the above-cited passages describe a continuing state of non-repentance in the one case and a blasphemous denunciation so perverse that God would never forgive in the other case, neither situation seems to be the matter discussed here. Further, a "once lost — always lost" view would be just as contrary to the teaching of Scripture as "once saved — always saved."

What "impossible to renew" must mean. In keeping with our interpretation of verses 1-3, a much simpler explanation appears to be the correct one. And it is in harmony with the context of the book. The passage was written to Hebrew Christians warning them not to fall away as some had already done. They were in danger of reverting to the Old Testament Levitical system with its priesthood and sacrifices. The purpose of the book was to prevent them from doing this. Therefore, Hebrews was written to demonstrate the superiority of Christ and Christianity over Judaism, to warn them against falling back to the Jewish system, and to exort them to renew their spiritual diligence.

A key section of the book emphasizes that Jesus' high priesthood is better than the Aaronic or Levitical priesthood and that the New Covenant replaced the Old. Since the one great sacrifice has now replaced the many sacrifices of the Levitical ritual, the writer's point in Hebrews 6:4-8 is that the Jewish sacrificial system cannot spiritually renew his Hebrew-Christian readers if they should happen to go back to it. The warning, both here and in the similar passage of 10:26-31, is not just against falling away in general but specifically against falling back to Judaism!

Even when the Old Covenant was still in force as God's religion, there was "a remembrance made of sins year by year" (Heb. 10:3). This was a remembrance of *all* past sins, even those previously atoned for, because it was actually "impossible that the blood of bulls and goats should take away sins" (v. 4). It was a faulty or limited covenant (He. 8:7) under which God had to continually find fault with his people (v. 8). But under the New Covenant no such "remembrance" kept coming up. When God forgave he forgot. With Jesus as the sin offering, God promised that all forgiven sins he would "remember no more" (Je. 31:34; He. 8:12; 10:17).

Now that the New Covenant has replaced the Old, the Levitical system cannot even do what it once did with its limited accomplishments. The Old can now do nothing at all for it has been taken away (He. 10:9). Therefore, with the Old Covenant it is now "impossible to renew them again unto repentance" (6:6) because under that system "there remaineth no more a sacrifice for sins" (10:26). For now "in none other is there salvation" except in Jesus (Acts 4:12). It is not that it is "impossible" for such apostates to return to *Christianity*, but rather it is "impossible" for them to be saved under *Judaism*.

Such people as those mentioned "crucify to themselves the Son of God" (He. 6:6) either by reverting to sacrifices which called for the death of Christ (10:5-10) or by associating themselves with an apostate nation and rejecting "the blood of the covenant" (10:29). Ultimately, such fallen ones can only have "a certain fearful expectation of judgment" (10:27). When they finally "fall into the hands of the living God" (10:31), their "end is to be burned" (6:8) in the "fierceness of fire which shall devour the adversaries" (10:27).

CONCLUSION

The Hebrew Christians had become "dull of hearing" (He. 5:11) because of continuing to be "inexperienced in the word of righteousness" (v. 13). We may not be in danger of reverting to Judaism as they were, but we always face the danger of reverting to worldly ways or some false religion and be lost at the end. A continual exposure to the "solid food" of God's Word, including difficult passages such as this one, will build us up (Acts 20:32) and keep our "senses exercised to discern good and evil" (He. 5:14). In case any interpretation of ours contained in this chapter should be incorrect after all, we will close by saying with Jesus — "let him that readeth understand."

ENDNOTES

1. Arthur W. Pink, *An Exposition of Hebrews* (Baker, 1954), p. 285.

2. F. F. Bruce, *The Epistle to the Hebrews* (Eerdmans, 1964), p. 112.

3. Neil R. Lightfoot, *Jesus Christ Today* (Baker, 1976), p. 120.

4. Philip Hughes, *A Commentary on the Epistle to the Hebrews* (Eerdmans, 1977), p. 195.

5. Herwart Vorlander, "Forgiveness," *The New International Dictionary of New Testament Theology* (Zondervan, 1967), vol. I, p. 697.

6. Arndt and Gingrich (eds.), *Greek-English Lexicon* (Univ. of Chicago, 1963), p. 125.

7. *Ibid.*

8. Rudolf Bultmann, *"Aphiemi,"* *Theological Dictionary of the New Testament* (Eerdmans, 1964), vol. I, p. 510.

9. Joseph H. Thayer, *Greek-English Lexicon* (Zondervan, 1975), p. 77.

10. Pink, *op. cit.*, p. 275.

11. Kenneth S. Wuest, *Hebrews in the Greek New Testament* (Eerdmans, 1947), p. 110.

12. Lothar Coenen, "Death, Kill, Sleep," *NIDNTT*, vol. I, p. 446.

13. Richard Trench, *Synonyms of the New Testament* (National Foundation for Christian Education, n.d.), pp. 346-347.

14. Hughes, *op. cit.*, p. 202.

15. Hughes, *op. cit.*, p. 199.

16. Hughes, *op. cit.*, p. 202.

17. W. F. Moulton, "The Epistle to the Hebrews," *A New Testament Commentary*, Charles J. Ellicott, ed. (Cassell & Co., 1884), vol. III, p. 303.

18. James MacKnight, *Apostolic Epistles* (Baker, n.d.), p. 532.

19. Adam Clarke, *Clarke's Commentary* (Abingdon-Cokesbury, n.d.), vol. II, p. 725.

20. W. E. Vine, *The Epistle to the Hebrews* (Oliphants, 1952), p. 57.

21. Wuest, *op. cit.*, pp. 115, 118.

22. Clarke, *op. cit.*, p. 724.

23. B. F. Westcott, *The Epistle to the Hebrews* (Eerdmans, 1965), pp. 148, 150.

24. Cf. MacKnight, *loc. cit.*

25. A. T. Robertson, *Word Pictures in the New Testament* (Baker, 1932), vol. V, p. 375.

26. Bruce, *op. cit.*, p. 124.

27. Guy N. Woods, *Questions and Answers* (Freed-Hardeman, 1976), pp. 133-135.

28. Hughes, *op. cit.*, pp. 214-222.

DIFFICULT PASSAGES IN HEBREWS
No. IV

HEBREWS 9:3-4	**WHY IS THE GOLDEN ALTAR IN THE HOLY OF HOLIES?**
HEBREWS 9:15	**HOW DOES THE BLOOD OF CHRIST REDEEM THE TRANSGRESSIONS UNDER THE FIRST COVENANT?**
HEBREWS 10:7	**WHAT IS THE "ROLL OF THE BOOK?"**
HEBREWS 10:25	**WHAT IS "THE DAY DRAWING NIGH?"**

By JOHN WADDEY

Nashville, TN native. Local preaching work in Mississippi, Colorado and Tennessee has spanned 26 years. Gospel meeting work in 29 states. Has visited mission works in 19 foreign nations. Director of annual World Missions Workshop, Knoxville, TN. Has conducted weekly radio broadcast for 11 years. Author of 20 books, hundreds of newspaper and gospel paper articles. Local evangelist with Karns Church, Knoxville, TN and instructor in East Tennessee School of Preaching conducted by Karns. Speaker, *First Annual Denton Lectures.*

INTRODUCTION

Anything of value which challenges the minds of wise men will of necessity contain some problem areas not of simple solution. The book of Hebrews abounds with such "difficult" passages, four of which we will now attend to.

WHY IS THE GOLDEN ALTAR IN THE HOLY OF HOLIES? (9:3-4)

In Hebrews 9:3-4 the author is describing the tabernacle, its furnishings and ritual: "And after the second veil, the

tabernacle which is called the Holy of holies; having a golden
altar of incense and the ark of the covenant . . ." The problem
here is two-fold: (1) What does the Greek word *thumiaterion*
mean? Is it correctly rendered "censer" or "altar of incense?"
(2) Where was the *thumiaterion* located?

Those rendering the term "censer" include the King James
translation, the English Revised (1881), the Septuagint, Latin
Vulgate and the Syriac Peshitta. The American Standard,
Revised Standard and most recent translations give us "altar
of incense." This was the understanding of Philo, Josephus
and the Greek translators Symmachus and Theodotion.

The Greek term simply means "something on which or in
which incense is placed" and thus could be rendered either
censer or altar of incense. The context must decide the matter.

First, the author is discussing the furnishings of the tabernacle. He mentions the candlestick, the table of showbread, the
veil, and the ark of the covenant. In the midst of that he
mentions the *thumiaterion* which in context would most certainly be the other item of furniture, the altar of incense. It is
not likely he would omit such an important item.

Second, Moses also writes,

> and thou shalt make an altar to burn incense upon . . . and thou
> shalt put it before the veil that is by the ark of the testimony . . .
> and Aaron shall burn thereon incense of sweet spices . . . (Ex. 30:1,
> 6-7).

"And Aaron shall make atonement upon the horns of it [the
altar of incense] once in the year; with the blood of the sin-
offering of atonement . . ." (Ex. 30:10).

The purposes and uses of the altar:

Every day of the year the high priest burned incense
thereon:

> And Aaron shall burn thereon incense of sweet spices; every morn-
> ing, when he dresseth the lamps, he shall burn it. And when Aaron
> lighteth the lamps at even, he shall burn it, a perpetual incense be-
> fore Jehovah . . . (Ex. 30:7-8).

This would require daily access to the altar. Since the high
priest could enter the holy of holies only one day per year, that
necessitated the altar's being placed in the holy place (Ex.
30:10). Even he was not allowed to enter at other times (Le.
16:2): "And Aaron shall make atonement upon the horns of it

once in the year; with the blood of the sin-offering of atonement. . ." (Ex. 30:10). Additionally on the Day of Atonement,

> And he shall take a censer full of coals of fire from off the altar be-
> fore Jehovah, and his hands full of sweet incense beaten small, and
> bring it within the veil; and he shall put the incense upon the fire
> before Jehovah, that the cloud of the incense may cover the mercy-
> seat. . . that he die not (Le. 16:12-13).

The blood on the horns of the altar was an important
aspect of the atonement for sins of the nation. The cloud of
incense filling the room shielded the high priest from divine
wrath as he stood before the mercy seat and the presence of
Jehovah.

The altar and its incense had additional atoning powers.
When a plague of judgment was sent upon the murmuring
Israelites,

> And Moses said unto Aaron, Take thy censer, and put fire therein
> from off the altar, and lay incense thereon, and carry it quickly unto
> the congregation, and make atonement for them . . . And he stood
> between the dead and the living; and the plague was stayed (Nu. 16:
> 46-48).

Possible explanations:

In addition to the altar of incense there was a golden "fire
pan" for incense on the day of atonement. This might be in-
ferred from Leviticus 16:12-13.

A second possibility is that the word *thumiaterion* refers to
the golden altar of incense alone which stood in the holy place,
before the veil hiding the mercy seat. The context supports
this. The high priest thus had daily access to the altar for
morning and evening offerings. On the Day of Atonement with
the curtains drawn back, then the altar would literally be
before the mercy seat. Lenski sees the solution in I Kings 6:22
which says, "the whole altar that belonged to the oracle (*i.e.,*
the holy of holies) . . ." which means that the golden altar was
by the oracle, standing before the veil that shielded the most
holy place.[1] Arthur Pink notes the writer's careful choice of
words. In verse two he speaks of the tabernacle (the holy place)
wherein was the candlestick and table . . . but in verses three
and four it is the Holy of holies; *having* a golden altar of
incense . . . "because this utensil did not form part of the
furniture of the holy of holies."[2]

A third possibility is that since the altar of incense was a movable object, on the Day of Atonement it could have been moved from its regular station in the holy place on into the holy of holies. We concede that no mention of this is made.

Finally, some scholars dismiss the problem by saying that the author was confused or mistaken. Dr. Gottlieb Lunemann in the H. A. Meyers Commentary on Hebrews held this view.[3]

Also Moffatt in *The International Critical Commentary on Hebrews*, p. 115, says that "the irregularity of placing it on the wrong side of the curtain is simply another of his inaccuracies in describing what he only knew from the text of the LXX."[4] In the words of Franz Delitzsch, it would take "a monster of ignorance" to make such a gross mistake. Clearly, we repudiate this simplistic approach of unbelievers.

This author opts for solution number two as the most consistent within the total context.

HOW DOES THE BLOOD OF CHRIST REDEEM THE TRANSGRESSIONS UNDER THE FIRST COVENANT? (9:15)

And for this cause he is the mediator of a new covenant, that a death having taken place for the redemption of the transgressions that were under the first covenant, they that have been called may receive the promise of the eternal inheritance (He. 9:15).

This passage, which is a mystery to some, contains wonderful lessons to him who rightly divides the word of truth (II Ti. 2:15).

The ninth chapter of Hebrews contrasts the old and new covenants, stressing the superiority of the new. Five points of contrast are noted: First, the old system had an earthly sanctuary, the new a heavenly one (9:1, 11). Second, the old was typical of something greater that was to come (9:2-5). The new is one of fulfillment. It is the reality of which the old was typical (9:23-28). Third, the old tabernacle was inaccessible to the people (9:6-7). In the new all Christians are priests (I Pe. 2:5, 9). Fourth, the old system was temporary (9:8), the new is final and complete (9:25-28). Fifth, the old ministry dealt with externals and ceremony (9:9-10). Christ's ministry is able to deal with sin effectively (9:12-15). His sacrifice is superior to animal sacrifices (9:16-23). The new sacrifice can cleanse the conscience, while the old offered only outward ceremonial cleansing. The old offered temporal blessings while the new offered eternal spiritual blessings (9:15).

An overview:

The contents of verse 15 are effectively summarized by John Owen as follows (cited by Arthur Pink):

> (a) God designed an "eternal inheritance" for certain individuals. (b) The title to this inheritance was conveyed by "promise." (c) Those to whom this promise was given have been "called." (d) Their enjoyment of this inheritance was being hindered by their "transgressions." (e) Because none of the sacrifices of the Mosaic system could take away the guilt of their transgressions so they could enjoy their inheritance, God gave a "new covenant." (f) The effectiveness of this new covenant was its Mediator who was a great "high priest," Jesus, God's Son. (g) This high priest forgave the transgressions of the first covenant by means of his own death. This was also necessary because this covenant was also a "testament" which required a death for validation. (h) The death of this Mediator/priest has paid an adequate price for, or "redeemed the transgressions that were under the first covenant" and ours as well. (i) Thus the promise is sure to all.[5]

The unresolved problem:

Sin has been with man since Eden. All sinned and fell short of God's glory (Ro. 3:23). The animal sacrifices of the Patriarchal and Mosaic system could not adequately deal with sin: "For it is impossible that the blood of bulls and goats should take away sins" (He. 10:4);

> For the law having a shadow of the good things to come, not the very image of the things, can never with the same sacrifices year by year, which they offer continually, make perfect them that draw nigh (He. 10:1).

Their animal sacrifices could "sanctify unto the cleanness of the flesh" (He. 9:13), *i.e.*, they could take away ceremonial defilement but not moral guilt.

We ask, "Why then did they offer these unavailing sacrifices?" Because God so instructed them. Their faithful compliance was evidence of their trusting faith in God and his word (John 14:15).

The meaning of this passage is illustrated more clearly in Romans 3:24-26:

being justfied freely by his grace through the redemption that is in
Christ Jesus: whom God set forth to be a propitiation through faith
in his blood, to show his righteousness because of the passing over
of the sins done aforetime, in the forbearance of God; for the showing, I say, of his righteousness at this present season; that he might
himself be just, and the justifier of him that hath faith in Jesus.

God's passing over the sins done before Christ came is
vividly illustrated by the ceremonies of the annual day of
atonement described in Leviticus 16. On that holy day the high
priest having first offered a "bullock of the sin-offering" for
himself, selected "two goats, and set them before Jehovah at
the door of the tent of meeting." Lots were cast upon them,
one being chosen for Jehovah's sacrifice, one for Azazel, *i.e.,* to
symbolically bear away their sins into the wilderness. "And
Aaron shall lay both his hands upon the head of the live goat,
and confess over him all the iniquities of the children of Israel,
and all their transgressions, even all their sins . . ." (16:21).
"And this shall be an everlasting statute unto you, to make
atonement for the children of Israel because of all their sins
once in the year . . ." (16:34).

Each year the sins of the people came due. This solemn
ritual reminded every Hebrew of his undone condition; of the
debt he owed because of his sin. Yet each year God deferred the
judgment due, by reason of their faithful observance of the
atonement. This system continued until Christ came and made
his ultimate sacrifice which alone could "cleanse [their] conscience from dead works" (He. 9:14).

Every lamb slain on the altars of Israel was a typical
prediction of the coming Christ who was the true "Lamb of
God, that taketh away the sin of the world" (John 1:29).

Thus those who lived and died in faith under that system
were counted among the saved of God. He passed over the
judgment of death due them because of their sins (Ro. 6:23).
But some might ask how could God be a just judge and
withhold the punishment due to those offenders? He could do
so because he knew that his own innocent Son would one day
die in the place of those guilty ones. Peter explains that we
were redeemed

. . . with precious blood, as of a lamb without blemish and without
spot, even the blood of Christ who was foreknown indeed before the

foundation of the world, but was manifested at the end of the times
for your sake (I Pe. 1:19-20).

His life was sufficient so that "once at the end of the ages
hath he been manifested to put away sin by the sacrifice of
himself" (He. 9:26).

The great truth of it all is that Christ's death was retro-
active in its saving power, forgiving the sins of all faithful
saints from Eden to the end of time. Paul preached:

Be it known unto you therefore, brethren, that through this man is
proclaimed unto you remission of sins: and by him every one that
believeth is justified from all things from which ye could not be
justified by the law of Moses (Acts 13:38-39).

Our basis for salvation:

Paul reasons that all men of all ages are saved "freely by
his grace," "through faith" in Romans 3:23-25. He proceeds to
show his Hebrew readers that even Abraham was thus saved
(Ro. 4:3-4) and so was David (Ro. 4:6-8). "For this cause it is of
faith, that it may be according to grace; to the end that the
promise may be sure to all . . ." (Ro. 4:16). While the details of
obedience varied from covenant to covenant, the basis for
salvation was always the same: God in grace, offering
salvation to every obedient believer (Ga. 5:6). Thus forgiveness
in every age was made possible by the death of Christ on
Calvary: whether in prospect for men before Christ or in retro-
spect for us.

An awesome thought:

Had Christ not emptied himself and taken the form of a
servant; had he not humbled himself becoming obedient unto
death, yea, the death of the cross (Ph. 2:5-8), all the sins of all
the ages would yet stand unremitted. Unforgiven, all would
face the penalty of death for their transgressions (Ro. 6:23). No
other sacrifice would have availed to forgive man. We would
have been hopelessly lost forever.

With the heavenly host we sing: "Worthy art thou . . . for
thou wast slain, and didst purchase unto God with thy blood
men of every tribe, and tongue, and people and nation . . ."
(Rev. 5:9). "Thanks be to God for his unspeakable gift" (II Co.
9:15).

WHAT IS THE ROLL BOOK?
(10:7)

"Then said I, Lo, I am come (in the roll of the book it is written of me) to do thy will, O God" (He. 10:7).

Looking first at the general context, we note the following: First, the law's being "a shadow of the good things to come . . . can never with the same sacrifices year by year . . . make perfect them that draw nigh" (10:1). Second, it was impossible that the blood of bulls and goats should take away sins (10:4). Third, when Christ came down to dwell with man he fully understood that all those animal sacrifices were insufficient to save man; that God had always wanted man's faithful obedience, not just his sacrifices and offerings (I Sa. 15:22-23; He. 10:5). Fourth, the Messiah's incarnation was planned in the councils of heaven long generations before he was born of the virgin—for David had predicted it in Psalms 40:6-8 (10:5-7). Fifth, he had come down to earth to do the Father's will by offering his body as the ultimate atoning sacrifice and thus to take away the first covenant that he may establish the second (10:9-10).

"In the roll of the book it is written of me:" likely refers not to one specific prediction but rather to the many predictions of and allusions to Messiah in the Old Law.

When David penned the 40th Psalm the only part of God's book written was the five books of Moses, Joshua, Judges, a few of the Psalms and perhaps Job.

Moses had written of the seed of the woman who would bruise Satan's head (Ge. 3:15). God had said to Abraham "and in thy seed shall all the nations be blessed" (Ge. 22:18). To Israel God said: "I will raise them up a prophet from among their brethren, like unto thee; and I will put my words in his mouth, and he shall speak unto them all that I shall command him" (De. 18:18). Time fails me to enumerate all the sacrifices which foreshadowed his coming: Passover, Atonements and Sin offerings, etc. The angel told John on Patmos that "the testimony of Jesus is the spirit of prophecy" (Re. 19:10).

As a note of passing interest, the Greek for "the roll of the book," derived from *kephalis,* refers to the head or knob of a stick on which a manuscript was rolled. Hebrew books were usually written so they could be rolled up on a spindle. When read, they were rolled from one and rolled up on another spindle at the other end. Each spindle had a small head for holding and for ornamentaion. The word "head" came to be used metaphorically for the whole volume. We see a similar use in the word "hands" for workers or "head" for cattle.

WHAT IS "THE DAY DRAWING NIGH?"
(10:25)

"Not forsaking our own assembling together, as the custom of some is, but exhorting one another: and so much the more, as ye see the day drawing nigh." Three possible interpretations are seen:

First, it might refer to the Christian's day of worship. But in other passages that day is designated the Lord's Day (Re. 1:10) or the first day of the week (Acts 20:7; I Co. 16:2). Few if any scholars hold this view.

Second, it could refer to the day of God's judgment on Jerusalem in 70 A.D. Since the book was written to Hebrew Christians around 60-65 A.D., the recipients would soon be facing this momentous calamity which would be a "day of the Lord."

Third, some take it to be the final day of judgment when Christ returns. Most recent commentators tend to accept this view. They reason that the final day of judgment is in the author's mind. In 9:28, "So Christ . . . shall appear a second time, apart from sin, to them that wait for him, unto salvation." In 10:37, he writes: "For yet a very little while, He that cometh shall come, and shall not tarry."

It is also observed that the writer uses the same word *engizo*, "drawing nigh," that in other places speaks of the coming of the final day of judgment. "The night is far spent, and the day is *at hand (engizo)*" (Ro. 13:12). Similar use is made in I Peter 4:5-7 and James 5:8.

Some of those who insist on the "day of judgment" rather than the destruction of Jerusalem do so because they would date the book after 70 A.D. and/or because they hold it was sent to Hebrew Christians outside of Palestine. While we acknowledge the plausibility of this view, the evidence is not compelling.

Albert Barnes offers six reasons why the day was the fall of Jerusalem.[6] To the present author they seem to make the strongest case. Assuming the date to be prior to 70 A.D. and the recipients to be Palestinian Hebrews, the case appears convincing.

1. The word "day" can refer to a local day of judgment as well as a universal judgment (compare Zep. 1:14).

2. Christ had specifically predicted a day of judgment upon Jerusalem in that generation (Ma. 24:1-34).

3. The destruction of Jerusalem and the temple would be of signal importance to those Hebrew Christians who were clinging to that old system or were tempted to leave Christ and return to it. That was one of the main problems discussed in the epistle.

4. At the time of composition, social and political events leading up to that awesome day were already in motion.

5. There was no more evidence that Christ was to soon appear for a final judgment then than now.

6. Such a fearful day of impending judgment would remind the readers of the dangers of neglect and apostasy.

Since God's local judgments on wicked people typify the coming "great day of judgment," that which the Hebrews writer held before them typifies the Lord's second coming. Today, no harm would be done if we exhort brethren to faithfulness in view of the day when Jesus shall come in glory to judge the living and the dead (Ma. 25:31-32).

CONCLUSION

As fascinating as the study of these difficult texts may be, we should remind ourselves that if we never arrived at a full understanding of them it would not affect our salvation. Such problems are excellent for provoking diligent study and that alone produces multitudinous benefits. The seeking sinner or the young Christian should not be intimidated by such difficulties. Faith in Christ and willingness to obey his gospel are the prerequisites of salvation (Ga. 5:6). We must love God's word and believe every line of it even when we cannot fully explain every difficulty. With David in Psalms 119 we sing:

> Oh how love I thy law!
> It is my meditation all the day (v. 97).
>
> For I have believed in thy commandments (v. 66).
>
> Give me understanding, and I shall keep the law;
> Yea, I shall observe it with my whole heart (v. 34).
>
> Open thou mine eyes, that I may behold
>   wondrous things out of thy law (v. 18).

ENDNOTES

1. R. C. H. Lenski, *The Interpretation of the Epistle to the Hebrews and the Epistle of James,* (Minneapolis: Augsbury Publishing House, 1963), p. 277.

2. Arthur Pink, *An Exposition of Hebrews,* (Grand Rapids: Baker Book House, 1968), pp. 467-468.

3. Gottlieb Lunemann, *Meyer's Commentary on the New Testament,* (New York: Funk & Wagnals, Publishers, 1885), p. 604.

4. James Moffatt, *A Critical and Exegetical Commentary on the Epistle to the Hebrews,* (Edinburgh: T & T Clark, 1968).

5. Pink, *op. cit.,* p. 504.

6. Albert Barnes, *Notes on the New Testament, Hebrews,* (Grand Rapids: Baker Book House, 1955), p. 238.

DIFFICULT PASSAGES IN HEBREWS

No. V

HEBREWS 10:26	**WHAT DOES IT MEAN TO SIN "WILFULLY?"**
HEBREWS 12:5-11	**WHAT IS THE LORD'S "CHASTENING," AND DOES HE STILL DO IT?**
HEBREWS 12:17	**WHOSE REPENTANCE IS REFERRED TO — ESAU'S OR ISAAC'S?**
HEBREWS 12:23	**WHAT IS MEANT BY "CHURCH OF THE FIRST-BORN?"**

By T. B. CREWS

Born in Lawrence County, Tennessee, 1916. Graduated from high school in Davis, Oklahoma; married Mary Riddle in 1937. Attended Business College intending to become an accountant, worked five years for Weingarten Stores in Houston. Started preaching fulltime for the Garden Oaks church in Houston in 1943. Since then has served churches in Texas and Oklahoma; spoken on various lectureships, and has done some writing for religious journals. Has one daughter. Serves as local evangelist, Northwest Church, Fort Worth, Texas.

WHAT DOES IT MEAN TO SIN "WILFULLY?" (10:26)

Hebrews 10:26 doesn't teach that one wilful act of sin will condemn us for all eternity. It is very apparent that the writer is not referring to one isolated act of misconduct. Neither does the passage refer to the unpardonable sin (Ma. 12:31-32). It is the strongest statement in the New Testament against the doctrine of "once in grace always in grace, once saved always saved."

There are those who would deny the impact of this verse by saying, "There is a difference in receiving a knowledge of the truth and really being a child of God." Their argument says the writer does not refer to Christians falling away and being lost. They say the writer refers to those who have learned the truth but have refused it. This is far-fetched indeed. Take a look at the preceding verses of the chapter: Verse 22 says, "Let *us* draw near . . .;" verse 23 says, "Let *us* hold fast . . .;" verse 24 says, "let *us* consider one another. . . ." To whom does "us" refer? It refers to those who are holy brethren, and partakers of the heavenly calling (He. 3:1). When the writer switches from "us" in these verses to "we" in verse 26, he has reference to the same ones. Thus there is the *danger* that brethren might fall away.

Problems arise if we equate one act of wilful sin that we commit to the one Adam and Eve committed in the Garden of Eden. We note that they wilfully and deliberately ate of the forbidden tree, and as a result they lost their place in that garden. We must understand that they had a law with only one specific command. When they broke this law, they violated the trust God had in them. They introduced sin by breaking this law (Ro. 5:12). Since that time Genesis 3:15 has been fulfilled, and the blood has been shed for the purpose of redeeming us. We live under a far more diversified law, that of the New Covenant. The New Covenant does not uphold sin, but our hope of heaven is not taken away forever when we deliberately commit one act of sin. The church at Corinth made many mistakes (I Corinthians), but corrected those mistakes, and Paul wrote a second epistle commending them for it (cf. II Co. 7:9-10).

It could well be that many of our members are burdened with a "guilt complex" because they are aware that they sin. But they are unaware that God is not chalking up our sins against us as he did before we became Christians (I John 1:7).

So we ask the question, "What does the writer refer to when he writes 'if we sin wilfully'?" If by one wilful act of sin we forever shut the doors of heaven on our chances, then all of us are lost. Which one of us has never deliberately done anything wrong? I am not willing to accept such a fatalistic view.

All will admit that Peter deliberately denied three times that he knew our Lord (Ma. 26:57-75), and Paul faced him with another mistake which evidently was deliberate (Ga. 2:11). But I expect Peter to be in heaven because he gained forgiveness for his wilful mistakes.

To "sin wilfully" literally means to be habitually engaged in sin. Here it has reference to a wilful abandonment of Christianity for Judaism. Thus it simply means to keep on sinning. One violates these instructions when he wilfully returns to his old life after obeying the gospel. Peter, who made some mistakes, wrote, "As obedient children, not fashioning yourselves according to the former lusts in your ignorance . . ." (I Pe. 1:14). Anyone who returns to the sinful lusts he once practiced after obeying the truth is lost — unless he repents. To remain or live in this state is to destroy forever the Christ who once lived through his word in him. Paul, the one recognized as the writer of Hebrews, seems to return to the warning he issued in chapter 6, verses 1-6. There he warns of the danger of so killing Christ, one can never return. I think I have dealt with a few who had gone so far back into their past life they could find no way back.

One cannot help taking note of what Paul says of what such a one has deliberately done. He has trodden under foot the Son of God, counted the blood of the covenant unholy, and done despite unto the Spirit of grace (v. 29). This is the consequence of wilfully returning to the life outside of Christ. Few who have forsaken their Christian vows would admit that they have done these things. But Paul, by divine inspiration, says they have. It is past time for us preachers to paint the picture of such a one as God paints it. "Sugar coated" lessons which ignore the apparent also fail to fulfill our responsibility to declare the whole counsel of God.

There are some other serious matters to consider. The decision to return to a life of sin, or to one's former religious belief, is seldom a spontaneous act. More often the decision comes about gradually. One thing leads to another, as one drink leads to another drink, and then another, and then alcoholism. So it is in returning to our past life. Throughout the book it is made very clear that the new covenant is far better than the old one, under which the Jew had lived for around sixteen hundred years. In his arguments, Paul often refers to the various ceremonies of that old covenant and to their symbolic nature. Apparently many of the Jewish converts to Christianity were finding it difficult to give up the pomp and splendor of these ceremonial rites for the simplicity of the Christian worship. Thus the urge was strong from their former religious partners, and from within, to go back. We face that same problem today as converts from some other religious groups find our services too simple. But those Christians had another pressure, the pressure of persecution. They often had to worship in secret. Many times they had to face ridicule from the Jews still in Judaism. So what was happening? The easiest thing to do would be to give it all up. So these Christians habitually began to miss the meeting together of the saints. Evidently this had become a gradual process. They would miss a period of worship, and because it was so easy to do, thus avoiding the persecution and criticism, they would miss more and more, until they fell completely away.

In not meeting with the saints they were guilty of another matter. They were not being considerate of others who needed their encouragement. As they became more and more negligent, they were more and more in danger of complete apostasy. They were wilfully forsaking the assembly, and they were habitually living the life they had lived before. Just as the phrase "committeth sin" (I John 3:8-9) means to "keep on sinning" so does "sin wilfully" mean "to wilfully return to sin."

Thus the appeal: brethren and sisters in Christ, don't drift into the habit of missing the assembling of the saints. This may well become habit-forming, and the danger of returning to one's old life is ever-present. One who faithfully attends all periods of worship is not likely to fall under the condemnation of Hebrews 10:26.

WHAT IS THE LORD'S "CHASTENING" AND DOES HE STILL DO IT? (12:5-11)

Now let us take up the question of chastening, and whether the Lord still does it. I could simply say, "Yes," and save a lot of time, but this is a question that has been bandied about in so many ridiculous ways we do need to study it. First of all we must not confuse chastisement, which means to "discipline or correct," with punishment. It seems that the word "chaste" and the word "chastise" are kindred words. Thus to be chaste is to be pure. To be chastised is to be brought back to purity. What does the Lord have in mind when he chastens us? He is striving to bring us back to a purity of life or trying to keep us from drifting back into a life of impurity.

So the big question is, "What is this chastening?"

First of all, I call your attention to an erroneous idea. A denominational preacher boldly proclaimed, "If a man is born again, no matter what he does — if he lies, steals, gets drunk, commits adultery, or whatever he does — the Lord will chasten him, whip him back in line, for God will not permit one of his children to be lost." We have already noted, from Hebrews 10:26, that a child of God can, and often does, go back into a life of sin. The Lord will whip us back in line again, *but not without our willingness to be brought back in line.*

Chasten, as used in Hebrews 12:6, 7, and 10, is from the Greek word *paideuo*. It means to instruct, or train up. The instructions of verse 5 are from Proverbs 3:11-12. The thought is that we should not despise the correction of Jehovah, nor murmur at his reproof. The thought of discipline is involved, but not merely a laying on of the rod. At least three reasons are implied for this correction: (1) to correct our faults, (2) to strengthen our faith, and (3) to make us more ready for eternity. These are reasons of love (v.6). It is out of love that the Lord chastens.

The great need of the church today is for more men who will stand in the pulpit and preach it like it is. The need is to reprove, rebuke, and exhort (II Ti. 4:1-4). When we preach the word, we are chastening with that word those who need to be more pure in their lives and in the teachings they have accepted. After all, the scriptures are profitable for doctrine, reproof, correction, and instruction (II Ti. 3:16-17). Any man who is apart from these is incomplete and in need of being chastened. Our Lord does chasten us today by way of his word.

All of us are familiar with the fact, "as we sow, so shall we reap" (Ga. 6:7-8). Some might say, "Now wait a minute, that is punishment, and you just said that we are not to confuse punishment with chastisement." But, is this punishment? It depends on what you are looking for. It is a lesson, a lesson from which we cannot get away. A simple fact remains: one cannot violate the laws of nature and get away with it. If I drink poison, I will either get sick or die. This is not so much punishment as it is a fact that continues to teach us. The same is true with God. I cannot violate his word and get by with it. When I do, his word is ever there to remind me of what I have done, and of what I am. If we read punishment into this thought, we are enlarging what *appears* to be punishment. But the real purpose is to teach us a lesson.

Then our Lord chastises us in another way. God gave us five senses. These five senses might be called the policemen of our bodies (He. 5:12-14). But these senses are controlled by our hearts, or minds. Built within us is a little thing we call "conscience." When we misuse our senses or our mind, our conscience chastises us. This is God's built-in way of trying to correct us.

In this there is one thing we cannot afford to overlook, and that is God's divine providence. This word "providence" occurs only one time in the Bible (Acts 24:2), and here it literally means "forethought." I do not use the word in this fashion here, but use it as it involves the care and help God affords us by using natural means to bring about the unusual. God does interfere in the lives of men and nations. Just when he does, and exactly how it is done, may not be ours to interpret; but based upon these words, I accept it:

> Be careful for nothing; but in every thing by prayer and supplication with thanksgiving let your requests be made known unto God. And the peace of God which passeth all understanding, shall keep your hearts and minds through Christ Jesus. (Ph. 4:6-7).

From this statement and others, we see that God does intervene. It is not easy for us to discern just when God may use physical means to chasten us. God's divine providence is not to be confused with "miracles." Something coming out of nothing is one thing; using the natural to bring about the unusual is another. As God may answer our prayers in guiding the hands of doctors and nurses to care for the ill for whom we pray, he may well use means to awaken his tottering children to their responsibilities.

We may be discouraged because the events of life seem to be going against us. This could be God chastening us. The besetting sin of the Jews, like ours, is that of "unbelief" (He. 12:1). We often place too much emphasis on the visible things of life. This could be God's way of bringing us back to reality. But, things pass.

The church is called upon to execute another means of chastisement. Punishment is involved in the action taken; this is done to shame and bring about restoration rather than merely spank. Action is taken to mark those who cause division (Ro. 16:17). We are to avoid the company of fornicators (I Co. 5). And we are to withdraw ourselves from those who walk disorderly (II Th. 3:6). God demands that we take this action; God is using us for his purpose of chastisement. This is not done to destroy or drive people further away from God. It is an act of love intended to awaken the fallen and to restore them. We are falling short in keeping the church pure according to God's method of ridding it of those who divide or weaken the church through immoral conduct. If we had been more zealous in our efforts to rid the church of those who would divide it asunder or weaken its influence through immoral conduct than we have been in building up large memberships, the church would be far stronger than it is — and I believe even stronger numerically. There are some who would brand us as just another denomination and be right in one respect. If we don't strive to keep the church pure, will that which evolves really be the church?

WHOSE REPENTANCE IS REFERRED TO — ESAU'S OR ISAAC'S? (12:17)

We know that godly sorrow worketh repentance (II Co. 7:10). We also know that the goodness of God leads us to repentance (Ro. 2:4). But we understand that these are not repentance. Because of this we might be quick to assume that Esau was the one who made the mistake; therefore, Esau was the one who needed to repent. But there is far more to this than just the rash act of Esau. Esau gave up, for one meal, all the rights which go to the firstborn. Could Jacob have claimed Esau's birthright without deceit? Esau knew that he would not die. He also knew that the giving of the blessing would still come from his father. Being the firstborn, the birthright had belonged to him. But Esau treated his birthright lightly.

Let us keep in mind that three people are involved in this matter. First is Esau who sold the birthright, second is Jacob who bought it, and third is Isaac who bestowed it. Now, who had to repent in order for Esau to get back what he had given away? I'm sure Esau changed his mind about what he had done and wanted it back. But could he get back what he had counted so cheap? Jacob did not actually receive the blessing until he received it from Isaac. Jacob could have changed his mind and forgotten the whole matter, but once he had what he wanted, he was not likely to give it up. The one who really gave it would have to be the one to change it all, and since he had given the blessing to Jacob, he could not in honesty change it. Since repentance refers to a change of mind, more than a change of one's spiritual relationship, it seems to me that the place of repentance would have to be in the heart of Isaac. Jacob did not want any change here, and since Esau had proved himself unworthy of becoming the father of a great nation, God surely wanted no change. Esau wanted the change, but there was no way for him to bring that about.

Let me use an example anyone can understand. A young lady is born. God's plan for woman is for her to be a help mate for man, to work beside man, and to bear his children. This is not to say that a woman who does not marry and does not bear children is lost. It does suggest, though, that the woman has not chosen the purpose for which Eve was created. Her birthright is to save her virginity for the man she loves and intends to live with in wedded bliss; but in a moment of passion she sells her birthright for a few minutes of sexual pleasure. She has sold something she can never reclaim — her virginity, her birthright. After she realizes what she has done, she weeps, she mourns, she is filled with remorse but there is no way she can go back to where she was.

Involved in this is the girl who sold her virginity, the boy to whom she gave it, and God. The girl cannot get it back, there is no way the boy can give it back, and the only one who can restore it is God. For God to do it he would have to turn back the pages of time, and this he will not do. The change of mind would have to come from God. However, God has put certain laws in motion and in these laws there is no variableness nor shadow of turning (Jam. 1:17). The young lady must live with the fact that she sold something (in one sense gave away something, because the price paid was so cheap: a few moments of satisfied passion) that only God can give back. She cannot change his mind. She can be forgiven, she can still marry, and she can still bear children, but the body she gives to her husband will be a body already used. Young ladies, or for that matter, young men, do not sell your virginity. Those few moments of pleasure may well become a lifetime of regret.

There are some things we can lose for life so easily. In a moment our reputation can be gone forever. God does not retract laws which are settled in heaven (Ps. 119:89). "Whatsoever a man soweth, that shall he also reap" (Ga. 6:7) stands unchanged. God will forgive, but where the tree has fallen, there it will have to lie (Ec. 11:3). One may be forgiven for murder, but his debt to society must still be paid. The state may pardon one who has committed murder, but the murderer must still live with what he has done.

Esau needed to be sorry for what he had done. He needed to repent. But he needed to recognize that he had given Jacob his birthright. Therefore when Isaac gave the blessing to Jacob (even in deceit) he did what Esau agreed to let him do. Isaac could not change his mind, and Esau could find no way to persuade him to do so.

Note the use of the word "repent" in Hebrews 7:21, "The Lord sware and will not repent, Thou art a priest forever after the order of Melchisedec." God simply would not change his mind. So it was with Isaac; he simply would not and did not change his mind.

WHAT IS MEANT BY "CHURCH OF THE FIRSTBORN?"
(12:23)

When I began preaching it seems that almost every preacher had a sermon entitled "Is There Anything In a Name?" They were trying desperately to give the church a name.

Romans 16:16 was almost worn out for this purpose. But when we read the passage, "churches" is still spelled with a small "c." We have a designation rather than a name. The church is designated as "the church which belongs to Christ," just as the statement "the wife of T. B. Crews" designates my wife as belonging to me.

Then we saw many trying to get a name from Romans 7:1-4. We are spoken of as being married to Christ. The argument goes like this: "When a woman marries a man she takes his name. Since we are married to Christ we naturally take his name. Therefore, the name of the church is the Church of Christ." This argument runs into problems with we consider the practice of then and now. Although Mary was married to Joseph, she was never known as Mrs. Joseph. She maintained her name, "Mary," but I'm sure was later known as "the wife of Joseph" just as the church is the church of Christ. If these words had been written in our age when the woman does take the name of the husband, the argument might be a good one, but they weren't. The only name I know given to us is the name "Christian" (Acts 11:26). I will be the first one to admit that every person who rightfully wears the name "Christian" must be in the church of Christ, but I cannot see the advisability of using this marriage reference as proof of the name we should wear.

Then others used Hebrews 12:23 as proof for our name. The argument follows: Jesus is referred to as "the firstborn among many brethren" (Ro. 8:29). He is also called "the firstborn of every creature" (Col. 1:15); and in that same chapter, verse 18, "the firstborn from the dead." Thus, since Jesus is the "firstborn" and the church is his, it wears his name. Because Christ is the "firstborn," the name of the church would thus be "Church of Christ." This too seemed to be a good argument. But further examination of other matters leads us to study more on this subject. It became more and more evident that we were reaching for straws to prove something that didn't need to be proved. This was like the "Elijah Argument." To say that John the Baptist was Elijah and God forbade the building of a church honoring John means that the Baptist church is unscriptural. We don't need this kind of argument to prove anything. Also, I Corinthians 2:9 has been quoted as a reference to heaven, but the very next verse takes care of that.

It is true that the church does belong to Jesus who is called the firstborn, and in conversation there is nothing wrong in referring to the church as "the church of the firstborn," nor are we wrong in referring to it as "the church of Christ." But let us be careful in saying that this is our proof for the name.

Consider a very personal view from "Crews' book of personal observations." Jesus was the first person to talk about "being born again" (John 3:3, 5). These were to be born of water and the Spirit. On the day of Pentecost (Acts 2), three thousand were born again, and were added to the church. These were the very first to be so born; thus they were the "firstborn." Since I belong to the same church they were added to, I am a member of the church of the firstborn or the church to which these firstborn ones were added.

But moving from a personal observation, we note that James uses this expression: "That we should be a kind of first fruits of his creatures" (Jam. 1:18). In Old Testament times the first fruits belonged to God. Since we are gathered into the church as children of God, we are thus "first fruits." In a true sense, we are the first fruits of the whole human race.

I am convinced that the "church of the firstborn" refers to the whole body of baptized believers, and that the word "firstborn" refers to them, not to Christ. Why? Primarily, "firstborn" is a plural term referring to those enrolled in heaven. In addition to the thoughts just expressed, let us remember that the book of Hebrews was a book written to the Hebrew people who were normally Jews. They had turned from Judaism to Christianity. This letter was written to those who were literally the "firstborn" because they were truly among the first Jews to be born again. But I doubt that Paul had this in mind. Study Exodus 22:29; 13:2, 12, and like passages. God demanded the firstborn of man and beast. They belonged to him. We belong to God. Since we belong to God we are the "firstborn" and we are his.

This reference to the "firstborn" goes back to Esau. As the firstborn, Esau had the birthright belonging to the firstborn. He sold his right to it. All those in the church who retain their birthright make up the church of the firstborn. We are even referred to as "the Israel of God" (Ga. 6:16). Whether we can agree as to whether the statement "firstborn" refers to Christ or to those in Christ, we can agree on the fact that heaven will be our home if we hold on to our birthright in Christ.

CONCLUSION

These difficult passages from the book of Hebrews have some great lessons for us if we can see the lessons in them rather than the difficulties. One of our problems has always been that we become too deeply concerned in controversy and we lose sight of the lesson. The argument over "The Man or the Plan" took up pages of our Christian journals several years ago. After I had read one article after another, I wasn't sure that there was much difference in what seemed to be two extremes. My thought is to look for the true lesson in these passages.

First of all, be careful about drifting into any dangerous practice. As one false move may well lead to another, the missing of one meeting of the saints without reason can easily lead to the missing of another, and another, and soon a complete forsaking. When we wilfully go back to our former life, the influence of Christ is destroyed.

Second, do not become angry when you hear a lesson that touches on one of your weaknesses. Don't become discouraged just because everything does not go exactly as you want it. It could be that these things are God's way of chastening you and trying to keep you from drifting back into a life of impurity.

Third, don't risk the loss of something very precious to you, such as your reputation or virginity, by treating it lightly. Once you have lost that which is precious, you might have to face up to the fact that it is gone forever.

Fourth, we as Christians are the church of the firstborn. We ourselves are "firstborn individuals," "first fruits," "firstborn," etc. Our allegiance must be to Christ who made it all possible. Live by his word, die by his word, and heaven will be the result.

SECTION IV

CONTROVERSIAL ISSUES
DISCUSSION FORUM

HOW THE WORLDS WERE FRAMED

DISCUSSION FORUM — No. I-A

**HEBREWS 11:3: The Biblical account of creation allows
for a very ancient earth.**

By JACK WOOD SEARS

Born in Cordell, Oklahoma 1918, married Mattie
Sue Speck. They have three children. Educated at
Harding College, and the Universities of Texas,
Minnesota, Chicago, Wisconsin, Colorado, and
Puerto Rico. Taught in the University of Texas,
now teaches biology and Bible at Harding Univer-
sity. Chairman, Biology Department, Harding
University, Searcy, Arkansas. Has preached for
churches in Arkansas, Texas, Mississippi and
Tennessee. Conducts meetings and speaks to youth
groups. Author of a book, *Conflict and Harmony
Between Science and Religion.*

INTRODUCTION

The topic assigned to me and that I have accepted as a
discussion topic is a very important topic in today's religious
world. There are those who maintain that the Bible demands a
young earth, from six to ten thousand years old only, and there
are those who, as I contend, find no biblical limitations on the
age of the earth. Both groups are sincere and nothing I say in
this talk should be construed to imply that they are not or that
I do not respect their views. I just disagree with some of the
conclusions reached by some. Of course, there are those who
ignore the Bible entirely and with those I will not be concerned
in this lesson.

Before I begin this discussion I want to make it perfectly
clear that I believe the Bible in its original autographs to be
inerrant and infallible, the inspired word of God Almighty.
Despite some manuscript problems and some translations as

we have it today is accurate, reliable and authorative, the inspired message from God. I recognize as you do that there are some translations that adhere more closely to the "original" text than others and that there are some so-called translations that are not that at all, but are mere human paraphrases of scriptures. I believe our differences and our difficulties are due not to the Bible but with our interpretations of Scripture. It is imperative that we get the message of Scripture as God intended we should when the Holy Spirit directed the writing of the message. We dare not twist the meaning of Scripture to accommodate any human theory, scientific or otherwise.

WHAT THE BIBLE SAYS

Now let us go to the Bible and try earnestly to see what God has told us there. "By faith we understand that the worlds have been framed by the word of God, so that what is seen hath not been made out of things which appear" (He. 11:3). I chose this beginning scripture because this lectureship is based on the book of Hebrews and also because this is one of the clearest and most beautiful statements of the doctrine of creation found in the Scriptures or elsewhere. I thrill each time I read this passage. Let us notice some of the things that are revealed here. First, it is stated that we "*understand* that the worlds have been framed. . . " This is faith. Always we must come back to the fact that faith is basic. All of our understanding is based on faith. We can *know* what the Bible says but we accept it by faith. In fact, I might almost say that all of our *knowledge* is based on faith. This is true in science and history as well as in religion. So the Holy Spirit through the pen of the writer of the book of Hebrews makes this very plain, "we *understand* . . ." We were not there when it occurred. We have no human witnesses who were there. Human knowledge, of which there was very little in this area at the time of the writing of the book, could not supply pertinent information. Only from God could this be obtained. We have not progressed essentially in our human information concerning the *beginning* even today. Science has hypotheses and theories but little else to offer. Some scientists and others have formed elaborate conjectures but these are of little value.

Today, as in the day of the writing of the book we call "Hebrews","we *understand* that the worlds have been framed by the word of God. . ."

Second, this statement tells us that ". . . so that what is *seen* hath not been made out of things which *appear.*" God did not take something that was already present to make the worlds, but he is the source of all that is. God and only God is eternal. Only He is ever-existing. All else must in some way have been derived from Him. This is a very biblical concept but foreign to the Greek thought of the day[1] and to much of the thought of the modern world. It is diametrically opposed to the materialistic philosophy. This is *creatio ex nihilo.*

Third, God did it and he did it be speaking the word. "By the word of Jehovah were the heavens made, and all the host of them by the breath of his mouth. . . For he spake, and it was done; He commanded, and it stood fast" (Ps. 33:6, 9). Of course, to say that God spoke the worlds into existence gives us no mechanism, scientific or otherwise, to explain creation, not mechanism.

In the first chapter of Hebrews we are told that Christ was the instrument through whom the worlds were made (He. 1:2). This is in harmony with the statement of the Apostle John who wrote:

> In the beginning was the Word, and the Word was with God, and the Word was God. The same was in the beginning with God. All things were made through him; and without him was not anything made that hath been made (John 1:1-3).

The Apostle Paul supported this concept when he wrote:

> For in him were all things created, in the heavens and upon earth, things visible and things invisible, whether thrones or dominions or principalities or powers; all things have been created through him; and unto him; and he is before all things, and in him all things consist (Col. 1:16-17).

The worlds were created by God through Christ but no mechanism is given to help man understand the "how" of creation. Neither is there given any indication of time. The "when" of creation is not of concern to the authors of these passages.

In Genesis the first chapter there is more information. There God reveals that he made the world and all that is in it. "In the beginning God created the heavens and the earth" (Ge. 1:1). But here again the emphasis is upon the creative act of a pre-existing, eternal God who by his power and by his authority brought into being this world of matter and energy rather than upon the time when it occurred. The emphasis is that God is first - matter, energy, the worlds all were derived from him. When the beginning was is not stated.

As one reads further we notice the orderly acts of creation as they occur by divine fiat. All of this from verse 3 through chapter 2:3 is in a setting of a week of seven days. Much has been said about these days. I do not wish to deal exhaustively with this controversy. As one reads the account it appears that these were seven 24-hour days. I have generally taken this to be so, but I refuse to make an issue of it. In scripture things are not always what they seem on the surface. Jesus said, "Destroy this temple, and in three days I will rainse it up" (John 2:19). This was thought by those that heard to refer to Herod's temple which had taken 46 years to build. But, of course, that was not at all his meaning. From the passage in Genesis 1 it is impossible to be certain as to the length of these days. I think I can say without fear of contradiction that the days of Genesis chapter 1 cannot be harmonized with the geological ages of the geologists without doing damage either to the Scriptures or to the science of geology. Many attempts have been made to bring harmony but all have been unsuccessful. Of course, the geologist is constantly changing his understanding of the geological ages with each new discovery in his field but the task of harmonizing the days of Genesis chapter 1 and geology is yet not possible. Immediate difficulties arise when we attempt to do so. If the third day and those following were each millions of years and each divided into similar periods of darkness and light, it is impossible to conceive how the green plants could live through nights of hundreds and thousands of years. This is one of the most obvious of the difficulties.

Since our God could create in a second, in the twinkling of an eye, all that has been made, if he so desired, just as well as he could create in six 24-hour days or in any period he might choose, the problem of the length of the days of Genesis 1 is not a great problem. It is impossible from the text, in spite of some dubious grammatical references to the contrary, to determine the length of these days, especially before day four when the sun and moon were placed in their positions and given a divine purpose. It seems to me unwise to make any issue of the length of days. Let us wait until we have more light. In the meantime let us not make the length of days in Genesis chapters 1 and 2 a test of fellowship.

WHAT SCIENCE SAYS

The real problem seems to involve the age of the earth itself and tht age of life on the earth. Modern science, by remarkably good methods of determination, estimate the age of the universe of which our earth is a part, to be at least 10 billion years old.[2] The methods used be the scientists are sound and reasonable and the age determinations reproducible by scientists at different places and at different times. Of course, all of this, as is true of all science, is based on certain assumptions but these are very reasonable and as far as the scientific communtty is concerned, acceptable. One must always remember, however, that science is an ever-changing approach to truth. Tomorrow we may discover something that will require a re-evaluation of the assumptions upon which these methods of dating arc based and so change the statements of science as to the age of the earth and of the universe.

Let me digress a moment. The scientists who are making these age determinations are often unaware of and unconcerned by the conflicts between their statements and the interpretations of Biblical passages, but they are "good scientists" and careful in their work. In the main, they are not attempting to disprove the Bible, but they are interested in trying to find the truth as to the age of the earth and of the universe. Of course, they are working under the assumption of the uniformitarian hypothesis but this does not allow them to ignore scientific facts or twist evidence. They understand the limitations of their methods perhaps better than most of their critics and are careful to guard against mistakes. I have heard many criticisms of the various scientific dating methods but by and large the criticisms are wide of the mark. When scientists say the beginning of the Cambrian was 600 million years ±50 million years, they are being very honest and expressing the limitations of their dating methods.[3] But bear in mind that it would require more than a 99% error in the methods they use to bring them into line with a 6000 year old earth, and such a degree of error is not at all conceivable.

Carbon-14 has been used to date certain artifacts but has such a short half-life it cannot be used to date the age of life on earth, nor can it be used to date the earth itself. It is interesting to notice that it has been used to date the Dead-Sea Scrolls with great benifit to the Bible record and it has shown that the ice-ages in North America ended only ten thousand years ago rather than the 100 thousand that had formerly been supposed. All of this has pleased the critics of dating methods, and they have accepted these findings readily, but they are still unduly critical, it seems to me, in other areas. But so much for the scientific methods of dating the past. These methods are not perfect but are the best available and are improving as we learn more and more. As we examine the earth, the mountain ranges, the canyons, the deltas, and the geological strata in many different places it becomes apparent that this earth looks old. But what does the Bible say?

> In the beginning God created the heavens and the earth. And the earth was waste and void; and darkness was upon the face of the deep: and the Spirit of God moved upon the face of the waters. And God said, Let there be light: and there was light. And God saw the light, that it was good: and God divided the light from darkness. And God called the light Day, and the darkness he called Night. And there was evening and there was morning, one day (Ge. 1:1-5).

If you continue this reading through the complete chapter and on through the second chapter you will find that the Bible is silent as to the age of the universe and as to the age of the earth. Nowhere does the Bible date the beginning. Some of the conflicts between the scientists and those of us who believe the Bible have come about because scientists have spoken dogmatically about their theories and "facts" as if they were absolute. Some difficulties have come about because Bible believers have spoken where God has not spoken and have drawn unwarranted conclusions and made these matters of "Bible Truth" and tests of fellowship.

GENEALOGICAL DATING

Archbishop Ussher (1581-1656 A.D.) of the Chruch of England, studied the genealogies given in Genesis chapters 5 and 11. He then added the ages of the patriarchs as given in the Hebrew manuscripts, and with certain other information obtained from the Bible and from profane history calculated that Adam was created in 4004 B.C. Bishop Lightfoot (1606-1675 A.D.) followed Archbishop Ussher's lead and made his own calculations. He said that, "Creation took place the week of October 18-24, 4004 B.C., with Adam created on October 23 at 9:00 A.M., forty-fifth meridian time."[4]

The difficulties with this approach are pointed out by an article by Dr. Hales in which he lists 120 different dates that have been computed in the manner of Archbishop Ussher. These dates vary from 6985 B.C. to 3616 B.C. Dr. Hales used the Septuagint text, and using the same method, came up with 5411 B.C.[5] There are many other difficulties with this type of approach to the age of the earth and of life on earth. First, it is obvious from a careful study of the genealogies in the Bible that abridgment is the general rule. ". . . Jesus Christ, the son of David, the son of Abraham" (Ma. 1:1), is an extreme case, but abridgment is common. In the genealogy of Christ as given by Matthew when compared with the lists of kings in II Kings and II Chronicles it is plain that Matthew has omitted four kings, Ahaziah, Joash and Amaziah between Joram and Uzziah, and Johoiakim between Josiah and Jechoniah. Yet Matthew had records available to correctly list all of the kings. A study of Matthew's account indicates that he did not make a mistake but rather that for purposes of aids to memory, perhaps, he groups his list of kings into three groups of fourteen generations each. To do this he even has to include one name in two lists. His purpose was not to give a chronological account but to indicate that the Christ was a descendant of David and Abraham and as such had a right to the throne of David and therefore could fulfill the prophecies.

If one compares the genealogies given in Ezra 7:3-4 with that recorded in I Chronicles 6:6-10, we find that Ezra omits six of the descendants of Aaron between Meraioth and Azariah (Amariah, Ahitub, Zadok, Ahimaaz, and Johanan). The omission of these six names cannot be attributed to a mistake on Ezra's part since the records were available to him (and his record was inspired, I believe). Rather, it did not serve the purpose of his message toi include all of the names. If the only purpose of genealogies was to record completely each individual in a lineage, this would not be permissable and Ezra would be defective and would have to be discarded as uninspired. The purpose of this list was to show that Ezra was a descendant of Aaron, the first high priest.

Again, in Luke's account of the genealogy of Jesus he lists the name of Cainan the son of Arphaxad (Luke 3:36) but when we examine the genealogy as given in Genesis, Cainan is not listed. Rather, Arphaxad's son is called Shelah (Ge. 11:12). That this is not another name for Cainan is made clear when we read in Luke's account (Luke 3:35) that Shelah is the son of Cainan. Does this mean that Genesis is not inspired and is in error? Most certainly not! Rather, I think, it is God's way of telling us these genelogical lists are not meant to be complete, that people have been omitted. How many? Only God knows.

I had always assumed that these genealogies had been handed down, generation after generation and that it was in this manner that Moses received the genealogies he recorded in chapters 5 and 11. Certainly the Hebrew people did memorize genealogies and hand them down. This was the only way they had of knowing who they were. They valued these family lines for often their only right to property was dependent upon proving their family relationship. At the time of the return from Babylonian captivity, a number of priests were denied the right to serve as priests because they could not show their lineage. Another purpose of the genealogies, especially of the descendants of Abraham and David, was to assure that the Messiah had the right genealogy. It is for this reason that both Matthew and Luke give genealogies of Jesus. But did Moses receive the genealogies he recorded in Genesis 5 and 11 through this human chain? I do not know. Certainly, I believe he was inspired of God to write. I know God must have inspired the writing of the account of creation, since no man was there to remember all of that. Perhaps God also gave him the record of the genealogies. I am sure inspiration insured that they were recorded as God wished them to be.

There is another problem with using the genealogies to give chronological age determinations. When we examine the genealogies in Genesis chapters 5 and 11, we see that too much is given. If the numbers given were to be used to make possible the calculation of the date of creation, what was the purpose of the other numbers? They certainly can not be used in that way. "And Seth lived after he begat Enos *eight hundred and seven years,* and begat sons and daughters" (Ge. 5:7). Why include the *eight hundred and seven years*? Perhaps, and I only make this as a suggestion, the purpose of the numbers given in the genealogies is to emphasize that things have changed! The nine persons mentioned before the flood who lived until their "natural" death (omitting Enoch whom God *took*) had an average age of 912.2 years, whereas, the eight mentioned after Shem and after the flood (including Abraham) had an average age of 292.6 years. The first three after Shem, after the flood had an average age of 445 years, but the next five listed had an average age of 201.2 years. It is very obvious that things had radically changed in the lives of men since the flood!

The final difficulty with using the genealogies to obtain a date for creation which I will mention is that there is no computation in the Scripture of the time from the creation to any other time, nor is there computation from the flood to any other time. But there is computation of the time from the descent into Egypt to the exodus (Ex. 12:40-41). And there is computation from the exodus to the building of the temple (I Ki. 6:1), etc. Is this God's way of letting us know that this time cannot be so computed? Or perhaps such computation from the time of creation or from the time of the flood to some other time would be unprofitable or give erroneous conclusions.

It is my conclusion, after much study, that the Bible says nothing about the date of creation of the earth, of the universe, or of life on earth. It gives only the simple, straightforward account in Genesis chapters 1 and 2 in which a brief history of creation is given, emphasizing that God created and that he did it systematically and with purpose. No time is given at all!

I know that some sincere believers disagree with me. I respect them but I believe they have been misled. Some have held to a young earth theory because they erroneously think that if we give the evolutionists enough time he will win the argument. I am opposed to the general theory of evolution. I believe it is wrong scientifically and is very hurtful theologically. I am not an evolutionist, and I have no desire to be one. But give the evolutionist all the time he asks and evolution cannot be true. It is impossible for any evolutionary process yet conceived to provide for the origin of matter, of life, of rational thought, of altruistic love and of human personality, to name only a few things. Time does nothing! Without God evolution cannot get started, and with God evolution is unnecessary.

"SCIENTIFIC CREATIONISM"

Today there is much said about "Scientific Creationism" and the Creation Research Society is in the lead in the anti-evolution campaigns in this country. The very term "Scientific Creation" is a misnomer and a contradiction. Creation by its very nature requires a creator and the only acceptable creator is Jehovah God. Creation is not scientific. It was the act of a Supernatural Being. Science is purely a human enterprise and by its very nature cannot deal with, investigate, or even speak about the supernatural or the actions of God. Science cannot deal with the beginning for that was before men were, and we cannot reach back and *experiment* with the beginning. We can theorize about it and we can attempt to find a mechanism or mencanisms that might have been used by a creator but we in science cannot *scientifically* speak about the beginning of the universe or of life on earth. There are facts that can be observed by the scientist that point to the necessity of a divine creative act. But this is not science. We do a disservice to the cause of creation by attempting to make it *scientific*! "Scientific Creationism" is really an extension of the theology of the people in the Creation Research Society which is not Biblical. It demands a young earth, not because of Biblical statements, but because of human theology. It demands flood geology, which is poor geology, not because of Biblical statements, but because of human theology. It demands a restoration of earth's pristine state, not because of Biblical statements, but because of human theology. It demands a final millennial reign of Christ on earth, not because of Biblical statements, but because of human theology. If you have some reservation concerning the statements I have made, I suggest you read Henry Morris' statements in *Impact No. 85*[6]. I do not doubt the sincerity of these men, but I am concerned that they hurt the cause of truth by their insistence upon human theology read into the Scriptures. Today in Arkansas, because the action of the courts in the matter of the "Scientific Creation" bill passed by the State Legislature, many believe that creation has been proved wrong and the Bible is relegated to the collection of outmoded, disproved relics of a superstitious age.

CONCLUSION

In conclusion let me urge that we not be dogmatic. The Bible does not really say when it was that God created the first life. Let us not make is a point of controversy or a matter of Christian fellowship. To do so can be very harmful. I spoke about the age of the earth at a large assembly of our brethren one Wednesday evening. The next Sunday morning a man who had been attending services for a number of years came forward in response to Christ's invitation, confessing his faith in Jesus and was baptized into Christ. He later said, "I have long believed in Christ but I thought one had to believe the earth was only 6,000 years old before he could become a Christian, and I could not believe that." I do not know who had given him that idea, but as well meaning as they may have been, they nearly caused the eternal damnation of a human soul. Brethren, we must not, we cannot, require of any person that which Christ through his word, the Bible, has not required! Let us pray for wisdom and understanding as we study God's work and let us practice the virtues of Christian love and tolerance.

ENDNOTES

1. Robert Milligan, *The New Testament Commentary, Epistle to the Hebrews* (Cincinnati, Ohio: Christian Board of Publication, 1875), Vol. IX, p. 302; Joseph Augustus Seiss, *Lectures On Hebrews* (Grand Rapids, Mich.: Baker 1954), pp. 315-317; F. F. Bruce, *The New International Commentary on the New Testament, The Epistle to the Hebrews* (Grand Rapids, Mich.: Eerdmans, 1964), pp. 280-281.

2. Methods of dating the age of the Universe involve the following:

Method	Determined Age
The red shift in the spectrum of the stars as they recede.	10 billion years for age of universe!
U^{238}/Pb^{206}; U^{235}/Pb^{207}; Pb^{206}/Pb^{207}; K^{40}/Ar^{40}	3 to 6 billion years for age of earth

3. Some scientists say life has been on earth more than 500-600 million years, having originated in the Pre-Cambrian; and the man similar to modern man first appears on earth nearly 3 million years ago. *But science does not know when life began on earth!* It is very difficult to date the fossils with definiteness. We have used various methods in our attempts to date the fossils, among these are the following:

     a. Key fossils and geological strata

     b. Strata sedimentation rates

     c. Carbon-14 (half-life = 5730 years) (At present useful for only 30 to 40,000 years).

     d. K^{40}/Ar^{40} (Half-life = 1,300 million years) (Difficult to date anything more recent than 2 million years).

The Geological Time Scale as generally presented is based mainly on methods (a) and (b) listed above. Most geological strata cannot be dated by radio-active methods.

4. Bernard Ramm, *The Christian View of Science and the Scriptures* (Grand Rapids, Eerdmans, 1954), p. 174.

5. J. D. Thomas, *Evolution and Antiquity* (Abilene, Tex.: Biblical Research Press, 1965), p. 56-57.

6. Henry M. Morris, *Impact Series #85* (Creation Research Society, 1980).

HOW THE WORLDS WERE FRAMED

DISCUSSION FORUM — No. I-B

HEBREWS 11:3: GOD CREATED THE UNIVERSE AND ALL THAT IS IN IT
IN A MATURE STATE IN SIX LITERAL DAYS OF APPROXIMATELY 24
HOURS EACH. HE DID NOT EMPLOY A SYSTEM REQUIRING VAST
PERIODS OR LONG AGES OF TIME TO BRING THE MATERIAL WORLD TO
ITS PRESENT STATE.

By BERT THOMPSON

Professor of Bible and Science at Alabama Christian School of Religion, Montgomery, Alabama.
Ph.D., Texas A&M University. Has been included in
many listings of outstanding people in his field. Has
done extensive lecturing and writing in field of
Christian apologetics and evidences. Author of
several books and series of cassette tapes dealing
with evolution and creation. Co-founder of Apologetics Press, co-editor of *Reason and Revelation*, a
monthly journal devoted to apologetics and evidences. Married, two sons. Speaker, *First Annual
Denton Lectures.*

INTRODUCTION —
THE IMPORTANCE OF THIS INQUIRY

For almost as long as some of us can remember, there have
been those among us who apparently have been working
overtime to find ways to compromise the plain, literal, historical creation account as given by Moses through inspiration in
Genesis 1 and 2, and as corroborated by various other inspired
writers in both the Old and New Testaments. The situation is
no better today and, in fact, has gotten progressively worse.
Especially hard hit have been those areas of Scripture dealing
with *time.* Those who have as their goal the adoption of evolutionary timetables, geologic time, etc. have attempted to
"squeeze" these alleged "eons of time" into the Biblical text in
any number of ways. It appears, as we have said before, that

417

intimidation is the name of the game! The Bible-believer is so intimidated by the scientist with his flowing laboratory coat, volumes of impressive data, technical methodology and fancy instruments that he capitulates, giving up *inspired testimony* for today's scientific *theories* (which may, in fact, turn out to be tomorrow's *superstitions*). While we ought to be holding all the more steadfastly to the inerrant, infallible, authoritative word of God, we are instead giving up inspired testimony for "scientific theory."

This attitude, which has for some time been prevalent among denominations, is not creeping into the Lord's church as well. It has fostered the "Double Revelation Theory," which states that God has given two revelations of truth, each fully authoritative in its own realm: the revelation of God in nature, and the revelation of God in Scripture. Whenever there is an apparent "conflict" between the scientist and the theologian, it is supposedly the Bible which must then be brought into harmony with science — never the reverse. We have dealt with this false notion elsewhere.[1] It is palpably false, yet it has become increasingly popular.[2] Bible must be "strained" through science to see if it can be accepted. Again, among the hardest hit have been those areas of Scripture dealing with *time*.

It is *not* the purpose of this paper to deal with the alleged scientific "proofs" of the age of the earth and related matters. The topic assigned deals specifically with the Biblical, not the scientific, information regarding the time associated with God's creation. For those interested, however, we have dealt elsewhere with the so-called "scientific proofs" of the age of the earth.[3]

What are the options open to the Bible-believer regarding the time element in God's creation? *First*, one may accept the clear statements, inferences, deductions and implications of Scripture that the universe and all that is in it was created in six literal days of approximately 24 hours each some few thousand years ago. *Second*, one may attempt to somehow manipulate the Biblical text and "force" evolutionary eons of time into the Bible. Or, *third*, one may simply suspend judgment and draw no conclusions at all.

With these things stated, note the following statement made by my opponent in this discussion, Dr. Jack Wood Sears, Chairman of the Department of Biology at Harding University, in his book, *Conflict and Harmony in Science and the Bible*:

> . . . When conflicts do occur, the part of wisdom is to *withhold judgment* until the facts are all in. For example, there is difficulty with the age of life on the earth. Science, as I indicated earlier, has seemed to indicate that life has been here much longer than we have generally interpreted the Bible to indicate. However, scientific determination of the ages of geological strata is not absolute and is subject to much difficulty and uncertainty. The Bible, as we have shown, *does not date creation,* and *the intimations it seems to present may not be properly understood.* Since I hold science to be a valid approach to reality, and since I have concluded, upon much and sufficient evidence, that the Bible is inspired and therefore true, the only rational recourse, it seems to me, *is to withhold judgment about a seeming contradition.* Wait and see. . . .[4]

I find these statements both *incredible* and quite *revealing! First,* the reader will immediately note that Dr. Sears plainly *admits* that the intimations of the Bible toward a young earth "seem to" be present. *Second,* if Dr. Sears does indeed hold the attitude, as expressed in this quotation, that the best part of wisdom is to *withhold judgment, why* has he then accepted this opportunity to fill the polemic platform *to defend the concept of an ancient earth?* Does that sound like he is "withholding judgment" to you? Indeed, it does not! But *third,* and most important, the question *must* be raised: *Why* "suspend judgment" to "wait and see?" Does Dr. Sears mean to indicate that we are to wait upon *additional revelation from God* to clear up the matter? Since he holds the Bible to be inspired,[5] and since the Bible plainly tells us that what we have is the final and last revelation God plans to give (Jude 3, Ga. 1:6-10), I assume this is not what Dr. Sears is "waiting on." *What,* then, *is Dr. Sears waiting on? Why* has he "suspended judgment?" What is he "waiting to see?" I suggest that it is nothing more than what the latest pronouncements of science will be! It is the attitude of "straining Bible through science" first, and *then* accepting the Bible *if* it fits with the current scientific thought. It is clear that Dr. Sears suggests we "wait" on something. I *must* press this issue home: for *what* are we waiting? If we are not waiting on additional revelation, then I see few other possibilities except that we are somehow to "wait" on science to make its pronouncement on this subject. Hear this: "science" (and here I am talking about the pseudo-science of evolutionary thought) has made its "pronouncement," and *that pronouncement is plainly at odds with Biblical revelation!* I *deny* that we must "wait and see" or "withhold judgment." I *affirm* that we have at our fingertips, in the pages of divine revelation, all the evidence we will ever need to draw the only conclusion God ever intended us to draw: the universe was created in a mature state in six literal days — not over vast periods of time as Dr. Sears and certain others[6] have suggested! The remainder of this paper will examine the evidence upon which this conclusion is to be based, and will refute the false theories that have been proposed which supposedly allow an ancient earth and a multi-billion-year-ago creation.

TO THOSE WHO DO NOT WISH TO ACCEPT THE BIBLICAL STATEMENTS REGARDING THE AGE OF THE EARTH AND THE TIME OF CREATION, THERE ARE BUT THREE OPTIONS LEFT OPEN

Error is always its own worst enemy! In attempting to answer the question, "How old is the earth?," with a response that says the earth is extremely ancient, proponents of such a view find that they are left with but three options which can be used to defend such a system of thought. And all three can easily be shown to be *false!* I must press Dr. Sears, and those of like mind, with this singular question: If the universe (creation) is ancient (and I remind you that this is the proposition he has agreed to defend!), *where* in the Biblical text is this time to be placed? As in the case recorded in Matthew 21:23-27 when Jesus asked the chief priests and elders about the baptism of John, so it is with this question: *any* answer except the correct answer leaves one with *no* answer!

The *correct* answer, of course, is that there is *no place* in the Biblical text for the concept of an "ancient" earth. But Dr. Sears has signed a proposition that affirms that the earth *is* ancient. He *must*, therefore, answer this question. He knows, as all who have investigated this field of study well know, that there are now only three options open to him in answering this piercing question. (A) The "eons" of time needed to make the creation "ancient" might be placed *before* the creation. (B) The time needed might be placed *during* the creation. (C) Or, the time needed might be placed *after* the creation account as given in Genesis 1. *These are the only three options open!* If the time needed to account for an "ancient" earth cannot successfully be placed in one of these three places, then it is obvious that such a time frame is unscriptural. Indeed, that is exactly the case! Consider the following.

THE ATTEMPT TO PLACE THE TIME NEEDED FOR AN ANCIENT EARTH BEFORE THE CREATION WEEK

THE GAP THEORY[7]

In Genesis 1:1-2 we find the following statements: (1) "In the beginning, God created the heavens and the earth. (2) And the earth was waste and void; and darkness was upon the face of the deep; and the Spirit of God moved upon the face of the waters." For over 100 years Bible-believers who were determined to insert the time necessary to have an "ancient" earth studied Genesis 1 with the intent of doing just that. They came to the conclusion that it might be possible to insert these alleged "eons of time" *before* the creation week, between Genesis 1:1 and 1:2. This came to be known as the Gap Theory (synonyms: Ruin and Reconstruction Theory, Ruination/Re-creation Theory, Pre-Adamic Cataclysm Theory, Restitution Theory, etc.). It was made popular by G. H. Pember in his book *Earth's Earliest Ages* and by Harry Rimmer in his book, *Modern Science and the Genesis Record.* The *Scofield Reference Bible* helped popularize it in the footnotes on Genesis 1. Dr. Arthur C. Custance wrote what many consider to be the most avid defense of the theory, in his work *Without Form and Void.* Several of our own brethren have championed the Gap Theory or modifications of it, including John Clayton,[8] Robert Milligan,[9] George Klingman,[10] and others. The theory states that a vast "gap" of time existed between Gensis 1:1 and 1:2, which may be accommodated to the geological time scheme of modern theorists. During this proposed gap, there lived successive generations of plants, animals, and even pre-

Adamic men. According to this view, God destroyed the original creation because of a Satanic rebellion and so Genesis 1:2 is translated to suggest that "the earth 'became' waste and void." The creation week is then said to be actually a "*re*creation" in six literal days. It is sad indeed when men who are supposedly Bible-believers must stoop to such "exegetical hocus-pocus" to pervert the plain teachings of the Bible so as to accommodate evolutionary presuppositions. The Gap Theory (and modifications of it) are false!

First, Exodus 20:11 (cf.: Ex. 31:17) plainly states, "for in *six days* Jehovah made heaven and earth, the sea, and *all* that in them is, and rested the seventh day . . ." (emp. added). Notice all that this statement includes. If *everything* was made in *six days,* then *nothing* was created prior to those six days! The Bible is its own best interpreter, as always. This one verse demolishes the Gap Theory, and all modifications of it. [*Note:* More will be said below concerning the supposed "difference" between the Hebrew words *asah* and *bara* as suggested by Gap theorists.]

Second, Adam (I Co. 15:45) is called the "*first man.*" That excludes any pre-Adamic race of men! Adam was the *first.*

Third, at the conclusion of the sixth day, God saw *everything* that he had made, and behold it was "*very good*" (Gen. 1:31; Emp. added.). If God's original creation had become contaminated through Satan's rebellion, and thus was subsequently destroyed — and the new creation rested on a veritable graveyard of corruption — it is difficult indeed to see how God could have surveyed the situation and then used the expression "very good" to describe it!

Fourth, gap theorists suggest that the Hebrew word for "was" (*hayetha*) should be translated "became" or "had become," indicating a change of state from the original perfect creation to a chaotic condition (v. 2). Yet none of the scholarly translations of the Bible so translate the verse. A few years ago, 20 leading Hebrew scholars were polled to see if there was exegetical evidence of a "gap" between Genesis 1:1 and 1:2. They *unanimously* responded "NO!"[11] Noted Hebrew scholar J. W. Watts stated: "In Genesis 1:2a the verb is perfect. It indicates a fixed and completed state. In other words, original matter was in a state of chaos when created; it came into being that way."[12] Harold Stigers, in his commentary on Genesis, states:

> The cataclysmic theory (also called the restitution theory) respecting v. 2 can have no place in a proper translation. The construction of "became void," etc., is not justified by Hebrew syntax. When the verb "to be" (*hayah*) is to be constructed as "became," the addition of the prepositional *lamedh* is required with the following word to provide this meaning, and this preposition is absent here.[13]

Fifth, we know the Gap Theory to be false because it implies death and destruction in the world prior to Adam. This is in direct contradition to New Testament teaching (I Co. 15:21; Ro. 8:20-22; Ro. 5:12) which states that sin and death entered into the world through the human race because of Adam's sin. If the Gap Theory is true, Paul is a liar!

Sixth, gap theorists assert that the phrase, "without form and void" of Genesis 1:2 (Hebrew, *tohu wabohu*) can refer only to something once in a state of repair, but now ruined. To that Dr. John Whitcomb replies:

> Many Bible students, however, are puzzled with the statement in Genesis 1:2 that the Earth was without form and void. Does God create things that have no form and are void? The answer, of course, depends on what those words mean. "Without form and void" translate the Hebrew expression *tohu wabohu*, which literally means "empty and formless." In other words, the Earth was not chaotic, not under a curse of judgment. It was simply empty of living things and without the features that it later possessed, such as oceans and continents, hills and valleys — features that would be essential for man's well-being. In other words, it was not an appropriate home for man. . . .[14]

Seventh, gap theorists assert that in order for their theory to be true the two Hebrew words *asah* and *bara* used in the creation account (meaning to "create" or "make") must refer to *different* things, and can never be used interchangeably. For example, *bara* supposedly means "to create" whereas *asah* means "to make, re-make, or make over again." The conclusion we are supposed to draw is, of course, that the "original creation" was "created" while the creation of the six days was "made" (*viz:* "made over"). This, however, is patently false. The two words are, on occasion, used interchangeably. Dr. Henry Morris calls our attention to this and much more when he says:

The Hebrew words for "create" (*bara*) and for "make" (*asah*) are very often used quite interchangeably in Scripture, at least when God is the one referred to as creating or making. Therefore the fact that *bara* is used only three times in Genesis 1 (vv. 1, 21 and 27) certainly does not imply that the other creative acts, in which "made" or some similar expression is used, were really only acts of restoration. For example, in Genesis 1:21, God "created" the fishes and birds; in 1:25 He "made" the animals and creeping things. In verse 26, God speaks of "making" man in His own image. The next verse states that God "created" man in His own image. No scientific or exegetical ground exists for distinction between the two processes, except perhaps a matter of grammatical emphasis. . . .

The natural reading of the whole account surely conveys the understanding of real creation throughout, with no intimation that the actual story is one of reconstruction of a devastated world. Finally, the summary verse (Genesis 2:3) clearly says that *all* of God's works, both of "creating" and "making" were completed with the six days, after which God "rested."[15]

If anyone is impressed by the fact that "made" (Hebrew *asah*) is used in Exodus 20:11 instead of "created" (Hebrew *bara*), the "all that in them is" should make it plain that the whole earth structure — not just the earth's surface — is included in the entities that were "made" in the six days.[16]

Dr. Weston W. Fields, in his classic response to Custance's works in this regard, demolishes the so-called "distinction" between *bara* and *asah* as it pertains to potential support for the Gap Theory. I highly recommend Dr. Fields' book, *Unformed and Unfilled.*[17]

If space permitted, there is much more that could be said to show the fallacious nature of the Gap Theory. I hope, however, that this will be enough to show that any attempt to "squeeze" the time necessary for an ancient earth *prior* to the creation week is doomed to failure.

THE ATTEMPT TO PLACE THE TIME NEEDED FOR AN ANCIENT EARTH DURING THE CREATION WEEK

THE DAY-AGE THEORY

Since the time required for an ancient earth cannot be placed *before* the creation week, some have then asserted that it might therefore be placed *during* the creation week. The "days" of Genesis 1, we are told, aren't "days" at all, but rather extended periods (eons) of time. While denominational-ists have advocated this theory (*e.g.,* Dr. Wilbur M. Smith in his book, *Therefore Stand!,* Dr. Davis A Young in his book, *Creation And The Flood,* Dr. Edward J. Carnell in his work, *The Case For Orthodox Theology,* etc.), some in the church have not hesitated to accept it as well. My opponent in this matter regarding the Biblical creation account and the age of the earth, Dr. Sears, is on record as advocating this particular viewpoint, in fact.[18] The Day-Age Theory, however, can easily be shown to be false. Consider the following.

First, we know the days of Genesis 1 are literal 24-hour days because the Hebrew word *yom* which is translated "day" is used *and* defined in Genesis 1:5.

> As added proof, the word is clearly defined the first time it is used. God defines His terms! "And God called the light Day, and the darkness He called Night. And the evening and the morning were the first day" (Gen. 1:5). *Yom* is defined here as the light period in the regular succession of light and darkness, which, as the earth rotates on its axis, has continued ever since. This definition obvious-ly precludes any possible interpretation as a geologic age.[19]

God plainly said that "the evening and the morning were the first day." That settles the matter! Amazingly enough, how-ever, we have a built-in scheme for interpreting the length of each of these days. Genesis 1:14 states that God created the lights to divide the day from the night, and that they were to be for signs, for seasons, for *days* and for years. If the "days" were "ages," then pray tell, what are the *years?* If a "day" is an "age," what is a night? Marcus Dods, writing in the *Expositor's Bible,* says: "If the word 'day' in this chapter does not mean a period of 24 hours, the interpretation of Scripture is hopeless."[20]

Second, the Day-Age Theory is false because whenever the Hebrew word *yom* is preceded in a non-prophetical passage, by a numeral, it *always* carries the meaning of a 24-hour day. *Yom* occurs over 100 times in the Old Testament in this manner, and *always* the meaning of a 24-hour day is conveyed. Dr. Arthur Williams, writing in the *Creation Research Annual,* says: "We have failed to find a single example of the use of the word 'day' in the entire Scripture where it means other than a period of twenty-four hours when modified by the use of the numerical adjective."[21]

Third, in addition, whenever the Hebrew word *yom* occurs in the plural (*yamim*), in a non-prophetical passage, it *always* refers to a literal 24-hour day.

> When the word "days" appears in the plural (Hebrew *yamin*) as it does over 700 times in the Old Testament, it *always* refers to literal days. Thus, in Exodus 20:11, when the Scripture says that "in six days the Lord made heaven and earth, the sea, and all that in them is," there can be no doubt whatever that six literal days are meant.[22]

Fourth, the Hebrew phrase translated "evening and morning" is used over 100 times in the Old Testament with the word *yom*. Each time it is used in a non-prophetical passage, it refers to a literal 24-hour day. "The Hebrew words for 'evening' and 'morning' occur over 100 times each in the Old Testament, and *always* in the literal sense."[23]

Fifth, had Moses wanted us to understand that these "days" were actually long, geological periods of time, he could have used words that so specified this point. But he did not! He could have used the Hebrew word *olam*, or the word *dor*, both of which would indicate indefinite periods of time. He could have modified the Hebrew word *yom* by the adjective *rab* (*yom rab* — a "long" day), but again, he did not. As Larry Chouinard points out, if God said that he created everything in six days, but really used six eons, wouldn't that make God a deceptive, tricky, sneaky, deceitful God?[24] Good point!

Sixth, if the "days" of Genesis were not days at all, but long geological periods of time, then a problem of no little significance arises in the field of botany. Guy N. Woods mentions this problem when he says:

> Botany, the field of plant-life, came into existence on the third day. Those who allege that the days of Genesis 1 may have been long geological ages, must accept the absurd hypothesis that plant-life survived in periods of total darkness through half of each geologic age, running into millions of years.[25]

Indeed, if there were periods of "evening and morning" — as the text so states after each of the creation days — then how did the plant life survive in extended periods of total darkness, and extended periods of nothing but light?!

Seventh, the days of Genesis 1 are plainly 24-hour days, because of God's explicit command to the Israelites to observe the Sabbath. God plainly told them not only *what* to do, but *why* to do it. The Sabbath command in Exodus 20:8-11 can be adequately understood only when the days of Genesis are considered to be 24-hour days. As Dr. John Whitcomb says:

> Genesis chapter one is explained by Exodus 20:8,11 when God spoke to Israel and said, "Six days shalt thou labor and do all thy work. . . . For in six days the Lord made heaven and earth, the sea, and all in them is." Obviously God was speaking in terms of literal days. No Jew in his right mind would think that God meant "six indefinite periods shalt thou labor and rest a seventh indefinite period." God, of course, could have created the universe in one moment, but as a matter of fact, He stretched it out over six whole days in order to serve as a pattern for man's cycle of work and rest.[26]

There are other arguments equally as damaging as these to the false concept of the Day-Age Theory, but space precludes us from examining each of them. It should be obvious, even to the most casual reader, that the time needed for an "ancient" earth cannot be placed *during* the creation week. There are simply too many safeguards to allow it!

THE ATTEMPT TO PLACE THE TIME NEEDED FOR AN ANCIENT EARTH AFTER THE CREATION WEEK

Failing in attempts to place the needed time for an ancient earth either *before* or *during* the creation week, a few have attempted to place such time *after* that week. But these attempts have indeed been few, because it is at this point that one major obstacle to *all* attempts to "squeeze" evolutionary time into the Bible comes clearly into view. That major obstacle has to do with the Biblical genealogies! Rarely will people try to place time *after* the creation week, for two reasons: (a) One of the main reasons for putting the time in is to allow for geologic ages to be possible. But if the creation has already taken place, what good is time "after the fact?" (b) The genealogies provide such tremendous "protection" of the text that there is simply no way around the message they tell. That message is this: *Man has been on the earth since the very beginning, and that beginning was not very long ago!* There have been those who have suggested that the genealogies cannot, and do not, provide reliable information which can be used to help establish relative dates for man's existence upon the earth, etc.[27] Dr. Sears, in his book, *Conflict and Harmony in Science and the Bible,* has made it clear that he falls in that category![28] But perhaps he has not considered the following information.

First, concerning Adam and Eve, Jesus declared: "But from the beginning of the creation, male and female made he them" (Mark 10:6; cf.: Ma. 19:4). Christ dates the first human couple from the creation week. "Beginning" *(arche)* here is used of "absolute, denoting the beginning of the world and of its history, the beginning of creation," and "creation" *(ktiseos)* denotes "the sum-total of what God has created."[29] Unquestionably, Jesus places the first humans at the very dawn of creation. To reject this clear truth, one must either contend that: (a) Christ knew that the universe was in existence billions of years prior to man, but, accommodating himself to the ignorances of that age, deliberately misrepresented the situation, or; (b) the Lord himself, living in pre-scientific times, was uninformed about the matter (despite the fact that he was there as Creator — Col. 1:16). Either of these allegations is blasphemous![30]

Second, we are told over and over again that the genealogies cannot be used for anything relating to chronology because there are "gaps" in them. But there are some important points that are conveniently overlooked by those who suggest such. One is this:

> We are told again and again that some of these genealogies contain gaps: but what is never pointed out by those who lay the emphasis on these gaps, is that they only know of the existence of these gaps because the Bible elsewhere fills them in. How otherwise could one know of them? But if they are filled in, they are not gaps at all! Thus in the final analysis the argument is completely without foundation.[31]

Furthermore, and this point needs to be driven home (!), *even if there were gaps in the genealogies, there would not necessarily be gaps in the chronologies therein recorded. The question of chronology is not that same as that of genealogy!*[32]

Gaps in genealogies, however, do not prove gaps in chronologies. The known gaps all occur in non-chronlogical genealogies. Morover, even if there were gaps in the genealogies of Genesis 5 and 11, this would not affect the chronological information therein recorded, for even if Enosh were the greatgrandson of Seth, it would still be the case that Seth was 105 years old when Enosh was born, according to a simple reading of the text. Thus genealogy and chronology are distinct problems with distinct characteristics. They ought not to be confused.[33]

Notice also that the "gaps" occur in derivative genealogies, not original ones. Matthew is at liberty to arrange his genealogy of Christ in three groups of 14, making some "omissions," because his genealogy is derived from the complete lists found in the Old Testament and elsewhere. In the genealogies of Genesis 5 and 11, remember also that the inclusion of the father's age at the time of his son's birth is wholly without meaning or use unless chronology is intended! Else why would the Holy Spirit give us such irrelevant information?

Third, man, according to the Lord himself, has been here "since the beginning of the creation." But some, wishing to have their "ancient earth," are then faced with a serious problem. It can be archaeologically demonstrated that the genealogy of Jesus from Mary back to Abraham spans, at most, about 2,000 years.[34] No one would doubt, of course, that from the present back to Jesus it has been roughly 2,000 years as well. The only time span in "doubt," then, is the span from Abraham back to Adam. How many generations does that cover? From Abraham back to Adam in Luke's record there will be found only twenty generations. Are there serious "gaps" in that record? Apparently not! Jude, by inspiration, corroborates the first seven, when he says (Jude 14) that Enoch was the seventh from Adam. That leaves, then, olny 13 generations into which all those eons of time can be "squeezed." I repeat: man, remember, has been here on the earth, according to the Lord, since the beginning! How could multiplied millions or billions of years be "squeezed" into just thirteen generations? It is impossible![35]

Fourth, Paul, in Romans 1:20, wrote: "For the invisible things of him since the creation of the world are clearly seen, being perceived through the things that are made, even his everlasting power and divinity; that they may be without excuse . . ." The term "perceived" is from the Greek, *noeo*, a word used for rational intelligence, while the phrase "clearly seen" (*kathoratai*) is an intensified form of *horao*, a term which "gives prominence to the discerning mind."[36] Paul's point is perfectly clear: the power and divinity of God, as revealed in the things that he made, have been observable to *human intelligence* since the creation of the world. Man has thus existed from the very beginning. The earth is *not* billions of years older than mankind!

Fifth, though the Genesis account does not declare how long Adam and Eve were in the garden of Eden prior to their fall, we know it was not long. This is revealed by the fact that Christ, referring to the curse of death upon the human family, said that the devil "was a murderer *from the beginning*" (John 8:44). Once again, human existence is placed near "the beginning."

Sixth, in Luke 11:45-52, the Lord rebuked the rebellious Jews of that day and foretold the horrible destruction that would come upon them. He charges them with following in the footsteps of their ancestors and hence announces that upon them will come "the blood of all the prophets, which was shed from the foundation of the world." Then, with parallelism characteristic of Hebrew expression, Christ re-phrases the thought by saying, "from the blood of Abel unto the blood of Zachariah. . . ." Here is the important point: Jesus places the murder of Abel back near the *foundation of the world.* Granted, Abel's death occurred some years after the initial creation, but was close enough to that creation for Jesus to state that it was associated with "the beginning of the world." If the world came into existence several billion years before the first family, how could the shedding of human blood be declared to extend back to the foundation of the world?

Seventh, chronology is the backbone of history. And Christianity is the religion of the true God — a religion *steeped in history*. This being the case, should we not then *expect* chronology from the Bible writers? And that is, in fact, exactly what we get:

. . . Chronology *is* of concern to the writers of the Bible. From this perspective we should be *surprised* if the Bible did *not* include chronological data regarding the period from Creation to Abraham, especially since such data can now be obtained from no other source. That chronology is of concern to the Bible (and to its Author) can also be seen from the often difficult and confusing chronology of the Kings of Israel. Thus, we find that it is the *intention* of the Bible to provide us with chronology from Abraham to the Exile. Some of that chronology is given in summary statements . . . but some is also given interspersed in the histories of the Kings. Is it therefore surprising or unreasonable that some should be given along with genealogies as well?[37]

It is easy enough to say, "Oh, but the genealogies have 'gaps' in them which render them useless for chronological purposes." But upon deeper examination, the "gaps" seem to disappear, and the fact that because a gap *might possibly* exist still does not destroy the *chronology* of the statements. Oh, if we could just understand this point!

CONCLUSION

"But the earth is measured scientifically to be *so* old," comes the objection. Again, this is *not* a treatise on the scientific methods used to "prove" the age of the earth. However, one last item *must* be considered, and that is the Biblical doctrine of the apparent age. How old was Adam two seconds after God created him? Well, of course, he was two seconds old. That was his *literal* age. What was his *apparent* age? That is, how old did Adam *look?* How old did he *appear* to be? He was old enough to reproduce, for that is the command God gave him (Ge. 1:28). Similarly with Eve — how old did she *appear* to be two seconds after her creation? She was *literally* two seconds old, but she must have *appeared* much older. She, too was able to reproduce. The same may then be said as well of the plants and animals. In fact, the same would apply in principle to the whole creation! Think about this: if God created plants, animals, and man with the "appearance of age," does it make sense that he would act any differently in regard to the earth that was to be their home? Of course not. God is the God of order, not confusion (I Co. 14:33). And consider this: how could God create *anything* without it's having the appearance of some age? If God had created an atom, how would he have made it look like it had not already been there? If he had wanted to create a sapling, how would he have made it so it did not appear to have some "age" attached to it? The point is this: the doctrine of apparent age is intrinsically linked to the creation account. And it does *not* lay God open to the charge, as some have said, of being deceptive or tricky or deceitful. After all, God *told* us exactly what he did. He can then hardly be charge with deception or deceit!

How old is the earth? One thing we know from the Bible: it is *five days older than man!* And relatively speaking it is very young — with an age measured in a few thousand years, not multiplied billions. The Bible is factual in its clear statements and its implied deductions regarding the history of man. Let us not be stampeded into accepting anything less than God's word on the subject. Above all, let us not be destroyed "for lack of knowledge" (Ho. 4:6).

ENDNOTES

1. See: *Studies in I Corinthians,* Dub McClish, editor (Denton, Tex.: Valid Publications, 1982), pp. 218ff.

2. See: *Evolutionary Creationism: A Review of the Teaching of John Clayton,* Wayne Jackson and Bert Thompson (Montgomery, Ala.: Aplogetics Press, Nov., 1982, Jan., 1983).

3. See: *Reason and Revelation* (Montgomery, Ala.: Apologetics Press, Nov., 1982, Jan., 1983).

4. Jack Wood Sears, *Conflict and Harmony in Science and the Bible* (Grand Rapids, Mich.: Baker Book House, 1969), p. 97 (emp. added).

5. *Ibid.*

6. See: *The Source,* John N. Clayton (South Bend, Ind.: John N. Clayton, 1978), pp. 109-111, 137-138.

7. The author acknowledges that a portion of the material used here in regard to the Gap Theory has been published previously (cf. endnote, No. 1). However, the topic assigned necessitated the reuse of it in this manuscript.

8. Clayton, *loc. cit.*

9. Robert Milligan, *The Scheme of Redemption* (Nashville, Tenn.: Gospel Advocate Co., 1972 reprint), pp. 23ff.

10. George Klingman, *God Is* (Nashville, Tenn.: Gospel Advocate Co., 1929), p. 128.

11. See: "Fundamental Christianity and Evolution," *Modern Science and the Christian FAith* (Wheaton, Ill.: Van Kampen Press, 1950), p. 49, n. 30.

12. J. W. Watts, *A Survey of Old Testament Teaching* (Nashville, Tenn.: Broadman Press, 1947), vol. I, p. 16.

13. Harold Stigers, *A Commentary on Genesis* (Grand Rapids, Mich.: Zondervan, 1976), p. 49.

14. John C. Whitcomb, "The Gap Theory," *And God Created*, K. L. Segraves, editor (San Diego, Calif.: Creation-Science Research Center, 1973), vol. II, pp. 69-70.

15. Henry M. Morris, *Studies in the Bible and Science* (Grand Rapids, Mich.: Baker Book House, 1966), p. 32 (emp. his).

16. Henry M. Morris, *Scientific Creationism* (San Diego, Calif.: Creation-Life Publishers, 1974), pp. 236-237.

17. W. W. Fields, *Unformed and Unfilled* (Grand Rapids, Mich.: Baker Book House, 1976).

18. In December, 1977, Dr. Sears and the author shared the platform at a week-long lecture series in Zimbabwe (then Rhodesia). During said series in Salisbury, the author responded to a question from the audience, stating that the days of creation in Genesis 1 were literal 24-hour periods. Dr. Sears, in his lecture the next day, took issue with the author's statements.

19. Morris, *op. cit.*, p. 224.

20. Marcus Dods, "Genesis," *The Expositor's Bible*, W. R. Nicoll, editor (Grand Rapids, Mich.: Eerdmans and Sons, 1948), vol. I, pp. 4-5.

21. Arthur Williams, *Creation Research Annual* (Ann Arbor, Mich.: Creation Research Society, 1965), p. 10.

22. Henry M. Morris, *Biblical Cosmology and Modern Science* (Grand Rapids, Mich.: Baker Book House, 1970), p. 59 (emp. his).

23. *Ibid.*, p. 58 (emp. his).

24. Larry Chouinard, "A Review of the 'Does God Exist?' Series," *Christian Courier*, Wayne Jackson, editor (Stockton, Calif.: Main St. Church of Christ, 1975), pp. 2-3.

25. Guy N. Woods, *Questions and Answers: Open Forum* (Henderson, Tenn.: Freed-Hardeman College, 1976), p. 17.

26. Whitcomb, *op. cit.*, pp. 63-64.

27. John N. Clayton, 1977), les. 4, p. 3.

28. Sears, *op. cit.*, pp. 17-20.

29. H. Cremer, *Biblico-Theological Lexicon of New Testament Greek* (London, England: T and T Clark Co., 1962), pp. 113-114, 381.

30. The author is indebted to Wayne Jackson for much of this material on the genealogies, used with his permission and assistance.

31. Arthur C. Custance, *The Genealogies of the Bible* (Ottawa, Canada: Doorway Papers, no. 24, 1967), p. 3.

32. The author is indebed to James Jordan and his articles, "The Biblical Chronology Question: An Analysis," published in the *Creation Social Sciences and Humanities Quarterly* (Wichita, Kan.), vol. II, no. 2, Winter, 1979, pp. 9-15 and vol. II, no. 3, Spring, 1980. pp. 17-26. for ideas and suggestions regarding the chronology of the Biblical genealogies.

33. *Ibid.*

34. See: K. A. Kitchen and T. C. Mitchell, *The New Bible Dictionary,* J. D. Douglas, editor (publisher n. a., 1974), p. 213.

35. See: "The Antiquity of Human History," Wayne Jackson, *Words of Truth* (Jasper, Ala.: Sixth Ave. Church of Christ), vol. XIV, no. 18, April 14, 1978, p. 1.

36. J. H. Thayer, *Greek-English Lexicon of the New Testament* (Edinburgh, Scotland: T and T Clark Co., 1958), p. 452.

37. Jordan, *loc. cit.,* (emp. his).

THE AUTHORITY OF ELDERS

DISCUSSION FORUM — No. II-A

HEBREWS 13:7, 17, 24: The role of elders is best defined as spiritual shepherds of the flock rather than authoritative rulers.

By WAYMON D. MILLER

Native of Little Rock, Arkansas. Educated at Harding University, the University of Central Arkansas and other universities. Author of twelve books. Has been preaching for more than 46 years, with local work in Arkansas, Oklahoma and Texas. Five years of mission work in the Union of South Africa. Has traveled in 28 foreign countries, preached on four continents. Now retired, living in Tulsa, OK.

INTRODUCTION

"Obey them that have the rule over you, and submit yourselves: for they watch for your souls . . ." (He. 13:17).

A highly respected brother expressed this opinion: "One of the major problems that confronts churches of Christ today is that of the eldership."[1] Another brother concurs: "The greatest bottleneck hindering growth in the churches of Christ is in the eldership."[2]

The first statement was made about 40 years ago by the lamented H. Leo Boles! The second was made just about three years ago by Dr. Flavil R. Yeakley, Jr. They both reveal deep concern over the status of the eldership — a concern spanning four decades. The deficiencies in our eldership have not yet been resolved, which fact justifies an intensive examination of the issue. And it is possible that few issues have been discussed with greater frequency or concern in our time than the eldership issue.

435

The material presented here is not to be understood as depreciating elders and their valuable role in the church. We certainly have no vendetta with elders. We entertain but the profoundest respect for those who serve the Lord with humility and dedication. Little else has created more disrespect for elders, however, than those who are tyrannical, despotic, dictatorial and overbearing.

A few years ago I became interested in making a more thorough study of scriptural teaching on the role of elders. At that time I held the view of the authoritative role of elders, sincerely believing them to be the ruling hierarchy in the local congregation. This view I had espoused all my preaching career — at that time more than 40 years. My sole concern was to examine in depth all of the scriptures bearing on the subject. As the study progressed it became apparent that some of the texts used, and the applications made, did not support our contentions. An honest treatment of these texts, therefore, required a modification of our views, some of which will be presented here. Our only motive in the presentation of these things is to challenge others to a study and a reassessment of these texts. Growth in grace and knowledge requires a constant pursuit of truth, and learning is a changing process.

A conclusion reached in our study was that we had fashioned the eldership into a ruling hierarchy, a setting in which they are not viewed in the scriptures. We have conceived the eldership to function like a corporate board of directors, whose chief duty it is to formulate policy and hand down top-level decisions for the church to unfailingly obey. While decision-making is necessary in the ministry of elders, many members conceive this to be their sole responsibility, for they pray more often for the elders to make the right decisions than anything else. These are concepts of the elders and their work which I do not believe are in harmony with the scriptures.

It should be clearly understood that we raise no objection to the exercise of legitimate authority by elders. Whether elders have authority to function in their role is not the issue. Any position requires the necessary authority to perform its duties, whether it be elder, deacon, minister, teacher, song leader, secretary or janitor. There is no disagreement over the fact that elders must lead the flock, oversee it, protect it, exhort it, admonish it, and nurture it. In the performance of these duties they must make whatever judgments as are necessary, and which would be in the best interests of the congregation. It is when elders disregard the wishes of the congregation, and dictate to it in an arbitrary and despotic manner that we believe to be unscriptural.

Brother Yeakley stated the matter well:

> Elderships which practice an authoritarian style of leadership function as though they had the authority of lords. They make their decisions in total isolation from the congregation. . . . And once the decision has been made, these elderships simply announce the decisions as orders which the members are expected to obey without question.[3]

It is this sort of ruling, dictatorial procedure that prompts these questions: (1) Where in the New Testament is it clearly stated that elders have this sort of "authority?" (2) Where is the passage that defines the nature and scope of an elder's "authority?" (3) Where is the passage that demands absolute obedience to the decisions of elders in matters of judgment?

WHO IS REFERRED TO IN HEBREWS 13:7, 17, 24?

Interestingly, one of the passages that required a revision of our thinking was Hebrews 13:17. We have accepted this as a classic text in affirming: (1) elders are endowed with special ruling authority, and (2) all other Christians are required to obey them implicitly. Upon careful scrutiny of the text, we were surprised to find that it did not mention elders at all! Yet we have appealed to the text as though it actually states: "Obey the elders, who are appointed to rule over you, and submit yourselves to their authority." It was observed further that elders are not mentioned at all in this chapter. Nor are they mentioned in the whole of the Hebrews document, with its 13 chapters and more than 300 verses!

Furthermore, in applying the text to elders the assumption must be made that the Greek terms translated "obey," "rule," and "submit" have the same meaning as their current English usage.

A question of fundamental importance is: "Who is referred to in Hebrews 13:17?" We have asserted the passage refers to elders, though the text does not clearly express this. A great deal more than supposition is necessary to establish a scriptural truth.

Several views have been proposed as to whom the text refers. (1) It is thought by some that the text refers to former leaders among the Hebrews, who had left a heritage of heroic martyrdom, since the last part of verse seven could be literally rendered "the spirit of their dying."[4] (2) One brother maintains that the text refers to Christian political rulers of that day. (3) Another view is that the text refers to "those who planted this community of Christians."[5] And of course (4) it is maintained that elders are referred to.

There are three verses in Hebrews 11 with almost identical language. The first (verse 7) exhorts: "Remember them which have the rule over you, who have spoken unto you the word of God: whose faith follow, considering the end of their conversation." The concluding verse exhorts: "Salute all them that have the rule over you . . ." (verse 24).

A comparison of several versions of verse seven is beneficial. "Remember your leaders, those who spoke to you the word of God; consider the outcome of their life, and imitate their faith" (R.S.V.). "Remember your leaders, who spoke the word of God to you" (N.I.V.). "Remember your leaders, those who first spoke God's message to you . . ." (N.E.B.). "You must not forget your former leaders, for it was they who brought you the message of God" (Williams). It is likely that the ones "who have the rule over you" are the same persons referred to in all three passages since this expression is identical in each of them. Who they are seems to be identified in verse seven as ones "who have spoken unto you the word of God." The above versions are clear in styling these persons as "leaders," with nothing being indicated of a rulership or exerting an authority of office. So the persons involved in all three verses could have been the ones who had preached the gospel to the Hebrews. That these verses refer to elders is speculation and assertion, supported only by human reason.

THE MEANING OF "OBEY" IN HEBREWS 13:17

Another problem in contending that this passage refers to absolute subservience to elders lies in the meaning of the term "obey." This is not the usual word used most frequently in the New Testament to suggest submission to authority. The Greek word commonly used for obedience is *hupakouo,* and it means "to harken to a command; *i.e.,* to obey, to be obedient unto, submit to."[6] This is the word used with reference to obedience to God (He. 5:9), to the faith (Acts 6:7), to the gospel (Ro. 10:16), of children to parents (Ep. 6:1), of servants to masters (Ep. 6:5).

But a different term is employed in Hebrews 13:17. It is the Greek term *peitho,* which has a totally different meaning from the term above. It means "to persuade," to win over, to be persuaded, to listen to." Further: "The obedience suggested is not by submission to authority, but resulting from persuasion."[7] This word is closely related to the word "trust" *(pisteuo),* and suggests a response that is inspired by trust. It would mean, then, that the persons of the text should be followed because they are trusted. They were not required to follow obediently because this was commanded!

This word for "obey" *(peitho)* is simply defined as "persuasiveness, persuasion."[8] And: "To persuade, induce one by persuasion to do something, to listen to, obey, yield to, comply with."[9] This is drastically different from submitting to command authority. The text means, then, that the leaders are to be followed because of their persuasive influence, not because they had issued a command. They are not spiritual lords, but spiritual leaders! Leaders do not command obedience; they are followed voluntarily and gladly.

Instances where *peitho* is used will confirm that it does not mean submission to authority. When Gamaliel referred to the charlatan Theudas in his speech to the Sanhedrin, he cited that "as many as *obeyed him* ("as many as had been *trusting him*" —Rotherham) were scattered" (Acts 5:36). The Sanhedrin then *agreed* (a form of the same word in He. 13:17) with the viewpoint of Gamaliel (v. 40). Warning authorities of the subversive plot of the Jews to kill Paul, his nephew appealed "but do not thou *yield unto them*" — that is, do not *be persuaded* by

them (Acts 23:21). When Paul warned of the impending ship-
wreck, "the centurion *believed* ("was more *persuaded by*"—
Rotherham; "was more *influenced* by"—T.C.N.T.) the master
and owner of the ship" more than Paul (Acts 27:11).

In all of these passages citing the same word for "obey" as
in Hebrews 13:17, we see a meaning totally different from the
concept of commanded obedience. The "obedience" under view
is, as Vine explained, not "submission to authority," but
"resulting from persuasion." If it were conceded that Hebrews
13:17 refers to elders, the attitude required is to follow them
because of trusting them and of yielding to their persuasive influence, not the response of command obedience. This passage,
therefore, does not support the idea at all of the absolute
authority of elders. If they do have an "authority" which must
be obeyed, this passage does not prove it. Where then is the
passage that teaches that elders possess supreme authority
over other Christians?

THE MEANING OF "RULE" IN HEBREWS 13:17

To presume "rule" in this text means the authoritative
exercise of power by elders is not correct. A brother presents
these salient thoughts on the issue:

> Confusion has existed concerning the "rule" of bishops-presbyters.
> Translations such as the King James Version leave the impression
> that ruling is an important function of elders. . . . The Greek words
> in the New Testament texts are forms of *proistemi* (Rom. 12:8; I
> Thess. 5:12; I Tim. 3:4-5, 12; 5:17) and forms of *hegoumenos* (Heb.
> 13:7, 17, 24). As will be shown, reading into these texts the idea of
> ruling comparable to political rule will not be justified by the mean-
> ing of the Greek words.[10]

And also:

> The elders "rule" in the sense of being over the church, just as the
> father is over the family (I Tim. 3:4f — the same Greek word), but
> they are never said to have "authority" (*exousia*) or "power"
> (*dunamis*) over the church.[11]

If the Hebrews author had intended to convey the idea that
elders exercise a rule like a civil official, the Greek word
exousia would have been used. This word means "the power of
rule or government, the power of one whose will and
commands must be obeyed by others."[12] The last part of this

definition sounds precisely like what brethren contend who affirm the authoritative role of elders.

The word for "rule" in Hebrews 13:17 is *hegeomai,* which W. E. Vine defines as "guides." Thayer defines the term as "leading as respects influence, controlling in counsel . . . so of the overseers or leaders of Christian churches."[13] It is significant to observe that Thayer gives as illustrations of this definition the very texts in our study: Hebrews 13:7, 17, 24! This is the basis as to why many translations since the King James Version quite correctly render the term as "guides" or "leaders" instead of "rulers."

Dr. Jack P. Lewis presents this appropriate observation on the word "authority" *(exousia),* citing that it is "never once used in connection with either the discharge of the function of an elder or with the attitude the Christian is to have toward elders."[14] If elders are "rulers" in the literal sense, then they would be vested with "authority" with which to rule. But since the New Testament never once states they have "authority," then elders are not "rulers" in the political sense.

Barnes adds these words:

> "Them which have the rule over you . . ." The word here used means properly *leaders, guides, directors.* It is often applied to military leaders. Here it means *teachers*— . . . . It does not refer to them so much as *rulers* or *governors* as *teachers* or *guides.*"[15]

THE MEANING OF "SUBMIT" IN HEBREWS 13:17

The Greek term for "submit" *(hupeiko)* in Hebrews 13:17 is defined as "to retire, withdraw, hence, to yield; submit is used metaphorically in Heb. 13:17, of submitting to spiritual guides in the church."[16] To show that this term does not mean just "submission" to constituted "authority," Christians are urged: "Submitting yourselves to one another in the fear of God" (Ep. 5:21; I Co. 16:15-16). Christians must exhibit a spirit of *deference* or *yielding* to one another, but this does not require any sort of slavish submission or obedience. Consequently, Dr. Roberts remarks: "The words for the attitude of members toward elders are those of deference and submission to their reasoned leading, not of obedience."[17] If then inspiration had intended members to "submit" to the "authority" of elders, why is this idea nowhere clearly stated in the New Testament?

THE AUTHORITY OF THE ASSEMBLY

The Lord selected a term for his people that has important significance—the term "church" (Ma. 16:18). We have ordinarily appealed to the literal meaning of the Greek term *ekklesia*, which so interpreted means "called out" (*ek* = "out of," *kalao* = "to call"). While our emphasis has been on the *called out* aspect, it is likely that emphasis should be placed upon the result of being "called out": that is, an *assembly*.

It appears that the prominent emphasis in Greek lexicons is upon the *assembly*. Just so *ekklesia* is defined as "assembly, meeting, congregation, church."[18] Again: "To summon forth, a popular assembly, the congregation . . ., the church."[19] Further: "Properly, a gathering of citizens called out from their homes into some public place; an assembly, a company of Christians."[20]

Among the Greek people the *ekklesia* was the assembly of the citizens of a city. Such an assembly had authority to formulate laws, appoint or discharge officials, make decisions regarding war, peace, finance, contracts, and other internal and external matters. The assembly was democratic, delegating authority to officials appointed by it. It is more than a coincidence that the Lord selected this term to describe his people.

The church as a decision-making, authoritative assembly is illustrated several times in the New Testament. We have this concept in view when we define the congregation as autonomous. The idea of autonomy means that a body has the right of self-government. It has the right to elect its own leaders, who function in behalf of the whole body. An autonomous body is in reality a democracy — a "government in which the supreme power is retained by the people and exercised either directly or indirectly through a system of representation." If we are correct in stating that the congregation is an autonymous body, then we must accept also *that it is a self-governing body,* not a body governed by a board of autocratic officials.

Jesus taught that the assembly has certain authority not possessed by individuals. He said if a brother sins against us and refuses to hear us, or two or three other brethren, then the matter is to be laid before the whole church. If he refuses to hear the church, he should be disfellowshipped (Ma. 18:15-17). Here it is clear that the assembly is endowed with power of action not possessed by an individual or several brethren.

When the Grecian widows complained about being neglected, "the twelve called the multitude of disciples unto them," and recommended appointment of seven brethren to attend these grievances. When the apostles established guidelines for the men who should so serve, "the saying pleased *the whole multitude*" (Acts 6:1-6). The church is here seen functioning as a assembly, an autonomous body, selecting those who would be its public servants. These men were not selected by the elders, and presented to the congregation for approval, as is often our custom. The selection was made by the collective action of the assembly, moving in an authoritative manner which individuals were not authorized to do. So the scholarly McGarvey commented: "No ingenuity of argument can evade the conclusion that this gives the authority of apostolic precedent for the popular election of church officers."[21]

The Jerusalem conference is another prime example of entire Christian communities exercising their right of determination (Acts 15). When the Antioch church was disturbed by false teachers who demanded circumcision of Gentiles, "they (the church) determined that Paul and Barnabas, and certain other of them, should go up to Jerusalem" to confer about this matter (v. 2). Reaching Jerusalem, they were received "of the church and of the apostles and elders" (v. 4). In the assembly where the Gentile issue was discussed, a "multitude" was present (v. 12). With deliberations concluded, "the apostles and elders, with the whole church" composed a letter to send to Antioch. Upon arriving in Antioch, those bearing the letter "gathered the multitude together," and "delivered the epistle" (vv. 22-23, 30). Now, if the church then had been "governed" as it is today, why didn't the elders of Antioch confer with the elders of Jerusalem, and formulate a decree which would be imposed upon the churches? Luke explicitly states that the church as a body participated in this decision-making. "The mass of the church did participate (in decision-making) in the apostolic age."[22] This was not an issue resolved in a private caucus of elders alone. How very different from our procedure today!

Finally, to show that the New Testament illustrates congregational decision-making action, we refer to the Corinthian case of the incestuous brother (I Co. 5). Paul directed that "when ye are gathered together" to "deliver such an one unto Satan" — that is, excommunicate him (vv. 4-5). Again is seen the fact that an assembly is assigned authority and power to make a determination in matters affecting its interests. In this instance it was whether a certain sinful brother was to be considered a part of the fellowship and assembly any longer. Our current procedure would be very different, for the decision of disfellowship is made by the elders and announced to the congregation for its approval.

AUTHORITY IN THE KINGDOM

The mother of James and John requested Jesus to bestow upon her sons favored positions in the kingdom. When the other apostles learned of this they were "indignant," and "there was also a strife among them, which of them should be accounted the greatest" (Luke 22:24). Jesus rebuked this dissension and power struggle with these pungent remarks:

> Ye know that the princes of the Gentiles exercise dominion over them, and they that are great exercise authority upon them. But it shall not be so among you: but whosoever will be great among you, let him be your minister; and whosoever will be chief among you, let him be your servant: even as the Son of man came not to be ministered unto, but to minister, and to give his life a ransom for many (Ma. 20:25-28).

In this monumental passage, which we are inclined to overlook in studying "authority" in the kingdom, Jesus established the criterion for greatness in the kingdom — that of *service!* Assuredly, he was not concerned with the *abuse* of authority, as some would contend, but of the *use* of it. Jesus positively declared that in regard to the "great exercise of authority," that "it shall not be so among you!" In the Lord's kingdom there are no positions of power and prestige, no high authoritative offices, and none issuing commands that others must obey. Greatness is not realized by attaining the "highest office in the church" — the eldership. The Lord would teach us that true spiritual greatness is to be attained by wielding a towel and a basin, not a crown and scepter!

What the Lord taught about Gentile princes "exercising dominion" is of great importance here. Appeal to other versions may assist in clarity of this expression. "You know that the rulers of the Gentiles lord it over them" (N.I.V.); "the rulers of the pagans exercise despotic powers" (E. V. Rieu). It is extremely important to observe that the expression "exercise dominion" in this text is precisely the same Greek expression employed by Peter where he forbids elders from being "lords over" God's people (I Pe. 5:3). These two passages, utilizing identical terminology, declare that there is not to be the sort of authority exercised in Christ's kingdom as in civil offices. Yet this is the very thing asserted by the concept of the authoritative rule of elders! It is precisely the sort of officialdom and exercise of authority Jesus said would not exist in his kingdom! The authoritative view contends that elders possess an authority of office like that of civil rulers; that elders *rule*, and members *must be obedient* to them. It is contended that the decrees of elders must be obeyed implicitly, and that even the opinions of elders become binding authority upon the congregation. This view asserts in effect that the elders are a *ruling hierarchy*, and when elders utter *ex cathedra* edicts the church must obey fully and without question.

In an attempt to lend dignity to the position of elders, we have distorted the view out of scriptural perspective. In an eagerness to urge members to follow the leadership of elders, we've in fact transformed leadership into dictatorship. In such exaggerated views it has been contended that the "authority of the eldership in the church is the authority of Christ," and that if members "rebel against these decisions then they, in fact, rebel against God." Brethren, we issue a call back to a sane and moderate view of the position of elders, such as can unquestionably command scriptural support. To contend "to oppose them (the elders) is to oppose God" is but shades of Roman Catholicism. Pope Leo XIII, in his *Great Encyclical Letters*, made the identical claim in asserting that the church owed the same "submission and obedience" to "the Roman

Pontiff as to God Himself." And, brethren, let us be reminded of history: it was a corruption of the eldership that led to the first great apostasy, and ultimately to the papacy.

Brother McGarvey commented thus on Matthew 20:25-28:

> To sit on his right and on his left in the kingdom would not only be an honor, but would give authority. Jesus informs them that while the princes among the Gentiles exercise dominion and authority, it is not to be so in his kingdom, but the post of honor is to be the post of service.[23]

E. G. Sewell added: "There shall be none in the church that have authority over others. The great ones in the church are not to be officers over others, but simply to serve for others; not to exercise dominion over them."[24] This text declares, therefore, that there are no authoritarian positions in the kingdom of Christ, but that the highest honor is the place of greatest service. To maintain the authoritative view is to contend that the highest position in the kingdom is the eldership!

"OFFICES" AND "OFFICERS"

The view is prevalent that elders are "officers" in the church (they are even called "the *highest officers*"), and if "officers" they must occupy some "office." It seems understood that when elders are ordained they by virtue of their "office" are vested with some special "authority." After installation into "office" elders are thought to then speak with *ex cathedra* authority. Such ideas are nowhere presented in the New Testament.

Regarding the notion of "office," "officers" and "authority," David Lipscomb wrote: "The word 'officer' is never in the Scriptures applied to a member of a church of Christ."[25] Lipscomb further added:

> We believe that no office in the church invests with a particle of authority. Controlling the church by virtue of authority of office is unknown of the scriptures. Whenever a man in the church of Christ claims authority or exercise of power merely on official grounds, is essentially a Pope.[26]

Dr. Jack Lewis concludes: "The Greek terms we've considered (elder, pastor, bishop) from the viewpoint of the elder emphasizes images of sacrifice and service that he is to discharge rather than images of authority."[27]

CONCLUSION

A woman once remarked to a minister: "I really enjoy your preaching, because you always seem to get so much more out of a text than is really there!" Brethren, we must not be guilty of doing so in the issue of the eldership. We must not formulate views regarding elders, and return to the scriptures and read into them much more than is really there! What can we actually justify about the role of elders by what is in truth found in the scriptures, instead of what we say they teach?

ENDNOTES

1. H. Leo Boles, *The Eldership of the Churches of Christ* (Nashville, TN: Gospel Advocate Co., n.d.), p. 1.

2. Flavil R. Yeakley, Jr., *Church Leadership and Organization* (Tulsa, OK: Christian Communications, Inc., 1980), p. 17.

3. *Ibid.,* p. 22.

4. *The Interpreter's Bible,* (Abingdon Press, n.d.), vol. II, p. 755.

5. F. F. Bruce, *Epistle to the Hebrews* (Grand Rapids, MI: Eerdmans, n.d.), p. 395.

6. Joseph H. Thayer, *Greek-English Lexicon* (New York, NY: American Book Co., 1889), p. 638.

7. W. E. Vine, *Expository Dictionary of New Testament Words* (London, England: Oliphants, Ltd., n.d.), vol. III, p. 124.

8. *Analytical Greek Lexicon* (London, England: S. Bagster and Sons, 1912), p. 313.

9. Thayer, *op. cit.,* p. 497.

10. William Conley, "The Nature and Basis of Episcopal Authority," *Christian Bible Teacher* (February, 1974), p. 62.

11. J. W. Roberts, "The Rulership of Elders," *Firm Foundation* (April 1, 1958), p. 170.

12. Vine, *op. cit.,* vol. I, p. 89.

13. Thayer, *op. cit.,* p. 276.

14. Jack P. Lewis, *Harding Graduate School of Religion Bulletin* (June, 1978), p. 1.

15. Albert Barnes, *Notes on the New Testament — Hebrews* (Grand Rapids, MI: Baker Book House, 1949), p. 318.

16. Vine, *op. cit.,* vol. IV, p. 87.

17. Roberts, *op. cit.*, p. 179.

18. Colin Brown, *New International Dictionary of New Testament Theology* (Grand Rapids, MI: Zondervan Publishing Co., n.d.), vol. I, p. 291.

19. Bagster, *op. cit.*, p. 125.

20. Thayer, *op. cit.*, pp. 195-196.

21. J. W. McGarvey, *New Commentary on Acts of Apostles* (Des Moines, IO: Gospel Broadcast, 1892), pp. 104, 105.

22. J. W. McGarvey, *A Treatise on the Eldership* (Murfreesboro, TN: DeHoff Publications, 1950), p. 40.

23. J. W. McGarvey, *The New Testament Commentary* (Des Moines, IO: Gospel Broadcast, 1875), vol. I (Matthew and Mark), p. 177.

24. E. G. Sewell, *The Gospel Advocate,* 1898, p. 280.

25. David Lipscomb, *The Gospel Advocate,* 1874, p. 294.

26. David Lipscomb, *The Gospel Advocate,* 1892, p. 292.

27. Jack P. Lewis, Harding University Graduate School of Religion Bulletin (April, 1979), p. 5.

THE AUTHORITY OF ELDERS

DISCUSSION FORUM — No. II-B

HEBREWS 13:7, 17, 24: Elders have been given delegated, decision-making authority in matters of expediency in the local church by the New Testament, and members of the local church have a responsibility to abide by their decisions that are in harmony with the New Testament.

By GARY WORKMAN

(See picture and biographical sketch at beginning of author's previous chapter.)

Within the last few years there has developed a growing controversy regarding the authority of elders. This is not a new turn of events, though, for the Restoration Movement. Certain "pioneer" voices of the past espoused the idea that elders have no real authority. Tolbert Fanning appears to have been the first to take such a view.[1] Fanning wrote, in part, against J. W. McGarvey's *Treatise on the Eldership,* a book which Christians today would do well to study.[2] In his efforts to oppose denominational systems of church government, Fanning over-reacted and took a radical departure both from his brethren and from the New Testament in his anti-authority stance.

Other names associated with a limitation of elders' authority would include those of David and William Lipscomb and E. G. Sewell.[3] However, a survey of their writings leaves the impression that they may have had in mind elders' lack of authority to make decisions in matters of doctrine more than in matters of judgment. If such is indeed the case, we can only concur, for doctrine has already been decided by the Lord

(John 16:13; Jude 3). Clearer statements against the authority of elders appeared twenty-five years ago in the pages of the *Firm Foundation*, written by the late J. W. Roberts. Following a long period of relative silence on this issue, Roberts' two-part series seems to have sown the seed for much of today's anti-authority syndrome. But what really precipitated the current rash of sermons, articles and books on the subject was a discussion of "Who Calls the Shots?" by Reuel Lemmons. That August 1977 editorial in the *Firm Foundation* followed by two more over the next several months and occasional re-mention of the subject until the close of his editorship in August 1983, stirred up a controversy that is still raging.

Many articles and several books appeared which dealt with elders and their authority.[4] The Harding Graduate School conducted a "Preachers Forum" on the subject in April of 1980.[5] And this writer and Reuel Lemmons expressed opposing views on the authority and function of elders on the "Issues Forum" of 1982's Pepperdine Lectureship.[6] Right in the middle of this current six-year stir on the subject, Waymon Miller published his book on the anti-authority side of the issue.[7] His book is the most thorough discussion to date espousing the negative view. It is therefore fitting that he be selected to represent that side of the issue in this "Discussion Forum" of the *Second Annual Denton Lectures*. We consider brother Miller to be a worthy disputant for this occasion but must take strong exception to his position.

BIBLICAL MATERIAL SUPPORTING THE AUTHORITY OF ELDERS

The basic terms. There are three basic terms for the men under consideration, all three referring to the same group. *Elders* are *bishops* who *pastor* (Tit. 1:5, 7; Acts 20:17, 28; I Pe. 5:1-2). An authoritative role is pictured in each of these terms.

"Elder" (*presbuteros*) occurs 66 times in the New Testament, some 15 of these in reference to elders of a church. The word's basic meaning (and that of its Hebrew equivalent) is "older." Appearing first in Exodus 12:21, it came to designate an official position (Ex. 24:1; Num. 11:16) of "office-bearers,"[8] namely the "heads" (ASV) or "rulers" (KJV) of the people (De.

1:13). They were "the ruling class of the individual tribes . . . and of Israel as a whole."[9] There is thus a "twofold meaning of the word," namely "age" and "title of office."[10] In the New Testament, the Jewish "elders" referred to the members of the Sanhedrin (Mark 8:31) and synagogue rulers (Luke 7:3). This is the background of the "elders" of the New Testament churches (Acts 11:30, etc.). The term was therefore easy for Jewish Christians to understand since it came from the synagogue pattern of government.

Since elders in Christian congregations were always an appointed plurality of men (Acts 14:23; Jam. 5:14; Tit. 1:5), the term "eldership" (*presbuterion*) was used. Referring first to the Jewish Sanhedrin — the "assembly of the elders" (Luke 22:66, ASV) or "estate of the elders" (Acts 22:5), this word also came to be used of the Christian "presbytery" (I Ti. 4:14) or "body of elders" (NIV). The term "eldership" is the nearest English equivalent,[11] and it is so rendered in the American Bible Union Version. The terms "elder" and "eldership" therefore plainly denote authority in New Testament churches, specifying "certain persons appointed to hold office . . . and to exercise spiritual oversight."[12]

"Bishop" also speaks of authority. The noun (*episkopos*) occurs five times in the New Testament — once of Christ (I Pe. 2:25) and elsewhere of elders of churches (Acts 20:28; Ph. 1:1; Tit. 1:7; I Ti. 3:2). Jesus is therefore the chief bishop with others appointed under him. This word "bishop" means an overseer or superintendent. Used in Greek history for "men who had a responsible position in the state," certain "officials" with "minor judicial functions,"[13] the word came also to be applied by the Holy Spirit to elders (Acts 20:17, 28). Elders are commanded to tend their flock by taking or exercising the "oversight" of it (I Pe. 5:2), literally "bishoping" (from the verb *episkopeo*). Therefore, they have an official function, an *episkope* (I Ti. 3:1) — "a definite function or a fixed office."[14]

"Pastor" is another word that reveals authority. The noun (*poimen*) occurs 18 times in the New Testament, rendered "shepherd" by the KJV in all but one passage. Eleven of those passages refer to Jesus who is the "great shepherd of the sheep" (He. 13:20), the "shepherd and bishop of your souls" (I

Pe. 2:25). There is the "chief shepherd" (*archipoimen*, I Pe. 5:4). and the undershepherds — the "pastors" whom he has left in charge (Ep. 4:11). The word "pastor" or "shepherd" came from a rich background where it was "frequently used in metaphorical senses: leader, ruler, commander."[15] Joshua was appointed as Moses' successor "over the congregation" of God's people as a "shepherd," and the children of Israel were required to "obey" him (Num. 27:17-20). Likewise, elders in the church are commanded to "shepherd" (tend, feed) the flock (I Pe. 5:2) or the church (Acts 20:28). Shepherding (*poimaino*) — to "be shepherd" (ASV) or "rule" (KJV) — is said to be the role of a "governor" (Ma. 2:6). It involves "authority" sufficient to "rule" (*poimaino*) with whatever "rod of iron" is necessary (Re. 2:26-27).

Brother Miller in his book on elders attempts to evade the authoritative force of "elder," "bishop" and "pastor" by saying that we cannot depend on lexical definitions, for example those of Thayer who speaks of the "presiding officer of a Christian church."[16] The singular occurrence of the word "bishop" in I Timothy 3:2 or Titus 1:7 may have led Thayer to think that the New Testament prescribes one-man rule or that a single bishop would be sufficient. But this does not mean that Thayer misunderstood the meaning of the words themselves. Miller himself quoted an article in the *NIDNTT*, a source which rejects the notion of a monarchical bishop yet still speaks of the "episcopal office."[17] One cannot overthrow the basic meaning of these words.

Other revealing terms. There are certain other words used in the New Testament which reveal the authoritative role of elders.

"Rule" (*proistemi*) is a word that occurs eight times in the New Testament. It is found in passages that speak of "elders that rule well" (I Ti. 5:17) and of those who are "over you in the Lord" (I Th. 5:12). Brother Miller would not admit that this latter passage refers to elders.[18] His efforts are wasted, though, since the former passage specifies them! Miller's approach was to evade the force of the word "rule" or "over" by quoting a writer who mistakenly thought that at the time Paul wrote to the Thessalonians "there was as yet no institutionalized or precisely differentiated offices in the church" (since elders were not mentioned specifically) so that the word "over" suggested only "an activity rather than an office."[19] Miller failed to tell us, though, that the *same* writer in the *same* article concluded that "by the time of the Pastoral Epistles" things had changed so that I Timothy 5:17 "refers to presiding elders," with the term "elders" referring to "an organized system of offices."[20]

Though Miller maintains that "the idea of ruling . . . will not be justified by the meaning of the Greek words,"[21] the lexicons indicate differently. Thayer says the word *proistemi* means "to be over, to superintend, preside over."[22] Arndt-Gingrich defines it as "be at the head of, rule, direct . . ., manage, conduct" and says the word refers to "officials and administrators in the church."[23] Liddell and Scott tell us that from the time of Herodotus (a fifth-century B.C. Greek historian) the word referred to political rulers and that its meaning is "to govern, direct, manage."[24] The *TDNT* says that the word "rule" in these passages speaks of "care on the part of those in authority."[25]

The above lexical definitions make the meaning plain. But notice also that the word "rule" (*proistemi*) is found three other times in I Timothy (3:4, 5, 12) where the word speaks not only of the care but also of "the authority of the head of the household."[26] Verse 5 specifies that to "rule" well in one's family shows qualification to "take care of the church." If "rule" in 5:17 does not indicate authority, neither does it in regard to ruling one's family. But it does. The father's rule of the family with "children in subjection" (3:4) reveals also the authoritative rule of elders.

Another word for "rule" (*hegeomai*) occurs 28 times in the New Testament, used only in the present participle. This is the word which is found in Hebrews 13:7, 17 and 24 where the Hebrew Christians were commanded to remember, obey, submit to, and salute those who "have the rule over you." Here again brother Miller resists finding any reference to elders.[27] He thinks it far more likely that the Hebrews were commanded to obey and submit to preachers! He says it is "assumption" to make any of these verses refer to elders since none of the basic terms for elders are mentioned here. Therefore, since verse 7 "apparently" refers to preachers, verse 17 must also. (That word "apparently" sounds very much like some *assumption* on the part of Miller.)

Lexical definitions will reveal why verses 17 and 24 *must* refer to elders, and why verse 7 *cannot* refer to preachers (apostles perhaps, but not preachers). Thayer says the word indicates a "leader" in the sense of "to rule, command; to have authority over."[28] Arndt and Gingrich give it as "ruler, leader" in a sense opposite to *diakonos* ("servant"). They say the word applies to "leaders of religious bodies" and, in particular, "heads of a Christian church."[29] These "heads" are the elders-bishops-pastors, not the preacher! The *TDNT* tells us that the word translated "have the rule over" refers in this chapter to "human officers with divinely given pastoral authority" and that the other members "owe them obedience."[30]

That the above lexicography is correct can be demonstrated by other occurrences of the word *hegeomai* in the New Testament. It speaks of Jesus as "governor" (Ma. 2:6) which Thayer says indicates "a prince, of regal power."[31] The quotation in Matthew is from Micah 5:2 where the Hebrew word *mashal* is translated "ruler" both in the KJV and ASV. Another New Testament passage speaks of Joseph as "governor" over Egypt (Acts 7:10), a position of definite authority. The corresponding noun (*hegemon*) is used in reference to imperial governors such as Pilate (Ma. 27), Felix (Acts 23-24) and Festus (26:30), one to whom belonged "power and authority" (Luke 20:20). This is why Christians are told to "obey" and "submit" to them (He. 13:17).

But we are told by brother Miller that "obey" and "submit" are not to be interpreted as "submission to authority." Instead, the words are said to simply mean being "persuaded" and showing "deference." Admittedly, the word "obey" (*peitho*) is sometimes used of voluntary compliance (Acts 5:36-37) and agreement (Acts 5:40). However, it must not be overlooked that Christians are *commanded* to do this. It is not optional in this case! As long as elders do not attempt to add to divine law (since we have only one lawgiver — Jam. 4:12), and as long as their decisions are not in violation of God's will (Acts 5:29), we cannot *refuse* to obey elders and still be faithful to God!

Peitho is the word used of Christians who "obey the truth" (Gal. 5:7) and of horses who "obey us" because of bridles in their mouths (Jam. 3:3). One cannot *force* a horse with a bridle; neither can an elder *force* a Christian to obey. But the Christian who will not be persuaded is in rebellion! He is under obligation to "submit" (*hupeiko*) — a word that lexicographers tell us means to "yield to authority."[32] It is therefore demonstrated that elders *have* been given authority in matters of judgment and expediency and that members are obligated to abide by their decisions.

OBJECTIONS TO THE AUTHORITY OF ELDERS

"No one has any authority at all." One of the prime arguments used against the authority of elders is to say that Jesus taught in Matthew 20:25-28 that no one in the kingdom has any authority at all. Brother Miller refers to this passage over and over in his book as specifying "no authoritative offices," and he calls it "the fundamental text" that all other passages must be harmonized with.[33] Miller's interpretation of this text is well summed up by Sewell, whom he quotes as follows: "There shall be none in the church that have authority over others."[34] Any interpretation of other passages which conflicts with this, says Miller, is "perversion."

However, the passage in question is the one that is being perverted. The statement of Jesus speaks of the *abuse* of authority, not the proper use of it. Miller, however, calls this interpretation "presumption" because it is "not the obvious meaning of the text."[35] Yet, he does not explain why his view is so "obvious." The problem here is twofold: (1) Miller does not seem to have carefully analyzed the words of the passage for their precise meaning, and (2) he does not seem to have noticed the context to which the statement is addressed. Over and over Miller denounces the "assumption" he thinks is involved in supposing elders to have authority, yet *assumption* is precisely the basis on which he has interpreted this passage!

There are two key terms to notice in the statement of verse 25 (and the parallel in Mark 10:42): *katakurieuo* and *katexousiazo*. The first term is the one found also in I Peter 5:3 where Peter instructs elders not to be "lording it over" the church.

This would be an abuse of power such as characterized tyrants or despots, not benign rulers. The second term is not the word which simply means to "have authority" (*exousiazo*) but rather a compound found only here in the New Testament. Various lexicons propose that it means "tyrannize,"[36] "to exercise lordship over, domineer over" as opposed to the ordinary exercise of authority,[37] a "tendency towards compulsion or oppression."[38] And various translations render it as "vaunt their power" (Knox), "oppress" (Berkeley), "tyrannize" (Goodspeed), and "rule as dictators" (Norlie).

Commentators have explained the word similarly. Robertson, perhaps the greatest of all Greek grammarians, defined it as "play the tyrant."[39] And Clarke said that "those who understand the genius of the language" will see that the word means *"exercise arbitrary power"* rather than the "simple" use of authority.[40] Plumptre referred to it as having a "forcible" meaning which "implies a wrong exercise of authority."[41] The *Pulpit Commentary* says it is to "use authority harshly and severely," and the comment is given that "our Lord does not find fault with that power or authority . . . which is exercised by princes or bishops. . . . What he condemns is the arbitrary and tyrannical exercise of such power."[42]

But why did Jesus make this statement? It was because of the request of James and John for special position among the apostles. As Guy Woods observed, "Matthew 20 is not an example of elders usurping authority. It's an example of preachers trying to do so."[43] Luke recounts a similar situation at the last supper (Luke 22:24-30) where there was "rivalry" among the apostles and a question of "which of them" should be the greatest. Both statements were spoken to the apostles. They would indeed have authority — even to the point of sitting on thrones (Luke 22:30; Ma. 19:28), but they were not to have *authority over each other:* "not so shall it be among you" (Ma. 20:26). All apostles were to be equal (cf. II Co. 12:11). Any attempt at a "greatest" and "first" among them would be usurpation. This is what the passage militates against.

If this passage denies authority to elders, it also denies it to apostles. But apostles *were* given authority (Ma. 18:18-20) and could "command" (I Th. 4:11; II Th. 3:4, 6, 10, 12). If it denies authority to elders, it denies it also to parents. But we know that parents *do* have authority because children are instructed to "obey" them (Eph. 6:1). And if it denies authority to elders, it denies it also to Jesus, for the hearers were to conduct themselves "even as" he did (Ma. 20:28). But we know that Jesus *did* have authority (Mark 2:10; Ma. 28:18). The truth is that this passage does not deny rightful authority to apostles or elders or anyone else!

"Elders are not said to have authority." Brother Miller in his book asks, "Where is the passage that clearly states that when one is installed as an elder that this 'office' endows him with 'authority'?" He says that "not a verse of inspired Scripture clearly states that elders have authority" but that one brother "succeeded in showing that nearly everyone in the church is said to have authority except elders."[44] At least the brother admittedly demonstrated the rightful existence of authority among Christians — a fact that Miller repeatedly denies.

The word "authority" (*exousia*) is found 103 times in the New Testament. Those questioning the authority of elders are like the chief priests and scribes who asked Jesus where he got his "authority" (Luke 20:1-2). It came from God (John 5:27; 17:2), and this is where the authority of others has come from as well. Jesus' having "all authority" (Ma. 28:18) does not mean that there is no authority left to be given to anyone else, as some have foolishly argued. Jesus has "all authority" in the sense of *supreme* authority "far above" all others (Ep. 1:20-21), other "authorities" being subject to him (I Pe. 3:22), but he can delegate authority to whomever he chooses.

While Jesus was still on earth he gave his *apostles* a measure of "authority" (Luke 9:1). Then he taught in a parable about his going back to heaven and giving his *servants* "authority" and "to each one his work" (Mark 13:34). This speaks of authority being given to various categories of individuals (not excluding elders) in their own sphere of activity. Consequently, apostles had authority despite brother Miller's claim that they were "not to exercise authority."[45] Paul told the Corinthians of his "authority" as an apostle (II Co. 10:8; 13:10).

There is "authority" in the civil realm (John 19:11; Ro. 13:1), in the marital realm (I Co. 7:4), and in the personal realm (I Co. 9:4-5). The fact that "authority" is not specifically ascribed to fathers does not mean they are without it. Likewise, the fact that the word "authority" is not specifically mentioned in connection with elders does not mean they are without it either. The various terms used of their position and activity, as well as the commanded subjection to them on the part of other Christians, affirms their authority to be God-given.

An elder is a "steward" (Tit. 1:7), which means "manager" — one who is a "ruler" (KJV) or who is "set over" (ASV) the household (Luke 12:42), a "master" appointed by the Lord over that house (v. 39, ASV). Just as Jesus at the end of time will give "authority" to Christians over cities (Luke 19:17), nations (Re. 2:26) and the tree of life (Re. 22:14), so now he gives political authority to rulers, domestic authority to husbands and fathers, and spiritual authority to apostles and elders.

"Elders have no office." It is often said that elders have no "office." Brother Miller makes this claim, though he will occasionally (and inconsistently) use the word "office" and "officers" for elders.[46] He denounces the appearance of the English word "office" in I Timothy 3:1 as "an inaccurate rendition of one verse in the King James text," saying that "if there is no 'office' then there can be no 'authority.' "[47] Translators and lexicographers disagree with Miller's position on this. The word "office" there (*episkope*) is the same word rendered "bishoprick" (KJV) or "office" (ASV) in reference to the apostleship of Judas in Acts 1:20. The word indicates a position vested with authority. So the word "office" is used in I Timothy 3:1 by the KJV, ASV, RSV and NASB translators, to mention only a few. The *TDNT* calls it "a distinct office."[48] The Arndt-Gingrich lexicon defines the Greek word as the "position or office as an overseer . . . the office of a bishop."[49] McGarvey well said, "The fact that it is a work makes it none the less an office." He said, "We regard the distinction as one between words rather than ideas" and added that elders are "officers of the church in the fullest sense of the term."[50] McGarvey was right.

Various other objections have been levelled against the authority of elders. Space prohibits a separate treatment of them here, but all are equally invalid.

CONCLUDING OBSERVATIONS

It is interesting to notice that often those who take a position against the authority of elders inadvertently reveal that an ungodly *abuse* of authority is their real complaint. In his book, brother Waymon Miller characterizes the authority of elders as autocratic, absolute and supreme, sovereign, totalitarian, lordly, despotic, and such like. This is not the way that *any* kind of authority should be manifested, and such terms are prejudicial to the issue.

We do not defend the abuse of authority in any realm. If brother Miller is really writing against inept, undesirable, egotistic, bossy, inconsiderate, ruthless, brutal, dictatorial and overbearing elders (as he describes them in his book) who are nothing more than "tyrants and despots," we wish he would put the issue in its proper light as the *abuse* of authority. And we would concur against such elders, wherever they may be. We would also be opposed to politicians, employers, husbands and fathers who display such characteristics. But the rightful *use* of authority in any of these positions cannot be so characterized.

Much of what is being written today starts out by criticizing elders who, in a dictatorial manner, lord it over the flock in violation of I Peter 5:3. But by the time the writer gets through, it becomes clear that he believes elders "lord it over" when they will not surrender to a democratic voting process on the part of the congregation. It is blatantly and rebelliously wrong to accuse the church's many humble and godly elders of "lording it over the flock" simply because they are obediently fulfilling God's directive to be "exercising the oversight."

Brother Miller is confusing "authoritarian" (which he mentions over 40 times in his book) with "authoritative" (which he denounces on pages 14, 20, 31, 36, 40 and 51). A wrongful "authoritarian" attitude and manner *cannot* be defended. But the "authoritative" role of elders *can* and *must* be defended, for that is what the New Testament presents.

ENDNOTES

1. Fanning presented his views in a series of 13 articles entitled "The Church of Christ" which appeared in *The Religious Historian*, a paper he edited from 1872 to his death in 1874. Many years later the articles were reprinted in the *Firm Foundation*.

2. J. W. McGarvey, *A Treatise on the Eldership* (DeHoff, 1962). This book, first published in 1870, is a collection of articles which had previously appeared in the weekly *Apostolic Times*, McGarvey being one of the editors.

3. A collection of miscellaneous writings from these and other men, selected principally from the first sixty years of the *Gospel Advocate*, is found in *Restoration Ideas on Church Organization*, edited and published by J. Ridley Stroup.

4. Highly recommended for further reading is Robert R. Taylor's *The Elder and His Work* (Lambert, 1978) and the April 1978 issue of *The Spiritual Sword*. See also Flavil R. Yeakley's *Church Leadership and Organization* (Christian Communications, 1980).

5. Tapes are available from Patterson-Hale Productions, 1356 S. White Station, Memphis, TN 38117.

6. Tapes are available from Christian Communications Inc., 2001-B W. Detroit, Broken Arrow, OK 74012.

7. Waymon D. Miller, *The Role of Elders in the New Testament Church* (Plaza Press, 1980).

8. Gunther Bornkamm, *"Presbus, Presbuteros,"* *Theological Dictionary of the New Testament*, Gerhard Kittel, ed., (Eerdmans, 1968), vol. VI, p. 656.

9. Lothar Coenen, *"Bishop, Presbyter, Elder,"* *The New International Dictionary of New Testament Theology*, Colin Brown, gen. ed., (Zondervan, 1967), vol. I, p. 195.

10. Bornkamm, *op. cit.*, p. 654.

11. Cf. McGarvey, *op. cit.*, p. 9.

12. A. C. Grant, "Elder in the New Testament," *The International Standard Bible Encyclopedia* (Eerdmans, 1939), vol. II, p. 924.

13. Coenen, *op. cit.*, p. 189.

14. Arndt and Gingrich, eds., *Greek-English Lexicon* (University of Chicago, 1963), p. 299.

15. Erich Beyreuther, "Shepherd," *NIDNTT*, vol. III, p. 564.

16. Joseph Henry Thayer, *Greek-English Lexicon* (Zondervan, 1975), p. 243; Miller, *op. cit.*, p. 32.

17. Coenen, *op. cit.*, pp. 192, 190.

18. Cf. Miller, *op. cit.*, p. 41.

19. Miller, pp. 41-42.

20. Coenen, *op. cit.*, p. 198.

21. Miller, *op. cit.*, p. 36.

22. Thayer, *op. cit.*, p. 539.

23. Arndt and Gingrich, *op. cit.,* p. 713.

24. Henry George Liddell and Robert Scott, *Greek-English Lexicon* (Clarendon, 1869), p. 1344.

25. Bo Reicke, *"Proistemi,"* *TDNT,* vol. VI, p. 702.

26. *Ibid.*

27. Miller, *op. cit.,* pp. 34-40.

28. Thayer, *op. cit.,* p. 276.

29. Arndt and Gingrich, *op. cit.,* p. 344.

30. Friedrich Buchsel, *"Hegeomai,"* *TDNT,* vol. II, p. 907.

31. Thayer, *loc. cit.*

32. Thayer, *op. cit.,* p. 638; cf. Arndt and Gingrich, *op. cit.,* p. 846.

33. Miller, *op. cit.* p. 30; cf. pp. 14, 17, 19, 22, 32, 35, 42, 46, 56, 63, 70.

34. Miller, *op. cit.,* p. 16.

35. Miller, *op. cit.,* p. 17.

36. Arndt and Gingrich, *op. cit.,* p. 472.

37. *The Analytical Greek Lexicon* (Harper, n.d.), p. 223.

38. Werner Foerster, *"Katexousiazo,"* *TDNT,* vol. II, p. 575.

39. Archibald Thomas Robertson, *Word Pictures in the New Testament* (Baker, 1930), vol. I, p. 162.

40. Adam Clarke, *Clarke's Commentary* (Abingdon-Cokesbury, n.d.), vol. I, p. 199.

41. E. H. Plumptre, "Matthew," *A New Testament Commentary,* Charles J. Ellicott, ed. (Cassell & Co., 1839), vol. I, p. 125.

42. A. Lukyn Williams, "Matthew," *Pulpit Commentary* (Eerdmans, 1950), vol. XV, sect. 2, p. 282; E. Bickersteph, "Mark," *Pulpit Commentary,* vol. XVI, sect. 2, p. 65.

43. Guy N. Woods, "Elders Have Authority By Divine Decree," *Harding Preachers' Forum* (Patterson-Hale, 1980).

44. Miller, *op. cit.,* pp. 24, 37. Strangely, on p. 94 Miller said that elders are "a group of men who are vested with the authority to oversee a congregation. . . ."

45. Miller, *op. cit.,* p. 21.

46. Miller, *op. cit.,* pp. 48, 61, 95; cf. pp. 49-50, 96.

47. Miller, *op. cit.,* pp. 27-29, 54-55.

48. Herman W. Beyer, *"Episkopos,"* *TDNT,* vol. II, p. 617.

49. Arndt and Gingrich, *op. cit.,* p. 299.

50. McGarvey, *op. cit.,* pp. 10, 17.

THE NATURE OF BIBLICAL FAITH

DISCUSSION FORUM — No. III-A

HEBREWS 11:1-3, 6: IN GENERAL MATTERS OF HUMAN KNOWLEDGE, THINGS NOT PERCEIVED THROUGH THE SENSES ARE MATTERS OF FAITH AND DO NOT PROVIDE THE CERTAINTY OF EMPIRICAL KNOWLEDGE.

By ARLIE J. HOOVER

Born 1936, Slaton, Texas. Married Gloria Kay Garrison, and they have two daughters. Holds M.A., and Ph.D. degrees; has done post-doctoral research in Germany. Professor of History and Philosophy at Pepperdine University 1964-1977; academic dean, Columbia Christian College; presently professor of History at Abilene Christian University. Recipient of Woodrow Wilson National Fellowship, Fulbright Grant, Exchange Fellowship from University of Texas, and a Research Grant from the National Association of Arts and Humanities.

INTRODUCTION

We are in the field of *epistemology* when we take up the question of knowledge and faith. Epistemology is the study of knowledge, especially the grounds and limits of knowledge. The first question you ask in this field, "Do we know anything at all?" If the answer to that is yes — which it usually is — the next question is, "How?" What are the processes of knowledge?

If you work with epistemological questions for a number of years you will probably come up with a systematic approach to various kinds of propositions. I maintain that most propositions fall into three major classes and I shall explain them here and lay the groundwork for our discussion of the difference between faith and knowledge.

CLASSES OF PROPOSITIONS

The three classes of propositions are deductive, demonstrative, and inferential. Let us look at them in some detail.

First, *deductive propositions* are absolutely certain, but this is a deceptive certainty because it is built into the definition of such statements. I have used the term "deductive" from logic because it refers to a process of reasoning where the conclusion is inescapable if the premises are true and the argument is formally correct. For example, if I argue,

> All crows are black.
> Jack is a crow,
> Therefore, Jack is black.

. . . the conclusion is absolutely certain if the premises are true. But this certainty is a built-in certainty because you still have to go out and prove the two premises, which gets you out of deduction.

Another kind of deductive proposition would be what Kant called analytical judgments, such as "Blind men can't see," or "Deaf men can't hear," or "Bachelors have no wives." All you need to do is to analyze the subject to get the predicate, hence the name, "analytical judgment." Such statements are absolutely certain but singularly uninformative. They are redundant, tautological, definitionally true.

Throughout the history of philosophy deductive propositions have been preferred by the rationalists and the mathematicians like Plato, Augustine, Descartes, Leibniz, and Spinoza.

Second, *demonstrative propositions* are empirical judgments, statements you prove by direct, concrete, empirical contact with the world. You have to use your senses to prove the premise, "All crows are black," hence you must have some demonstrative propositions in order to use deduction in the real world.

I use the term "demonstrative" because I like the old proverb from jurisprudence, "What can be demonstrated need not be debated." If we get into an argument over the boiling point of water the way to settle the argument is to boil some actual water, not argue with non-empirical data. Demonstrative propositions are verified or falsified with empirical data.

Up to this point we have the agreement of the positivists in philosophy. They admit that man uses these two types of propositions, but they stop here and they are wrong when they do. We must establish a third category.

Third, *inferential propositions* are established by implication from demonstrative propositions. Hence you may call them "remotely demonstrative," if you like. They are seen indirectly, not directly. The object of such a proposition may be real and objective, like an historical event in the past, but it is not immediately objective.

For exampke, in a court of law you must work with inferential propositions. The jury may not see directly the event affirmed (*e.g.*, "Jones killed Brown"), but it can see the event indirectly. We see remote events through the eyes of competent witnesses. We have cases on record where a defendant was executed for a crime that no one saw directly. The jury convicted him strictly on circumstantial evidence. Surely this should convince us of the importance and validity of inferential propositions. Positivists have belittled them through history, but they are vital. Rejecting them would destroy all history writing, close all newspapers, and terminate most court proceedings.

A good example of the difference between demonstrative and inferential propositions would be the big hole near Flagstaff, Arizona, called Meteor Crater. From all evidence in this case — the crater, the metal fragments, the crushed rock strata — we can infer that indeed a meteor caused this great hole in the ground, although no one saw the meteor fall about 6,000 years ago, as they estimate. We can almost say, "I am certain that a meteor caused this crater."

But which is more certain — the hole in the ground or the meteor? You can walk right up and see the hole; you can even climb down into it. You can examine the metal fragments and view the crushed rock strata. But can you examine directly the meteor? No, so we would say that the empirical data pointing to the meteor is "more certain" than the meteor.

A. N. Whitehead once coined a nice name for a fallacy — the Fallacy of Misplaced Concreteness. You commit it when you assume that your theory is as concrete (certain) as the facts it is proposed to explain. You would commit it here if you assumed that the meteor was as certain as the hole. We see the hole directly but we see the meteor fall "by faith," as it were. This is what we mean when we say that we can see something "by the eye of faith." There is a great deal of evidence for the meteor, but the evidence is inferential, not demonstrative.

FAITH NOT IRRATIONAL

Yet faith is not something irrational. It is supported by good evidence. We must always oppose those unbelievers who try to define faith as a "leap in the dark," with no supporting evidence. Scientists use faith just as much as we do, though they might not call it that.

We must conclude, therefore, that in our usual experience inferential propositions are not as certain as demonstrative propositions. Now, my main point in this discussion is that we *ordinarily* use the terms "know" and "believe" in these two senses. When we say we know something we mean (loosely) that we have more or less direct empirical contact with it. Conversely, when we say we believe something we mean (loosely) that we have indirect evidence for it.

Sometimes an inference may be so highly probable that we say we know it. For example, I'm so thoroughly persuaded that a meteor caused Meteor Crater that I could be caught saying that I know it! But this only shows how loosely we use these terms. When you get down to a precise epistemological analysis you'll have to say that you know the hole and believe in the meteor.

There is a passage in the Gospel of John which shows that the people in the New Testament observed this same distinction. Speaking of the woman at the well near Sychar, John says:

> And from that city many of the Samaritans believed on him because of the word of the woman, who testified, He told me all things that I ever did. So when the Samaritans came unto him, they besought him to abide with them: and he abode there two days. And many more believed because of his word; and they said to the woman, Now we believe, not because of thy speaking: for we have heard for ourselves, and know that this is indeed the Saviour of the world (John 4:39-42).

The Greek word for "know" here is *oida*, which is a stronger word for know than the customary verb, *ginosko*. It implies a certain knowledge based on observation. Here it could be translated, "know for sure." This certain knowledge based on direct contact is contrasted with belief based on the woman's testimony. The contrast is obviously between direct and indirect evidence.

Yet we note something puzzling in this passage: these people who said they knew for sure were called *believers* and used the expression, *"we believe."* If they knew for sure, why use the term believe? I think the harmony lies in the fact that the New Testament often uses believe (*pisteuo*) to mean trust in Christ to the point of complete commitment. To believe in Christ usually means to become a Christian, to trust fully in him, not to give just a bare mental assent to him.

What about people, like most Christians since the first century, who have never had the privilege of meeting Jesus Christ directly? Would we say that they must just believe and never know? No, I think not. Paul said, "I know whom I have believed," and I feel every Christian since Paul's day can say the same: "I know the Christ in whom I have placed my trust."

But, you ask, if we are limited to inferential propositions about Christ, if we don't have direct contact, how can we say we now?

This is an excellent question and indeed is the crux of our issue here today. None of us has seen Christ or his resurrection so how can we say we know it? We can't in the usual meaning of the word "know," if all you have is inference in history. Those who say that they know Christ arose from the dead are saying that New Testament history is demonstrative, that remote history is as certain as current empirical experience. This is not how we usually use the word "know." In my judgment, remote history can be highly probable, but never as certain as immediate empirical observation.

Yet, the Christian has certainty! Jesus assured us that those who believed without seeing are blessed; he implied that our certainty is as good as that of Thomas (John 20:29). Paul told the Colossians that Christians are expected to have "the full assurance of understanding" of the gospel (Col. 2:2).

HOLY SPIRITS PROVIDES CERTAINTY

If we have certainty and it doesn't come from history, where did we get it? I reply: *from the Holy Spirit!* This is taught, I feel, in a number of passages which we shall now analyze. I will not quote each passage in full but will give a few comments on the contents.

I Corinthians 2:11-16. In a context discussing the wisdom of God which man in his wisdom can never discover, Paul tells us that it was the Spirit that brought us the thoughts of God. He states plainly that we received the Spirit of God so that we might understand (*oida* — know for sure) what God has given us. Checking the context you can see that these gifts of God refer to his thoughts, his wisdom, his gospel, his revelation. So the Spirit is the one who helps us understand the gospel; he is given for this express purpose.

On the other hand, the natural or unspiritual man rejects the divine revelation. Why? The answer here is crucial. Paul says it is because the gospel is foolishness to him and he can't understand the revelation because it is "spiritually judged" ("discerned" — NIV). The Greek word for "judge" here is *anakrino*, which means in various contexts to judge, examine, scrutinize, question, or evaluate. It means to investigate for the purpose of determining the excellence or defects of a person or thing. Paul says the non-Christian can't possibly understand the gospel because it is spiritually evaluated, that is, investigated with the help of, or under the auspices of, the Spirit.

I John 2:20, 27. In a context warning about the Antichrist and his followers, John assures Christians that they have an anointing (Greek: *chrisma*) from the Holy One, evidently the Holy Spirit. Because of this anointing we know the truth and don't need anyone to teach us and should therefore have no fear of those who are trying to lead us astray.

John says something in I John 4:13 that repeats this point: "Hereby we know that we abide in him and he in us, because he hath given us of his Spirit."

Romans 8:15-16. Paul says that when we as children of God cry, *"Abba* Father," it is the Holy Spirit acting as our agent.

Further, Paul says that the Spirit himself testifies with our spirit that we are God's children. Here some people object and argue that Paul said only that the Spirit testifies *with* our spirit, not *to* our spirit. But if you meditate for a moment on the meaning of "testify with" you will see, I think, that it necessarily implies "testify to." The Spirit is our co-witness in proving the proposition that we are children of God.

The Greek word here is *summartureo*, "to witness with." It is used only four times in the New Testament and three of these are by Paul in Romans. The other two times in Romans (2:15; 9:1) Paul uses it to refer to the Gentiles who keep the law and then to himself in his feelings for Israel. In both cases it is a matter of the conscience bearing witness with the person. Now, surely when the conscience bears witness it is *to* the person possessing the conscience, is it not?

Matthew 16:17. When Peter confessed that Jesus was the Messiah, Jesus responded: "Blessed are you, Simon Bar-Jona! For flesh and blood has not revealed this to you, but my Father who is in heaven" (RSV). "Flesh and blood" refers to basic humanity, man with his natural cognitive equipment, unaided reason. Peter would not have arrived at his conviction concerning Jesus without God's helping him. Something more than regular empirical confrontation was needed.

This agrees with our exegesis of I Corinthians 2 — the unspiritual man can't receive the revelation of God because it is foolishness to him and it is spiritually evaluated.

CHRISTIAN FAITH AND "GENERAL FAITH"

Here we must make a critical point: Christian faith is different from "general faith," chiefly because of the work of the Holy Spirit. Faith is usually described as inferior to knowledge by the New Testament never says this. This is why we can say, like Paul, "I know whom I have believed." In "general faith," demonstrative facts are more certain than inferences; the crater is more certain than the meteor. But this distinction breaks down when we get to Christian faith, because the Christian has certainty and if this certainty doesn't come from history then it must come from the Holy Spirit. The passages we have analyzed seem to teach this very thing.

Please don't panic and call this "creeping Calvinism!" The work of the Spirit is not irresistible or overpowering. John exhorts us to remain in him (I John 2:27). Paul tells us not to quench the Spirit (I Th. 5:19), which implies that you can, by your free will, control the degree of the Spirit's influence in your life.

Once we've mentioned the work of the Spirit, we must re-balance the equation and go back to say a good word for the objective, external evidences. When we say the Spirit gives certainty, we don't mean to imply that the resurrection can't be defended. Not at all. The historical evidence for the resurrection is very strong, so strong that a non-Christian would have to say, I feel, that it is highly probable. Since we use all these terms loosely he might even say it is certain, as certain as any event in ancient history.

But some unbelievers could still say that it is not absolutely certain. Rene Descartes once said, "Give unqualified assent to no propositions but those the truth of which is so clear and distinct that they cannot be doubted." If you followed this advice to the letter you would be what we call a *rationalist*. A rationalist would not believe in the resurrection because you can always doubt an inferential proposition.

SUMMARY OF POSITION

Allow me to sum up my position as it relates to the discipline of Christian apologetics. My position says that the external evidence for the faith is important and that the Holy Spirit uses that evidence to produce faith in the unbeliever. The unbeliever may choose to frustrate this work of the Spirit. We have here a fugue, as it were, with two movements working together, external and internal: First, the external evidence, inferential propositions like the resurrection, provide high probability, but not absolute certainty. Their high probability may induce the unbeliever to believe in Jesus Christ and accept his claims as the Son of God. Second, the internal evidence, the work of the Spirit, whom God gives to all those who obey him (Acts 5:32), provides certainty to the obedient Christian, allowing him to say, with Paul, "I know whom I have believed."

As a Christian apologist, I must say a word about the vital importance of the external evidences. The work of the Spirit in no way makes the external evidences unimportant, as some people are prone to conclude. The Spirit works with the Word (I Th. 1:5). Jesus said the Spirit would testify, not of himself, but of Christ (John 16:14). Thus, the internal Spirit works *in connection with* the external Scriptures and the historical Jesus. If we didn't have good solid evidence for the resurrection of Jesus then the work of the Spirit would be to no avail; in fact, the Spirit would have nothing to work *with*, to witness *to!*

I've been searching for years for a way to relate the external and the internal and the best way I've found is to use the difference between two kinds of causes: *necessary* and *sufficient*. An illustration will be better than a formal definition: Suppose a room is full of light and you ask, "Why is this room full of light? What causes this illumination?" Well, the sun is the real cause of the light, but while we're looking for causes we notice that the room has a hole in the ceiling through which the sunlight can come into the room. In a real sense the hole in the ceiling is a cause of the illumination — we call it a necessary cause. It is necessary to the final effect. The sun we call a sufficient cause — the real cause, we usually say.

Before you belittle the necessary cause in comparison to the sufficient cause, ask yourself: What would happen if we closed up the hole? Would any light get into the room? No. Consequently, necessary causes are very important. The thing you should remember about a necessary cause is that you could prevent the effect by its *absence* but not cause the effect by its mere *presence*.

Applied to our case here, we can say that highly probable external evidence is necessary for our certainty, but the Holy Spirit is the sufficient cause of our certainty. However, you would destroy our certainty if the external evidence were proved to be of low quality. It takes both: the external evidence and the internal Holy Spirit.

CONCLUSION

Perhaps one reason that we as a brotherhood have thought that the inferential propositions provided our certainty is that we have had a low view of the Holy Spirit throughout our history. I think you can have the Spirit operating as a witness in your heart and not know it. If you have a low view of the Spirit you make take the certainty he imparts and attribute it to the external evidence. Our certainty has come from the Spirit, who graciously gives us "full assurance," even though we might not have known where the assurance came from.

In a question like this were the data are varied and complex you always have more than one possible explanation of the material. I have suggested a hypothesis that I think throws all the available data into a coherent and consistent paradigm. It is not perfect but, then, no theory is. All theories leave a few threads dangling. You have to go with the one that does the best job of integrating the material at hand, and this is what I have done. I may change tomorrow, but to do so I will have to see a better paradigm.

THE NATURE OF BIBLICAL FAITH

DISCUSSION FORUM — No. III-B

HEBREWS 11:1-3, 6: SOME NON-EMPIRICAL PROPOSITIONS MAY BE KNOWN WITH GREATER CERTAINTY THAN EMPIRICALLY-PERCEIVED THINGS.

By DICK SZTANYO

Converted in 1970, began preaching about three months later. B.A. from Harding College, M.A. from Harding Graduate School. Graduate work at Andrews University in Michigan, University of Dallas, and International Academy of Philosophy in Irving. Teaches at Brown Train Preacher Training School, Hurst, Texas. Preached part-time at the Polytechnic congregation in Fort Worth; now preaches part-time for the Alvord congregation. Writes for several gospel papers. He and his wife have three children.

INTRODUCTION

One apologist for atheism says about the faith-reason issue: "it is logically impossible to reconcile reason and faith."[1] Again,

Reason and faith are opposites, two mutually exclusive terms: there is no reconciliation or common ground. Faith is belief without, or in spite of, reason.[2]

If reason can tell us anything there is to know, there is no longer a job for faith. *The entire notion of faith rests upon and presupposes the inadequacy of reason.*

This explains why discussions in favor of faith are always accompanied by references to the limits of reason.[3]

Another one of their apologists stated:

> We are told that ultimately nothing can be proven true and that consequently we must rely on faith throughout our lives.. . . .
>
> The theist argues that we have to rely on some faith in our everyday lives and then, using this statement as a springboard, he leaps to the conclusion that faith in anything is somehow justified — fairies, leprechauns, walking on air, and God. But the fact remains that we do not have good reasons for believing any of these things. Faith or not, proof or not — we still have to decide on the basis of whether there are good reasons available for our beliefs.[4]

Challenges like these cannot be ignored. But, I am convinced that, for a number of our brethren who have written — or are writing on the faith-reason issue, these problems are insurmountable!

PRELIMINARY CONSIDERATIONS

This discussion forum is ultimately designed to help us learn how to correctly understand this problem, and then to adequately formulate our response. Relative to this question, my distinguished opponent and I have fundamentally different positions. For instance, he holds that there is a basic difference between "general matters of human knowledge and faith" and "Biblical knowledge and faith." I hold that they are basically the same, and that the human mind works the same way in both the natural and supernatural spheres. From this first distinction, my opponent also holds that *no things not perceived through the senses* (excluding analytic propositions, mathematics, and geometrical axioms) *provide as great a certainty as empirical knowledge.* I hold the exact contradictory to this position, namely, *some things not perceived through the senses* (excluding analytic propositions, mathematics, and geometrical axioms) *provide as great a certainty as empirical knowledge.* In fact, I hold that some non-empirically known things (given the exceptions already noted) provide a greater certainty than empirical knowledge. But, my proposition obligates me only to show that some non-empirically known things are known at least *as* certainly as empirically known things.

Some Crucial Distinctions: At this point some important distinctions should be made. *First,* one should distinguish between *psychological certitude* and *intellectual certainty.*

Certainty is epistemological, whereas certitude is psychological. Certainty is the intellectual apprehension of an objective state of affairs, while certitude is subjective assurance with reference to an object whose reality status is problematic at best. Mark Hanna explains:

> If a state of affairs is not as one believes it to be, then one has only certitude, no matter how intense his conviction. Believing something to be the case is a necessary but not a sufficient condition of certainty. Certainty also requires that a state of affairs actually be the case.[5]

A *second* crucial distinction is between *inductive generalizations* and *necessary and/or self-evident states of affairs*. An inductive generalization depends for its truth on (1) the real existence of at least one member of the class spoken about, and (2) repeated observations. An example would be, "All the horses I have ever observed or read about have had tails, so, it is *likely* the case that all horses which will ever be observed will have tails. However, I cannot say for sure." In the very nature of the case, *no* inductive generalization (which, by the way, is the same as the hypethetico-deductive method of modern science) can be known with absolute certainty. Since exceptions are always possible, they could not possibly be known to be universally and necessarily true! On the other hand, necessary and/or self-evident states of affairs do not (1) depend on the real existence of the class described (although such does not alter or diminish their truthfulness) and (2) they are highly intelligible, universally applicable, and absolutely necessary. For instance, I know with indubitable certainty that "it is always wrong at all places for all persons in all periods of history to murder their fathers for money." It may be that such has never occurred and never will occur, but the proposition is nonetheless true.

To demonstrate the truth of my proposition, I will appeal first to some *philosophical considerations,* and finally, to some *scriptural considerations.*

PHILOSOPHICAL CONSIDERATIONS

First, I will mention the principle of non-contradiction, a *metaphysical* principle which has important applications also in logic. Laws of logic are actually derived from the metaphysical first principles of being. That is, the laws that govern human thinking are a reflection of the necessities found in nature (reality). As such, there is an important parallel between thought, being, and language! The *metaphysical* principle is, "a being cannot both be and not be at the same time and taken in the same sense." This principle holds even for those things which I will never see at all (such as "hell"). I know that the universe cannot both exist and not exist at the same time and taken in the same sense. Hence, any proposition I formulate about the universe logically, will be either true or false. It cannot be both. That is, if I assert, "the universe does not exist," my assertion will be either true or false. It cannot be both! And, the reason it cannot be both true and false is because such does not obtain in reality. If it could, then the logical principle of non-contradiction ("contradictory propositions cannot both be true") could not hold. No one can deny this principle without appealing to the principle in order to formulate his denial. If I say, "The principle of non-contradiction is false," then my statement is either true or false. It cannot be both true and false! And, unless I am prepared to affirm that contradictory propositions are either *always* both true or that they may *possibly* both be true, then my denial is self-defeating. Now, all *perceived objects* are distinguished on the "background" of this principle. For example, no perceived object can be both "a door" and "not a door" at one and the same time and taken in the same sense. The object is either a door or it is not! It is impossible to make distinctions in perceived objects without an intuitive awareness of the principle of non-contradiction. It is, in short, a necessary and self-evident state of affairs.

Second, there is a strict impossibility that any perception is grasped with a greater degree of certainty than the one who is the subject of such a perception. Since perception is an act of a conscious subject distinct from other acts of a conscious subject (such as willing, feeling, thinking, remembering, etc.), it shares the same *basic* characteristics of all such conscious activity. "I" am the one who *thinks,* who *wills,* who *feels* emotionally, who *remembers,* and who *perceives!* In spite of the fact that each perception is totally new even with reference to the same object of perception at different times, it is still one and the self-same "I" who perceives. I am always immediately aware of my own existence (and its unity) as well as my own conscious activity. The acts of consciousness which I, as a conscious subject *perform*, literally *cannot* be known with greater certainty than my own self-awareness. Such is patently absurd. Any act of consciousness presupposes a conscious subject who performs such an act.

Furthermore, one's reason is the power and function of grasping *necessary connections*. Many things in the world could have been otherwise. The pen with which I composed this paper was red; but it could have been black (or some other color). Whatever color my pen happens to be, it could have been colored differently, but it is *necessarily* the case that my pen could not have been red all over and black all over at the same time and in the same sense. The necessary truth that my pen is red all over and not at the same time black all over *cannot* be a function of sense experience. Sense experience may be able to report what is the case at a *particular time*. But, sense experience is incapable of grasping what *must* be at *all times*.

Additionally, whatever *criteria* are used to distinguish perceived objects from one another (so as to separate illusion, delusion, and deception from reality, and one real object from another) are non-empirical and operate in the "background" of any perception. Even if I have an illusory experience, or I am either deluded or deceived, still it is "I" who have the illusory experience; it is "I" who am deluded; and it is "I" who am deceived. Any acts of a conscious subject presuppose an intuitive awareness of self-existence. And, such is known by that person both *non-empirically* and *absolutely!* To summarize, I have attempted to show that it is strictly impossible for an act of consciousness to be known with greater certainty than the *conscious performance by* and *self-existence of* the subject of those acts. In other words, I know with *undeniable certainty* that I do exist and that I perform certain conscious activities, including *acts of perception!* This knowledge contradicts my opponent's proposition and, though I am only obligated to show that I can know such a non-empirical state of affairs *at least as* certainly as "empirical knowledge," I believe that I have shown that my case is actually stronger than what I am obligated to show.

Third, I will simply list a number of propositions which are known with absolute certainty and which are all "non-empirical truths." But, since my proposition only obligates me to show that these are known with a greater degree of certainty than "empirical knowledge," I shall argue only for this. And, I challenge anyone to deny that the following are known with greater certainty than "empirical knowledge:" (1) "Justice cannot be attributed to impersonal beings;" (2) "moral virtue presupposes freedom;" (3) "every judgment (statement or proposition) makes a claim to be either true or false;" (4) "responsibility presupposes freedom;" (5) "every change presupposes a sufficient cause;" (6) "an impersonal being cannot embody a moral virtue, such as humility;" (7) "moral values cannot be attributed to an impersonal being;" (8) "every value demands an adequate response on the part of the person to whom it is revealed;" (9) "love implies interest in the happiness of the beloved;" etc. Both space and time prohibit an adequate treatment of any of these; nevertheless, I insist that each of these represents a necessary state of affairs. As such, they are all capable of being known with a greater degree of certainty than empirical forms of knowledge, which *never* represent necessary states of affairs!

Fourth, it should be pointed out that my opponent's proposition is a *non-empirical* truth claim (as is my own). Since he holds that no empirical truth may be known with *absolute* certainty, and all non-empirical propositions are known with less certainty than empirical propositions, it follows that his proposition cannot be *known to be true!* He may hold that it is *possibly* true or *probably* true, but he cannot know it to be as certain as the *weakest* empirical perception! And, since my proposition contradicts my opponent's proposition, since contradictory propositions are so related that, if one is true, the other is *necessarily* false, and since he cannot know that his proposition is true, it follows that he can neither prove nor know that my proposition is false.

SCRIPTURAL CONSIDERATIONS

If that which is sensorily perceived is known more certainly than that which is not, then, since the only sensory perception most persons had of the Christ was that of a mere man, it follows that no man could know that he was the Christ (God-man) except to a much lesser degree of certainty than they knew that he was a man. In fact, since no one today even has empirical knowledge of Jesus, the only *possible* position regarding his deity is that of uncertainty. That is, no one could know for sure that he is the Christ! This is an agnostic position! But, it seems to me that this is refuted by Matthew 16:1-4, which reads:

> The Pharisees also with the Sadducees came, and tempting desired him that he would shew them a sign from heaven. He answered and said unto them, when it is evening, ye say, it will be fair weather: for the sky is red. And in the morning, it will be foul weather to day: for the sky is red and lowring. O ye hypocrites, ye can discern the face of the sky; but can ye not discern the signs of the times? A wicked and adulterous generation seeketh after a sign; and there shall no sign be given unto it, but the sign of the prophet Jonas.

Here, Jesus explains that they had evidence enough to establish a correct conclusion to be drawn concerning his true identity. *They wanted an empirical sign!* Some may think that a greater certainty would have been the result if he had given them such a sign, but there is no indication at all that such would have been the case. And, remember, no one could possibly *give an empirical sign of a non-empirical Being (God)* except by way of furnishing evidence so that a correct inference could be drawn about the identity of the non-empirical Being. If one modifies the original assertion to maintain that he infers the truth of the proposition (*i.e.,* Jesus is the Anointed One of God — the God-man) from things perceived or that he infers them from inviolable principles, then I inform him that such is precisely the move made in Christianity, and that such is the kind of evidence upon which faith is built. But, then, the original assertion (*i.e.,* that things sensorily perceived are known with a greater degree of certainty than things which are not subject to sensory perception) *no longer holds!*

As a *second* consideration, I would have you notice Acts 2:36 in conjunction with 2:22:

> Ye men of Israel, hear these words; Jesus of Nazareth, a man approved of God among you by miracles and wonders and signs, which God did by him in the midst of you, as *ye yourselves also know.* . . . Therefore let all the house of Israel *know assuredly,* that God hath made that same Jesus, whom ye have crucified, both Lord and Christ (emphasis mine, DS).

The term "know" in verse 22 translates *eido,* which means basically "I see (or, perceive) and therefore know" (see also Acts 3:16: "whom ye see and know"). On the other hand, "know" in verse 36 translates *ginosko* which refers to the process of "coming to know" a thing by whatever means (type of evidence) is necessary. In this context, Peter argues from *empirical evidence* and *fulfilled prophecy,* and maintains that the Israelites could know *assuredly* (from *asphalos,* meaning "with certainty" or "securely" or "assuredly") that Jesus is both Lord and Christ. That is, they could "accept as certain" (Acts 2:36, NEB) the fact that Jesus of Nazareth is the God-man — the Son of God! And, they knew this *prior* to becoming Christians. On the basis of the evidence at hand, they could make their commitment *to* Christ. In spite of this, however, one author says:

> The final proof of any pudding, Agnos, is in the eating. "Taste and see" (Ps. 34:8) is the ultimate test of any worldview. I can lead you to Christ, but I can't force you to commit your life to him. . . . commitment to Christ brings you the final proof of the Christian faith. The final proof is an inward, spiritual testimony that comes only with decision and obedience.
>
> If a person hasn't committed himself to Christ yet, he may find this final proof difficult to understand.[6]

This author means for us to understand that such a final proof necessarily comes *after* and *not before* conversion. And, as this next statement shows, he also holds that "certainty" (which is what he means by "final proof") cannot be attained until *after* conversion.

> I . . . mean . . . that he undergirds his objective revelation in Scripture and in Christ with an internal psychological certitude. This inner certainty, created by God himself, is the psychological equivalent of deduction and empirical immediacy. With the inductive, objective evidences we can never say, "It is certain," but with the Holy Spirit in us we can say, "I am certain," or as one great Christian said, "I know whom I have believed" (II Tim. 1:12).[7]

Again, I would have you notice that my opponent's position holds only with reference to "general knowledge." That is, there is supposedly a great difference between "general matters of human knowledge and faith" and "Biblical knowledge and faith." I deny that there is this difference. The only

possible way to defend it is to appeal to the inward testimony
of the Holy Spirit in the Christian's life, but I have already
shown you that certainty is possible prior to conversion. This
is evidence contradictory to my opponent's premise.

Third, please notice the text of John 4:39, 41-42:

> And from that city many of the Samaritans believed on him be-
> cause of the word of the woman, who testified, He told me all things
> that ever I did. . . . And many more believed because of his word;
> and they said to the woman, Now we *believe,* not because of thy
> speaking: for we have *heard (akeikoamen)* for ourselves, and *know
> (oidamen)* that this is indeed the Saviour of the world (emphasis
> mine, DS).

There are two groups here under consideration. In both cases,
there is a *claim* ("Jesus is the Savior of the world"), *evidence* to
show that the claim is true, and *belief* in the Christ based upon
a knowledge of the truth of the claim (see also John 8:32). The
woman and the second group of Samaritans came to a knowledge of the truth of the claim (which was the basis for their
belief), upon the conjoining of testimony plus sight. The first
group believed on the strength of the testimony of the woman,
without visual evidence. In both cases, the evidence was sufficient to show that the claim made was true. And, in both cases,
they *knew* that it was true (cf. John 2:21-22 for a similar
example). There is no indication anywhere that the degree of
certainty is different for these people, in spite of the fact that
the evidence was given to them in different ways. If the evidence was interpreted correctly (given the totality of Biblical
evidence), they would have been able to determine that Jesus
of Nazareth was indeed God incarnate (see John 1:1-14, etc.).
Now, since the Holy Spirit was virtually unknown to them at
this time (see Acts 19:1-6), there is no question of an "inward,
spiritual testimony" being given to them. Yet, they were able
to come to a knowledge of the truth, and, because of this
knowledge, they were able to make a commitment *to* the
Christ, the "Saviour of the world." In addition to the passage
considered above think of John 20:26-31, which clearly teaches
that the word was written to produce *belief,* whether by *visual
inspection* (as in Thomas' case) or in the *absence* of such (as
with you and me). Then, recall I John 5:13 which indicates that
the same word was also written to produce *knowledge* (which
translates *ginosko)!*

Fourth, in Luke 16:19-31, we have the narrative of the rich man and Lazarus. You will recall that the rich man desired to have Lazarus return from the dead to warn his brothers of the terrible fate awaiting them if they did not amend their ways. The text records the conversion in verses 29-31:

> Abraham saith unto him, They have Moses and the prophets; let them hear them. And he said, Nay, father Abraham: but if one went unto them from the dead, they will repent. And he said unto him, If they hear not Moses and the prophets, neither will they be persuaded, though one rose from the dead.

Remember, my opponent is obligated to defend the following proposition: *In general matters of human knowledge, things not perceived through the senses are matters of faith and do not provide the certainty of empirical knowledge.* He holds that the situation is different for the Christian (in fact, the situation is exactly reversed) precisely because the Holy Spirit is a special witness for the obedient Christian. But, there is no question at all of the inward testimony of the Holy Spirit in this case, since these men were *not* right with God at all. Abraham insists that they could have the benefit of empirical knowledge (a man whom they knew to be dead, but who communicated directly to them about their spiritual condition), but that this evidence would be no more convincing or compelling than Moses and the prophets (clearly a form of "non-empirical" evidence, since the things stated in "Moses and the prophets" would have been withdrawn from their own sense perception). In short, they would *not* be more greatly persuaded by the visual evidence than by the Scriptural evidence. I argue, therefore, that the supposed "greater degree of certainty" of empirical knowledge is refuted by this one passage alone.

The *fifth* passage which I wish to consider is Luke 1:1-4, which reads as follows:

> Forasmuch as many have taken in hand to set forth in order a declaration of those things which are most surely believed among us, even as they delivered them unto us, which from the beginning were eyewitnesses, and ministers of the word; it seemed good to me also, having had perfect understanding of all things from the very first, to write unto thee in order, most excellent Theophilus, that thou mightest *know the certainty* of those things, wherein thou hast been *instructed* (emphasis mine, DS).

From this text it is evident that Theophilus is a lover of God (the literal meaning of his name would be, "friend of God"), and that he *had been* instructed in the fundamental doctrines of Christianity (the term "instructed" translates *katecheo,* which means detailed and rigorous instruction, and from which our English word "catechism" derives). Furthermore, it seems to be evident that Theophilus was *not* an eyewitness of those things about which he was instructed. Moreover, the evidence which he received from Luke is in the form of *written testimony from a credible source!*

Now, there is no possible way to determine the exact identity of Theophilus, nor is it possible to determine whether or not he was, in fact, a *Christian* at the time Luke wrote to him. Let us suppose for a moment that Theophilus *was* a Christian at the time Luke wrote to him. If this were the case, then, since there is nothing to indicate a rebellious spirit in him, the Holy Spirit should certainly be providing an "inner certainty" for him. The problem of his lack of certainty could not have been blamed on the instruction he had received, for Luke simply means to give additional evidence to uphold the truth of that instruction! If my opponent's proposition is correct, then Theophilus should already be in possession of this "inner certainty," and Luke is performing a useless task. But, this cannot be the case, because Luke writes (*non-empirical* testimony) so that Theophilus might know with *certainty* (from *epiginosko*) the truths of the gospel.

If, on the other hand, Theophilus *was not* a Christian, then it becomes clear that the whole problem of *certainty* without the inward testimony of the Holy Spirit becomes an insurmountable problem for my opponent. That is, Luke would be affirming what my distinguished opponent says cannot occur until *after* conversion! Either alternative (Theophilus *was* or *was not* a Christian at the time Luke wrote to him) is evidence against the proposition affirmed by my opponent!

CONCLUSION

I have attempted to show three things in this lecture. *First,* the two propositions for this particular forum were shown to be contradictory. This means that, if one is true, then the other is necessarily false, and, if one is false, the other is necessarily true! *Second,* I have provided *philosophical* evidence designed to sustain my proposition and falsify that of my opponent. *Third,* I have introduced *Scriptural* evidence which was intended to accomplish the same end. I have purposely selected passages which affirm certainty is possible in religious matters (*i.e.,* in those matters which may have or may fail to have empirical elements) *prior* to conversion. In this way I have tried to show that the human mind works in basically the same way in matters of knowledge. The difference is in the types of evidence with which the human mind is confronted. At the same time, I have sought to set forth (as I have done in several other articles) an epistemology which is in harmony with Scriptural information, and, which is in harmony with philosophical exploration. Truth, regardless of where one discovers it, will not contradict truth found in some other way or in some other sphere!

ENDNOTES

1. George H. Smith, *Atheism: The Case Against God,* The Skeptic's Bookshelf (Buffalo, NY: Prometheus Books, 1979), p. 101.

2. *Ibid.,* p. 98.

3. *Ibid.,* p. 104.

4. B. C. Johnson, *The Atheist Debater's Handbook* (Buffalo, NY: Prometheus Books, 1981), pp. 95-96.

5. Mark M. Hanna, *Crucial Questions in Apologetics* (Grand Rapids, MI: Baker Book House, 1981), p. 80.

6. A. J. Hoover, *The Case for Christian Theism: An Introduction to Apologetics,* 2nd ed. (Grand Rapids, MI: Baker Book House, 1976), p. 267.

7. *Ibid.,* p. 269.

THE KINGDOM AND REIGN OF CHRIST

DISCUSSION FORUM — No. IV-A

HEBREWS 10:12-13; 12:28: THE PROPHECIES OF THE MESSIANIC KINGDOM AND THRONE REQUIRE A LITERAL POLITICAL MILLENNIAL KINGDOM AND THRONE OF CHRIST ON EARTH FOR FULFILLMENT.

By ROBERT SHANK

Author of several books in the field of Biblical theology, which are used in seminaries and colleges of many denominations. Twenty-two years a Baptist preacher and six years in the Christian Church, identified with churches of Christ in 1971. Associated with Restoration Leadership Ministry for ten years. Has spoken on many lectureships and at colleges and churches throughout the nation. Now devotes his time largely to writing and occasional preaching missions from his home in Mt. Vernon, Missouri.

INTRODUCTION

In his final encounter with the religious authorities before his arrest, trial, and crucifixion, Jesus told a parable of a landowner who planted a vineyard and let it out to tenants, and then went away to a far county. At harvest time, he sent servants to collect his share of the profit. But the tenants beat one, stoned another, and killed the third. The landowner then sent more servants, who received the same treatment. Finally he sent his son, assuming that they would respect his son and pay what they owed. But the tenants, hoping to gain possession of the vineyard, killed the son. "When therefore the Lord of the vineyard comes," said Jesus, "what will he do unto those husbandmen?"

They say unto him, He will miserably destroy those miserable men, and will let out the vineyard unto other husbandmen, who shall render him the fruits in their seasons. Jesus saith unto them, Did ye never read in the scriptures, The stone which the builders rejected, the same was made the head of the corner; this was from the Lord, and it is marvellous in our eyes? Therefore say I unto you, The kingdom of God shall be taken away from you, and shall be given to a nation bringing forth the fruits thereof (Ma. 21:41-43).

The meaning of the parable is clear. The landowner is God, and the vineyard is his kingdom on earth. The wicked tenants are Israel, the servants are the prophets whom they persecuted and killed, and the son is Jesus the Messiah, whom Israel rejected and crucified. The kingdom was taken from Israel and given "to a nation bringing forth the fruits thereof." That nation is the church.

The church is the kingdom of Christ on earth today, over which he now reigns from heaven. Men enter the kingdom through faith and obedience to Christ and the gospel, being thus delivered "out of the power of darkness" and translated "into the kingdom of the Son of his love" (Col. 1:13). Baptized into Christ and his body, the church, men become citizens of "a kingdom which cannot be moved" (He. 12:28), a kingdom as enduring as its King, "Jesus Christ, the same yesterday, and today, and forever" (He. 13:8). The King is "not ashamed" to own his citizens as brethren, "saying, I will declare thy name unto my brethren, in the midst of the church will I sing praise unto thee" (He. 2:11-12).

The church is no afterthought or expedient to which Jesus resorted when Israel "surprised" him by rejecting him in his first advent. The rejection and crucifixion came as no surprise to the Father or the Son, but rather as the fulfillment of prophecy in the accomplishment of the eternal redemptive purpose of God (cf. John 3:14-15). Like the rejection, death, and resurrection of Jesus, the church was in the plan and counsel of God from the beginning (cf. Ma. 16:18). Paul declared that to heavenly "principalities and powers" God is making known through "the church the manifold wisdom of God, according to the eternal purpose which he purposed in Christ Jesus our Lord" (Ep. 3:10-11). The church was eternally in the purpose of God.

The church is now the kingdom of Christ in the world, over which he reigns from heaven. But the reign of Christ over his churches does not fulfill all that God promised to his Son nor most of what the prophets foretold concerning the reign of Messiah the King. Jesus is to reign, not only over his churches, but also over Israel and the nations in a reign yet future. We are not under the necessity of choosing whether to believe that the church is now the kingdom of Christ on earth over which he reigns from heaven, or to believe instead that the reign of Christ awaits his return to earth to reign over Israel and the nations. Both things are disclosed in the Scriptures, and neither great truth contradicts or militates against the other.

The prophecies of the Messianic kingdom and throne require a literal political millennial kingdom and throne of Christ on earth for fulfillment.

JESUS WILL REIGN AS KING OVER ISRAEL

To Mary, the angel Gabriel said of Jesus, "the Lord God shall give unto him the throne of his father David: And he shall reign over the house of Jacob for ever; and of his kingdom there shall be no end" (Luke 1:32-33). Micah prophesied, "But thou, Bethlehem Ephrata . . . out of thee shall he come forth unto me who is to be ruler in Israel" (5:2). Isaiah prophesied,

> For unto us a child is born, unto us a son is given; and the government shall be upon his shoulder: . . . Of the increase of his government and peace there shall be no end, upon the throne of David, and upon his kingdom, to order it and to establish it with judgment and with justice from henceforth even for ever. The zeal of the Lord of hosts will perform this (9:6-7).

Jeremiah prophesied,

> Behold, the days come, saith the Lord, that I will raise unto David a righteous Branch, and a King shall reign and prosper, and shall execute judgment and justice in the earth. In his days Judah shall be saved, and Israel shall dwell safely: . . . [And the Lord shall gather] . . . the seed of the house of Israel out of the north country, and from all countries whether I had driven them; and they shall dwell in their own land (23:5-8).

The things prophesied by Jeremiah (and other prophets) did not happen in the first advent, when Jesus "came to his own, and his own received him not" (John 1:11). Jesus knew from the beginning that he would be rejected and crucified; but he knew also that the promised gathering of Israel and his reception and reign as King over Israel (and "the earth" — all nations) will indeed occur at his second advent. In his sad farewell in the temple, Jesus cried,

> O Jerusalem, Jerusalem, . . . how often would I have gathered thy children together, even as a hen gathers her chickens under her wings, and ye would not! Behold, your house is left to you desolate. For I say to you, Ye shall not see me henceforth, till ye shall say, Blessed is he that cometh in the name of the Lord [a Messianic designation, cf. Ma. 21:9; Ps. 118:26, 22f] (Ma. 23:37-39).

Israel will not see Jesus again until a sufficient number of the God-fearing remnant acknowledge their offense and call for him to return. Hosea portrays Messiah as saying, "I will go and return to my place till they acknowledge their offence, and seek my face: in their affliction [Israel's coming Tribulation — RS] they will seek me earnestly" (5:15). Hosea pictures the godly remnant as saying,

> Come, and let us return unto the Lord: for he hath torn, and he will heal us; he hath smitten, and he will bind us up. . . . His going forth is prepared as the morning; and he shall come unto us as the rain, as as the latter and former rain unto the earth. (6:1, 3).

After his rejection, death, and resurrection, Jesus "returned to his place" at God's right hand in heaven to await the time when Israel will "acknowledge their offence" and call for him to return. Soon after Pentecost, Peter preached to men of Israel that

> . . . the things which God foreshadowed by the mouth of all the prophets, that his [Messiah — RS] should suffer, he thus fulfilled. Repent ye therefore, and turn again, that your sins may be blotted out, that so there may come seasons of refreshing from the presence of the Lord; and that he may send the [Messiah — RS] who hath been appointed for you, even Jesus: whom the heaven must receive until the times of restoration of all things, whereof God spake by the mouth of his holy prophets that have been from of old (Acts 3:18-21).

Included in the "restoration of all things," foretold by the prophets, will be the restoration of the Davidic kingdom to Israel. After his 40-day post-resurrection ministry to his apostles, in which Jesus spoke of "the things pertaining to the

kingdom of God" (Acts 1:3), the apostles asked only one question about the kingdom: "Lord, wilt thou at this time restore
again the kingdom to Israel?" (v. 6). Jesus did not charge
them with entertaining "a false concept of the kingdom," as
some interpreters have done. He did not ask how, in view of all
this teaching about the kingdom, they could still retain such
an expectation. He did nothing to divest them of their
anticipation of the restoration of the kingdom to Israel.
Instead, he further confirmed it. The question was not *whether*
the kingdom will be restored to Israel, but rather *when* it will
be restored. By replying to the question of *when*, Jesus
confirmed the apostles' expectation of the restoration of the
kingdom to Israel, an expectation he had confirmed during his
ministry (cf. Ma. 19:28). Christ's reply leaves no room for some
later "clarification" through further disclosures which would
constitute a negation of the apostles' concept and expectation.
Any such negation would be in radical contradiction of
Christ's categorical declaration that the Father "hath set
within his own authority" the time when the kingdom will
indeed be restored to Israel (v. 7). The Scriptures disclose that
it will be at the time of the coming of our Lord Jesus, the
Messiah.

Jerusalem will not see Jesus again until the remnant of
Israel "acknowledge their offence" and "seek him earnestly"
(Ho. 5:15) in penitence and faith, ready to welcome him with
praise and the Messianic acclamation, "Blessed is he who
comes in the name of the Lord!" (Ma. 23:39).

The prophetic Song of Moses (De. 32), one of the great
foundation prophecies in the Bible, projects the course of the
redemptive history of Israel from the time God chose them to
be a special people and nation until the time when finally Israel
will become all that God intended from the beginning. Chosen
of God, established in the land, and abundantly blessed, Israel
became disobedient and unfaithful, bringing on themselves
God's chastening. The chastening eventually included being
driven from their land and scattered among the nations (in the
Exile which began with the Assyrian and Babylonian captivi-
ties and was reiterated in the Dispersion of A.D. 70). The
chastening will continue until finally in "the day of their
calamity" (the climax of the Tribulation, "the time of Jacob's

trouble," Je. 30:7), when "their power is gone" and they are totally helpless and in utter peril, they will acknowledge that God alone can deliver them (De. 32:35-39), whereupon God will rise to their defense to bring deliverance: "I will render vengeance to mine enemies, and will reward them that hate me" (Armageddon — RS), ". . . and will be merciful unto his land and to his people" (the Restoration of the faithful remnant — RS), for which cause the nations at last will "rejoice . . . with his people" Israel (vv. 40-43).

The Song of Moses contains the first categorical prophecy of the church. God declares that because Israel "moved me to jealousy with that which is not God . . . I will move them to jealousy with those which are not a people; I will provoke them to anger with a foolish nation" (v. 21). According to Peter and Paul, that nation is the church, now vested with the spiritual privileges and obligations God intended (and still intends) for Israel (cf. I Pe. 2:9-10; Ro. 10:19; 11:11). For a correct understanding of the total prophetic and eschatological disclosure of the Bible, it is essential to recognize that the first prophecy of the church is set in the context of a great foundation prophecy which affirms the ultimate recovery and restoration of Israel to the favor and blessing of God in the land. The popular assumption that the church has forever supplanted Israel in the ongoing redemptive purpose of God is without foundation in the Bible. The church is now the kingdom of Christ on earth; but Israel, restored, is also to become the kingdom of Messiah on earth in a far more overt manifestation in the eyes of the nations than the church has experienced in this present age.

From both the prophetic Ode of Moses and the total New Testament disclosure, it is evident that God's purpose for the church is two-fold: (1) to be a people and "nation" of God, his spiritual "Israel of God" (Ga. 6:16) and the kingdom of Christ on earth in the present age, to gather from the nations a special people for his name (Acts 15:14); and (2) to be a factor in the recovery and restoration of Israel for the realization of their appointed destiny as the nucleus of the kingdom of Messiah on earth in the coming Messianic Age (together with the church) for the great gathering of the nations into the kingdom of God (Acts 15:15-18).

Peter admonishes Christians now in the kingdom of Christ, the church, to "give diligence to make your calling and election sure" so that "an entrance shall be ministered unto you abundantly into the everlasting kingdom of our Lord and Savior Jesus Christ" (II Pe. 1:10-11), the kingdom in the Messianic Age, still future, to be inaugurated by "the power and coming of our Lord Jesus Christ" (v. 6), of which advent in power and glory the Transfiguration was a preview and pledge (vv. 16-19).

As the prophetic Ode of Moses affirms, Israel is ultimately to be restored to the favor and blessing of God in the Land (De. 32:43). Paul writes that the present partial blindness of Israel will pass, and then "all Israel" will be saved when "there shall come out of Zion the Deliverer, and shall turn away ungodliness from Jacob: for this is my covenant unto them, when I shall take away their sins" (Ro. 11:25-27; cf. Is. 59:20-21). Israel is still beloved of God "for the fathers' sake," and their corporate election ("the gifts and calling of God") is irrevocable (Ro. 11:28-29).

At the coming of Messiah, the remnant of Israel who believed God for the covenants and for the coming of Messiah and prepared their hearts to receive him (Ma. 23:39) will be brought under the new covenant (Je. 31:31-34; He. 8:8-12). God will give them "a new heart and a new spirit" (Eze. 36:26) and "will open your graves, and cause you to come up out of your graves, O my people, and I will bring you into the land of Israel. . . . And I will put my Spirit in you, and you will live, and I will place you in your own land: . . . And my servant David [Messiah, Son of David — RS] shall be king over them" (Eze. 37:12-14, 24). Israel is to be a nation for ever:

> Thus saith the Lord, which giveth the sun for a light by day, and the ordinances of the moon and of the stars for a light by night, which divideth the sea when the waves thereof roar; The Lord of hosts is his name: If those ordinances depart from before me, saith the Lord, then the seed of Israel also shall cease from being a nation before me forever (Je. 31:35-36).

God will keep his promise to his Son: "The Lord God shall give unto him the throne of his father David: And he shall reign over the house of Jacob for ever; and of his kingdom there shall be no end" (Luke 1:32-33). God has appointed the time when he will restore again to Israel the kingdom (Acts

1:6-7), and Jesus will reign as king over Israel from the throne of David in Jerusalem. (The throne of David is not in heaven. The throne in Jerusalem on which David and Solomon sat was indeed *Jehovah's* throne, for kings sat on it *only by God's leave as his vice regents.* But God's throne in heaven is not *David's* throne or Solomon's, for God does not occupy his eternal throne by leave of David or Solomon or any other. To call God's glorious holy throne "David's throne" is an insult to Almighty God who has said, "My glory will I not give to another" [Is. 42:8; 48:11].

JESUS WILL REIGN OVER THE NATIONS

From heaven, Jesus now reigns over his present kingdom on earth, the church, joined to him in the everlasting "new covenant." What Jesus accomplished in his first advent as the great High Priest who offered himself and his body and blood as the perfect everlasting sacrifice for the sins of all humanity, and what he now performs in his ministry of intercession as our High Priest before the mercy seat of God in heaven, shows that all that was performed in prior dispensations and generations for atonement was only prelude and prolepsis. All that preceded Christ under the old covenant was shadow; Christ and his divine ministry under the new covenant is substance. The new covenant has forever superseded the old. Such is the theme of the writer to the Hebrews.

Jesus is the High Priest and agent of the new covenant, "the mediator of a better covenant . . . established on better promises" than the old covenant (He. 8:6). But he is *more:* as Messiah, he is himself the *Living Covenant* whom God has "given for a covenant of the people, to *establish the earth*" (Is. 49:8; cf. 42:6, 4; Ps. 2:8).

As Messiah, Jesus bears a special relation to the earth. By the Father's appointment, he is "heir of all things" (He. 1:2), including the earth. "All things were created by him, and *for* (emp. mine — RS) him" (Col. 1:16). Above all men, Jesus is *the* son of Man, to whom God has given First Dominion over the earth, "the works of thy hands" (He. 2:6-7). His dominion will be implemented and made manifest in his reign on earth in the Messianic kingdom in "the world to come," for to him God has "put in subjection the world to come" (He. 2:5, *oikoumene*, the inhabited earth, same word in 1:6). God has "put all things in subjection under his feet," though "now we see not yet all things put under him" (2:8), which will occur at his triumphant coming in judgment, power, and glory.

Jesus, "after he had offered one sacrifice for sins for ever, sat down on the right hand of God, from henceforth expecting till his enemies be made his footstool" (He. 10:12-13; cf. Ps. 110:1). To his Son at his right hand, God has said, "Ask of me, and I shall give thee the nations for thine inheritance, and the uttermost parts of the earth for thy possession" (Ps. 2:8). How is this to be accomplished? How will "his enemies be made his footstool?" How will Jesus take possession of the earth to rule over the nations? The answer is Armageddon, as many Scriptures indicate — including Psalms 110 and 2:

> The Lord at thy right hand shall strike through kings in the day of his wrath. He will judge among the heathen, he shall fill the places with the dead bodies; he shall wound the heads over many countries [cf. Je. 25:29-33]. Thou shalt break them with a rod of iron; thou shalt dash them in pieces like a potter's vessel (Ps. 110:5-6; Ps. 2:9).

The word *Armageddon* is symbolic. But men who lightly treat Armageddon as "mentioned only once in the Bible, in a book filled with symbols" are unaware of the vast Bible content devoted to this cardinal theme of Bible prophecy. The event of Armageddon, a cataclysmic Day of divine intervention and judgment inaugurating the reign of Messiah on earth, appears many times in the Bible from Moses to the Revelation. The final passage concerning Armageddon, Revelation 19:11-21, is especially significant as the context of Revelation 20:1-6.

Revelation 20:1-6 foretells a thousand-year reign of Christ with the "blessed and holy" who share in "the first resurrection," during which time Satan is "bound a thousand years . . . that he should deceive the nations no more till the thousand years should be fulfilled." Many have asserted that the passage lends no support to premillennialism because "nothing is said in Revelation 20:1-6 about Christ's coming to earth to reign over the nations," etc. (The argument is the same sorry dodge to which many resort in their opposition to the place of baptism in conversion: "There is nothing about baptism in John 3:16; nothing about baptism in Acts 16:30-31," etc.) No passage stands alone. We are not at liberty to isolate Revelation 20:1-6 from its context — both the context of the total eschatological disclosure of the Bible, and also its immediate context in the Revelation. Revelation 19:11-21, which is an integral part of the complete episode (Re. 19:11-20:15), posits the coming of Christ to earth in power and righteous judgment to "smite the nations" and to "rule them with a rod of iron" (19:15). In the prophetic episode, the reign of Christ over the nations (the central thesis of 20:1-6) follows his coming in power and judgment. If Revelation 20:1-6 were to be expunged from the Bible, the integrity of the episode would be destroyed, for 19:15 posits that after "smiting the nations" in righteous judgment, Christ will "rule them with a rod of iron," and without 20:1-6 there remains no place in the episode for such a reign to occur. Thus 20:1-6 is essential to the continuity and integrity of the episode, and its position in the episode posits premillennialism.

For opponents of premillennialism, Revelation 19:11-21 poses a crucial problem: if the passage depicts the second advent, it predicates a realistic understanding of 20:1-6 and establishes premillennialism. To defend their allegorical interpretation of 20:1-6, amillenarians must assume that the second advent is not in view in Revelation 19:11-21.

The popular allegorical interpretation of Revelation 19:11-21 offered by amillenarians is that the passage symbolizes Christ's conquest of evil through the preaching of the gospel (the sharp sword's proceeding from his mouth, v. 15), whereby he now rules the nations through his churches. All such fanciful interpretations are forbidden by the significance of cognate passages.

In II Thessalonians 2 (an epistle, containing no apocalyptic symbolism), Paul writes of "the coming of our Lord Jesus Christ and our gathering together unto him" (v. 1) when he comes in power in "the day of the Lord" (v. 2). Christ will destroy the "man of sin" (v. 3, the antichrist) whose coming to power at the end of the age, shortly before the coming of Christ, will be accomplished by "the working of Satan with all power and signs and lying wonders" (v. 9). Christ will destroy him "by the manifestation of his coming," slaying him "with the breath of his mouth" (v. 8) — the spoken command, which in Revelation 19:15 is "the sharp sword proceeding out of his mouth" with which Christ will "smite the nations" and dispatch the beast (antichrist) and the false prophets and the remnant of the armies of the beast (vv. 20,21, cf. Is. 11:4 and context). Paul pictures Christ's conquest, not as an "agelong struggle between good and evil, with victory won at last through the long process of the preaching of the gospel" (as some have said of Revelation 19:11-21), but as a cataclysmic *event* when "by the manifestation of his coming" Christ will destroy "the man of sin" by his spoken command. Revelation 19:11-21 and II Thessalonians 2:1-8 forbids the figurative interpretation of Revelation 19:11-21 by which opponents of premillennialism propose to nullify its significance as the context of Revelation 20:1-6.

The coming of Christ in view in II Thessalonians 2:1 and 8 is in view also in 1:7-10, and the obvious parallel between II Thessalonians 1:7-10 and Revelation 19:11-21 will not be lost to any candid reader. In II Thessalonians 1:7-10 and 2:1-8 the coming of Christ is a spectacular cataclysmic *event* at the end of the age. The same great end-of-the-age event — the second advent — is in view in the cognate passage Revelation 19:11-21. The significance of Revelation 19:11-21 as context of Revelation 20:1-6 posits a realistic rather than an allegorical understanding of 20:1-6, and thus confirms the truth of premillennialism.

From the foregoing considerations, it is evident that the reign of Christ over the nations (which the faithful will share) is not from heaven in this present age, but will be on earth following his return in power and judgment, when "the world to come" will be "put in subjection" to him (He. 2:5-8) and the nations will be his "inheritance, and the uttermost parts of the earth [his] possession" (Ps. 2:8). The reign of Christ and the saints in view in Revelation 20:4-6 is precisely the reign in view in the promise of Jesus to the faithful of his churches in Revelation 2:25-29:

> But that which ye have already [the true faith — RS] hold fast till I come. And he that overcometh, and keepeth my works unto the end,

to him will I give power over the nations: and he shall rule them with a rod of iron; as the vessels of a potter shall they be broken to shivers:even as I received of my Father [cf. Ps. 2:8-9]. And I will give him the morning star [cf. Re. 22:16]. He that hath an ear, let him hear what the Spirit saith unto the churches.

Let us compare the two passages, Revelation 19:11-20:6 and 2:25-29:

In Revelation 19:11-20:6, Christ comes to earth with righteous judgment, and then rules over the nations. Please read the passage and observe three things: 1. Christ comes to earth to "smite the nations" in judgment and to "rule them with a rod of iron" (19:15). 2. Christ's reign over the nations follows his coming (as context indicates). 3. Those who take part in "the first resurrection" (the faithful) will share Christ's reign over the nations (20:4-6). In Revelation 2:25-29, Christ speaks "to the churches" concerning his coming to judge and to rule the nations. Please read the passage and observe three things — precisely the three things observed in 19:11-20:6: 1. Christ will come to judge ("break in pieces") the nations and to "rule them with a rod of iron" as the Father has promised him (v. 27, cf. Ps. 2:8-9). 2. Christ's reign over the nations will follow his coming (vv. 25-27). 3. The faithful of the churches who "overcome and keep my works to the end" will share Christ's reign over the nations (vv. 26,27, cf. Re. 5:9,10).

From the above passages four things are established: (1) the reign of Christ and the faithful of his churches is future, beyond our present life pilgrimage of faith; (2) the reign will follow the coming of Christ in judgment at the end of the age; (3) the reign will follow "the first resurrection;" and (4) the reign will be over the nations on earth.

Why the millennium? What could be the purpose of a millennial Messianic kingdom, an interim age before the beginning of the final age of the new heaven and earth? The Bible discloses that the millennium will be the time of the great gathering of the nations into the kingdom of God (Is. 11:10-12; Mi. 4:1-8; Je. 3:17; Ze. 2:10-12; Acts 15:14-18), for which purpose both restored Israel and the faithful of the churches will be priests of God for the instruction of the nations (Ze. 8:20-23; Re. 5:9-10). Christ and the faithful of his churches will shepherd the nations for their blessing and salvation, but it will be "with a rod [sceptre] of iron," with firmness against evil. (The word *rule, poimaino,* Revelation 19:15 and 2:27, means both to shepherd and to govern.) The millennial age is not "a second chance" and takes nothing away from the urgency of the gospel in the present age.

The millennium is a gracious age in which God will gather multitudes from the nations (cf. Re. 21:24-22:2) to dwell with him forever in the eternal kingdom in the new heaven and earth. The kingdom of God will find its eternal dimension in the "new heaven and earth" (Re. 21 and 22), the ultimate merger of heaven and the new earth. "The holy city, new Jerusalem" which "comes down from God out of heaven" (Re. 21:2,10) is "the bride, the Lamb's wife" (v. 9) and bears the names both of the tribes of Israel and the apostles of the church, for Messiah is King of both Israel and the church. The eternal kingdom in the new heaven and earth is the ultimate destiny of all the redeemed.

CONCLUSION

In the years when he was a "stranger and pilgrim on earth" and "sojourned in the land of promise, as in a strange country, dwelling in tents," Abraham "looked for a city which has foundations, whose builder and maker is God" (He. 11:9-10,13). Like Abraham, we too are pilgrims now and "here have we no continuing city, but we seek one to come" (He. 13:14). Our destination is "the city of the living God, the heavenly Jerusalem" (He. 12:22). Inheriting the heavenly Jerusalem, we will also "inherit the earth" (Ma. 5:5) when God merges the heavenly Jerusalem (his present dwelling place), "the Jerusalem which is above" (Ga. 4:26), with the new earth in "the new heaven and earth," to be the eternal dwelling place of God and his people (Re. 21:1-3). Dwelling among his people forever, in the endless ages to come God will "show the exceeding riches of his grace in his kindness toward us through Christ Jesus (Ep. 2:7).

THE KINGDOM AND REIGN OF CHRIST

DISCUSSION FORUM — NO. IV-B

Hebrews 10:12-13; 12:28: The prophecies of the Messianic kingdom and throne are fulfilled in the establishment of the church of Christ, the ascension of Christ and the present reign of Christ in heaven. Therefore, there will be no earthly millennial kingdom or throne.

By WAYNE JACKSON

Educated at David Lipscomb College, The College of Evangelists, Stockton College, Sacramento Baptist College, and holds the M.A. degree from Alabama Christian School of Religion. Honorary Doctorate in Literature from Graduate School of Religion of the American Christian Bible College. Served the East Main Street church of Christ in Stockton, California for the past twenty-two years. Experienced debater. Editor of *Christian Courier*, associate editor of *Reason and Revelation*, co-founder of Apologetics Press. Contributor to numerous other religious journals. Author of eight books and fifteen tracts.

INTRODUCTION

It will be the burden of this presentation to affirm that certain Old Testament prophecies which foretell the coming of the *Messianic kingdom*, as well as numerous New Testament declarations which assert its imminence, are fulfilled in the establishing of the church of Jesus Christ. It is thus affirmed that Christ is presently reigning on David's (spiritual) throne and, consequently, there is no future, earthly, political throne, as alleged by premillennialists.

In connection with this presentation, special consideration will be given to the views of millennialist Robert Shank, as recently set forth in his book entitled, *Until — The Coming of*

Messiah and His Kingdom, which, if we may respectfully say so, contains "some of the most fanciful and ludicrous conjectures and interpretations ever offered as serious 'exposition'."[1] (If the foregoing words sound harsh, attribute the bluntness to Shank, for the words are *his,* aimed at those who oppose his premillennial notions.)

THE PROPHECY OF DANIEL 2

In chapter 2 of that remarkable book that bears his name, the prophet Daniel was chosen of God to interpret a dream for the Babylonian king, Nebuchadnezzar. The dream involved a great image of four principal components — a head of gold, breast and arms of silver, belly and thighs of brass, and legs and feet of iron (the feet being partially clay). A stone, fashioned without hands, smote the image upon its feet and brake them in pieces. Eventually, the stone became a great mountain and filled the earth.

In his interpretation of the dream, Daniel noted that the image represented four empires. The head of gold was the Babylonian kingdom (2:37-38). After it another was to arise, which history reveals was the empire of the Medes and Persians (2:39; cf. 5:28). A third nation was to follow — that of the Greeks (2:39; cf. 8:20-21). Finally, a fourth kingdom would arise, symbolized by the legs and feet (2:40-41). It is very crucial to observe at this point that *only four* empires are suggested by the image. The fourth (Roman) was to be partly strong and partly weak (legs of iron and feet of iron and clay), but it was the *final* kingdom of the dream, and it signified but a *single* nation.

Well, of the time of the Roman empire, the prophet declared:

> And in the days of those kings shall the God of heaven set up a kingdom which shall never be destroyed, nor shall the sovereignty thereof be left to another people; but it shall break in pieces and consume all these kingdoms, and it shall stand for ever (2:44).

Now it is a known historical fact that the Roman empire fell in 476 A.D. (though its weaknesses were easily discernable long before its demise). Accordingly, there are but three ways of viewing Daniel 2:44. (1) The kingdom here described is the

church (Ma. 16:18-19), which was established during the days
of the Roman empire (Luke 3:1). (2) The kingdom of Daniel 2:44
is the millennial kingdom which the Lord will set up at his
return, hence, there must be a *literal resurrection* of the kings
of the old Roman empire prior to Christ's advent. Or, finally,
(3) Daniel was a false prophet. Obviously, those who have
respect for the integrity of the Bible will reject number three.
It is equally clear, however, that number two is also patently
false as we will subsequently show.

Robert Shank contends that the kingdom of Daniel 2:44 is
the Messiah's millennial reign, which, he alleges, is to be set up
in the not-too-distant future of our own generation.[2] But how
could such a theory possibly be harmonized with the plain
historical fact that the *Roman empire* has been buried in the
dust of oblivion for more than fifteen centuries?! Here is how
the magic is performed. Shank claims that the "ten toes" of
that great metalic image represent a "federation" of ten
nations that are "fragments" of the old Roman kingdom. The
nations are not necessarily to be literally resurrected, "but
more especially nations which are the ideological and cultural
heirs of the empire."[3]

The theory is seriously flawed at several places. First, the
indications of Daniel 2 are that God's kingdom is *of a different
nature* than the political kingdoms with which it is contrasted.
The heavenly kingdom "cut out of the mountain without
hands"[4] was to be *spiritual* in nature (cf. John 6:15; 18:36;
Luke 17:21[5]). Second, Daniel's prophecy does not speak of the
kingdom's being established during the time of ten "nations"
(plural), but rather, during the time of the "fourth kingdom"
(singular — note the "it," 2:40-41). Third, there is absolutely
no indication that the "ten toes" of the image represent anything. *They are not even mentioned!* Perhaps the millennialists
can tell us what the "ten fingers" of the two arms symbolize![6]
Fourth, the Bible declares that God's kingdom would be set up
"in the days of those kings;" not merely in a time when their
"ideological and cultural heirs" would exercise influence. Such
is a woeful mishandling of the Biblical text![7] Finally, it is quite
clear that the "kingdom" of 2:44 was one that would stand *for
ever*, not merely for *one thousand years!* The premillennial
concept of Daniel 2:44 is false.

THE PROPHECY OF II SAMUEL 7:12-13

In II Samuel 7:12-13, the prophet Nathan informed king David:

> When thy days are fulfilled, and thou shalt sleep with thy fathers, I will set up thy seed after thee, that shall proceed out of thy bowels, and I will establish his kingdom. He shall build a house for my name, and I will establish the throne of his kingdom for ever.

There is no question but that this prophecy ultimately refers to Christ (cf. He. 1:5). The question is, though, does it allude to the establishment of the Lord's spiritual kingdom, the church, and his enthronement at the right hand of God after his ascension, or does it denote an earthly, political regime wherein Christ reigns upon David's throne from the city of Jerusalem? Erroneously, the premillennialists contend for the latter.

The truth of the matter is, II Samuel 7:12-13 simply cannot be forced into the mold of premillennial eschatology. Note: premillennialism alleges that when Christ returns to earth, he will first raise all of the righteous dead (including David), and then, subsequent thereto, he will sit down to rule upon David's throne. This passage, however, declares that Christ will receive the throne and the kingdom *while David is still asleep with his fathers.* This is *too soon* for the premillennialists! Robert Shank makes a pitifully feeble response to this argument: "The passage affirms that the Messiah will reign on David's throne. But it does not require that he reign on David's throne while David remains in the grave. All that is required with respect to *time* is that David's Seed be 'set up' while David sleeps in his grave."[8] That is amazing! The divine text says, "thou shalt sleep with thy fathers, I will set up thy seed after thee . . ., *and* I will establish thy kingdom. . . ." By what rule of exegesis is it determined that the seed is to be "set up" while David sleeps in the grave, but the kingdom is to be "established" after he awakes, when the verbals are joined with the coordinating "and?" Shank would squeeze *two thousand years* into the comma (,) between "bowels" and "and" in 2:12![9]

One of the problems of the premillennialists is that they just will not let the New Testament be the interpreter of Old

Testament prophecy. They have their own eschatological scheme mentally set and the Bible must be made to harmonize with that. The New Testament makes it abundantly plain that Jesus became heir to David's throne when he ascended to the Father's right hand.

In Isaiah 55:3, the prophet foretold the coming of an "everlasting covenant" which is described as "the sure mercies of David" (an obvious allusion to the promise made to David in II Samuel 7:12-13; cf. Psalms 89:3-4). Though premillennialists misapply these prophecies to that alleged future, political kingdom on earth,[10] the inspired Paul, in Acts 13:32ff, shows that God "hath fulfilled" (the perfect tense reveals that the fulfillment *had already been accomplished* and the results were continuing) the "good tidings of the promise made unto the fathers," which included the "holy and sure blessings of David." This had been accomplished by the resurrection of Christ and the subsequent proclamation of remission of sins in his name. F. F. Bruce says: "Paul regards the resurrection of Christ as the fulfillment of the 'sure mercies' or 'holy and sure blessings' (RV) promised to David."[11]

The angel Gabriel informed Mary that she would bear the Christ child and that unto him would be given "the throne of his father David." He would "reign over the house of Jacob for ever; and of his kingdom there shall be no end" (Luke 1:32-33). But *when* was this promise to be fulfilled? The premillennialists contend that it has not yet been fulfilled, but its accomplishment awaits the return of Christ to the earth. The apostle Paul, however, did not so view the matter. He declares in Acts 2:30ff that God had sworn with an oath that of the fruit of David's loins would one be appointed to sit upon David's throne. Having foreseen such (*viz.,* the enthronement of our Lord), David, in Psalms 16:8ff, spoke of the Savior's resurrection. Unless one is totally blinded by a preconceived theory, he could scarcely fail to see the *chronological connection* between the Lord's resurrection and his exaltation to David's throne.[12] J. W. McGarvey (whom Shank has erroneously labeled as a "premillennialist") comments upon this context: "It also corrected their (the Jews) conception of an *earthly reign* of Christ, and showed them that he was to sit on David's throne after his resurrection, and not before his death" (emp. WJ).[13]

Moreover, it is also significant that Peter stresses that Christ's exaltation to the right hand of God was a fulfillment of that prophetic psalm (110) which foretold of the dual kingdom/priesthood with which the Lord was to be endowed simultaneously (cf. Ze. 6:12-13), which offices, incidentally, could not be filled *on earth* (cf. He. 8:4 — more on this later). And so, Acts 2:30ff makes it absolutely certain that Christ's occupation of David's throne was a *heavenly* matter! Shank's cursory treatment of this most vital context was revealing indeed!

THE PROPHECY OF ZECHARIAH 6:12-13

A few moments ago we mentioned the prophecy of Zechariah 6:12-13. We will now give more detailed attention to that context.

> Thus speaketh Jehovah of hosts, saying, Behold, the man whose name is the Branch: and he shall grow up out of his place; and he shall build the temple of Jehovah; . . .[14] and he shall bear the glory, and shall sit and rule upon his throne;[15] and he shall be a priest upon his throne; and the counsel of peace shall be between them both.

This passage positively affirms that Christ will serve as both a king and priest upon his throne, and that simultaneously. Now, according to the book of Hebrews there was only one *earthly* priesthood, and that was the Levitical priesthood. Since Jesus was not of the proper tribe to serve in the Levitical priesthood (He. 7:14), he thus could not be a priest on earth (He. 8:4). Let us arrange the argument logically:

1. Christ could not be a priest on earth (He. 8:4).
2. But he is to be priest and king simultaneously (Ze. 6:13).
3. Thus, he cannot be a king on earth.

1. Christ cannot be a king on earth.
2. But he is king upon his (David's) throne (Luke 1:32).
3. Thus, his (David's) throne is not on earth.

All of this is, of course, perfectly consistent with Peter's declaration on the day of Pentecost (see Acts 2:30ff).

Robert Shank recognizes the force of this argument and with it he struggles desperately! In spite of overwhelming evidence to the contrary, the gentleman's solution is to assert that Christ *did serve as a priest on earth*. He suggests that Hebrews 8:4 merely means that he could not function as a *Levitical* priest; but, he argues, Jesus served on earth as a priest after the order of Melchizedek. Since the Lord so served as an earthly priest before his ascension, he can do so again when he returns.[16] It would be difficult to imagine a concept more riddled with error. Surely the man has not thought the matter through. Let us analyze his position on this point.

First, one should note the logical consequences that result from Shank's contention that Christ was functioning as a priest on earth. If that were the case, then God had *two* priesthoods operating on the earth at the same time. Too, if the Lord functioned as a priest on earth, and yet he is priest upon his *throne*, then he must have already had a throne on earth. This, of course, is too early for the millennialists and is in contradiction to Acts 2:30ff. Finally, if the priesthood "after the order of Melchizedek" was already operative while Jesus was still on earth, then the new law was operative at that time, for a change of the priesthood necessitates a change of the law (He. 7:12). Yet, such a conclusion would contradict Hebrews 9:17 which declares that the new covenant could never avail before the death of Jesus.

Second, we recognize, of course, that Christ "offered up" himself while on earth (where else could he have died? in heaven?!), but from the vantage point of the New Testament, his priestly function was strictly *heavenly*. Note the following: (1) According to Hebrews 5:5, Christ's assumption of the priesthood was not an act of *self*-glorification; rather, he was glorified to be high priest by God. But when was the Lord glorified that he might be a priest? Not until after his death and ascension! (Cf. Luke 24:26; John 7:39; 12:16). (2) Since the "word of the oath" — by which Christ was appointed high priest — was made "after the law" (He. 7:28), and as the law was abrogated at the cross (Col. 2:14), Jesus could not have been appointed priest until after his death. (3) The ministry of the new priesthood is in the "true tabernacle" and is administered by him who "sat down on the throne of the Majesty in the heavens" (He. 8:1-2). (4) Christ was to function as a priest on his throne (Ze. 6:13), thus, over his kingdom. But he did not receive his kingdom until he entered the "far country" (Luke

19:12), which was heaven. Thus, his priesthood was conferred in heaven. Professor Leon Morris has summed up the matter well:

> We must be clear that Christ's priesthood is not one of this earth (though his offering of himself took place here). There are divinely appointed earthly priests, and Jesus has no place among them. On earth Jesus was a layman. He performed no priestly functions in any earthly sanctuary. Those functions were performed by the priests to whom God entrusted them. Christ's priestly functions must obviously, then, be exercised elsewhere, in the true sanctuary in heaven.[17]

The argument, therefore, based upon Zechariah 6:12-13 and Hebrews 8:4, demonstrating that Christ's throne *could not be on earth* stands! It is untouched!

NEW TESTAMENT EVIDENCE

As one turns to the New Testament record, he finds ample evidence that the imminence of the coming kingdom was proclaimed during the time of Christ's earthly ministry. Moreover, from Acts 2 onward, there are numerous affirmations that the kingdom had arrived. Consider the following:

Some six months before his death, our Lord, speaking to Peter, declared: "I will build by church" (Ma. 16:18). Continuing, he announced that unto Peter would be given the "keys of the kingdom of heaven." Well, the apostle used those "keys" (a symbol of the authority to open [cf. Re. 1:18]) on the day of Pentecost (Acts 2) and at the house of Cornelius (Acts 10), and by the proclamation of the gospel "of the kingdom" (Ma. 4:23) he introduced both the Jews and Gentiles into the church. With the establishment of the church, therefore, *the kingdom had come!* In view of this, just what would possess a man to state that the church "is not the kingdom of which Jesus spoke in Caesarea Philippi"?[18]

Shortly thereafter Christ exclaimed: "Verily I say unto you, There are some here of them that stand by, who shall in no wise taste of death, till they see the kingdom of God come with power" (Mark 9:1; cf. Ma. 16:28[19]). Either the kingdom came within the lifetime of those to whom he referred, or they are getting very old! Observe the logic:

1. Jesus promised that the kingdom would come with power (Mark 9:1).
2. But that power would accompany the reception of the Holy Spirit (Acts 1:8).[20]
3. Thus, the kingdom would come with the arrival of the Spirit.
4. But, the Spirit came on the day of Pentecost (Acts 2:4).
5. Hence, the kingdom was established at that time.

In one of the most incredible examples of Biblical manipulation imaginable, Robert Shank attempts to overthrow the force of the foregoing argument. First, he asserts that the "kingdom" of Mark 9:1; Matthew 16:28[21] is to arrive at Christ's "triumphant coming at the end of the age."[22] One could only conclude, then, that some of those standing nearby as Christ spoke would not die until the Lord's millennial kingdom came! But Shank does not believe such to be the case, for on the same page as cited above, he contends that the Lord's prediction of the coming kingdom (Ma. 16:28; Mark 9:1) *"was fulfilled in the Transfiguration six days later"* (emp. WJ). Try to fathom the logic if you can! Shank's eschatological theory has him in deep trouble here. He knows the prediction of these passages must find a fulfillment within the lifetime of the Lord's auditors. Yet his doctrinal stance requires that the millennial kingdom be the focus of the prophecy. He is thus caught in a contradiction from whence there is simply no escape! But how does he attempt to extract himself? Well, he claims that since the three apostles at the Transfiguration scene were "eyewitnesses of his (Christ's) majesty" (II Pe. 1:16), this event served as "proof" of the future coming of the Lord, and hence *somehow* fulfilled the Lord's promise that the kingdom would come before some of them died — which will actually come in the "end time." Now wasn't that simple?! If you are totally bewildered, welcome to the group. That just has to be one of the most shocking examples of bizarre exegesis ever — an embarrassment to every serious Bible student.

That the kingdom of our Lord was established on Pentecost day, has continued since that time, and thus is a present reality, is a truth that is repeatedly rehearsed in the New Testament. The following is suggested for your careful study.

The King: At his ascension, Christ was exalted to the throne of God — also called his throne and the throne of David (Luke 1:32; Acts 2:30ff; Re. 3:21) — where he was given authority, rule, power, and dominion (Ma. 28:18; Ep. 1:21-22; Ph. 2:9-10; Col. 2:10). He is "prince" (*archegos*[23] — Acts 3:15; 5:31), "ruler" (*archon* — Re. 1:5), and "king" (*basileus* — Re. 17:14).

The Kingdom Received: When the Lord left this earth and entered into heaven, he received his kingdom. In a certain parable (Luke 19:12ff) Jesus declared: "A certain nobleman [Christ] went into a far country [heaven], to receive for himself a kingdom [the church], and to return [the Second Coming]." Without question, therefore, Christ *has* received his kingdom, and he received it in heaven.[24]

The Kingdom Entered: In their famous evening conversation, Jesus informed Nicodemus that, "Except one be born of water and the Spirit, he cannot enter into the kingdom of God" (John 3:5). The implication, of course, is that if one does submit to the conditions of the new birth, he can enter the kingdom. We subsequently learn that the kingdom is the church. This is demonstrated by the fact that the same process that introduces a person into the kingdom of the Lord also makes him a member of the body, the church. Observe the following diagram of cognate passages:

(John 3:5)	Spirit + water	=	kingdom
(I Co. 12:13)	Spirit + baptism	=	body
(Ep. 5:25-26)	Word + washing of water	=	cleansed church

Further, when Paul wrote to the Colossians, he affirmed that God "delivered us out of the power of darkness, and translated [a past tense form] us into the kingdom of the Son of his love" (1:13). And in John's book of Revelation, he informed the saints of the "seven churches that are in Asia" (1:4) that they had been loosed from their sins by the blood of Christ and had been made "to be a kingdom" (1:6). Additionally, he was a "partaker" with them in that kingdom (1:9). In view of these final two passages especially, I cannot understand why Robert Shank would claim that when John penned the Revelation from Patmos, "the coming of the Messianic kingdom was still future, awaiting the coming of Messiah in power and righteous judgment (Re. 11:15-19, 19:11-20:6)."[25] A careful reading of these passages cited by Shank will reveal, however, that the term "kingdom" is but twice used in our English translation.[26] And concerning that matter the Greek text exclaims that the "kingdom of the world is become (egeneto — aorist)" that "of our Lord, and of his Christ" (Re. 11:15). And there is, of course, a sense in which that reign will continue for ever (see later). But from the viewpoint of Christ's return, his earthly reign has already been accomplished and is completely victorious (cf. Ps. 2:8; 110:5-6; I Co. 15:25). (Note: I am still wondering why Shank [Until, p. 116] cites Revelation 11:15 thusly: "the kingdom of this world will become the kingdom of our Lord . . . ." Just what possessed him to change a past tense form to a future tense? I have been unable to find any translation which justifies this!)

Kingdom Instruction: Our Lord Jesus, in much of his parabolic teaching, anticipated the imminent establishment of the kingdom of heaven. For example: In the parable of the sower Christ taught of varying attitudes toward the gospel of the kingdom (Ma. 13:3ff); the story of the tares recognizes the presence of evil in the kingdom and speaks of an ultimate purging at the judgment (Ma. 13:24ff; cf. 13:47-50); the narrative of the mustard seed predicted the extensive growth of the kingdom (13:31-32); the parable of the leaven foretold of the kingdom's great influence (13:33); and, that of the hidden treasure and pearl of great price emphasized the value of the Lord's kingdom and the necessary sacrifices for obtaining it (13:44-45). Surely the sincere Bible student can see the wonderful kingdom truths in these parables that apply to us now.

Kingdom Worship: Shortly before his death, the Savior promised his disciples, ". . . ye may eat and drink at my table in my kingdom . . ." (Luke 22:30). The Lord's table was to be placed within his kingdom. If one can find disciples partaking of that table, it will amount to a demonstration of the kingdom's existence. Now, notice: when Paul wrote to "the church . . . at Corinth" (I Co. 1:2), he rebuked them for their abuses in partaking of the "table of the Lord" (10:21). It is thus quite evident that the Corinthian Christians were in the kingdom. The truth of the matter is, anyone who alleges that the kingdom has not come, and yet who attempts to observe the Lord's supper, is woefully inconsistent.

508   STUDIES IN HEBREWS

Kingdom Consummation: Finally, let it be noted that at the "end" (*viz.*, the time of Christ's coming) (I Co. 15:23-24) the Lord will "deliver up the kingdom to God" (not receive it *from* him). In the meantime, he "must reign" (present tense — "continue to reign") until all his enemies are vanquished (v. 25).

CIRCUMVENTION OF KINGDOM TRUTHS

Dispensational premillennialism utterly denies the present existence of the kingdom, alleging it was postponed because of the Jewish rejection of Christ. This notion is patently false and is infidelic in its implications.[27] To his credit, Shank does not adopt this preposterous doctrine; to his discredit, he invents a whole new vocabulary to justify his theory that the Messianic kingdom has not come. According to Shank, the kingdom *is* here, but it *isn't.* Now you see it, now you don't! Here is the way he explains it. When Jesus ascended to heaven, he merely received the "investiture" of the kingdom, but he will be "inaugurated" as king when he returns at the end of the age, and his "coronation" will occur when he assumes David's throne at Jerusalem.[28] Now get this: Shank says that "the Church is not the promised Messianic kingdom, but instead is a *proleptic manifestation* of the kingdom of God on earth in anticipation of the Messianic kingdom of Christ yet to come. . . ."[29] So the church is but a "proleptic manifestation" of the kingdom! According to Webster, a prolepsis is "the describing of an event as taking place before it could have done so, the treating of a future event as if it had already happened." So, in the final analysis, though Shank glibly speaks as though a "kingdom" was in existence from Pentecost onward, his vocabulary camouflage suggests otherwise. Perhaps Matthew 16:18 could be re-translated in a new premillennial version of the Bible thusly: ". . . upon this rock I will build my proleptic manifestation (my investiture) of the kingdom . . . and I will give unto thee the keys of the end-time, Messianic, inaugural, coronated kingdom . . ."! As Robert would say:

> What incredible subtleties good men sometimes impose on a simple text of Scripture in an effort to accommodate it to what they believe to be the general teaching of the Bible. Many exegetical (?) and theological constructions, like David's body, are "fearfully and wonderfully made."[30]

A FUTURE KINGDOM?

In his chapter, "Was Pentecost the Coming of the Kingdom?" (a question which he answers negatively), Shank thinks he has found a number of New Testament passages which reveal that the kingdom is yet in the future.[31] For example: at his return Christ will say to the faithful, "Come, ye blessed of my Father, inherit the kingdom prepared for you from the foundation of the world" (Ma. 25:34). In Acts 14:22 Paul announced that "through many tribulations we must enter into the kingdom of God." And what of II Peter 1:11, "for thus shall be richly supplied unto you the entrance into the eternal kingdom of our Lord and Saviour Jesus Christ?" Do not these passages indicate that the kingdom is yet future?

Here is an important fact that must be noted. Though Christ will end his reign over the earthly phase of his kingdom (*viz.*, his subjects on earth) at the time of his return (cf. I Co. 15:23-24), nonetheless, there is a sense in which Christ will reign for ever and his kingdom extend into the endless ages of eternity. John says, "to him [Christ] be the glory and the dominion for ever and ever" (Re. 1:6). The eternal throne is the "throne of God and of the Lamb" (Re. 22:1). So, similarly, there is a sense in which the kingdom is forever (Dan. 2:44); it is the eternal kingdom (II Pe. 1:11). But the question is, "*Is that kingdom into which we are to enter at the time of the Lord's coming earthly or heavenly?*" Premillennialists contend that it is earthly; the Bible teaches that it is *heavenly*.

Let us examine one of the passages which Shank introduced as proof of the future earthly kingdom (Acts 14:22), and we will let Paul, with one of his cognate passages, explain the matter for us.

Acts 14:22	II Timothy 4:18
"through many tribulations we must enter into the kingdom"	"the Lord will deliver me from every evil work, and will save me unto his *heavenly kingdom*"

In this latter passage (a verse, incidentally, about which Shank was strangely silent in his discussion of this matter), it can be clearly seen that the kingdom into which God's saints enter at the time of the Lord's return is the *heavenly*, eternal realm of the divine kingdom.

CONCLUSION

There simply is no Biblical justification for a future millennial reign of Christ upon this earth!

ENDNOTES

1. Robert Shank, *Until — The Coming of Messiah and His Kingdom* (Springfield, MO: Westcott, 1982), p. 324.

2. *Ibid.,* p. 316. " 'Signs of the time' are on every hand in the world today, indicating the imminence of the coming of our Lord."

3. *Ibid.,* p. 113.

4. Note the similar terminology used by the apostle — "a house not made with hands" (II Co. 5:1) — to suggest the *spiritual* nature of the resurrected body.

5. Shank vigorously opposes the idea that Luke 17:21 — "the kingdom of God is within you" — limits the kingdom of Christ to a *spiritual* regime (*Ibid.,* p. 358). He contends that *entos,* rendered "within you" really means "in your midst" (but was the millennial kingdom already in their midst?). However, *entos* clearly means "within" (note Matthew 23:26 — the only other NT usage of the term). Too, another expression, *en meso humon* (John 1:26), is employed to convey the idea of "in your midst."

6. There is not a shred of evidence that the "ten [unmentioned] toes" of Daniel 2 are analogous to the "ten horns" of Daniel 7, and those of the beast in Revelation 13 and 17 (*Ibid.,* p. 112).

7. Shank (*Ibid.,* 114, 115) contends that the "kings" of 2:44 represent not a succession of rulers, but concurrent nations. Not so. Does the phrase "in the days when the judges ruled" (Ruth 1:1), mean that they ruled successively or concurrently? Christ came to earth in the days of Claudius Caesar, and his kingdom was established in the time of Tiberias (cf. Luke 2:1; 3:1).

8. *Ibid.,* p. 33.

9. The premillennialists have the unusual ability of finding many "gaps" where the Bible indicates none. They jam 2,000 years between Isaiah 9:6 and 7; between Daniel 2:43 and 44; and, between the 69th and 70th weeks of Daniel 9:24-27. They squeeze 1,000 years between the resurrection of the righteous and the wicked (John 5:28-29; Acts 24:15), and between the Lord's coming to judge those who "obey not the gospel" and his glorification "in his saints" in II Thessalonians 1:8, 10.

10. *Ibid.,* p. 84.

11. F. F. Bruce, *The Acts of the Apostles* (Grand Rapids: Eerdmans, 1951), p. 270.

12. Shank (*op. cit.,* p. 33) sees no chronological proximity between Jesus' resurrection and his ascension to David's throne. He says that "Christ's assumption of the throne of David need not immediately follow his resurrection in order to establish the fact that his resurrection was for that purpose."

He thus admits that Christ was raised from the dead *for the purpose* of occupying David's throne, but contends that enthronement has been delayed *two millennia!* His example of David's anointing is entire irrelevant in view of Peter's comments in Acts 2:30ff.

13. J. W. McGarvey, *New Commentary on Acts of Apostles* Delight, AR: Gospel Light Pub. Co., n.d.), p. 33.

14. This is obviously the church (cf. I Co. 3:16; Ep. 2:21-22).

15. "His" throne is the "throne of David" which was *given* to him (cf. Luke 1:32).

16. Shank, *op. cit.*, pp. 31-32.

17. Leon Morris, "Hebrews," *The Expositor's Bible Commentary,* Frank E. Gaebelein & J. D. Douglas, Eds. (Grand Rapids: Zondervan, 1981), Vol. XII, p. 75.

18. Shank, *op. cit.*, p. 359.

19. If Matthew 16:28 was fulfilled on Pentecost, *how* did Christ "come" at that time? Jesus had informed the sorrowing disciples that he would not leave them desolate, but he would send the Comforter, the Holy Spirit (John 14:16-18, 26; 15:26); yet, in that connection, Christ promised, "I *come* to you" (14:18). *How* was he thus to come to them? Not personally, but *representatively,* in the Person of the Spirit whom he would send (15:26).

20. The connection between the coming of the kingdom, power and Spirit is here (Acts 1:6-8) plainly indicated. The disciples asked when the *kingdom* would be restored to Israel, and the Lord replied that such would be accomplished with the coming of the Spirit. In a valuable comment, H. B. Hackett notes: "The question of the disciples, as Bengal observes, related merely to the time when Christ would establish his kingdom; and his answer, as here given, he confines to the same point. Their remaining misconceptions as to the nature of that kingdom were soon to be removed more effectually than by any formal instruction" (*A Commentary on the Original Text of the Acts of the Apostles* [Andover: John Draper, 1879], p. 31). That the true "restoration of Israel was to be *spiritual* in emphasis, and not political, is evidenced by a consideration of Isaiah 49:5-13 (see "restore," v. 6) in the light of inspired New Testament interpretation (cf. Acts 13:47; II Co. 6:2).

21. The fact that Christ mentions his Second Coming in passages adjacent to Mark 9:1 and Matthew 16:28 does not necessarily identify the two as referring to the same event. The Lord simply summarizes the entire span from the *coming* of the kingdom to the *consummation* of the kingdom. See William Hendricksen, *Exposition of the Gospel According to Matthew* (Grand Rapids: Baker, 1973), p. 659.

22. Shank, *op. cit.*, p. 359.

23. This term carries the idea of *"originator, founder."* Of *what* is Christ the founder?

24. Shank (*Ibid.*, p. 266) claims that Christ only received his "investiture as king" in heaven (a jargon of human invention — cf. R. C. Trench, *Notes on the Parables,* p. 513), but he will not be "inaugurated" until he returns. "His citizens" (the Jews) were unaware of any such distinction for, *from earth,* they

said: "We will not (present tense) that this man *reign* over us" (Luke 19:14). It was their refusal of his reign that earned them the epithet "enemies" when he returned (19:27). Additionally, there is not the slightest hint in this context of a "national conversion" of the Jews; in fact, just the reverse impression is left!

25. Shank, *Ibid.*, p. 115.

26. The second use of the noun "kingdom" — in italics in our English versions — is implied by the grammatical structure.

27. See my booklet, *"Premillennialism — A System of Infidelity (Christian Courier,* 3906 East Main St., Stockton, CA 95205).

28. Shank, *op. cit.,* pp. 255, 256.

29. *Ibid.,* p. 356.

30. *Ibid.,* p. 362.

31. *Ibid.,* pp. 356, 357.